2003 LEVEL III READINGS
CONTENTS

Study
Session

ETHICAL AND PROFESSIONAL STANDARDS

02-02   "Case Study: Suitability," *Standards Reporter*   3

INVESTMENT TOOLS

04-01A   "Using Economic Models," *Economic Analysis for Investment Professionals*   7

04-01B   "Economic Forecasts and the Asset Allocation Decision," *Economic Analysis*   12
          for Investment Professionals

04-02   "What Determines the Exchange Rate: Economic Factors or Market Sentiment?"   23
         Business Review

04-03A   "The Nature of Effective Forecasts," *Improving the Investment Decision*   36
          Process—Better Use of Economic Input in Securities Analysis and
          Portfolio Management,

04-03B   "Developing a Recommendation for a Global Portfolio," *Improving*   44
          the Investment Decision Process—Better Use of Economic Input in Securities
          Analysis and Portfolio Management

ASSET VALUATION

05-01   "Security Market Indicator Series," *Investment Analysis and Portfolio*   58
         Management, 6th Edition

05-02   "Twenty Years of International Equity Investing," *The Journal of*   85
         Portfolio Management

05-04   "International Portfolio Investment," *Foundations of Multinational Financial*   99
         Management, 3rd Edition

Study
Session

ASSET VALUATION (continued)

06-01   "A Framework for Assessing Trading Strategies," *Fixed Income Analysis for the Chartered Financial Analyst Program*   118

08-01A   "The Real Estate Portfolio Management Process," *The Handbook of Real Estate Portfolio Management*   152

08-01B   "International Real Estate Investment: A Realistic Look at the Issues," *The Handbook of Real Estate Portfolio Management*   213

08-02   "Leverage in a Private Equity Real Estate Portfolio," *Modern Real Estate Portfolio Management*   251

08-03   "Real Estate Investment Performance and Portfolio Considerations," *Real Estate Finance and Investments,* 11th Edition   262

08-04   "The Economics of the Private Equity Market," *Economic Review*   284

08-05   "The Reality of Hedge Funds," *The Journal of Investing*   298

08-06A   "Controlled Risk Strategies," *Alternative Investing*   317

08-06B   "Market Neutral: Engineering Return and Risk," *Alternative Investing*   329

08-07   "The Search for Alpha Continues: Do Fund of Hedge Funds Managers Add Value?" *UBS Warburg Global Alternative Investment Strategies*   339

ISBN 0-935015-80-9

Printed in the United States of America

Case Study: Suitability

The United States Securities and Exchange Commission recently upheld sanctions imposed by the New York Stock Exchange on a former Shearson Lehman Brothers broker for unsuitable recommendations and excessive trading. According to the SEC, the broker, Stephen T. Rangen, used his influence over his clients to pursue aggressive, short-term trading strategies that were inconsistent with his clients' investment objectives.

According to the SEC opinion, four unsophisticated, inexperienced individual investors with limited means opened accounts with Rangen at Shearson Lehman seeking safe, income-producing investments. Despite these client profiles, the SEC found that Rangen made unsuitable recommendations and excessively traded in the three accounts opened by the investors (two of the investors were an elderly couple who opened one account). The SEC found that Rangen's method of trading was contrary to their goals in several ways:

According to the SEC, control of accounts may be established "when a client relies upon the broker to such an extent that the broker is in a position to control the volume and frequency of the transactions in the account."

- ❖ The U.S. Treasury strips and over-the-counter stocks purchased for one or more of the accounts did not produce income as sought by the clients.

- ❖ Rangen's use of margin accounts was inappropriate in this case because it increased the risk of loss and required clients to pay interest on the margin loan, adding to the cost to maintain the account.

- ❖ Rangen increased the risk of loss for the clients beyond that consistent with the client objectives by concentrating so much of their equity in particular securities (as much as 80 percent of the equity in one account was concentrated in one stock over a five-month period).

- ❖ All three accounts had extremely high turnover rates. The SEC found that the three account values would have had to increase annually by 236 percent, 48 percent, and 80 percent simply to break even.

According to the SEC, Rangen admitted that the clients were investing in a manner that was not suitable to them but contended that the clients were aware of the risks and that for him to refuse their orders merely because he felt that the investments were not suitable would have been wrong. Rangen also claimed that he did not have control over the accounts. Finally, Rangen stated that Shearson's research department recommended the purchase of the Treasury strips and that the stocks recommended to the clients were all in the "top rated categories of the Lehman Research Division."

The SEC rejected all of Rangen's arguments. According to the SEC, control of accounts may be established "when a client relies upon the broker to such an extent that the broker is in a position to control the volume and frequency of the transactions in the account." The SEC also indicated that none of the clients initiated any transactions in their respective accounts and all relied heavily on and followed Rangen's advice in overseeing the accounts.

Further, even if the clients wanted to speculate and were aware of the risks (a claim rejected by the SEC in this case), the SEC stated that the issue is not whether the clients considered the transactions in their account to be suitable. The test, according to the SEC, is whether Rangen fulfilled the obligation he assumed when he undertook to counsel the clients: to make only such recommendations as would be consistent with their financial needs. In this case, the SEC found that Rangen did not.

Finally, the SEC rejected Rangen's attempt to shift the blame to his employer when he argued that Shearson's research department had recommended the purchase of the securities. The commission stated that "Rangen cannot shift his responsibility as an investment counselor to his employer. It was Rangen's duty to make only such recommendations as were in the best interests of his clients. Rangen was obligated not only to consider Shearson's recommendations, but his clients' investment objectives and financial situations which he failed to do."

As an investment adviser, Rangen had a fiduciary duty to each client. The responsibilities to individual clients are especially important because the knowledge and information of the professional investment manager may be greater than the knowledge and information of the client, as the SEC found in this case. The disparity places the individual client in a vulnerable posi-

tion of trust. Particular care should be taken to ensure that the goals of the investment professional in selling products or executing security transactions do not conflict with the best interests of the client.

The Commission found that Rangen placed his own interests above those of his clients by excessively trading in the accounts, contrary to the NYSE's just and equitable principles of trade. The SEC upheld the NYSE's censure of Rangen and their decision to suspend him from membership, allied membership, approved person status, and employment or association in any capacity with any NYSE member or member organization for four years.

AIMR Standard of Professional Conduct IV(B.2), Portfolio Investment Recommendations and Actions, states that members must consider the appropriateness and suitability of investment recommendations or actions for each portfolio or client. In determining appropriateness and suitability, members shall consider applicable relevant factors, including the needs and circumstances of the portfolio or client, the basic characteristics of the investment involved, and the basic characteristics of the total portfolio. Members shall not make a recommendation unless they reasonably determine that the recommendation is suitable to the client's financial situation, investment experience, and investment objectives.

Rangen's conduct, as described in the SEC opinion, constituted a clear violation of Standard IV(B.2). To prevent suitability questions from arising, members should

❖ obtain such client information as financial circumstances, income, investment objectives, liquidity needs, tax considerations, and time horizon and should update this information no less frequently than annually;

❖ pay special attention to assessing the client's tolerance for risk;

❖ when appropriate, diversify a client's portfolio;

❖ ensure that the client understand the basic characteristics of each investment considered and how that investment will fit into the portfolio to meet the client's investment objectives.

———— ❖ ————

4

Investment Tools

Using Economic Models

Avery B. Shenfeld
Senior Economist
CIBC Wood Gundy

> Economic models come in various forms. But no matter the form, all models have potential problems. Investment professionals must be aware of the various types of models and the problems associated with them, so that when they look at research, they can better judge its validity.

We all get inundated with research—reports produced by brokerage firms, journal articles, etc.—and have grown used to being skeptical of whether or not we can get any payoff from it. I will provide some guidelines for looking at statistical research—information with all sorts of equations, charts, and features that appear very impressive. Armed with these guidelines, as investment professionals you should be able to look behind the pretty wrappings to test whether the research is something that you might actually put money behind or something that can go in the filing cabinet under your desk. I will also describe how we use models at CIBC Wood Gundy to look at particular sectors of the economy.

FORECASTING APPROACHES

Economic forecasting can be divided into five groups based on the differing methodologies:
- econometric, or structural, models,
- leading-indicator approaches,
- technical analysis,
- judgmental techniques, and
- mixed analysis.

■ *Econometric models.* Econometric models are generally large-scale structural models of the economy. These structural models are the most formal examples of modeling and often run to hundreds of equations. For example, the research from places such as DRI/McGraw-Hill is based on models with hundreds or even thousands of equations and thousands of individual variables, which is very costly to maintain. Most investment professionals would find it extremely difficult to duplicate that type of research effort.

A structural model usually takes a group of "exogenous" variables—variables for which the modeler has to make assumptions—and uses those variables to project other variables that the model solves for. So, typically, a structural model has an equation or a group of equations for each part of the economy—for the consumer sector, for the business sector, for housing demand, for government spending, and so on—and it adds all the equations together. The model creates a picture of the economy, which in turn influences other equations that give such things as interest rates.

In addition to these complex models, some very straightforward methods of econometric modeling are in use. For example, a basic regression analysis, in which a line is fitted to the data to try to ascertain the influence of one particular variable on another, can serve as a form of econometric modeling.

■ *Leading-indicator approaches.* In the leading-indicator approach, forecasters try to develop lists of variables that predict the variable of interest. The lists are not necessarily built into any formal statistical model but rather are used as signposts of upcoming changes in bond yields, equity prices, and so on. The government publishes some leading indexes, and individual researchers and consulting firms have devised some composite indexes to try to capture what they think are advance warning signals for economic trends.

■ *Technical analysis.* Technical analysis looks at chart points, Elliot waves, etc., to generate forecasts. This approach is quite common, so I will not delve into the details.

■ *Judgmental techniques.* The judgmental method of forecasting uses the investment professional's judgment about economic trends by taking a hodgepodge of indicators and trying to build a story of what the economy is likely to do. From that story, the movements of bond yields and stock prices, for example, are forecasted.

■ *Mixed analysis.* The mixed approach is essentially the approach that we use at Wood Gundy. Broadly speaking, we use a judgmental approach but supplement it with models to serve as a test of the story created by our judgmental approach. So, for example, we might use a model that looks at how long-bond yields should respond to changes in short-term interest rates and then use that model to check whether or not our story on long rates and short rates is broadly consistent with the data.

WHY USE MODELS?

Using models, either exclusively or as part of a forecasting effort, allows for the testing of hypotheses and ideas. Examples of what can be tested include determining how much low interest rates stimulate growth and whether wages can be used as a predictor of inflation. One advantage of using a model is that it puts hypotheses to a formal test instead of simply looking at the data and trying to see whether some trend exists.

Models are also helpful in estimating sensitivities. Researchers may be quite confident that one thing affects another—that inflation affects interest rates, for example—but they want to know by how much. How much, for example, would a 1 percentage point rise in the U.S. Consumer Price Index typically translate into 10-year bond yields? Statistical techniques can be used to try to isolate that effect.

Using models and statistical techniques also helps in developing internally consistent forecasts. For example, when researchers are using a judgmental approach, they may fail to see that something they are implying about income growth does not jibe with their assumptions on employment growth. One benefit of a big, formal model is it makes sure that everything adds up.

Models are also used for running simulations of complex scenarios. For example, a government economist may need to find out what happens if interest rates and government spending are both cut. Often, estimating the combined impact of good news and bad news is difficult. The U.S. growth rate may pick up, but inflation may stay flat. Statistical modeling lets a researcher try to balance the various influences.

Finally, sometimes models are used because variables have an underlying statistical process that has information in it. For example, something may have a tendency to revert back to its mean, and the researcher may be able to use that tendency to develop a better forecast.

PROBLEMS IN THE USE OF MODELS

The basic problem with all models is reliability. If a particular model suggests gold is going to $500 an ounce, investment professionals need to know whether they should believe the model and buy gold. If I am going to impart any message, it is that as investment professionals you should be critical readers of research. One has to look for what could be wrong before accepting the research as valid. I will talk here about a number of the things that can go wrong that would leave the research looking good but the underlying data are suspect—in effect, cases in which you cannot judge the book by the cover.

Implausible Results

One common problem arises from a model with a lot of variables that then attempts to isolate one of them. Although the model claims to have found that the one particular variable influences a second, other variables do not seem to be working correctly. Take an absurd illustration: The model is indicating that the higher inflation goes, the lower interest rates should go. The tendency should be to be skeptical about the rest of the research, because what that error is implying is that something is not working in this model; therefore, the model's predictions might be quite unreliable.

Statistical versus "Real World" Significance

Another issue arises when researchers say they have found a statistically significant relationship, say between the price of gold and inflation. The key is to look at the statistical significance, which is the technical term for saying that the statistics indicate that the variable has an influence. But that significance has to be contrasted with the questions, "Does the variable matter in the real world? Does it have enough of an influence to matter?"

Let me give an example. A colleague of mine spent a great deal of effort attempting to develop a model to predict the monthly nonfarm payrolls report, because if he knew what nonfarm payrolls were going to be, he could certainly make a lot of money. The obvious variable that people look at to predict nonfarm payrolls is the initial claims for unemployment benefits. People also use a continuing claims variable that measures the number of people who are still receiving benefits after the initial claim.

So, my colleague built a model. He had lots of statistical work, and he came up with something that he thought looked good. In other words, all the statistics seemed to be pointing to a reasonable amount of explanatory power in predicting monthly nonfarm payrolls, and it looked like something usable.

Next, he conducted a test for real-world significance. He asked whether the model explained the data any better than a naive forecast of assuming that this month's nonfarm payrolls was simply the average of the three preceding months' nonfarm payrolls. The answer unfortunately was no, it did not. Sometimes a model can look good on the surface, have lots of statistical explanatory power, but still not be of any use because it does not beat a naive approach; the model just does not have what it takes to truly capture the underlying data.

Errors in Underlying Data

Variables that are subject to massive revisions create another problem when using models. Charts usually show that in the past, a certain variable appears to have been a good predictor of some other variable of interest, such as long-bond yields. The problem is, the chart shows the final revised data, not the data that would have been available at the time. You should be very careful about research that uses data that are subject to large revisions, such as the payrolls reports and Canadian merchandise trade surplus. You need to know if the predictive relationship holds for the initially released data as well as it does for the revised data.

Assumptions

Assumptions, assumptions, assumptions. That is what people always say the economists of the world make. No model predicts every variable, so every model has to have some starting points. Unfortunately, for the Canadian economy, one starting point often is what the U.S. economy is going to do, which is as tough to forecast as the Canadian economy. Modelers do not want a model that uses variables that are themselves as tough to forecast as the variable they are trying to forecast.

Let me give an example. When I was in consulting, I did some modeling for a group of luxury car companies that wanted me to forecast the demand for luxury cars in Canada. When I talked to them about what variables they thought influenced the demand, they all agreed that the stock market is an important variable. When the stock market is doing well, people go out and buy Porsches. The problem with that variable is the inability to predict the stock market. You have to be careful when the assumed variables are themselves as difficult to forecast as the variable you are trying to get out of the model.

Structural Changes

Another problem is with structural changes in the economy. All models assume that past relationships have some validity in predicting future relationships. In the case of economies that are changing rapidly, where fundamental structural changes are taking place, one does not know whether or not those past situations have much validity in predicting the future.

For example, some people argue that with heightened international competition and more layoffs and turnover in the economy now, the unemployment rate can go a lot lower than it has in the past without stimulating inflation. Well, that prediction cannot be tested because it is a new phenomenon. We do not have enough data on this post-transition economy, high-layoff world to determine whether or not wage inflation will take place.

Robert Lucas, a Nobel Prize winning economist, poked some holes into a lot of the work on economic modeling. His argument is essentially that the very fact that people can observe a change in policy influences their behavior in response to it. He argued that an economic model that, for example, tries to simulate what happens if interest rates are cut, is in theory wrong, because the model cannot account for the fact that individuals in the economy, having seen in the past how interest rates affected the economy, would then change their behavior in response to interest rate changes. People would be trying to run ahead of what the policymakers were doing.

To some extent, this theory sounds farfetched. It makes it sound as if individuals are running their own little economic models to determine what they are doing, but it is not that farfetched. Think about the fact that the world is filled with economic commentators who are watching closely what is going on and are providing insights into what is likely to happen. Lucas may be right. Using past responses to policies, for example, to assess how the economy will perform in the future may be fundamentally flawed.

Simultaneity

A common error that sometimes creeps into modeling is "simultaneity," which is the technical term for trying to measure the influence of one variable on another when that second variable also influences the first one. This phenomenon can cause statistical models to entirely mess up relationships.

For example, suppose the researcher is looking at the Canadian dollar. The tendency is to think that the narrower the Canada–U.S. interest rate spread, the weaker the Canadian dollar. A less generous spread or even a negative spread at the short end should dissuade people from putting short-term assets into the Canadian dollar, which would tend to weaken the currency. Running a statistical estimate of that theory and looking at spreads would show absolutely nothing. In other words, the statistical model would indicate that spreads do not influence the Canadian dollar at all, so the Bank of Canada could cut interest rates by another 300 basis points (bps), get them down to basically zero, and the Canadian dollar should not be affected.

That intuition is wrong because the strength of the Canadian dollar also influences interest rate spreads. In periods when the Canadian dollar was strengthening, the Bank of Canada might have chosen to take advantage of that situation by cutting Canada–U.S. interest rate spreads. Spreads influence the Canadian dollar; the Canadian dollar influences spreads. A more complicated model is needed to capture both of those relationships at once, which essentially gets into a model with a couple of equations. An equation is needed to explain the Canadian dollar as function of a number of factors, such as resource prices and interest rate spreads. A separate equation is also needed that explains the Canada–U.S. interest rate spread and allows the spread to be a function of a number of variables, including, of course, the Canadian dollar.

Robustness

Another problem with models, and unfortunately assessing this problem is often difficult, is what is called the lack of "robustness," which comes down to a matter of trust. If someone gets a piece of research from Avery Shenfeld at Wood Gundy, that person does not know how many different versions of the model I tried until I got one that worked. That is, I could have tried all kinds of variables, attempted a logarithmic form of the equation, and so on until finally I got the statistics showing a model that fits the data and also showing the effect that I was trying to investigate.

For example, if I am trying to argue that gold is a predictor of inflation, I could vary the start date of the data until I find a period when my hypothesis works. If I start the series in the first quarter of 1971, this theory works. But if I start the series in the third quarter of 1971 or in 1982, this theory may not work at all. In doing research, those seemingly minor choices about how the model is constructed should not affect the basic results.

As the reader of research, you have to be very careful and skeptical if you think the modeler tried lots of things before coming up with the results, but understanding the modeling process is very difficult. What you should look for are odd choices in how the model is set up, such as the starting date for the analysis. Robustness is tough to assess when reading the research, so it is somewhat a matter of trust.

Data Mining

Robustness gets at the general issue of data mining—making multiple calculations with the data in order to get something that works. We have all heard arguments and seen papers that claim to have found profound statistical evidence with a tremendous explanatory power showing that years ending in a seven are good for the stock market. The question is, did these researchers test years ending in zero, one, two, and so on, finding only a relationship in years ending in a seven so that is what they chose to present? If so, the statistical tests are, in effect, cheating, because what the statistical tests indicate is a 90 percent confidence interval—the researchers are 90 percent sure that the relationship is not because of chance. In other words, what they are saying is a 1-in-10 chance exists that this relationship would have been found purely by chance. Well, if the researcher tries 10 such 1-in-10 chances, that person is likely to find a relationship. Those relationships, however, have no validity. That researcher has merely kept trying until lucking out, in effect, finding something totally unrelated to the data.

Time-Series Data

Time-series data sometimes have a number of problems. Unfortunately for economists and investment professionals, we cannot rerun the world and observe how the economy performs; we cannot rerun the 1980s and do something a little different. We have only this one set of data to work with, the data over time. Data over time present a number of problems for statisticians. For one, the data tend to violate many textbook assumptions on the purity of statistical tests.

A classic example of data problems occurs when variables have a trend to them. Most economic variables are trending up over time because the economy is growing, the population is growing, and so on. Variables that are trending over time often show relationships with each other. So, I could pick two variables that are trending up—say, the population of Japan and Canadian car sales. What I conclude from my statistical tests, if I want to predict Canadian car sales in the year 2000, is that I simply need to know the population of Japan. Well, that result cannot be right. What is wrong is that those variables have an underlying trend to them. A variety of statistical methods can be used to try to eliminate those spurious relationships between variables that have a trend, thus separating out the influences of trends and divergences from trends.

Vector Autoregressive Equations

Models called vector autoregressive equations, which have very little structure imposed on them, are sometimes used. Vector autoregressive equations do not try to impose too much structure on the data in terms of which variables influence which other variables. Rather, they take some variables and assume that their historical values are related to some of the other variables' historical values in the model. In the extreme case, this approach is like statistical work without theory.

USING MODELS

At Wood Gundy, models are an integral part of our work and our forecasts. One model that we use looks at the demand for Canadian commodities and tries to assess the influence of global industrial production on commodity prices. We also use a number of other variables that we think influence commodity prices. Because the prices are in U.S. dollars, we take a look at the value of the U.S. dollar against the G–10 index of other exchange rates. We then look at inflation, as measured by the U.S. Producer Price Index, as a predictor of gold prices. Finally, we use one of those complicated structural models—in this case something called an autoregressive moving-average process, which allows for trends and the tendency for commodity prices to overshoot and revert back to the trend. This approach seems to work reasonably well. When we ran it in February 1996, it indicated a weakening of base metal prices and a strengthening in energy prices. Many of the broad predictions that the model made seemed to pan out.

Another approach we take is what I referred to earlier as the mixed approach. That is, we look at a judgmental model and then test it to see if the data support the story that the judgmental model produced. For example, I often heard our foreign exchange traders say that they were surprised that the Canadian dollar did well because the U.S. dollar had weakened against the German mark. Many people in Canada believe that if the U.S. dollar weakens against international currencies, the Canadian dollar will weaken against the U.S. dollar. A test of this judgmental model revealed that no such relationship existed. Thus, sometimes statistical methods invalidate the old canards of forecasting.

Another approach we take is the leading-indicator approach. The Granger causality test attempts to answer a very simple question: "Do trends in one variable lead movements in another variable?" We used a Granger causality test to look at provincial bond spreads—for example, the spread between Ontario bonds and Canadian bonds in the Canadian market—to determine whether those spreads lead or lag the spread in the U.S. market for the same credits. We found that a leading relationship does exist in which the Canadian spreads are a little bit ahead of the U.S. spreads.

CONCLUSION

The bottom line on models is, do they tell us anything at all? I would argue that they do, but they are better at testing hypotheses than forecasting per se, because they do not seem to do any better than judgmental forecasts on average. Having said that, models do have some value in terms of simulating complex issues and testing to see whether one's intuition is correct that a particular variable has in fact had an influence on another one. A problem with all of this analysis is, we can have the best economic forecasts and still be wrong on the markets. The problem that we often face as investment professionals and advisors is that, although we may have a model that perfectly predicts nonfarm payrolls, for example, deciding what the market has already assumed is often difficult. The ultimate problem with models is that sometimes translating what they indicate into good financial investments is difficult.

Economic Forecasts and the Asset Allocation Decision

Abby Joseph Cohen, CFA
Managing Director
Goldman, Sachs & Company

The origins of the current bull market can be traced to structural changes for the good taking place in the United States. These structural changes in demographics, corporate management, fiscal policy, and inflation have led to a sustained slow-growth economy that has fueled various sectors and affected both domestic and international markets.

The key behind my long-standing bullish outlook has been the structural changes that have taken place in the U.S. economy since the late 1980s. I will provide a quick survey of several of those changes and then discuss how they affect equity market forecasts. Specific industry examples are provided to illustrate my points.

STRUCTURAL CHANGES

The extremely strong U.S. equity markets of recent years are, in my opinion, directly related to major structural changes for the good that have been taking place in the United States. Key structural changes have occurred in demographics, corporate management, fiscal policy, and inflation.

Demographics

In the early 1990s, the Baby Boomers—the single largest population cohort in modern history—began to move from their prime spending and borrowing years to being more inclined to save and invest. This change in Baby Boomer spending habits has implications for consumption growth (lower), savings growth (higher), and stock selection.

Corporate Management

The late 1980s witnessed the early stages of a corporate renaissance in the United States. During the preceding two decades, corporate managements in the United States had taken their comparative advantages for granted and allowed previously substantial leads in factors such as productivity and R&D spending to erode. In the 1960s, for example, many corporate managements in the United States were

paid on the basis of top-line growth, or revenues. If someone managed a big company, he or she was typically well paid, regardless of that company's level of profitability. This focus on size rather than results may have encouraged the move toward corporate conglomeration in the 1960s and 1970s. Now, the focus has returned to bottom-line growth, or return on those assets, which is an incentive system more in keeping with shareholder interests.

Corporate managements have also had to learn to manage in the low-inflation environment of the 1990s, which is much less forgiving of loose management practices. When inflation was consistently high and rising, its presence could always be counted on, and company managements learned to hide behind the smoke screen it produced. They could be sloppy in decision making, with impunity. They could produce too much, hire too many workers, or pay too much for supplies, and it did not matter; most mistakes could be passed on to the customer. That has certainly not been the case since the beginning of this decade, a period of low inflation and low-inflation expectations.

Fiscal Policy

A real sea change has taken place with regard to the way fiscal policy is approached. By the early 1990s, U.S. citizens showed a determination to get the budget deficit down. In keeping with this conviction, the Clinton administration's record was excellent in the first term, actually tightening fiscal policy contrary to the actions of most first-term presidents. The deficit shrank dramatically in terms of dollars, and it has collapsed as a percentage of GDP, which is the right way to look at it. In President George Bush's last year in office, the U.S. budget deficit was 6 percent of our national income; it is now 1.5 percent.

Inflation

Perhaps the most important structural change has been the reduction in inflation and inflation expectations. A secular updrift in inflation began in the 1960s, exacerbating each cyclical upturn linked to the usual factors such as capacity utilization and labor costs. Each cyclical peak in inflation was higher than the one before, and each cyclical trough in inflation was higher than the one before. A period of secular disinflation began in the 1980s. The impact of that disinflation on economic decision making is still being felt.

The late 1970s was a period of not only high inflation but also high-inflation expectations. Everyone was certain that inflation would continue to rise—a box of tissues would be 5 cents more expensive then the week before. People did not refuse to buy the box of tissues; they bought two, anticipating the next price hike. When inflation expectations are high and rising, consumption occurs in anticipation of future need and also in anticipation of future income. There was little reluctance to borrow because consumers believed they would be paying the money back in cheaper dollars later on. The item or service that was wanted would be more expensive in the future anyway. Businesses made similar decisions.

The current environment is the opposite: low inflation and low-inflation expectations. For example, people do not buy cars unless they receive rebates. In terms of business investment, the inventory-to-sales ratio in the United States is the lowest it has been in decades. Some say it is because of the computerized systems to control inventory. Certainly, such just-in-time systems have facilitated tighter inventory controls, but the motivation behind the low inventory-to-sales ratio is the absence of profits in inventory. If pricing is inflexible and the cost of carry to borrow money to keep those inventories is positive, why have a large inventory?

ECONOMIC ANALYSIS OF STRUCTURAL CHANGES

In a period of high inflation and high-inflation expectations, the economy moves faster than expected because consumers are consuming in anticipation of future need and businesses are building inventories in anticipation of future demand. In an environment of low-inflation expectations, things slow down. This slowdown in economic growth combined with the aging of the Baby Boomers, which slows down consumption growth, results in what we have been refer-

ring to for six years at Goldman Sachs as the "Silly Putty" economic cycle, so called because it does not exhibit the usual upside-down "V" pattern. Another way to look at the cycle is that it has a series of interim peaks and interim valleys, but the sine curve is much more moderate than in previous cycles. It is as if the cycle has been stretched horizontally and decreased vertically, as when playing with Silly Putty.

Profits

In the typical economic cycle, whether looking at year-on-year GDP growth or year-on-year profit growth, the curve looked like an upside-down "V". It would start in recession and have a notable build in momentum. Then, at the peak of the cycle, consumers and business people would be very confident, and pricing would begin to rise dramatically, which would not thrill the Federal Reserve. So, typically, the brakes would be slammed on the economy through higher interest rates, and economic activity would slide down the curve.

Figure 1 shows the profit expansion cycle since 1986 compared with the typical economic cycle. The "Silly Putty" cycle that we are in now displays a very different pattern from the typical cycle. First, it is not particularly vigorous. It is moving in the right direction but in slow motion. Second, this profit cycle has already lasted dramatically longer than almost any other profit cycle in U.S. economic history. Third, the cumulative profit growth (the area under the curve) has been absolutely fabulous; it is true that the U.S. equity market has risen more than ever before in terms of stock prices, but it is also true that profits have gone up more than ever before. Cumulative profit growth has already exceeded 100 percent, compared with an average of 75 percent for other time periods of equal length.

This period of profit growth has happened without an explosion in economic activity, simply a long-lasting period of moderate activity. Real GDP growth since the last recession (66 months) has been 14.6 percent, which is lower than the 22.8 percent experienced by the average cycle for the same number of months, but the growth was achieved without the usual "wind at the back" of corporate profits that occurs in more vigorous cycles. Companies have done an excellent job with the macroeconomic environment that they have been given: Without a vigorous economy and without pricing flexibility, they have generated record profits. This current period is extraordinary in part because the quality of earnings has surged.

Return on equity (ROE) in the United States, illustrated in **Figure 2**, has been rising since mid-1991, largely in response to improved corporate profitability. Average ROE in the current profit cycle can be

Figure 1. The "Silly Putty" Profit Expansion: S&P 500 Earnings per Share, Actual Data for First Quarter 1986 to Fourth Quarter 1996 plus Forecast

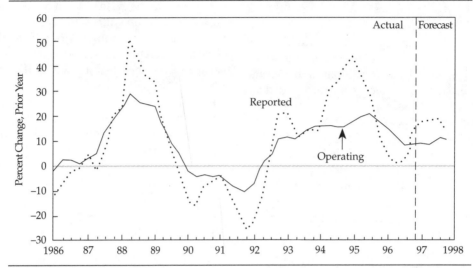

Source: Goldman, Sachs & Company, based on data from Standard & Poor's and Goldman Sachs Portfolio Strategy.

viewed as an all-time best for the United States, and it compares quite favorably with results in other industrial economies. In most other large economies, ROE is currently below 10 percent: ROE is below 5 percent in Japan. Other periods in which ROE looked good were in some cases an optical illusion. Consider that ROE was boosted in the late 1970s by high inflation and in the late 1980s by the dramatic reduction in equity capital. The current high-level ROE is yet another indication of strong returns generated by U.S. corporations.

Labor Costs

Labor costs have also displayed a stretched-out pattern in the "Silly Putty" cycle. **Figure 3** shows the employment cost index, which is a measure of total compensation. Historically, good economic growth led to tighter labor markets and rising wage inflation. The pattern has been slow to develop in the current economic cycle. Inflation expectations are down, and the employment cost index has been rising much more slowly than many economists had expected. Job creation, although cumulatively strong, has again

Figure 2. S&P 500 ROE, First Quarter 1978 to Fourth Quarter 1996

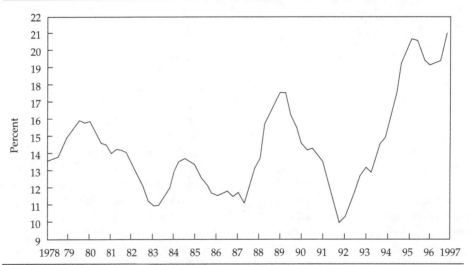

Note: Calculations are based on reported earnings.

Source: Goldman, Sachs & Company, based on data from Standard & Poor's and Goldman Sachs Portfolio Strategy.

©Association for Investment Management and Research

Figure 3. Employment Cost Index, Second Quarter 1982 to Fourth Quarter 1996

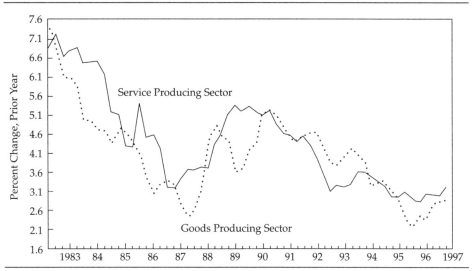

Source: Goldman, Sachs & Company, based on data from the Bureau of Labor Statistics.

not been as vigorous as usual. In this new slow-growth, low-inflation environment, wages are not necessarily the number one priority on workers' agendas. For example, recent collective bargaining agreements in the United States show that the first issue is job security, the second is retention of benefits, and the third is increasing wages. This statement does not mean that wages are not rising in the United States; they are, but they are rising more slowly than they have in the past. It will take longer than usual before wage inflation becomes problematic.

Good economic news will eventually turn into bad inflation news, but fears since 1994 that it will happen "soon" have been spectacularly premature for

two reasons: First, the wages themselves are not rising quickly, and second, wages are only part of the picture. Changes in productivity must also be considered.

Unit costs are a function of wage trends and productivity improvements. Since 1992, modest increases in compensation, combined with continuing productivity gains, have pushed unit labor costs down in the manufacturing sector, as shown in **Figure 4**, which has been to the benefit of corporate profit margins. Very simply, paying workers 3 percent more is affordable if productivity gains are also 3 percent, because the employer's net cost is zero.

Many economists, including those at the Federal Reserve, believe that published data understate the

Figure 4. Unit Labor Costs for the Manufacturing Sector, Second Quarter 1982 to Fourth Quarter 1996

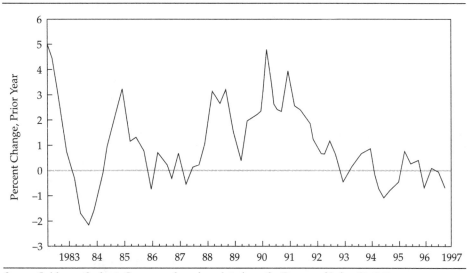

Source: Goldman, Sachs & Company, based on data from the Bureau of Labor Statistics.

Economic Analysis for Investment Professionals

27

true gains in labor productivity. Several methodology problems are involved; perhaps the most important one relates to the service sector, in which productivity is hard to measure. In the U.S. economy, a significant shift away from the manufacturing sector into the service sector has taken place, and this change worsens the data quality. Productivity change is hard to measure in about 70 percent of the U.S. economy, much of it service related, leading some analysts to conclude that economy-wide data are unreliable. Consider, for example, FIRE (finance, insurance, and real estate)—which is 20 percent of the service sector. This industry has seen billions of dollars invested by banks and insurance companies in new computer systems and telecommunication equipment. Although a considerable number of people have lost their jobs, the transactions being processed have absolutely boomed. According to the government data, productivity change in FIRE over the past six years has been zero, which makes the data somewhat suspect.

Inflation

Cyclical inflation has yet to rise in the United States despite several years of economic expansion. When it does rise (and it will), inflation will build more slowly than in other cycles. Although jobs are being created, no significant pressure yet exists in most industries for significant wage increases, and even in cases in which compensation has begun to accelerate, dramatic offsets from productivity change still exist.

This view on inflation, which is tied to the structural change in the economy, has a very important impact on the financial markets: When inflation is low, P/E multiples tend to be high. Investors are willing to pay more for a given level of earnings when inflation is low because little inflation padding is in the earnings and investors are more confident in the durability of the profit expansion. **Table 1** shows the relationship between P/E multiples for the S&P 500 Index and inflation. During the last 75 years, the average P/E multiple for the U.S. market has been about 14, but this average is not a helpful guide to

Table 1. Inflation as Measured by the CPI and P/E Multiples, 1950–95

Inflation	Average S&P 500 P/E
Less than 3.5%	16.2×
Less than 4.5%	15.3
4.5–5.5%	15.6
5.5–6.5%	12.1
6.5–7.5%	10.0
Greater than 7.5%	8.6

Source: Goldman, Sachs & Company.

investors. When inflation has been 3.5 percent or less, the average multiple has been 16.2. As inflation goes higher and higher, the multiple goes lower and lower. In periods of high inflation, the multiple has been well less than 10. Averaging different experiences together is not helpful. Rather, comparing current P/E multiples with those from similar inflation environments produces a clearer picture. On that basis, a market with a P/E of 15.5 (based on current price and our estimate of 1997 earnings) is undervalued relative to past periods when inflation has been less than 3.5 percent. The notable inverse relationship between the market's P/E ratio and inflation is illustrated in **Figure 5.**

Dividend Payouts

Periods of moderate inflation have also been associated with "below-average" nominal dividend yields. **Figure 6** shows a very strong normal correlation between the dividend yield and inflation. When inflation is low, so is the dividend yield. The decline in dividend yields during the past 10 or 15 years is not dramatically out of the ordinary relative to inflation. Even so, the current dividend yield has been somewhat lower than during other periods of moderate inflation. This situation raises the issue of another structural change: dividend payouts. If companies are well managed and if they are generating good returns on assets and equity, they should be reinvesting their money back into their businesses rather than paying dividends, which is exactly what these companies are doing. Payout ratios in the United States are at their lowest levels in decades. For the S&P 500, the payout ratio is now 36 percent, compared with the normal range of 50–75 percent. And return on equity, at 20 percent, is at its highest level.

EFFECTS OF STRUCTURAL CHANGES ON SECTORS

The structural changes that have taken place in the United States have had a significant impact on several sectors of the economy. These structural changes affect the relative attractiveness of specific industries.

Technology

One of the major changes in the structure of the U.S. economy has been the significant increase in the importance of technology and other equipment-related production and spending. Industrial production in technology-related sectors has grown several times faster than the total industrial production since 1990, as **Figure 7** shows. Thus, technology stocks have outperformed the market because technology companies have dramatically outperformed the economy.

Figure 5. Inflation and S&P 500 P/E Multiples, First Quarter 1950 to Fourth Quarter 1996

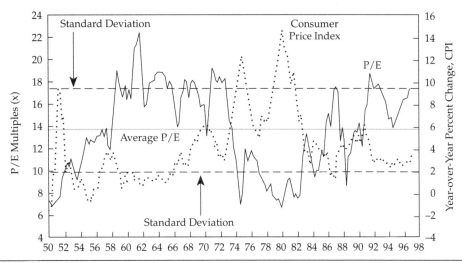

Note: Operating earnings per share are used to calculate P/E multiples beginning in the first quarter 1985.

Source: Goldman, Sachs & Company, based on data from Standard & Poor's, Bureau of Labor Statistics, and Goldman Sachs Portfolio Strategy.

Investment in producers durable equipment has grown as a percentage of GDP since the early 1960s, as **Figure 8** shows. The surge in spending on computer equipment, telecommunications systems, and other productivity enhancements since 1990 is clearly seen in Figure 8. During this period, the relative importance of investment in structures (that is, bricks and mortar) has declined. We believe this shift represents, in large part, a structural change in the U.S. economy, not a short-term cyclical phenomenon. Figure 8 begins in 1960 because prior to that time, two

distinct trends were not apparent. At the end of an economic cycle, business managers were enthusiastic and raised capital spending budgets, and both lines (equipment and structures) would move up as a percentage of GDP; at the beginning of a recession, both lines would go down. Thus, prior to 1960, no specific secular trend existed.

Recent trends in equipment investing are extremely important. Between 1960 and 1990, the increase in spending on equipment was related to the increased sophistication of the U.S. manufacturing

Figure 6. Inflation and S&P 500 Dividend Yields, First Quarter 1960 to Fourth Quarter 1996

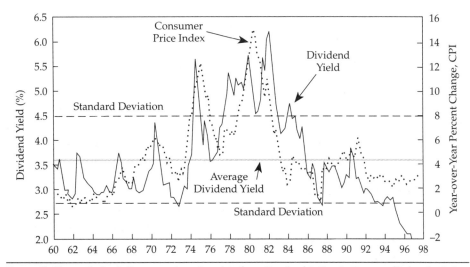

Source: Goldman, Sachs & Company, based on data from Standard & Poor's, Bureau of Labor Statistics, and Goldman Sachs Portfolio Strategy.

Figure 7. Growth of Technology-Related Goods and Services Relative to Total Industrial Production, Monthly Data from January 1990 to January 1997

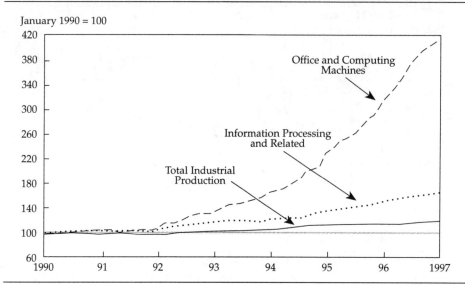

January 1990 = 100

Source: Goldman, Sachs & Company, based on data from the Federal Reserve Bank.

Figure 8. Investment in Equipment, First Quarter 1960 to Fourth Quarter 1996

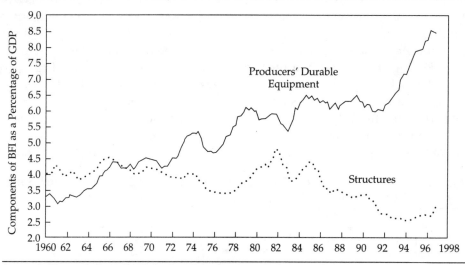

Source: Goldman, Sachs & Company, based on data from the Bureau of Economic Analysis.

sector, which went from heavy-duty metal bending to something a little more complicated. The exponential portion of the curve beginning in 1990 is related to the point in time when the service sector, which has had little measurable productivity change because the government does not know how to measure it, began to spend heavily on equipment; this change accounts for the dramatic upward shift. Seventy percent of computer-related expenditures in the United States since 1990 have come from the service side of the economy.

Financial Services

With the exception of a short period in the 1970s, bank stocks have underperformed the market, but they look attractive now because of several favorable structural changes. First, the downshift in inflation and inflation expectations during the past five years have led to a happy bond market for most of the past five or six years. This benign interest rate environment is good news for financial stocks but will not be a permanent feature.

Second, in the 1980s, discussion centered on whether the banking sector was going out of business, and those stocks got extraordinarily cheap. Now, people recognize that the U.S. banking sector is strong and healthy. Reduced global trade barriers allow U.S. companies to compete outside the United States.

The third structural change in the financial services industry is consolidation. When I started my career as a junior economist at the Federal Reserve, the United States had 16,700 banks; there are now 10,500, which is still a large number. Canada has six. Regulatory changes in the United States have allowed consolidation to go forward, with a significant impact on the investment outlook for these companies.

The fourth structural change is higher demand for financial services. For many reasons, individuals are now in need of companies that can provide them with financial services. One reason is that the Baby Boomers have gotten older and are now buying life insurance and investing for retirement and their children's university educations. Inflation has also affected how individuals save and invest. During a high-inflation environment, such as the 1970s and early 1980s, individual investors had barbell-shaped portfolios: They typically owned residential real estate and short-term fixed income, such as money market mutual funds, and little in between. In a low-inflation environment, there is less demand for tangible assets and more demand for financial assets, particularly long-duration assets. Furthermore, because corporate employers have been shifting to defined-contribution plans from defined-benefit pension schemes since early in the decade, individual employees are now responsible for making the investment decisions. Consequently, the need for financial intermediaries, such as mutual funds, has increased dramatically.

Retail Stocks

Maturing Baby Boomers and milder inflation have combined to slow down consumption growth in the 1990s. Therefore, consumption-related companies no longer generate above-average earnings growth. As a result, the relative performance of retail stocks, in general, has been declining since the early 1990s. In today's environment, some cynics argue that consumers are putting money in mutual funds rather than consuming goods. Nevertheless, specific investment opportunities do exist in the sector, owing to factors such as industry consolidation, attractive niche markets, and strong management.

Commodities

This "Silly Putty," stretched-out economic cycle has also affected whether and when investors want to own commodity-related stocks. In the typical economic cycle, investors knew that they wanted to be heavily exposed to economically sensitive, commodity-sensitive stocks before the cycle reached the top of the "V". Finding that point has been much harder in the current economic cycle, which is underscored by the relatively unimpressive performance of this sector recently. Some might find it surprising that the commodity-sensitive stocks have seen periods of underperformance when the U.S. economy has been growing reasonably well, but the answer is that the United States is no longer the only market. Global capacity utilization rates help track supply/demand trends.

Small-Capitalization Stocks

Another aspect of this slow-moving economy is the performance of small-cap stocks versus large-cap stocks. The S&P 500 has done extremely well but without encouraging the performance of small-cap stocks. This bull market has not been pushed ahead by a vigorous pace of economic growth but by a moderate pace of growth accompanied by moderate inflation in a calm bond market. There has not been much enthusiasm about the pace of aggregate profit generation. Why own small-cap stocks when larger companies may offer more consistent and visible earnings trends? The strong relative performance of large-cap issues has led to the relative undervaluation of smaller-cap stocks.

International Investing

Structural changes in the United States have also had a significant impact on non-U.S. markets. The fastest-growing sector of the U.S. economy since the mid-1980s has been exports, as **Figure 9** shows. Ten years ago, exports were about 5 percent of total GDP. They are now up to about 12 percent, which is a significant increase. For some industries, foreign-related activity is 50 percent or higher. Business fixed investment has been a leading sector for the past five years as corporations have directed much of their capital spending toward labor-productivity-enhancing equipment; its growth rate has been similar to that of exports during this period. The strength of these two sectors has had enormous implications for the way business is conducted.

One reason this cycle has been stretched out is the desynchronization of major economies: When the United States has been strong, many of its foreign trade partners have been weak. For example, Japan and Germany—the world's second and third largest economies—have been sluggish in recent months. When trying to explain the ebbs and flows of the U.S.

Figure 9. Components of U.S. GDP, Fourth Quarter 1987 to Fourth Quarter 1996

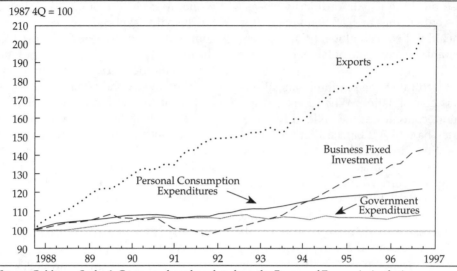

Source: Goldman, Sachs & Company, based on data from the Bureau of Economic Analysis.

economy, many investors focus only on domestic conditions. Yet, the real incremental change may be seen among our trade partners. Another moderating factor in this economic cycle has been the desynchronized pattern of global monetary policy. For example, the United States has followed stimulative monetary policy when other countries followed tight monetary policy, and when the United States moved to tight policy, others moved to stimulative policy.

Foreign participation in the U.S. fixed-income markets increased during much of the 1980s. Non-U.S. investors currently own 6 percent of the total

U.S. equity market, which is not very significant and thus not very influential. The bond market, however, is a different story. Non-U.S. investors own about 15 percent of U.S. corporate bonds and about 28 percent of U.S. Treasury issues. When forecasting U.S. interest rates, one must consider the impact of foreign demand for U.S. Treasury securities.

For the flip side (U.S. investors investing outside the United States), **Figure 10** shows a dramatic trend in the United States toward globalizing portfolios, beginning around 1991. One factor supporting this globalization is the desire for diversification. Another

Figure 10. U.S. Stock Price Performance and Net Purchases of Foreign Equities

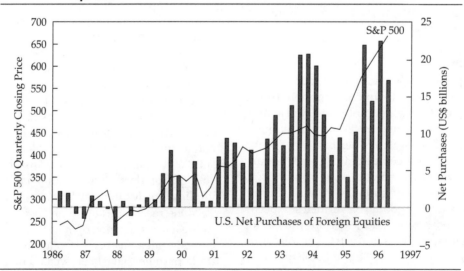

Note: Data for second quarter 1996 are preliminary.

Source: Goldman, Sachs & Company, based on data from the Federal Reserve Board and Standard & Poor's.

©Association for Investment Management and Research

is the belief that investors can get better expected returns and, under the appropriate circumstances, currency exposure in international markets. The correlations between the U.S. market performance and non-U.S. market performance increased dramatically for many markets in 1993 and 1994 because U.S. investors became a more important factor in those markets. A strong relationship exists between good performance in the U.S. market and willingness to invest in foreign markets, attributable to investor confidence. This relationship can have an impact on the other markets because flows outside the United States can increase as they did in 1993 and 1996.

Table 2 shows net U.S. flows into selected foreign equity markets. Notice the small numbers prior to 1991; they reflect a period when U.S. investors were not investing internationally to the extent that they are today. There were significant increases beginning in 1992. Data for 1993 clearly show U.S. investors' enthusiasm for non-U.S. equities. In the second half of that year, 50 percent of the U.S. money invested outside the United States went into the world's smallest markets. U.S. investors were like a big elephant that stuck its foot into a little tub of water. A lot of liquidity going into small markets had a very interesting effect. In 1993, U.S. investors put $6.2 billion to work in Japan and $6.4 billion in Hong Kong (the Japanese market is 10 times larger than the Hong Kong market). One can guess what happened to Hong Kong when U.S. investors went in, and guess what happened when they came out. Thus, a structural change in the United States has had a significant effect on other markets.

CONCLUSION

The structural changes in the U.S. economy have contributed to the very strong equity market. Goldman Sachs' current recommended model portfolio is still bullish but not as bullish as it was 18 months ago. The Dow Jones Industrial Average is now at 6,300, so the valuation is not as attractive as it was. For several years, we thought the market was dramatically undervalued. Now, equities are reasonably priced given the fundamental strengths of the economy and corporations.

Several risks can be identified. The first (a downside risk) is the pace of economic activity. My concern is not the North American economy but the rest of the world. The statistics on exports described earlier explain only part of the picture because they do not take into account the operations that U.S. companies have in other nations and so do not fall into the trade balance numbers. It is not an import/export issue.

Table 2. Net U.S. Flows into Selected Foreign Equity Markets
($ millions)

Market	1987	1988	1989	1990	1991	1992	1993	1994	1995	1996 1Q	1996 2Q[a]
Canada	$2,357	($ 462)	$ 1,267	$ 131	($ 375)	($ 344)	$ 5,121	$ 2,447	($ 228)	$ 1,503	$ 1,476
Total Europe	3,484	1,752	10,294	4,378	14,701	18,094	26,627	16,589	21,014	7,688	10,018
United Kingdom	3,274	406	5,032	1,444	8,299	11,495	11,177	6,165	9,685	2,412	6,585
Germany	(399)	254	393	725	1,521	787	2,705	1,491	382	1,605	826
France	(178)	456	1,948	(292)	1,556	498	2,049	2,077	1,413	997	2,164
Total Latin America	396	(88)	361	2,256	2,662	5,003	12,532	4,062	1,882	668	1,149
Mexico	18	12	8	1,064	2,078	2,765	5,135	1,205	159	305	(165)
Brazil	(6)	149	372	22	326	1,067	1,780	844	1,402	603	817
Argentina	5	(3)	(42)	7	64	12	2,337	1,727	398	69	260
Total Asia	(7,257)	1,046	968	1,832	15,386	8,931	17,234	21,761	26,441	11,707	4,042
Japan	(6,490)	747	974	616	13,922	4,444	6,237	14,715	19,472	7,944	2,617
Hong Kong	(698)	319	(262)	557	1,069	2,832	6,389	2,404	2,179	2,518	108
Malaysia	94	22	27	137	(25)	235	1,101	26	(145)	106	162
Singapore	(32)	(28)	403	527	(165)	508	1,350	9	854	(250)	(132)
Korea	11	(28)	38	(31)	0	466	1,253	1,680	1,637	285	728
Indonesia	0	1	0	27	90	175	302	967	687	22	29
Taiwan	(22)	(19)	(12)	(6)	38	14	80	(111)	155	132	79
India	0	0	0	(1)	3	0	107	422	343	206	114
Thailand	30	134	(3)	42	89	121	48	192	(10)	138	(74)
Mainland China	(2)	1	0	1	0	(4)	107	588	160	64	(12)
The Philippines	(32)	21	7	21	28	219	122	460	491	71	96
Grand total	($1,081)	$1,959	$13,097	$9,205	$31,967	$32,295	$63,340	$47,236	$50,291	$22,240	$17,237

[a]1996 second quarter data are preliminary and are not annualized.

Source: Goldman, Sachs & Company, based on data from the U.S. Department of the Treasury.

Thirty percent of the revenues of S&P 500 companies have to do with activities outside the United States. I am most concerned that the rest of the industrial world still looks pretty punk—economic conditions are sluggish and remain sluggish—which has an impact on the profit outlook.

The second concern is the outlook for future government policies. The United States has enjoyed good policies for several years, although perfection is not a reasonable goal. Fiscal policy has moved in the right direction. Trade policy has focused on opening markets in which U.S. companies enjoy a competitive advantage, such as technology and financial services.

A third issue is the long-term need to invest adequately in technology and education. I am concerned that these priorities may be hurt as politicians strive to reduce the budget deficit further.

U.S. investors typically fixate on the actions of our policymakers—the Federal Reserve, the president, and Congress. Yet, in a global economy, it is wise to pay attention to all the critical policymakers. For example, I believe that decisions made in 1997 by the Japanese and German governments will play an important role in the performance of the U.S. economy and financial markets. This will be true of both monetary and fiscal policies.

The Federal Reserve has already demonstrated its willingness to raise interest rates preemptively during this economic expansion. Unlike previous cycles, when Fed action triggered economic downturns, higher interest rates will likely serve to stretch out the "Silly Putty" cycle still further.

One final observation has to do with the market itself. People have the sense, which is incorrect, that the U.S. stock market always moves in a straight line; that is, it zigs up and zags down, etc. The U.S. stock market, in fact, moves like a staircase. During the past few years, a structural bull market has prevailed that has been driven by structural economic changes in the United States. Even so, the market has not moved straight up. A tendency exists in the S&P 500 and the Dow to experience a notable price increase telescoped into a short period that is followed by a trading range. Since July 1996, an increase of about 15 percent in stock prices has occurred. That period of increase is almost ending, and it will be followed by a trading range, perhaps a choppy trading range. What will determine the start of the next bear market will be the usual factors. The first precondition for a bear market is significant overvaluation, which is not present. The second important precondition is a dramatic deterioration in economic fundamentals—a ramping-up of inflation and a dramatic decline in corporate profits—which is not in the cards for 1997 or 1998 either.

Finally, this analysis is not a science. Those of us in economics and investment management have lots of numbers to work with. We have crackerjack computers and software, and we think that we are scientists. But we are not.

What Determines the Exchange Rate: Economic Factors or Market Sentiment?

Gregory P. Hopper*

Readers of the financial press are familiar with the gyrations of the currency market. No matter which way currencies zig or zag, it seems there is always an analyst with a quotable, ready explanation. Either interest rates are rising faster than expected in some country, or the trade balance is up or down, or central banks are tightening or loosening their monetary policies. Whatever the explanations, the

―――――――

*When this article was written, Greg Hopper was a senior economist in the Research Department of the Philadelphia Fed. He is now in the Credit Analytics Group at Morgan Stanley, Co., Inc., New York.

underlying belief is that exchange rates are affected by fundamental economic forces, such as money supplies, interest rates, real output levels, or the trade balance, which, if well forecasted, give the forecaster an advantage in predicting the exchange rate.

What is not so well known outside academia is that exchange rates don't seem to be affected by economic fundamentals in the short run. Being able to predict money supplies, central bank policies, or other supposed influences doesn't help forecast the exchange rate. Economists have found instead that the best forecast of the exchange rate, at least in the short run, is whatever it happens to be today.

17

In this article, we'll review exchange-rate economics, focusing on what is predictable and what isn't. We'll see that exchange rates seem to be influenced by market sentiment rather than by economic fundamentals, and we'll examine the practical implications of this fact. Sometimes, there are situations in which market participants may be able to forecast the direction but not the timing of the movement. We'll also see that volatility of exchange rates and correlations between exchange rates are predictable, and we'll examine the implications for currency option pricing, risk management, and portfolio selection.

THE EXCHANGE RATE AND ECONOMIC FUNDAMENTALS

The earliest model of the exchange rate, the monetary model, assumes that the current exchange rate is determined by current fundamental economic variables: money supplies and output levels of the countries. When the fundamentals are combined with market expectations of future exchange rates, the model yields the value of the current exchange rate. The monetary model might also be dubbed the "newspaper model." When analyzing movements in the exchange rate, journalists often use the results of the monetary model. Similarly, when Wall Street analysts are asked to justify their exchange-rate predictions, they will typically resort to some variant of the monetary model. This model is popular because it provides intuitive relationships between the economic fundamentals and it's based on standard macroeconomic reasoning.

The reasoning behind the monetary model is simple: the exchange rate is determined by the relative price levels of the two countries. If goods and services cost twice as much, on average, in U.S. dollars as they do in a foreign currency, $2 will fetch one unit of the foreign currency. That way, the same goods and services will cost the same whether they are bought in the U.S. or in the foreign country.[1]

But what determines the relative price levels of the two countries? The monetary model focuses on the demand and supply of money. If the money supply in the United States rises, but nothing else changes, the average level of prices in the United States will tend to rise. Since the price level in the foreign country remains fixed, more dollars will be needed to get one unit of foreign currency. Hence, the dollar price of the foreign currency will rise: the dollar will depreciate--it's worth less in terms of the foreign currency.

Money supplies are not the only economic fundamentals in the monetary model. The level of real output in each country matters as well because it affects the price level. For example, if the level of output in the United States rises, but other fundamental factors, such as the U.S. money supply, remain constant, the average level of prices in the United States will tend to fall, producing an appreciation in the dollar.[2] Future economic fundamentals also matter because they determine the market's expectations about the future exchange rate. Not surprisingly, market expectations of the future exchange rate matter for the current exchange rate. If the market expects the dollar price of the yen to become higher in the future than it is today, the dollar price of the yen will tend to be high today. But if the market expects the dollar price of the yen to be lower in the future than it is today, the dollar price of the yen will tend to be low today.

Here's an example of how to use the monetary model: suppose we wanted to predict the

[1]When purchasing power parity holds, particular goods and services cost the same amount in the domestic country as they do in the foreign country. There is an extensive literature that documents that purchasing power parity doesn't hold except perhaps in the very long run.

[2]In the monetary model, the price level must fall in this situation to ensure that money demanded by consumers is the same as money supplied by the central bank.

FEDERAL RESERVE BANK OF PHILADELPHIA

dollar-yen exchange rate. The first thing we need to do is think about the relationships between the fundamentals and the exchange rate. The monetary model implies that if the U.S. money supply is growing faster than the Japanese money supply, the dollar price of the yen will rise: the dollar will depreciate and the yen will appreciate. So, the analyst needs to assess monetary policy in the two countries. The monetary model also implies that if output is growing faster in the United States than it is in Japan, the dollar price of the yen will tend to fall: the dollar will appreciate and the yen will depreciate. Finally, the analyst must assess expectations about the future exchange rate. If the market's expectation of the future exchange rate were to change, the current exchange rate would move in the same direction. When making an exchange-rate forecast based on the monetary model, the analyst must consider the effect of all the fundamentals simultaneously. He can do this by using a statistical model or by combining judgment with the use of a statistical model.

In practice, using the monetary model to make exchange-rate forecasts is difficult because the analyst never knows the true value of the economic fundamentals. At any time, money supply and output levels are not known with certainty; they must be forecast based on the available economic data. Of course, expectations about the future of the exchange rate are even harder to assess because these expectations are unobservable. The analyst can always survey market participants about their expectations, but he can never be sure if the surveys accurately reflect the market's views. If we assume the monetary model is valid, the goal of the successful exchange-rate forecaster is to predict the values of the fundamentals better than the competition and then use the monetary model or some variant to derive forecasts of the exchange rate.

The fatal flaw in this strategy is the assumption that the monetary model can be used to successfully forecast the exchange rate once the values of the fundamentals are known. Although the monetary model had some early success, economists have established that the model fails empirically except perhaps in unusual periods such as hyperinflations.[3] For one thing, research did not establish a strong statistical relationship between exchange rates and the values of the fundamentals. Moreover, a key assumption of the model was found to be false: the model assumes that the price level can move freely. Yet the price level seems to be "sticky," meaning that it moves very slowly compared with the movement of the exchange rate.

What about other models? After the failure of the monetary model became apparent, economists went to work developing other ideas. Rudiger Dornbusch developed a variant of the monetary model called *the overshooting model,* in which the average level of prices is assumed to be fixed in the short run to reflect the real-world finding that many prices don't change frequently. The effect of this assumption is to cause the exchange rate to overshoot its long-run value as a result of a change in the fundamentals; eventually, however, the exchange rate returns to its long-run value. Ultimately, this model was shown to fail empirically: economists couldn't find the strong statistical relationships between the fundamentals and the exchange rate that should exist if the model were true.[4]

Another extension of the simple monetary model is called *the portfolio balance model.* In this approach, the supply of and demand for foreign and domestic bonds, along with the

---

[3]See the papers by Frenkel (1976, 1980), Bilson (1978), and Hodrick (1978) for empirical analysis of the monetary model.

[4]For an empirical treatment of the overshooting model, see the paper by Backus (1984).

supply of and demand for foreign and domestic money, determine the exchange rate. Early tests of the model were not very encouraging.[5] Later, economists formulated a more sophisticated version of the portfolio balance model, in which investors were assumed to choose a portfolio of domestic and foreign bonds in an optimal way. According to the more sophisticated portfolio balance theory, the degree to which investors are willing to substitute domestic for foreign bonds depends on how much investors dislike risk, how volatile the returns on the bonds are, and the extent to which the returns on the different bonds in the portfolio move together. Unfortunately, economists did not find much empirical support for the more sophisticated version of the portfolio balance model.[6]

Economic News. Thus, the three major models of the exchange rate—the monetary, the overshooting, and the portfolio balance models—do not provide a satisfactory account of the exchange rate. Nonetheless, it is possible that *news about the fundamentals* affects the exchange rate even if the fundamentals themselves don't influence the exchange rate in the manner suggested by the three major exchange rate models.

The news about the fundamentals can be defined as the difference between what market participants expect the fundamentals to be and what the fundamentals actually are once their values are announced. For example, market participants form expectations about the value of the money supply before the government announces the money supply figures, and

these expectations are translated into decisions to buy or sell currency. These decisions ultimately help to determine the current level of the exchange rate. Once the government announces the value of the money supply, market participants buy or sell currencies as long as the news is different from what they expected. Thus, news about fundamentals, under this view, is an important determinant of the exchange rate.

The difficulty in testing this view is that economists don't know how to measure the news because they don't know how to measure the market's expectations. One solution is to assume that market participants form their expectations using a statistical device called linear regression. Using linear regression, an econometrician could estimate the expected level of a fundamental, such as the U.S. money supply, for each quarter during the past 20 years. He could then subtract the value of the estimated expected money supply from its actual value in each quarter to generate an estimate of the news about the quarterly U.S. money supply. The news for other fundamentals can be estimated in a similar way.

Once the econometrician has estimated each fundamental's news for each quarter during the last 20 years, he can check to see if it explains the level of the exchange rate. Studies by economists who have carried out this procedure generally indicate that news about the fundamentals explains the exchange rate better than the three major exchange-rate models.[7] However, two factors make this result hard to interpret. First, we have no direct evidence suggesting that market participants form their expectations using linear regression models or that they form their expectations as if they were using these models. Second, these

---

[5]See, for example, the paper by Branson, Halttunen, and Masson (1977).

[6]See the papers by Frankel (1982) and Lewis (1988) for empirical analysis of the more sophisticated portfolio balance model. The fundamental problem with the model is that investors must have an implausibly high aversion to risk to explain the exchange rate.

[7]For empirical analysis of news models, see the papers by Branson (1983), Edwards (1982, 1983), and MacDonald (1983).

FEDERAL RESERVE BANK OF PHILADELPHIA

studies use the final values of the fundamentals, values released by governments months, if not years, after the forecasts were made. Yet, forecasters must use the government's preliminary estimates of the fundamentals when they make their predictions. In other words, the econometrician is assuming that market participants are making forecasts using information they don't have. Hence, the result that news about the fundamentals seems to explain the level of the exchange rate better than the models is hard to interpret.

One way to avoid the problem of using final values of fundamentals is to collect the initial estimates from newspapers, government announcements, and wire services and examine their ability to affect the level of the exchange rate. Studies that have done this have found that *announcements about fundamentals* affect the exchange rate only in the very short run: the effects of announcements generally disappear after a day or two.

When we look at the evidence from the three major exchange-rate models, from the news analysis, and from the effects of announcements, it is hard not to be pessimistic about the fundamentals' ability to explain the exchange rate. But the evidence we have examined so far is backward-looking: the fundamentals don't seem to explain exchange-rate behavior over the past couple of decades. However, we can also do a forward-looking analysis: do the fundamentals help us forecast the level of the exchange rate?

The surprising answer to this question, given by economists Richard Meese and Kenneth Rogoff in the early 1980s, is no. Meese and Rogoff examined the ability of the fundamentals to predict the level of the exchange rate for horizons up to one year. They considered fundamentals-based economic models as well as statistical models of the relationship between the fundamentals and the exchange rate that did not incorporate economic assumptions. They found that a *naive strategy* of using today's

exchange rate as a forecast works at least as well as any of the economic or statistical models. Worse, they found that when they endowed the economic or statistical models with final values of the fundamentals—giving the models an advantage that forecasters could not possibly match—the naive strategy still won the forecasting contest. Despite many attempts since the publication of Meese and Rogoff's results, economists have not convincingly overturned their findings.

Thus, if we look backward or forward over periods of up to a year, the fundamentals don't seem to explain the exchange rate, contrary to what standard models in international finance textbooks imply. But this result might be dismissed by claiming that only the models tested have failed to explain the exchange rate. Perhaps economists will discover a model that works in the future.

Although a fundamentals-based model that works is a possibility, evidence from other countries suggests otherwise. In the European Exchange Rate Mechanism (ERM), exchange rates between major European currencies are kept relatively stable by the countries' central banks. If fundamentals are closely associated with the currencies, they should be stabilized as well. However, when we examine European fundamentals, we find that they fluctuate about as much as do the fundamentals of nonstabilized currencies, such as the U.S. dollar. Hence, the evidence from the European experience does not suggest a close connection between the fundamentals and the exchange rate, leading one to suspect that no fundamentals-based model will predict the short-run exchange rate.[8]

It's possible that the fundamentals really do explain the exchange rate, but we can't see the relationship because we can't observe the true fundamentals. Perhaps if economists discov-

---

[8]See Rose (1994) for a detailed discussion of this point.

ered different economic models that use fundamentals other than money supplies and real output levels, the exchange rate could still be explained in terms of basic economic quantities. For example, some economic models imply that the true fundamentals are business technologies and tastes and preferences of consumers. However, the evidence from European countries renders this potential solution implausible. According to such a model, stabilization of European currencies in the ERM corresponds to stabilization of the true fundamentals. But why should business technologies and tastes and preferences of consumers change less in Europe than they do in the United States? At present, economists have found no evidence to suggest they do and, indeed, have little reason to suppose that they will ever find such evidence.

THE ALTERNATIVE VIEW: MARKET SENTIMENT MATTERS

The alternative view is that exchange rates are determined, at least in the short run (i.e., periods less than two years), by *market sentiment*. Under this view, the level of the exchange rate is the result of a self-fulfilling prophecy: participants in the foreign exchange market expect a currency to be at a certain level in the future; when they act on their expectations and buy or sell the currency, it ends up at the predicted level, confirming their expectations.

Even if exchange rates are determined by market sentiment in the short run, the fundamentals are still important, but not in the commonly supposed way. From reading the newspapers, we know that market participants take the fundamentals very seriously when forming exchange-rate expectations. Thus, if we wish to understand the level of the exchange rate, we need to know the values of the fundamentals and, more important, how market participants interpret those levels. However, the evidence we reviewed shows no pattern or necessary connection between the fundamentals and the level of the exchange rate. When market participants use the fundamentals to form expectations about the exchange rate, they don't use them in any consistent way that could be picked up by an economic or statistical model. As we have seen, we can do as well forecasting the exchange rate by quoting today's rate.

Although the naive forecast is at least as accurate as statistical or model-based forecasts, it's still not very good. It's just that statistical or model-based forecasts are so bad that even the naive forecast can do at least as well. How can we improve our forecast? Unfortunately, economists are just starting to build models of market sentiment, so we can't get much guidance from economic theory just yet. Nonetheless, we know that exchange rates are likely determined by market sentiment, so it seems reasonable to try to understand the psychology of the foreign exchange market to improve forecasts of the short-run exchange rate.

To understand the psychology of the foreign exchange market, we need to know about the various economic theories. Even if they aren't very accurate, their implications may still influence expectations in the market, although we would not expect any particular model to have any consistent influence. We also need to find out what the market is thinking. Probably the best way to do so is to be an active participant in the foreign exchange market and to talk to other participants to learn which events they think are important for a particular currency's outlook. These events might be announcements of fundamentals, political events, or some other factors. The analyst could then concentrate on forecasting those events. Of course, there will probably be no pattern to which events are important. For example, the U.S. budget deficit may well be important for the dollar one year and unimportant the next.

Speculative Attacks. In some cases, the forecaster might be able to make a reasonable guess about the direction of the exchange rate's

22

movement, even if he can't be precise about the timing. As an example, let's review what happened to the exchange rate between the Swedish krona and the German deutsche mark in the early 1990s.

Sweden applied to enter the ERM in May 1991 in a bid to stabilize its currency. To stabilize the krona-deutsche mark exchange rate, interest rates in Sweden and Germany had to be the same. Therefore, the Swedish and German central banks couldn't independently use monetary policy—that is, change short-term interest rates—if they wanted to keep the exchange rate stable.[9] If Sweden wanted to act independently, it had to use fiscal policy (tax and government spending policies) to stimulate the country's growth rate.

However, a weak Swedish economy provoked speculators, who mounted an attack on the krona in September 1992. Speculators knew that the weak economy would tempt Sweden to abandon its fixed exchange rate and use monetary policy to cut short-term interest rates, especially since the new Swedish government was adopting restrictive fiscal policy. Speculators believed that if the Swedish central bank cut the short-term interest rate, the krona wouldn't be as attractive to investors. Thus, the speculators thought that after interest rates were cut, the currency would depreciate with respect to other ERM currencies. But since speculators expected the depreciation to happen, they decided to sell the currency immediately, i.e., mount a speculative attack on the currency.

This attack put the Swedish central bank in an uncomfortable position. To combat the currency's depreciation, the central bank raised short-term interest rates temporarily to repel

the speculative attack—exactly the policy it didn't want in the face of sluggish economic growth. In fact, the Swedish central bank raised the short-term interest rate to an astonishing 500 percent and held it there for four days.[10]

The speculators were deterred, but not for long. The speculators understood that the Swedish central bank had to raise short-term interest rates temporarily to support the currency. But they were betting that the central bank wouldn't fight off the attack for long, especially in the face of disquiet in the country resulting from weak economic growth and the higher interest rates needed to fight the speculative attack. The high short-term interest rates had made the economic situation in Sweden even more precarious, so, in November, the speculators attacked again, selling the krona in favor of other ERM currencies. This time the Swedish central bank did not aggressively raise interest rates and the krona depreciated.

Profit opportunities such as this one can sometimes be exploited by speculators who recognize that a country's exchange-rate policy is inconsistent with the monetary policy needed, given a country's domestic situation. By paying careful attention to a country's economic and political developments, a speculator can sometimes forecast the direction of a

---

[9]If a central bank can't change the short-term interest rate independently, it can't use monetary policy independently to stimulate the economy. Hence, countries with stabilized exchange rates must give up the independent use of monetary policy.

[10]If speculators expect the value of the currency to fall, and they are right, speculators can profit by selling the currency short. As an example, suppose a speculator anticipates that the value of the Swedish krona with respect to the deutsche mark will fall in one week. The speculator could borrow krona and sell them for deutsche marks at the current exchange rate. If the speculator is correct and the krona does depreciate, at the end of the week the speculator can buy back the krona for fewer deutsche marks than he sold them for. Provided the krona fell enough over the week, the speculator can repay the loan with interest and make a profit in deutsche marks. However, if the central bank makes short-term interest rates high enough, it can make this transaction unprofitable. Thus, one defense against a speculative attack is to dramatically raise short-term interest rates.

23

currency's move when it breaks out of a stabilized exchange rate system. But the timing is not easily forecast; it is probably determined by market sentiment.[11]

WHAT ABOUT TECHNICAL RULES?

Many market participants don't rely on the fundamentals. Instead, they use technical rules, which are procedures for identifying patterns in exchange rates. A simple technical rule involves looking at interest rates in two countries. Suppose the first country is the United States and the second is Canada. If the one-month U.S. interest rate is higher than the one-month rate in Canada, the U.S. dollar will tend to appreciate with respect to the Canadian dollar. But if the one-month Canadian interest rate is higher, the U.S. dollar will tend to depreciate with respect to the Canadian dollar. Economists and foreign exchange participants have often noted this fact.[12]

Indeed, it is possible to make money, on average, by using this rule. The problem is that implementing this rule carries risk. There is an ongoing debate about how big this risk is, and whether the average profits are explained by the level of risk. After all, it would not be surprising that the market pays a premium to those willing to assume substantial risk. Furthermore, the profits may have occurred only by chance and may not recur. Sometimes, economists report other technical rules that seem to make money in the foreign exchange market.[13] However, the considerations noted in the interest-rate differential rule apply to any tech-

nical rule. Even if the rule makes profits on average, the profits might be explained by the level of risk assumed in applying the rule. Moreover, the profits may well disappear when we account for technical statistical problems. Since economists are undecided at present about whether technical rules really do make money, it seems prudent to be cautious when evaluating the merits of any such rule.

WHAT ABOUT LONG-RUN FORECASTING?

Even though economic models or the fundamentals don't help us understand the exchange rate in the short run (except to the extent that they influence market psychology), there is evidence that models do better in the long run. For example, economists Martin Eichenbaum and Charles Evans report that currencies react as theory would suggest to unanticipated movements in the money supply, but only in the long run, after a period of about two years. Standard monetary theories would imply that an unanticipated decline in the U.S. money supply would lead to an appreciation of the dollar with respect to other currencies. Eichenbaum and Evans found that the dollar does, in fact, appreciate in response to an unanticipated monetary contraction; however, the full effects on the dollar are not registered until two years after the contraction, suggesting that models may well work in explaining the exchange rate in the long run.[14]

IS ANY ASPECT OF THE EXCHANGE RATE PREDICTABLE IN THE SHORT RUN?

Although the level of the exchange rate in the short run is not very predictable, volatilities and correlations of currencies are much

---

[11]For further discussion of the myriad problems that can arise when countries attempt to fix their exchange rates, see the article by Obstfeld and Rogoff (1995).

[12]See my 1994 *Business Review* article for a nontechnical discussion.

[13]For an example, see Sweeney (1986).

---

[14]For further evidence on the effects of unanticipated monetary contractions on the exchange rate, see Schlagenhauf and Wrase (1995).

FEDERAL RESERVE BANK OF PHILADELPHIA

more predictable. The daily volatility of a currency measures the extent to which the currency's value in terms of another currency fluctuates each day. The value of high-volatility currencies fluctuates more each day than that of low-volatility currencies. Correlations measure the extent to which currencies move together. In general, volatilities and correlations vary with time, rising or falling each day in a somewhat predictable way.

The time-varying nature of the daily volatility of the dollar in terms of the deutsche mark can be seen in the figure. Notice that, in 1991, days on which the volatility of the dollar is high tend to cluster together, and in 1990, days with lower volatility follow one another. Since daily volatility clusters together, it is predictable. If we want to predict tomorrow's volatility, we need only look at the recent past. If daily volatility has been high over the recent past, we can be reasonably sure that it will be high tomorrow.

This idea forms the basis for statistical mod-

els of a currency's volatility. The GARCH model, developed by economist Tim Bollerslev, who built on work by economist Robert Engle, uses the volatility-clustering phenomenon to predict future volatility. In essence, a GARCH model measures the strength of the relationship between recent volatility and current volatility. Once this strength is known, it can be used to forecast volatility. GARCH models have good empirical support for exchange rates and are being used in practical applications in the foreign exchange market.[15]

GARCH models can be extended to handle two or more currencies, and they can measure the strength of recent correlations in predict-

---

[15]GARCH stands for Generalized Autoregressive Conditional Heteroskedasticity. For the technical details of how GARCH models work, see Bollerslev (1986). Examples of technical applications of GARCH models of exchange rates include Bollerslev (1990) and Kroner and Sultan (1993). Heynen and Kat (1994) use GARCH to forecast volatility.

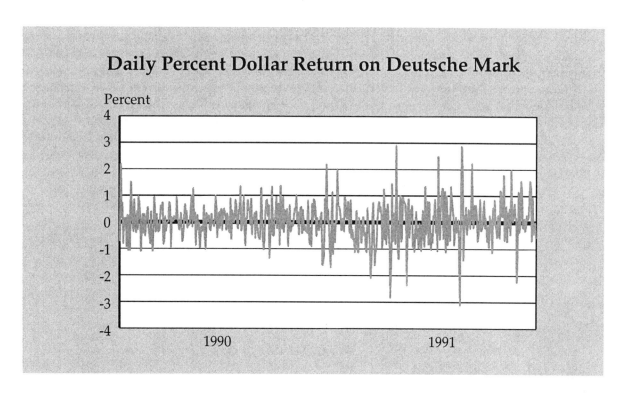

Daily Percent Dollar Return on Deutsche Mark

ing current ones. Once this strength is understood, it can be used to forecast correlations.

USES OF VOLATILITY AND CORRELATION FORECASTS

Volatility and correlation forecasts have important uses in finance. First, currency derivatives, securities whose value depends on the value of currencies, require measures of volatility and sometimes correlations to price them. GARCH models can supply estimates of these volatilities and correlations. Second, volatilities of individual currencies coupled with correlations between currencies can be combined to determine the volatility of a portfolio of currencies. Since the volatility of a portfolio measures the extent to which the portfolio's value fluctuates, the volatility can be used to assess a portfolio's risk. Portfolios with higher volatilities are riskier because they have a tendency to lose more per day—or gain more per day—than do portfolios with lower volatilities (see *Using GARCH to Measure Portfolio Risk*). Finally, knowledge of volatilities and correlations can help an investor choose the proportions of each currency to hold in a portfolio. For example, knowing a portfolio's volatilities and correlations may show an investor how to rearrange

Using GARCH to Measure Portfolio Risk

Here, we illustrate the use of a GARCH model to manage risk in a simple portfolio of two currencies, the yen and the deutsche mark. Using daily data on the yen and the deutsche mark from January 2, 1981, to June 30, 1996, the time-varying volatilities and correlations were estimated using Engle and Lee's (1993a,b) GARCH model. Suppose we have a portfolio with $1 million invested in yen and $1 million invested in deutsche marks. Then we can calculate the value at risk (VaR) of the portfolio. The VaR is the maximum loss the portfolio will experience a certain fraction of the time during a specific period. For example, we can see from the table that daily VaR at the 95 percent confidence level is $12,000. That means that 95 percent of the time, the largest daily loss on the portfolio will be $12,000. But 5 percent of the time, the loss will be bigger, sometimes by a substantial amount. The daily loss measures the difference between the value of the portfolio at the end of one trading day and its value at the end of the next trading day.

As another example, consider weekly VaR at the 98 percent confidence interval. The numbers indicate that 98 percent of the time, the loss over five trading days will not exceed $35,000. But 2 percent of the time, the losses will be bigger. See Hopper (1996) for more discussion.

Value at Risk of a Currency Portfolio with $1 Million Invested in Both Yen and Deutsche marks

	One-Day Horizon	Five-Day Horizon
95 percent	$12,000	$27,000
98 percent	$15,000	$35,000
99 percent	$18,000	$41,000

These numbers for the value at risk apply to the risk in the portfolio on July 1, 1996, the day after the end of the data period. However, the reason for using a GARCH model is that volatility varies over time. The value at risk would be higher in times of greater volatility and lower when the market is less volatile.

the proportions of currencies in a portfolio so that he has the same return, on average, but a lower risk of loss.

CONCLUSION

The evidence discussed in this article suggests that economic models and indeed fundamental economic quantities are not very useful in explaining the history of the exchange rate or in forecasting its value over the next year or so. This fact has important implications for market participants. It is all too common to encounter private-sector foreign exchange economists who tell very cogent stories designed to buttress their short-term forecasts for the values of currencies. These stories are often based on plausible economic assumptions or models. These economists hope that market participants will act on their forecasts and trade currencies. However, if these forecasts are justified by a belief that economic models or fundamentals influence the exchange rate in the short run, it's likely they are not very good. Indeed, we have seen that these forecasts will probably be outperformed by the naive forecast: tomorrow's exchange rate will be what it is today.

On the other hand, to the extent that these forecasts reflect market sentiment or a self-fulfilling prophecy, they may be useful. Unfortunately, it is difficult to judge when this is the case. The difficulty is accentuated by the unobservability of market expectations. A forecaster might be using a model he believes in, and his forecast might turn out to be correct if the market also temporarily believes the implications of the model. But it is hard, if not impossible, to know what the market expects; hence, it is hard to judge the merits of a forecast.

Fortunately, the situation is better regarding volatilities and correlations, which follow predictable patterns. The GARCH model and its more sophisticated variants can be used to price derivatives, assess currency portfolio risk, and set allocations of currencies in portfolios. Economists are continually discovering new empirical facts about volatility and correlations. No doubt the GARCH model will eventually be supplanted by an alternative, but for now, economists will use the GARCH model, or some variation of it, to forecast volatilities and correlations of currencies.

REFERENCES

Backus, David. "Empirical Models of the Exchange Rate: Separating the Wheat from the Chaff," *Canadian Journal of Economics* (1984), pp. 824-46.

Bilson, John. "The Monetary Approach to the Exchange Rate—Some Empirical Evidence," IMF *Staff Papers*, 25 (1978), pp. 48-75.

Bollerslev, Tim. "Generalized Autoregressive Conditional Heteroskedasticity," *Journal of Econometrics*, 31 (1986), pp. 307-27.

Bollerslev, Tim. "Modelling the Coherence in Short-Run Nominal Exchange Rates: A Multivariate Generalized ARCH Model," *Review of Economics and Statistics*, 72 (1990), pp. 498-505.

27

REFERENCES (continued)

Branson, William. "Macroeconomic Determinants of Real Exchange Rate Risks," in R.J. Herring, ed., *Managing Foreign Exchange Risk*. Cambridge, U.K.: Cambridge University Press, 1983.

Branson, William, Hannu Halttunen, and Paul Masson. "Exchange Rates in the Short Run: The Dollar-Deutschemark Rate," *European Economic Review*, 10 (1977), pp. 303-24.

Dornbusch, Rudiger. "Expectations and Exchange Rate Dynamics," *Journal of Political Economy*, 84 (1976), pp. 1161-76.

Edwards, Sebastian. "Exchange Rates and News: A Multi-Currency Approach," *Journal of International Money and Finance*, 1 (1982), pp. 211-24.

Edwards, Sebastian. "Floating Exchange Rates, Expectations, and New Information," *Journal of Monetary Economics*, 11, (1983), pp. 321-36.

Eichenbaum, Martin, and Charles Evans. "Some Empirical Evidence on the Effects of Monetary Policy Shocks on Exchange Rates," NBER Working Paper 4271 (1993).

Engle, Robert F. "Autoregressive Conditional Heteroskedasticity with Estimates of the Variance of U.K. Inflation," *Econometrica*, 50 (1982), pp. 987-1008.

Engle R., and G. Lee. "A Permanent and Transitory Component Model of Stock Return Volatility," Discussion Paper 92-44R, Department of Economics, University of California, San Diego (1993a).

Engle R., and G. Lee. "Long Run Volatility Forecasting for Individual Stocks in a One Factor Model," Discussion Paper 93-30, Department of Economics, University of California, San Diego (1993b).

Frankel, Jeffrey. "In Search of the Exchange Rate Risk Premium: A Six Currency Test Assuming Mean-Variance Optimization," *Journal of International Money and Finance*, 1 (1982), pp. 255-74.

Frenkel, Jacob. "A Monetary Approach to the Exchange Rate: Doctrinal Aspects and Empirical Evidence," *Scandinavian Journal of Economics*, 78 (1976), pp. 200-24.

Frenkel, Jacob. "Exchange Rates, Prices, and Money: Lessons From the 1920s," *American Economic Review*, 70 (1980), pp. 235-42.

Heynen, Ronald C., and Harry M. Kat. "Volatility Prediction: A Comparison of the Stochastic Volatility, GARCH (1,1), and EGARCH (1,1) Models," *The Journal of Derivatives*, 2 (1994), pp. 50-65.

Hodrick, Robert. "An Empirical Analysis of the Monetary Approach to the Exchange Rate," in J. Frenkel and H.G. Johnson, eds., *The Economics of Exchange Rates*. Reading, Mass.: Addison Wesley, 1978, pp. 97-116.

Hopper, Greg. "Is the Foreign Exchange Market Inefficient?" Federal Reserve Bank of Philadelphia *Business Review* (May/June 1994).

Hopper, Greg. "Value at Risk: A New Methodology For Measuring Portfolio Risk," Federal Reserve Bank of Philadelphia *Business Review* (July/August 1996).

Kroner, Kenneth F., and Jahangir Sultan, "Time-Varying Distributions and Dynamic Hedging with Foreign Currency Futures," *Journal of Financial and Quantitative Analysis*, 28 (1993), pp. 535-51.

Lewis, Karen. "Testing the Portfolio Balance Model: A Multi-lateral Approach," *Journal of International Economics*, 7 (1988), pp. 273-88.

MacDonald, Ronald. "Some Tests of the Rational Expectations Hypothesis in the Foreign Exchange Markets," *Scottish Journal of Political Economy*, 30 (1983), pp. 235-50.

Meese, Richard, and Kenneth Rogoff. "Empirical Exchange Rate Models of the 1970s: Do They Fit Out of Sample?" *Journal of International Economics*, 14 (1983), pp. 3-24.

Obstfeld, Maurice, and Kenneth Rogoff. "The Mirage of Fixed Exchange Rates," *Journal of Economic Perspectives*, 9 (1995), pp. 73-96.

Rose, Andrew. "Are Exchange Rates Macroeconomic Phenomena?" Federal Reserve Bank of San Francisco *Economic Review*, 1 (1994), pp. 19-30.

Schlagenhauf, Don, and Jeffrey Wrase. "Liquidity and Real Activity in a Simple Open Economy Model," *Journal of Monetary Economics*, 35 (1995), pp. 431-61.

Sweeney, Richard J. "Beating the Foreign Exchange Market," *Journal of Finance* (1986), pp. 163-82.

29

The Nature of Effective Forecasts

David B. Bostian, Jr., CFA
Chief Economist and Investment Strategist
Herzog, Heine, Geduld, Inc.

Any technique for making economic forecasts should have a discipline to help avoid psychological pitfalls and those related to erroneous data and theories. A discipline serves as a frame of reference to force the forecaster to identify decision points. This discipline is required to take available data and bring them into coherent focus.

Forecasting is both a science and an art. On the surface, that statement does not sound very profound. But the longer you are in this business, the more you will see the truth in it. No sure technique and no one econometric model can forecast the economy or select individual stocks, construct portfolios, or even allocate assets. At some point, a model that has worked well in the past will suddenly cease working. This is primarily because in forecasting, we are dealing with human behavior.

You should read the *Economic Report of the President*, published annually by the Government Printing Office, not only for its substance but also for its interweaving of politics and economics. Economics is political. It is not a quantitative or statistical discipline that can be analyzed in a vacuum, free from what happens on the political front.

Over the years, these economic reports have varied substantially in their degree of cockiness or humility. The following is from the 1992 *Economic Report*: "Economic forecasting is an imprecise science. . . . Unexpected events and policy changes can cause actual events to be substantially different from the forecast. Forecasts are based largely on predictions about human behavior, usually taking previous patterns of behavior as a guide. But human behavior is complex, difficult to predict, and subject to change. People do not always respond the same way, or with the same speed, in what appear to be similar circumstances. Hence, uncertainty remains about the outlook for the economy." Having this statement come from the *Economic Report of the President* is important because it emphasizes the art of forecasting. It has a human element.

The art-form aspect of forecasting reflects the blending of statistical facts with judgments about human behavior based on insights derived from both experience and intuition. One might conjecture, as we develop fifth-generation computers and artificial intelligence systems, that the science element will become more dominant. An intriguing article in a recent issue of the *Financial Analysts Journal* pointed out the exciting potential of using "fuzzy neural systems" for forecasting.[1] These systems use fifth-generation computers and artificial intelligence, in which the machine starts to think, possibly even in the irrational ways humans think. Conceivably, we will develop fuzzy neural systems for forecasting the economy, and maybe then it will become more science than art. This remains to be seen.

Forecasting the economic cycle is the dominant challenge. Forecasting interest rates and inflation is important, but they derive from the movement of the economic cycle itself. The data that go into the forecast are a tremendous challenge in timeliness. To have any element of science, you must grapple with data, and a major challenge is to determine the data's quality. Assume you have developed some data that appear to forecast the economy, interest rates, or inflation. The validity of the data deteriorates over time. For example, about a decade ago, many people focused on weekly money supply figures. Using these figures, they tried to figure out whether to buy or sell stocks and bonds or the implications for the economy. We have moved away from money supply figures and now look at payroll employment or other data. Eventually forecasts will be proven wrong because we are dealing with a human element and/or erroneous data.

[1]F.S. Wong, P.Z. Wang, T.H. Goh, and B.K. Quek, "Fuzzy Neural Systems for Stock Selection," *Financial Analysts Journal* (January/February 1992):47–52, 74.

5

Understanding Risks in Economic Forecasting

Many economic forecasters fail because of three human weaknesses. First is *linear perception*—the human tendency to remember the past and extrapolate it into the future in a straight line. The stock market went up from 1982 to 1987, with similar trends for the bond market, corporate profits, and so forth. Events since autumn 1987 make obvious that most things do not move in straight lines.

Second is *group think*. This deals with the human tendency to want to feel comfortable. Whether economists, strategists, or analysts, people tend to gravitate toward a consensus view because it is comfortable. The problem is the risk that comes from subconsciously gravitating into a consensus view because you do not want to appear to be an outsider.

The third human weakness is the *messenger syndrome*. If the message is good, this is not necessarily a problem, but in Greek and Roman times, the messenger who brought bad news to the emperor was "shot" (i.e., speared). Many economists had given up forecasting a recession by late 1989 and early 1990 to avoid the discomfort of delivering unpleasant messages that had repeatedly proven incorrect.

Another type of risk in economic forecasting is the data. Erroneous data can lead to trouble no matter how sophisticated the model or skilled the intuition about the data. For example, the financial press carried much commentary about how, as the current recession approached, the Labor Department was creating phantom jobs by extrapolating the past into the future based on newly started businesses. Based on this information, the Commerce Department decided these jobs created personal income, and if personal income was growing, the economy was healthy. Unfortunately, the whole concept was a statistical mirage. Michael Boskin, chairman of President Bush's Council of Economic Advisers, has spearheaded an effort to upgrade the accuracy of government statistics. That may do as much for our ability to have better forecasts in the future as anything mentioned thus far.

A third type of risk in economic forecasting is faulty economic theories. Not every economic theory is false, but the truth is so complex in an advanced economy in which many humans have different dispositions that no single economic theory can encompass everything. Thus, we have many economic theories. Keynesian economics, for example, basically deals with government spending. With the deficit at its current size, the government cannot stimulate the economy as it did in the past. Another theory, monetarist economics, focuses on money supply: The growth rate of the monetary aggregates is the primary determinate of economic growth, the rate of inflation, and so forth. Milton Friedman, based on his monetary observations, forecasted in the mid-1980s soaring inflation and a relapse into recession. This forecast preceded a period of economic growth and declining inflation. Still other economists cling to supply-side economics.

Many economists develop their own economic theory, and mine is called productivity economics, which appears alien to other theories. This approach emphasizes knowledge, motivation, investment, and energy as the driving forces of economic growth. It could be called liberal arts economics. To understand and forecast the economy, do not look at it in Keynesian, monetary, or supply-side frameworks; try to figure out how the economy really works. It functions because of knowledge, motivation, and investment—whether in people, plant, or machinery—and in inverse relation to the cost of energy.

Effective Economic Forecasts

To be effective, an economic forecast must be reasonably accurate. Any forecasting technique for the economy should have a discipline to help avoid psychological pitfalls and those related to erroneous data and theories. This does not contradict my commentary about the importance of art or judgment or even intuition in the forecasting process. Instead, a discipline serves as a frame of reference to force the forecaster to identify decision points. Some discipline is needed to take whatever data are available and bring them into coherent focus.

The discipline I use, the Macro-Economic Index (MEI), consists of 26 independent economic variables. Its record is exceptional in signaling both recessions and recoveries. **Figure 1** is the monthly plot of the MEI since 1950. The top panel shows the coincident economic index, which is based on industrial production, employees on nonagricultural payrolls, and so forth. It is a real-time measure of the economy, much more so than gross national product (GNP) or gross domestic product (GDP). The shaded bands represent recessions as officially defined after the fact by the National Bureau of Economic Research (NBER).

The MEI represents an attempt to avoid the pitfalls most economists encounter. It differs from the government's Leading Economic Indicators (LEI) by incorporating a wider array of data—26 components as opposed to 11—including measures of interest rates and profits, and using a rate-of-change rather than cumulative basis to calculate the components.

The lower panel of Figure 1 shows how the cyclical turning points are identified. Based on history,

6

Figure 1. Composite Index of Four Coincident Indicators
(with Bostian Macro-Economic Index signals)

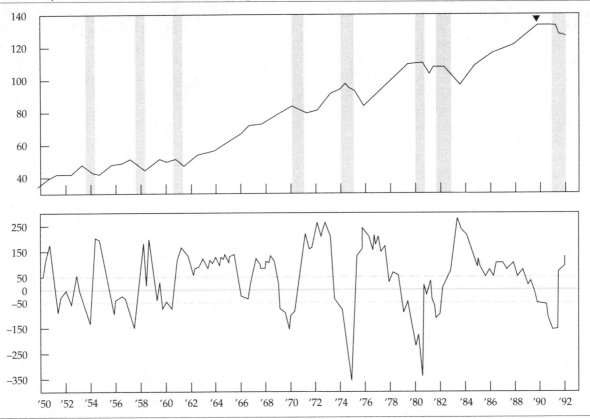

Source: Bostian Economic Research.

Notes: Data based on information from Bureau of Economic Analysis. Last observations January 1992 (top graph) and February 1992 (bottom graph). Shaded areas represent recessions as defined by the National Bureau of Economic Research.

I developed two thresholds: +50, where the index moves into an expansion mode, and −50, where it moves into a recession mode. These signals, of course, are not perfect. Figure 1 shows a down arrow in August 1989, in advance of the date when the recession officially began. NBER has not officially determined when and if the recession ended.

The MEI removes emotion from the forecasting process and, based on the breadth of its measurement of the real and financial economy, it is able to circumvent bad data that distort various individual economic variables from time to time. Nonetheless, judgment is still required in assessing the probable amplitude and duration of cyclical movements and other unique characteristics of each economic cycle. For example, I considered excessive debt to be the unique characteristic of the recent economic downturn.

I am not suggesting you must use the MEI. My message is to have a discipline that uses data on a rate-of-change basis. The MEI's forecasting profile can be approximated by expressing the movement of the leading indicators on a rate-of-change basis. The upper panel of **Figure 2** shows the LEI, which missed

the onset of the most recent recession. In the lower panel, the data are expressed on a year-to-year percent change basis. Although the signals are not always clearly defined, this rate-of-change approach revealed extremely weak economic momentum in the summer of 1990, even though the reported leading indicators data were still making new highs as the recession approached.

Considering that the post-November 1982 economic expansion was setting longevity records in the summer of 1990, and with a progressively weaker response to even greater increments of corporate and consumer indebtedness, forecasting a recession should not have been difficult for most economists. In retrospect, the fact that so many economists missed the recession is amazing. Probably one problem was that they had forecast two or three recessions that did not occur during the record-setting expansion, so they became gun-shy. Apparently, the recession was difficult to forecast because, in combination with other perceptual problems, economists focused on the upward movement of the leading indicators. Although the Middle East conflict did not

7

Figure 2. Leading Indicators Index

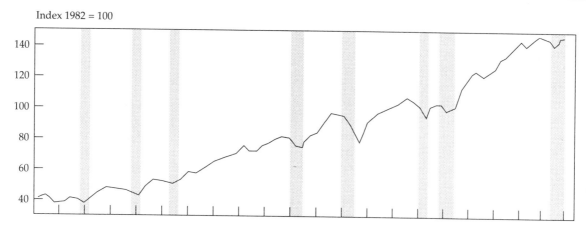

Index 1982 = 100

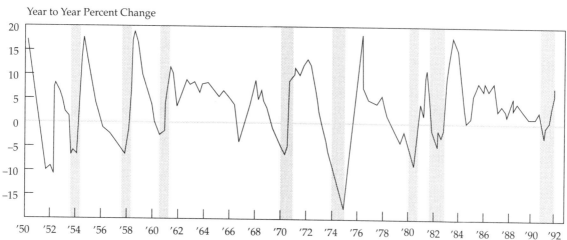

Year to Year Percent Change

Source: Crandall, Pierce & Co.

Notes: Data based on information from Bureau of Economic Analysis. Last observation January 1992. Shaded areas represent recessions as defined by the National Bureau of Economic Research.

cause the recession, it did initially exacerbate it.

Accurate forecasting of the economic cycle requires a decision-oriented discipline. One of the best methods for expressing such a discipline is on a rate-of-change basis. Looking at things on a rate-of-change basis identifies when an absolute series is about to change direction. A business needs time to prepare for a recession or a recovery, and in the investment business, you frequently need time to change your portfolio stance.

Knowing what is and is not possible in forecasting is important. Forecasting the economic cycle is possible. Forecasting the amplitude and duration of an economic expansion or an economic contraction is more difficult. These particular points require several judgmental observations. Certainly the amplitude, or the strength of the recovery, has much to do with whether it reaches extremes. Experience has taught me never to forecast individual statistics, such

as payroll employment, because the numbers are continually revised. Forecasting exogenous events also is not possible. Think about what would happen if a sudden coup occurs in Russia and Yeltsin goes to the Gulag. Geopolitical shocks cannot be forecast.

Alternative Forecasting Methods

Economists use a variety of methods for forecasting the economy and market behavior. *Consensus forecasting* has become popular in recent years. The consensus for 1992 was only 1.6 percent growth in real GDP. Consensus forecasting helps in understanding the "mind of the market." When something different from what the market thinks occurs, the result is big moves in stock and bond markets or in individual securities. But the mind of the market can be right.

8

The weakness of consensus forecasting is that it can miss critical turning points. The challenge is to try to look at the mind of the market and understand what it is. To use consensus forecasting to explore the mind of the market, ask "What is wrong with this?" If something is wrong with the consensus, that is where the markets move when the adjustment occurs. *Blue Chip Economic Indicators*, a monthly survey of more than 50 economists, has become widely recognized for its consensus economic forecasts. Nevertheless, the *Blue Chip* consensus missed the severe economic downturn in 1982 and the onset of the 1990–91 recession. Otherwise, the record is good.

Scenario analysis is a sophisticated way to manipulate economic variables, often with the aid of a computer, to create different outcomes to which probabilities can be assigned. Strategically, it is useful to consider scenarios that are at odds with a most probable forecast so as to be alert to adverse events and cognizant of the risk that might attend such adverse outcomes. Unfortunately, the multiple scenarios can also lead to a paralysis in decision making because of the many computer printouts reflecting different events that could happen. Which do you act on?

Historical methods assume the past can be used to predict the future. The past is not always prologue, but it provides norms against which to judge what is happening. **Figure 3** presents six indicators. The average for the past six cycles is considered the norm. The leading indicators moved up a little more sharply than the norm, then went laterally, and now they are moving up again, but they are basically tracking history. Real durable goods orders, industrial production, and total employment look different from the norm, but now they are right on the historical track.

Some of these indicators reflect an artificial spurt of euphoria following the apparent success of Operation Desert Storm. This surge in economic activity spiked some of the series up from what would have been a normal recessionary path. When they came back down to where they would have been without Desert Storm, economists said, "Here comes a double-dip recession." It was not a double dip; it was the economic data moving back into a normal recessionary pattern.

The index of consumer sentiment and the housing starts series are tracking below their historical paths, which may reflect some longer term secular problems dealing with debt, demographics, and so forth.

The consensus, scenario, and historical approaches have value, but they seldom provide actionable conclusions about the future. Judgment is still required. Such approaches allow comparisons of a forecast with what has been the historical norm and identification of possible bias in the deviations, which may be justified.

Evaluating Forecasts

Evaluating forecasts is a continuous process. To be successful in applying economics, focus on what will happen in the future, not what happened in the past. Ask whether something is different out there. In forecasting market data or economic data, ask whether the data contain some knowledge you may not have. This is the continuing battle between what you perceive and know and what the market perceives and knows, and both can be right on occasion.

The easiest way to identify trend change is to use rate-of-change data. Take any series important to an analyst's or portfolio manager's success, and use some method to smooth the data—a 10-day, 10-week, or 10-year moving average, perhaps—and plot the differential between the data and the moving average. Look at the performance of that data during the past 10 or 20 years or however long the history is available. This simple approach is the ultimate pragmatism. If something starts to happen in the data, it will keep you asking why.

Occasionally, the data can be wrong and you can be right. Checking forecasts for consistency and bias is difficult but important. An econometric approach permits a history-based check to be made. If the economy is supposed to expand and interest rates are supposed to go up, but your forecast has interest rates coming down, you may be right. Figure out why something that is historically inconsistent appears to be occurring. Clearly, judgment is the ultimate criterion.

Use of Economic Inputs in Security Analysis

Economic inputs are obviously useful in the analysis of individual securities and the construction of portfolios, as well as in asset allocation. As stated earlier, however, with regard to economic forecasting, use of economic inputs involves as much art (or judgment) as science. Economic relationships can be quantified in almost limitless correlations if mathematical sophistication is more important than accurate forecasts.

Trying to quantify an economic input in forecasting an individual security is a tricky exercise. For example, the revenues of a capital goods company can be correlated with a component of the national income accounts such as capital spending. Nonetheless, capital spending must be accurately projected,

9

Figure 3. The Business Cycle: Selected Indicators

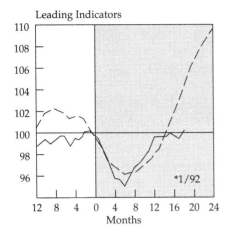

Leading Indicators

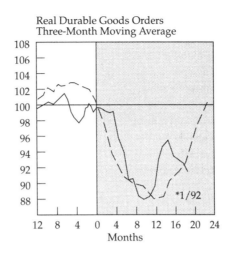

Real Durable Goods Orders
Three-Month Moving Average

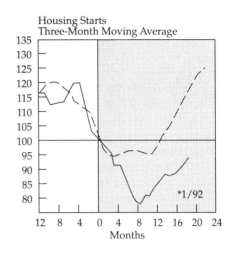

Housing Starts
Three-Month Moving Average

Total Employment
Nonagricultural, Establishment

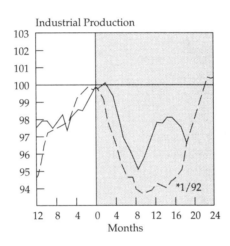

Industrial Production

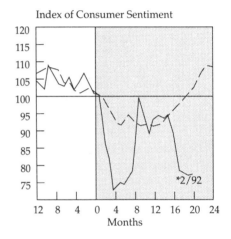

Index of Consumer Sentiment

——— Current Cycle
– – – Average of Previous Six Cycles
0 = Business Cycle Peak

Source: Crandall, Pierce & Co.

Notes: Shaded areas represent the 24 months after the business cycle peak. Current cycle peak = July 1990.

*Indicates last observation of current cycle.

and then, assuming the historical correlation holds with revenues, judgments must be made about possible changes in margins, tax rates, and so forth. Finally, it is necessary to judge what price–earnings multiple the market will apply to the resulting earnings assumption. In my opinion, accurately quantifying the macroeconomic inputs to security analysis will always be difficult. Successful stock selection will always have its "artistic" elements.

John Maynard Keynes addressed the security selection problem by comparing investing to a beauty contest: "Each competitor (investor) has to pick, not those faces which he himself finds the prettiest, but those he thinks likeliest to catch the fancy of the other competitors, all of whom are looking at the problem from the same point of view."[2]

Group and sector selection will become more dominant in professional money management in the 1990s. When portfolios are constructed based on

[2]Peter Bernstein and David Bostian, in *Methods and Techniques of Business Forecasting*, eds. William F. Butler, Robert A. Kavesh, and Robert B. Platt (Englewood Cliffs, N.J.: Prentice Hall, 1974).

10

group or sector themes, economic inputs may become more statistically significant in the selection process. The factors affecting capital goods stocks, consumer stocks, or oil stocks are much more easily correlated than influences on individual stocks in a larger universe. One company might have problems, but if the group or sector correlation has merit, it might do well.

Figure 4 shows the ratio of prices of capital goods stocks to prices of consumer goods stocks during the past several decades. An unsustainable market disequilibrium has developed between these two major sectors. Capital goods relative performance surpassed that of consumer goods at the end of the 1970s, and then the pendulum swung to an even more extreme position favoring consumer goods stocks in the 1980s. Capital goods stocks may have gone up, but their upward movement is so minute that this ratio has continued to plunge.

Now that the mathematical relationship between the capital goods sector and the consumer goods sector has reached an unsustainable extreme, a weighty array of fundamental factors argues for a major reversal, in favor of overperformance of capital goods equities. These fundamental factors range from market measures to economic factors to demographic trends to government policies. The risk–reward matrix in **Table 1** highlights the reasons portfolio managers should seriously consider increasing the portfolio weighting in the capital goods sector and reducing the weighting in the consumer goods sector. The six factors (market, economics, productivity, profit, demographics, and government policy) imply negative conclusions about the outlook for consumer stocks, possibly mitigated by new markets

abroad, and positive conclusions for the capital goods sector. The implications of this potentially major portfolio shift are incredible risk and reward.

Whether this transition to capital goods stocks will be gradual or more sudden is difficult to ascertain. One possible "sudden" catalyst could be a sustained rise in industrial commodity prices. Capital goods profitability could be surprisingly strong even in the slow economic recovery most economists anticipated. A vigorous economic expansion could produce astounding earnings gains for many capital goods companies.

Most people on Wall Street value the equity market using dividend discount models, historical price–earnings multiples, normalized price–earnings multiples, dividend yields, book values, and so forth, all of which indicate the market has been overvalued. I look at stocks relative to GNP (now GDP), or the ongoing value of the economy. **Figure 5** shows the occasional secular overvaluation and undervaluation of equities. Overvaluation is considered to occur when the market value of all New York Stock Exchange stocks exceeds 70 percent of GNP; undervaluation is below 40 percent. We are now headed back toward overvaluation.

Figure 5. Bostian Equity Valuation/GNP Model
(GDP optional)

Source: Bostian Economic Research.

Notes: Data based on information from the New York Stock Exchange and the U.S. Commerce Department. Last observation February 1992 est.

Figure 4. Ratio of Capital Goods/Consumer Goods Stock Prices

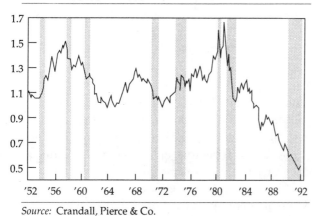

Source: Crandall, Pierce & Co.

Notes: Data based on information from Standard & Poor's Corp. Last observation February 1992. Shaded areas represent recessions as defined by the National Bureau of Economic Research.

International events also influence domestic forecasting, but mixing domestic and international forecast variables can be confusing. I first make forecasts based on variables that have been valid from a domestic standpoint. Then, as a separate exercise, I modify the forecast based on pertinent international considerations. The international realm introduces many unpredictabilities because some economies and political structures have no precedent domesti-

11

Table 1. Factors Affecting Consumer and Capital Stocks

Consumer Stocks Risk Factors	Capital Stocks Reward Factors
Market	Market
• High relative P/E[a]	• Low relative P/E[a]
• Lower dividend yield	• Higher dividend yields
• 10-year overperformance	• 10-year underperformance
• Institutions overweighted now	• Institutions underweighted now
Economics (consumer spending)	Economics (capital spending)
• Consumer heavily indebted implies weaker spending in recovery	• Corporate competitiveness heavily dependent on capital investment
• Consumer purchase mix downscaled by necessity	• Emerging world economy implies need for capital exports
• Home real estate weak	• Infrastructure rebuilding needed
Productivity	Productivity
• Low-productivity industries	• High-productivity industries
• Higher labor costs (services)	• Lower labor costs (manufacturing)
Profit	Profit
• Profit vulnerability to consumer and government action	• Profit resilience in recession implies strong rebound
Demographics	Demographics
• Aging population implies weaker consumer economy and slower household formation	• Aging population implies higher savings and capital investment
Government Policy	Government Policy
• Anticonsumption tax policy expected	• Pro-investment initiatives expected

Source: Bostian Economic Research.

[a]Relative to S&P 500 Index P/E.

cally. International influences, however, should make investing in the 1990s more challenging.

Conclusion

Investment management and research will experience a period of unprecedented innovation and excitement as the 21st century approaches. New disciplines and techniques will be developed and for brief periods will appear to be ultimate solutions to the investment challenges we all face. Keep in mind, however, that the human element in both the economic and investment realms will remain. Implicit in that advice is the need to remember that judgment will always be necessary in achieving "effective forecasts."

12

Developing a Recommendation for a Global Portfolio

Charles I. Clough, Jr., CFA
Chief Investment Strategist
Merrill Lynch & Co.

Any set of disciplines a financial analyst uses to drive a global portfolio has to be designed to recognize change. Traditional approaches can provide a sense of intellectual complacency, particularly at important turning points in economic and financial market behavior. Missing those turning points can lead to underperformance.

The purpose of this presentation is not to bring another quantitative valuation model to the table or describe in detail how Merrill Lynch designs global portfolios, but rather to discuss the principles we use in investing across markets, and for that matter, in investing within a single market. Merrill Lynch, like most organizations, has the capability to build some fairly complicated models. Unfortunately, the more complicated the analysis, the more likely it is to miss the forest for the trees.

Any set of disciplines used to drive a global portfolio has to be designed to recognize change. Traditional approaches based simply on trend growth rate and interest rate levels often provide a sense of intellectual complacency, particularly at important turning points in economic and financial market behavior. Missing those turning points can lead to underperformance.

Anticipating Change in Fundamental Trends

We use a number of important principles in designing a global investment portfolio. First is the need to understand what we do not know. Not only are the more traditional domestic inputs of investment activity, such as yield curve behavior and credit market activity, important to global decision making but also currency values and different accounting conventions must be considered. It is easy to extrapolate all the domestic ambiguities and uncertainties. Second is the need to assess where important secular changes may have occurred that could accelerate or decelerate a region's growth, where the valuation formulas, especially the inputs, might be wrong.

Change always occurs at the margin, and as recent events in Latin America and China suggest, it can be profound. Third is the need for a series of disciplines to help determine where the consensus might be wrong. If consensus estimates about earnings, growth rates, risk premiums, and so forth are pumped into the discipline, the models produce consensus output and, probably, subpar returns.

Two experiences I had as a portfolio manager suggest reasons for skepticism about popular types of analysis—particularly unidimensional analysis, such as simple dividend discount modeling—when important changes are afoot. By early 1979, valuation formulas or dividend discount models during the late stages of the energy boom of the 1970s suggested underweighting energy stocks. The growth rate and earnings estimates were based on the experience investors had viewing the industry over the postwar period. By March 1979, the oil service stocks and many international and domestic integrated stocks were emerging as extremely overvalued on our internal valuation models. As events turned out, two-thirds of the rise in the sector's stock prices still lay ahead. The stocks did not peak until almost 18 months later. Because of the unprecedented rise in energy prices, the earnings momentum dynamic carried earnings, profit margins, and stock market valuations much higher than historical patterns. The models could not predict change, and something had changed.

The second event was in 1985, at the bottom of the paper stock price cycle. As the industry moved out of recession, our valuation model indicated that on the basis of its price–earnings ratio (P/E), even when the measure was based on peak earnings and peak returns on investment in a future time frame, one particular container board company's stock was fairly valued. (Cyclical stocks tend to rise sharply at the beginning of their cycles. They will take a big jump off their lows and appear to have already discounted the cycle, even though much of the earnings gains lie ahead). Despite the appearance of overvaluation, the stock subsequently increased in price nearly 10 times. It had moved ahead from $10 to $28 but then moved to more than $200 a share on the then-outstanding stock. The company's balance sheet was highly leveraged, so the pricing and leverage dynamics combined to carry nominal earnings up dramatically. Again, something had changed.

In international investing, the possibility of change increases exponentially. At Merrill Lynch, domestic and international portfolio strategy is based on a number of complementary observations:

▓ *Markets are rational.* This is true even though they can sustain abnormally high or low P/Es or the appearance of overvaluation or undervaluation for extended periods of time. This is the basis by which securities markets, particularly equity markets, direct capital flows. High risk premiums or low risk premiums are a way of controlling capital flows. A combination of value, liquidity, and earnings momentum techniques is used to attempt to capture the dynamic element of change and to determine what is happening in industries and in markets to weave an understanding of economic and industry dynamics. A portfolio is then designed around those disciplines.

▓ *Some inputs must be conjectural rather than quantitative.* Conjectural judgments are necessary and often are difficult to put into quantitative terms. In 1987, for example, the Japanese central bank engineered a dramatic decline in the cost of capital as part of a coordinated central bank policy of dollar support. That move unleashed a torrent of liquidity into the Japanese real estate and stock markets, creating a speculative explosion in prices and a subsequent bust (which is still working itself out). These markets were substantially overvalued long before they peaked, both in time and levels. Their peaks occurred when market liquidity began to deteriorate, but by that time they had gone well beyond levels anyone thought possible. Being underweight in Japan hurt a diversified international portfolio dramatically for a long period of time. Liquidity, if it is powerful and long lasting, can drive both valuation and themes to excess. More important is to recognize when those forces have peaked. Recognizing that markets are overvalued simply is not enough.

▓ *We look at markets from a top-down and bottom-up perspective simultaneously.* This is particularly true

if a major international investment theme is emerging across several markets. The practice is important in dealing with smaller markets, such as Switzerland or Malaysia, in which capitalization constraints limit the ability to diversify within the market. Portfolio representation in a particular market may not be based on that market's valuation parameters but on a theme, such as technology or infrastructure, that is highly represented in that market.

▓ *In the 1990s, most of the world's growth will occur outside the industrialized nations.* Trends in demography and in debt suggest growing deflationary patterns will hinder earnings in many large equity markets. Currently, Merrill Lynch's global portfolios are overweighted in Hong Kong, Latin America, and to a lesser extent, France, and they are underweighted in Japan, Germany, and some of the smaller Asian markets.

▓ *Evidence suggests that a major worldwide credit contraction is under way.* This will affect economic growth, bank rates, bond yields, and P/Es in much of the industrialized world. Credit cycles have peaked almost everywhere. Bank deposit rates have declined to surprisingly low levels in North America. If the debt deflation persists, returns to household deposits will fall to low levels—with the United States in the lead—and remain low in most industrialized nations throughout much of the decade.

▓ *The dollar is likely to be a strong currency in this credit contraction.* At the moment, it is weak against those European Monetary System currencies tied to the deutsche mark, where currency rates are at stranglehold levels. The dollar, however, is not being inflated. More fairly stated, the deutsche mark is strong rather than the dollar is weak. In fact, the absence of domestic credit expansion could be the source of a dollar shortage in the 1990s. The United States is further along the declining phase of the credit curve than most other nations, and the availability of dollar liquidity in the world is shrinking, leaving us somewhat overweighted in the U.S. market in global portfolios. By 1993, recovery cycles are likely to emerge in the rest of the industrialized world, particularly Europe. Recovery is already somewhat visible in North America, but in Japan, Europe, and other countries, economies are still weakening. The upcoming cycle, however, will be tame by postwar period standards. The demographics of aging are beginning to play a major role in all industrialized nations, and interest rates will probably continue to decline in the 1990s as in the 1980s. Consequently, the 1990s will bring lower financial market returns and even lower cash returns than the 1980s.

▓ *By the middle of the decade, capital will flow to*

obvious places. These include Eastern Europe, Latin America, India, and China. P/Es in most industrialized stock markets will be at higher levels because credit will not be used speculatively, freeing up domestic savings for investment capital. Capital will flow to developing areas at astonishingly low costs relative to the yields at the long end of the yield curves in most industrialized nations.

Money Supply and a Credit Contraction

Slower rates of growth in borrowing will affect the way money grows in all industrialized nations. The United States is a prime example, but the same monetary patterns are emerging in other economies. Declining worldwide money growth will affect valuation and how equities and fixed-income instruments will be priced. The narrow U.S. monetary aggregates are up. M1 is up 12 percent year-on-year. In contrast, as **Figure 1** shows, M3 is contracting. In fact, the year-on-year growth of M3 is at the lowest level ever. M3 is the critical monetary aggregate because (1) it eliminates the distortions that arise as the result of people changing the way they hold deposits, and (2) it measures the totality of the banking system's deposit base. To transaction balances in M1, M3 adds small-time deposits that are in M2. Most international money supply measures basically break down the same way. To M2, M3 adds overnight repos, Eurodollar term deposits, and large time deposits. Those are the deposits for which banks must aggressively bid. To increase its total deposit base, or the liability side of its balance sheet, a bank must aggressively expand its M3-type deposits. That is a signal that a real credit upcycle is beginning. Currently, the credit cycles in the United States and other nations are still headed the other way.

In the United States, a banking system consolidation process is under way. When Manufacturers Hanover and Chemical merged, for example, a number of events occurred in New York. First, a headquarters building and its related real estate proved excessive. Branch offices were closed and employment fell, but those were rather superficial events. Most important was the banking system's downsizing of its balance sheet. The reason the two banks had to merge was that the New York metropolitan area did not produce enough loans or assets to support the size of the banking system that had evolved there. When the banks stopped lending to build excessive real estate, they were forced to downsize their assets and liquidate liabilities.

This is happening globally as well. In Canada, for example, some banks are holding assets of lesser value than they think. Likewise, in the United Kingdom and Japan, as real estate assets shrink, so do the banks' liabilities, which are primarily household deposits.

The banking system is consolidating because the demand for credit is not likely to grow much in the future. The United States has had a production bounce in the economy that indicates it will lead to expansion, but as **Figure 2** shows, that is not happening in credit. In a credit contraction, the broad money supply does not grow much. Before earlier upcycles, M3 grew faster than M1 or M2. Now, not only is M3 the slowest growing aggregate but it also is at the lowest rate of growth ever. Even though the economy appears to be several months into an expansion, money and credit are still not growing much.

A second characteristic of a credit contraction is that nominal income growth is not rapid. U.S. nominal disposable income grew only 3 percent in 1991—the slowest rate since 1960. The two-year moving average for disposable income growth, shown in **Figure 3**, has declined to less than 6 percent. The last time the Federal Reserve Board reduced the discount rate from 4.5 percent to 3.5 percent, which probably kicked off this credit cycle, was in 1930. Thus, this

Figure 1. U.S. Broad Money Supply (M3), 1961–91
(year-to-year percent change)

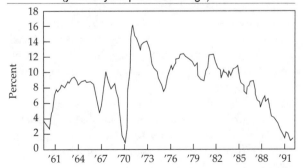

Source: Federal Reserve System.

Figure 2. U.S. Private Nonfinancial Debt, 1956–91
(year-to-year percent change)

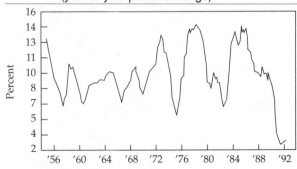

Source: Federal Reserve System.

60

Figure 3. U.S. Nominal Disposable Income, 1962–91
(year-to-year percent change, two-year
moving average)

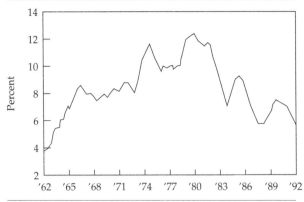

Source: U.S. Department of Commerce, Bureau of Economic Analysis.

recession has produced record-low interest rates, record-low nominal activity, and record-low short-term yields.

Demographic Trends and Labor Costs

Slow labor force growth may lead long-term interest rates lower in the 1990s in the industrialized world. How the demographic trends in the United States affect the labor force and employment is shown in **Figure 4**. Similar trends are found in Japan, the United Kingdom, and many other Western European nations. Most populations are becoming older, and growth rates are declining, particularly in Western Europe.

Employment growth is sluggish in this cycle because demand for labor is in a secular decline. The corporate sector is doing something perfectly rational: Companies are downsizing their need for labor because labor will become less available in the 1990s and because labor cost is exorbitant.

According to most demographic studies, U.S. labor force growth will slow to somewhere between 0.5 percent and 1 percent a year in the 1990s, which is down from 1.75 percent in the 1980s and 2.75 percent in the 1970s. Labor force growth is declining in Europe. Some observers have suggested this may lead to labor shortages in the 1990s. Business will bid up the price of labor, and a cost-push form of inflation will develop, especially with all the social pressures for universally available health care and higher retirement costs for an aging work force. History suggests a different scenario may evolve. As Figure 4 shows, yields tend to follow demographics with a notable lag, and demographics and credit cycles appear to be positively correlated.

Population growth will be slow not only in the United States but also in other industrialized nations. The labor force has already absorbed the postwar baby boomers, their offspring, and a high percentage of women. If demand for consumer goods and services grows correspondingly more slowly, the extra airport, office, and mall space that has been built will take longer to be absorbed. Concerns are mounting that even Hong Kong's long-anticipated airport may be a white elephant. Personal employment growth is slow because many service industries are overstaffed. Nominal income and spending growth will both slow. Economics may be systemically slower in the industrialized world because fewer people are entering the borrowing and spending times of their lives.

Population dynamics may be playing a role in credit cycles around the world. If so, corporations will shift back from heavy use of labor to greater emphasis on capital. Labor has already become so expensive that corporations have every incentive to substitute capital for labor. **Figure 5** shows trends in U.S. manufacturing labor compensation per hour relative to output per hour—unit labor costs stated crudely. This ratio moved up sharply in the 1970s

Figure 4. U.S. Labor Force Growth, 1952–91
(year-to-year percent change, two-year
moving average)

Total Labor Force Growth and Treasury Yields

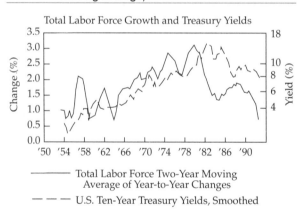

——— Total Labor Force Two-Year Moving
Average of Year-to-Year Changes

– – – U.S. Ten-Year Treasury Yields, Smoothed

Two-Year Moving Average of the
Year-to-Year Labor Force Growth Rate

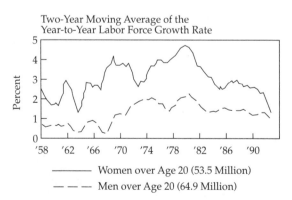

——— Women over Age 20 (53.5 Million)

– – – Men over Age 20 (64.9 Million)

Source: U.S. Department of Labor, Bureau of Labor Statistics.

Figure 5. Unit Labor Cost, U.S. Manufacturing Sector, 1948–90
(ratio of compensation per hour to output per hour)

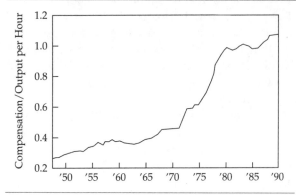

Source: U.S. Department of Labor, Bureau of Labor Statistics.

and 1980s. As long as the manufacturing sector could pass those costs through in prices, the cost-push inflationary pattern fed on itself. Once the dollar became overvalued and U.S. manufacturers could not raise prices to cover higher labor costs, the manufacturing sector hit the wall. Massive cash flow deficits resulted, along with a long-term process of "restructuring" (reducing the labor component of costs).

The U.S. manufacturing sector has been fairly successful in controlling labor costs. Manufacturing employment declined during the 1980s, as shown in **Figure 6**. It peaked in the late 1970s, and during the longest peacetime expansion we have had on record, manufacturing employment declined 15 percent from its peak. General Motors, for example, has the capacity to manufacture 5.5 million automobiles, but it only sells 3 million. It is hemorrhaging cash at the rate of about $15 million a day. No matter how large your balance sheet, if you lose cash that fast, sooner or later you run out of it. So, Mr. Stempel has to close

Figure 6. Total Employment, U.S. Manufacturing Sector, 1948–90
(millions)

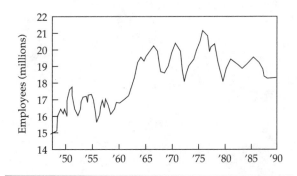

Source: U.S. Department of Labor, Bureau of Labor Statistics.

plants sooner than he thought. If he closes 21 plants, reportedly, 75,000 additional layoffs will take place. The growing trend around the world toward the establishment of trading blocs will only intensify pressures for greater productive efficiency, lower costs, and higher quality. The emergence of Europe and North America as regional trading blocs will create a great deal of redundant production capacity. This represents another change in investment equation inputs.

Figure 7 shows what is happening to labor costs in the services sector. Most advanced economies are service driven, and labor costs are still accelerating in that sector. The impending peak in U.S. service-sector employment **(Figure 8)** may be occurring in a number of economies. In the four largest services segments—finance, insurance, retail and wholesale trade, and defense—employment is contracting, which will probably slow the growth of the services labor force. As in manufacturing, service-sector businesses will make a more concentrated attempt to reduce the labor component of their costs—another change in economic inputs.

Figure 7. Unit Labor Cost, U.S. Services Sector, 1964–91
(ratio of weekly payroll index to output)

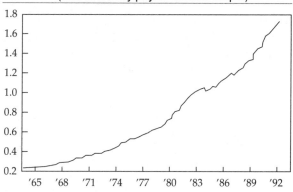

Source: U.S. Department of Labor, Bureau of Labor Statistics.

Credit Demands

An often-heard concern earlier this year was that as the economy starts to recover, private-sector credit demands would soar. The common perception is that heavy public-sector financing by the U.S. government will force higher interest rates. On the contrary, I believe long-term bond markets offer substantial value, not only in the United States but also around the world.

Again, using the United States as an example that can be extrapolated internationally, the total U.S. credit structure includes about $11 trillion of nonfi-

62

Figure 8. Total Employment, U.S. Services Sector, 1948–90
(millions)

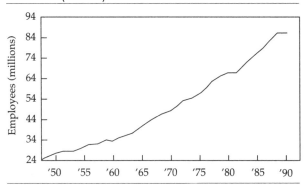

Source: U.S. Department of Labor, Bureau of Labor Statistics.

nancial debt, which is defined as debt outside the banking system. This debt, broken down by maturity, is shown in **Figure 9**. The economy's short-term debt, defined as M4 or liquidity, consists primarily of bank deposits and Treasury bills. The size of this type of debt—$5 trillion—shows the effect of a positive yield curve: A dynamically positive yield curve inhibits the creation of long-term debt and pulls more liquidity to the short end of the curve. This is also happening in other industrialized nations.

The vast bulk of the long-term credit in today's society consists of mortgage debt—loans used to fund real estate. Real estate developers in every industrialized country borrow more money than any other entity, including governments. In the process, they have created more than $4 trillion of mortgage credit in the United States.

The remaining debt amounts to about $2 trillion. About $400 billion, or 4 percent of the nation's credit structure, is long-term government debt, or 5- to 30-year paper. Although government debt is not a large component of the nation's debt, it is important because prices of other debt types, such as mortgages, are based on the long-term government yield. About $600 billion dollars represents long-term corporate debt—investment-grade and high-yield bonds. The remaining debt stock consists of various forms of personal debt—consumer installment credit, for example, which may not extend out more than a year, but the Federal Reserve data include it in the "other" category because these are not large debt aggregates.

Figure 9 presents an extrapolated picture of the banking system's balance sheet. M4 consists largely of banking system liabilities such as certificates of deposits, money funds, and guaranteed investment contracts sitting in life insurance companies. These liabilities are used to fund mortgage debt. If the financial sector cannot inflate real estate credit, it

cannot pay high returns on the deposits held by the household sector. If igniting a mortgage-driven real estate credit cycle proves impossible, credit growth will be very sluggish. Two-thirds of mortgage debt consists of one- to four-family home mortgages. These are great credit instruments to a fiduciary or investor because the household sector generally pays the rent on time. Default rates are low, and the duration or maturity of these credit instruments tends to be stable. Homeowners will not suddenly try to exchange 9 percent fixed-rate mortgages for adjustable rate mortgages. That is exactly what they should do, but unless interest rates collapse, people tend to hold onto their long-term mortgages. The problem is that we are not creating many new residential mortgages. The creation of residential credit is experiencing a sharp slowdown. The demographics are such that we are no longer inflating the housing stock in most of the industrialized world.

The large stock of commercial mortgages outstanding is what will give the U.S. banking and insurance sector, the Japanese banking system, and part of the Canadian and U.K. banking systems a run for their money in the next few years. Many of these

Figure 9. U.S. Debt, 2Q1991
(trillions of dollars)

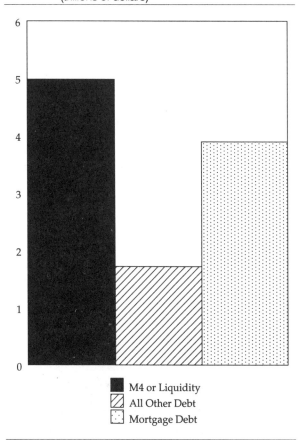

- ■ M4 or Liquidity
- ▨ All Other Debt
- ▥ Mortgage Debt

Source: Federal Reserve System, Flow of Funds.

63

are first mortgages on existing structures that may produce a cash flow; the lessees are actually paying the rent. As the leases on buildings built between 1982 and 1986 run out, however, those cash flows will start to collapse. Many current facilities are backed by single-payment, "bullet" mortgages that will mature between 1993 and 1996. Although carried on the books at full value in most instances, many of these mortgages will default. New leases are being written at rental rates that are fractions of the rates built into the original leases. In short, a lot of loan restructurings lie ahead. The "Canary Wharf" problem in London and Tokyo's real estate horror stories suggest that worldwide defaults are on the way.

The problems with commercial mortgage credit have been well chronicled. What is less understood is the impact of these defaults on the yield curve. As mortgages default or liquidate, the duration or maturity of the credit market shrinks. The value of long-term mortgage credit declines, and investors have trouble locking in duration or yield. The same event is unfolding in Japan and the United Kingdom. As leases run out, the value of the buildings and the underlying mortgages collapses. Not only will this continue to depress commercial mortgage activity but also it will force banks holding such mortgages to reduce the yield on their deposit liabilities. This is the downside of the credit cycle.

The volume of high-quality long-term corporate credit will similarly shrink if current trends persist. Of the $600 billion of corporate bonds currently outstanding, about 25 percent, or $166 billion, are likely to be called in 1992. Much of that will not be refunded in the long-term bond market because borrowing there is so expensive. Funding is cheaper in equities, in the commercial paper market, or along the five- to seven-year part of the curve. In a period of credit deflation, as banks reduce their funding rates, the yield curve will remain steeply positive. The fact that the bank rate fell below 3 percent is perfectly consistent with the beginning of a credit contraction. Lower rates of borrowing will likely translate into far lower rates paid on U.S. money market securities, and sooner or later, those abroad as well.

The Structure of Savings

Changing demographics also affect savings rates, as **Figure 10** shows. As the number of people between the ages of 40 and 64 rises as a percentage of the total adult population, the U.S. savings rate will start to rise. That is already beginning and is reflected in the dollar's stability in the face of a severe arbitrage

64

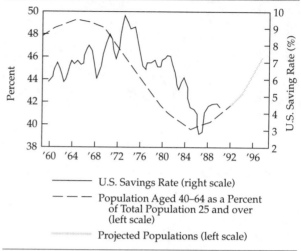

Figure 10. U.S. Savings Rate and the Proportion of the Population Likely to be Savers, 1959–99 (estimated)

——— U.S. Savings Rate (right scale)

– – – Population Aged 40–64 as a Percent of Total Population 25 and over (left scale)

·········· Projected Populations (left scale)

Source: Federal Reserve System, Flow of Funds.

exchange rate discount, particularly with respect to the German mark. The U.S. bank rate is 3 percent, Germany's is 9 percent, and the dollar is no lower relative to the German currency than it was in 1988. That is only possible if we, as a nation, are throwing off excess savings.

The composition of household financial assets is changing, albeit slowly. Liquid assets as a percent of household financial assets are declining, as **Figure 11** shows. This implies that a major restructuring of the nation's savings pattern is under way. **Figure 12** suggests a migration from certificates of deposit to bonds and stocks is in an early stage. As of the third quarter of 1991, low percentages of household financial assets were still held in the forms of savings

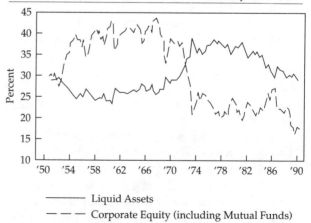

Figure 11. U.S. Ownership of Equities as a Percent of Household Financial Assets, 1951–91

——— Liquid Assets

– – – Corporate Equity (including Mutual Funds)

Source: Federal Reserve System, Flow of Funds.

Figure 12. Securities as a Percent of Household Financial Assets, 1954–91

Sources: Federal Reserve System, Flow of Funds; Merrill Lynch Strategy.

Note: Securities included are savings; government, tax-exempt, and corporate bonds; equities; and mutual funds.

bonds, government bonds, tax-exempt bonds, equities, and mutual funds. **Figure 13** shows that despite record-low money market rates, the household sector is still increasing its holdings of money-fund-type assets such as insurance policies and guaranteed investment contracts. Changing liquidity preferences is a long-term process. So long as the household sector insists on holding its assets at the 90-day bank rate and the banking system faces lower credit demands, the rate paid on household deposits will continue to fall. In the 1990s, bank rates should be astonishingly low. Eventually, that will force savers out on the yield curve and into equities, an event that could change the long-term valuation parameters characterizing most of the world's equity markets during the postwar period.

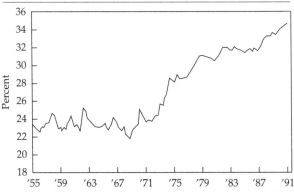

Figure 13. The "Other Financial Assets" Category as a Percent of U.S. Household Financial Assets

Sources: Federal Reserve System, Flow of Funds; Merrill Lynch Strategy.

Note: Other financial assets include private life insurance and pension reserves (insured and noninsured), government insurance, and miscellaneous financial assets.

Two forms of credit can grow. One is commercial and industrial loans—working-capital lending—which in the United States amounts to about $280 billion. The other is consumer installment credit, which is now $600 billion. Consumers have been liquidating credit for the first time in history during this recession, but it could pick up a little in 1993. So about $900 billion of credit might grow. Mortgages outstanding total $4 trillion. Without a real estate inflation, whether it is based on an inflating value of the housing stock or a commercial credit cycle, no credit expansion is likely to be significant enough to absorb the credit capacity in the banking system.

The banking and insurance sectors will be shrinking on three continents. As that happens, these institutions must liquidate their liabilities. This should lead to very low bank rates through the 1990s, first in the United States and eventually in Europe and Japan. Short-term notes' interest rates may bounce a bit as production gains in the middle of 1992, but beyond that bounce, rates will settle at much lower levels. The long end of the curve will have to take care of itself. That will take a while longer simply because of all the indigenous fears in the minds of investors, from government deficits to inflation, but the economics we see will clearly sustain downward pressure on the 90-day bank rate.

Future Issues

The equity markets of the world face three risks. The first is that central banks will overstay tight credit policies. Again, in a domestic credit contraction, tight central bank policies are neither likely nor helpful. **Figure 14** illustrates an indicator of the banking system's balance sheet that correlates fairly well with stock prices. This indicator plots the ratio of nonborrowed reserves plus extended credit to required reserves on a 13-week rate-of-change basis. When the ratio moves up, banking system liquidity is increasing, and the result is generally a bottom in equity prices. The last one was on November 19, 1991. A fall in the indicator would be a cause for concern about a sharper market correction, but as the bottom panel of Figure 14 suggests, bank liquidity is picking up systemically.

The second risk is the possibility of a trade war with Europe, Japan, or the Southeast Asian "tiger" economies. World capital markets probably would not like that. A trade war could be a serious event because all industrialized nations are leveraged, and a trade war would impede the flow of capital.

The third risk for the financial markets is bad fiscal policy, a possibility that must be taken seri-

65

Figure 14. Bank Liquidity and Stock Prices, 1982–91

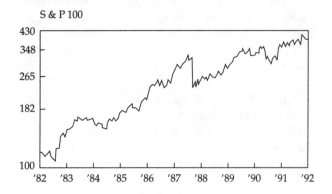

S & P 100

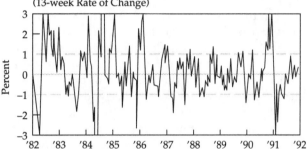

Nonborrowed Reserves and
Extended Credit/Required Reserves
(13-week Rate of Change)

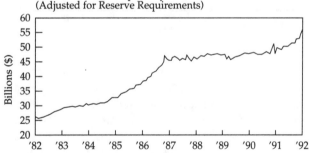

Total Reserves of Depository Institutions
(Adjusted for Reserve Requirements)

Source: Federal Reserve System, Release H.3.

Figure 15. U.S. Economic Rate of Change and Bank Reserves, 1959–91
(year-to-year percent change)

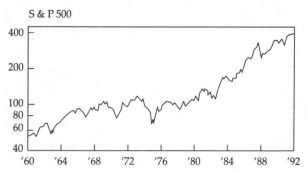

S & P 500

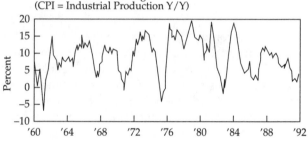

Economic Rate of Change
(CPI = Industrial Production Y/Y)

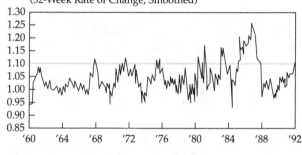

Total Bank Reserves
(52-Week Rate of Change, Smoothed)

Sources: Federal Reserve System; Standard & Poor's; Merrill Lynch Investment Strategy.

ously in an election year. A constituency for a major effort to expand public-sector deficits has not surfaced as yet, however.

A modest cyclical expansion appears to be under way in the United States. **Figure 15** shows that bank reserves are starting to expand, which usually precedes a rise in spending and production. The economic rate of change is the consumer price index multiplied by industrial production. Industrial production has bottomed, and so our equity strategy, not only domestically but around the world, is becoming more focused on companies that are tied to the level of economic activity.

Liquidity as a Determinant of Equity Exposure

On a worldwide basis, liquidity available to the financial markets peaked in the late 1980s and has been at least stable since then. No new sustained peaks in the world equity index will occur without liquidity growth (see **Figure 16**). The reason for this is shown in **Figure 17**, which shows the pattern of real broad money supply growth in four of the major G-7 countries with large capital markets. The broad money supply in Japan is defined as M2 plus certificates of deposits; in the United Kingdom, it is M4; and in Germany and the United States, it is M3. The worldwide pattern has been one of consistent deceleration in inflation-adjusted money supply growth. One

66

Figure 16. World Equity Index, 1978–91

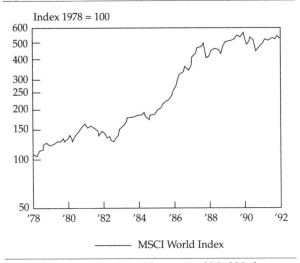

Index 1978 = 100

MSCI World Index

Source: Morgan Stanley Capital International World Index.

reason is that, on a worldwide basis, economies are not creating liquidity. Liquidity builds when somebody borrows, and very little of that is happening anywhere. At the same time, however, the economies are absorbing very little liquidity because no one is spending. So we are in a stalemate. Yield curves, on balance, are becoming positive.

As borrowing slows, the world appears to be moving toward a systematically positive yield curve. **Figure 18** illustrates the ratio of the long-term government bond yield to the three-month Eurocurrency rate. Each market is weighted by the size of its bank deposits. Gradually, positive yield curves are

Figure 17. Real Broad Money Growth and Industrial Production, Four G-7 Countries, 1977–91
(year-to-year percent change)

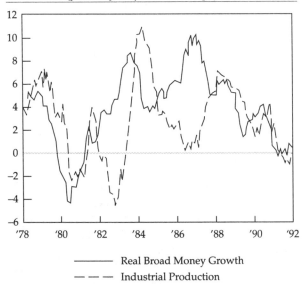

——— Real Broad Money Growth
– – – Industrial Production

Source: Federal Reserve Board.

being reestablished everywhere. Germany is the laggard because the Bundesbank has to deal with the one-shot blip in the Germany money supply stemming from reunification. The credit cycle in Japan is not too far behind that of the United States. The world will see lower growth and less inflation in the 1990s in most of the industrialized economies. Many economies are facing the same slowing demographic patterns as the United States. They are also burdened with an overbuilt services sector and excess employment. The positive in all of this is that a lot of liquidity is parked at the short end of the yield curve in all markets, and that tendency is being exacerbated in Germany.

The concern a year ago was that the Japanese would sell their foreign bonds and bring home the money to forestall a real estate deflation. The Japanese have been liquidating their holdings of U.S. Treasury bonds since 1986, and now 88 percent of the Treasury's debt is held domestically, largely because U.S. domestic savings rates have been picking up for the past several years. Would Somitono Bank sell its last remaining dollar-earning asset to lend to a real estate developer in Tokyo or to try to bail somebody out? I doubt it. In fact, the trade numbers imply that the Bank of Japan is trying to let that nation's credit deflation down easy. An aggressive liquidation of dollar bonds on the part of Japanese banking institutions is highly unlikely.

In the meantime, the Japanese household sector sits on a vast stock of savings, which Japan is starting to export again. Japan is running an $85 billion current account surplus and continues to export capital. The difference is that the United States is also a capital exporter for the first time in decades. That is

Figure 18. Ratio of Long-Term Government Bond Yield to the Three-Month Eurocurrency Rate, 1977–91

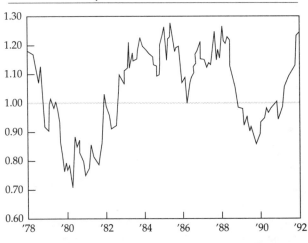

Source: Federal Reserve Board.

not likely if we are importing it.

These dominant changes in the use of money and credit will have a dramatic effect on national growth rates and capital flows and on how well traditional valuation models work. The cost of capital worldwide is falling because virtually all the industrialized nations are experiencing the downside of the great postwar real estate credit cycles. In the final analysis, real estate drives credit. As we go into the 1990s, the bank rate will continue to fall, with cyclical variations, in most industrialized nations.

The final question is whether developing world credit needs will overwhelm world credit markets. We think not. As the industrialized nations stem the speculative use of borrowing, capital will be available for those parts of the world that need it. Even though the focus of these investment flows will be on decade-long investment patterns, capital should be available at astonishingly low rates.

Capital cycles that provide investment for building up an underdeveloped nation's industrial stock or an investment base usually are accompanied by low capital costs. Cycles dominated by speculative capital uses or that are consumption based—used to build casinos or golf courses—are characterized by high capital costs.

Outlook for the Financial Markets

In designing a global portfolio with state-of-the-art valuation and interest rate markets, we monitor the relationship of broad money growth to industrial production in various economies. The strong markets tend to be liquidity driven; domestic money supplies are growing more rapidly than industrial production. The United States is the only industrialized nation beginning to rebuild liquidity. We believe modest credit expansion and recovery is under way, and the recovery is unlikely to be strong enough to build inflationary pressures into the system.

Broad money growth in the United Kingdom still seems to be decelerating. Industrial production is not growing; it has only stopped declining. Japan seems to be in a state of virtual liquidity collapse. It is in the process of unwinding several heavy inflationary bubbles in several sectors. One is the securities markets. Another is real estate, which became terribly overvalued. Even the industrial stock became overbuilt. A tremendous boom took place in industrial capital spending, to a large extent in sunset industries, such as automobiles and consumer electronics, and that cycle is unwinding as well. Borrowing is now collapsing, and Japan's banking system is in the process of downsizing.

Germany is almost comatose. The Bundesbank is trying to offset the money supply growth caused by reunification, but industrial production is starting to decline, and the real money supply is beginning to pick up. A decline in interest rates and an increase in money supply should stabilize the stock market, perhaps later in 1992.

The U.S. equity markets are overvalued relative to bonds and undervalued relative to cash, and that will continue to be the real investment enigma of the 1990s. This pattern will soon be repeated in other nations. The equity markets will look overvalued relative to the fixed-income side because bonds are discounting such possibilities as inflation and excessive credit demands, which we doubt will happen. The cash rate will stay low if we encourage worldwide credit contracts. In the long run, low cash rates would probably drive stock markets to the point that P/Es will begin to look uncomfortably high. Stock markets will not fit the patterns of the past 30 years, because that period captured a major increase in the use of credit to power economic cycles and asset inflation. Before the expansion was far along, some nonmarket asset was inflating and driving liquidity out of the financial markets.

The stock markets will probably start to discount a declining cost of capital, and high P/Es will become more common. The markets would be very rational in doing this. They are pricing down the cost of capital, especially for those sectors of the economy that require investment. The economic cycles in the 1990s will be investment driven, and your guess is as good as mine as to where that investment will flow.

The Japanese stock market is coming closer to a better valuation pattern as the central bank brings the bank rate down. Credit deflations are tricky; where they will bottom out is hard to predict. We would rather see Japanese stocks go fully undervalued before we step back in.

The model for the U.K.'s stock market is neutral. Before we will increase our U.K. weightings, interest rates will have to fall or the money supply expand, suggesting a coming expansion. Germany's market is still overvalued because yields are very high. We would rather stay on the fixed-income side of most European capital markets right now. Once we see clear signs of substantial economic weakness, those markets will probably move toward undervaluation. Currently, France looks like the best value. It has artificially high rates because they have to stay in line with Germany's rates. Once rates decline, market opportunities should improve in Japan, Spain, and Hong Kong. The most interesting part of the world is southern Asia, although those markets also entail risks, many of which are political.

68

Conclusion

Bank rates are likely to be in systemic decline throughout the world in the 1990s, which will change the way historic valuation models work. The U.S. market might see a temporary bounce at the short end of the curve, but borrowing or spending will probably not be sufficient to allow the banks to use their credit capacity, so they are unlikely to bid aggressively for deposits. In two or three years, the 90-day certificate of deposit may become extinct. It is a creature of the 1970s, when banks were given the flexibility to expand their balance sheets by building deposit liabilities because a major, once-in-a-lifetime credit cycle was under way.

The psychology of banking is changing. With low bank rates in one industrialized nation after another, the correct investment strategy will be to shift to long-term financial assets in these countries. At the margin, bonds may currently offer better value than stocks. In recovering economies, particularly in the United States, we lean modestly toward stocks because of the outlook for higher earnings in 1993. Stocks will appear systemically overvalued as long as the credit cycle is unwinding.

(This page intentionally left blank.)

Asset Valuation

Chapter

5

SECURITY-MARKET INDICATOR SERIES

After you read this chapter, you should be able to answer the following questions:

- What are some major uses of security-market indicator series (indexes)?
- What are the major characteristics that cause alternative indexes to differ?
- What are the major stock-market indexes in the United States and globally, and what are their characteristics?
- What are the major bond-market indexes for the United States and the world?
- What are some of the composite stock–bond market indexes?
- Where can you get historical and current data for all these indexes?
- What is the short-run relationship among many of these indexes (monthly)?

A fair statement regarding **security-market indicator series**—especially those outside the United States—is that everybody talks about them, but few people understand them. Even those investors familiar with widely publicized stock-market series, such as the Dow Jones Industrial Average (DJIA), usually know little about indexes for the U.S. bond market or for non-U.S. stock markets such as Tokyo or London.

Although portfolios are obviously composed of many different individual stocks, investors typically ask, "What happened to the market today?" The reason for this question is that if an investor owns more than a few stocks or bonds, it is cumbersome to follow each stock or bond individually to determine the composite performance of the portfolio. Also, there is an intuitive notion that most individual stocks or bonds move with the aggregate market. Therefore, if the overall market rose, an individual's portfolio probably also increased in value. To supply investors with a composite report on market performance, some financial publications or investment firms have developed stock-market and bond-market indexes.[1]

The initial section discusses several ways that investors use market indicator series. An awareness of these significant functions should provide an incentive for becoming familiar with these series and indicates why we present a full chapter on this topic. The second section considers what characteristics cause alternative indexes to differ. In this chapter, we discuss numerous stock-market and bond-market indexes. You should understand their differences and why one of them is preferable for a given task because of its characteristics. The third section presents the most well-known U.S. and global stock market series separated into groups based on the weighting scheme used. The fourth section considers bond-market indexes, which is a relatively new topic, not because the bond market is new, but because the creation and maintenance of total return bond indexes are new. Again, we

---

[1]Throughout this chapter and the book, we will use *indicator series* and *indexes* interchangeably, although *indicator series* is the more correct specification because it refers to a broad class of series; one popular type of series is an index, but there can be other types and many different indexes.

153

consider international bond indexes following the domestic indexes. In section five, we consider composite stock market–bond market series. Our final section examines how these indexes relate to each other over monthly intervals. This comparison demonstrates the important factors that cause high or low correlation among series. With this background, you should be able to make an intelligent choice of the indicator series that is best for you based upon how you want to use the index.

USES OF SECURITY-MARKET INDEXES

Security-market indexes have at least five specific uses. A primary application is to use the index values to compute total returns for an aggregate market or some component of a market over a specified time period and use the rates of return computed as a *benchmark* to judge the performance of individual portfolios. A basic assumption when evaluating portfolio performance is that any investor should be able to experience a rate of return comparable to the market return by randomly selecting a large number of stocks or bonds from the total market; hence, a superior portfolio manager should consistently do better than the market. Therefore, *an aggregate stock- or bond-market index can be used as a benchmark to judge the performance of professional money managers.* You should recall from our earlier discussion that you should also analyze the differential risk for the portfolios being judged as compared to the risk inherent in the benchmark.

Indicator series are also used to develop an index portfolio. As we will discuss later, it is difficult for most money managers to consistently outperform specified market indexes on a risk-adjusted basis over time. If this is true, an obvious alternative is to invest in a portfolio that will emulate this market portfolio. This notion led to the creation of *index funds,* whose purpose is to track the performance of the specified market series (index) over time, that is, derive similar rates of return.[2] The original index fund concept was related to common stocks. Subsequently, development of comprehensive, well-specified bond-market indexes and similar inferior performance relative to the bond market by most bond portfolio managers have led to a similar phenomenon in the fixed-income area (bond index funds).[3]

Securities analysts, portfolio managers, and others use security-market indexes to examine the factors that influence aggregate security price movements (that is, the indexes are used to measure aggregate market movements). A similar use is to analyze the relationship among stock and bond returns of different countries. An example is the analysis of the relationship among U.S., Japanese, and German stock or bond returns.

Another group interested in an aggregate market series is "technicians," who believe past price changes can be used to predict future price movements. For example, to project future stock price movements, technicians would plot and analyze price and volume changes for a stock market series like the Dow Jones Industrial Average.

Finally, work in portfolio and capital market theory has implied that the relevant risk for an individual risky asset is its *systematic risk,* which is the relationship between the rates of

---

[2]For a discussion of developments in indexing, see "New Ways to Play the Indexing Game," *Institutional Investor* 22, no. 13 (November 1988): 92–98; and Sharmin Mossavar-Rahmani, "Indexing Fixed-Income Assets," in *The Handbook of Fixed Income Securities,* 5th ed., ed. Frank J. Fabozzi (Chicago: Irwin Professional Publishing, 1997).

[3]See Fran Hawthorne, "The Battle of the Bond Indexes," *Institutional Investor* 20, no. 4 (April 1986); and Chris P. Dialynas, "The Active Decisions in the Selection of Passive Management and Performance Bogeys," in *The Handbook of Fixed Income Securities,* 5th ed., ed. Frank J. Fabozzi (Chicago: Irwin Professional Publishing, 1997).

return for a risky asset and the rates of return for a market portfolio of risky assets.[4] Therefore, it is necessary when computing the systematic risk for an individual risky asset (security) to relate its returns to the returns for an aggregate market index that is used as a proxy for the market portfolio of risky assets.

In summary, security market indexes are used:

- As benchmarks to evaluate the performance of professional money managers
- To create and monitor an index fund
- To measure market rates of return in economic studies
- For predicting future market movements by technicians
- As a proxy for the market portfolio of risky assets when calculating the systematic risk of an asset

DIFFERENTIATING FACTORS IN CONSTRUCTING MARKET INDEXES

Because the indicator series are intended to reflect the overall movements of a group of securities, it is necessary to consider which factors are important in computing an index that is intended to represent a total population.

THE SAMPLE   The size of the sample, the breadth of the sample, and the source of the sample used to construct a series are all important.

A small percentage of the total population will provide valid indications of the behavior of the total population *if* the sample is properly selected. In fact, at some point the costs of taking a larger sample will almost certainly outweigh any benefits of increased size. The sample should be *representative* of the total population; otherwise, its size will be meaningless. A large biased sample is no better than a small biased sample. The sample can be generated by completely random selection or by a nonrandom selection technique that is designed to incorporate the characteristics of the desired population. Finally, the *source* of the sample is important if there are any differences between segments of the population, in which case samples from each segment are required.

WEIGHTING SAMPLE MEMBERS   Our second concern is with the weight given to each member in the sample. Three principal weighting schemes are used: (1) a price-weighted series, (2) a value-weighted series, and (3) an unweighted series, or what would be described as an equally weighted series.

COMPUTATIONAL PROCEDURE   Our final consideration is selecting the computational procedure. One alternative is to take a simple arithmetic average of the various members in the series. Another is to compute an index and have all changes, whether in price or value, reported in terms of the basic index. Finally, some prefer using a geometric average of the components rather than an arithmetic average.

STOCK-MARKET INDICATOR SERIES

As mentioned in the introduction to this chapter, we hear a lot about what happens to the Dow Jones Industrial Average (DJIA) each day. In addition, you might also hear about

---

[4]This concept and its justification are discussed in Chapters 8 and 9. Subsequently, in Chapter 10 we consider the difficulty of finding an index that is an appropriate proxy for the market portfolio of risky assets.

other stock indexes, such as the NYSE Composite, the S&P 500 index, the NASDAQ index, or even the Nikkei Average. If you listen carefully, you will realize that these indexes change by differing amounts. Reasons for some differences are obvious, such as the DJIA versus the Nikkei Average, but others are not. This section will briefly review how the major series differ in terms of the characteristics discussed in the prior section. As a result, you should come to understand that the movements over time for alternative indexes *should* differ and you will understand why they differ.

The discussion of the indexes is organized by the weighting of the sample of stocks. We begin with the price-weighted series because some of the most popular indexes are in this category. The next group is the value-weighted series, which is the technique currently used for most indexes. Finally, we will examine the unweighted series.

PRICE-WEIGHTED SERIES

A **price-weighted series** is an arithmetic average of current prices, which means that index movements are influenced by the differential prices of the components.

DOW JONES INDUSTRIAL AVERAGE   The best-known price-weighted series is also the oldest and certainly the most popular stock-market indicator series, the Dow Jones Industrial Average (DJIA). The DJIA is a price-weighted average of 30 large, well-known industrial stocks that are generally the leaders in their industry (blue chips) and are listed on the NYSE. The DJIA is computed by totaling the current prices of the 30 stocks and dividing the sum by a divisor that has been adjusted to take account of stock splits and changes in the sample over time.[5] The divisor is adjusted so that the index value will be the same before and after the split. This is demonstrated in Table 5.1.

$$DJIA_t = \sum_{i=1}^{30} p_{it}/D_{adj}$$

where:

> $DJIA_t$ = **the value of the DJIA on day** t
> p_{it} = **the closing price of stock** i **on day** t
> D_{adj} = **the adjusted divisor on day** t

| TABLE 5.1 | EXAMPLE OF CHANGE IN DJIA DIVISOR WHEN A SAMPLE STOCK SPLITS |

		Before Split	After Three-for-One Split by Stock A	
		Prices	Prices	
	A	30	10	
	B	20	20	
	C	10	10	
		60 ÷ 3 = 20	40 ÷ X = 20	X = 2 (New Divisor)

---

[5]A complete list of all events that have caused a change in the divisor since the DJIA went to 30 stocks on October 1, 1928, is contained in Phyllis S. Pierce, ed., *The Business One Irwin Investor's Handbook* (Burr Ridge, Ill.: Dow Jones Books, annual). Prior to 1992, it was the *Dow Jones Investor's Handbook.* In May 1996 the DJIA celebrated its 100th birthday, which was acknowledged with two special sections entitled "A Century of Investing" and "100 Years of the DJIA," *Wall Street Journal,* 28 May 1996.

| TABLE 5.2 | DEMONSTRATION OF THE IMPACT OF DIFFERENTLY PRICED SHARES ON A PRICE-WEIGHTED INDICATOR SERIES |

| | Period T | Period T + 1 | |
		Case A	Case B
A	100	110	100.7
B	50	50	50
C	30	30	33
Sum	180	190	183
Divisor	3	3	3
Average	60	63.3	61
Percentage change		5.5	1.7

In Table 5.1, three stocks are employed to demonstrate the procedure used to derive a new divisor for the DJIA when a stock splits. When stocks split, the divisor becomes smaller as shown. The cumulative effect of splits can be derived from the fact that the divisor was originally 30.0, but as of July 1999 it was 0.197405.

The adjusted divisor ensures that the new value for the series is the same as it would have been without the split. In this case, the pre-split index value was 20. Therefore, after the split, given the new sum of prices, the divisor is adjusted downward to maintain this value of 20. The divisor is also changed in the rare instances of a change in the sample makeup of the series.

Because the series is price weighted, a high-priced stock carries more weight than a low-priced stock, so, as shown in Table 5.2, a 10 percent change in a $100 stock ($10) will cause a larger change in the series than a 10 percent change in a $30 stock ($3). In Case A, when the $100 stock increases by 10 percent, the average rises by 5.5 percent; in Case B, when the $30 stock increases by 10 percent, the average rises by only 1.7 percent.

The DJIA has been criticized on several counts. First, the sample used for the series is limited. It is difficult to conceive that 30 nonrandomly selected blue-chip stocks can be representative of the 3,000 stocks listed on the NYSE. Beyond the limited number, the stocks included are the largest and most prestigious companies in various industries. Therefore, it is contended that the DJIA probably reflects price movements for large, mature, blue-chip firms rather than for the typical company listed on the NYSE. Several studies have pointed out that the DJIA has not been as volatile as other market indexes and that the long-run returns on the DJIA are not comparable to the other NYSE stock indexes.

In addition, because the DJIA is price weighted, when companies have a stock split, their prices decline, and therefore their weight in the DJIA is reduced—even though they may be large and important. Therefore, the weighting scheme causes a downward bias in the DJIA, because the stocks that have higher growth rates will have higher prices, and because such stocks tend to split, they will consistently lose weight within the index.[6] Regardless of the several criticisms made of the DJIA, a fairly close relationship exists between the *daily* or monthly percentage changes for the DJIA and comparable price

---

[6]For discussions of these problems, see H. L. Butler, Jr., and J. D. Allen, "The Dow Jones Industrial Average Reexamined," *Financial Analysts Journal* 35, no. 6 (November–December 1979): 37–45. For several articles that consider the origin and performance of the DJIA during its 100 years, see "100 Years of the DJIA," section in the *Wall Street Journal,* 28 May 1996, R29–R56. For a recent discussion of differing results, see Greg Ip, "What's Behind the Trailing Performance of the Dow Industrials vs. the S & P 500?" *Wall Street Journal,* 20 August 1998, C1, C17.

changes for other NYSE indexes, as shown in a subsequent section of this chapter. Dow Jones also publishes an average of 20 stocks in the transportation industry and 15 utility stocks. Detailed reports of the averages are contained daily in the *Wall Street Journal* and weekly in *Barron's,* including hourly figures.

NIKKEI–DOW JONES AVERAGE Also referred to as the Nikkei Stock Average Index, the Nikkei–Dow Jones Average is an arithmetic average of prices for 225 stocks on the First Section of the Tokyo Stock Exchange (TSE). This is the best-known series in Japan, and it has been used to show stock price trends since the reopening of the TSE. Notably, it was formulated by Dow Jones and Company, and, similar to the DJIA, it is a price-weighted series, so a large price change for a small company will have the same impact as a similar price change of a large firm. It is also criticized because the 225 stocks that are included comprise only about 15 percent of all stocks on the First Section. The results for this index are reported daily in the *Wall Street Journal* and the *Financial Times* and weekly in *Barron's.*

VALUE-WEIGHTED SERIES

A **value-weighted series** is generated by deriving the initial total market value of all stocks used in the series (Market Value = Number of Shares Outstanding × Current Market Price). This initial figure is typically established as the base and assigned an index value (the most popular beginning index value is 100, but it can vary—say, 10, 50). Subsequently, a new market value is computed for all securities in the index, and the current market value is compared to the initial "base" value to determine the percentage of change, which in turn is applied to the beginning index value.

$$\text{Index}_t = \frac{\Sigma P_t Q_t}{\Sigma P_b Q_b} \times \text{Beginning Index Value}$$

where:

Index$_t$ = index value on day t
P$_t$ = ending prices for stocks on day t
Q$_t$ = number of outstanding shares on day t
P$_b$ = ending price for stocks on base day
Q$_b$ = number of outstanding shares on base day

A simple example for a three-stock index is shown in Table 5.3. As you can see, there is an *automatic adjustment* for stock splits and other capital changes with a value-weighted index because the decrease in the stock price is offset by an increase in the number of shares outstanding.

In a value-weighted index, the importance of individual stocks in the sample depends on the market value of the stocks. Therefore, a specified percentage change in the value of a large company has a greater impact than a comparable percentage change for a small company. As shown in Table 5.4, assuming the only change is a 20 percent increase in the value of Stock A, which has a beginning value of $10 million, the ending index value would be $202 million, or an index of 101. In contrast, if only Stock C increases by 20 percent from $100 million, the ending value will be $220 million or an index value of 110. The point is, price changes for the large market value stocks in a value-weighted index will dominate changes in the index value over time. This value-weighting effect was prevalent during 1998 when the market was being driven by large growth stocks—that is, almost all of the gain for the year was attributable to the largest 50 of the S&P 500 Index.

Table 5.5 is a summary of the characteristics of the major price-weighted, market-value-weighted, and equal-weighted stock price indexes for the United States and the major

TABLE 5.3	**EXAMPLE OF A COMPUTATION OF A VALUE-WEIGHTED INDEX**

Stock	Share Price	Number of Shares	Market Value
December 31, 1999			
A	$10.00	1,000,000	$ 10,000,000
B	15.00	6,000,000	90,000,000
C	20.00	5,000,000	100,000,000
Total			$200,000,000
			Base Value Equal to an Index of 100
December 31, 2000			
A	$12.00	1,000,000	$ 12,000,000
B	10.00	12,000,000[a]	120,000,000
C	20.00	5,500,000[b]	110,000,000
Total			$242,000,000

$$\frac{\text{New}}{\text{Index Value}} = \frac{\text{Current Market Value}}{\text{Base Value}} \times \frac{\text{Beginning}}{\text{Index Value}}$$

$$= \frac{\$242,000,000}{\$200,000,000} \times 100$$

$$= 1.21 \times 100$$

$$= 121$$

[a]Stock split two-for-one during the year.

[b]Company paid a 10 percent stock dividend during the year.

TABLE 5.4	**DEMONSTRATION OF THE IMPACT OF DIFFERENT VALUES ON A MARKET-VALUE-WEIGHTED STOCK INDEX**

		DECEMBER 31, 1999		DECEMBER 31, 2000			
				CASE A		CASE B	
Stock	Number of Shares	Price	Value	Price	Value	Price	Value
A	1,000,000	$10.00	$ 10,000,000	$12.00	$ 12,000,000	$10.00	$ 10,000,000
B	6,000,000	15.00	90,000,000	15.00	90,000,000	15.00	90,000,000
C	5,000,000	20.00	100,000,000	20.00	100,000,000	24.00	120,000,000
			$200,000,000		$202,000,000		$220,000,000
Index Value			100.00		101.00		110.00

foreign countries. As shown, the major differences are the number of stocks in the index, but more important, the *source* of the sample (stocks from the NYSE, the OTC, the AMEX, or from a foreign country, such as the United Kingdom or Japan).

Figure 5.1 shows the "Stock Market Data Bank" from the *Wall Street Journal* of May 27, 1999, which contains values for many of the U.S. stock indexes we have discussed. To gain an appreciation of the differences among indexes, you should examine the different 12-month percentage changes of alternative indexes in the third column from the left. Figure 5.2 shows a similar table for alternative indexes created and maintained by the *Financial Times*.

TABLE 5.5 SUMMARY OF STOCK MARKET INDEXES

Name of Index	Weighting	Number of Stocks	Source of Stocks
Dow Jones Industrial Average	Price	30	NYSE
Nikkei–Dow Jones Average	Price	225	TSE
S&P 400 Industrial	Market value	400	NYSE, OTC
S&P Transportation	Market value	20	NYSE, OTC
S&P Utilities	Market value	40	NYSE, OTC
S&P Financials	Market value	40	NYSE, OTC
S&P 500 Composite	Market value	500	NYSE, OTC
NYSE			
Industrial	Market value	1,420	NYSE
Utility	Market value	227	NYSE
Transportation	Market value	48	NYSE
Financial	Market value	864	NYSE
Composite	Market value	2,559	NYSE
NASDAQ			
Composite	Market value	4,879	OTC
Industrial	Market value	3,019	OTC
Banks	Market value	320	OTC
Insurance	Market value	107	OTC
Other finance	Market value	646	OTC
Transportation	Market value	91	OTC
Telecommunications	Market value	141	OTC
AMEX Market Value	Market value	900	AMEX
Dow Jones Equity Market Index	Market value	2,300	NYSE, AMEX, OTC
Wilshire 5000 Equity Value	Market value	5,000	NYSE, AMEX, OTC
Russell Indexes			
3,000	Market value	3,000	NYSE, AMEX, OTC
1,000	Market value	1,000 largest	NYSE, AMEX, OTC
2,000	Market value	2,000 smallest	NYSE, AMEX, OTC
Financial Times Actuaries Index			
All Share	Market value	700	LSE
FT100	Market value	100 largest	LSE
Small Cap	Market value	250	LSE
Mid Cap	Market value	250	LSE
Combined	Market value	350	LSE
Tokyo Stock Exchange Price Index (TOPIX)	Market value	1,800	TSE
Value Line Averages			
Industrials	Equal (geometric average)	1,499	NYSE, AMEX, OTC
Utilities	Equal	177	NYSE, AMEX, OTC
Rails	Equal	19	NYSE, AMEX, OTC
Composite	Equal	1,695	NYSE, AMEX, OTC
Financial Times Ordinary Share Index	Equal (geometric average)	30	LSE
FT-Actuaries World Indexes	Market value	2,275	24 countries, 3 regions (returns in $, £, ¥, DM, and local currency)
Morgan Stanley Capital International (MSCI) Indexes	Market value	1,375	19 countries, 3 international, 38 international industries (returns in $ and local currency)
Dow Jones World Stock Index	Market value	2,200	13 countries, 3 regions, 120 industry groups (returns in $, £, ¥, DM, and local currency)
Euromoney—First Boston Global Stock Index	Market value	—	17 countries (returns in $ and local currency)
Salomon-Russell World Equity Index	Market value	Russell 1000 and S-R PMI of 600 non-U.S. stocks	22 countries (returns in $ and local currency)

FIGURE 5.1	STOCK MARKET DATA BANK

STOCK MARKET DATA BANK 5/26/99

MAJOR INDEXES

†12-MO HIGH	LOW		DAILY HIGH	LOW	CLOSE	NET CHG	% CHG	†12-MO CHG	% CHG	FROM 12/31	% CHG
DOW JONES AVERAGES											
11107.19	7539.07	30 Industrials	10721.33	10518.70	x10702.16	+ 171.07	+ 1.62	+1765.59	+ 19.76	+1520.73	+ 16.56
3783.50	2345.00	20 Transportation	3477.01	3426.21	x3453.88	+ 0.55	+ 0.02	+ 121.38	+ 3.64	+ 304.57	+ 9.67
330.63	271.67	15 Utilities	331.20	327.64	x330.63	+ 2.15	+ 0.65	+ 53.21	+ 19.18	+ 18.33	+ 5.87
3366.13	2411.00	65 Composite	3255.20	3210.08	x3251.23	+ 35.55	+ 1.11	+ 434.66	+ 15.43	+ 380.40	+ 13.25
1296.00	900.71	DJ Global-US	1235.88	1210.32	1235.88	+ 19.27	+ 1.58	+ 204.17	+ 19.79	+ 66.54	+ 5.69
NEW YORK STOCK EXCHANGE											
651.35	477.20	Composite	624.94	615.41	624.84	+ 7.50	+ 1.21	+ 60.91	+ 10.80	+ 29.03	+ 4.87
808.78	593.49	Industrials	777.69	767.66	777.30	+ 7.36	+ 0.96	+ 77.48	+ 11.07	+ 33.65	+ 4.52
479.79	354.33	Utilities	472.98	465.05	472.15	+ 5.69	+ 1.22	+ 107.49	+ 29.48	+ 26.21	+ 5.88
560.33	351.13	Transportation	511.41	503.61	510.14	+ 1.76	+ 0.35	+ 17.53	+ 3.56	+ 27.76	+ 5.75
599.15	399.19	Finance	550.18	536.19	550.18	+ 12.16	+ 2.26	+ 9.11	+ 1.68	+ 28.76	+ 5.52
STANDARD & POOR'S INDEXES											
1367.56	957.28	500 Index	1304.85	1278.43	1304.76	+ 20.36	+ 1.59	+ 212.53	+ 19.46	+ 75.53	+ 6.14
1635.22	1134.73	Industrials	1566.10	1536.65	1565.37	+ 20.62	+ 1.33	+ 288.67	+ 22.61	+ 86.21	+ 5.83
269.21	229.71	Utilities	269.43	266.54	269.21	+ 2.07	+ 0.77	+ 37.17	+ 16.02	+ 9.59	+ 3.69
409.63	275.93	400 MidCap	393.88	387.48	393.88	+ 2.41	+ 0.62	+ 38.94	+ 10.97	+ 1.57	+ 0.40
194.44	128.70	600 SmallCap	176.38	174.48	175.38	− 0.30	− 0.17	− 13.03	− 6.92	− 1.99	− 1.12
287.08	200.77	1500 Index	274.24	268.93	274.24	+ 3.96	+ 1.47	+ 41.25	+ 17.70	+ 14.19	+ 5.46
NASDAQ STOCK MARKET											
2652.05	1419.12	Composite	2427.18	2339.12	2427.18	+ 46.28	+ 1.94	+ 646.08	+ 36.27	+ 234.49	+ 10.69
2260.66	1128.88	Nasdaq 100	2053.04	1960.55	2053.04	+ 54.00	+ 2.70	+ 843.58	+ 69.75	+ 217.03	+ 11.82
1534.20	882.40	Industrials	1451.02	1405.90	1449.93	+ 15.37	+ 1.07	+ 130.22	+ 9.87	+ 145.68	+ 11.17
2372.33	1346.58	Insurance	2364.71	2337.80	2361.15	+ 16.96	+ 0.72	+ 563.46	+ 31.34	+ 564.36	+ 31.41
2198.81	1486.32	Banks	1825.85	1810.36	1825.75	+ 6.74	+ 0.37	− 364.43	− 16.64	− 12.25	− 0.67
1381.92	690.19	Computer	1206.75	1151.37	1206.68	+ 30.81	+ 2.62	+ 451.58	+ 59.80	+ 72.49	+ 6.39
700.12	310.74	Telecommunications	643.65	619.21	643.42	+ 15.42	+ 2.46	+ 268.96	+ 71.83	+ 142.51	+ 28.45
OTHERS											
800.39	563.75	Amex Composite	783.13	775.97	782.66	+ 3.82	+ 0.49	+ 73.82	+ 10.41	+ 93.67	+ 13.60
713.04	494.35	Russell 1000	680.00	666.48	680.00	+ 10.16	+ 1.52	+ 107.78	+ 18.84	+ 37.13	+ 5.78
463.64	310.28	Russell 2000	436.94	429.71	435.41	+ 0.96	+ 0.22	− 14.85	− 3.30	+ 13.45	+ 3.19
734.62	509.10	Russell 3000	701.24	687.72	701.24	+ 9.81	+ 1.42	+ 100.90	+ 16.81	+ 36.97	+ 5.57
483.72	346.66	Value-Line(geom.)	450.14	446.14	449.71	+ 1.01	+ 0.23	− 28.11	− 5.88	+ 12.56	+ 2.87
12549.05	8620.80	Wilshire 5000	...	...	11969.09	+ 156.51	+ 1.32	+1665.02	+ 16.16	+ 651.50	+ 5.76

†-Based on comparable trading day in preceding year.

Source: *Wall Street Journal*, 27 May 1999, C2.

UNWEIGHTED PRICE INDICATOR SERIES

In an **unweighted index**, all stocks carry equal weight regardless of their price or market value. A $20 stock is as important as a $40 stock, and the total market value of the company is unimportant. Such an index can be used by individuals who randomly select stock for their portfolio and invest the same dollar amount in each stock. One way to visualize an unweighted series is to assume that equal dollar amounts are invested in each stock in the portfolio (for example, an equal $1,000 investment in each stock would work out to 50 shares of a $20 stock, 100 shares of a $10 stock, and 10 shares of a $100 stock). In fact, the actual movements in the index are typically based on *the arithmetic average of the percent changes in price or value for the stocks in the index.* The use of percentage price changes means that the price level or the market value of the stock does not make a difference—each percentage change has equal weight. This arithmetic average of percent changes procedure is used in academic studies when the authors specify equal weighting.

FIGURE 5.2

FINANCIAL *TIMES* ACTUARIES SHARES INDICES

FTSE Actuaries Share Indices   UK Series
Produced in conjunction with the Faculty and Institute of Actuaries

	£ Stlg May 27	Day's chge%	Euro Index	£ Stlg May 26	£ Stlg May 25	Year ago	Actual yield%	Cover	P/E ratio	Xd adj. ytd	Total Return
FTSE 100	6199.5	−0.6	7386.1	6236.8	6249.3	5862.3	2.26	1.62	27.31	71.85	2776.71
FTSE 250	5667.7	+0.3	6752.6	5652.4	5653.7	5898.5	2.81	1.85	19.20	70.11	2497.38
FTSE 250 ex Inv Co	5721.4	+0.3	6816.5	5703.1	5703.5	5965.0	2.93	1.90	17.94	73.66	2533.48
FTSE 350	2968.4	−0.5	3536.5	2982.2	2987.4	2860.9	2.34	1.66	25.63	34.77	2718.12
FTSE 350 ex Inv Co	2973.6	−0.5	3542.7	2987.7	2992.9	2863.6	2.35	1.67	25.40	35.12	1396.81
FTSE 350 Higher Yield	2970.7	−0.7	3539.3	2991.3	2985.1	2787.5	3.02	1.50	22.02	41.46	2342.38
FTSE 350 Lower Yield	2958.9	−0.2	3525.2	2965.5	2982.7	2941.5	1.61	1.99	31.09	27.24	2185.77
FTSE SmallCap	2551.68	+0.1	3040.10	2549.94	2557.36	2769.58	2.75	1.81	20.16	27.70	2280.07
FTSE SmallCap ex Inv Co	2524.96	+0.1	3008.27	2523.28	2531.40	2774.96	2.91	1.91	18.01	28.94	2283.30
FTSE All-Share	2882.07	−0.4	3433.73	2894.77	2899.95	2798.68	2.36	1.67	25.30	33.63	2678.59
FTSE All-Share ex Inv Co	2890.24	−0.5	3443.47	2903.31	2908.60	2803.28	2.38	1.68	24.98	34.09	1382.30
FTSE Fledgling	1403.99	......	1672.73	1404.47	1405.05	1501.28	2.77	1.23	29.43	15.21	1599.46
FTSE Fledgling ex Inv Co	1419.95	−0.1	1691.75	1421.21	1421.77	1533.94	3.13	1.26	25.33	17.27	1624.56
FTSE All-Small	1448.40	......	1725.64	1447.73	1451.16	1567.07	2.75	1.68	21.63	15.72	1652.18
FTSE All-Small ex Inv Co	1460.65	......	1740.24	1460.15	1463.99	1599.39	2.96	1.77	19.15	16.95	1679.23
FTSE AIM	978.0	−0.1	1165.2	979.0	980.9	1138.5	0.99	30.00†	0.14	3.41	899.83

Source: *Financial Times*, 28 May 1999, 36.

TABLE 5.6

EXAMPLE OF AN ARITHMETIC AND GEOMETRIC MEAN OF PERCENTAGE CHANGES

	SHARE PRICE			
Stock	**T**	**T + 1**	**HPR**	**HPY**
X	10	12	1.20	0.20
Y	22	20	.91	−0.09
Z	44	47	1.07	0.07

$\Pi = 1.20 \times 0.91 \times 1.07$ $\Sigma = 0.18$

$= 1.168$ $0.18/3 = 0.06$

$1.168^{1/3} = 1.0531$ $= 6\%$

Index Value (T) $\times$ 1.0531 = Index Value $(T + 1)$

Index Value (T) $\times$ 1.06   = Index Value $(T + 1)$

In contrast to computing an arithmetic average of percentage changes, both Value Line and the *Financial Times* Ordinary Share Index compute a *geometric* mean of the holding period returns *and* derive the holding period yield from this calculation. Table 5.6 contains an example of an arithmetic average and a geometric average. This demonstrates the downward bias of the geometric calculation. Specifically, the geometric mean of holding period yields (HPY) shows an average change of only 5.3 percent versus the actual change in wealth of 6 percent.

GLOBAL EQUITY INDEXES

As noted in this chapter's appendix, there are stock-market indexes available for most individual foreign markets similar to those we described for Japan (the Nikkei and TOPIX) and the United Kingdom (the several *Financial Times* indexes) described in Table 5.5. While these local indexes are closely followed within each country, a problem arises in comparing the results implied by these indexes across countries because of a lack of consistency among them in sample selection, weighting, or computational procedure. To solve these comparability problems, several groups have computed a set of country stock indexes with consistent sample selection, weighting, and computational procedure. As a result, these indexes can be directly compared and can be combined to create various regional indexes (for example, Pacific Basin). We will describe the three sets of global equity indexes.

FT/S&P-ACTUARIES WORLD INDEXES   The FT/S&P-Actuaries World Indexes are jointly compiled by the Financial Times Limited, Goldman Sachs and Company, and Standard and Poor's (the "compilers") in conjunction with the Institute of Actuaries and the Faculty of Actuaries. Approximately 2,461 equity securities in 30 countries are measured, covering at least 70 percent of the total value of all listed companies in each country. Actively traded medium- and small-capitalization stocks are included along with major international equities. All securities included must allow direct holdings of shares by foreign nationals.

The indexes are market-value weighted and have a base date of December 31, 1986 = 100. The index results are reported in U.S. dollars, U.K. pound sterling, Japanese yen, German marks, and the local currency of the country. Performance results are calculated after the New York markets close and are published the following day in the *Financial Times* as shown in Table 5.7. In addition to the individual countries and the world index, there are several geographic subgroups, as shown in Table 5.7.

MORGAN STANLEY CAPITAL INTERNATIONAL (MSCI) INDEXES   The Morgan Stanley Capital International Indexes consist of 3 international, 19 national, and 38 international industry indexes. The indexes consider some 1,375 companies listed on stock exchanges in 19 countries with a combined market capitalization that represents approximately 60 percent of the aggregate market value of the stock exchanges of these countries. All the indexes are market-value weighted. Table 5.8 contains the countries included, the number of stocks, and market values for stocks in the various countries and groups.

In addition to reporting the indexes in U.S. dollars and the country's local currency, the following valuation information is available: (1) price-to-book value (P/BV) ratio, (2) price-to-cash earnings (earnings plus depreciation) (P/CE) ratio, (3) price-to-earnings (P/E) ratio, and (4) dividend yield (YLD). These ratios help in analyzing different valuation levels among countries and over time for specific countries.

Notably, the Morgan Stanley group index for Europe, Australia, and the Far East (EAFE) is being used as the basis for futures and options contracts on the Chicago Mercantile Exchange and the Chicago Board Options Exchange. Several of the MSCI country indexes, the EAFE index, and a world index are reported daily in the *Wall Street Journal,* as shown in Figure 5.3.

DOW JONES WORLD STOCK INDEX   In January 1993, Dow Jones introduced its World Stock Index with results beginning December 31, 1991. Composed of more than 2,200 companies worldwide and organized into 120 industry groups, the index includes 33 countries representing more than 80 percent of the combined capitalization of these countries. In addition to the 33 countries shown in Figure 5.4, the countries are grouped into three regions: Asia/Pacific, Europe/Africa, and the Americas. Finally, each country's index is calculated in its own currency as well as in the U.S. dollar. The index is reported daily in the *Wall Street Journal* (domestic), in the *Wall Street Journal Europe,* and in the *Asian Wall Street Journal.* It is published weekly in *Barron's.*[7]

COMPARISON OF WORLD STOCK INDEXES   As shown in Table 5.9, the correlations between the three series since December 31, 1991, when the DJ series became available, indicate that the results with the alternative world stock indexes are quite comparable.

---

[7]"Journal Launches Index Tracking World Stocks," *Wall Street Journal, 5* January 1993, C1.

TABLE 5.7   FT/S&P ACTUARIES WORLD INDEXES

FT/S&P ACTUARIES WORLD INDICES

The FT/S&P Actuaries World Indices are owned by FTSE International Limited, Goldman, Sachs & Co. and Standard & Poor's. The Indices are compiled by FTSE International and Standard & Poor's in conjunction with the Faculty of Actuaries and the Institute of Actuaries.

NATIONAL AND REGIONAL MARKETS (Figures in parentheses show number of lines of stock)	WEDNESDAY MAY 26 1999								TUESDAY MAY 25 1999					DOLLAR INDEX		
	US Dollar Index	Day's Change %	Pound Sterling Index	Yen Index	Euro Index	Local Currency Index	Local % chg on day	Gross Div. Yield	US Dollar Index	Pound Sterling Index	Yen Index	Euro Index	Local Currency Index	52 week High	52 week Low	Year ago (approx)
Australia (75)	216.51	-1.3	201.01	166.79	237.95	221.99	0.0	3.39	219.34	203.05	170.15	238.08	221.90	236.98	163.86	198.26
Austria (21)	174.75	-1.0	162.24	134.62	169.47	169.47	0.2	2.20	176.53	163.42	136.94	169.08	169.08	253.73	165.27	253.73
Belgium (22)	340.85	-2.1	316.45	262.58	323.63	323.63	-0.8	2.27	348.04	322.19	269.99	326.37	326.37	446.95	322.79	357.37
Brazil (29)	145.72	5.4	135.28	112.25	160.14	463.48	4.0	5.18	138.23	127.97	107.23	150.04	445.53	239.10	89.32	206.79
Canada (124)	219.22	-1.2	203.52	168.88	240.92	233.87	-0.2	1.58	221.83	205.35	172.08	240.78	234.36	242.37	159.94	242.37
Denmark (34)	420.54	-0.6	390.43	323.97	462.18	405.73	0.6	1.86	423.27	391.83	328.34	459.42	403.40	537.33	406.62	511.69
Finland (26)	637.68	-1.2	592.01	491.24	759.41	759.41	0.1	1.54	645.20	597.27	500.50	758.86	758.86	719.62	338.49	443.99
France (72)	328.55	-1.5	305.03	253.10	322.65	322.65	-0.3	2.09	333.59	308.81	258.77	323.54	323.54	354.45	253.86	328.64
Germany (53)	254.07	-0.9	235.88	195.73	246.56	246.56	0.3	1.61	256.38	237.34	198.88	245.73	245.73	325.61	226.35	303.12
Greece (35)	441.68	-3.8	410.05	340.25	485.41	982.51	-2.7	1.22	459.27	425.16	356.27	498.50	1009.66	467.85	211.47	300.61
Hong Kong, China (69)	371.64	0.4	345.03	286.29	408.43	370.01	0.4	3.00	370.05	342.56	287.06	401.66	368.43	407.18	196.64	285.43
Indonesia (21)	74.96	-4.5	69.59	57.74	82.38	372.47	-3.2	1.07	78.47	72.64	60.87	85.17	384.63	80.38	19.04	38.28
Ireland (14)	497.12	-1.5	461.52	382.96	526.51	526.51	-0.3	2.01	504.74	467.25	391.54	527.97	527.97	605.85	396.15	521.11
Italy (53)	161.32	-1.0	149.77	124.28	222.65	222.65	0.2	1.74	162.94	150.83	126.39	222.09	222.09	192.64	128.68	174.10
Japan (443)	110.93	0.4	102.98	85.45	121.91	85.45	-0.3	0.81	110.48	102.27	85.70	119.92	85.70	119.02	76.83	93.20
Mexico (29)	1668.64	1.8	1549.15	1285.45	1833.85	17669.39	3.5	1.60	1639.38	1517.61	1271.71	1779.41	17069.17	1870.23	787.15	1451.45
Netherlands (26)	498.21	-1.4	462.54	383.80	478.25	478.25	-0.2	2.03	505.27	467.74	391.95	479.03	479.03	562.73	394.92	529.83
New Zealand (19)	62.40	-1.6	57.93	48.07	68.58	62.19	0.4	3.73	63.38	58.67	49.17	68.80	61.94	72.33	45.68	69.59
Norway (37)	253.63	-0.8	235.46	195.38	278.74	270.27	0.1	1.72	255.69	236.70	198.35	277.54	270.00	323.73	181.86	323.73
Philippines (22)	107.79	-0.2	100.07	83.04	118.46	204.39	0.4	0.74	107.96	99.94	83.75	117.18	203.64	120.36	42.48	93.30
Portugal (18)	210.89	-0.7	195.79	162.46	276.19	276.19	0.6	2.32	212.32	196.54	164.70	274.62	274.62	296.74	194.13	291.55
Singapore (40)	269.20	-0.3	249.93	207.38	295.86	214.53	0.1	1.22	269.90	249.85	209.37	292.95	214.36	297.82	102.45	181.99
South Africa (31)	224.98	-1.4	208.87	173.32	247.26	308.24	-0.8	3.46	228.09	211.15	176.94	247.58	310.59	298.93	151.55	298.93
Spain (29)	368.85	-1.7	342.44	284.15	443.73	443.73	-0.4	1.63	375.16	347.29	291.02	445.74	445.74	435.19	290.81	396.60
Sweden (41)	560.12	-1.6	520.01	431.49	615.58	709.54	-0.7	1.92	568.98	526.72	441.38	617.58	714.37	628.19	379.18	611.47
Switzerland (29)	366.63	-1.0	340.38	282.44	402.93	345.51	0.1	1.35	370.21	342.72	287.19	401.84	345.04	441.65	307.73	414.95
Thailand (26)	35.03	0.2	32.52	26.98	38.49	50.52	0.4	1.64	34.95	32.35	27.11	37.93	50.30	42.39	8.15	21.73
United Kingdom (199)	389.65	-0.5	361.74	300.17	428.22	361.74	-0.2	2.34	391.62	362.54	303.79	425.08	362.54	417.04	307.96	385.50
USA (605)	538.04	1.6	499.52	414.48	591.31	538.04	1.6	1.25	529.81	490.46	410.99	575.07	529.81	564.34	390.12	446.35
Americas (787)	479.08	1.5	444.78	369.06	526.52		1.5	1.28	472.14	437.07	366.25	512.47	400.15	503.06	347.59	403.57
Europe (709)	349.84	-1.0	324.79	269.50	384.48	343.92	-0.1	1.98	353.40	327.15	274.14	383.58	344.36	386.24	282.63	367.09
Eurobloc (334)	99.15	-1.3	92.05	76.38	104.14	104.14	0.0	1.86	100.43	92.97	77.91	104.19	104.19	113.92	81.53	106.34
Nordic (138)	518.59	-1.2	481.46	399.50	569.94	565.25	-0.2	1.78	525.16	486.16	407.38	570.02	566.45	555.97	360.04	531.26
Pacific Basin (715)	120.55	0.2	111.92	92.87	132.49	95.04	-0.2	1.27	120.30	111.37	93.32	130.58	95.23	129.86	82.88	101.33
Euro-Pacific (1424)	215.56	-0.6	200.13	166.06	236.90	188.50	-0.2	1.76	216.92	200.81	163.27	235.45	188.78	227.88	166.00	212.11
North America (729)	516.50	1.4	479.52	397.89	567.64	517.04	1.5	1.26	509.13	471.31	394.94	552.62	509.47	541.76	374.92	433.41
Europe Ex. UK (510)	319.22	-1.3	296.36	245.91	350.83	325.12	-0.1	1.79	323.35	299.33	250.83	350.83	325.38	366.32	260.93	345.25
Europe Ex. Eurobloc (375)	97.52	-0.7	90.53	75.12	107.17	101.72	-0.2	2.10	98.23	90.94	76.20	106.62	101.94	103.93	77.40	100.08
Europe Ex. UK Ex. Eurobloc (176)	93.78	-1.3	87.07	72.25	103.07	98.16	-0.2	1.52	94.98	87.92	73.68	103.09	98.35	109.21	75.16	104.20
Pacific Ex. Japan (272)	211.13	-0.5	196.01	162.65	232.03	213.44	0.2	2.94	212.19	196.43	164.60	230.31	213.07	230.69	128.26	177.75
World Ex. Eurobloc (1908)	111.29	0.9	103.32	85.74	122.31	111.28	0.9	1.43	110.33	102.14	85.59	119.76	110.26	116.77	83.09	97.48
World Ex. US (1637)	216.25	-0.6	200.76	166.59	237.66	194.25	-0.1	1.78	217.55	201.39	168.76	236.14	194.45	228.52	165.95	215.04
World Ex. UK (2043)	313.21	0.7	290.79	241.29	344.22	286.73	0.9	1.40	311.13	288.02	241.35	337.70	284.18	327.39	236.11	280.46
World Ex. Japan (1799)	424.03	0.6	393.67	326.65	466.01	423.31	0.9	1.58	421.65	390.33	327.08	457.66	419.50	443.90	320.58	386.81
The World Index (2242)	319.83	0.6	296.93	246.38	351.50	293.70	0.8	1.49	318.09	294.46	246.75	345.26	291.42	335.13	242.36	289.35

Source: Financial Times, 28 May 1999, 37.

TABLE 5.8	**MARKET COVERAGE OF MORGAN STANLEY CAPITAL INTERNATIONAL INDEXES AS OF AUGUST 26, 1998**					
	GDP EAFE	**Weights[a] World**	**Companies in Index**	**U.S. $ Billion**	**Free EAFE[b]**	**World**
Austria	1.5	0.9	20	24.1	0.4	0.2
Belgium	1.8	1.1	17	123.1	1.9	0.9
Denmark	1.3	0.8	22	64.1	1.0	0.5
Finland	1.0	0.6	20	70.0	1.1	0.5
Finland (free)	1.0	0.6	20	70.0	1.1	0.5
France	10.7	6.5	67	639.2	9.9	4.6
Germany	16.2	9.9	62	728.9	11.3	5.3
Ireland	0.5	0.3	17	31.6	0.5	0.2
Italy	9.4	5.7	52	331.0	5.1	2.4
The Netherlands	2.7	1.7	23	369.4	5.7	2.7
Norway	1.2	0.7	30	30.5	0.5	0.2
Norway (free)	1.2	0.7	30	30.5	0.5	0.2
Spain	4.2	2.6	31	207.6	3.2	1.5
Sweden	1.7	1.0	38	197.2	3.0	1.4
Sweden (free)	1.7	1.0	38	197.2	3.0	1.4
Switzerland	2.1	1.3	32	523.3	8.1	3.8
United Kingdom	9.7	5.9	136	1,466.4	22.7	10.6
Europe 14 (free)	64.6	39.4	587	4,849.8	74.9	35.2
Europe 14	64.6	39.4	587	4,849.8	74.9	35.2
Australia	2.6	1.6	54	147.6	2.3	1.1
Hong Kong	1.2	0.8	34	114.0	1.8	0.8
Japan	29.9	18.3	308	1,292.7	20.0	9.4
Malaysia	0.5	0.3	72	23.3	0.4	0.2
New Zealand	0.5	0.3	9	12.7	0.2	0.1
Singapore	0.7	0.4	35	32.1	—	0.2
Singapore (free)	—	—	35	32.8	0.5	—
Pacific	35.4	21.6	512	1,622.3	—	11.8
Pacific (free)	—	—	512	1,623.0	25.1	—
EAFE (free)	100.0	61.0	1,099	6,472.1	—	46.9
EAFE	—	—	1,099	6,472.8	100.0	—
Canada	—	24	78	264.1	—	1.9
United States	—	36.6	383	7,059.9	—	51.2
The World Index (free)	—	100.0	1,560	13,796.1	—	100.0
The World Index	—	—	1,560	13,796.8	—	—
Nordic countries	5.1	3.1	110	361.8	—	2.6
Europe 14 ex UK	54.9	33.5	451	3,383.3	—	24.5
Far East	32.3	19.7	449	1,462.0	—	10.6
Far East (free)	—	—	449	1,462.7	22.6	—
EASEA (EAFE ex. Japan)	70.1	42.7	791	5,179.4	—	37.5
North America	—	39.0	461	7,324.0	—	53.1
Kokusai (World ex. Japan)	—	81.8	1,252	12,503.4	—	90.6

[a]GDP weight figures represent the initial weights applicable for the first month. They are used exclusively in the MSCI "GDP weighted" indexes.

[b]*Free* indicates that only stocks that can be acquired by foreign investors are included in the index. If the number of companies is the same and the value is different, it indicates that the stocks available to foreigners are priced differently from domestic shares.

Source: Morgan Stanley Capital International (New York: Morgan Stanley & Co., 1998).

BOND-MARKET INDICATOR SERIES[8]

Investors know little about the several bond-market series because these bond series are relatively new and not widely published. Knowledge regarding these bond series is

---

[8]The discussion in this section draws heavily from Frank K. Reilly and David J. Wright, "Bond Market Indexes," *The Handbook of Fixed-Income Securities,* 5th ed., ed. Frank J. Fabozzi (Chicago: Irwin Professional Publishing, 1997).

FIGURE 5.3 **LISTING OF MORGAN STANLEY CAPITAL INTERNATIONAL STOCK INDEX VALUES FOR MAY 27, 1999**

Morgan Stanley Indexes			
	MAY 25	MAY 24	% FROM 12/31/98
U.S.	1255.6	ʼ1277.5	+ 4.9
Britain	1837.6	1858.8	+ 5.4
Canada	807.3	827.0	+ 8.2
Japan	830.1	837.1	+ 19.3
France	1384.6	1394.8	+ 10.6
Germany	677.6	691.1	+ 2.73
Hong Kong	7206.8	7253.2	+ 21.3
Switzerland	866.4	886.10	– 2.8
Australia	584.8	593.5	+ 2.3
World Index	1185.4	1200.1	+ 3.1
EAFE MSCI-p	1414.7	1423.6	+ 0.7

As calculated by Morgan Stanley Capital International Perspective, Geneva. Each index, calculated in local currencies, is based on the close of 1969 equaling 100.

Source: *Wall Street Journal,* 27 May 1999, C12.

becoming more important because of the growth of fixed-income mutual funds and the consequent need to have a reliable set of benchmarks to use in evaluating performance.[9] Also, because the performance of many fixed-income money managers has been unable to match that of the aggregate bond market, interest has been growing in bond index funds, which requires the development of an index to emulate.[10]

Notably, the creation and computation of bond-market indexes is more difficult than a stock-market series for several reasons. First, the universe of bonds is much broader than that of stocks, ranging from U.S. Treasury securities to bonds in default. Second, the universe of bonds is changing constantly because of numerous new issues, bond maturities, calls, and bond sinking funds. Third, the volatility of prices for individual bonds and bond portfolios changes because bond price volatility is affected by duration, which is likewise changing constantly because of changes in maturity, coupon, and market yield (see Chapter 16). Finally, significant problems can arise in correctly pricing the individual bond issues in an index (especially corporate and mortgage bonds) compared to the current and continuous transactions prices available for most stocks used in stock indexes.

The subsequent discussion is divided into three subsections: (1) U.S. investment-grade bond indexes, including Treasuries; (2) U.S. high-yield bond indexes; and (3) global government bond indexes. Notably, all of these indexes indicate total rates of return for the portfolio of bonds, including price change, accrued interest, and coupon income reinvested. Also most of the indexes are market-value weighted using current prices and outstanding

---

[9]For a discussion of benchmark selection, see Chris P. Dialynas, "The Active Decisions in the Selection of Passive Management and Performance Bogeys," and Daralyn B. Peifer, "A Sponsor's View of Benchmark Portfolios," in *The Handbook of Fixed-Income Securities,* 5th ed., ed. Frank J. Fabozzi (Chicago, Ill.: Irwin Professional Publishing, 1997).

[10]For a discussion of this phenomenon, see Fran Hawthorne, "The Battle of the Bond Indexes," *Institutional Investor* 20, no. 4 (April 1986); and Sharmin Mossavar-Rahmani, "Indexing Fixed-Income Investments," in *The Handbook of Fixed-Income Securities,* 5th ed., ed. Frank J. Fabozzi (Chicago: Irwin Professional Publishing, 1997).

FIGURE 5.4 **DOW JONES WORLD STOCK INDEX LISTING**

DOW JONES GLOBAL INDEXES

5:30 p.m., Wednesday, May 26, 1999

REGION/ COUNTRY	DJ GLOBAL INDEXES, LOCAL CURRENCY	PCT. CHG.	IN U.S. DOLLARS								
			5:30 P.M. INDEX	CHG.	PCT. CHG.	12-MO HIGH	12-MO LOW	12-MO CHG.	PCT. CHG.	FROM 12/31	PCT. CHG.
Americas			**301.23**	**+ 4.60**	**+ 1.55**	**316.29**	**219.47**	**+ 45.89**	**+ 17.97**	**+17.44**	**+ 6.15**
Brazil†	1139 + 5.75		256.09	+18.11	+ 7.61	406.24	155.25	−113.82	− 30.77	+17.50	+ 7.33
Canada	206.64 − 0.29		162.40	− 0.80	− 0.49	174.70	117.73	− 11.53	− 6.63	+16.15	+11.05
Chile	211.02 + 1.28		159.43	+ 1.86	+ 1.18	174.92	96.32	+ 0.40	+ 0.25	+28.49	+21.76
Mexico	414.17 + 3.45		132.16	+ 2.78	+ 2.15	147.81	60.60	+ 19.88	+ 17.71	+43.13	+48.45
U.S.	1235.88 + 1.58		1235.88	+19.27	+ 1.58	1296.00	900.71	+204.17	+ 19.79	+66.54	+ 5.69
Venezuela	391.49 + 2.37		40.40	+ 0.89	+ 2.25	56.43	23.01	− 15.86	− 28.19	+ 0.47	+ 1.18
Latin America			**159.27**	**+ 6.11**	**+ 3.99**	**187.21**	**90.39**	**− 18.14**	**− 10.22**	**+30.95**	**+24.12**
Europe/Africa			**228.05**	**− 3.00**	**− 1.30**	**251.61**	**185.07**	**− 6.66**	**− 2.84**	**− 6.95**	**− 2.96**
Austria	123.58 + 0.26		100.19	− 1.32	− 1.30	137.08	93.22	− 36.86	− 26.89	− 5.13	− 4.87
Belgium	289.21 − 0.82		234.68	− 5.66	− 2.36	307.75	225.59	− 8.89	− 3.65	−54.73	−18.91
Denmark	199.31 + 0.18		167.78	− 0.54	− 0.32	210.95	156.84	− 31.26	− 15.70	−22.35	−11.75
Finland	918.75 − 0.27		668.40	−12.40	− 1.82	752.22	365.19	+194.64	+ 41.09	+63.88	+10.57
France	269.06 − 0.03		221.86	− 3.57	− 1.58	238.23	173.04	+ 10.15	+ 4.80	+ 0.85	+ 0.39
Germany	284.33 + 0.26		229.97	− 3.03	− 1.30	280.68	195.52	− 20.64	− 8.23	−18.05	− 7.28
Greece	594.50 − 2.71		336.33	−12.69	− 3.64	358.78	181.78	+ 95.39	+ 39.59	+54.34	+19.27
Ireland	373.68 − 0.73		295.97	− 6.88	− 2.27	369.89	247.45	− 9.57	− 3.13	−39.67	−11.82
Italy	319.59 + 0.30		212.59	− 2.72	− 1.26	252.46	169.16	− 4.74	− 2.18	−21.83	− 9.31
Netherlands	398.83 − 0.17		322.60	− 5.64	− 1.72	366.66	258.60	− 16.62	− 4.90	−23.43	− 6.77
Norway	174.59 + 0.32		132.81	− 0.88	− 0.66	170.80	96.85	− 33.90	− 20.33	+16.69	+14.37
Portugal	354.23 + 0.54		249.32	− 2.58	− 1.02	352.93	221.49	− 84.19	− 25.24	−48.57	−16.30
South Africa	188.45 − 0.71		82.58	− 0.97	− 1.16	116.10	57.78	− 30.31	− 26.85	+11.88	+16.80
Spain	405.01 − 0.48		247.94	− 5.13	− 2.03	293.48	194.86	− 6.99	− 2.74	−22.68	− 8.38
Sweden	431.36 − 0.76		279.43	− 4.63	− 1.63	317.82	190.08	− 21.45	− 7.13	+25.98	+10.25
Switzerland	392.41 + 0.15		348.55	− 5.66	− 1.60	421.91	295.28	− 46.16	− 11.69	−47.38	−11.97
United Kingdom	237.51 − 0.34		202.85	− 1.43	− 0.70	217.02	162.40	+ 3.99	+ 2.01	+ 4.28	+ 2.15
Europe/Africa (ex. South Africa)			**236.36**	**− 3.11**	**− 1.30**	**260.76**	**191.94**	**− 5.26**	**− 2.18**	**− 8.03**	**− 3.29**
Europe/Africa (ex. U.K. & S. Africa)			**257.50**	**− 4.14**	**− 1.58**	**292.44**	**210.59**	**− 10.82**	**− 4.03**	**−15.39**	**− 5.64**
Asia/Pacific			**90.97**	**− 0.02**	**− 0.02**	**98.15**	**62.38**	**+ 15.92**	**+ 21.22**	**+ 9.94**	**+12.27**
Australia	181.14 + 0.54		154.35	− 0.93	− 0.60	168.20	112.56	+ 24.60	+ 18.95	+13.34	+ 9.46
Hong Kong	248.81 + 0.47		249.55	+ 1.16	+ 0.47	272.00	134.48	+ 65.61	+ 35.67	+45.49	+22.29
Indonesia	244.80 − 2.88		60.31	− 3.17	− 4.99	63.48	15.47	+ 28.26	+ 88.18	+19.87	+49.11
Japan	79.89 − 0.25		81.52	− 0.24	− 0.29	87.96	57.38	+ 12.55	+ 18.19	+ 7.33	+ 9.87
New Zealand	137.75 + 0.42		135.66	− 1.47	− 1.07	157.99	99.94	− 13.46	− 9.02	+ 6.26	+ 4.84
Philippines	228.74 + 0.62		156.04	+ 0.01	+ 0.01	175.79	60.68	+ 26.20	+ 20.17	+28.75	+22.59
Singapore	142.28 + 0.42		133.30	+ 0.32	+ 0.24	145.54	59.89	+ 40.94	+ 44.32	+23.89	+21.84
South Korea	125.82 + 3.13		80.12	+ 2.16	+ 2.77	89.81	25.38	+ 51.65	+181.43	+18.90	+30.86
Taiwan	181.11 + 0.41		142.42	+ 0.48	+ 0.34	147.37	106.17	+ 0.17	+ 0.12	+19.13	+15.52
Thailand	77.82 + 3.11		49.43	+ 1.42	+ 2.96	56.76	20.88	+ 15.49	+ 45.64	+ 9.67	+24.32
Asia/Pacific (ex. Japan)			**154.35**	**+ 0.85**	**+ 0.55**	**166.45**	**91.45**	**+ 34.64**	**+ 28.93**	**+23.65**	**+18.10**
World (ex. U.S.)			**150.49**	**− 1.14**	**− 0.75**	**159.31**	**115.37**	**+ 4.48**	**+ 3.07**	**+ 3.47**	**+ 2.36**
DJ WORLD STOCK INDEX			**210.25**	**+ 0.99**	**+ 0.47**	**220.75**	**160.36**	**+ 20.91**	**+ 11.04**	**+ 7.46**	**+ 3.68**

Indexes based on 6/30/82=100 for U.S., 12/31/91=100 for World.
†Local currency index shown in 000s.

Source: *Wall Street Journal,* 27 May 1999, C12.

TABLE 5.9	**CORRELATIONS OF PERCENT PRICE CHANGES OF ALTERNATIVE WORLD STOCK INDEXES 12/31/91–12/31/98**

	U.S. Dollars
FT–MS:	0.998
FT–DJ:	0.997
MS–DJ:	0.996

par values publicly held. Table 5.10 is a summary of the characteristics for the indexes available for these three segments of the bond market.

INVESTMENT-GRADE BOND INDEXES

As shown in Table 5.10, four investment firms have created and maintain indexes for Treasury bonds and other bonds considered investment grade; that is, the bonds are rated BBB or higher. As demonstrated in Reilly and Wright and shown in Chapter 4, the relationship among the returns for these bonds is strong (that is, the correlations among the returns average about 0.95), regardless of the segment of the market. This implies that the returns for these investment-grade bonds are being driven by aggregate interest rates—that is, shifts in the government yield curve.

HIGH-YIELD BOND INDEXES

One of the fastest-growing segments of the U.S. bond market during the past 15 years has been the high-yield bond market, which includes bonds that are not investment grade—that is, they are rated BB, B, CCC, CC, and C. Because of this growth, four investment firms and two academicians created indexes related to this market. A summary of the characteristics for these indexes is included in Table 5.10. As shown in a study by Reilly and Wright, the relationship among the alternative high-yield bond indexes is weaker than among the investment-grade indexes, and this is especially true for the bonds rated CCC.[11]

MERRILL LYNCH CONVERTIBLE SECURITIES INDEXES In March 1988, Merrill Lynch introduced a convertible bond index with data beginning in January 1987. This index includes 600 issues in three major subgroups: U.S. domestic convertible bonds, Eurodollar convertible bonds issued by U.S. corporations, and U.S. domestic convertible preferred stocks. The issues included must be public U.S. corporate issues, have a minimum par value of $25 million, and have a minimum maturity of one year.

GLOBAL GOVERNMENT BOND MARKET INDEXES

Similar to the high-yield bond market, the global bond market has experienced significant growth in size and importance during the recent five-year period. Unlike the high-yield bond market, this global segment is completely dominated by government bonds because few non-U.S. countries have a corporate bond market, much less a high-yield corporate bond market. Once again, several major investment firms have responded to the needs of investors and money managers by creating indexes that reflect the performance for the global bond market, certain individual countries, and several regions. As shown in Table 5.10, the various indexes have several similar characteristics, such as measuring total rates of return, using market-value weighting, and using trader pricing. At the same time, the total sample sizes differ as do numbers of countries included.

---

[11]Frank K. Reilly and David J. Wright, "An Analysis of High-Yield Bond Benchmarks," *Journal of Fixed Income* 3, no. 4 (March 1994): 6–24. The uniqueness of CCC bonds is demonstrated in Frank K. Reilly and David J. Wright, "High-Yield Bonds and Segmentation in the Bond Market," mimeo (January 1999).

| TABLE 5.10 | SUMMARY OF BOND MARKET INDEXES |

Name of Index	Number of Issues	Maturity	Size of Issues	Weighting	Pricing	Reinvestment Assumption	Subindexes Available
U.S. Investment-Grade Bond Indexes							
Lehman Brothers	5,000+	Over 1 year	Over $100 million	Market value	Trader priced and model priced	No	Government, gov./corp., corporate, mortgage-backed, asset-backed
Merrill Lynch	5,000+	Over 1 year	Over $50 million	Market value	Trader priced and model priced	In specific bonds	Government, gov./corp., corporate, mortgage
Ryan Treasury	300+	Over 1 year	All Treasury	Market value and equal	Market priced	In specific bonds	Treasury
Salomon Brothers	5,000+	Over 1 year	Over $50 million	Market value	Trader priced	In one-month T-bill	Broad inv. grade, Treas.-agency, corporate, mortgage
U.S. High-Yield Bond Indexes							
Blume-Keim	233	Over 10 years	Over $25 million	Equal	Trader priced	Yes	Only composite
First Boston	423	All maturities	Over $75 million	Market value	Trader priced	Yes	Composite and by rating
Lehman Brothers	624	Over 1 year	Over $100 million	Market value	Trader priced	No	Composite and by rating
Merrill Lynch	735	Over 1 year	Over $25 million	Market value	Trader priced	Yes	Composite and by rating
Salomon Brothers	299	Over 7 years	Over $50 million	Market value	Trader priced	Yes	Composite and by rating
Global Government Bond Indexes (Initial Date of Index)							
Lehman Brothers (January 1987)	800	Over 1 year	Over $200 million	Market value	Trader priced	Yes	Composite and 13 countries, local and U.S. dollars
Merrill Lynch (December 1985)	9,736	Over 1 year	Over $50 million	Market value	Trader priced	Yes	Composite and 9 countries, local and U.S. dollars
J. P. Morgan (12/31/85)	445	Over 1 year	Over $100 million	Market value	Trader priced	Yes in index	Composite and 11 countries, local and U.S. dollars
Salomon Brothers (12/31/84)	400	Over 1 year	Over $250 million	Market value	Trader priced	Yes at local short-term rate	Composite and 14 countries, local and U.S. dollars

Source: Frank K. Reilly, Wenchi Kao, and David J. Wright, "Alternative Bond Market Indexes," *Financial Analysts Journal* 48, no. 3 (May–June, 1992): 14–58; Frank K. Reilly and David J. Wright, "An Analysis of High-Yield Bond Benchmarks," *Journal of Fixed Income* 3, no. 4 (March 1994): 6–24; and Frank K. Reilly and David J. Wright, "Global Bond Markets: Alternative Benchmarks and Risk–Return Performance," mimeo (May 1997).

An analysis of performance in this market indicates that the differences mentioned have caused some large differences in the long-term risk–return performance by the alternative indexes.[12] Also, the low correlation among the various countries is similar to stocks. Finally, there was a significant exchange rate effect on volatility and correlations.

COMPOSITE STOCK–BOND INDEXES

Beyond separate stock indexes and bond indexes for individual countries, a natural step is the development of a composite series that measures the performance of all securities in a given country. A composite series of stocks and bonds makes it possible to examine the benefits of diversifying with a combination of asset classes such as stocks and bonds in addition to diversifying within the asset classes of stocks or bonds.

MERRILL LYNCH–WILSHIRE U.S. CAPITAL MARKETS INDEX (ML–WCMI)

A market-value-weighted index called Merrill Lynch–Wilshire Capital Markets Index (ML–WCMI) measures the total return performance of the combined U.S. taxable fixed-income and equity markets. It is basically a combination of the Merrill Lynch fixed-income indexes and the Wilshire 5000 common-stock index. As such, it tracks more than 10,000 stocks and bonds. The makeup of the index is as follows (as of December 1997):

Security	$ in Billions	Percent of Total
Treasury bonds	$1,085	20.89%
Agency bonds	166	3.20
Mortgage bonds	467	8.99
Corporate bonds	453	8.72
OTC stocks	331	6.37
AMEX stocks	105	2.02
NYSE stocks	2,586	49.92
	$5,193	100.00%

BRINSON PARTNERS GLOBAL SECURITY MARKET INDEX (GSMI)

The Brinson Partners GSMI series contains both U.S. stocks and bonds, but also includes non-U.S. equities and nondollar bonds as well as an allocation to cash. The specific breakdown is as follows (as of January 1999):

	Percent
Equities	
U.S. large capitalization	35
U.S. small and mid-cap	15
Non-U.S.	17
Fixed Income	
U.S. domestic investment grade	18
International dollar bonds	2
Nondollar bonds	8
Cash	5
Total	100

---

[12]Frank K. Reilly and David J. Wright, "Global Bond Markets: Alternative Benchmarks and Risk–Return Performance," mimeo (May 1997).

Although related to the relative market values of these asset classes, the weights specified are not constantly adjusted. The construction of the GSMI used optimization techniques to identify the portfolio mix of available global asset classes that matches the risk level of a typical U.S. pension plan. The index is balanced to the policy weights monthly.

Because the GSMI contains both U.S. and international stocks and bonds, it is clearly the most diversified benchmark available with a weighting scheme that approaches market values. As such, it is closest to the theoretically specified "market portfolio of risky assets" referred to in the CAPM literature.[13]

COMPARISON OF INDEXES OVER TIME

This section discusses price movements in the different series for various monthly or annual intervals.

CORRELATIONS AMONG MONTHLY EQUITY PRICE CHANGES

Table 5.11 contains a matrix of the correlation coefficients of the monthly percentage of price changes for a set of U.S. and non-U.S. equity-market indexes during the 25-year period from 1972 to 1997.[14] Most of the correlation differences are attributable to sample differences, that is, differences in the firms listed on the alternative stock exchanges. Most of the major series—except the Nikkei Stock Average—are market-value-weighted indexes that include a large number of stocks. Therefore, the computational procedure is generally similar and the sample sizes are large or all-encompassing. Thus, the major difference between the indexes is that the stocks are from different segments of the U.S. stock market or from different countries.

There is a high positive correlation (0.92) between the alternative NYSE series (the S&P 500 and the NYSE composite). These indexes are also highly correlated with the Wilshire 5000 index that is value weighted, which means it is heavily influenced by the large NYSE stocks in the index.

In contrast, there are lower correlations between these NYSE series and the AMEX series (about 0.72) or the NASDAQ index (about 0.78). Further, the relationship between the Russell 2000 Index and the other U.S. series ranges from 0.73 to 0.91, which reflects the fact that the Russell 2000 series includes a sample of small-cap stocks from all exchanges.

The correlations among the U.S. series and those from Canada, the United Kingdom, Germany, and Japan support the case for global investing. The relationships among the two TSE series were correlated about 0.87 even though the sample sizes, weightings, and computations differ. These within-country results attest to the importance of the basic sample. In contrast, the U.S.–Canada and U.S.–U.K. correlations, which averaged about 0.73, and the U.S.–Japan correlations, which were about 0.30, confirm the benefits of global diversification because such low correlations reduce the variance of a portfolio.

---

[13]This GSMI series is used in a study that examines the effect of alternative benchmarks on the estimate of the security market and estimates of individual stock betas. See Frank K. Reilly and Rashid A. Akhtar, "The Benchmark Error Problem with Global Capital Markets," *Journal of Portfolio Management* 22, no. 1 (fall 1995). Brinson Partners has a Multiple Markets Index (MMI) that also contains venture capital and real estate. Because these assets are not actively traded, the value and rate of return estimates tend to be relatively stable, which reduces the standard deviation of the series.

[14]In earlier editions of the text, the correlations examined daily percentage price changes. The shift to monthly percentage price changes made it possible to consider a wider range of non-U.S. equity indexes. Notably, the monthly price change correlation results among U.S. indexes are similar to the daily results.

TABLE 5.11 CORRELATION COEFFICIENTS AMONG MONTHLY PERCENTAGE PRICE CHANGES IN ALTERNATIVE EQUITY MARKET INDICATOR SERIES: JANUARY 1972 (WHEN AVAILABLE) TO DECEMBER 1997

	S&P 500	NYSE	AMEX	NASDAQ Industr.	Wilshire 5000	Russell 2000[a]	Toronto SE 300	Tokyo SE	Nikkei	FAZ[b]	FT All-Share[b]	M-S World	FT/S&P World[c]
S&P 500	—												
NYSE	0.919	—											
AMEX	0.719	0.801	—										
NASDAQ Ind.	0.783	0.881	0.824	—									
Wilshire 5000	0.906	0.987	0.817	0.906	—								
Russell 2000	0.731	0.848	0.764	0.913	0.870	—							
Toronto 300	0.687	0.761	0.768	0.740	0.768	0.723	—						
Tokyo SE	0.302	0.299	0.245	0.251	0.284	0.249	0.269	—					
Nikkei	0.358	0.350	0.280	0.308	0.335	0.325	0.293	0.872	—				
FAZ	0.501	0.534	0.381	0.404	0.515	0.440	0.452	0.279	0.330	—			
FT All-Share	0.615	0.712	0.591	0.620	0.693	0.618	0.627	0.266	0.379	0.514	—		
M-S World	0.763	0.821	0.658	0.704	0.808	0.669	0.714	0.588	0.631	0.525	0.651	—	
FT/S&P World	0.590	0.695	0.508	0.589	0.666	0.572	0.616	0.664	0.731	0.505	0.617	0.960	—

[a]Russell 2000 series starts in 1979.
[b]FAZ and FT All-Share series start in 1983.
[c]FT/S&P World Index series starts in 1986.

CORRELATIONS
AMONG MONTHLY
BOND INDEXES

The correlations among the monthly bond return series in Table 5.12 consider a variety of bond series, including investment-grade bonds, U.S. high-yield bonds, and government bond indexes for several major non-U.S. countries (GE–Germany, JA–Japan, and UK–the United Kingdom). The correlations among the U.S. investment-grade bond series ranged from 0.90 to 0.99, confirming that although the *level* of interest rates differs due to the risk premium, the overriding factors that determine the rates of return for investment-grade bonds over time are *systematic* interest rate variables.

The correlations among investment-grade bonds and HY bonds are significantly lower (0.40 to 0.54), caused by definite equity characteristics of HY bonds.[15] Finally, the low and diverse relationships among U.S. investment-grade bonds and non-U.S. government bond series (0.14 to 0.33) reflect different interest-rate movements and exchange-rate effects (these non-U.S. government results are U.S. dollar returns). Again, these results support the concept of global diversification.

MEAN ANNUAL
STOCK PRICE
CHANGES

The mean and standard deviation of annual percentage of price changes for the major stock indexes is contained in Table 5.13. One would expect differences among the price changes and measures of risk for the various series due to the different samples. For example, the NYSE series should have lower rates of return and risk measures than the AMEX and OTC series. The results generally confirm these expectations. For example, the Russell 2000 reflects the results for the small-capitalization segment of the U.S. stock market. This series, which began in 1979, shows higher returns and higher risk measures than the large-cap NYSE series during most individual years.

Regarding non-U.S. results, the Canadian results on the Toronto Exchange had higher average returns than the NYSE, and lower risk than the NASDAQ. The United Kingdom (that is, the FT All-Share) had higher returns than the NYSE indexes, but much larger variability, while Germany (the FAZ) had lower returns than the United States, but similar volatility. Finally, the Japanese markets experienced lower returns and slightly lower volatility than the U.S. markets. Remember, these non-U.S. stock results reflect the domestic price changes and do not consider the exchange-rate effect.

These results for the Japanese market were significantly affected by poor results during 1990 to 1997. Because the Japanese stock market had relatively low correlation with alternative U.S. stock-market indexes (Table 5.11), it indicates that Japan would have been a prime source of diversification benefits even with the higher volatility.

ANNUAL BOND RATES
OF RETURN

Table 5.14 shows the mean and standard deviation of annual total rates of return for the Lehman Brothers bond-market indexes.[16] You cannot directly compare the bond and stock results because the bond results are *total* rates of return versus annual percentage price change results for stocks (most of the stock series do not report dividend data).

The major comparison for the bond series should be among the average rates of return and the risk measures, because although the monthly rates of return are correlated, we would expect a difference in the level of return due to the differential risk premiums. The results generally confirm our expectations (that is, there typically are lower returns and risk measures for the government series followed by higher returns and risk for corporate and mortgage bonds).

---

[15]For a detailed analysis of this point, see Frank K. Reilly and David J. Wright, "High Yield Bonds and Segmentation in the Bond Market," mimeo (June 1999).

[16]Because of the high correlations among the monthly rates of return as shown in Table 5.12, the results for various bond-market segments (government, corporate, mortgages) are similar regardless of the source (Lehman Brothers, Merrill Lynch, Salomon Brothers, Ryan). Therefore, only the Lehman Brothers risk–return results are presented in Table 5.14.

TABLE 5.12   **CORRELATIONS AMONG MONTHLY BOND RETURNS FOR U.S. INVESTMENT-GRADE BONDS, U.S. HIGH-YIELD BONDS, AND NON-U.S. GOVERNMENT BONDS: 1985–1997**

	LBGC	LBG	LBC	LBM	LBA	MLHYM	SBGE	SBJA	SBUK
LBGC	—								
LBG	0.997	—							
LBC	0.976	0.958	—						
LBM	0.919	0.905	0.927	—					
LBA	0.995	0.990	0.978	0.952	—				
MLHYM	0.457	0.419	0.548	0.454	0.465	—			
SBGE	0.308	0.321	0.259	0.298	0.308	−0.031	—		
SBJA	0.183	0.196	0.159	0.142	0.178	0.043	0.486	—	
SBUK	0.280	0.297	0.227	0.235	0.276	−0.013	0.656	0.455	—

TABLE 5.13   **MEAN AND STANDARD DEVIATION OF ANNUAL PERCENTAGE PRICE CHANGE FOR STOCK PRICE SERIES 1972–1997**

	Geometric Mean	Arithmetic Mean	Standard Deviation	Coefficient of Variation
DJIA	8.79	10.09	16.70	1.66
S&P 400	9.29	10.58	16.44	1.55
S&P 500	9.06	10.35	16.49	1.59
AMEX Value Index	10.04	12.26	22.07	1.80
NASDAQ Comp.	11.89	13.94	20.81	1.49
Russell 2000[a]	15.61	17.00	18.05	1.06
Wilshire 5000	9.29	10.69	17.07	1.60
Toronto S.E. Comp.	11.32	12.54	16.52	1.32
FT All-Share	10.37	14.36	31.94	2.22
FAZ	7.58	10.16	24.27	2.39
Nikkei	6.97	9.74	25.77	2.65
Tokyo S.E. Index	6.86	9.84	27.15	2.76
MS World	8.58	9.82	16.19	1.65

[a]The Russell 2000 index was initiated in 1979.

TABLE 5.14   **MEAN AND STANDARD DEVIATION OF ANNUAL RATES OF RETURN FOR LEHMAN BROTHERS BOND INDEXES 1976–1997**

	Geometric Mean	Arithmetic Mean	Standard Deviation	Coefficient of Variation
Government/Corporate	9.68	9.95	8.04	0.81
Government	9.65	9.77	7.15	0.73
Corporate	10.17	10.60	10.25	0.97
Mortgage-Backed	9.94	10.35	10.07	0.97
Yankee	10.34	10.73	9.63	0.90
Aggregate	9.75	10.02	8.17	0.82

THE INTERNET | *Investments Online*

We've seen several previous Web sites which offer online users a look at current market conditions in the form of a time-delayed market index (some sites offer real-time stock and index prices, but only at a cost to their customers). Here are a few others:

www.bloomberg.com   The site is somewhat of an Internet version of the "Bloomberg machine," which is prevalent in many brokerage house offices. It offers both news and current data on a wide variety of global market securities and indexes as well as information on interest rates, commodities, and currencies.

www.stockmaster.com   The Stockmaster Web site offers information on a number of U.S. and overseas market indexes.

www.asx.com.au   Australian Stock Exchange

www.bolsamadrid.es   Madrid Stock Exchange; Web site is in Spanish

www.tse.com   Toronto Stock Exchange

www.nikko.co.jp:80/SEC/index_e.html   Nikko Stock Market index (Japan)

www.exchange.de/realtime/dax_d.html   German Stock Exchange information

Here's a test of your Web information-seeking skills: see if you can find Web pages for some of the country stock exchanges listed in the Chapter 5 appendix.

Summary

- Given the several uses of security-market indicator series, you should know how they are constructed and the differences among them. If you want to use one of the many series to learn how the "market" is doing, you should be aware of what market you are dealing with so you can select the appropriate index. As an example, are you only interested in the NYSE or do you also want to consider the AMEX and the OTC? Beyond the U.S. market, are you interested in Japanese or U.K. stocks, or do you want to examine the total world market?[17]
- Indexes are also used as benchmarks to evaluate portfolio performance.[18] In this case, you must be sure the index (benchmark) is consistent with your investing universe. If you are investing worldwide, you should not judge your performance relative to the DJIA, which is limited to 30 U.S. blue-chip stocks. For a bond portfolio, the index should match your investment philosophy. Finally, if your portfolio contains both stocks and bonds, you must evaluate your performance against an appropriate combination of indexes.
- Whenever you invest, you examine numerous market indexes to tell you what has happened and how successful you have been. The selection of the appropriate indexes for information or evaluation will depend on how knowledgeable you are regarding the various series. The purpose of this chapter is to help you understand what to look for and how to make the right decision.

Questions

1. Discuss briefly several uses of security-market indicator series.
2. What major factors must be considered when constructing a market index? Put another way, what characteristics differentiate indexes?
3. Explain how a market indicator series is price weighted. In such a case, would you expect a $100 stock to be more important than a $25 stock? Why?
4. Explain how to compute a value-weighted series.
5. Explain how a price-weighted series and a value-weighted series adjust for stock splits.

---

[17]For a readable discussion on this topic, see Anne Merjos, "How's the Market Doing?" *Barron's*, 20 August, 1990, 18–20, 27, 28.

[18]Chapter 27 includes an extensive discussion of the purpose and construction of benchmarks and considers the evaluation of portfolio performance.

6. Describe an unweighted price-indicator series and describe how you would construct such a series. Assume a 20 percent price change in GM ($40/share; 50 million shares outstanding) and Coors Brewing ($25/share and 15 million shares outstanding). Explain which stock's change will have the greater impact on this index.

7. If you correlated percentage changes in the Wilshire 5000 equity index with percentage changes in the NYSE composite, the AMEX index, and the NASDAQ composite index, would you expect a difference in the correlations? Why or why not?

8. There are high correlations among the monthly percentage price changes for the alternative NYSE indexes. Discuss the reason for this similarity: is it size of sample, source of sample, or method of computation?

9. Compare stock price indicator series for the three U.S. equity-market segments (NYSE, AMEX, OTC) for the period 1972 to 1997. Discuss whether the results in terms of average annual price change and risk (variability of price changes) were consistent with economic theory.

10. Discuss the relationship (correlations) between the two stock price indexes for the Tokyo Stock Exchange (TSE). Examine the correlations among the TSE series and two NYSE series. Explain why these relationships differ.

11. You learn that the Wilshire 5000 market-value-weighted series increased by 16 percent during a specified period, whereas a Wilshire 5000 equal-weighted series increased by 23 percent during the same period. Discuss what this difference in results implies.

12. Why is it contended that bond-market indexes are more difficult to construct and maintain than stock-market indexes?

13. The Wilshire 5000 market-value-weighted index increased by 5 percent, whereas the Merrill Lynch–Wilshire Capital Markets Index increased by 15 percent during the same period. What does this difference in results imply?

14. The Russell 1000 increased by 8 percent during the past year, whereas the Russell 2000 increased by 15 percent. Discuss the implication of these results.

15. Based on what you know about the *Financial Times* (FT) World Index, the Morgan Stanley Capital International World Index, and the Dow Jones World Stock Index, what level of correlation would you expect among monthly rates of return? Discuss the reasons for your answer based on the factors that affect indexes.

Problems

1. You are given the following information regarding prices for a sample of stocks:

Stock	Number of Shares	PRICE T	PRICE T + 1
A	1,000,000	60	80
B	10,000,000	20	35
C	30,000,000	18	25

   a. Construct a *price-weighted* series for these three stocks, and compute the percentage change in the series for the period from T to $T + 1$.

   b. Construct a *value-weighted* series for these three stocks, and compute the percentage change in the series for the period from T to $T + 1$.

   c. Briefly discuss the difference in the results for the two series.

2. a. Given the data in Problem 1, construct an equal-weighted series by assuming $1,000 is invested in each stock. What is the percentage change in wealth for this equal-weighted portfolio?

   b. Compute the percentage of price change for each of the stocks in Problem 1. Compute the arithmetic average of these percentage changes. Discuss how this answer compares to the answer in 2a.

   c. Compute the geometric average of the percentage changes in 2b. Discuss how this result compares to the answer in 2b.

3. For the past five trading days, on the basis of figures in the *Wall Street Journal,* compute the daily percentage price changes for the following stock indexes:
   a. DJIA
   b. S&P 400
   c. AMEX Market Value Series
   d. NASDAQ Industrial Index
   e. FT-100 Share Index
   f. Nikkei Stock Price Average

   Discuss the difference in results for a and b, a and c, a and d, a and e, a and f, e and f. What do these differences imply regarding diversifying within the United States versus diversifying between countries?

4.

Company	PRICE			SHARES		
	A	B	C	A	B	C
Day 1	12	23	52	500	350	250
Day 2	10	22	55	500	350	250
Day 3	14	46	52	500	175[a]	250
Day 4	13	47	25	500	175	500[b]
Day 5	12	45	26	500	175	500

[a]Split at close of Day 2
[b]Split at close of Day 3

   a. Calculate a Dow Jones Industrial Average for Days 1 through 5.
   b. What effects have the splits had in determining the next day's index? (Hint: Think of the relative weighting of each stock.)
   c. From a copy of the *Wall Street Journal,* find the divisor that is currently being used in calculating the DJIA. (Normally this value can be found on pages C2 and C3.)

5. Utilizing the price and volume data in Problem 4,
   a. Calculate a Standard & Poor's Index for Days 1 through 5 using a beginning index value of 10.
   b. Identify what effects the splits had in determining the next day's index. (Hint: Think of the relative weighting of each stock.)

6. Based on the following stock price and shares outstanding information, compute the beginning and ending values for a price-weighted index and a market-value-weighted index.

	DECEMBER 31, 1999		DECEMBER 31, 2000	
	Price	Shares Outstanding	Price	Shares Outstanding
Stock K	20	100,000,000	32	100,000,000
Stock M	80	2,000,000	45	4,000,000[a]
Stock R	40	25,000,000	42	25,000,000

[a]Stock split two-for-one during the year

   a. Compute the percentage change in the value of each index.
   b. Explain the difference in results between the two indexes.
   c. Compute the results for an unweighted index and discuss why these results differ from the others.

7. a. Assume a base index value of 100 at the beginning of 1972. Using the returns in Table 5.13, what would be your ending index value if you owned the stocks in the Nikkei Average through 1998?
   b. In addition to knowing this domestic rate of return, you are told that the exchange rate at the beginning of 1972 was ¥200 to the dollar and it was ¥120 to the dollar at the end of 1998. Compute the compound return in U.S. dollars.

References   Fisher, Lawrence, and James H. Lorie. *A Half Century of Returns on Stocks and Bonds.* Chicago: University of Chicago Graduate School of Business, 1997.

Ibbotson Associates. *Stocks, Bonds, Bills and Inflation.* Chicago: Ibbotson Associates, annual.

Lorie, James H., Peter Dodd, and Mary Hamilton Kimpton. *The Stock Market: Theories and Evidence.* 2d ed. Homewood, Ill.: Richard D. Irwin, 1985.

Reilly, Frank K., and David J. Wright, "Bond Market Indexes." In *The Handbook of Fixed-Income Securities,* 5th ed., ed. Frank J. Fabozzi. Chicago, Ill.: Irwin Professional Publishing, 1997.

Chapter 5

APPENDIX   FOREIGN STOCK-MARKET INDEXES

Index Name	Number of Stocks	Weights of Stocks	Calculation Method	History of Index
ATX-index (Vienna)	All stocks listed on the exchange	Market capitalization	Value weighted	Base year 1967, 1991 began including all stocks (Value = 100)
Swiss Market Index	18 stocks	Market capitalization	Value weighted	Base year 1988, stocks selected from the Basle, Geneva, and Zurich Exchanges (Value = 1500)
Stockholm General Index	All stocks (voting) listed on exchange	Market capitalization	Value weighted	Base year 1979, continuously updated (Value = 100)
Copenhagen Stock Exchange Share Price Index	All stocks traded	Market capitalization	Value weighted	Share price is based on average price of the day
Oslo SE Composite Index (Sweden)	25 companies			Base year 1972 (Value = 100)
Johannesburg Stock Exchange Actuaries Index	146 companies	Market capitalization	Value weighted	Base year 1959 (Value = 100)
Mexican Market Index	Variable number, based on capitalization and liquidity		Value weighted (adjustment for value of paid-out dividends)	Base year 1978, high dollar returns in recent years
Milan Stock Exchange MIB	Variable number, based on capitalization and liquidity		Weighted arithmetic average	Change base at beginning of each year (Value = 1000)
Belgium BEL-20 Stock Index	20 companies	Market capitalization	Value weighted	Base year 1991 (Value = 1000)
Madrid General Stock Index	92 stocks	Market capitalization	Value weighted	Change base at beginning of each year
Hang Seng Index (Hong Kong)	33 companies	Market capitalization	Value weighted	Started in 1969, accounts for 75 percent of total market
FT-Actuaries World Indexes	2,212 stocks	Market capitalization	Value weighted	Base year 1986
FT-SE 100 Index (London)	100 companies	Market capitalization	Value weighted	Base year 1983 (Value = 1000)
CAC General Share Index (French)	212 companies	Market capitalization	Value weighted	Base year 1981 (Value = 100)

Index Name	Number of Stocks	Weights of Stocks	Calculation Method	History of Index
Morgan Stanley World Index	1,482 stocks	Market capitalization	Value weighted	Base year 1970 (Value = 100)
Singapore Straits Times Industrial Index	30 stocks	Unweighted		
German Stock Market Index (DAX)	30 companies (Blue Chips)	Market capitalization	Value weighted	Base year 1987 (Value = 1000)
Frankfurter Allgemeine Zeitung Index (FAZ) (German)	100 companies (Blue Chips)	Market capitalization	Value weighted	Base year 1958 (Value = 100)
Australian Stock Exchange Share Price Indices	250 stocks (92 percent of all shares listed)	Market capitalization	Value weighted	Introduced in 1979
Dublin ISEQ Index	71 stocks (54 official, 17 unlisted). All stocks traded	Market capitalization	Value weighted	Base year 1988 (Value = 1000)
HEX Index (Helsinki)	Varies with different share price indexes	Market capitalization	Value weighted	Base changes every day
Jakarta Stock Exchange	All listed shares (148 currently)	Market capitalization	Value weighted	Base year 1982 (Value = 100)
Taiwan Stock Exchange Index	All ordinary stocks (listed for at least a month)	Market capitalization	Value weighted	Base year 1966 (Value = 100)
TSE 300 Composite Index (Toronto)	300 stocks (comprised of 14 subindexes)	Market capitalization (adjusted for major shareholders)	Value weighted	Base year 1975 (Value = 1000)
KOSPI (Korean Composite Stock Price Index)	All common stocks listed on exchange	Market capitalization (adjusted for major shareholders)	Value weighted	Base year 1980 (Value = 100)

Twenty Years of International Equity Investing

Still a route to higher returns and lower risks?

Richard O. Michaud, Gary L. Bergstrom, Ronald D. Frashure, and Brian K. Wolahan

RICHARD O. MICHAUD is senior vice president at Acadian Asset Management in Boston (MA 02110).

GARY L. BERGSTROM is president of Acadian Asset Management.

RONALD D. FRASHURE is executive vice president at Acadian Asset Management.

BRIAN K. WOLAHAN is senior vice president at Acadian Asset Management.

International equity portfolio diversification is now well accepted by investors around the world. It was a novel concept, and perceived as unusually risky, when proposed originally in this Journal by Bergstrom [1975]. In the twenty years since, many other writers have described the risk reduction and return enhancement of carefully diversifying portfolios across different international equity markets. A comprehensive summary of the extensive literature appears in Solnik [1988].

In these two decades, the benefits of global portfolio diversification have been largely accepted by the academic and professional investment communities. At this point, it is of interest to consider two critical questions:

1. Has international equity diversification achieved its original objectives of raising return per unit of risk for U.S.-based and other global investors?
2. What new routes are open to future global investors?

THE CASE FOR GLOBAL INVESTING

The arguments for global portfolio diversification are — as laid out in the mid-1970s — centered on decreasing portfolio risk or increasing portfolio expected return relative to a comparable domestic portfolio. The seed of the argument was planted in Markowitz's [1959] classic work on portfolio efficiency.

Theory

A prudent investor is concerned with a portfolio's expected return and its risk. Expected portfolio return is the weighted sum of each security's expected return. One widely used measure of portfolio risk is the variance. Portfolio variance depends on the variance of each security and the correlations among securities.

A portfolio is said to be Markowitz mean-variance efficient if it has the highest level of expected return at a given level of portfolio risk or, equivalently, the lowest level of risk for a given level of expected return. The curve describing all efficient portfolios is called the Markowitz mean-variance efficient frontier. By definition, all stocks and portfolios lie below or on the mean-variance efficient frontier.

These concepts are illustrated in Exhibit 1. Suppose a portfolio manager invests only in domestic stocks. In this case, the "domestic efficient frontier" reflects the optimal set of portfolios available. In the exhibit, the domestic portfolio A has maximum expected return for the given level of risk.

Now consider a global equity manager, whose stock universe is not confined to stocks in the domestic market. Typically, global managers invest in stocks in ten, twenty, or more countries. In this case, the global stock universe may include stocks with both higher and lower risks and expected returns than those in the domestic universe.

To account for differences in trading costs in foreign markets, expected returns in a global context are defined net of expected transaction and other costs for a domestic investor. Given the expanded set of stocks, the "global efficient frontier" generally plots above, as well as extends at either end of, the domestic efficient frontier.

Consequently, as illustrated in Exhibit 1, there is an efficient global portfolio B that will have less risk at the same level of expected return as portfolio A. Also, there is an efficient global portfolio C that will have more expected return for the same level of risk as portfolio A.

Globally diversified portfolios hold out the very real promise of less risk for the same level of expected return, or more return for the same level of risk, or both, than can be achieved with domestic portfolios. This is true for a U.S.-based investor as well as for one domiciled in Japan, Australia, the Netherlands, or any other country.

Markowitz's arguments provide a sound theoretical rationale for the obvious intuitive benefits of global portfolios: significant expansion of investment opportunities over those of a purely domestic investor. Global investment vastly widens the number of investment choices, leading to many opportunities for significantly improving performance.

Note that Markowitz theory is a normative theory of investment management. Consequently, active global strategies are potentially the major beneficiaries of the increased opportunities associated with global equity investment.

Grinold [1989] provides a noteworthy extension of Markowitz theory that can be applied to quantifying the theoretical superiority of active global to domestic investing. He shows that the value-added of an active investment strategy is approximately proportional to the square of the manager's information level times the number of independent decisions.

For a global active manager, the over- and underweighting of country markets relative to a global benchmark provides a number of opportunities for relatively independent investment decisions not available to a purely domestic investor. Consequently, the value of a global active investment strategy is potentially far richer than one based purely on domestic markets.

Empirical Results

Empirical studies of international portfolio performance are inevitably country-, investment strategy-, and time period-dependent. One natural test is to com-

EXHIBIT 1
GLOBAL VERSUS DOMESTIC
PORTFOLIO EFFICIENCY

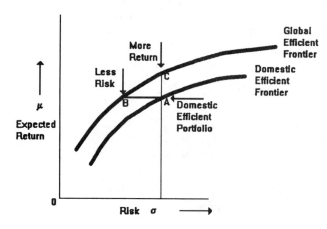

pare the performance of a passive international investment strategy in international developed markets to the performance of U.S. equities since 1975.[1] This is a true out-of-sample test of the original thesis. We represent the performance of U.S. stocks with the S&P 500 stock index and the U.S. dollar returns of international stocks with the capitalization-weighted Morgan Stanley Capital International Europe, Australia, and Far East (MSCI EAFE) index.

In Exhibit 2, the annualized average return and risk of the S&P 500 and MSCI EAFE indexes are plotted at the end points of the curve. The international index returns are net dividends, which is a more appropriate comparison for a U.S.-based investor than gross dividends. The data show that an international index portfolio provides slightly more return, and more risk, than a domestic index over the period.

The performance of various passive global portfolios is illustrated by points along the curve. Each point represents a fixed and decreasing proportion of assets in the MSCI index and a corresponding increasing proportion of assets in the domestic index.

The data show that a passive global portfolio consisting of a 70% international/30% domestic mix of portfolios would have had nearly the same level of risk as the S&P 500 index and slightly more return. Exhibit 2 also shows that a global passive portfolio

with roughly a 40/60 mix would have had significantly less risk, and slightly more return, than a purely domestic index portfolio.

In summary, publicly available empirical data for the last twenty years for passive global strategies provide a simple out-of-sample test that is consistent with the original thesis — international portfolio diversification increases return per unit of risk relative to a comparable U.S.-only portfolio. For passive global strategies, the empirical data are much more convincing as a way of lowering risk than enhancing return.

It is useful to note that the optimal ex post risk-minimizing level of international equity diversification over this period for a U.S.-based investor — a 40% allocation to international securities — is much higher than allocations to international equities typically found at present in domestic investors' portfolios (not to mention the levels of international diversification that would have been considered institutionally prudent in the mid-1970s).

UPDATE ON GLOBAL EQUITY RETURNS

Bergstrom [1975] presents U.S. dollar total return data for twenty major world equity markets for two periods ending June 30, 1975. Exhibit 3 provides similar returns for each of these same twenty equity

EXHIBIT 2
PORTFOLIO RETURN AND RISK — S&P 500 AND MSCI EAFE
JANUARY 1976-DECEMBER 1995

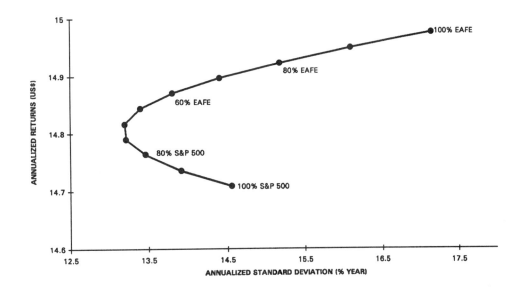

EXHIBIT 3
Compound Annual Total Returns —
Percent per Year in U.S. Dollars

Market	Returns 1959-1975	Returns 1976-1995	Standard Deviation 1976-1995
Hong Kong	14.9	20.1	32.6
Netherlands	7.7	17.5	16.9
Sweden	11.5	16.3	23.4
Japan	14.9	16.1	23.4
U.K.	7.1	15.3	21.6
Belgium	8.9	15.2	19.7
Singapore	14.9	15.1	25.6
Switzerland	11.3	14.5	18.0
U.S.	6.8	14.2	14.4
France	6.3	12.8	23.9
Norway	12.2	12.0	27.1
Germany	11.4	11.9	20.7
Denmark	9.5	11.9	18.6
Australia	7.7	11.2	25.2
Austria	12.7	10.3	23.0
Italy	1.9	9.7	27.3
Canada	6.7	9.5	18.9
Brazil[a]	22.0	8.4	58.0
South Africa[b]	15.6	6.6	42.8
Spain	12.5	6.1	24.0

[a]Data source for Brazil is International Finance Corporation (IFC); for all other data, source is MSCI.
[b]1976-1992 performance based on MSCI SA Gold Mines; 1993-1995 based on MSCI South Africa equity index.

Note: Rank order correlation of 1959-1975 and 1976-1995 return series: −0.02.

markets for January 1959-December 1975 and January 1976-December 1995.

In the recent period, the U.S. market ranks ninth, with an annualized compound return of 14.2%. Hong Kong provided the strongest return of 20.1% annually, while Spain lagged, with a 6.1% annual return. Brazil, the best-performing market for the sixteen and a half years through mid-1975, provided a mediocre 8.4% return in U.S. dollars for the next twenty years. Likewise, the MSCI South Africa Gold Mines index, which ranked second through mid-1975, returned only 6.6% per year subsequently.

More formally, the rank order correlation of returns between the two time periods is −0.02, sug-

gesting there is essentially no relationship between returns in the pre- and post-1975 intervals. This evidence indicates that simple extrapolation of historical returns has not been an effective methodology for predicting future country returns during the past two decades. These results also illustrate the substantial opportunities both to enhance returns from global investment, if return prediction frameworks can be developed, and mitigate some of the risks.

GLOBAL MARKET CORRELATIONS

The size and stability over time of correlations between country indexes impact the likely benefits of international investment. The analysis in Exhibit 4 provides estimates of the monthly correlations between the U.S. equity market, the MSCI EAFE index, and many MSCI foreign equity market indexes over the twenty-year period January 1976-December 1995. These estimates can be contrasted directly with similar correlations from the pre-1975 period estimated by Lessard [1976] for the period 1959 through 1973.

Of the fifteen markets for which there are correlations for both pre- and post-1975 periods, eight have higher correlations for the last twenty years, while six have lower correlations. There are some interesting differences.

For example, markets that were relatively highly correlated with the U.S. in the earlier period — Canada, Netherlands, and Switzerland — show somewhat lower numbers over the latest period, while Spain and Denmark (almost unrelated to the U.S. market in the earlier period) have higher correlations over the last two decades. Looked at in statistical terms, the rank order correlation between these two sets of long-term correlation estimates is 0.71, suggesting a surprisingly strong continuity in the long-term relationships among these equity markets.

While this very long-term evidence suggests there have not been dramatic changes in correlations between the U.S. and most important foreign equity markets, a frequently heard opinion is that the correlations between global equity markets have been increasing more recently. This view may have its origin in the belief that world equity markets are increasingly subject to common influences, and that global economies are becoming more highly synchronized. At least anecdotally, world equity markets do seem to have become more correlated in their movements during some

EXHIBIT 4
Comparison of Correlations to the U.S. Market — Monthly MSCI U.S. Dollar Total Returns*
January 1959-October 1973 and January 1976-December 1995

Market	Correlations for 1976-1995	Correlation Rank 1976-1995	Correlations for 1959-1973*	Correlation Rank 1959-1973
Australia	0.40	7	0.23	9
Austria	0.12	15	0.12	13
Belgium	0.40	8	0.46	4
Canada	0.68	1	0.80	1
Denmark	0.32	11	0.04	14
France	0.42	6	0.25	8
Germany	0.33	10	0.38	5
Italy	0.20	14	0.21	10
Japan	0.23	13	0.13	12
Netherlands	0.58	2	0.61	2
Norway	0.47	4	0.17	11
Spain	0.29	12	0.04	14
Sweden	0.39	9	0.33	6
Switzerland	0.46	5	0.49	3
U.K.	0.50	3	0.29	7

*Rank correlation between periods: 0.71.

recent periods, such as the October 1987 equity market crash and the decline in world bond markets that began in February 1994 when the U.S. Federal Reserve began to hike interest rates.

To address this question, we estimate the correlations of weekly returns for U.S. equities and the MSCI EAFE index by calendar quarter from 1980 forward. The correlation of U.S. to international stocks has averaged about 0.3 during this period. Although this correlation rises sharply in certain quarters (as in the fourth quarter of 1987), it is not at all clear from these data that there has been any significant secular trend in correlations, or that upsurges in correlations are more than episodic.[2]

A related claim is that international diversification is not as effective during declining markets, reducing the benefit when it would be most advantageous. To examine this issue, we estimate the correlations of weekly returns between international and U.S. equity indexes in two environments: 1) when the U.S. market is up or flat for a given week; and 2) when the U.S. market is down. The correlations are computed separately for each of these two return categories for each calendar year from 1980 through 1995.

The average correlation between U.S. and MSCI EAFE returns is roughly 0.3 when the U.S. market is up for the week, and 0.2 when the U.S. market is down. During this sixteen-year interval, there are only four years when the correlation of weekly returns was greater during a declining U.S. market than during a rising U.S. market. This evidence is consistent with the view that there has not been a significant reduction in the benefits of international diversification, even during periods when the U.S. market has declined.

EMERGING MARKETS

The term "emerging market" is typically applied to a number of country equity markets not included in major international equity market indexes yet that have significant economic activity and that may be suitable for institutional investment.[3] In recent years, many of these markets have become popular investment vehicles individually and collectively.

The rationale for investment in emerging markets is a natural extension of that for international diversification and is consistent with the argument described in Exhibit 1. Including emerging markets in a global portfolio will increase the opportunity set and can provide numerous occasions to add value. Such countries represent investment opportunities today in the same way that many now-developed markets did twenty years ago.

It is often convenient to think of emerging markets as a separate asset class rather than as an extension of the global investment opportunity set. While both approaches are fundamentally equivalent, many institutional investors prefer to separate their decision processes for developed and emerging markets. This choice is attributable in part to the relative novelty of emerging markets and heightened perceptions of risk. More substantively, emerging markets may require special expertise to deal with issues that are either unique or far more prominent than in developed markets. Such issues include transfer risks, property rights, settlement risks, liquidity risk, informational risks, and shareholder treatment (see Rowley [1995]).

Comprehensive performance data for emerging market indexes are generally available beginning in 1985. Exhibit 5 shows the impact on realized risk and return of adding different allocations of an emerging markets index to an EAFE index portfolio for the 1985 to 1995 period.[4] Empirically, adding emerging markets to an EAFE index portfolio has provided substantial opportunity to increase return per unit of risk significantly over this recent period.

Emerging markets represent many interesting challenges for institutional investors. There is no particular homogeneity to country markets included in the indexes. Long-term correlations, both to other emerging markets and to developed ones, have been quite var-ied. Differences in economic development, industry composition, and local political factors, as well as fundamental perceptions of the sources of economic growth, have led to substantial divergences in return even over long periods of time. Of course, such risks are likely to be consistent with the investment opportunities available to thoughtful and disciplined investors.[5]

These risks and opportunities are further illustrated in Exhibit 6, which provides historical risks and returns for a variety of emerging and developed market countries over the last ten years.

SMALL-CAPITALIZATION INTERNATIONAL EQUITIES

Investment in international small-capitalization stocks, once considered too risky or illiquid for institutional investors, is an additional avenue of potential portfolio diversification that was little explored twenty years ago. Following extensive academic and professional research in the 1980s, domestic small-capitalization equities have found a well-defined role in many

EXHIBIT 6

Annualized Equity Returns and Standard Deviation (%)
Major Developed and Emerging Markets
1986 Through 1995 in U.S. Dollars

	Return	Standard Deviation
U.S.	15.0	14.9
Canada	8.6	15.7
France	16.3	22.7
Germany	12.2	22.5
Japan	15.7	27.6
U.K.	16.2	20.5
Argentina	45.3	70.3
Brazil	32.3	71.0
Chile	43.6	27.7
Greece	33.7	43.6
Korea	20.3	29.3
Malaysia	19.1	27.2
Mexico	42.5	46.2
Philippines	42.8	37.8
Taiwan	33.6	51.0
Thailand	33.4	31.8

Note: Developed markets returns from MSCI with net dividends, except U.S. with total dividends. Emerging markets from IFC Global (total return) 1986-1987 and MSCI EM Free (total return) 1988-1995.

EXHIBIT 5
PORTFOLIO RETURN AND RISK —
EMERGING MARKETS AND MSCI EAFE
JANUARY 1985-DECEMBER 1995

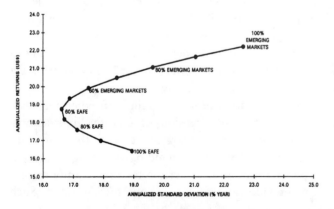

institutional portfolios (see Banz [1981]). Indeed, many sophisticated institutions consider domestic small-capitalization stocks a separate asset class in their asset allocation decisions.

International small-capitalization stocks are a natural extension of the domestic small-capitalization concept for portfolio diversification. Publicly available historical data for small-capitalization international indexes have been available only since 1987 when the Financial Times-Actuaries (FT-A) Euro-Pacific medium- and small-capitalization index was established.

Exhibit 7 compares the annualized quarterly returns for the FT-A medium- and small-capitalization index to the FT-A Europe and Pacific region index, for the 1987 to 1995 period. It also shows the risk/return characteristics of various passive allocations to medium- and small-capitalization equities relative to the large-capitalization index. While the data are for a more limited period than those for emerging markets, the empirical results suggest that international small-capitalization portfolios in the developed markets would have provided meaningful diversification benefits for global investors.

At a minimum, international small-capitalization stocks represent an extension of the investment opportunity set for global investors and a means of enhancing return or minimizing risk in the spirit of the relationships shown in Exhibit 1. Beyond this important point, however, and in spite of the support of long-term empirical data in many markets, the theoretical underpinnings of the small-stock premium and its implications for active management remain unsettled.

EXHIBIT 7
PORTFOLIO RETURN AND RISK
FT-A EUROPE AND PACIFIC INDEX WITH
FT-A SMALL EUROPE AND PACIFIC INDEX
JANUARY 1987-DECEMBER 1995

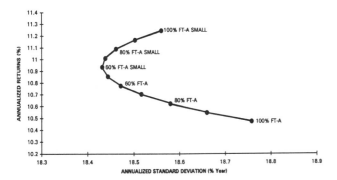

GLOBAL STOCK PRICING ANOMALIES

Over the last twenty years, considerable evidence has accumulated to indicate the existence of statistically significant "market anomaly" relationships between beginning-of-period values of various stock characteristics and ex post returns. These stock factors include: earnings-to-price ratio (E/P), book-to-price ratio (B/P), dividend yield, and firm size or market capitalization.[6] While most of the original studies were performed for the U.S. equity market, many have been extended to non-U.S. markets and similar relationships reported (see, for example, Hawawini and Keim [1997]). As a consequence, institutional active equity management is often based on portfolios tilted toward various market anomaly factors.

There are a number of key questions concerning the nature of the observed factor relationships with return. One of the most critical ones is whether they are economically significant and likely to persist. These and related issues have a direct impact on their practical value for active management.

The investment significance of these results is controversial (see Berk [1995], for example). If such factors are indicative of unmeasured or time-varying systematic risk, then they are likely to be persistent but not economically meaningful for active management. If the relationships are true market inefficiencies, their investment value may be significant, but they may not persist.

Even the long-term evidence of many academic studies may provide little confidence in their future economic significance. This is because, as Lo and MacKinlay [1990] note, for any time period, however long, some factor is likely to be found that is statistically significantly related to return. Because many long-term studies reuse the same data, they are likely to find similar "confirming" results with little out-of-sample reliability.

From a practical investment point of view, many of the academic controversies on market anomalies have little relevance. Experienced investors are well aware that few simple factor-return relationships persist period-by-period. It is of little investment value to know that a factor has worked well at forecasting return for the last fifty years if it has not worked for the last three years. Successful active management must also be concerned with dealing with the shorter-term dynamic character of markets.

The data in Exhibit 8 provide simple illustrations

EXHIBIT 8
Factor Correlations with Subsequent One-Year Total U.S. $ Return — Japan

	Cap*	E/P	B/P	CE/P	DDM	NE/P
1975	0.22	0.19	0.14	−0.03	0.24	0.19
1976	0.11	−0.01	0.03	−0.11	0.00	−0.05
1977	0.19	0.08	0.46	0.27	−0.06	0.01
1978	0.32	−0.02	0.26	0.12	0.09	0.10
1979	−0.08	0.03	0.12	0.13	0.02	0.08
1980	−0.02	0.16	0.06	0.16	0.14	0.09
1981	−0.33	0.19	0.25	0.21	0.11	0.17
1982	−0.07	0.25	0.08	0.03	0.31	0.26
1983	0.16	0.11	0.01	−0.05	0.24	0.23
1984	−0.10	0.0	0.02	0.02	−0.09	−0.06
1985	0.08	0.06	0.25	0.12	0.01	0.08
1986	−0.13	−0.02	−0.07	−0.02	−0.14	−0.15
1987	0.19	0.12	0.26	0.13	0.13	0.20
1988	0.07	0.06	0.12	0.09	−0.06	0.07
1989	0.52	0.03	0.13	−0.03	0.00	0.05
1990	0.11	0.15	0.16	0.11	0.17	0.16
1991	0.11	−0.01	0.07	0.03	0.05	0.04
1992	0.03	−0.01	0.04	0.03	0.02	0.02
1993	−0.18	0.11	0.27	0.23	0.23	0.27
1994	0.33	−0.17	0.25	−0.07	0.05	0.14
1995	−0.12	0.21	0.07	0.13	0.18	0.19
Average	0.07	0.07	0.14	0.07	0.08	0.10
Standard Deviation	0.20	0.10	0.12	0.10	0.12	0.11
T-Statistic	1.56	3.32	5.27	3.13	2.96	4.13

*Defined as the negative of the natural log of market capitalization.

of these and other important practical investment issues. Exhibit 8 provides twenty-one years of correlations of annual U.S. dollar total returns with six beginning-of-period stock factors for all stocks in the Japan MSCI country index. The stock factors are: 1) market capitalization (size); 2) earnings-to-price ratio; 3) book-to-price ratio; 4) cash earnings-to-price ratio; 5) dividend discount model return; and 6) normalized earnings-to-price ratio.[7] The average, standard deviation, and t-statistic (of the average) of annual correlations for each factor are given at the end of the table.

Except for firm size, all stock factors have statistically significant average correlation t-statistics over the 1975-1995 period. This indicates that a portfolio tilted toward positive values of these five significant factors is likely to have performed well over this period. Yet even a manager who chose (in hindsight) the single best predictive factor over this period in Japan — book-to-price ratio — would have experienced two recent consecutive years (1991-1992) and three additional consecutive years (1982-1984) with little added-value.

Such performance could have serious business consequences in the practical world of institutional investment management. In the case of the popular earnings-to-price ratio, only two of the last five years show correlations of sufficient size to provide significant positive performance (see Bergstrom and England-Markun [1982]). Similar situations pertain with other factors and in three other markets.

There are additional noteworthy issues illustrated in such data. Factors can differ significantly in predictive power in the same time period. In 1994, while book-to-price, capitalization, and normalized-earnings-to-price have positive correlations with return in Japan, the earnings-to-price correlation is large negative, and the correlations for cash earnings-to-price and

DDM are insignificant.

Also, the predictive power of factors has varied markedly from one market to another. Using similar analyses, while book-to-price is important in predicting returns in Japan and the United Kingdom, it is unimportant in Germany and of only marginal importance in France.

ADDRESSING CHALLENGES OF GLOBAL MANAGEMENT

The idiosyncratic nature of capital markets and their dynamic characteristics largely define the challenge to active global management, but there are some tools of the trade for addressing such issues.

Multiple Valuation Forecasts

The practical investment issue of interest is how to use historical market anomalous factors to forecast active return and add value. The challenge is to deal with the fact that no single factor is beneficial in all time periods, and that factors can vary significantly in their predictive power by market and time period. The question is: What principles can be brought to bear to guide in the choice of factors and to help define their weights?

The benefits of stock pricing anomalous relationships are most likely to be observed in a multiple valuation setting that conforms to principles of optimal design. These principles are based on the pioneering work of Ambachtsheer and Farrell [1979] and developed in Michaud [1990].

Assume two factors are positively correlated with return and not strongly correlated with each other. Then it can be shown empirically (Ambachtsheer and Farrell) and theoretically (Michaud) that a combination of the two factors can have a higher correlation with return than the weighted average of the correlations of the two factors, and often a larger correlation than either of the two factors, with less variability. Consequently multiple valuation models, properly defined, can be information-synergistic and enhance predictive power while reducing forecast risk.

Multiple valuation models are not a free lunch. It is unlikely that simply adding factors will synergistically enhance information. The key conditions for synergy — factors with significant positive correlations with future return and low correlations with other factors — severely limit the number of factors that are likely to be useful and put a high premium on choosing the optimal set of factors and factor weights. Some statistical methods, such as factor analysis, can sometimes be employed to help define factors that enhance information synergy.

Transaction Costs

Some of the most serious concerns with respect to international investing in the 1970s relate to low liquidity and high transaction costs in non-U.S. equity markets. The encouraging news is that there has been much improvement. Transaction costs in most non-U.S. equity markets have declined substantially, while trading volumes have increased dramatically. One simple but suggestive positive indication of this trend is the decline in commission costs in many global markets. The 1984 estimates in Bergstrom et al. [1986] are four to ten times current estimates in many cases.

Commission costs are normally a small portion of the total cost of trading. The three components of total trading costs are fixed costs (commissions, fees, taxes), market impact (price change from the decision to trade), and opportunity costs (price change of stocks not traded). There are many factors that can have a significant effect on trade costs. These include: country market, broker, measures of liquidity, buy versus sell transactions, stock price momentum, or investment style.

Exhibit 9 presents recent estimates of the three major components of trading costs, as well as total costs, based on actual institutional activity in four major developed markets. They illustrate the differences and similarities in implementation costs that can be incurred in different countries over the same time period.[8] While the reliability of the data is necessarily limited, due in part to the short time period and the number of trades, the results suggest that opportunity and market impact costs can vary widely by market.

Global active managers can use the results of such empirical analyses to improve their trading processes and optimize investment performance. The recent availability of data may lead to customizing valuation processes to the expected trade cost characteristics of individual stocks. This is one of the largely unexplored vistas of modern global investing.

Currency Hedging Policy[9]

For the last two decades, the impact of currency exchange rates has been a much more important issue for global equity investors than in the pre-1975 era

EXHIBIT 9
Sample of Total Trade Costs (basis points) for 1993Q2 through 1995Q4[a]

	Sample Size (U.S. $ million)	Commission	Market Impact[b]	Opportunity Cost[b]	Total Cost
France	688	−10	−76	−18	−104
Germany	205	−10	−27	−7	−43
Japan	3,073	−10	−54	−44	−108
U.K.	1,731	−12	−66	−13	−91

[a]Source: "Plexus Global Monitor," Santa Monica, California.
[b]Market impact is measured as the difference between execution price and the market price at the time the order is initially placed. Opportunity cost is the price change over thirty trading days from initial order date for orders not completed. Note that, as package trades, taxes are not explicitly included by market in these estimates.

when most exchange rates were fixed and changes infrequent. One issue of interest is definition of an appropriate currency hedging policy for an internationally diversified equity portfolio.

Hedging policy defines the desired benchmark for a passive currency management program as well as for measuring active currency management performance, much as equity market indexes are typically used as performance measurement benchmarks. This policy decision is separable from the potential benefits of actively managing currencies.

A fairly broad consensus on currency hedging policy appears to be emerging, according to recently available research. We cite a few key articles spanning the policy spectrum of approaches to hedging policy to frame the issues.

The pioneering case for the optimality of 100% currency hedging is given in Perold and Schulman [1988]. Their examination of ten years of quarterly data (1978-1987) shows that a 100%-hedged equity portfolio for various countries would have experienced roughly 20% less volatility than an unhedged portfolio. Since currencies, in their argument, have a zero long-term expected return, 100% hedging reduces volatility at no loss of expected return (except for the cost of hedging). The impact of hedging policy on risk reduction depends on the proportion and kinds (equities, bonds, and so on) of non-domestic assets held.

Criticism of these results focuses on the time period-dependent character of the data. The 1978-1987 time period may not be representative of the long-term currency market environment. An additional open issue is the reliability of the dimension of the risk reduction estimates.

Froot [1993] challenges the view that currency exposure of international investments should be hedged. Using nearly 190 years of data, he shows that, while a 100%-currency hedged policy reduces risk substantially over short horizons, hedging often does not reduce risk at all over long horizons, and may in fact increase it. The basic reason is that hedge returns are driven by different factors over different time horizons, and hedges do not protect against the risk factors affecting long-term exchange rates.

Froot shows that the benefit of short-term hedging for equities diminishes significantly beyond a year or two. Because most pension plans and many other institutional investors have long investment horizons, a 100% hedging policy, or indeed any significant hedging policy, may have limited benefits.

An important limitation of Froot's analysis is that the long-term benefits of 0% hedging may have limited practical value for many institutional investors. This is because fund sponsors may need to consider near-term portfolio volatility in meeting funding objectives.

Jorion [1989] focuses on the impact of currencies on portfolio — instead of asset — volatility, and describes how hedging policy may be conditional on asset mix. This is an important practical issue, as most U.S.-based investors are invested primarily in U.S. assets. Using data for the eleven-year period 1978-1988, Jorion finds that the addition of international assets decreases portfolio risk whether or not the assets are hedged. The effect of hedging currencies reduces asset volatility and increases correlation with U.S. assets. Both the lower volatility and the higher correlation together imply that hedging barely reduces aggregate portfolio risk unless non-domestic assets are a substantial part of total assets.

Roughly, Jorion finds that 20% (of the overall

portfolio) is the minimum level of investment in non-domestic assets required to make currency hedging valuable. As with Perold and Schulman, Jorion's results can be critiqued because they are highly time period-dependent.

Black [1989] develops a single-period universal hedging policy formula that implies that hedging increases expected return for both participants. His results are independent of the level of non-domestic assets or investor risk aversion. Black's formula is controversial. Adler and Solnik's [1990] critique centers on Black's non-standard framework and a number of restrictive key assumptions. Froot [1993] also notes that investors must be willing to bear more than normal risk if they wish to take advantage of the positive expected returns described in Black.

Investment policy ideally depends on the nature of a fund's liabilities, funding status, institutional risk tolerance, and investment objectives. Many pension plan sponsors are likely to find that short-term asset and portfolio risk is an important corporate concern in the context of asset management monitoring, projected cash flows, and overall corporate objectives. In such cases, investment horizon, risk aversion, and other assumptions are likely to impact hedging policy.

From a purely investment perspective, assuming a fund with roughly 20% or less of non-domestic assets, a zero hedging policy benchmark may often be desirable. This policy is consistent with Jorion's and Froot's results.

If the percentage of non-domestic assets is significantly larger, a non-zero hedge policy may be appropriate in order to reduce some of the short-term currency risk. As a simple heuristic, a hedging benchmark of 50% of non-domestic assets may be a useful compromise policy that balances a pension plan's long-term investment interests with shorter-term corporate and plan funding requirements. Allowing managers to hedge up to perhaps 30% of their non-domestic assets seems a practical guideline for investors who wish to pursue some active management opportunities in currency markets.

Finally, it may be of interest to note that hedged U.S. investors would have experienced substantial underperformance relative to an unhedged position over the last twenty years, as the U.S. dollar has generally declined versus major foreign currencies.

Global Equity Asset Allocation

It is of interest for many global equity investors to define an efficient allocation among the three major global equity asset classes: domestic, developed, and emerging markets. The classic approach to this problem is to solve for Markowitz [1959] mean-variance efficient allocations using historical data.

As noted earlier, useful and consistent emerging market index data have been available only since 1985. Exhibit 10 illustrates the efficient frontier and historical annualized risk and average return of total monthly returns for these three asset classes adjusted for monthly U.S. T-bill return (return premiums).

Unsurprisingly, given the relatively large average return premium for emerging markets over this period, the efficient allocations include a large proportion in emerging markets at most risk levels. The question is, given data limitations and the character of portfolio optimization technology, whether useful investment information can be derived from this data (see Michaud [1989]).

It is convenient to define three reference portfolios — index, typical, and equal-weighted. The "index" portfolio has a 40/50/10% weighting in domestic, developed, and emerging markets, and represents an asset allocation roughly consistent with the current capitalization of a comprehensive global equity index. While standards are changing rapidly, a "typical" institutional global equity portfolio might include approximately 20% of assets in developed non-U.S. markets and none in emerging markets. Finally, an equally weighted portfolio is often a useful reference

EXHIBIT 10
RETURN PREMIUM EFFICIENT FRONTIER

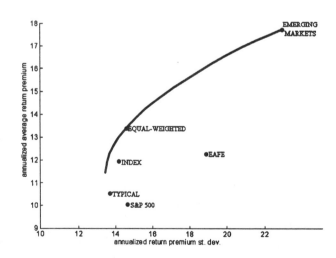

EXHIBIT 11
INDEX-RELATIVE RETURN EFFICIENT FRONTIER

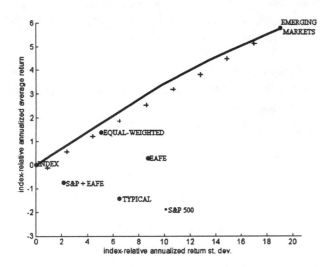

point. The performance of all three reference portfolios illustrated in Exhibit 10 reflects the benefits of international diversification over this period.

For many institutional investors, the most appropriate measure of portfolio risk is not total risk but residual risk relative to the return of a given equity benchmark. An institutional active manager mandate is often defined by guidelines that specify a 3%-6% annual residual or index-relative risk target. The historical index-relative risk and average returns and efficient frontier for the asset classes and portfolios in Exhibit 10 are given in Exhibit 11.

Exhibit 11 shows that portfolios with substantial allocations to emerging markets significantly outperformed over the January 1985-December 1995 period. For example, for an annual residual risk of 5%, the efficient asset allocation is approximately 50% EAFE, 15% S&P, and 35% emerging markets. Such an allocation is likely to appear excessively risky to many institutional investors because of its large underweighting in U.S. securities. It is also likely to be unreliable, as the efficient frontier solutions are, in general, "error-maximized."[10] Note, however, that the equal-weighted portfolio is nearly efficient with a residual risk of about 5%.

To analyze the data further, define a portfolio "S&P + EAFE" consisting of an equal weighting in the S&P and EAFE indexes. The index-relative risk and average return of the S&P + EAFE portfolio is also displayed in Exhibit 11. The sequence of +s in the Exhibit moving upward from the S&P + EAFE portfolio indicates the residual risk and return of an increasing allocation to emerging markets, in steps of 10%, relative to the S&P + EAFE portfolio.

This sequence of portfolios shows that an asset mix consisting of an equal weighting in the U.S. and developed markets plus a minimum of 10% in emerging markets is nearly efficient. Consequently, efficient frontier portfolios are well-approximated by an equal weighting of EAFE and U.S. markets with the remainder (10% minimum) in emerging markets.

This result indicates that, roughly, an efficient asset allocation's active risk can be viewed as associated with the degree of allocation to emerging markets. Finally, allocations to emerging markets of 10% to 30% appear to be consistent with levels of active risk normally associated with institutional global equity mandates.

SUMMARY AND CONCLUSION

As anticipated, marketplace evidence for the last twenty years indicates that thoughtful international equity diversification can improve the risk/return characteristics of investors' portfolios. Much of the potential improvement in return is in the form of increased opportunities to add value with active management; passive global investing may be most useful for reducing risk.

Although the challenges of successfully implementing international equity programs are clearly different now from two decades ago, the current opportunities are also considerably greater. The availability of many additional equity markets, especially rapidly growing emerging markets, the enormous growth in the number of available stocks, particularly of smaller companies, and great improvements in marketplace liquidity, trading methods, and quality of information are some of the most noteworthy and positive changes.

Looking forward, we envision the development of larger and more accurate data bases that will support increasingly sophisticated research on the behavior of capital markets and the development of more advanced risk measurement and forecasting tools. While global portfolio diversification is no longer a *new* route to higher returns and lower risks, as it was two decades ago, the decades ahead are likely to see the globalization of portfolios become the norm for investment management.

ENDNOTES

[1] By developed markets we mean the approximately

twenty equity markets included in indexes such as the Morgan Stanley Capital International EAFE index, the Financial Times-Actuaries Europac index, or the Salomon Brothers Europe and Pacific index.

[2]All correlation data are available upon request.

[3]The list of markets normally considered to be "emerging" may vary significantly by investment institution and index provider. A current list might include Argentina, Brazil, Chile, China, Colombia, Czech Republic, Greece, India, Indonesia, Israel, Jordan, Korea, Malaysia, Mexico, Nigeria, Pakistan, Philippines, Portugal, Taiwan, Thailand, Turkey, Venezuela, and Zimbabwe. Over time the list is likely to be expanded to include additional markets in Eastern Europe, the Pacific Basin, the Middle East, and Africa.

[4]Emerging markets are represented by the International Finance Corporation's (IFC) Global Index for 1985-1987 and by the Global Investable Index after its inception in 1988.

[5]For accessible discussions of some "economic growth" controversies that impact perceptions of financial value, see Krugman [1996] and "Economic Growth" [1996].

[6]For the P/E ratio, see Basu [1977]; for dividend yield, see Litzenberger and Ramaswamy [1979]; for market capitalization, see Banz [1990]; for P/E and size, see Reinganum [1979]; and for book-to-price and market capitalization, see Fama and French [1992].

[7]DDM is a variation of a standard dividend discount model used by many investment organizations. See Michaud and Davis [1982]. NE/P is the inverse of current price-to-book ratio divided by time-weighted average return on equity.

[8]The data are estimated trade costs dollar-weighted over the indicated time period from buy and sell trades. The data are average costs for a variety of trade types, and may not reflect all attempted trades.

[9]This discussion is based on Michaud [1994].

[10]A term coined in Michaud [1989] to describe the investment impact of the instability of mean-variance optimization on optimized portfolios.

REFERENCES

Adler, Michael, and Bruno Solnik. "The Individuality of 'Universal' Hedging." Letter to *Financial Analysts Journal*, May–June 1990.

Ambachtsheer, Keith, and James L. Farrell, Jr. "Can Active Management Add Value?" *Financial Analysts Journal*, November–December 1979.

Banz, Rolf. "The Relation Between Return and Market Value of Common Stocks." *Journal of Financial Economics*, March 1981.

Basu, Sanjoy. "The Investment Performance of Common Stocks in Relation to Price–Earnings Ratios: A Test of the Efficient Market Hypothesis." *Journal of Finance*, June 1977.

Bergstrom, Gary. "A New Route to Higher Returns and Lower Risks." *Journal of Portfolio Management*, Fall 1975.

Bergstrom, Gary, and Mark England-Markun. "International Country Selection Strategies." *Columbia Journal of World Business*, Summer 1982.

Bergstrom, Gary, Donald Lessard, John Koeneman, and Martin Siegel. "International Securities Markets." In Frank Fabozzi and Frank Zarb, eds., *Handbook of Financial Markets: Securities, Options and Futures*, 2nd edition. Homewood, IL: Dow Jones-Irwin, 1986.

Berk, Jonathan. "A Critique of Size-Related Anomalies." *Review of Financial Studies*, June 1995.

Black, Fischer. "Universal Hedging." *Financial Analysts Journal*, July–August 1989.

"Economic Growth." *The Economist*, May 1996.

Fama, Eugene, and Kenneth French. "The Cross-Section of Expected Returns." *Journal of Finance*, June 1992.

Froot, Kenneth. "Currency Hedging Over Long Horizons." Working paper No. 4355, National Bureau of Economic Research, May 1993.

Grinold, Richard. "The Fundamental Law of Active Management." *Journal of Portfolio Management*, Spring 1989.

Hawawini, Gabriel, and Donald Keim. "On the Cross-Sectional Behavior of Common Stock Returns: A Review of the Evidence Around the World." In William Ziemba and Donald Keim, eds., *Security Market Imperfections in Worldwide Equity Markets*. Cambridge: Cambridge University Press, 1997, forthcoming.

Jorion, Philippe. "Asset Allocation with Hedged and Unhedged Foreign Assets." *Journal of Portfolio Management*, Summer 1989.

Krugman, Paul. *Pop Internationalism*. Cambridge: MIT Press, 1996.

Lessard, Donald. "World, Country, and Industry Relationships in Equity Returns." *Financial Analysts Journal*, January–February 1976.

Litzenberger, Robert H., and Krishna Ramaswamy. "The Effect of Personal Taxes and Dividends on Capital Asset Prices: Theory and Empirical Evidence." *Journal of Financial Economics*, 1979.

Lo, Andrew, and A. Craig MacKinlay. "Data-Snooping Biases in Tests of Financial Asset Pricing Models." *Review of Financial Studies*, 3, 3 (1990).

Markowitz, Harry. *Portfolio Choice: Efficient Diversification of Investments*. New York: John Wiley & Sons, 1959.

Michaud, Richard. "Currency Hedging Policy." Acadian Asset Management, January 1994.

——. "Demystifying Multiple Valuation Models." *Financial Analysts Journal*, January–February 1990.

———. "The Markowitz Optimization Enigma: Is 'Optimized' Optimal?" *Financial Analysts Journal*, January–February 1989.

Michaud, Richard, and Paul Davis. "Valuation Model Bias and the Scale Structure of Dividend Discount Returns." *Journal of Finance*, March 1982.

Perold, André, and Evan Schulman. "The Free Lunch in Currency Hedging: Implications for Investment Policy and Performance Standards." *Financial Analysts Journal*, May–June 1988.

Reinganum, Mark. "A Misspecification of Capital Asset Pricing: Empirical Anomalies Based on Earnings Yields and Market Values." *Journal of Financial Economics*, March 1979.

Rowley, Ian. "Finding New Criteria for Global Investing: Beyond Emerged and Emerging Markets." Presented at Global Investment Management Conference, Geneva, 1995.

Solnik, Bruno. *International Investments*. Reading, MA: Addison-Wesley, 1988.

INTERNATIONAL PORTFOLIO INVESTMENT

Key Terms

American Depository
  Receipts (ADRs)
American shares
cross-border equity investment
efficient frontier
emerging markets
foreign market beta
global fund
IFC Emerging Markets
  Index
international asset allocation
international diversification
international fund
international investing
liquidity
Morgan Stanley Capital
  International Europe,
  Australia, Far East (EAFE)
  Index
Morgan Stanley Capital
  International World Index
regional fund
risk-return trade-off
single-country fund
total dollar return

Capital now flows at the speed of light across national borders and into markets once deemed impregnable.

Citicorp Annual Report (1991)

CHAPTER LEARNING OBJECTIVES

- To calculate the return associated with investing in securities issued in different markets and denominated in various currencies
- To calculate the currency risk associated with investing in securities issued in different markets and denominated in various currencies
- To describe the advantages of international investing
- To explain how international investing can allow investors to achieve a better risk-return trade-off than by investing solely in U.S. securities
- To identify the barriers to investing overseas
- To describe the various ways in which U.S. investors can diversify into foreign securities
- To explain why investing in foreign stocks and bonds provides a better risk-return trade-off than investing in either foreign stocks or bonds alone

At one time, investors treated national boundaries as impregnable barriers, limiting their reach and financial options to predominantly domestic and regional markets. Times have changed. Just as companies and consumers are going global, so are increasing numbers of investors. American investors are buying foreign stocks and bonds and foreign investors are purchasing U.S. securities. The purpose of this chapter is to examine the nature and consequences of international portfolio investing. Although the chapter focuses on international investing from an American perspective, its lessons are applicable to investors from around the world.

459

Foundations of Multinational Financial Management, 3rd edition, by Alan C. Shapiro. Copyright © 1998, John Wiley & Sons, Inc. Reprinted by permission of John Wiley & Sons, Inc.

THE BENEFITS OF INTERNATIONAL EQUITY INVESTING

The advantages of **international investing** are several. For one thing, an international focus offers far more opportunity than a domestic focus does. About 60% of the world's stock market capitalization is in non-U.S. companies, and this fraction has generally increased over time (see Exhibit 17.1). In fact, if you want to invest in certain products with huge global markets, you'll find that most of the big, highly profitable manufacturers are overseas. For example, videotape recorders are the world's best-selling consumer electronics product, and 95% of them are made in Japan; over 80% of all cars are made abroad, 85% of all stereo systems, and 99% of all 35mm cameras. The Japanese dominance of these and other consumer product markets helps explain why in recent years Japan's market capitalization actually exceeded that of the United States. The 60% plunge in the Tokyo Stock Exchange between 1990 and 1995 has evened up market capitalizations.

International Diversification

International investing yields a better risk/return trade-off.

The expanded universe of securities available internationally suggests the possibility of achieving a better **risk-return trade-off** by investing in international securities as well as U.S. securities rather than by investing solely in U.S. securities; that is, expanding the universe of assets available for investment should lead to higher returns for the same level of risk or less risk for the same level of expected return. This relation follows from the basic rule of portfolio diversification: *The broader the diversification, the more stable the returns and the more diffuse the risks.*

Prudent investors know that diversifying across industries leads to a lower level of risk for a given level of expected return. A fully diversified U.S. portfolio is only about

EXHIBIT 17.1 • STOCK MARKET CAPITALIZATION AS PERCENT OF WORLD TOTAL (20 MAIN STOCK MARKETS)

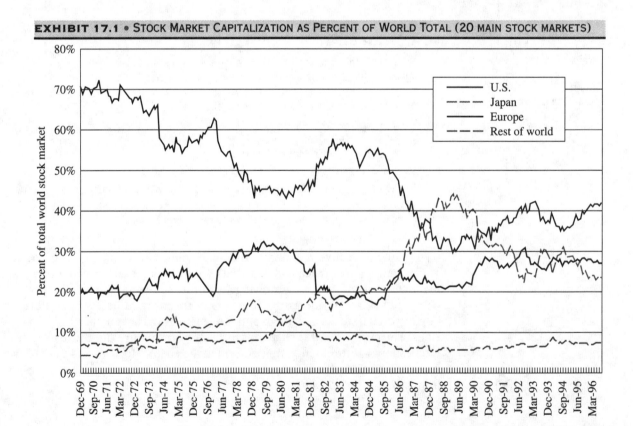

EXHIBIT 17.2 • ANNUALIZED MONTHLY RETURNS AND STANDARD DEVIATIONS OF RETURNS: 1981–1996

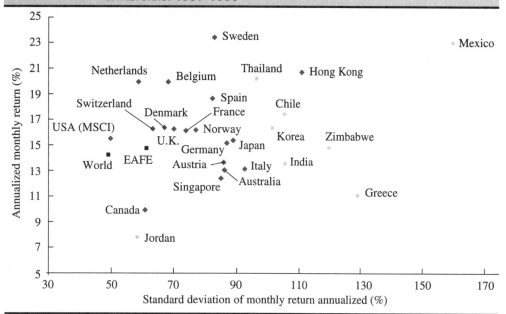

Note: Circles are emerging markets, diamonds are developed markets, and squares show EAFE and MSCI world indices.

Domestic diversification reduces risk, but the degree of risk reduction is limited.

27% as risky as a typical individual stock. Put another way, about 73% of the risk associated with investing in the average stock can be eliminated in a fully diversified U.S. portfolio. Ultimately, though, the advantages of such diversification are limited because all companies in a country are more or less subject to the same cyclical economic fluctuations. Through **international diversification**—that is, by diversifying across nations whose economic cycles are not perfectly in phase—investors should be able to reduce still further the variability of their returns. In other words, risk that is systematic in the context of the U.S. economy may be unsystematic in the context of the global economy. For example, an oil price shock that hurts the U.S. economy helps the economies of oil-exporting nations, and vice versa. Thus, just as movements in different stocks partially offset one another in an all-U.S. portfolio, so movements in U.S. and non-U.S. stock portfolios cancel each other out to some degree.

The possibility of achieving a better risk-return trade-off by investing internationally is supported by Exhibit 17.2, which shows the annualized returns and standard deviations of returns for a variety of developed and emerging stock markets over the 16-year period 1981–1990.[1] Exhibit 17.2 illustrates three points:

1. Historically, national stock markets have wide differences in returns and risk (as measured by the standard deviation of annual returns).
2. **Emerging markets** (shown as circles)—a term that encompasses all of South and Central America; all of the Far East with the exception of Japan, Australia, and New Zealand; all of Africa; and parts of Southern Europe, as well as Eastern Europe and countries of the former Soviet Union—have had higher risk and return than the developed markets (shown as diamonds).

---

[1]The standard deviations used in this chapter are all monthly standard deviations annualized (multiplied by 12). They are significantly larger than annual deviations calculated using yearly data because monthly returns are more volatile than yearly returns (monthly ups and downs often cancel each other out).

3. The **Morgan Stanley Capital International Europe, Australia, Far East (EAFE) Index** (which reflects all major stock markets outside of North America, 20 altogether) has had lower risk than most of its individual country components.

> The value of international equity diversification appears to be substantial.

Empirical research bears out the significant benefits from international equity diversification suggested by Exhibit 17.2. Bruno Solnik and Donald Lessard, among others, have both presented evidence that national factors have a strong impact on security returns relative to that of any common world factor.[2] They also found that returns from the different national equity markets have relatively low correlations with one another. More recent research shows that differences in industrial structure and currency movements account for very little of the low correlation between national stock market returns.[3] The more likely explanation for the low degree of international return correlation is that local monetary and fiscal policies, differences in institutional and legal regimes, and regional economic shocks induce large country-specific variation in returns.

EXHIBIT 17.3 • HOW FOREIGN MARKETS WERE CORRELATED WITH U.S. MARKET AND WORLD INDEX, 1970–1996

Country	Correlation with U.S. Market	Standard Deviation of Returns[1] (%)	Market Risk (Beta) from U.S. Perspective	Correlation with World Index	Market Risk (Beta) from World Perspective
United States	1.00	49.52	1.00	0.82	0.83
Canada	0.70	60.65	0.86	0.70	0.87
Australia	0.46	86.46	0.81	0.55	0.97
Hong Kong	0.30	110.87	0.68	0.41	0.92
Japan	0.25	86.37	0.44	0.68	1.21
Singapore	0.45	85.29	0.77	0.53	0.92
Austria	0.12	86.16	0.22	0.29	0.52
Belgium	0.42	68.25	0.57	0.62	0.86
Denmark	0.31	66.99	0.42	0.48	0.65
France	0.43	77.00	0.67	0.62	0.98
Germany	0.34	73.76	0.51	0.55	0.83
Italy	0.21	92.58	0.40	0.42	0.81
Netherlands	0.57	58.56	0.67	0.73	0.88
Norway	0.43	88.51	0.78	0.50	0.91
Spain	0.28	82.44	0.47	0.48	0.81
Sweden	0.41	83.02	0.68	0.55	0.94
Switzerland	0.49	63.22	0.62	0.67	0.87
United Kingdom	0.50	69.88	0.71	0.68	0.97
EAFE index[2]	0.47	61.27	0.58	0.87	1.09
World index[3]	0.82	48.75	0.81	1.00	1.00

[1]Monthly standard deviation annualized.

[2]The Morgan Stanley Capital International Europe, Australia, Far East (EAFE) Index is the non-North American part of the world index and consists of 20 major stock markets from these parts of the world.

[3]The Morgan Stanley Capital International World Index has a combined market value of $8.6 trillion, covers 22 countries including the United States, and includes about 1,600 of the largest companies worldwide.

Source: Reprinted with permission from *Morgan Stanley Capital International.*

[2]Bruno H. Solnik, "Why Not Diversify Internationally Rather Than Domestically?" *Financial Analysts Journal,* July–August 1974, pp. 48–54; and Donald R. Lessard, "World, Country, and Industry Relationships in Equity Returns: Implications for Risk Reduction through International Diversification," *Financial Analysts Journal,* January–February 1976, pp. 32–38.

[3]Steven L. Heston and K. Geert Rouwenhorst, "Does Industrial Structure Explain the Benefits of International Diversification?" *Journal of Financial Economics,* August 1994, pp. 3–27.

Correlations and the Gains from Diversification. Exhibit 17.3 contains some data on correlations between the U.S. and non-U.S. stock markets. **Foreign market betas,** which are a measure of market risk derived from the capital asset pricing model (see Chapter 16), are calculated relative to the U.S. market in the same way that individual asset betas are calculated:

$$\textit{Foreign market beta} = \textit{Correlation with U.S. market} \times \frac{\textit{Standard deviation of foreign market}}{\textit{Standard deviation of U.S. market}}$$

For example, the Canadian market beta is $0.70 \times 60.7/49.5 = 0.86$. Market risk is also calculated from a world perspective, where the correlations are calculated relative to the world index. Notice that the betas calculated relative to the world index are higher than the betas calculated relative to the U.S. market for all but the U.S. market.

Measured for the 27-year period 1970–1996, foreign markets in developed (EAFE) countries were correlated with the U.S. market from a high of 0.70 for Canada to a low of 0.12 for Austria. The relatively high correlation for Canada reveals that this market tracked the U.S. market's ups and downs. Austria's low correlation, on the other hand, indicates that the Austrian and U.S. markets have tended to move largely independently of each other.

Notice also that the investment risks associated with these different markets can be quite different—with the Hong Kong market showing the highest level and the Dutch market the lowest. Indeed, all the markets had a higher level of risk, as measured by the standard deviation of returns, than the U.S. market. Yet the internationally diversified **Morgan Stanley Capital International World Index** had the lowest level of risk—lower even than the U.S. market. The reason, of course, is that much of the risk associated with markets in individual countries is unsystematic and so can be eliminated by diversification, as indicated by the relatively low betas of these markets.

> Much of the risk associated with individual markets is unsystematic and so can be diversified away.

These results imply that international diversification may significantly reduce the risk of portfolio returns. In fact, the standard deviation of an internationally diversified portfolio appears to be as little as 11.7% of that of individual securities. In addition, as shown in Exhibit 17.4, the benefits from international diversification are significantly

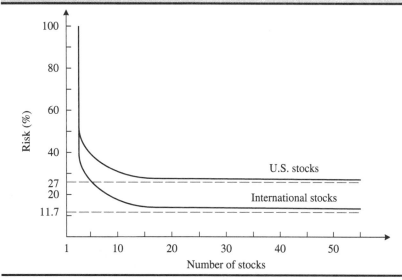

EXHIBIT 17.4 • THE POTENTIAL GAINS FROM INTERNATIONAL DIVERSIFICATION

Source: Bruno H. Solnik, "Why Not Diversify Internationally Rather Than Domestically?" Reprinted with permission from Financial Analysts Federation, Charlottesville, VA. All rights reserved. *Financial Analysts Journal,* July–August 1974.

EXHIBIT 17.5 • THE U.S. MARKET LAGS BEHIND THE EAFE INDEX: 1970–1997

Source: Reprinted with permission from *Morgan Stanley Capital International.*

greater than those that can be achieved solely by adding more domestic stocks to a portfolio. Specifically, an internationally diversified portfolio appears to be less than half as risky as a fully diversified U.S. portfolio.

> **Foreign investing has been more profitable than investing in the United States in recent decades.**

Moreover, from 1970 through 1996, the compound annual return for the *EAFE Index* was 12.9% compared with 11.8% for the U.S. market. Further, the EAFE Index outpaced the U.S. market 19 times during the 30-year period 1961–1990. In the 27 years ended February 1997, the U.S. portion of Morgan Stanley Capital International's world stock index was up 2,082%, while the cumulative return for the EAFE Index was 2,542% (see Exhibit 17.5). Even more astounding, from 1949 to 1990, the Japanese market soared an incredible 25,000%. Even with the recent plunge in the Tokyo Stock Exchange, an investor in the Japanese stock market would still be way ahead.

The obvious conclusion is that international diversification pushes out the **efficient frontier**—the set of portfolios that has the smallest possible standard deviation for its level of expected return and has the maximum expected return for a given level of risk—allowing investors simultaneously to reduce their risk and increase their expected return. Exhibit 17.6 illustrates the effect of international diversification on the efficient frontier.

> **International diversification pushes out the efficient frontier.**

One way to estimate the benefits of international diversification is to consider the expected return and standard deviation of return for a portfolio consisting of a fraction a invested in U.S. stocks and the remaining fraction, $1 - a$, invested in foreign stocks. Define r_{us} and r_{rw} to be the expected returns on the U.S. and rest-of-world stock portfolios, respectively. Similarly, let σ_{us} and σ_{rw} be the standard deviations of the U.S. and rest-of-world portfolios. The expected return r_p can be calculated as

$$r_p = ar_{us} + (1 - a)r_{rw} \qquad (17.1)$$

EXHIBIT 17.6 • INTERNATIONAL DIVERSIFICATION PUSHES OUT THE EFFICIENT FRONTIER

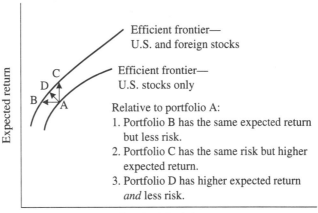

To calculate the standard deviation of this portfolio, we need to know that the general formula for the standard deviation of a two-asset portfolio with weights w_1 and w_2 ($w_1 + w_2 = 1$) is

$$\text{Portfolio standard deviation} = [w_1^2\sigma_1^2 + w_2^2\sigma_2^2 + 2w_1w_2\sigma_{12}\sigma_1\sigma_2]^{1/2} \qquad (17.2)$$

where σ_1^2 and σ_2^2 are the respective variances of the two assets, σ_1 and σ_2 are their standard deviations, and σ_{12} is their correlation. We can apply Equation 17.2 to our internationally diversified portfolio by treating the domestic and foreign portfolios as separate assets. This operation yields a portfolio standard deviation σ_p equal to

$$\sigma_p = [a^2\sigma_{us}^2 + (1 - a)^2\sigma_{rw}^2 + 2a(1 - a)\sigma_{us}\sigma_{rw}\sigma_{us,rw}]^{1/2} \qquad (17.3)$$

where $\sigma_{us,rw}$ is the correlation between the returns on the U.S. and foreign stock portfolios.

An internationally diversified portfolio is less risky than a diversified U.S. stock portfolio.

To see the benefits of international diversification, assume that the portfolio is equally invested in U.S. and foreign stocks, with the EAFE Index representing the foreign stock portfolio. Using data from Exhibit 17.3, we see that $\sigma_{us} = 49.5\%$, $\sigma_{rw} = 61.3\%$, and $\sigma_{us,rw} = 0.47$. According to Equation 17.3, these figures imply that the standard deviation of the internationally diversified portfolio is

$$\begin{aligned}\sigma_p &= [0.5^2(49.5)^2 + 0.5^2(61.3)^2 + 0.5^2 \times 2 \times 49.5 \times 61.3 \times 0.47]^{1/2}\\ &= 0.5(9,060.2)^{1/2}\\ &= 47.6\%\end{aligned}$$

Here the risk of the internationally diversified portfolio is below the risk of the U.S. portfolio. Moreover, as indicated earlier, the expected return is higher as well.

Recent Correlations. The benefits of diversification depend on relatively low correlations among assets. Investors often assume that as the underlying economies of national capital markets become more closely integrated and cross-border financial flows accelerate, these markets will become more highly correlated, significantly reducing the benefits of international diversification. Indeed, the correlations between the U.S. and non-U.S. stock markets are generally higher today than they were during the 1970s. But Exhibit 17.7 shows that contrary to intuition, these correlations have, if anything, fallen in recent years. Using four-year periods—1981–1984, for instance, versus 1993–1996—correlations are

EXHIBIT 17.7 • CORRELATION OF MONTHLY RETURNS WITH THE U.S. MARKET: DEVELOPED COUNTRY MARKETS

	1981–1996	1981–1984	1985–1988	1989–1992	1993–1996
Canada	0.71	0.71	0.79	0.70	0.66
Australia	0.42	0.43	0.37	0.47	0.49
Hong Kong	0.34	0.08	0.55	0.41	0.49
Japan	0.25	0.38	0.19	0.31	0.16
Singapore	0.48	0.41	0.54	0.63	0.29
Austria	0.13	0.10	0.09	0.14	0.28
Belgium	0.42	0.30	0.27	0.28	0.26
Denmark	0.32	0.38	0.41	0.40	0.39
France	0.45	0.27	0.29	0.28	0.25
Germany	0.36	0.28	0.29	0.28	0.26
Italy	0.22	0.14	0.20	0.19	0.20
Netherlands	0.59	0.56	0.58	0.60	0.59
Norway	0.49	0.38	0.42	0.43	0.42
Spain	0.35	−0.10	0.01	0.01	0.00
Sweden	0.42	0.29	0.31	0.30	0.29
Switzerland	0.49	0.50	0.50	0.49	0.46
United Kingdom	0.56	0.47	0.47	0.46	0.43
World	0.76	0.88	0.89	0.89	0.88

Source: Computed using data from Ibbotson Associates Encorr Software © 1997, Chicago, IL. Used with permission. All rights reserved.

almost uniformly lower in more recent periods, particularly during the 1990s, when economic integration has presumably increased.

In addition to the somewhat higher correlations today relative to the 1970s, the U.S. market has outperformed the Japanese and European markets in recent years (see Exhibit 17.5 over the period 1990–1996), reducing the expected return on the EAFE Index relative to the U.S. market.

International diversification is of limited value when financial markets are very volatile.

Recent research points to another problematic aspect of international investing as well: When markets are the most volatile, and investors most seek safety, global diversification is of limited value.[4] In particular, Exhibit 17.8 shows that the correlations among markets appear to increase when market volatility is at its highest. Even worse, the markets appear to move in synchrony only when they're falling, not when they're rising. In other words, only bear markets—not bull markets—seem to be contagious.

Taken together, these changes have diminished the risk-return benefits of international investing. Nonetheless, these benefits still exist, particularly for those who have patience to invest for the long term. Exhibit 17.9 calculates the standard deviations and annualized returns of different mixes of the S&P 500 and the EAFE Index using quarterly data for the 27-year period 1970–1996. Shifting from a portfolio invested 100% in the S&P 500 to one that contains up to 20% invested in the EAFE Index, an investor reduces risk and at the same time sees returns increase. As the percentage invested in the EAFE Index is increased past 40%, both portfolio risk and return rise.

[4]See Patrick Odier and Bruno Solnik, "Lessons for International Asset Allocation," *Financial Analysts Journal*, March–April 1993, pp. 63–77.

EXHIBIT 17.8 • NO PLACE TO HIDE?

World markets seem to be most in step with each other when volatility is greatest. Correlation among markets is measured here on a scale of 0 to 1, where 1 indicates that markets track each other perfectly and 0 means they are completely independent. Volatility is measured on the basis of "standard deviation"—how much prices vary from the mean.

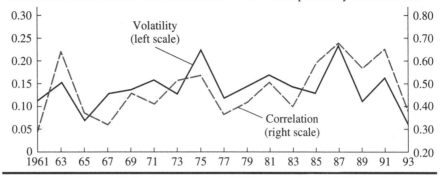

Source: Bruno Solnik, Hautes Etudes Commerciales in the *Wall Street Journal,* April 14, 1994, p. C1. Reprinted by permission of the *Wall Street Journal,* ©1994 Dow Jones & Company, Inc.. All rights reserved worldwide.

EXHIBIT 17.9 • AVERAGE RETURNS AND STANDARD DEVIATION OF RETURNS, 1970–1996

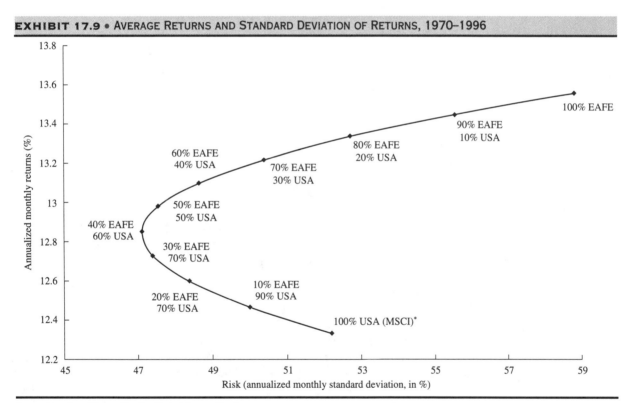

Source: Data from Morgan Stanley Capital International.

Investing in Emerging Markets

We have already seen in Exhibit 17.2 some of the high risks and rewards historically associated with investing in emerging markets. It should come as no surprise, then, that these countries, with their volatile economic and political prospects, are often the ones that

EXHIBIT 17.10 • RISK AND RETURN FOR EMERGING MARKETS, 1987–1996

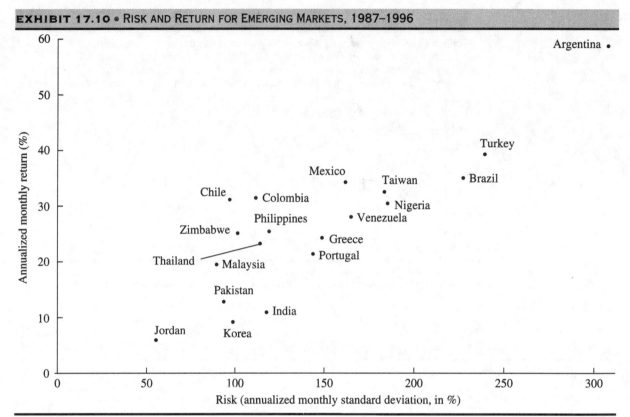

Source: Data from Morgan Stanley Capital International.

Emerging markets present attractive investment opportunities.

offer the greatest degree of diversification and the highest expected returns.[5] Exhibit 17.10 shows how some of these "emerging markets" performed over the ten-year period ending December 31, 1996. As the graph shows, historically, no other stock markets so lavishly rewarded investors. Gains of 30% to 40% a year were not unusual. In response to figures such as these, since 1989, private capital flows to emerging stock markets have expanded from less than $10 billion a year to between $60 billion and $80 billion a year.

But the high returns possible in emerging markets are matched by some breathtaking risks. To begin, these are small markets, representing in the aggregate less than 10% of the world's stock market capitalization. Hence, they are subject to the usual volatility and lack of liquidity associated with small markets. But they face some unique risks as well: relatively unstable governments, the risk of nationalization of businesses, less protection of property rights, and the threat of abrupt price movements. For example, in February 1990, when the newly elected Brazilian president froze most personal bank accounts, the São Paulo exchange plummeted 70% in a few days. Similarly, Taiwan's market rose more than 1,000% from January 1987 to its peak in February 1990. It then gave back most of these gains, falling nearly 80% by October 1990. The Indian stock market has also taken a roller-coaster ride. In the euphoria that accompanied the liberalization of the Indian economy, the Bombay stock index rose 458% between June 1991 and April 1992. It then fell

[5]See, for example, Vihang R. Errunza, "Gains from Portfolio Diversification into Less Developed Countries," *Journal of International Business Studies*, Fall–Winter 1977, pp. 83–99, and Warren Bailey and Rene M. Stulz, "Benefits of International Diversification: The Case of Pacific Basin Stock Markets," *Journal of Portfolio Management*, Summer 1990, pp. 57–62.

30% in April and May following disclosure of a scandal in which a broker cheated financial institutions out of at least half a billion dollars to play the market. The more recent debacle in the Mexican Bolsa will remain fresh in the minds of investors for some time to come.

Despite their high investment risks, however, emerging markets can reduce portfolio risk because of their low correlations with returns elsewhere. That is, most of their high total risk is unsystematic in nature.

Emerging markets tend to have low correlations with the U.S. market.

Exhibit 17.11 shows how some emerging markets were correlated with the U.S. market for the same four-year periods shown in Exhibit 17.7. For the four-year period 1993–1996, these correlations range from a high of 0.43 for Argentina to a low of –0.10 for Colombia. Moreover, as the composite indices show, these correlations have generally fallen in more recent years. Although not shown here, these emerging markets also have a low correlation with the MSCI World Index.

Most of the emerging markets, as a group as well as individually, have low correlations with the U.S. market and the MSCI World Index; this status indicates their potential for significant diversification benefits. Exhibit 17.12 shows for the ten-year period 1987–1996 the risk and return of a global portfolio that combines in varying proportions the MSCI World Index with the **IFC Emerging Markets Index,** published by the International Finance Corporation (an international lending organization discussed in Chapter 14).

We see that shifting from a portfolio invested 100% in the MSCI World Index to one that contains up to 20% invested in the IFC Emerging Markets Index reduces risk and at

EXHIBIT 17.11 • CORRELATIONS OF MONTHLY RETURNS WITH THE U.S. MARKET: EMERGING MARKETS

	1985–1996	1985–1988	1989–1992	1993–1996
Greece	0.12	0.23	0.02	0.14
Jordan	0.03	–0.20	0.26	0.02
Nigeria	0.04	0.14	–0.04	0.00
Portugal	N/A	N/A	0.34	0.21
Turkey	N/A	N/A	–0.20	–0.05
Zimbabwe	–0.02	–0.12	0.08	0.05
India	–0.08	0.00	–0.19	–0.06
Indonesia	N/A	N/A	N/A	0.52
Korea	0.20	0.26	0.22	0.02
Malaysia	0.44	0.51	0.55	0.20
Pakistan	0.01	–0.07	0.05	0.00
Philippines	0.25	0.16	0.45	0.18
Taiwan	0.13	0.12	0.17	0.11
Thailand	0.30	0.27	0.39	0.31
Argentina	0.05	0.00	0.04	0.43
Brazil	0.11	0.04	0.20	0.11
Chile	0.26	0.37	0.14	0.22
Colombia	0.07	0.15	0.10	–0.10
Mexico	0.35	0.42	0.36	0.20
Venezuela	–0.06	–0.08	–0.08	0.00
Composite	0.30	0.33	0.28	0.27
Asia	0.25	0.31	0.22	0.22
Latin America	0.27	0.30	0.24	0.24

Source: Computed using data from Ibbotson Associates Encorr Software © 1997, Chicago, IL. Used with permission. All rights reserved.

EXHIBIT 17.12 • RISK AND RETURN FOR VARIOUS MIXES OF MSCI WORLD AND IFC EMERGING MARKETS INDICES, 1987–1996

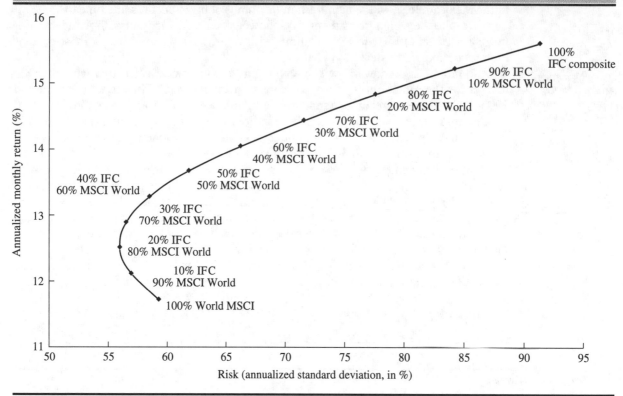

Source: Arjun B. Divecha, Jaime Drach, and Dan Stefek, "Emerging Markets: A Quantitative Perspective," *Journal of Portfolio Management,* Fall 1992, p. 49. This copyrighted material is reprinted with permission from *Journal of Portfolio Management,* Institutional Investor Inc., 488 Madison Avenue, New York, NY 10022.

Despite their high individual risks, emerging markets can reduce portfolio risk.

the same time increases expected return. Beyond that point, portfolio risk starts increasing as the higher volatility of the Emerging Markets Index more than offsets the benefits of diversification. Thus, even if one did not expect the emerging markets to outperform the developed country markets, risk reduction alone would dictate an investment of up to 20% in the emerging markets. Because the emerging markets outperformed the developed country markets during this period, a 20% investment in the IFC Index would have reduced the annual standard deviation by 3.34% and increased the annual return by 0.78% as well.

ILLUSTRATION *Latin American Stocks Were Hotter than Salsa*

A conversion to free-market economics in much of Latin America did wonders for their stock markets in the early 1990s. Investors expected that tighter monetary policies, lower tax rates, significantly lower budget deficits, and the sale of money-losing state enterprises would go a long way toward curing the sickly Latin economies. These expectations, in turn, helped stock markets to soar during the early 1990s in all countries shown in Exhibit 17.13 except Brazil—the one country that has backslid on instituting serious market-oriented reforms. Overall, from 1984 through 1996, the six Latin American stock markets depicted in Exhibit 17.13 rose an average 2,300%, far exceeding the returns available in any other region of the world. Note, however, that these gains reflect the markets'

EXHIBIT 17.13 • LATIN AMERICAN STOCK MARKETS TAKE OFF, 1985–1996

Source: ©1992 The Economist Newspaper Group, Inc. Reprinted with permission. Further reproduction prohibited.

low starting points as much as the success of the economic reforms. Most Latin American markets took a tumble in 1994, led by the Mexican market, as interest rates rose in the United States and as investors began to understand that the payoffs from the economic changes would take more time than earlier thought to be realized and would be riskier than expected.

Emerging markets appear to respond with a lag to events that affect developed-country markets immediately.

We should note one caveat to the data presented on the low correlations between U.S. and emerging country stock market returns, which are based on monthly data: Monthly return correlations have tended to understate the long-run interrelatedness of emerging markets and their developed-country counterparts. A recent study shows that correlations between developed and developing-country markets are much higher when these correlations are computed using yearly data instead of monthly data.[6] In contrast, correlations between developed nation markets do not vary significantly when computed with yearly instead of monthly data. These results suggest that because of various impediments to capital mobility in emerging markets, events that affected developed country returns immediately tended to affect emerging market returns with a lag. With the reduction of these impediments to capital mobility—which include government restrictions on capital flows and a lack of liquidity—the low monthly correlations between developed and developing markets are likely to rise in the future.

Barriers to International Diversification

The benefits to international diversification will be limited, however, to the extent that there are barriers to investing overseas. Such barriers do exist. They include legal, informational, and economic impediments that serve to segment national capital markets, deterring investors seeking to invest abroad. The lack of **liquidity**—the ability to buy and sell securities efficiently—is a major obstacle on some overseas exchanges. Other barriers include currency controls, specific tax regulations, relatively less-developed capital markets abroad, exchange risk, and the lack of readily accessible and comparable

[6]John Mullin, "Emerging Equity Markets in the Global Economy," *Federal Reserve Bank of New York Quarterly Review,* Summer 1993, pp. 54–83.

EXHIBIT 17.14 • BUYING STOCKS ABROAD

Net cross-border equity flows, in billions of dollars

*Estimate

Source: Baring Securities Ltd. in the *Wall Street Journal,* April 14, 1994, p. C1. Reprinted by permission of the *Wall Street Journal,* ©1994 Dow Jones & Company, Inc. All rights reserved worldwide.

information on potential foreign security acquisitions. The lack of adequate information can significantly increase the perceived riskiness of foreign securities, giving investors an added incentive to keep their money at home.

Barriers to investing overseas are being eroded.

Some of these barriers are apparently being eroded. Money invested abroad by both large institutions and individuals is growing dramatically. For the world as a whole, investors purchased a total of $159.2 billion of stock in other countries in 1993, triple the amount of **cross-border equity investment** in 1992 and well above the previous record of $100.6 billion, set in 1991 (see Exhibit 17.14). Overall, at the end of 1993, overseas investors held an estimated $1.2 trillion worth of foreign stocks.[7]

Despite this growth in the level of foreign investing, these holdings still represent a relatively minor degree of international diversification. For example, in 1993, Americans held 94% of their equity investments in domestic stocks. Nonetheless, discussions with U.S. institutional investors indicate that many intend to have 20%–25% of their funds invested overseas by the year 2000 (in contrast to only 7% in 1993).[8]

U.S. investors are not well diversified internationally.

U.S. investors can diversify into foreign securities in several ways. A small number of foreign firms—fewer than 100—have listed their securities on the New York Stock Exchange (NYSE) or the American Stock Exchange. Historically, a major barrier to foreign listing has been the NYSE requirements for substantial disclosure and audited financial statements. For firms that wished to sell securities in the United States, the U.S. Securities and Exchange Commission's (SEC) disclosure regulations have also been a major obstruction. However, the gap between acceptable NYSE and SEC accounting and disclosure standards and those acceptable to European multinationals has narrowed substantially. Moreover, Japanese and European multinationals that raise funds in international capital markets have been forced to conform to stricter standards. This change may encourage other foreign firms to list their securities and gain access to the U.S. capital market.

Investors can always buy foreign securities in their home markets. One problem with buying stocks listed on foreign exchanges is that such buying can be expensive,

[7]This estimate appeared in Michael R. Sesit, "Americans Pour Money into Foreign Markets," *Wall Street Journal,* April 4, 1994, p. C12.
[8]These discussions were reported by Michael R. Sesit, "Foreign Investing Makes a Comeback," *Wall Street Journal,* September 1, 1989, pp. C1 and C14.

primarily because of steep brokerage commissions. Owners of foreign stocks also face the complications of foreign tax laws and the nuisance of converting dividend payments into dollars.

Instead of buying foreign stocks overseas, investors can buy foreign equities traded in the United States in the following form:

U.S. investors have several ways to diversify into foreign securities.

1. **American Depository Receipts (ADRs)**: These receipts are certificates of ownership issued by a U.S. bank as a convenience to investors in lieu of the underlying shares it holds in custody. The investors in ADRs absorb the handling costs through transfer and handling charges. American Depository Receipts for about 1,000 companies from 33 foreign countries are currently traded on U.S. exchanges.
2. **American shares:** These shares are securities certificates issued in the United States by a transfer agent acting on behalf of the foreign issuer. The foreign issuer absorbs part or all of the handling expenses involved.

Internationally diversified mutual funds provide a low-cost vehicle for international investing.

The easiest approach to investing abroad is to buy shares in an internationally diversified mutual fund, of which a growing number are available. There are four basic categories of mutual fund that invest abroad:

1. **Global funds** can invest anywhere in the world, including the United States.
2. **International funds** invest only outside the United States.
3. **Regional funds** focus on specific geographical areas overseas, such as Asia or Europe.
4. **Single-country funds** invest in individual countries, such as Germany or Taiwan.

The greater diversification of the global and international funds reduces the risk for investors, but it also lessens the chances of a high return if one region (for example, Asia) or country (for example, Germany) suddenly gets hot. The problem with this approach is that forecasting returns is essentially impossible in an efficient market. Most investors would be better off buying an internationally diversified mutual fund. Of course, it is possible to construct one's own internationally diversified portfolio by buying shares in several different regional or country funds.

INTERNATIONAL BOND INVESTING

Internationally diversified bond portfolios offer superior investment performance.

The benefits of international diversification extend to bond portfolios as well. Barnett and Rosenberg started with a portfolio fully invested in U.S. bonds and then replaced them, in increments of 10%, with a mixture of foreign bonds from seven markets.[9] They then calculated for the period 1973–1983 the risk and return of the 10 portfolios they created. Their conclusions were as follows:

1. As the proportion of U.S. bonds fell, the portfolio return rose—a result of foreign bonds outperforming U.S. bonds over this 10-year period.
2. As the proportion of U.S. bonds fell from 100% to 70%, the volatility of the portfolio fell—reflecting the low correlation between U.S. and foreign bond returns.
3. By investing up to 60% of their funds in foreign bonds, U.S. investors could have raised their return substantially while not increasing risk above the level associated with holding only U.S. bonds.

Other studies examining different time periods and markets have similarly found that an internationally diversified bond portfolio delivers superior performance.

[9]G. Barnett and M. Rosenberg, "International Diversification in Bonds," *Prudential International Fixed Income Investment Strategy,* Second Quarter 1983.

OPTIMAL INTERNATIONAL ASSET ALLOCATION

The evidence clearly indicates that both international stock diversification and international bond diversification pay off. Not surprisingly, expanding the investment set to include stocks and bonds, both domestic and foreign, similarly pays off in terms of an improved risk-return trade-off.

The most detailed study to date of the advantages of international stock and bond diversification is by Bruno Solnik and Bernard Noetzlin.[10] They compared the performances of various investment strategies over the period 1970–1980. Exhibit 17.15 shows the outcome of their analysis. The right-hand curve is the efficient frontier when investments are restricted to stocks only. The left-hand curve is the efficient frontier when investors can buy both stocks and bonds. All returns are calculated in U.S. dollars.

The conclusions of their study were as follows:

> International stock and bond diversification together offer a better risk/return trade-off than either alone.

1. International stock diversification yields a substantially better risk-return trade-off than does holding purely domestic stock.
2. International diversification combining stock and bond investments results in substantially less risk than international stock diversification alone.
3. A substantial improvement in the risk-return trade-off can be realized by investing in internationally diversified stock and bond portfolios whose weights don't conform to relative market capitalizations. In other words, the various market indices used to measure world stock and bond portfolios (e.g., Capital International's EAFE Index and World Index) don't lie on the efficient frontier.

As indicated by Exhibit 17.15, optimal **international asset allocation** makes it possible to double or even triple the return from investing in an index fund without taking on

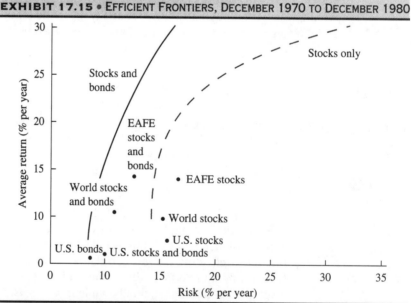

EXHIBIT 17.15 • EFFICIENT FRONTIERS, DECEMBER 1970 TO DECEMBER 1980

Source: Bruno H. Solnik and Bernard Noetzlin, "Optimal International Asset Allocation," *Journal of Portfolio Management*, Fall 1982. This copyrighted material is reprinted with permission from *Journal of Portfolio Management*, Institutional Investor, Inc., 488 Madison Avenue, New York, NY 10022.

[10]Bruno H. Solnik and Bernard Noetzlin, "Optimal International Asset Allocation," *Journal of Portfolio Management*, Fall 1982, pp. 11–21.

more risk. Although Solnik and Noetzlin had the advantage of hindsight in constructing their efficient frontier, they concluded that the opportunities for increased risk-adjusted returns are sizable and that the performance gap between optimal international asset allocations and passive investing in simple index funds is potentially quite large.

MEASURING THE TOTAL RETURN FROM FOREIGN PORTFOLIO INVESTING

The total dollar return on a foreign investment consists of dividend/interest income, capital gains, and currency gains.

This section shows how to measure the return associated with investing in securities issued in different markets and denominated in a variety of currencies. In general, the **total dollar return** on an investment can be decomposed into three separate elements: dividend/interest income, capital gains (losses), and currency gains (losses).

Bonds

The one-period total dollar return on a foreign bond investment $R_\$$ can be calculated as follows:

$$\underset{\text{return}}{\text{Dollar}} = \underset{\text{return}}{\text{Foreign currency}} \times \underset{\text{gain (loss)}}{\text{Currency}}$$

$$1 + R_\$ = [1 + \frac{B(1) - B(0) + C}{B(0)}](1 + g) \tag{17.4}$$

where $B(t)$ = foreign currency (FC) bond price at time t

C = foreign currency coupon income

g = percent change in dollar value of the foreign currency

Suppose the initial bond price is FC 95, the coupon income is FC 8, the end-of-period bond price is FC 97, and the local currency appreciates by 3% against the dollar during the period. According to Equation 17.4, the total dollar return is 13.8%:

$$R_\$ = [1 + (97 - 95 + 8)/95](1 + 0.03) - 1$$
$$= (1.105)(1.03) - 1$$
$$= 13.8\%$$

Note that the currency gain applies to both the local currency principal and to the local currency return.

Stocks

Using the same terminology, the one-period total dollar return on a foreign stock investment $R_\$$ can be calculated as follows:

$$\underset{\text{return}}{\text{Dollar}} = \underset{\text{return}}{\text{Foreign currency}} \times \underset{\text{gain (loss)}}{\text{Currency}}$$

$$1 + R_\$ = [1 + \frac{P(1) - P(0) + DIV}{P(0)}](1 + g) \tag{17.5}$$

where $P(t)$ = foreign currency stock price at time t

DIV = foreign currency dividend income

Suppose the beginning stock price is FC 50, the dividend income is FC 1, the end-of-period stock price is FC 48, and the foreign currency depreciates by 5% against the dollar during the period. According to Equation 17.5, the total dollar return is −6.9%:

$$R_\$ = [1 + \frac{(48 - 50 + 1)}{50}](1 - 0.05) - 1$$
$$= (0.98)(0.95) - 1$$
$$= -6.9\%$$

In this case, the investor suffered both a capital loss on the FC principal and a currency loss on the investment's dollar value.

MEASURING EXCHANGE RISK ON FOREIGN SECURITIES

We have just seen that the dollar return on a foreign security can be expressed as

$$\begin{array}{ccc} \text{Dollar} & \text{Foreign currency} & \text{Currency} \\ \text{return} & = \text{return} & \times \text{gain (loss)} \\ 1 + R_\$ & = (1 + R_f)(1 + g) & \end{array}$$

(17.6)

where R_f is the foreign currency rate of return. Ignoring the cross-product term, $R_f g$, which should be quite small relative to the other terms (because R_f and g are usually much less than 1) we can approximate Equation 17.6 by Equation 17.7:

$$R_\$ = R_f + g$$

(17.7)

> *Currency fluctuations affect the risk of investing in foreign securities.*

Equation 17.7 says the dollar rate of return is approximately equal to the sum of the foreign currency return plus the change in the dollar value of the foreign currency. Foreign currency fluctuations introduce exchange risk. As we have already seen (in Chapter 7), the prospect of exchange risk is one of the reasons investors have a preference for home country securities.

Using Equation 17.7, we can see how exchange rate changes affect the risk of investing in a foreign security (or a foreign market index). Specifically, we can write the standard deviation of the dollar return, $\sigma_\$$, as

$$\sigma_\$ = [\sigma_f^2 + \sigma_g^2 + 2\sigma_f \sigma_g \sigma_{f,g}]^{1/2}$$

(17.8)

where σ_f^2 = the variance (the standard deviation squared) of the foreign currency return

σ_g^2 = the variance of the change in the exchange rate

$\sigma_{f,g}$ = the correlation between the foreign currency return and the exchange rate change

Equation 17.8 shows that the foreign exchange risk associated with a foreign security depends on both the standard deviation of the foreign exchange rate change and the covariance between the exchange rate change and the foreign currency return on the security.

Suppose the standard deviation of the return on Matsushita, a Japanese firm, in terms of yen is 23% and the standard deviation of the rate of change in the dollar:yen exchange rate is 17%. In addition, the estimated correlation between the yen return on Matsushita and the rate of change in the exchange rate is 0.31. According to Equation 17.8, the standard deviation of the dollar rate of return on investing in Matsushita stock is 32.56%:

$$\sigma_\$(Matsushita) = (0.23^2 + 0.17^2 + 2 \times 0.23 \times 0.17 \times 0.31)^{1/2} = 0.3256$$

Clearly, foreign exchange risk increases risk in this case. However, the foreign exchange risk is not additive; that is, the standard deviation of the dollar return—32.56%—is less than the sum of the individual standard deviations—23% + 17%, or 40%. Conceivably, the exchange risk could lower the risk of investing overseas. Lowering risk would require a sufficiently large negative correlation between the rate of exchange rate change and the foreign currency return.

SUMMARY AND CONCLUSIONS

As the barriers to international capital flows come down and improved communication and data-processing technology provide low-cost information about foreign securities, investors are starting to realize the enormous potential in international investing. We saw in this chapter that international stock and bond diversification can provide substantially higher returns with less risk than investment in a single market. A major reason is that international investment offers a much broader range of opportunities than domestic investment alone, even in a market as large as the United States. An investor restricted to the U.S. stock market, for example, is cut off, in effect, from over two-thirds of the available investment opportunities.

Even though a passive international portfolio—one invested in an index fund based on market capitalization weights—improves risk-adjusted performance, an active strategy can do substantially better. The latter strategy bases the portfolio proportions of domestic and foreign investments on their expected returns and their correlations with the overall portfolio.

Chapter 6

A FRAMEWORK FOR ASSESSING TRADING STRATEGIES

LEARNING OUTCOME STATEMENTS

After reading this chapter you should be able to:

- explain what leverage is.
- identify the advantages and disadvantages of leverage.
- explain what a repurchase agreement is.
- compute the dollar interest of a repurchase agreement.
- discuss the credit risks associated with a repurchase agreement.
- distinguish between special (or hot) collateral and general collateral.
- explain the factors that affect the repo rate.
- compute the total return for a bond over some investment horizon.
- describe what scenario analysis is.
- explain how interest rate risk is controlled in a trade.
- explain why total return analysis and scenario analysis should be used to assess the potential performance of a trade before the trade is implemented.

529

SECTION I
INTRODUCTION

Portfolio managers are inundated with trades suggested by sales people and in periodic publications by dealer firms. Moreover, managers develop trading strategies based on their historical analysis of yields and yield spreads. In this chapter, we will explain the framework for assessing a trade or trading strategy.

A manager may be permitted to use leverage as part of a trade or trading strategy. Leverage means borrowing funds to purchase a part of the securities involved in the strategy. So, we will begin this chapter with a discussion of the advantages and disadvantages of using leverage and then how managers can borrow funds using repurchase agreements. Then we show how to compute the total return for a trade and the use of scenario analysis in evaluating a trade. In the last section, we look at some trades and how to apply the framework developed in this chapter to assess them.

SECTION II
THE PRINCIPLE
OF LEVERAGE

The investment principle of borrowing funds in the hope of earning a return in excess of the cost of funds is called **leveraging**. The attractive feature of leveraging is that it magnifies the return that will be realized from investment in a security for a given change in the price of that security. That's the good news. The bad news is that leveraging also magnifies any loss.

To illustrate this, consider an investor who wants to purchase a 30-year U.S. Treasury bond in anticipation of a decline in interest rates six months from now. Suppose that the investor has $1 million to invest. The $1 million is referred to as the **investor's equity**. Assuming that the coupon rate for the 30-year Treasury bond is 8% with the next coupon payment six months from now and the bond can be purchased at par value, then the investor can purchase $1 million of par value of an 8% coupon 30-year Treasury bond with the equity available.

Exhibit 1 shows the return that will be realized assuming various yields six months from now at which the 8% coupon 30-year Treasury bond will trade. The dollar return consists of the coupon payment six months from now and the change in the value of the 30-year Treasury bond. (There is no reinvestment income.) At the end of six months, the 30-year Treasury bond is a 29.5-year Treasury bond. The percent return is found by dividing the dollar return by the $1 million of investor's equity and then annualizing by simply multiplying by 2 (so the return is computed on a bond-equivalent basis). Notice that the range for the annualized percent return based on the assumed yields six months from now ranges from −29.8% to +63.0%.

Exhibit 1: Annual Return from a $1 Million Investment in a 30-Year 8% Coupon Treasury Bond Held for Six Months

Assumed yield six months from now (%)	Price per $100 par value ($)*	Market value per $1 million par value ($)*	Semiannual coupon payment ($)	Dollar return ($)	Annualized percent return (%)**
10.00	81.12	811,200	40,000	−148,800	−29.8
9.50	85.23	852,300	40,000	−107,700	−21.5
9.00	89.72	897,200	40,000	−62,800	−12.6
8.50	94.62	946,200	40,000	−13,800	−2.8
8.00	100.00	1,000,000	40,000	40,000	8.0
7.50	105.91	1,059,100	40,000	99,100	19.8
7.00	112.41	1,124,100	40,000	164,100	32.8
6.50	119.58	1,195,800	40,000	235,800	47.2
6.00	127.51	1,275,100	40,000	315,100	63.0

* This is the price and market value six months later, rounded to the nearest $100.
** Annualized by doubling the semiannual return.

Exhibit 2: Annual Return from a $2 Million Investment in a 30-Year 8% Coupon Treasury Bond Held for Six Months Using $1 Million of Borrowed Funds

Assumed yield six months from now (%)	Market value per $100 par value ($)*	Market value per $2 million par value ($)*	Semiannual coupon payment ($)	Dollar return to equity ($)**	Annualized percent return (%)***
10.00	81.12	1,622,400	80,000	−342,600	−68.5
9.50	85.23	1,704,600	80,000	−260,400	−52.1
9.00	89.72	1,794,400	80,000	−170,600	−34.1
8.50	94.62	1,892,400	80,000	−72,600	−14.5
8.00	100.00	2,000,000	80,000	35,000	7.0
7.50	105.91	2,118,200	80,000	153,200	30.6
7.00	112.41	2,248,200	80,000	283,200	56.6
6.50	119.58	2,391,600	80,000	426,600	85.3
6.00	127.51	2,550,200	80,000	585,200	117.0

* This is the price and market value six months later, rounded to the nearest $100.
** After deducting interest expense of $45,000 ($1 million × 9%/2).
*** Annualized by doubling the semiannual return.

In our illustration, the investor did not borrow any funds. Hence, the strategy is referred to as an **unleveraged strategy**. Now let's suppose that the investor can borrow $1 million to purchase an additional $1 million of par value of the 30-year 8% coupon Treasury bond. Assume further that the loan agreement specifies that:

1. the maturity of the loan is six months
2. the annual interest rate for the loan is 9%, and
3. $1 million par value of the 30-year 8% coupon Treasury bond is used as collateral for the loan

Therefore, the loan is a collateralized loan. The collateral for this loan is the $2 million par value of the 30-year 8% Treasury bond purchased by the investor. The $2 million invested comes from the investor's equity of $1 million and $1 million of borrowed funds. In this strategy, the investor is using leverage. Since the investor has the use of $2 million in proceeds and has equity of $1 million, this amount of leverage is said to be "2-to-1 leverage." (This means $2 invested for $1 in investor's equity.)

Exhibit 2 shows the annual percent return for this leveraged strategy assuming the same yields at the end of six months as in Exhibit 1. The return is measured relative to the investor's equity of $1 million, not the $2 million. The dollar return on the $1 million of equity invested shown in the exhibit adjusts for the cost of borrowing.

By using borrowed funds, the range for the annualized percent return is wider (−68.5% to +117.0%) than in the case where no funds are borrowed (−29.8% to 63.0%). This example clearly shows how leveraging is a two-edged sword — it can magnify returns both up and down. Notice that if the market yield does not change at the end of six months for the 30-year Treasury bond, then the unleveraged strategy would have generated an 8% annual return. That is, for the $1 million invested the coupon interest is $40,000 for six months. Since there is no change in the market value of the security, this gives a 4% semiannual return and therefore 8% on a simple annual basis (i.e., a bond-equivalent basis). In contrast, consider what happens if $2 million is invested in the 2-for-1 leveraging strategy. Since $2 million is invested, the coupon interest is $80,000 for six months. But the interest cost of the $1 million loan for six month is $45,000 ($1 million × 9%/2). Thus, the dollar return after the financing cost is $35,000 ($80,000 − $45,000). Hence, the return on the $1 million equity of the investor is 3.5% for six months ($35,000/$1 million) and 7% annualized. Thus, without leverage the investor earns 8% if interest rates do not change but only 7% in the same scenario in the 2-for-1 leveraging strategy.

Suppose that instead of borrowing $1 million, the investor can find a lender who is willing to lend for six months $11 million at an annual interest rate of 9%. The investor can now purchase $12 million of 30-year 8% coupon Treasury bonds. That is, there will be $1 million of investor's equity and $11 million of borrowed funds. The lender requires that the $11 million of Treasury bonds be used as collateral for this loan. Since there is $12 million invested and $1 million of investor's equity, this strategy is said to have "12-to-1 leverage."

Exhibit 3 shows the annual return assuming the same yields for the 30-year Treasury six months from now as in Exhibits 1 and 2. Notice the considerably wider range for the annual return for the 12-to-1 leverage strategy compared to the 2-to-1 leverage strategy and the unleveraged strategy. In the case where the yield remains at 8%, the 12-to-1 strategy results in an annual return of −3%. This result occurs because the coupon interest earned on the $12 million invested for six months is $480,000 ($12 million × 8%/2) but the interest expense is $495,000 ($11 million borrowed × 9%/2). The dollar return to the investor for the 6-month period is then −$15,000 or −1.5% (−$15,000/$1 million). Doubling the −1.5% semiannual return gives the −3% annual return.

Exhibit 4 shows the range for different degrees of leverage. The greater the leverage, the wider the range of potential outcomes, and therefore the greater the risk of a leveraging strategy as measured by the greater dispersion of the possible outcomes.

PRACTICE QUESTION 1

Reconstruct Exhibit 2 assuming the investor has $1 million equity and borrows $5 million.

Exhibit 3: Annual Return from a $12 Million Investment in a 30-Year 8% Coupon Treasury Bond Held for Six Months Using $11 Million of Borrowed Funds

Assumed yield six months from now (%)	Price per $100 par value ($)*	Market value per $12 million par value ($)*	Semiannual coupon payment ($)	Dollar return to equity ($)**	Annualized percent return (%)***
10.00	81.12	9,734,900	480,000	−2,280,100	−456.0
9.50	85.23	10,227,900	480,000	−1,787,100	−357.4
9.00	89.72	10,766,000	480,000	−1,249,000	−249.8
8.50	94.62	11,354,700	480,000	−660,300	−132.1
8.00	100.00	12,000,000	480,000	−15,000	−3.0
7.50	105.91	12,708,800	480,000	693,800	138.8
7.00	112.41	13,489,100	480,000	1,474,100	294.8
6.50	119.58	14,349,600	480,000	2,334,600	466.9
6.00	127.51	15,301,200	480,000	3,286,200	657.2

* This is the price and market value six months later, rounded to the nearest 100.
** After deducting interest expense of $495,000 ($11 million × 9%/2).
*** Annualized by doubling the semiannual return.

Exhibit 4: Annual Return For Various Degrees of Leverage

Assumed yield six months from now (%)	Annual return for $1 million of equity and debt of $X million (%)					
	$0	$1	$2	$3	$5	$11
10.00	−29.8	−68.5	−107.3	−146.0	−223.6	−456.1
9.50	−21.5	−52.1	−82.6	−113.2	174.2	−357.5
9.00	−12.6	−34.1	−55.7	−77.2	120.4	−249.7
8.50	−2.8	−14.5	−26.3	−38.0	61.6	−132.1
8.00	8.0	7.0	6.0	5.0	3.0	−3.0
7.50	19.8	30.6	41.5	52.3	73.9	138.8
7.00	32.8	56.6	80.5	104.3	151.9	294.8
6.50	47.2	85.3	123.5	161.6	238.0	466.9
6.00	63.0	117.0	171.1	225.1	333.1	657.2

SECTION III BORROWING FUNDS VIA REPURCHASE AGREEMENTS

A **repurchase agreement** is the sale of a security with a commitment by the seller to buy the same security back from the purchaser at a specified price at a designated future date. The price at which the seller must subsequently repurchase the security is called the **repurchase price** and the date by which the security must be repurchased is called the **repurchase date**. Basically, a repurchase agreement is a **collateralized loan**, where the collateral is the security sold and subsequently repurchased.[1] The agreement is best explained with an illustration.

Suppose a government securities dealer has purchased $10 million of a particular Treasury security. Where does the dealer obtain the funds to finance that position? Of course, the dealer can finance the position with its own funds or by borrowing from a bank. Typically, however, the dealer uses the repurchase agreement or "repo" market to obtain financing. In the repo market the dealer can use the $10 million of the Treasury security as collateral for the loan. The term of the loan and the interest rate that the dealer agrees to pay are specified. The interest rate is called the **repo rate**. When the term of the loan is one day, it is called an **overnight repo** (or RP); a loan for more than one day is called a **term repo** (or RP). The transaction is referred to as a repurchase agreement because it calls for the sale of the security and its repurchase at a future date. Both the sale price and the purchase price are specified in the agreement. The difference between the purchase (repurchase) price and the sale price is the dollar interest cost of the loan.

Back to the dealer firm who needs to finance $10 million of a Treasury security that it just purchased and plans to hold for one day. Suppose that a customer of the dealer firm has funds of $10 million. The dealer firm would agree to deliver ("sell") $10 million of the Treasury security to the customer for $10 million and simultaneously agree to buy back (i.e., "repurchase") the same Treasury security the next day for $10 million plus interest. The amount of the interest is determined by the repo rate.

The dollar amount of the interest is based on the repo rate, the number of days that the funds are borrowed (i.e., the term of the loan), and the amount borrowed. The formula for the dollar interest is:

dollar interest = amount borrowed × repo rate × repo term/360

Notice that the dollar interest is computed on an actual/360-day basis.

In our example, if the repo rate is 5%, then we know

---

[1] There is a special type of repurchase agreement used in the mortgage-backed securities market. This arrangement is called a "dollar roll." For an explanation of a dollar roll, see Chapter 9 in Frank J. Fabozzi and David Yuen, *Managing MBS Portfolios* (New Hope, PA: Frank J. Fabozzi Associates, 1998).

$$\text{amount borrowed} = \$10,000,000$$
$$\text{repo rate} = 0.05$$
$$\text{repo term} = 1 \text{ day}$$

and therefore the dollar interest is

$$\text{dollar interest} = \$10,000,000 \times 0.05 \times 1/360 = \$1,388.89$$

So, our dealer would sell the Treasury security to the customer for $10 million and agree to repurchase it the next day for $10,001,388.89 ($10,000,000 + $1,388.89).

The advantage to the dealer of using the repo market for borrowing on a short-term basis is that the rate is lower than the cost of bank financing. (The reason for this is explained below.) From the customer's perspective, the repo market offers an attractive yield on a short-term secured transaction that is highly liquid.

While the example illustrates financing a dealer's long position in the repo market, dealers can also use the market to cover a short position. For example, suppose a government dealer sold short $10 million of Treasury securities two weeks ago and must now cover the position — that is, deliver the securities. The dealer can do a **reverse repo** (agree to buy the securities and sell them back). Of course, the dealer eventually would have to buy the Treasury security in the market in order to cover its short position. In this case, the dealer is actually making a collateralized loan to its customer. The customer (or other dealer) is then using the funds obtained from the collateralized loan to create leverage.

PRACTICE QUESTION 2

A dealer needs to finance $5 million of a Treasury security that it plans to hold overnight using a repurchase agreement. Assume that the overnight repo rate is 4% and the dealer can obtain 100% financing.

a. How much dollar interest would the dealer pay?
b. How much would the dealer agree to repurchase the security for the next day?

A. Industry Jargon

There is a good deal of Wall Street jargon describing repo transactions. To understand it, remember that one party is lending money and accepting a security as collateral for the loan; the other party is borrowing money and providing collateral to borrow the money. When someone lends securities (i.e., uses securities as collateral) in order to receive cash (i.e., borrow money), that party is said to be "reversing out" securities. A party that lends money with the security as collateral is said to be "reversing in" securities. The expressions "to repo securities" and "to do repo" are also used. The former means that someone is going to finance securities using the security as collateral; the latter means that the party is going to invest in a repo. Finally, the expressions "selling collateral" and "buying collateral" are used to describe a party financing a security with a repo on the one hand, and lending on the basis of collateral, on the other.[2]

In practice, the term repo transaction and reverse repo transaction are used in a special way in the industry. When a dealer uses a repo agreement to borrow funds,

---

[2] Note that the terms "buying collateral" and "selling collateral" do not mean the same thing in the mortgage-backed securities market as used here. Recall from Chapter 3 that passthroughs are used to create collateralized mortgage obligations. Consequently, passthroughs are referred to as "collateral." In the MBS market, buying collateral means buying passthroughs and selling collateral means selling passthroughs.

the dealer is said to do a **repo transaction**. When a non-dealer entity (such as a portfolio manager) uses a repo agreement to borrow funds, the non-dealer entity is said to do a **reverse repo transaction**. This is important to understand because the expression "repo" and "reverse repo" are used relative to who is borrowing the funds. *The same loan agreement is used whether a dealer or non-dealer is using the loan agreement to finance a position.* That is, it is a repurchase agreement. However, if the dealer needs to borrow funds and uses the repurchase agreement to obtain the funds, the dealer is said to be doing a "repo" or "repo transaction." If, instead, a non-dealer uses a repurchase agreement to obtain financing via a repurchase agreement the non-dealer is said to be doing a "reverse repo" or "reverse repo transaction."

Rather than using industry jargon, investment guidelines should be clear as to what a manager is permitted to do. For example, a client may have no objections to its portfolio manager using a repo as a short-term investment — that is, the portfolio manager may lend funds on a short-term basis. The investment guidelines will set forth how the loan arrangement should be structured to protect against credit risk. We'll discuss this below. However, if a client does not want a money manager to use the repo agreement as a vehicle for borrowing funds (thereby, creating leverage), it should state so.

B. Margin and Marking to Market

Despite the fact that there may be high-quality collateral underlying a repo transaction, both parties to the transaction are exposed to credit risk. Why does credit risk occur in a repo transaction? Consider our initial example where the dealer uses $10 million of government securities as collateral to borrow. If the dealer cannot repurchase the government securities, the customer may keep the collateral; if interest rates on government securities increase subsequent to the repo transaction, however, the market value of the government securities will decline, and the customer will own securities with a market value less than the amount it lent to the dealer. If the market value of the security rises instead, the dealer will be concerned with the return of the collateral, which then has a market value higher than the loan.

Repos should be carefully structured to reduce credit risk exposure. The amount lent should be less than the market value of the security used as collateral, thereby providing the lender with some cushion should the market value of the security decline. The amount by which the market value of the security used as collateral exceeds the value of the loan is called **repo margin** or simply **margin**. Margin is also referred to as the "haircut." Repo margin is generally between 1% and 3%. For borrowers of lower credit worthiness and/or when less liquid or more price sensitive securities are used as collateral, the repo margin can be 10% or more.

For example, consider the dealer who needs to borrow $10 million to finance the purchase of a Treasury security. Suppose that the repo margin is 2%. Then for a Treasury security with a market value of $10 million, only 98% of that amount, $9.8 million, will be lent. That is, the dealer will agree to deliver (sell) $10 million of the Treasury security to the customer for $9.8 million and agree to repurchase the $10 million of the Treasury security the next day for $9.8 million plus the dollar interest. The dollar interest in this transaction for an overnight repo assuming a repo rate of 5% is

$$\text{dollar interest} = \$9,800,000 \times 0.05 \times 1/360 = \$1,361.11$$

Note that the dollar interest is based on $9.8 million (the amount actually lent by the customer), not $10 million as in our earlier example.

Another practice to limit credit risk is to mark the collateral to market on a regular basis. (Marking a position to market means recording the value of a position at its market value.) When the market value changes by a certain percentage, the repo position is adjusted accordingly. The decline in market value below a specified amount will result in a **margin deficit**. In such cases, the borrower of funds typically has the option to take care of the margin deficit by either providing additional cash or by transferring additional acceptable securities to the lender of funds. In cases when the market value rises above the amount required, **excess margin** will result. When this occurs, the lender of funds has the option to give cash to the borrower of funds equal to the amount of the excess margin or to transfer purchased securities to the borrower of funds.

C. Delivery and Credit Risk

One concern in structuring a repo is delivery of the collateral to the lender. The most obvious procedure is for the borrower to deliver the collateral to the lender or to the cash lender's clearing agent. In such instances, the collateral is said to be "delivered out." At the end of the repo term, the lender returns the collateral to the borrower in exchange for the principal and interest payment. This procedure may be too expensive though, particularly for short-term repos, because of costs associated with delivering the collateral. The cost of delivery would be factored into the repo rate. The risk of the lender not taking possession of the collateral is that the borrower may sell the security, or go under and the lender has nothing to liquidate, or use the same security as collateral for a repo with another party.

As an alternative to delivering out the collateral, the lender may agree to allow the borrower to hold the security in a segregated customer account. Of course, the lender still faces the risk that the borrower may use the collateral fraudulently by offering it as collateral for another repo transaction. If the borrower of the cash does not deliver out the collateral, but instead holds it, then the transaction is called a **hold-in-custody repo** (HIC repo). Despite the credit risk associated with a HIC repo, it is used in some transactions when the collateral is difficult to deliver or the transaction amount is small and the lender of funds is comfortable with the reputation of the borrower.

Another method is for the borrower to deliver the collateral to the lender's custodial account at the borrower's clearing bank. The custodian then has possession of the collateral that it holds on behalf of the lender. This practice reduces the cost of delivery because it is merely a transfer within the borrower's clearing bank. If, for example, a dealer enters into an overnight repo with Customer A, the next day the collateral is transferred back to the dealer. The dealer can then enter into a repo with Customer B for, say, five days without having to redeliver the collateral. The clearing bank simply establishes a custodian account for Customer B and holds the collateral in that account. This specialized type of repo arrangement is called a **tri-party repo**. Tri-party repos account for about half of all repo arrangements.

The responsibilities of the third party are as follows. First, it is responsible for marking the collateral to market and reporting these values each day to the two parties. Second, if the borrower of funds wishes to substitute collateral (i.e., change the specific Treasury securities collateralizing the loan), the third-party agent verifies that the collateral satisfies the requirements set forth in the repo agreement.

D. Determinants of the Repo Rate

There is not one repo rate. The rate varies from transaction to transaction depending on a variety of factors:

- quality of collateral
- term of the repo

- delivery requirement
- availability of collateral
- prevailing federal funds rate
- seasonal factors

The higher the credit quality and liquidity of the collateral, the lower the repo rate. With respect to the term of the repo, it is important to understand that there is a repo rate based on the length of time of the repo agreement. This is basically the very short-end of the yield curve. The maturity of the security used as collateral for a repo transaction has nothing to do the repo rate. If delivery of the collateral to the lender is required, the repo rate will be lower. If the collateral can be deposited with the bank of the borrower, a higher repo rate is paid.

The more difficult it is to obtain the collateral, the lower the repo rate. To understand why this is so, remember that the borrower (or equivalently the seller of the collateral) has a security that lenders of cash want, for whatever reason. Such collateral is referred to as **hot collateral** or **special collateral** (or just as "on special"). (Collateral that does not have this characteristic is referred to as **general collateral**.) The party that needs the hot collateral will be willing to lend funds at a lower repo rate in order to obtain the collateral.[3]

While these factors determine the repo rate on a particular transaction, the federal funds rate determines the general level of repo rates in the United States. Banks borrow funds from each other via the federal funds market. The interest rate charged on such borrowing is called the **federal funds rate** (or "fed funds"). The repo rate generally will be a rate lower than the federal funds rate because a repo involves collateralized borrowing, while a federal funds transaction is unsecured borrowing.

SECTION IV
TOTAL RETURN

Now let's look at a framework for assessing trades. A trade is evaluated in terms of its performance. When comparing two possible trades or a trade of a security versus maintaining a current position, the relative performance of the alternatives must be assessed. But what does performance mean? It is the expected **total return** over the investment horizon of the trade. The total return consists of three sources: (1) coupon payments, (2) the change in the value of the bond, and (3) reinvestment income from reinvesting coupon payments and principal repayment (in the case of amortizing securities) from the time of receipt to the end of the investment horizon.

For example, suppose that an investor purchases a security for $90 and expects a dollar return over a 1-year investment horizon from the three sources to be $6. Then the expected total return is 6.7% (= $6/$90).

When a trade involves the borrowing of funds via a repo, the interest cost of the repo must be deducted from the dollar return of these three sources. The dollar return adjusted for the financial cost is then related to the dollar amount invested. For example, suppose the investor purchased the $90 security by borrowing $80 and investing his own funds of $10 (i.e., the investor's equity). Suppose also that the cost of the borrowed funds is 5% or $4. Then the dollar return after adjusting for the financing cost is $2 ($6 − $4). The total return is then 20% ($2 return after adjusting for the borrowing cost divided by the investor's equity of $10 funds invested). This is precisely what was done in Section II when we demonstrated how to compute the total return using various degrees of leverage.

---

[3] Bloomberg provides information on issues on special [Type NI RP<go>].

Below we discuss how to calculate the total return for assessing trades and discuss scenario analysis. At Level III, we discuss total return analysis for a portfolio.

A. Computing the Expected Total Return

The total return considers all three sources of potential dollar return over the investor's investment horizon. It is the return (interest rate) that will make the proceeds (i.e., price plus accrued interest) invested grow to the projected total dollar return at the end of the investment horizon.[4] The total return requires that the investor specify:

- an investment horizon
- a reinvestment rate
- a price for the bond at the end of the investment horizon.

More formally, the steps for computing a total return over some investment horizon are as follows:

Step 1: Compute the total coupon payments plus the reinvestment income based on an assumed reinvestment rate. The reinvestment rate is one-half the annual interest rate that the investor assumes can be earned on the reinvestment of coupon interest payments.[5]

Step 2: Determine the projected sale price at the end of the investment horizon. We refer to this as the **horizon price**. At Level I (Chapter 5) and in Chapters 2 and 5 we explained how the price of a bond is computed based on the term structure of default-free interest rates (i.e., the Treasury spot rate curve) and the term structure of credit spreads. Moreover, for bonds with embedded options, the price will depend on the option-adjusted spread (OAS). So, to determine the horizon price in the total return analysis it is necessary to use at the horizon date an assumed Treasury spot rate curve, term structure of credit spreads, and OAS. Obviously, the assumed values reflect changes in interest rates and spreads from the beginning to the end of the investment horizon. We shall refer to these rates as the **structure of rates at the horizon date**.
However, in the illustrations to follow, to simplify we will assume a single yield to price a security at the horizon date. This yield would reflect the Treasury rate plus a spread and we will refer to it as the **horizon yield**.

Step 3: Add the values computed in Steps 1 and 2. Reduce this value by any borrowing cost to obtain the total future dollars that will be received from the investment given the assumed reinvestment rate and projected structure of rates at the horizon date (or horizon yield in our illustrations to follow).

Step 4: Compute the *semiannual total return* using the following formula:

$$\left(\frac{\text{total future dollars}}{\text{full price of bond}}\right)^{1/h} - 1$$

where the full price is the price plus accrued interest and h is the *number of semiannual periods in the investment horizon*.

---

[4] The total return is also referred to as the **horizon return**.

[5] An investor can choose multiple reinvestment rates for cash flows from the bond over the investment horizon.

Exhibit 5: Graphical Depiction of Total Return Calculation

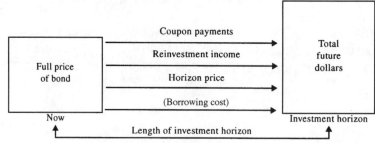

Total return is the interest rate that will make the full price of the bond grow to the total future dollars

Step 5: For semiannual-pay bonds, double the interest rate found in Step 4. The resulting interest rate is the total return expressed on a bond-equivalent basis. Instead, the total return can be expressed on an effective rate basis by using the following formula:

$$(1 + \text{semiannual total return})^2 - 1$$

A graphical depiction of the total return calculation is presented in Exhibit 5.

The decision as to whether to calculate the total return on a bond-equivalent basis or an effective rate basis depends on the situation. If the total return is being compared to a benchmark index that is calculated on a bond-equivalent basis, then the total return should be calculated in that way. However, if the bond is being used to satisfy liabilities that are calculated on an effective rate basis, then the total return should be calculated in that way.

To illustrate the computation of the total return, suppose that an investor with a 1-year investment horizon is considering the purchase of a 20-year 6% corporate bond. The issue is selling for $86.4365 for a yield of 7.3%. The issue will be purchased for cash (i.e., no funds will be borrowed). Assume that the yield curve is flat (i.e., the yield for all maturities is the same) and the yield for the on-the-run 20-year Treasury issue is 6.5%. This means that the yield spread over the on-the-Treasury issue for this corporate bond is 80 basis points. The investor expects that:

1. he can reinvest the coupon payments (there will be two of them over the 1-year investment horizon) at 6%.
2. the Treasury yield curve will shift down by 25 basis points and remains flat at the end of 1 year, so that the yield for the 19-year Treasury issue is 6.25% (6.5% minus 25 basis points)
3. the yield spread to the 19-year Treasury issue is unchanged at 80 basis points so the horizon yield is 7.05% (6.25% plus 80 basis points)

The calculations are as shown below.

Step 1: Compute the total coupon payments plus the reinvestment income assuming an annual reinvestment rate of 6% or 3% every six months. The semiannual coupon payments are $3. The future value of an annuity can be used or because the investment horizon is only one year, it can be computed as follows:

First coupon payment reinvested for six months = $3 (1.03)	=	$3.09
Second coupon payment not reinvested since at horizon date	=	$3.00
Total	=	$6.09

Step 2: The horizon price at the end of the 1-year investment horizon is determined as follows. The horizon yield is 7.05% by assumption. The 6% coupon 20-year corporate bond now has 19 years to maturity. The price of this bond when discounted at a flat 7.05% yield (the yield curve is assumed to be flat) is $89.0992.

Step 3: Adding the amounts in Steps 2 and 3 gives the total future dollars of $95.1892.

Step 4: Compute the following (*h* is 2 in our illustration):

$$\left(\frac{\$95.1892}{\$86.4365}\right)^{1/2} - 1 = 4.94\%$$

Step 5: The total return on a bond-equivalent basis and on an effective rate basis are shown below:

$$2 \times 4.94\% = 9.88\% \qquad \text{(BEY)}$$

$$(1.0494)^2 - 1 = 10.13\% \quad \text{(effective rate basis)}$$

PRACTICE QUESTION 3

Consider again the 6% coupon 20-year corporate bond. Assume again a 1-year investment horizon. However, assume that the investor expects that

1. he can reinvest the coupon payments at 4%.
2. the Treasury yield curve will shift down by 25 basis points and remain flat, so that the yield for the 19-year Treasury issue is 6.25% (6.5% minus 25 basis points)
3. the yield spread to the 19-year Treasury issue increases by 10 basis points

---

1. OAS-Total Return

The option-adjusted spread (OAS) can be incorporated into a total return analysis to determine the horizon price. This requires a valuation model. At the end of the investment horizon, it is necessary to specify how the OAS is expected to change. The horizon price can be "backed out" of a valuation model. This technique can be extended to the total return framework by making assumptions about the required variables at the horizon date.

Assumptions about the OAS value at the investment horizon reflect the expectations of the portfolio manager. It is common to assume that the OAS at the horizon date will be the same as the OAS at the time of purchase. A total return calculated using this assumption is referred to as a **constant-OAS total return**. Alternatively, managers or traders will take positions to reflect their views on how the OAS will change — either widening or tightening. The total return framework can be used to assess how sensitive the performance of a bond with an embedded option is to changes in the OAS.

2. Total Return for a Mortgage-Backed and Asset-Backed Security

In calculating total return of mortgage-backed and asset-backed securities, the total future dollars will depend on (1) the projected principal repayment (scheduled plus projected prepayments) and (2) the interest earned on reinvestment of the projected interest payments and projected principal payments. To obtain the total future dollars, a prepayment rate over the investment horizon must be assumed.

The monthly total return for a mortgage-backed security and an asset-backed security that makes monthly payments is computed using the formula:

$$\text{monthly total return} = \left(\frac{\text{total future dollars}}{\text{full price}}\right)^{\frac{1}{\text{number of months in horizon}}} - 1$$

The monthly total return can be annualized on a bond-equivalent yield basis as follows:

$$\text{bond-equivalent annual return} = 2[(1 + \text{monthly total return})^6 - 1]$$

Recall from our discussion in Chapter 5 that the calculation of a bond-equivalent yield for a monthly pay security such as a mortgage-backed or asset-backed security is to compute the effective 6-month yield and then annualize it by doubling the effective 6-month yield. This is precisely what the bond-equivalent annual return formula above does.

So, for example, if the monthly total return for a monthly pay mortgage-backed security or asset-backed security is 0.7%, the bond-equivalent annual return is

$$2[(1 + 0.007)^6 - 1] = 0.0855 = 8.55\%$$

Or, the effective annual return can be computed as follows:

$$\text{effective annual return} = (1 + \text{monthly total return})^{12} - 1$$

The effective annual return is just the compounding of the monthly return. For the previous example where the monthly total return is 0.7%, the effective annual return is:

$$(1 + 0.007)^{12} - 1 = 0.0873 = 8.73\%$$

As explained earlier, the decision as to whether to use the bond-equivalent annual return or the effective annual return depends on the situation.

3. Scenario Analysis

The computation of a total return is based on one or more assumptions regarding interest rates at the end of the investment horizon, spreads at the end of the investment horizon, and reinvestment rates available over the investment horizon. A manager would not want to rely on just one set of assumptions to make an investment decision. Instead, a manager will determine what happens to the total return under different sets of assumptions. A set of assumptions is referred to as a **scenario**. Evaluating what will happen to a strategy under several scenarios selected by the manager is called **scenario analysis**. Regulators also require certain institutions to perform scenario analysis based on assumptions specified by regulations.[6]

Exhibits 6 and 7 provide illustrations of scenario analysis. The bond used in the illustrations is the 6% 20-year corporate bond selling for $86.4365 for a yield of 7.3%. The assumptions in the scenario analysis in both exhibits is that the yield curve is flat and when it shifts it is a parallel shift in the yield curve. In Exhibit 6 it is assumed that only the Treasury yield curve shifts. In Exhibit 7 it is assumed that the yield spread changes and the change varies with how the Treasury yield curve shifts.

---

[6] Scenario analysis is referred to by some broker/dealers, vendors of analytical systems, and regulators as "simulation." They are not the same techniques. Simulation is a more powerful tool that takes into consideration the dynamics of interactions of the factors.

Exhibit 6: Scenario Analysis Assuming only the Treasury Yield Curve Changes (1-Year Investment Horizon)

	Scenario								
	1	2	3	4	5	6	7	8	9
At trade date									
Treasury rate	6.50%	6.50%	6.50%	6.50%	6.50%	6.50%	6.50%	6.50%	6.50%
Spread (bp)	80	80	80	80	80	80	80	80	80
Initial yield	7.30%	7.30%	7.30%	7.30%	7.30%	7.30%	7.30%	7.30%	7.30%
Coupon rate	6.00%	6.00%	6.00%	6.00%	6.00%	6.00%	6.00%	6.00%	6.00%
Maturity	20.0	20.0	20.0	20.0	20.0	20.0	20.0	20.0	20.0
Initial price	86.4365	86.4365	86.4365	86.4365	86.4365	86.4365	86.4365	86.4365	86.4365
At horizon date									
Treasury rate change (bp)	−150	−100	−50	−25	0	25	50	100	150
Spread change (bp)	0	0	0	0	0	0	0	0	0
Horizon yield	5.80%	6.30%	6.80%	7.05%	7.30%	7.55%	7.80%	8.30%	8.80%
Coupon rate	6.00%	6.00%	6.00%	6.00%	6.00%	6.00%	6.00%	6.00%	6.00%
Remaining maturity	19.0	19.0	19.0	19.0	19.0	19.0	19.0	19.0	19.0
Horizon price	102.2846	96.7035	91.5375	89.0992	86.7520	84.4920	82.3155	78.1993	74.3770
Reinvestment rate	6.0%	6.0%	6.0%	6.0%	6.0%	6.0%	6.0%	6.0%	6.0%
Interest + reinvest inc	6.09	6.09	6.09	6.09	6.09	6.09	6.09	6.09	6.09
Total future dollars	108.3746	102.7935	97.6275	95.1892	92.8420	90.5820	88.4055	84.2893	80.4670
Total return (SA)	11.97%	9.05%	6.28%	4.94%	3.64%	2.37%	1.13%	−1.25%	−3.51%
Total return (BEY)	23.95%	18.10%	12.55%	9.88%	7.28%	4.74%	2.27%	−2.50%	−7.03%
Total return (effective)	25.38%	18.92%	12.95%	10.13%	7.41%	4.80%	2.28%	−2.48%	−6.91%

Exhibit 7: Scenario Analysis Assuming Shift in Treasury Yield Curve and Change in Yield Spread (1-Year Investment Horizon)

	Scenario								
	1	2	3	4	5	6	7	8	9
At trade date									
Treasury rate	6.50%	6.50%	6.50%	6.50%	6.50%	6.50%	6.50%	6.50%	6.50%
Spread (bp)	80	80	80	80	80	80	80	80	80
Required yield	7.30%	7.30%	7.30%	7.30%	7.30%	7.30%	7.30%	7.30%	7.30%
Coupon rate	6.00%	6.00%	6.00%	6.00%	6.00%	6.00%	6.00%	6.00%	6.00%
Maturity	20.0	20.0	20.0	20.0	20.0	20.0	20.0	20.0	20.0
Horizon price	86.4365	86.4365	86.4365	86.4365	86.4365	86.4365	86.4365	86.4365	86.4365
At horizon date									
Treasury rate change (bp)	−150	−100	−50	−25	0	25	50	100	150
Spread change (bp)	40	25	20	10	0	−10	−20	−25	−40
Horizon yield	6.20%	6.55%	7.00%	7.15%	7.30%	7.45%	7.60%	8.05%	8.40%
Coupon rate	6.00%	6.00%	6.00%	6.00%	6.00%	6.00%	6.00%	6.00%	6.00%
Remaining maturity	19.0	19.0	19.0	19.0	19.0	19.0	19.0	19.0	19.0
Horizon price	97.7853	94.0708	89.5795	88.1496	86.7520	85.3858	84.0501	80.2191	77.4121
Reinvestment rate	6.0%	6.0%	6.0%	6.0%	6.0%	6.0%	6.0%	6.0%	6.0%
Interest + reinvest inc	6.09	6.09	6.09	6.09	6.09	6.09	6.09	6.09	6.09
Total future dollars	103.8753	100.1608	95.6695	94.2396	92.8420	91.4758	90.1401	86.3091	83.5021
Total return (SA)	9.62%	7.65%	5.21%	4.42%	3.64%	2.87%	2.12%	−0.07%	−1.71%
Total return (BEY)	19.25%	15.29%	10.41%	8.83%	7.28%	5.75%	4.24%	−0.15%	−3.42%
Total return (effective)	20.18%	15.88%	10.68%	9.03%	7.41%	5.83%	4.28%	−0.15%	−3.39%

SECTION V CONTROLLING FOR INTEREST RATE RISK

Unless the objective of a trade is to alter the duration exposure of a position, it is critical in assessing strategies to compare positions that have the same dollar duration. To understand why, consider two bonds, X and Y. Suppose that the price of bond X is 80 and has a duration of 5 while bond Y has a price of 90 and has a duration of 4. Since duration is the approximate percentage change per 100 basis point change in yield, a 100 basis points change in yield for bond X would change its price by about 5%. Based on a price of 80, its price will change by about $4 per $80 of market value. Thus, its dollar duration for a 100 basis point change in yield is $4 per $80 of market value. Similarly, for bond Y, its dollar duration for a 100 basis point change in yield per $90 of market value can be determined. In this case it is $3.6. So, if bonds X and Y are being considered as alternative investments in some strategy, the amount of each bond in the strategy should be such that they will both have the same *dollar* duration.

To illustrate this, suppose that a portfolio manager owns $10 million of par value of bond X which has a market value of $8 million. The dollar duration of bond X per 100 basis point change in yield for the $8 million market value is $400,000. Suppose further that this portfolio manager is considering exchanging bond X that it owns in its portfolio for bond Y. If the portfolio manager wants to have the same interest rate exposure (i.e., dollar duration) for bond Y that he currently has for bond X, she will buy a market value amount of bond Y with the same dollar duration. If the portfolio manager purchased $10 million of par value of bond Y and therefore $9 million of market value of bond Y, the dollar price change per 100 basis point change in yield would be only $360,000. If, instead, the portfolio manager purchased $10 million of market value of bond Y, the dollar duration per 100 basis point change in yield would be $400,000. Since bond Y is trading at 90, $11.11 million of par value of bond Y must be purchased to keep the dollar duration of the position from bond Y the same as for bond X.

Mathematically, the market value of bond Y necessary to have the same dollar duration (per 100 basis point change in rates) as bond X is:

$$\text{market value of bond Y} = \frac{\text{dollar duration of bond X}}{\text{duration of bond Y}/100}$$

The par value of bond Y that must be purchased to obtain the same dollar duration as bond X is then found by:

$$\text{par value of bond Y} = \frac{\text{market value of bond Y}}{\text{price of bond Y per \$1 of par value}}$$

Using our previous illustration to demonstrate how to use these two formulas, we know that:

$$\text{dollar duration of bond X} = \$400,000$$
$$\text{duration of bond Y} = 4$$

therefore,

$$\text{market value of bond Y} = \frac{\$400,000}{4/100} = \$10,000,000$$

This means that $10 million in *market* value of bond Y is needed in order to have the same dollar duration as the $8 market value position in bond X. The amount of the par value of bond Y that must be purchased given its assumed price of 90, or 0.90 per $1 of par value, is:

$$\text{par value of bond Y} = \frac{\$10,000,000}{0.90} = \$11.11 \text{ million}$$

Exhibit 8: Three Hypothetical Treasury Securities

Information on three Treasury securities:

Treasury issue	Coupon rate (%)	Price	Yield to maturity (%)	Maturity (years)
A	6.5	100	6.5	5
B	8.0	100	8.0	20
C	7.5	100	7.5	10

Calculation of duration and convexity (shock rates by 10 basis points):

Treasury issue	Value if rate changes by +10 bp	Value if rate changes by −10 bp	Duration	Convexity
A	99.5799	100.4222	4.21122	10.67912
B	99.0177	100.9970	9.89681	73.63737
C	99.3083	100.6979	6.94821	31.09724

Failure to adjust a trade based on some expected change in yield spread so as to hold the dollar duration the same means that the outcome of the trade will be affected by not only the expected change in the yield spread but also a change in the yield level. Thus, a manager would be taking a conscious yield spread view and possibly an undesired view on the level of interest rates.

Also note that equating the dollar durations of two positions only means that they will be equal for small changes in rates because of the convexity of a bond.

SECTION VI AN ILLUSTRATION

There is no shortage of trading strategies suggested by bond dealer firms or in the popular press. Also, investment management firms have developed what they believe to be proprietary trading strategies. All of these strategies are based on a set of assumptions regarding what will occur in the bond market over the investment horizon and they all involve risk. A trading strategy may involve borrowing funds in the repo market and/or shorting bonds. Some managers and dealers unfortunately use the term "arbitrage" to refer to trading strategies that they may tout to customers. The fact is that such strategies do incur risk, no matter how small that risk may be perceived to be by the proponent of the strategy.

The bottom line is that the potential performance of any trading strategy can be quantified using total return analysis. More specifically, scenario analysis is used to determine what the total return will be under different assumptions about what might occur over the investment horizon. Of course, this should be done before a trade is entered into. The scenario analysis will identify the range of possible outcomes and therefore provide the manager with a feel for the risk associated in a trade.

In this section, a basic illustration will be used to show how to evaluate a trade. We begin with three Treasury securities — A, B, and C. Information about each of these three securities is provided in Exhibit 8. Security A is the short-term Treasury, security B is the long-term Treasury, and security C is the intermediate-term Treasury. Each Treasury security is selling at par, and it is assumed that the next coupon payment is six months from now. The duration and convexity for each security are calculated in the exhibit. Since all the securities are trading at par value, the durations and convexities are then the dollar duration and dollar convexity per $100 of par value.

Suppose that the following two Treasury portfolios are constructed. The first portfolio consists of only security C, the 10-year issue, and shall be referred to as the **bullet portfolio**. (It is called a bullet portfolio because the principal for this portfolio is returned at one time — the maturity date of the 10-year issue.) The second portfolio consists of 51.86% of security A and 48.14% of security B, and this portfolio shall be referred to as the **barbell portfolio**. (It is referred to as a barbell portfolio because the maturity dates for the principal for this portfolio are both shorter than and longer than that of the bullet portfolio.)

As can be seen in Exhibit 8, the duration of the bullet portfolio is 6.94821. The duration of the barbell portfolio is the market value weighted average of the duration of the two Treasury securities in the portfolio and is computed below:

$$0.5186 \, (4.21122) + 0.4814 \, (9.89681) = 6.94826$$

The duration of the barbell is equal to the duration of the bullet. In fact, the barbell portfolio was designed to produce this result.

Duration is just a first approximation of the change in market value resulting from a change in interest rates. As explained at Level I (Chapter 7), the convexity measure provides an improvement to the duration estimate. The convexity measure of the bullet and barbell portfolios is not equal. We explained the issues associated with computing the convexity measure at Level I so we won't repeat them here. The only thing that is important to understand regarding the convexity measure in Exhibit 8 is the relative size of the convexity measures for the two portfolios. The convexity measure of the bullet portfolio is 31.09724. The convexity measure of the barbell is a market weighted average of the convexity measure of the two Treasury securities in the portfolio. That is,

$$0.5186 \, (10.67912) + 0.4814 \, (73.63737) = 40.98722$$

Thus, the bullet portfolio has a convexity measure that is less than that of the barbell portfolio. Below is a summary of the duration and convexity measures of the two portfolios:

	Treasury Portfolio	
Parameter	Bullet	Barbell
Dollar duration	6.94821	6.94826
Dollar convexity	31.09724	40.98722

Given these values, a manager is considering the following trade: buy one portfolio and sell the other. By selling the other it is meant that the manager **sells short** or **shorts** the security or securities in the portfolio. When a manager shorts a security, the coupon interest paid on the shorted security must be paid by the manager to the owner of the security.

Now both the barbell portfolio and the bullet portfolio have the same duration. Since the dollar value that will be invested in both portfolios will be the same, then the two portfolios will have the same dollar duration, but different convexities. Suppose that the manager believes that there will be significant interest rate volatility over the next six months and therefore anticipates a substantial change in interest rates. It is precisely under such circumstances that the a portfolio with higher convexity will benefit. Based on this expectation, suppose that the manager decides to buy the better convex portfolio, the barbell portfolio, because it has a higher convexity than the bullet portfolio, and short the bullet portfolio. Also assume that the manager is basing the trade on a 6-month investment horizon.

Let's assess this trade for the manager. The first thing to note is that expectations based on a large change in interest rates is vague. What is "large"? Can the manager be more specific about how much rates must change in order to benefit from the better convexity of the barbell portfolio relative to the bullet portfolio? Also, is there an implicit assumption about what happens to the shape of the yield curve at the end of the investment horizon? All of this can be quantified by using total return analysis and scenario analysis.

Based on a 6-month investment horizon, the last column of Exhibit 9 shows the total return for this trading strategy assuming that the yield curve shifts in a "parallel" fashion. By parallel it is meant that the yield for the short-term security (A), the intermediate-term security (C), and the long-term security (B) changes by the same number of basis points, as shown in the first column of the exhibit. Since the barbell portfolio is owned and the bullet portfolio is sold, then the difference between the next-to-the last two columns is the total return for this trading strategy. For example, if the yield curve shifts down by 150 basis points (i.e., the row indicating "−150" in the first column), the barbell portfolio would earn a 6-month total return of 29.26%. The bullet portfolio's total return — if it were owned — would be 28.99% for the same scenario of a 150 basis point decline in yield. However, the bullet portfolio was shorted; therefore, the manager must pay this return. Thus, the barbell portfolio earned 29.26% but the manager had to pay 28.99% to short the bullet portfolio, resulting in a 27 basis point 6-month total return for this trading strategy.

The total return for the trading strategy for the different scenarios is shown in the last column. This column helps the manager quantify how much the yield curve must shift (up or down) to realize a positive return from this trading strategy. Notice that the yield curve must change up or down in a parallel fashion by more than 100 basis points (the precise number of basis points is not shown in Exhibit 9) in order to benefit from the better convexity of the barbell portfolio relative to the bullet portfolio. Thus, the manager now knows more than just that he or she is taking a view on a "large" rate change, but a view that rates will change by more than 100 basis points if interest rates shift in a parallel fashion.

Exhibit 9: Performance of Trading Strategy Over a 6-Month Horizon Assuming a Parallel Yield Curve Shift: Scenario Analysis

Yield change (in b.p.)	Price plus coupon ($)			Total return (%)		
	A	B	C	Barbell	Bullet	Trading Strategy*
−300	115.6407	141.0955	126.7343	55.79	53.47	2.32
−250	113.4528	133.6753	122.4736	46.38	44.95	1.43
−200	111.3157	126.8082	118.3960	37.55	36.79	0.76
−150	109.2281	120.4477	114.4928	29.26	28.99	0.27
−100	107.1888	114.5512	110.7559	21.47	21.51	−0.05
−50	105.1965	109.0804	107.1775	14.13	14.35	−0.22
−25	104.2176	106.4935	105.4453	10.63	10.89	−0.26
0	103.2500	104.0000	103.7500	7.22	7.50	−0.28
25	102.2935	101.5961	102.0907	3.92	4.18	−0.27
50	101.3481	99.2780	100.4665	0.70	0.93	−0.23
100	99.4896	94.8852	97.3203	−5.45	−5.36	−0.09
150	97.6735	90.7949	94.3050	−11.28	−11.39	0.11
200	95.8987	86.9830	91.4146	−16.79	−17.17	0.38
250	94.1640	83.4271	88.6433	−22.01	−22.71	0.70
300	92.4686	80.1070	85.9857	−26.96	−28.03	1.06

* A negative sign indicates that the bullet portfolio outperformed the barbell portfolio; a positive sign indicates that the barbell portfolio outperformed the bullet portfolio.

Exhibit 10: Performance of Trading Strategy Over a 6-Month Horizon Assuming a Steepening of the Yield Curve: Scenario Analysis

Yield change for C (in bp)	Price plus coupon ($)			Total return (%)		
	A	B	C	Barbell	Bullet	Trading Strategy*
−300	116.9785	136.5743	126.7343	52.82	53.47	−0.65
−250	114.7594	129.4918	122.4736	43.70	44.95	−1.24
−200	112.5919	122.9339	118.3960	35.14	36.79	−1.65
−150	110.4748	116.8567	114.4928	27.09	28.99	−1.89
−100	108.4067	111.2200	110.7559	19.52	21.51	−1.99
−50	106.3863	105.9874	107.1775	12.39	14.35	−1.97
−25	105.3937	103.5122	105.4453	8.98	10.89	−1.91
0	104.4125	101.1257	103.7500	5.66	7.50	−1.84
25	103.4426	98.8243	102.0907	2.44	4.18	−1.74
50	102.4839	96.6046	100.4665	−0.69	0.93	−1.63
100	100.5995	92.3963	97.3203	−6.70	−5.36	−1.34
150	98.7582	88.4758	94.3050	−12.38	−11.39	−0.99
200	96.9587	84.8200	91.4146	−17.77	−17.17	−0.60
250	95.2000	81.4080	88.6433	−22.88	−22.71	−0.17
300	93.4812	78.2204	85.9857	−27.73	−28.03	0.30

Assumptions:
Change in yield of A = Change in yield of C minus 30 bp.
Change in yield of B = Change in yield of C plus 30 bp.
* A negative sign indicates that the bullet portfolio outperformed the barbell portfolio; a positive sign indicates that the barbell portfolio outperformed the bullet portfolio.

Moreover, there is another assumption made in this trade — that the yield curve will shift in a parallel fashion. Exhibit 10 shows what happens if the yield curve does not shift in a parallel fashion. The assumption made in computing the total return for the trading strategy in Exhibit 10 is that there is a steepening of the yield curve. There are an infinite number of ways that the yield curve may steepen. The scenario analysis in Exhibit 10 assumes that if there is a change in the yield for security C shown in the first column, the yield on A will change by the same amount less 30 basis points, whereas the yield on B will change by the same amount plus 30 basis points. The last column of Exhibit 10 shows that the trade will result in a loss for the scenarios analyzed in the exhibit except if there is a 300 basis point shift in the yield for C.

Thus, we see the power of using total return analysis and scenario analysis in sharpening our skills in assessing a trading strategy.

SECTION VII KEY POINTS

❑ *Treasury securities can be used as collateral to borrow funds via a repurchase agreement.*

❑ *Leveraging is the investment principle of borrowing funds in the hope of earning a return in excess of the cost of the borrowed funds.*

❑ *Leveraging magnifies the potential gain that will be realized from investing in a security for a given change in the price of that security but also magnifies the potential loss.*

❑ *A repurchase agreement is the sale of a security with a commitment by the seller to buy the security back from the purchaser at the repurchase price at the repurchase date.*

❑ *The difference between the repurchase price and the sale price is the dollar interest cost of the loan.*

❑ *An overnight repurchase agreement is one that has a maturity of one day; a term repurchase agreement is one that has a maturity of more than one day.*

❑ *Interest in a repurchase agreement is computed on a 360-day basis.*

❑ *In a repurchase agreement, the lender of funds is borrowing securities and is making a short-term investment.*

❑ *There is a good deal of Wall Street jargon describing repo transactions but basically one party is buying collateral (and making a short-term investment) and the other party is selling collateral (and obtaining financing).*

❑ *Rather than using industry jargon, investment guidelines should be clear as to what a manager is permitted to do with respect to repo transactions.*

❑ *In a repurchase agreement the lender is exposed to the risk that the borrower will default.*

❑ *To reduce credit risk there is over collateralization of the loan (i.e., there is a repo margin) and the collateral is marked to market on a regular basis.*

❑ *When the market value of the collateral declines by a certain percentage, a repo agreement can specify either a margin call or repricing of the repo.*

❑ *One concern in structuring a repo is delivery of the collateral to the lender.*

❑ *When the borrower must deliver the collateral to the lender or to the cash lender's clearing agent, the collateral is said to be "delivered out" and at the repurchase date the lender returns the collateral to the borrower in exchange for the principal and interest payment.*

❑ *If the lender agrees to allow the borrower to hold the security in a segregated customer account, then the transaction is called a hold-in-custody repo and exposes the lender to greater credit risk than delivering out the securities.*

❑ *A tri-party repo is an alternative to delivering out the collateral which requires that the borrower deliver the collateral to the lender's custodial account at the borrower's clearing bank.*

❑ *The repo rate for a particular transaction will depend on the quality of the collateral, term of the repo, delivery requirement, availability of collateral, and the prevailing federal funds rate.*

❑ *Collateral that is highly sought after by dealers is called hot or special collateral and can be used as a cheap source of repo financing.*

❑ *The three sources of potential return from investing in a bond are: (1) the coupon interest payments, (2) any capital gain (or capital loss), and (3) income from reinvestment of the coupon interest payments.*

❑ *Calculation of the total return to the maturity date requires specification of the reinvestment rate.*

❑ *Calculation of the total return to an investment horizon that is less than the maturity date requires specification of the reinvestment rate and the horizon yield.*

❑ *The horizon yield is needed to obtain the horizon price of the bond at the end of the investment horizon.*

❑ *A semiannual return can be annualized on a bond-equivalent basis or on an effective rate basis, the selection depending on the manager's investment objective.*

137

❑ *For a mortgage-backed security, total return requires an assumption about prepayment rates.*

❑ *Option-adjusted spread analysis can be incorporated into a total return analysis by specifying the OAS at the end of the investment horizon.*

❑ *When the OAS is not assumed to change from its initial value, the total return is said to be calculated on a constant OAS basis.*

❑ *Scenario analysis involves calculating the total return under different assumptions regarding the reinvestment rate and horizon yield.*

❑ *Total return analysis and scenario analysis should be used to assess the potential outcomes of a trading strategy.*

❑ *Total return analysis and scenario analysis allows the manager to quantify vague notions about what must happen for a trading strategy to be successful.*

END OF CHAPTER QUESTIONS

1. Suppose that an investor has $477,300 in funds to invest and is considering the purchase of a 7% coupon 15.5-year Treasury security. The security is selling for 95.46 (or $954.60 per $1,000 of par value). Assume that there is no accrued interest. The yield to maturity is 7.5%.

   a. How much in par value can this investor purchase with $477,300?

   b. If the investor purchases this bond, what is the annual return assuming the following horizon yield for the bond and the corresponding horizon price for a 6-month time horizon:

Horizon yield	Horizon price
9.00%	83.71
8.50%	87.42
8.00%	91.35
7.50%	95.54
7.00%	100.00
6.50%	104.75
6.00%	109.80

   c. Suppose that the investor borrows $477,300 to purchase an additional amount of the 7% coupon 15.5-year bond. Assume that the annual borrowing rate is 10.8%. What is the annual return for the same scenarios as in part b?

   d. Suppose that the investor borrows $1,909,200 to purchase an additional amount of the 7% coupon 15.5-year bond. Assume that the annual borrowing rate is 10.8%. What is the annual return for the same scenarios as in part b?

   e. Compare the annual return for the scenarios in part b for the cases where no funds are borrowed (part b), $477,300 is borrowed (part c), and $1,909,200 is borrowed and comment on the results.

2. What is the difference between a repo transaction and a reverse repo transaction?

3. In the investment guidelines for a pension fund, the following is specified:

   "The manager of the fund is permitted to enter into a repurchase agreement."

   Why is this provision in the investment guidelines confusing?

4. In an article in a popular daily publication, a statement similar to the following was made: "Repurchase agreements are extremely risky vehicles." Explain why this statement is ambiguous.

5. Suppose that an investor purchases $3 million market value of a bond. The investor decides to borrow the funds via a repurchase agreement and the dealer is willing to lend 97% of the market value of the bond. The overnight repo rate is 7% and the 30-day term repo rate is 7.3%.

   a. Assuming that the investor borrows the funds for 1 day, what is the dollar interest cost of this borrowing arrangement?

   b. Assuming that the investor borrows the funds for 30 days, what is the dollar interest cost of this borrowing arrangement?

6. Explain why you agree or disagree with the following statement: "The repo rate depends on the shape of the yield curve and the maturity of the security used as collateral for the loan."

7. An assistant portfolio manager is reviewing a daily printout of Treasury securities published by a government broker/dealer. He notices that the yield for the on-the-run 10-year Treasury note is trading at a yield considerably less than Treasury securities with a similar maturity or a similar duration. He believes that the issue is expensive (i.e., the price is too high). He asks you whether or not this Treasury issue is rich. What is your response?

8. Suppose that an investor owns a security that is on special in the repo market. If this investor wants to use this security to obtain financing, what will the repo rate be compared to generic collateral for the same term? (No calculation required.)

9. If the repo margin for a 30-day term repo agreement is 2% and the value of the collateral is $10 million, how much will the dealer lend?

10. a. Why is the lender of funds in a repo transaction exposed to credit risk?
    b. What is the credit risk of a hold-in-custody repo?
    c. How do lenders of funds in a repo transaction reduce credit risk?

11. Why is the overnight repo rate generally lower than the federal funds rate?

12. An investor is considering the purchase of an option-free corporate bond with a coupon rate of 7.25% and 15 years remaining to maturity. The price of the bond is 106.1301. The yield to maturity of this bond is 6.6%. Assume that the Treasury yield curve is flat at 6% and that the credit spread for this issuer is 60 basis points for all maturities. Compute the (a) 1-year total return on a bond-equivalent basis and (b) 1-year total return on an effective rate basis assuming:

    i. the reinvestment rate is 4%
    ii. the Treasury yield curve is flat at the horizon date at 5.65%
    iii. the credit spread for this issuer is 50 basis points for all maturities at the horizon date

13. An investor is considering the purchase of an option-free high-yield corporate bond with a coupon rate of 10% and 9 years remaining to maturity. The price of the bond is 95.7420. The yield to maturity of this bond is 10.75%. Assume that the Treasury yield curve is flat at 7.5% and that the credit spread for this issuer is 325 basis points for all maturities. Compute the (a) 1-year total return on a bond-equivalent basis and (b) 1-year total return on an effective rate basis assuming:

    i. the reinvestment rate is 5%
    ii. the Treasury yield curve does not change and therefore remains flat at the horizon date at 7.5%
    iii. the credit spread for this issuer declines by 200 basis points for all maturities at the horizon date

14. Explain why it is essential to have a good valuation model in order to perform total return analysis?

15. "The problem with total return analysis is that it assumes the option-adjusted spread does not change and that the yield curve is flat." Explain why you agree or disagree with this statement.

16. Depository institutions are typically required by regulators to test the sensitivity of their portfolios to an instantaneous parallel shift in the yield curve. Usually, regulators require a shift of ±100 basis points, ±200 basis points, and ±300 basis points. Why is this procedure a special case of total return analysis?

17. Typically, in the collateralized mortgage obligation market the option-adjusted spread (OAS) on planned amortization class tranches (PACs) increases with the average life of the tranche. That is, the OAS for short average life PACs trade tighter (i.e., lower spread) to the collateral than intermediate average life PACs, and intermediate average life PACs trade tighter than long average life PACs. By "collateral" it is meant the passthrough securities used to create the CMO.

In December 1998, the shape of the OAS for PACs became U-shaped such that short average life PACs offered a higher OAS than intermediate PACs. To benefit from this anomaly in the OASs, a portfolio manager could create a "barbell PAC" as a substitute for collateral. A barbell PAC involves buying a combination of a short and a long average life PAC. The PaineWebber Mortgage Group assessed this strategy using scenario analysis. Table A shows the analysis. The PAC barbell was created from 71% FHR 2105 PA and 29% from FHR 2105 PE. The comparison is to a 6% coupon FNMA passthrough. The bottom panel of Table A shows the total return for different scenarios.

Table A: Analysis of PAC Barbell versus 6.0% Collateral

	Face	Proceeds	%	Price	Dur	Cnvx	OAS
FHR 2105 PA	23,082	23,446	71	101:03	1.83	−1.46	70
FHR 2105 PE	10,000	9,762	29	97:04+	9.55	0.66	70
Barbell	—	33,208	100	—	4.10	−0.84	70
30 yr FNMA 6.0%	10,000	9,892	100	98:22+	4.53	−1.72	59

Total Rate-of-Return Analysis

	−200	−150	−100	−50	Unch	50	100	150	200	Steep	Flat
FHR 2105 PA	3.74	4.08	5.24	6.67	6.19	5.36	4.40	3.40	2.38	6.62	5.72
FHR 2105 PE	24.31	20.51	15.70	10.95	6.49	1.99	−2.47	−6.87	−11.13	6.21	6.71
Barbell	10.00	9.04	8.37	7.94	6.28	4.37	2.41	0.44	−1.50	6.50	6.01
30 yr FNMA 6.0%	7.34	7.34	7.68	7.75	6.29	4.19	1.77	−0.68	−3.13	6.57	5.99
Difference	2.66	1.70	0.69	0.18	−0.02	0.18	0.64	1.12	1.63	−0.07	0.03

Source: Table 3 in "PAC Barbells: The Way to Go," *PaineWebber Mortgage Strategist* (December 15, 1998), p.11.

a. How does the duration of the PAC barbell and the collateral suggest that they will perform if interest rates change?

b. What do the convexity measures of the collateral and the PAC barbell suggest about the performance of the two positions if interest rates change?

c. Suppose that a portfolio manager owns the collateral in her portfolio. What do the results of the scenario analysis in Table A suggest as a trade to enhance return?

d. What are some important assumptions that should be kept in mind when reviewing the results of the scenario analysis shown in Table A?

e. Explain why the results in Table A would not have been predicted by just considering duration alone.

141

18. Suppose that in June 1998 a portfolio manager was considering the purchase of either a 3-year average life nonagency mortgage-backed security or a home equity loan (HEL) issue. The nonagency MBS was a RAST 1998-A5 and the HEL issue was an Amresco 1998-2. Summary information about these two issues is given below:

	3-Year Nonagency MBS	3-Year Home Equity
Issue	RAST 1998-A5	Amresco 1998-2
Class	A2	A3
Speed	100 PPC (16% CPR in 12 Months)	24% PPC
Price	100:06+	100:08+
Yield	6.610	6.136
Avg. Life	3.19 yrs	2.96 yrs
Spread/AL	112 bps	65 bps

The table below shows the PPC (i.e., prospectus prepayment curve) and average life comparison for the two issues at the end of a 12-month investment horizon for different interest rate scenarios (assuming a parallel shift in interest rates):

Spread and Average Life Comparison

	Basis Point Shifts						
	+150	+100	+50	0	−50	−100	−150
Nonagency MBS: RAST 1998-A5 A2							
PPC	63	75	87	100	125	187	218
Avg. Life	5.20	4.25	3.65	3.19	2.57	1.72	1.48
Home Equity: AMRESCO 1998-2 A3							
PPC	75	83	92	100	108	121	133
Avg. Life	4.25	3.76	3.34	2.96	2.64	2.35	2.12

The following table provides a total return comparison for different interest rate scenarios based on a 12-month investment horizon assuming that the spread to the average life is unchanged for each scenario:

Total Return Comparison

	Basis Point Shifts							Wt. Avg.
	+150	+100	+50	0	−50	−100	−150	
Prob of Rate Chg. (%)	1.8	7.4	21.9	35.1	26.1	7.2	0.6	Total
Total Return								Return
Nonagency MBS	2.01	4.13	5.55	6.56	7.18	7.00	6.91	6.27
Home Equity	2.34	3.95	5.17	6.09	6.79	7.24	7.51	5.94
Advantage of Nonagency MBS	−0.33	0.18	0.38	0.47	0.39	−0.24	−0.60	0.33

Source: Adapted from Tables 2, 3, and 4 of "Short Alt-As: Alternative vs. Short Home Equities," *PaineWebber Mortgage Strategist* (June 23, 1998), pp. 10 and 11.

a. Based on the latest prepayment information at the time (June 1998) and the prevailing pricing levels, the PaineWebber Mortgage Group stated that it appeared that the 3-year average life nonagency MBS provides relative value compared to the 3-year average life HEL, especially for investors expecting a modest increase in rates ("Short Alt-As: Alternative vs. Short Home Equities," Paine-Webber *Mortgage Strategist* (June 23, 1998), pp. 8-9.) Explain why.

b. PaineWebber assigned probabilities to the different scenarios. These probabilities are shown below the interest rate scenario. Based on the weighted average total return, which is the better issue to purchase? (Note: The expected total return is simply the weighted average of the total return in each scenario. The weight for the total return for a given scenario is the probability of occurrence for that scenario.)

c. What are the critical assumptions in the relative analysis performed?

19. Explain why in attempting to neutralize two positions against a small parallel shift in interest rates it is necessary to match the effective dollar duration of two positions in a trade and not just the effective duration of the two positions.

20. Mr. Lenox is a portfolio manager who own $15 million of par value of bond ABC. The market value of the bond is $13 million and the effective dollar duration for a 100 basis point change in rates is $1.2 million. Mr. Lenox is considering swapping out of bond ABC and into bond XYZ. The market price of bond XYZ is $75 per $100 of par value and the effective duration is 7. How much of par value of bond XYZ would Mr. Lenox have to purchase to maintain the same exposure to a small parallel shift in interest rates as with bond ABC?

SOLUTIONS TO END OF CHAPTER QUESTIONS

1. a. Since the price per $100 of par value is $95.46, this means that $500,000 of par value [= $477,300/(95.46/100)] can be purchased.

b.

Assumed yield six months from now (%)	Price per $100 par value ($)*	Market value ($)	Semiannual coupon payment ($)	Dollar return ($)	Annualized percent return (%)
9.00%	83.71	418,550	17,500	(41,250)	−17.3%
8.50%	87.42	437,100	17,500	(22,700)	−9.5%
8.00%	91.35	456,750	17,500	(3,050)	−1.3%
7.50%	95.54	477,700	17,500	17,900	7.5%
7.00%	100.00	500,000	17,500	40,200	16.8%
6.50%	104.75	523,750	17,500	63,950	26.8%
6.00%	109.80	549,000	17,500	89,200	37.4%

We will illustrate one of the calculations. Consider the 8% horizon yield. The corresponding horizon price is 91.35. So, for $500,000 in par value, the value of the bonds would equal $456,750 [=$500,000 (91.35/100)].

The coupon interest (for all the scenarios) is $17,500 (=$500,000 multiplied by the semiannual coupon rate of 3.5%). The total proceeds are then the value of the bonds of $456,750 plus the coupon interest of $17,500 which is equal to $474,250.

Given the total proceeds, the dollar return is found by subtracting the initial investment of $477,300. The dollar return is then −$3,050. The semiannual rate of return is found by dividing the dollar return of −$3,050 by the initial investment of $477,300 giving −0.00639. Doubling this return gives an annual return of −0.01278 or −1.3% (rounded).

c.

Assumed yield six months from now (%)	Price per $100 par value ($)	Market value per $1 million par value ($)	Semiannual coupon payment ($)	Dollar return ($)	Annualized percent return (%)
9.00%	83.71	837,100	35,000	(108,274)	−45.4%
8.50%	87.42	874,200	35,000	(71,174)	−29.8%
8.00%	91.35	913,500	35,000	(31,874)	−13.4%
7.50%	95.54	955,400	35,000	10,026	4.2%
7.00%	100.00	1,000,000	35,000	54,626	22.9%
6.50%	104.75	1,047,500	35,000	102,126	42.8%
6.00%	109.80	1,098,000	35,000	152,626	64.0%

Once again, let's illustrate the 8% horizon yield scenario. There is now $1 million of par value invested. The value of the position is $913,500. The semiannual dollar coupon interest is $35,000 (= 3.5% semiannual coupon rate times the $1 million of par value). This is the same for each scenario. The total proceeds are equal to the dollar return (the value of the bonds plus the dollar coupon interest) reduced by the cost of borrowing $477,300. Since the borrowing rate is assumed to be 10.8%, the borrowing cost is $477,300 multiplied by 5.4%. The interest cost is therefore $25,774.20. This is the same interest cost for each scenario. The total dollar proceeds after the interest cost is then −$31,874. Dividing by the equity investment of $477,300 and then multiplying by 2 gives an annual return of −13.4%.

d.

Assumed yield six months from now (%)	Price per $100 par value ($)*	Market value per $1 million par value ($)*	Semiannual coupon payment ($)	Dollar return ($)	Annualized percent return (%)**
9.00%	83.71	2,092,750	87,500	(309,347)	−129.6%
8.50%	87.42	2,185,500	87,500	(216,597)	−90.8%
8.00%	91.35	2,283,750	87,500	(118,347)	−49.6%
7.50%	95.54	2,388,500	87,500	(13,597)	−5.7%
7.00%	100.00	2,500,000	87,500	97,903	41.0%
6.50%	104.75	2,618,750	87,500	216,653	90.8%
6.00%	109.80	2,745,000	87,500	342,903	143.7%

e. The annual returns for the three cases are summarized below.

Horizon yield	No borrowed funds	Borrowed 477,300	Borrowed 1,909,200
9.00%	−17.3%	−45.4%	−129.6%
8.50%	−9.5%	−29.8%	−90.8%
8.00%	−1.3%	−13.4%	−49.6%
7.50%	7.5%	4.2%	−5.7%
7.00%	16.8%	22.9%	41.0%
6.50%	26.8%	42.8%	90.8%
6.00%	37.4%	64.0%	143.7%

The results clearly indicate that borrowing is advantageous in that it offers upside return greater than in the unleveraged case. The advantage is greater the more borrowed. In contrast, the loss is much greater the more leverage that is used. This is the tradeoff when using leverage.

2. A repurchase agreement is a contract that allows a party to either borrow or lend funds using the securities purchased as collateral. In practice, the expression "repo transaction" is used when a dealer uses a repo agreement to borrow funds (i.e., finance a position). A "reverse repo" is a term used when a non-dealer is using the securities to borrow funds (i.e., finance a position).

3. A repurchase agreement can be used to lend funds (i.e., a high quality short-term investment or money market instrument) or as a financing vehicle (i.e., a vehicle to borrow funds). The provision is unclear because as stated, it would suggest that the manager of the funds can use a repurchase agreement as either a short-term investment or a vehicle for financing. This may or may not have been the intent of the trustees of the pension fund.

4. When a repurchase agreement is used to create leverage (i.e., when it is used as a financing vehicle), it is a risky vehicle because of the risk associated with leverage. In contrast, when it is used as a vehicle in which to invest funds on a short-term basis, if properly structured, it is a high quality money market instrument.

5. a. The dollar interest cost is

dollar interest = amount borrowed × repo rate × repo term/360

Since only 97% of the market value can be borrowed,

amount borrowed = $3,000,000 × 0.97 = $2,910,000

The appropriate repo rate is 7% and the term is one day. Therefore,

dollar interest = $2,910,000 \times 0.07 \times 1/360 = \$565.83$

b. Since the repo is for 30 days, the 30-day term repo rate of 7.3% is used. The dollar interest cost is

dollar interest = $2,910,000 \times 0.073 \times 30/360 = \$17,702.50$

6. This statement is incorrect. The repo rate depends on the number of days or term of the borrowing arrangement. It is this term — the number of days of the repo — not the maturity of the security that is important. That is, a 30-day repo in which the collateral is a Treasury bond with 10 years remaining to maturity and one with 20 years remaining to maturity will have the same repo rate (assuming neither is on special).

7. The Treasury security is not likely to be rich. One reason it will offer a lower yield than similar maturity or similar duration Treasury securities is because of the better liquidity since it is an on-the-run issue. However, the major reason it is trading at a yield considerably less than otherwise comparable Treasury issues is that it is probably on special — that is, it is "hot" collateral. As a result, the issue offers attractive financing and market participants are willing to pay more for this issue, thereby driving down its yield.

8. Because the security is on special, dealers are willing to offer cheaper financing in order to obtain the use of the collateral. Thus, for a given term for the repo, the repo rate will be less for this security than for generic collateral.

9. If the repo margin is 2%, then the dealer will lend 98% or $9.8 million.

10. a. The credit risk of the lender of funds is that the value of the collateral declines and the borrower defaults. As a result, the lender owns the collateral with a market value less than the amount lent. Also, if the borrower holds the collateral, there is the risk that the collateral can be fraudulently used in another borrowing and/or the collateral can be sold without the knowledge of the lender.

b. In a hold-in-custody repo, the borrower retains custody of the collateral. So, there is the risk associated with the collateral being fraudulently used in another borrowing and/or the collateral can be sold without the knowledge of the lender.

c. A lender in a repo can protect itself in several ways. First, it can remove the risk of the collateral disappearing by using a tri-party repo. Second, the loan is for less than the market value of the collateral. This is the repo margin or "haircut." Finally, the collateral is marked to market requiring that if the margin declines below a specified amount the borrower must either provide additional cash or transfer acceptable securities to make up any margin deficit.

11. The repo rate represents a collateralized loan. In contrast, the federal funds rate is a rate on a loan that is unsecured. Hence the repo rate will be less.

12. The horizon yield given the assumptions about the Treasury yield curve and the credit spread is 6.15%. This means that the yield for this corporate bond declined over the 1-year investment horizon from 6.6% to 6.15%. The calculations to compute the 1-year total return are shown below.

   Step 1: Compute the total coupon payments plus the reinvestment income assuming an annual reinvestment rate of 4% per year or 2% every six months. The semiannual coupon payments are $3.625. The value is

First coupon payment reinvested for six month = $3.625 (1.02)	=	$3.6975
Second coupon payment not reinvested since at horizon date	=	$3.6250
Total	=	$7.3225

   Step 2: The horizon price at the end of the 1-year investment horizon is determined as follows. The horizon yield is 6.15% by assumption. The 7.25% coupon 15-year corporate bond now has 14 years to maturity. The price of this bond when discounted at a flat 6.15% (a flat yield curve is assumed) is $110.2263.

   Step 3: Adding the amounts in Steps 2 and 3 gives the total future dollars of $117.5488.

   Step 4: Compute the following:

   $$\left(\frac{\$117.5488}{\$106.1301}\right)^{\frac{1}{2}} - 1 = 5.24\%$$

   Step 5: The total return on a bond-equivalent basis and on an effective rate basis are shown below:

   $$2 \times 5.24\% = 10.48\% \text{ (BEY)}$$

   $$(1.0524)^2 - 1 = 10.76\% \text{ (effective rate basis)}$$

13. The horizon yield given the assumptions about the Treasury yield curve and the decline in the credit spread is 8.75%. The calculations to compute the 1-year total return are shown below.

   Step 1: Compute the total coupon payments plus the reinvestment income assuming an annual reinvestment rate of 5% per year or 2.5% every six months. The semiannual coupon payments are $5. The value is

First coupon payment reinvested for six month = $5 (1.025)	=	$ 5.1250
Second coupon payment not reinvested since at horizon date	=	$ 5.0000
Total	=	$10.1250

   Step 2: The horizon price at the end of the 1-year investment horizon is determined as follows. The horizon yield is 8.75% by assumption. The 10% coupon 9-year corporate bond now has 8 years to maturity. The price of this bond when discounted at a flat 8.75% (a flat yield curve is assumed) is $107.0853.

   Step 3: Adding the amounts in Steps 2 and 3 gives the total future dollars of $117.2103.

Step 4: Compute the following:

$$\left(\frac{\$117.2103}{\$95.7420}\right)^{\frac{1}{2}} - 1 = 10.64\%$$

Step 5: The total return on a bond-equivalent basis and on an effective rate basis are shown below:

$$2 \times 10.64\% = 21.29\% \text{ (BEY)}$$

$$(1.1064)^2 - 1 = 22.42\% \text{ (effective rate basis)}$$

14. In calculating total return it is necessary to determine the value of a security at the end of the investment horizon. It is in this step of the total return calculation that a valuation model is used. If the valuation model is poor, the horizon price will not be an accurate estimate and the total return computed will be misleading.

15. The statement is incorrect. A total return analysis does allow the analyst to change the OAS at the horizon date. However, a valuation model to compute the horizon price based on the new OAS is required. Moreover, any type of yield curve shift can be accommodated. The yield curve at the horizon date would be a required input into the valuation model to obtain the horizon price.

16. This is a special case of total return analysis assuming that the investment horizon is the next moment in time. Consequently, there is no coupon income nor any reinvestment income. The only concern is with changes in the price of the securities in the portfolio.

17. a. The top panel of Table A shows that the duration of the PAC barbell is less than the duration of the 30-year FNMA 6% (4.10 versus 4.53). Thus, if interest rates increase, the PAC barbell should outperform (based solely on duration) the collateral. The reverse is true if interest rates decrease.

   b. Recall from Level I (Chapter 7) that different dealers and vendors of analytical services scale their convexity measures in different ways. The convexities in Table A — which were referred to as convexity measures at Level I — are based on the scaling used by PaineWebber. There is greater negative convexity for the collateral than the PAC barbell (−1.72 versus −0.84). This means that for large changes in interest rates, the collateral will underperform the PAC barbell.

   c. The results in Table A suggest that it is only in the scenario where rates are unchanged, or the yield curve steepened, that the collateral outperformed the PAC barbell and the underperformance is slight (only 2 and 7 basis points, respectively). Thus, if a manager owns the collateral, there is the potential to enhance return by selling the collateral and purchasing the PAC barbell.

   d. There are three important assumptions. First, it is assumed that the valuation model used to determine the horizon price of the three securities (the collateral and the two PACs) does a good job of estimating what the prices will be for each interest rate scenario. Second, it assumed that the OAS does not change. Third, it is assumed in the ±200 bp scenarios that the yield curve shifts in a parallel fashion.

e. The duration of the collateral is greater than the duration of the PAC barbell. Consequently, in declining interest rate scenarios, using just duration alone one would expect that the collateral would outperform the PAC barbell. This is not the case in Table A. The reason is due to the greater negative convexity of the collateral relative to the PAC barbell.

18. a. The total return comparison based on a 12-month investment horizon assuming a constant spread at the horizon date (i.e., a constant spread to the average life shown for the given scenario) indicates that if the rate change is between −50 basis points and +50 basis points, the 3-year nonagency MBS will outperform the 3-year HEL issue based on the underlying assumptions. Even if rates rise by 100 basis points, the nonagency MBS will outperform by 18 basis points. For a +150 basis point increase, the nonagency MBS underperforms. It also underperforms for a decline in rates of more than 100 basis points. (This is because while not shown in the information supplied for the question there is greater negative convexity for the nonagency MBS than the HEL issue.)

b. Based on the probabilities, there is a higher expected total return for the nonagency MBS than the home equity loan issue (6.27% versus 5.94%) and therefore the nonagency MBS would be the preferred investment if the investor agreed with these probabilities.

c. The critical assumptions are:

1. The yield curve shifts in a parallel fashion.
2. The spread to the average life is unchanged over the 12-month investment horizon.
3. The prepayment speeds for each interest rate scenario for each security are as expected.
4. The valuation model used to derive the horizon prices for each interest rate scenario is a good model.

When using the probability analysis, the assumption is that the probabilities are correct.

19. Matching the effective durations of two positions means only that they will have the same percentage price change for a change in rates. More specifically a small change in rates. However, if two positions have a different dollar value, the dollar price change will not be the same. What is sought in a trade that does not attempt to benefit from changes in interest rates is the neutralization of a trade against interest rate risk. Matching effective dollar durations will do this for a small change in rates.

20. The market value for bond XYZ that must be purchased is found as follows (where duration in the formula refers to effective duration):

$$\text{market value of bond XYZ} = \frac{\text{dollar duration of bond ABC}}{\text{duration of bond XYZ}/100}$$

Since

dollar duration of bond ABC　=　$1.2 million
duration of bond XYZ　　　　=　7

then

$$\text{market value of bond XYZ} = \frac{\$1,200,000}{7/100} = \$17,142,857.14$$

The par value that must be purchased of bond XYZ is equal to

$$\text{par value of bond XYZ} = \frac{\text{market value of bond XYZ}}{\text{price of XYZ per \$1 of par value}}$$

Since the price of XYZ is $75 per $100 of par value, the price per $1 of par value is 0.75 and therefore

$$\text{par value of bond XYZ} = \frac{\$17,142,857.14}{0.75} = \$22,857,142.86$$

SOLUTIONS TO PRACTICE QUESTIONS

1.

Assumed yield six months from now (%)	Market value per $100 par value ($)*	Market value per $2 million par value ($)*	Semiannual coupon payment ($)	Dollar return to equity ($)**	Annualized percent return (%)***
10.00%	81.12	4,867,200	240,000	(1,117,800)	−223.6%
9.50%	85.23	5,113,800	240,000	(871,200)	−174.2%
9.00%	89.72	5,383,200	240,000	(601,800)	−120.4%
8.50%	94.62	5,677,200	240,000	(307,800)	−61.6%
8.00%	100.00	6,000,000	240,000	15,000	3.0%
7.50%	105.91	6,354,600	240,000	369,600	73.9%
7.00%	112.41	6,744,600	240,000	759,600	151.9%
6.50%	119.58	7,174,800	240,000	1,189,800	238.0%
6.00%	127.51	7,650,600	240,000	1,665,600	333.1%

* This is the price and market value six months later, rounded to the nearest $100.
** After deducting interest expense of $225,000 ($5 million × 9%/2).
*** Annualized by doubling the semiannual return.

2. a. The dollar interest is

$$\$5,000,000 \times 0.04 \times 1/360 = \$555.56$$

b. The repurchase price is $5,000,555.56 (the amount borrowed of $5 million plus the dollar interest of $555.56).

3. The horizon yield is 7.15% (a decrease in the Treasury yield by 25 basis points to 6.25% and an increase in the yield spread by 10 basis points to 90 basis points).
    The calculations are as shown below.

Step 1: Compute the total coupon payments plus the reinvestment income assuming an annual reinvestment rate of 4% or 2% every six month. The semiannual coupon payments are $3. The value is

First coupon payment reinvested for six months = $3 (1.02) = $3.06
Second coupon payment not reinvested since at horizon date = $3.00
Total = $6.06

Step 2: The horizon price at the end of the 1-year investment horizon is determined as follows. The horizon yield is 7.15% by assumption. The 6% coupon 20-year corporate bond now has 19 years to maturity. The price of this bond when discounted at a flat 7.15% yield (the yield curve is assumed to be flat) is $88.1496.

Step 3: Adding the amounts in Steps 2 and 3 gives the total future dollars of $94.2096.

Step 4: Compute the following (*h* is 2 in our illustration):

$$\left(\frac{\$94.2096}{\$86.4365}\right)^{\frac{1}{2}} - 1 = 4.40\%$$

Step 5 The total return on a bond-equivalent basis and on an effective rate basis are shown below:

$$2 \times 4.40\% = 8.80\% \qquad (\text{BEY})$$

$$(1.0494)^2 - 1 = 8.99\% \qquad (\text{effective rate basis})$$

CHAPTER 25

THE REAL ESTATE PORTFOLIO MANAGEMENT PROCESS

Frederich Lieblich
Metlife Realty Group, Inc.

What is born will die,
What has been gathered will be dispersed,
What has been accumulated will be exhausted,
What has been built up will collapse,
And what has been high will be brought low.

Buddhist saying on impermanence

INTRODUCTION

The last several years have wrought dramatic changes in the real estate industry, the likes of which have not been seen since the Great Depression of the 1930s. The tremendous increase in supply and subsequent reduction in demand and capital inflows for real estate have caused lease pricing and ultimately property values to collapse. Few investors contemplated such dramatic changes, and fewer still repositioned their portfolios in anticipation of such changes. Exhibit 25–1 identifies some current uncertainties in the real estate market.

Where will these uncertainties take us? What can we do to properly assess ever-changing market risks and position our portfolios to be on the winning side of these changes? The answer to the first question is simple: *No one fully knows.* The answer to the second

I wish to express my deep appreciation to Joseph L. Pagliari, Jr. (editor), for his encouragement and his significant contribution in the chapter's development and refinement. I also wish to thank Michael Giliberto and Peter Colwell (consulting editors) for their many thoughts, ideas, and suggested improvements to the chapter.

998

EXHIBIT 25–1
Uncertainty in the Real Estate Markets

Capital Markets	Space Markets

• Global integration of capital markets; competition among asset classes
• Growth of international trade
• Growth of real estate securities
• Development and use of real estate derivatives
• High to low inflation environment
• High to low interest rate environment
• Tax Code revisions
	• Existing oversupply of space
	• Global competition:
	   Corporate downsizing
	• Electronic revolution:
	   Working at home, virtual company, and hoteling (office and apartment)
	   Home shopping (retail)
	   Just-in-time inventory (industrial)
	• Shifting demographics:
	   Aging of the population
	   Increased ethnic diversity
	   Continued shift to South and West
	   CBD to edge city to small town
	• Environmental issues

question, which is the theme of this chapter, is found in *the creation, integration, and implementation of a systematic and disciplined portfolio management process*. While investors can't change the past, they can hope to learn from it.

THE PARADIGM SHIFT

The need to implement a portfolio management process has caused a shift in the paradigm of real estate investment management. The old paradigm is represented by firms using an asset-by-asset process, whereas the new paradigm is represented by firms using a disciplined portfolio management process. This fundamental evolution has transformed real estate investment.

Until very recently, the asset-by-asset process dominated real estate portfolio allocation, construction, and management. From this perspective, the investment decision is based on the *individual* property's fundamentals (location, physical, economic, and legal characteristics, etc.), its sensitivity to local supply and demand market conditions, and the market's pricing of risky assets. In essence, portfolio allocation under this approach is determined by an ad hoc selection of assets that meet singular property criteria. It focuses the investment decision on the risk-return relationship of an individual property, with little or no understanding of how it influences the risk-return relationship of the entire portfolio.

The portfolio management process, on the other hand, concentrates on the aggregation of individual properties that, when combined into a *portfolio,* exhibit risk return characteristics. While the asset-by-asset investment analysis remains an essential element of a disciplined portfolio management process, it becomes an intermediate step in a more encompassing process.

Institutional real estate investors are now making this paradigm shift for several reasons: (1) the need to restore credibility lost in the recent industry collapse; (2) the lower cost and increased availability of national, regional, and local real estate market supply and demand information made possible by the proliferation of low-cost, computer-related applications; (3) asset class competition for capital inflows; (4) increased sophistication of real estate professionals corresponding to their attainment of advanced degrees and designations (e.g., MBA, PhD, CFA); and (5) their application of financial technologies initially developed for the bond and stock markets.

To address these market forces, most real estate investment management firms have adopted their own real estate portfolio approach or style, probably no fewer than one for each firm. However, equally important is the firm's dedication to a disciplined portfolio management approach. Only those firms that can develop a disciplined portfolio management process and can integrate and implement it within their organizations will have completed the paradigm shift. By creating a framework for understanding the changing real estate market, these firms can expect to have the upper hand in assessing market/portfolio opportunities and risks. Without this discipline, the firm loses perspective on the inherent risks in its portfolio, lacks the tools and techniques to identify opportunities for higher returns and risk reduction through diversification, and possibly becomes susceptible to the latest investment fad.

Also important to the real estate investment firm is its ability to remain flexible while adhering to a disciplined portfolio management process. The portfolio manager must understand the limitations and applications of many of the analytical tools and techniques (some of which are presented in this chapter) and must recognize that *judgment* must be applied and used as a "reality check" at all times.

It is this balance between the adherence to a disciplined portfolio management process and the need for flexibility and judgment that must be sought by the investment decision maker.

To introduce the steps involved in a disciplined portfolio management process this chapter overviews both the portfolio management process and the role of the portfolio manager. This chapter provides investors/portfolio managers with a pragmatic approach to creating, integrating, and implementing their own portfolio management process. To focus on the process itself, the chapter simply introduces several of the techniques and tools that accompany it. These analytical mechanisms are amply covered in other chapters of this book (for example, see Chapter 2, "Portfolio Management Concepts and Their Application to Real Estate"). In addition, the chapter does not dwell on the subtle, and sometimes not so subtle, differences created by the form of investment vehicle (e.g., direct investments such as joint ventures and (non)discretionary separate accounts and indirect investments such as commingled funds and REITs) on the portfolio management process. See Chapter 24, "Developing a Portfolio Strategy," for discussion of each form of investment vehicle, though the portfolio management process described below is generally independent of the form of the investment vehicle(s).

THE PORTFOLIO MANAGEMENT PROCESS

The concept, definition, and implementation of a portfolio management process has been evolving for many years. Like many new ideas, it has grown and evolved at different rates, depending on the market forces acting on it. The two main forces that have acted on the portfolio management process are (1) technological advances in computers, statistics, and theoretical finance and (2) the tremendous growth in institutional assets under a fiduciary framework. Both forces have greatly contributed to its evolution.

Technological Advances and Modern Portfolio Theory

The theoretical foundation underlying the portfolio management process began in earnest with Harry Markowitz. His seminal work in the early 1950s formalized the concept of diversification and, consequently, the importance of asset allocation to portfolio performance.

Moreover, Markowitz introduced the mathematical/statistical framework for identifying these efficient portfolios, which later became known as *modern portfolio theory (MPT)*. However, had it not been for the advances in the computer industry (in terms of speed, cost, accessibility, etc.), it is unlikely that Markowitz's framework for optimizing a portfolio would enjoy the wide use and acceptance that it does today.

Modern portfolio theory identifies sets of efficient portfolios. An *efficient portfolio* is one in which no other portfolio offers a higher expected return for the same or lower risk (or lower risk with the same or a higher expected return). The set of all efficient portfolios derived from a portfolio group of assets is called the *efficient frontier* (see Exhibit 25–2). As the portfolio manager moves up along the efficient frontier, two things happen: The asset mix of the portfolio changes, and the portfolio's expected return and risk change.

EXHIBIT 25–2
The Efficient Frontier

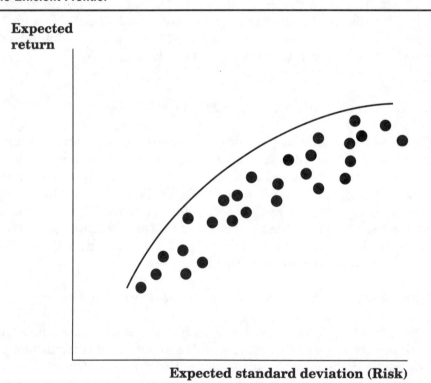

To derive the efficient frontier, estimates of the following three inputs are required for each asset over a specified time period:

1. *Expected return,* which is the summation of each of the asset's potential return conditions multiplied by the probability of that condition occurring.
2. *Expected standard deviation,* which is the variation of potential returns around the expected return.
3. *Expected correlation of returns,* or the degree to which each asset's returns are expected to move together over time with the returns from all other assets in the portfolio.

The investor's goal then becomes to move the portfolio to a point on the efficient frontier that fulfills the investor's objectives and constraints. However, the required inputs, and hence the efficient frontier, are constantly in flux. Consequently, the job of the investor/portfolio manager is to monitor these changing inputs and rebalance the portfolio accordingly. This rebalancing must be performed in light of the transaction costs involved, which in the case of real estate can be substantial. Therefore, a long-term view of these required inputs (and consequent portfolio construction) is usually taken.

Growth of Institutional Assets under a Fiduciary Framework

Around the same time Markowitz developed MPT, institutional investors (composed primarily of pension funds and insurance companies) began their phenomenal growth (see Exhibit 25–3). Furthermore, the enactment of the Employee Retirement Income Security Act of 1974 (ERISA) required the fiduciaries of private pension plans to use the same care, skill, prudence, and diligence in making investments that a prudent person who is familiar with such matters would use under similar circumstances (the "prudent man" rule). Along with the prudent man rule, ERISA required diversification of investment to minimize large losses. These fiduciary provisions of ERISA caused plan trustees to become much more focused on available portfolio management technologies (e.g., MPT) and the means to implement them.

Until ERISA's passage, real estate occupied a minuscule portion of institutional mixed-asset portfolios. However, many saw the passage of ERISA as a mandate to more completely diversify institutional

EXHIBIT 25–3
Institutional/Ownership of U.S. Financial Assets, 1950–90

Year	Owned by Institutions (millions)	Percent of Total
1990	$6,520	20.5%
1985	3,298	15.5
1980	1,769	13.5
1975	914	12.9
1970	569	12.3
1965	392	11.5
1960	256	10.8
1955	170	9.5
1950	107	8.4

Sources: Adapted from W. O'Barr and J. Conley, *Fortune and Folly: The Wealth and Power of Institutional Investing* (Homewood, IL: Business One Irwin, 1992). Data from the Federal Reserve, Columbia Institutional Investor Project, and New York Stock Exchange.

portfolios, which is consistent with the concepts of prudent behavior. Beginning in the late 1970s and early 1980s, institutional investors began to allocate a more meaningful portion of their assets to real estate. In fairness, note that this allocation to real estate was also spurred by the poor performance concurrently experienced in the stock and bond markets as inflation rose to unexpectedly high levels.

In essence, the real estate portfolio manager was the last to come to the party. During the last several decades, portfolio managers in the stock and bond markets have continued to develop and implement sophisticated tools, techniques, and processes to understand the dynamics of their markets and fulfill the needs of their investors. Meanwhile, the real estate investment manager, not subject to the same forces and not privy to the same wealth of historical data, was able to remain competitive without these technological improvements.

Steps in the Portfolio Management Process

Presently, the real estate portfolio manager faces many of the same forces that previously caused stock and bond portfolio managers to embrace a disciplined portfolio management process. That is, the collapse in stock and bond values (especially on an inflation-adjusted basis) led many stock and bond managers to abandon their old ways of doing business and adopt more sophisticated techniques (such as MPT) in a more integrated and disciplined fashion.

Exhibit 25–4 illustrates the dynamics of the real estate portfolio management process. The process is broken down into the following six steps:

1. Investor objectives and constraints.
2. Real estate market conditions and expectations.
3. Target portfolio determination.
4. Portfolio strategy determination.
5. Monitoring of investor objectives and constraints, market conditions and expectations, and portfolio rebalancing.
6. Portfolio performance measurement.

Each of these steps, along with the role of the portfolio manager, is discussed in detail in the remaining sections of this chapter.

EXHIBIT 25–4
Real Estate Portfolio Management Process

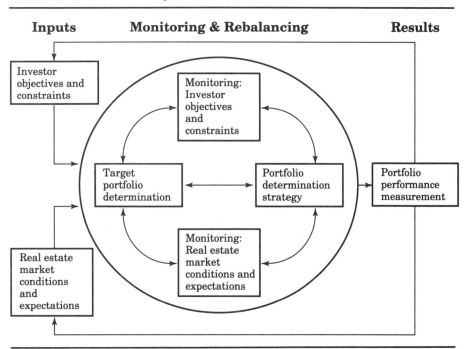

INVESTOR OBJECTIVES AND CONSTRAINTS

The most fundamental business precept is to understand and fulfill the needs of your customer. Real estate portfolio management is no different. Its first precept is "know thy investor." Therefore, before constructing a portfolio or repositioning an existing portfolio, it is essential to thoroughly understand the investor's objectives and constraints and develop a formal investment policy that encompasses them.

An investment policy is a statement of the investor's investment objectives and constraints, along with the method(s) by which they will be attained. Different investors will have (sometimes radically) different investment needs. Accordingly, as a means of more accurately understanding the investor's preference, the portfolio manager will interview the investor to determine the investor's specific needs. For example, defined benefit pension plans have significantly different investment needs depending on such factors as ratio of active to retired individuals, over- or under-funded benefits obligations, percentage of vested benefits, and so on. Likewise, insurance companies have their own internal lines of business (e.g., personal insurance, group insurance, and pensions), each requiring portfolios (i.e., portfolio segmentation) tailored to properly match its financial products and liabilities.

Although few portfolio managers would dispute the importance of developing and continuously updating an investment policy, they often do not give the policy the attention it deserves. Once initially developed, if developed at all, the investment policy often becomes a dormant document gathering dust on someone's back shelf instead of the effective and dynamic communication tool it is meant to be. By their nature, investors' investment needs are always changing. Consequently, even if portfolio managers satisfy the investor's initial objectives, they may unknowingly stray from the investor's changing investment needs if they do not constantly monitor those needs. The following sections briefly identify some areas that are typically addressed in an investment policy statement.

Portfolio Size

How much money does the investor want to allocate to equity real estate? Typically, investors use an optimization model that includes each major asset class (e.g., bonds, stocks, real estate) to determine the appropriate allocation to equity real estate. Thus, the equity real estate portfolio size is often known (or bounded by a range), and the real estate portfolio manager can then focus on the allocation within equity real estate.

Return Requirements

What are the required level and form of the return? Is there a minimum return requirement that must be met? Should the return level be measured in nominal or real terms? Should the form of return be mostly in current income or long-term capital gains? For example, income tax considerations and the durations of the fund's corresponding liabilities often influence the desired trade-off between current return and appreciation.

Risk Tolerance

How much volatility can the investor accept in his or her portfolio returns? Given the strong positive relationship between risk and return, the investor's risk tolerance will be a defining force behind the portfolio's long-term return. Exhibit 25–5 subjectively illustrates equity real estate's risk-return spectrum by core real estate property type. Furthermore, since factors other than property type have a powerful impact on portfolio return, they are often defined in the investment policy. For example, the investment policy of a *conservative* investor may specify relatively fixed percentages (i.e., little or no market timing) of the portfolio to be allocated to specific property types and require the properties to be fully leased, located in diversified and stable markets, and purchased without leverage. The investment policy of an *aggressive* investor may allow greater flexibility (i.e., market timing) in the allocation of the portfolio to various property types and allow the properties to be exposed to significant lease rollover, located in nondiversified markets with high vacancy rates, and/or purchased with substantial leverage.

Liquidity and Time Horizon Requirements

Given the inherent poor liquidity (e.g., 6 to 12 months to execute a trade) and lumpiness (i.e., the size of investment) in real estate private market transactions, it is essential that investors and portfolio man-

EXHIBIT 25–5
Estimate of Current Equity Real Estate Risk-Return Spectrum

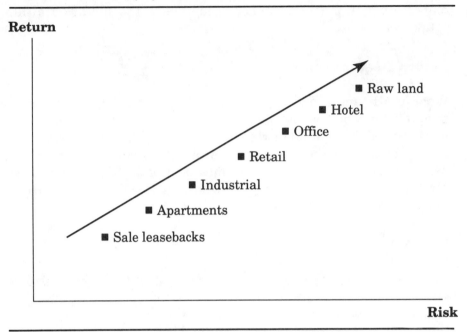

agers define the liquidity needs of the portfolio and continually reassess its cash requirements over an extended time horizon. For example, does a portion of the portfolio need to be liquidated to meet upcoming obligations? Most investors have come to understand (many the "hard way") the poor liquidity and extended time horizon requirements of investing in real estate and have already considered this when making their allocation decisions.

Given the recent explosion of real estate equity securities, many institutional investors are further partitioning their real estate allocations to include the traditional illiquid real estate investment vehicles along with some portion of liquid real estate equity securities from the emerging public market.

Tax and Legal Considerations

Assuming the investor is a taxable entity, the portfolio manager's goal is to maximize the investor's after-tax return. Legal considerations may include limiting the investor's liability from property-level incidence (environmental, personal injury, etc.) and regulatory considerations (e.g., ERISA).

To summarize, an understanding of the investor's investment objectives and constraints is the essential starting point in the portfolio management process. When the portfolio manager begins the process with a solid understanding of the investor's needs (portfolio size, return requirements, risk tolerance, liquidity, time horizon, and tax and legal considerations) and the knowledge that these needs are distinct and continually changing, the chance of success is greatly enhanced.

REAL ESTATE MARKET CONDITIONS AND EXPECTATIONS

Once the investor's objectives and constraints are understood, the portfolio manager's attention focuses on real estate market conditions. The real estate market is constantly evolving and changing, with discount rates and capitalization rates rising and falling along with investor sentiment for particular markets and property types. In the context of identifying the combination of properties that will lead to a portfolio located near or on the efficient frontier, which is consistent with the investor's objectives and constraints, the portfolio manager must *identify and analyze markets within the targeted investment universe.*

Investors and portfolio managers require an objective and analytical approach to identifying the factors that contribute to equity real estate return and risk. Accordingly, substantial time and resources are now being spent on the creation of "real estate market expectation models" that assist in estimating the inputs into the optimization process. Remember: Portfolio construction is based on estimates of future risk-reward parameters, which are inherently uncertain. Thus, portfolio managers are left with the unsettling task of subjectively—albeit heavily steeped in quantitative analysis—estimating these parameters. The question is how to do this.

Before beginning our discussion, it is imperative to mention the difficulty of obtaining high-quality, inexpensive, and consistent real estate market data. This shortcoming is especially apparent when comparing the availability of real estate market data to the abundance of data available for the bond and stock markets. However, there are hopeful signs that this is changing. Now a small number of real estate market information vendors and econometric firms have been able to assemble historical databases that capture the relevant local, regional, and national market conditions systematically through time. A systematic approach (i.e., employing a consistent, unbroken methodology) to gathering these data is essential to properly analyze property type and market performance over time. In addition, there is growing industry awareness that real estate investors, advisors, and managers need to share data to better understand real estate's risks and returns.

Another aspect of this lack of quality real estate market data merits mentioning. An increased amount of quality, inexpensively available data offers no guarantee of superior investment performance. For example, the availability of the vast amounts of market data is one of the primary reasons why the bond and stock portfolio managers have a very difficult time beating their respective portfolio benchmarks (e.g., market indices)—the crux of "adding value." Therefore, the real estate portfolio manager with access to "relatively" superior market information has the upper hand in beating the market indices, thereby adding the most value.

Given the preceding caveats, we now begin our discussion of real estate market conditions and expectations by introducing different portfolio/property analysis approaches and a general framework for analyzing real estate market conditions and expectations. Furthermore, we will attempt to explain the linkages among the approaches, tools, and techniques presented in this section and the portfolio process itself. This section is broken down into the following areas:

1. Market efficiency.
2. Portfolio management approaches.
3. Real estate market analysis.
4. Market segmentation.
5. The return factor model.
6. Fundamental analysis.
7. Scenario analysis/probabilistic forecasting.
8. Portfolio optimization: reconciliation and judgment.

Much of what follows focuses on the returns-generating process. Since risk-adjusted returns are typically considered the main determinant of portfolio performance, it seems to be a proper focus for portfolio managers.

Market Efficiency

At the start, portfolio managers must determine how they themselves view the question of market efficiency. How efficient is the market? Ultimately, how investors and portfolio managers view this question determines how the portfolio is to be managed: passively or actively. Once the portfolio manager answers this question, the portfolio/property analysis approaches to be employed become clearer.

An *efficient market* is a market with many participants in which market information is quickly and efficiently disseminated and asset prices adjust rapidly in accordance with the new information. In such markets, there is little benefit (net of transaction costs) to asset selection and/or market-timing approaches intended to identify mispriced opportunities. Exhibit 25–6 provides a spectrum of market efficiency and places both active and passive market approaches within this spectrum.

An *active portfolio approach* assumes low to moderate market efficiency, and thus mispriced market segments and properties are worth seeking out. A *passive portfolio approach* assumes moderate to high market efficiency, and consequently the costs of finding mis-

EXHIBIT 25–6
Market Efficiency Spectrum

Low	Moderate	High

Active Market Approach

Goal: Over/under allocate portfolio in certain market segments or individual properties in order to outperform broad market index

Assumes: Low to moderate market efficient; mispriced market segments and properties are worth seeking out

Passive Market Approach

Goal: Allocate portfolio to match broad market index

Assumes: Moderate to high market efficient; mispriced market segments and properties are not worth seeking out

priced market segments and properties are not justified. Under the passive portfolio approach, the portfolio manager should focus his or her energies on constructing and maintaining a low-cost index or index proxy portfolio that matches the investor's objectives and constraints.

Given the lesser quality and availability of real estate market information, few believe the real estate market is efficient. Thus, for real estate, an active portfolio approach that attempts to provide the potential to obtain "excess" or premium returns above what is justified by the risk assumed seems appropriate. However, as the real estate market becomes relatively more efficient, perhaps through real estate equity securities (REITs), and the cost of constructing and maintaining a passive portfolio decreases, passive equity real estate portfolio approaches will become more viable.

If investors and portfolio managers conclude that the equity real estate market is efficient and accordingly a passive portfolio approach is appropriate, they should focus their attention on ways to construct and monitor an index proxy portfolio. The balance of this section is for those investors and portfolio managers who have concluded that the equity real estate market is inefficient and for whom an active portfolio management approach is therefore appropriate. Consequently, we will now introduce portfolio management and asset selection approaches used within an active portfolio framework.

Portfolio Management Approaches

As in the stock and bond markets, the real estate portfolio manager will typically favor either a top-down or a bottom-up investment approach. For real estate, the *top-down approach* focuses the investment decision on the national market first. Then regions and local markets that are expected to outperform the overall market based on their forecasted economic cycle, current market strength, current pricing levels, and so on are identified. Finally, properties are selected in the local market based on their expected excess return. The *bottom-up approach* focuses the investment decision on the return and risk relationship of an individual property to determine if it is priced attractively. The goal is to purchase properties that can be bought at below their estimated intrinsic value and sell properties that can be sold above their estimated intrinsic value. If taken to its extreme, the bottom-up approach constitutes the asset-by-asset process perspective discussed earlier. The portfolio manager disregards what is happening in national and regional economies and how the property fits in within a portfolio context, and is content to receive the positive excess returns due from finding a mispriced asset.

In real estate portfolio management, more so than for stocks and bonds, the investor is to some degree directly responsible for the management of the asset (unless investing through a REIT or a similar vehicle). Therefore, it is essential that the portfolio managers also maintain accurate and timely information from the property/asset managers so that informed decisions can be made.

Exhibit 25–7 depicts an *interactive top-down/bottom-up approach* to real estate portfolio management. The local market is where both approaches interact, as this is where the real estate portfolio manager's knowledge of the market typically dissipates and the manager can no longer (nor should he or she attempt to) be expert in the

EXHIBIT 25–7
Interactive Top-Down/Bottom-Up Portfolio Management Approaches

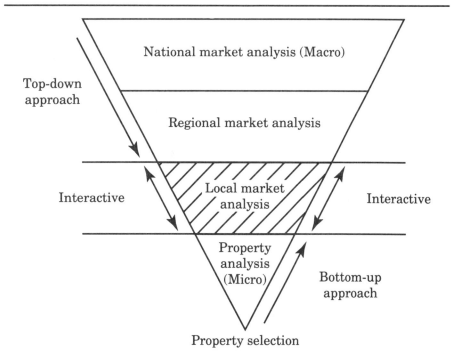

dynamics of all markets and the properties they contain. Accordingly, the portfolio manager must rely on the knowledge and experience of the internal organization (e.g., acquisition/disposition, property/asset management, architectural/engineering, and legal or external advisors) to obtain an understanding of local market and property dynamics. Likewise, the field organization (either internal or external) must rely on the portfolio manager to communicate and monitor investor objectives and constraints, capital market conditions and expectations, the portfolio strategy, and portfolio performance. Thus, as we can see, top-down and bottom-up approaches in real estate are not mutually exclusive; rather, they are interdependent.

Asset Selection Approaches

The property-level investment decision focuses on determining whether an existing property should be held or sold and whether a potential acquisition should be purchased or passed over. Active investors in the common stock arena have developed two approaches to making this decision: fundamental analysis and technical analysis.

Fundamental analysis assumes the markets are not efficient and mispriced assets[1] exist. This approach assumes an asset is worth the present value of all future cash flows. It therefore becomes the job of the investment analyst to assess the asset's (or, company's) fundamentals to estimate the amount and timing of cash flows, along with the appropriate discount rate to apply, to arrive at an estimate of the asset (or, stock) value. This value estimate is then compared to the current market price of the asset to determine whether it should be purchased or sold.

Technical analysis also assumes the market is not efficient and asset mispricing exists. This approach is based primarily on past prices and transaction volumes to determine the asset (or, stock's) future price behavior. Its basic assumption is that there are repeatable patterns and momentum in the market that persist over time that the investment analyst can identify and use in selecting under- and overpriced assets (or, stocks).

---

[1] Throughout this chapter, the term *mispriced assets* is used to identify assets (specifically properties) that have a positive expected net present value (i.e., their "intrinsic" value exceeds the current market price), either because investors' expectations differ substantially from the capital market's aggregate view or because the heterogeneity of investors causes them to price asset characteristics differently.

Since the fundamental approach is more compatible with accepted real estate analytics, we will now focus on it. However, this does not imply that, in the less efficient real estate market, all forms of technical analysis are without merit.

Real Estate Market Analysis

Determining real estate market condition and expectations and, accordingly, expected returns, volatility, and correlation is a complicated undertaking, but it can be made a little easier by developing a general framework for the real estate market. This framework, or model, helps us understand the many factors that interact to determine a market and/or property's return expectation.

Comparison between Stock and Real Estate Market Analysis
Exhibit 25–8 gives an overview of the stock market and real estate analysis process. As you can see, both analytical processes employ

EXHIBIT 25–8
Comparison of Stock Market and Real Estate Market Analysis

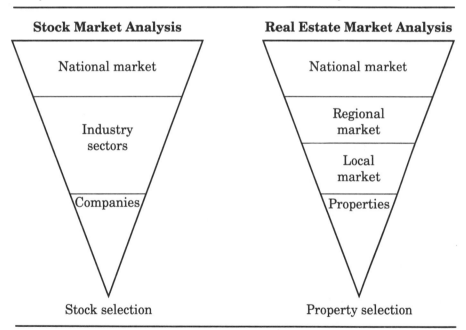

very similar approaches. Both stock and real estate returns are affected by changes in the capital markets and by specific company or property factors that define the asset. The main difference is due to the fixed/contractual nature of real estate leases. In essence, a property is a factory that provides "space" for sale or rent to its surrounding local market. Consequently, property performance can be viewed as having a bondlike component (relating to the lease contract[s]) and a reversionary value (upon the expiration of the lease[s]) that is directly linked to local supply and demand conditions. Companies, on the other hand, have greater flexibility in both the mobility of their factories and the markets they wish to supply. Therefore, a company's performance is directly linked to the industry (or industries) in which it competes, while a property's performance is directly linked to the market in which it competes.

Real Estate Markets, Linkages, and Potential Risk Factors

As shown in Exhibit 25–8, the stock market and real estate market analysis process is very similar. In comparison, Exhibit 25–9 focuses solely on real estate. It provides an overview of the unique nature of the real estate markets, the linkages among them, and the potential risk factors for each. Much of a portfolio manager's attention is given to understanding the risks inherent in the real estate market and how these risks can be managed. This section divides risk into its two components: *systematic risk* (factors that are not diversifiable) and *unsystematic risk* (factors that are diversifiable). Those firms that develop a framework with which to understand and manage risk factors will have a competitive advantage in assessing the market's opportunities and risks.

Systematic Risks

As noted above, systematic risk factors affect all assets in the market. Consequently, it is impossible for the portfolio manager to diversify these risk factors away completely. However, if the portfolio manager can determine the portfolio's sensitivity to these systematic risk factors and can reposition the portfolio according to its anticipated movements (up or down), the portfolio's risk-return performance can be improved.

National Market.   It is well documented that fiscal and monetary policies influence the national economy and the assets that are traded in them. Changes in fiscal policy (increases or decreases in

EXHIBIT 25–9
Real Estate Market Analysis, Risk Factors, and Diversification

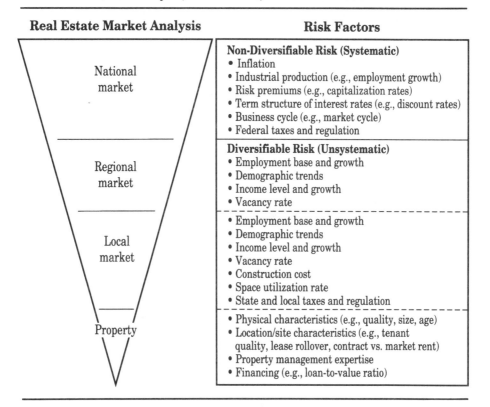

Real Estate Market Analysis	Risk Factors
National market	**Non-Diversifiable Risk (Systematic)** • Inflation • Industrial production (e.g., employment growth) • Risk premiums (e.g., capitalization rates) • Term structure of interest rates (e.g., discount rates) • Business cycle (e.g., market cycle) • Federal taxes and regulation
Regional market	**Diversifiable Risk (Unsystematic)** • Employment base and growth • Demographic trends • Income level and growth • Vacancy rate
Local market	• Employment base and growth • Demographic trends • Income level and growth • Vacancy rate • Construction cost • Space utilization rate • State and local taxes and regulation
Property	• Physical characteristics (e.g., quality, size, age) • Location/site characteristics (e.g., tenant quality, lease rollover, contract vs. market rent) • Property management expertise • Financing (e.g., loan-to-value ratio)

government taxes or spending) can have an impact on the entire national market and all the properties contained therein or a disproportionate impact on one area of the country. A poignant example is the impact of recently decreased federal spending on defense on southern California's property values. Similarly, the Tax Reform Act of 1986 (TRA '86) may have been more damaging (merely from a tax-advantaged viewpoint) to apartments than most other commercial property types. However, changes in monetary policy (increases or decreases in the supply of funds in the economy) that affect business cost of capital (interest rates) can have a broad impact on a variety of property types. Consequently, monetary policy affects "all" aspects of the economy, including the pricing of all assets. Furthermore, inflation, industrial production, risk premiums, and interest rates have broad implications for all asset pricing, with real estate potentially posing additional systematic risks for market cycles (vacancy rates), employment growth, and high information, transaction, and liquidity costs.

Unsystematic Risks

Unsystematic risks do not affect all properties in the market. Consequently, it is possible for the portfolio manager to diversify many of these risk factors away by properly combining properties. Exhibit 25–10 shows how the addition of properties (assuming their returns are less than perfectly correlated) reduces total portfolio risk. As mentioned earlier, this is the most cost-effective way to reduce overall portfolio risk without reducing portfolio return. Therefore, a diligent portfolio manager will always be looking for ways to combine real estate assets to maximize the benefits of diversification. Accordingly, diversification can become one of the dominant forces in the determi-

EXHIBIT 25–10
Portfolio Risk Reduction through Diversification

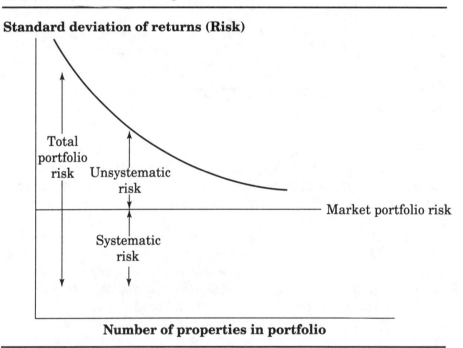

Standard deviation of returns (Risk)

Total portfolio risk

Unsystematic risk

Market portfolio risk

Systematic risk

Number of properties in portfolio

nation of the real estate portfolio's allocations to various property types and geographic locations.

Regional Market. The national real estate market is often broken down into regional markets that define a specific area of the country by some distinguishing economic characteristics, most typically by its underlying business activities (e.g., employment base). For example, the industrial Midwest region would encompass the cities and states around the Great Lakes that have a high dependence on the industrial employment sector. Behind this regional market breakdown is the hypothesis that economic regions behave very differently over time than the national market due to differences in their existing employment base, employment growth, demographics, income trends, market vacancy levels, and other factors. These differences provide the portfolio manager with the potential to identify regional opportunities for increases in real estate returns along with the diversification benefits of owning properties in several economic regions, thereby reducing regional risks in the portfolio.

The concept of the economic region is evolving away from the grouping of contiguous states and/or metropolitan areas to the grouping of metropolitan areas based on their respective economic concentrations (e.g., employment base). This allows for the grouping of noncontiguous areas into economic clusters. For example, metropolitan areas with a preponderance of jobs in the financial services sector may be grouped together even though they are located in divergent parts of the country.

Local Market. While the health of national and regional markets can have a significant impact on local property returns, they often seem a diluted force when compared to the dynamics of the local market. It is here where buyers and sellers of space consummate transactions and hence determine rent and property pricing. These transactions are based on the interaction of several factors, including current and expected local supply and demand, cost of new construction, and local taxes and regulations, along with a general knowledge of required rates of return in the capital markets.

Property. At the property level, the old axiom "no two properties are alike" applies. A property's own individual characteristics have a very significant impact on its returns over time. Property factors like physical condition, location, lease characteristics, and property management all affect a property's return. One way to view how a property is linked to its local market is to think of the local market as a "stream" of real estate cash flow determined by the national, regional, and local market factors described above. How affected the property is by this stream of cash flow depends on its sensitivity to the surrounding market.

Exhibit 25–11 lists some determinants of a property's sensitivity to local market conditions (see also Chapter 4, "Leases as a Key to Performance and Value"). Most of the sensitivity of a property's asset value is a function of the property's lease characteristics. The shorter the property's average lease term, the more equitylike its cash flows and, accordingly, the more sensitive it is to local market conditions. The longer the property's average lease term, the more bondlike its cash flows and the less sensitive its value is to local market conditions. For example, consider two adjacent class A office buildings. One is a multitenant building with an average remaining lease term of 1.5 years, and the other is a single-tenant building recently contracted on a 20-year, long-term lease. As the leases in the building with the average lease term of 1.5 years expire, the space is "marked to market," thus giving the building a high market sensitivity. The building with the long-term lease, assuming quality tenancy, has no exposure to the market for another 20 years and thus has low market sensitivity, but it does have high sensitivity to movements in interest and inflation rates.

From the preceding framework, we can see that one of the main goals of the portfolio manager is to identify and predict which risk factors will influence real estate returns and position the portfolio

EXHIBIT 25–11
Sensitivity of Property Value Determinants to Changing Market Conditions

Property Characteristic	Change in Characteristic	Property Value Sensitivity to Changing Market Conditions
Average time to lease rollover	Increase	Decrease
Difference between contract rent and effective market rent	Increase	Increase
Tenant quality	Increase	Decrease

accordingly. As the real estate market changes over time, the significance of each risk factor also changes. As we look back over the 1980s, we see the significant *macro* risk factors for office properties included the reduction in office employment growth, continued growth in office construction, and unjustifiably positive investor sentiment (as manifested by low capitalization rates). As we look forward into the remaining half of the 1990s, we see the significant risk factors may have again changed, perhaps to many of the uncertainties listed in Exhibit 25–1. This illustrates the potential pitfalls of using historical trends to forecast the future, along with underscoring the importance of diversification as the only prudent way to protect the portfolio against unexpected changes in market conditions.

Market Segmentation

To analyze the domestic real estate investment universe, we need to break it down into manageable, homogeneous pieces called *market segments,* or *diversification categories.* Essentially, market segmentation means the aggregation of individual assets into categories with similar return behavior over time. Statistically, a market segment should constitute an aggregation of assets with high correlations of returns but low correlations of returns to other market segments over time. Market segmentation has been used by stock market portfolio managers to help them capitalize on market trends and investment styles. Some stock market examples are industry sectors (utilities, automotive, technology, etc.), firm size (small, medium, and large capitalization), and cyclical (consumer, durable, etc.) goods. For real estate, some market segments that have been used are property type, geographic region, economic region, economic cluster, metropolitan area employment growth, type of tenancy, average lease rollover, density of land use, and property life cycle. (See also Chapter 23, "Portfolio Diversification Considerations.")

Once the market segments have been identified, the portfolio manager needs to understand as much as possible about what drives the returns for each segment. This understanding can be obtained from several complementary sources; including (1) a historical review of applicable data series and research literature; (2) interviews and discussions with other portfolio managers, researchers, and asset/property managers; and (3) creation of the investment firm's own knowledge base through analysis and development of market explanatory models. Once these steps have been completed, the investor/

portfolio manager will be better equipped to understand each market segment.

We now introduce some of the basic tools, techniques, and models that may enhance understanding of the dynamics of the real estate markets.

The Return Factor Model

While an in-depth discussion is beyond the scope of this chapter, we will briefly introduce the concept and benefits of return factor models. Factor models can be an effective analytical tool in identifying an asset's (or portfolio's) return-generating process and, accordingly, its potential risk (as measured by the standard deviation of its returns). For our purposes, we begin by discussing the components of the required rate of return and then introduce single- and multifactor return models.

Required Rate of Return

The *required rate of return* is the return an investor requires to be fairly compensated for assuming the risks of the asset or portfolio being acquired. For reasons described earlier, we have broken the real estate market into manageable, homogeneous market segments. Consequently, we will use market segments as our fundamental unit for market analysis.

To determine a real estate market segment's required rate of return, recall that a nominal rate of return has three components: (1) the rate of inflation, (2) the real risk-free rate, and (3) the risk premium. These relationships are multiplicative and are shown in equation (1):

$$k = (1 + p)(1 + r' + r'') - 1 \qquad (1)$$

where k = Nominal, required rate of return.
p = Inflation rate.
r' = Real risk-free rate.
r'' = Risk premium.

This return can be viewed on either an ex ante or ex post basis. On an ex ante basis, this input represents the investor's expectations. On an ex post basis, the inflation rate is known as is the nominal return (k) earned by the asset; accordingly, the real risk-free and risk premium rates can be determined.

As discussed earlier, all assets are affected by the real risk-free and inflation rates (i.e., the nominal risk-free rate). What differs for each asset is the uncertainty of the size and timing of expected cash flows. This uncertainty needs to be quantified in a market risk factor model to determine the market segment's risk premium and, accordingly, the required rate of return the investor needs to be fairly compensated for the inherent risk in the market segment.

A return factor model uses a single- or multiple-regression equation to measure risk and explain real estate returns. It can be used at the national, regional, local, and/or property level to estimate expected returns and identify the factors that are responsible for real estate returns. Essentially, it attributes real estate returns to factors that influence returns, thereby acting as a tool with which to further understand real estate risk and return and identify a property's (or portfolio's) sensitivities to these risk factors.

The two types of factor models used to determine an asset's expected return are the single-factor model and the multifactor model. The *single-factor model,* which has become one of the major paradigms in finance, is commonly referred to as the *capital asset pricing model (CAPM).* Its basic premise is that the required rate of return of an asset (or a portfolio) is dependent on the rate of return of the market and its sensitivity to changes in the market's return. The CAPM also states that the asset's (or portfolio's) return is based solely on its systematic risk (beta), since it is unsystematic risk (e_i) which can be diversified away. The market model form of the CAPM is presented in equation (2):

$$E(R_i) = R_f + B_i \times [E(R_m) - R_f] + e_i \qquad (2)$$

where $\quad E(R_i) =$ Required rate of return on ith asset (or portfolio).

$\qquad R_f =$ Risk-free rate of return.

$\qquad B_i =$ Sensitivity of the ith asset's (or portfolio's) return to the market return.

$\quad E(R_m) =$ Expected return on the market.

$\qquad e_i =$ Error term, or non-market-related (unsystematic) return.

The *multifactor model* is an extension of the single-factor model. Essentially, it includes additional factors to measure an asset's (or portfolio's) risk and commensurate expected return. The multifactor model is referred to as the *arbitrage pricing theory (APT).* Whereas the CAPM relies solely on a single factor, how the asset moves with the market portfolio (as measured by beta), APT asserts that an asset's return, and thus its riskiness, is a function of its "sensitivities" to unanticipated changes in several factors. A standard representation of a multifactor return model is presented in equation (3):

$$R_i = b_{i,0} + b_{i,1} \times F_1 + b_{i,2} \times F_2 + \ldots + b_{i,n} \times F_n + e_i \qquad (3)$$

where R_i = Return on the ith asset (or portfolio).

$b_{i,0}$ = Constant (or intercept) term.

$b_{i,n}$ = Sensitivity of the asset's return to factor n.

F_n = Value of factor n.

e_i = Error term, or non-factor-related (unsystematic) return.

A traditional applicaton of APT would include identifying unexpected changes in the following four economic factors that have been shown to influence returns on all assets: (1) inflation, (2) industrial production, (3) risk premiums, and (4) the term structure of interest rates. Because of real estate's unique nature, the portfolio manager may want to include factors specific to real estate, such as the influence of market cycles (vacancy rates), employment growth, and high information, transaction, and liquidity costs. (As with CAPM, the ex-ante version of APT assumes that the expected return to unsystematic risk equals zero.)

Following are some basic characteristics of a good factor model: First, when examining ex-post returns, the error term (e_i) should not be correlated to other significant factors in the model, for if it is, the factors may suffer from multicollinearity. Second, when examining ex-post returns, the error term (e_i) of the asset (or portfolio) should not be correlated with the asset's (or portfolio's) return; if it is, the factor model may be missing a significant systematic risk factor. Third, the model is parsimonious; that is, the selection of very few risk factors explains most of the return (a high R-squared).

Despite the apparent rigorousness of these models, several practical problems should be noted:

1. Which factors should be used? The absence of one or more significant factors might seriously impair the model.
2. These models are often developed using historical data. Their application to projecting future returns implicitly assume these factors (F_n) can be accurately predicted over time. This

may be a large leap of faith (e.g., can the future value of the factors driving the supply of and demand for CBD office space be accurately forecasted?).

3. The models assume the sensitivity (b_n) of these factors will remain constant (or nearly so) in the future (e.g., will the demand for CBD office space continue to be explained by the same factors, with the same relative magnitude, as those observed in the past?).

4. A scenario/probabilistic approach (expected factors and probability of outcome) is still needed to determine the variance and covariance of returns (which are needed inputs in the MPT process).

Assuming the portfolio manager has developed a multifactor model that has the required positive characteristics and has kept in mind the very practical problem with all factor models described above, the model may provide the portfolio manager with two potential uses. First, it may assist in developing a portfolio diversification, or allocation, strategy based on the portfolio's current factor "sensitivities" and market factor expectations. Second, it may generate the required inputs (i.e., expected return, standard deviation, and correlation) for each market segment for portfolio optimization.

Fundamental Analysis

We now move from single- and multifactor models to a market analysis model. We begin by exploring the concepts of intrinsic value and market value. *Intrinsic*, or *investment, value* (V_0) is the value an individual investor places on an asset. *Market value* (M_0) is the price the market places on the asset. As both a basic valuation model and one of the central tenets in finance, equation (4) states that the intrinsic value of any asset equals the present value of the asset's expected cash flows over the holding period:

$$V_0 = \sum_{n=1}^{N} \frac{CF_n}{(1 + k)^n} \qquad (4)$$

where V_0 = Current intrinsic value.
CF_n = Cash flow (including sales price) in period n.
N = Holding period.
n = Equal, discrete time periods.
k = Discount rate.

The discount rate can be determined through the multiplicative approach and/or the return factor models discussed earlier. In addition, equation (4) can be expressed in a form to which real estate practitioners (specifically real estate appraisers/underwriters) are more accustomed:

$$V_0 = \frac{CF_0(1 + g_1)}{(1 + k)^1} + \frac{CF_1(1 + g_2)}{(1 + k)^2} + \cdots$$
$$+ \frac{CF_{N-1}(1 + g_N)/(k - g_N)}{(1 + k)^N} \qquad (5)$$

where $\quad g_n$ = Growth in cash flow in period n.
$(k - g_N)$ = Reversionary capitalization rate (assuming long-term equilibrium).

Equation (5) expands equation (4) by breaking cash flow out to include growth rates and sales price. Equation (5) represents the *multistage dividend discount model,* which is often used by stock analysts to determine intrinsic stock prices. However, its use requires that cash flows grow at a constant rate (g_N) once equilibrium is experienced after the Nth period.

To determine whether a market is overpriced, underpriced, or fairly priced, an investor must derive his or her best estimate of the market's (1) expected cash flow, (2) growth in cash flows, (3) exit capitalization rate, and (4) required rate of return. If an investor's estimate of intrinsic value differs from the market value, in effect the investor is disagreeing with some or all of the market's consensus opinion of CF_n, g_n, or k.

Market Segment Pro Forma

To determine a real estate market segment's expected return, it is necessary to build an income and expense pro forma for the market segment and include these estimates in equation (4) and/or (5). This has only recently become possible with improvements in the gathering of real estate market information. Depending on the size of one's investment organization, one can obtain the needed market segment information from various vendors, the investor's field organization, or both.

A market segment pro forma is then established based on an average unit measure for the targeted market segment (e.g., average class A office space per square foot). The market segment pro forma would contain estimates of current market rent, occupancy, operating expenses (fixed and variable), and capital expenditures (leasing commissions, tenant improvements, etc.), along with growth rates in income and expenses, going-in/going-out capitalization rates, and the expected rate of return. Exhibit 25–12 presents an example of cash flow pro forma and assumptions for a hypothetical market segment. Potential rent and expense growth rates, changes in market vacancy, and exit capitalization rates are derived by forecasting changes in the space and capital markets.

This process culminates in a ranking of property markets by estimated returns. This ranking can be summarized as:

$V_0 > M_0$; market is underpriced (buy)

$V_0 < M_0$; market is overpriced (sell)

$V_0 = M_0$; market is fairly priced (hold)

However, estimates of the variance and covariance of returns are still needed as inputs to the MPT-based portfolio optimization approach.

Scenario Analysis/Probabilistic Forecasting

The scenario approach takes a probabilistic view of the market segment's anticipated performance rather than the single-point estimate approach presented in Exhibit 25–12. Scenario analysis applies estimated probabilities to a variety of asset (or portfolio) potential outcomes and can then be used to determine expected return, standard deviation, and correlation. It more accurately reflects the uncertain nature of future asset returns and can generate all three portfolio optimization inputs (expected return, standard deviation, and correlations).

Given the cost, sophistication, and capacity of today's computer hardware and software, the benefits of using a scenario approach to understand the dynamics of the real estate market can no longer be readily dismissed on the basis of excessive cost and/or time requirements. Today a scenario analysis can be performed inexpensively. Accordingly, there is very little justification for continuing to use the old, single-point estimate approach when a scenario approach provides substantially more insight. Moreover, the process of thinking through the different scenarios and how they affect each market segment's expected returns adds considerably to the portfolio

EXHIBIT 25–12
Hypothetical Retail Market Pro Forma

	Market Cash Flow Projections					Reversionary Proceeds	Growth Rate Assumptions					Comments
	Year 1	Year 2	Year 3	Year 4	Year 5	End of Year 5	Year 1	Year 2	Year 3	Year 4	Year 5	
Potential rent	$15.53	$16.23	$16.29	$17.20	$17.98	$17.98	0.0%	1.0%	-3.0%	2.0%	1.0%	Year-over-year percentage increase.*
Occupancy	86.0%	87.0%	85.0%	86.0%	85.0%	85.0%	1.0	1.0	-2.0	1.0	-1.0	Change in occupancy percentage points
Net rent	$13.35	$14.12	$13.85	$14.79	$15.28	$15.28						
Operating expenses:												
Variable expenses	1.05	1.11	1.09	1.16	1.20	1.20	7.8	7.8	7.8	7.8	7.8	Percentage of net rent
Fixed expenses	3.11	3.21	3.33	3.44	3.56	3.56	3.5	3.5	3.5	3.5	3.5	Year-over-year percentage increase†
Total	4.16	4.32	4.42	4.60	4.76	4.76						
Net operating income	$9.20	$9.80	$9.44	$10.19	$10.52	10.52						

1028

Reversionary capitalization rate					.09						
Capital expenses:											
Leasing commissions	0.52	0.54	0.54	0.55	0.55		3.5	3.5	3.5	3.5	Year-over-year percentage increase.†
Tenant improvements	1.04	1.07	1.07	1.11	1.11		3.5	3.5	3.5	3.5	Year-over-year percentage increase.†
Other	0.31	0.32	0.33	0.34	0.36		3.5	3.5	3.5	3.5	Year-over-year percentage increase.†
Total	1.87	1.93	1.94	2.00	2.02						
Net cash flow and reversionary proceeds	$7.34	$7.87	$7.50	$8.18	$8.50	$116.91					

Summary assumptions:

Initial purchase price	$100.00
Going-in capitalization rate	8.75%
Going-out capitalization rate	9.00%

Results:

Expected annual growth in cash flow	4.11%
Expected annual rate of return	10.56%

* Percentage change in real rents.
† Assumed inflation rate.
Note: Numbers may not add due to rounding.

1029

manager's appreciation of the intricacies and relationships of the various market segments. Good portfolio managers will use these insights to exploit market opportunities and minimize portfolio risk.

On the other hand, the accuracy of this approach is only as good as the user's capabilities. It is subject to arbitrariness in the selection of the scenarios and in the weights assigned to each. Moreover, it may be difficult to forecast the correlation among assets if the scenarios are incorrectly framed. For example, a rising market in one area of the country may be attributable to, say, the recent passage of a plethora of trade agreements (e.g., NAFTA, GATT), while another part of the country may suffer a falling market due to the same causes. Other examples might include military buildup versus reduction, tax law changes, and other market uncertainties listed in Exhibit 25–1. Accordingly, great care must be taken in framing these scenarios.

To illustrate how scenario/probabilistic forecasts can be used, we have extended the market pro forma presented in Exhibit 25–12 into a probabilistic forecast. Exhibit 25–13 summarizes initial market-based financial information and probability matrix and market expectations for each of six market outcomes for a hypothetical market segment. More specifically, there are three conditions for market vacancy—rising, steady, and falling—and two conditions for inflation—low and high. Thus, we have a 3 × 2 joint-probability matrix, or, in other words, a six-scenario analysis.

Exhibit 25–14 shows the return distribution resulting from weighting each of the six scenarios by its estimated probability of occurrence. Once the expected return is calculated, the standard deviation can be completed. Assuming that the expected return is normally distributed, the frequency distribution shown in Exhibit 25–14 can be plotted. Exhibits 25–15 through 25–20 show the derivation of expected return for each of the six scenarios. Finally, Exhibit 25–21 shows the computation of the scenario-based expected return and standard deviation for the hypothetical retail market segment.

Similar benefits can be obtained by using a Monte Carlo simulation approach to generating returns under uncertainty for which the mean return, standard deviation, and correlation parameters can be estimated. Fundamentally similar to a scenario-based approach, Monte Carlo simulation requires the portfolio manager to estimate the distribution of each significant variable (rental rates, vacancy,

EXHIBIT 25–13 Overview of Market Assumptions: Hypothetical Market Segment

Initial Market-Based Financial Information		Probability Matrix of Market Conditions				
	Actuals from Prior Year	Inflation Rate	Rising	Steady	Falling	Total
Potential rent	$15.00	Low	20.0%	40.0%	20.0%	80.0%
Occupancy	85.0%	High	5.0	10.0	5.0	20.0
Net rent	$12.75	Total	25.0%	50.0%	25.0%	100.0%

Operating expenses:		Market Expectations	
Variable expenses	1.00		
Fixed expenses	3.00	Real Changes in Rents	
Total	$4.00		

			Year 1	Year 2	Year 3	Year 4	Year 5
Net operating income	8.75						
Capital expenses:							
Leasing commissions	0.50	Rising	0.5%	1.0%	0.5%	1.0%	1.0%
Tenant improvements	1.00	Steady	0.0	1.0	−3.0	2.0	1.0
Other	0.30	Falling	−0.5	−1.0	−0.5	−1.0	−1.0
Total	1.80	(Year-over-year percentage increase.)					
Net cash flow	$6.95	Changes in Occupancy					

Summary assumptions:			Year 1	Year 2	Year 3	Year 4	Year 5
Initial purchase price	$100.00						
Going-in capitalization rate	8.75%	Rising	0.5%	1.0%	1.5%	1.0%	0.5%
Going-out		Steady	1.0	1.0	−2.0	1.0	−1.0
capitalization rate (at		Falling	−0.5	−1.0	−1.5	−1.0	−0.5
disposition)	9.00%	(Change in occupancy percentage points.)					

Scenario-Based Expected Result		Inflation Rate	
Return	11.12%	Low	3.5%
Standard deviation	2.54%	High	7.0

growth rate, etc.) to the return-generating process. From these distributions, a series of simulated "draws" are recorded and used to create a distribution of returns. However, space limitations preclude an extensive treatment here. Interested readers are referred to any graduate-level textbook on quantitative analysis with a thorough treatment of simulation technologies.

Portfolio Optimization: Reconciliation and Judgment

We now focus on obtaining the inputs into the optimization process in order to create an efficient frontier that formally represents the return, risk, and diversification expectations for each segment of the

EXHIBIT 25–14
Overview of Return Distribution: Hypothetical Market Segment

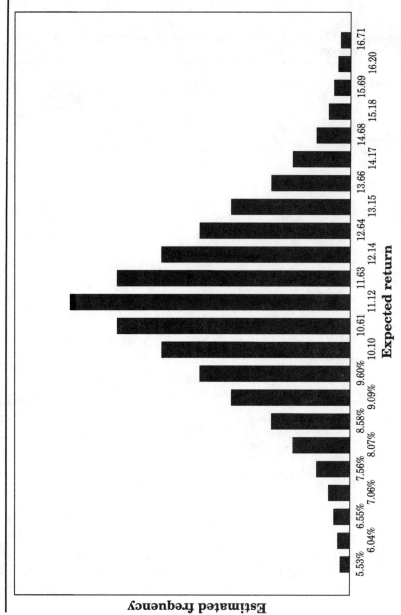

1032

EXHIBIT 25–15   Probability 20% (Rising Market/Low Inflation): Hypothetical Market Pro Forma

	Market Cash Flow Projections					Reversionary Proceeds
	Year 1	Year 2	Year 3	Year 4	Year 5	End of Year 5
Potential rent	$15.60	$16.31	$16.97	$17.73	$18.54	$18.54
Occupancy	85.5%	86.5%	88.0%	89.0%	89.5%	89.5%
Net rent	$13.34	$14.11	$14.93	$15.78	$16.59	$16.59
Operating expenses:						
Variable expenses	1.05	1.11	1.17	1.24	1.30	1.30
Fixed expenses	3.11	3.21	3.33	3.44	3.56	3.56
Total	4.16	4.32	4.50	4.68	4.86	4.86
Net operating income	9.19	9.79	10.43	11.10	11.73	$11.73
Capital expenses:						
Leasing commissions	0.52	0.54	0.54	0.55	0.55	
Tenant improvements	1.04	1.07	1.07	1.11	1.11	
Other	0.31	0.32	0.33	0.34	0.36	
Total	1.87	1.93	1.94	2.00	2.02	
Reversionary capitalization rate						.09
Net cash flow and reversionary proceeds	$7.33	$7.86	$8.49	$9.10	$9.71	$130.31

Summary assumptions:	
Initial purchase price	$100.00
Going-in capitalization rate	8.75%
Going-out capitalization rate	9.00%
Results:	
Expected annual growth in cash flow	6.91%
Expected annual rate of return	13.03%

Note: Numbers may not add due to rounding.

targeted market. However, we have a problem, and the problem is called *uncertainty*. There is little question that on an ex post basis, the efficient frontier creates nothing less than the exact answer. But as a tool to construct ex ante portfolios, the efficient frontier is only as good as its inputs. This is also why the efficient frontier has been nicknamed the "fuzzy" frontier by practitioners and academics alike. To improve our chances of deriving the best inputs to the optimization process, we employ four approaches, a reconciliation, and a strong dose of judgment. To recognize the inherent uncertainty of the inputs in addition to the lumpy nature of real estate private market transactions, target allocation ranges have been instituted.

EXHIBIT 25–16   Probability 5% (Rising Market/High Inflation): Hypothetical Market Pro Forma

	Market Cash Flow Projections					Reversionary Proceeds
	Year 1	Year 2	Year 3	Year 4	Year 5	End of Year 5
Potential rent	$16.13	$17.43	$18.75	$20.26	$21.89	$21.89
Occupancy	85.5%	86.5%	88.0%	89.0%	89.5%	89.5%
Net rent	$13.79	$15.08	$16.50	$18.03	$19.59	$19.59
Operating expenses:						
Variable expenses	1.08	1.18	1.29	1.41	1.54	1.54
Fixed expenses	3.21	3.43	3.68	3.93	4.21	4.21
Total	4.29	4.61	4.97	5.34	5.75	5.75
Net operating income	9.50	10.46	11.53	12.68	13.85	$13.85
Capital expenses:						
Leasing commissions	0.54	0.57	0.57	0.61	0.61	
Tenant improvements	1.07	1.14	1.14	1.23	1.23	
Other	0.32	0.34	0.37	0.39	0.42	
Total	1.93	2.05	2.08	2.23	2.26	
Reversionary capitalization rate						.09
Net cash flow and reversionary proceeds	$7.57	$8.40	$9.44	$10.45	$11.59	$153.89

Summary assumptions:

Initial purchase price	$100.00
Going-in capitalization rate	8.75%
Going-out capitalization rate	9.00%

Results:

Expected annual growth in cash flow	10.77%
Expected annual rate of return	16.88%

Note: Numbers may not add due to rounding.

In his seminal paper "Portfolio Selection," Markowitz notes the difficulty in determining the correct inputs for portfolio optimization:

> [W]e must have procedures for finding reasonable [means] and [variances]. These procedures, I believe, should combine statistical techniques and the judgment of practical men. My feeling is that the statistical computations should be used to arrive at a tentative set of [means] and [variances]. Judgment should then be used in increasing or decreasing some of these [means] and [variances] not taken into account by the formal computations.[2]

---

[2] Harry Markowitz, "Portfolio Selection," *Journal of Finance,* March 1952, p. 91.

EXHIBIT 25–17   **Probability 40% (Steady Market/Low Inflation): Hypothetical Market Pro Forma**

	Market Cash Flow Projections					Reversionary Proceeds
	Year 1	Year 2	Year 3	Year 4	Year 5	End of Year 5
Potential rent	$15.53	$16.23	$16.29	$17.20	$17.98	$17.98
Occupancy	86.0%	87.0%	85.0%	86.0%	85.0%	85.0%
Net rent	$13.35	$14.12	$13.85	$14.79	$15.28	$15.28
Operating expenses:						
Variable expenses	1.05	1.11	1.09	1.16	1.20	1.20
Fixed expenses	3.11	3.21	3.33	3.44	3.56	3.56
Total	4.16	4.32	4.42	4.60	4.76	4.76
Net operating income	9.20	9.80	9.44	10.19	10.52	$10.52
Capital expenses:						
Leasing commissions	0.52	0.54	0.54	0.55	0.55	
Tenant improvements	1.04	1.07	1.07	1.11	1.11	
Other	0.31	0.32	0.33	0.34	0.36	
Total	1.87	1.93	1.94	2.00	2.02	
Reversionary capitalization rate						.09
Net cash flow and reversionary proceeds	$7.34	$7.87	$7.50	$8.18	$8.50	$116.91

Summary assumptions:
Initial purchase price	$100.00
Going-in capitalization rate	8.75%
Going-out capitalization rate	9.00%

Results:
Expected annual growth in cash flow	4.11%
Expected annual rate of return	10.56%

Note: Numbers may not add due to rounding.

Given the historically poor quality of real estate market information and the short time these tools have been employed in the real estate market, Markowitz's warning seems particularly appropriate. In part because of these problems, there has been much debate regarding the usefulness of these approaches, including the benefits of applying MPT to real estate at all. Notwithstanding the shortcomings of using an MPT-based approach, the benefits of adhering to a disciplined portfolio optimization process, including multiple approaches reconciled with judgment, provide the practitioner with many benefits that cannot be easily dismissed.

EXHIBIT 25–18   Probability 10% (Steady Market/High Inflation): Hypothetical Market Pro Forma

	Market Cash Flow Projections					Reversionary Proceeds
	Year 1	Year 2	Year 3	Year 4	Year 5	End of Year 5
Potential rent	$16.05	$17.35	$18.00	$19.65	$21.23	$21.23
Occupancy	86.0%	87.0%	85.0%	86.0%	85.0%	85.0%
Net rent	$13.80	$15.09	$15.30	$16.90	$18.05	$18.05
Operating expenses:						
Variable expenses	1.08	1.18	1.20	1.33	1.42	1.42
Fixed expenses	3.21	3.43	3.68	3.93	4.21	4.21
Total	4.29	4.61	4.88	5.26	5.63	5.62
Net operating income	9.51	10.47	10.43	11.64	12.43	$12.43
Capital expenses:						
Leasing commissions	0.54	0.57	0.57	0.61	0.61	
Tenant improvements	1.07	1.14	1.14	1.23	1.23	
Other	0.32	0.34	0.37	0.39	0.42	
Total	1.93	2.05	2.08	2.23	2.26	
Reversionary capitalization rate						.09
Net cash flow and reversionary proceeds	$7.58	$8.41	$8.34	$9.41	$10.17	$138.06

Summary assumptions:	
Initial purchase price	$100.00
Going-in capitalization rate	8.75%
Going-out capitalization rate	9.00%
Results:	
Expected annual growth in cash flow	7.91%
Expected annual rate of return	14.34%

Note: Numbers may not add due to rounding.

Forecasting Approaches

To summarize, we have discussed several possible approaches to forecasting the three inputs (expected return, standard deviation, and correlation) needed to derive the efficient frontier. The first is based primarily on historical relationships, while the remaining three are based on subjective estimates about the future (which might be substantially influenced by historical relationships):

1. Factor models.
   a) single-factor,
   b) multi-factor
2. Fundamental analysis.

EXHIBIT 25–19   Probability 20% (Falling Market/Low Inflation): Hypothetical Market Pro Forma

	Market Cash Flow Projections					Reversionary Proceeds
	Year 1	Year 2	Year 3	Year 4	Year 5	End of Year 5
Potential rent	$15.45	$15.83	$16.30	$16.70	$17.11	$17.11
Occupancy	84.5%	83.5%	82.0%	81.0%	80.5%	80.5%
Net rent	$13.05	$13.22	$13.37	$13.53	$13.78	$13.78
Operating expenses:						
Variable expenses	1.02	1.04	1.05	1.06	1.08	1.08
Fixed expenses	3.11	3.21	3.33	3.44	3.56	3.56
Total	4.13	4.25	4.38	4.50	4.64	4.64
Net operating income	8.92	8.97	8.99	9.03	9.13	$9.13
Capital expenses:						
Leasing commissions	0.52	0.54	0.54	0.55	0.55	
Tenant improvements	1.04	1.07	1.07	1.11	1.11	
Other	0.31	0.32	0.33	0.34	0.36	
Total	1.87	1.93	1.94	2.00	2.02	
Reversionary capitalization rate						.09
Net cash flow and reversionary proceeds	$7.06	$7.04	$7.05	$7.02	$7.11	$101.48

Summary assumptions:

Initial purchase price	$100.00
Going-in capitalization rate	8.75%
Going-out capitalization rate	9.00%

Results:

Expected annual growth in cash flow	0.47%
Expected annual rate of return	7.31%

Note: Numbers may not add due to rounding.

3. Scenario analysis.
4. Monte Carlo simulation.

The difficulty with the historical relationships is the potential naive extension of historical statistics into the future, which runs contrary to the notions of the inevitability of change, investor fads, and so on.

While the factor models rely extensively on history, fundamental, scenario, and Monte Carlo analyses rely on forecasting to reflect the uncertain nature of future asset returns. The difficulty with these approaches is that their accuracy is only as good as the user's capabili-

EXHIBIT 25–20 **Probability 5% (Falling Market/High Inflation): Hypothetical Market Pro Forma**

	Market Cash Flow Projections					Reversionary Proceeds
	Year 1	Year 2	Year 3	Year 4	Year 5	End of Year 5
Potential rent	$15.97	$16.92	$18.01	$19.08	$20.21	$20.21
Occupancy	84.5%	83.5%	82.0%	81.0%	80.5%	80.5%
Net rent	$13.49	$14.13	$14.77	$15.45	$16.27	$16.27
Operating expenses:						
Variable expenses	1.06	1.11	1.16	1.21	1.28	1.28
Fixed expenses	3.21	3.43	3.68	3.93	4.21	4.21
Total	4.27	4.54	4.84	5.14	5.49	5.49
Net operating income	9.23	9.58	9.94	10.31	10.79	$10.79
Capital expenses:						
Leasing commissions	0.54	0.57	0.57	0.61	0.61	
Tenant improvements	1.07	1.14	1.14	1.23	1.23	
Other	0.32	0.34	0.37	0.39	0.42	
Total	1.93	2.05	2.08	2.23	2.26	
Reversionary capitalization rate						.09
Net cash flow and reversionary proceeds	$7.30	$7.52	$7.85	$8.08	$8.53	$119.84

Summary assumptions:
Initial purchase price $100.00
Going-in capitalization rate 8.75%
Going-out capitalization rate 9.00%

Results:
Expected annual growth in cash flow 4.17%
Expected annual rate of return 10.98%

Note: Numbers may not add due to rounding.

ties and are subject to arbitrariness in the selection of the scenarios, weights, distributions, and so on.

Having completed several approaches, the portfolio manager must now determine the best inputs to use to create the efficient frontier. This compares to the "mosaic" approach used by security analysts and the three approaches to value (cost, market, and income) reconciliation used by real estate appraisers. It is at this point that judgment must come into play in the selection of the inputs, or range of inputs, to derive the efficient frontier. It is hoped, however, that portfolio managers, through the completion of each approach and the thought process that accompanies it, will have gained additional knowledge and insight that will enhance their ability to select the

EXHIBIT 25–21

Computation of Expected Return and Standard Deviation for Hypothetical Market Segment

Market Conditions	Inflation Rate	Expected Return	Estimated Probability of Occurrence	Weighted Expected Probability Return	Deviation from the Mean	Squared Deviations	Estimated Probability of Occurrence	Weighted Squared Probability Deviations
Rising	Low	13.0%	20.0%	2.61%	1.91%	0.0365%	20.0%	0.0073%
Rising	High	16.9	5.0	0.84	5.76	0.3319	5.0	0.0166
Steady	Low	10.6	40.0	4.22	−0.56	0.0031	40.0	0.0012
Steady	High	14.3	10.0	1.43	3.22	0.1037	10.0	0.0104
Falling	Low	7.3	20.0	1.46	−3.81	0.1451	20.0	0.0290
Falling	High	11.0	5.0	0.55	−0.14	0.0002	5.0	0.0000
			100.0%	11.12% Mean			100.0%	0.0645% Variance

2.54% Standard deviation

1039

best inputs. Thus, the process of completing multiple approaches and reconciliation has the benefit of forcing a more explicit thought process, which should enhance the selection of the portfolio optimization inputs.

Other Optimization (MPT) Related Problems

In addition to the limitations and difficulties of each approach, at least two other MPT problems merit discussion. First, the results of MPT-generated efficient frontiers also depend on the classification scheme used (i.e., market segments). As the classification of market segments is not an exact science, the portfolio manager risks classifying them too broadly or too narrowly. Too broad a classification system will mask important (risk reduction) differences in the portfolio, while too narrow a classification system may result in an overly cumbersome analytical process. Second, the nature of the portfolio optimization process is such that if two assets offer nearly identical mean/variance characteristics but one is slightly more attractive, the optimization process will place a very large portfolio allocation on the one asset that is slightly more attractive to the virtual exclusion of the other asset. However, common sense tells us that the uncertainty of the inputs for both assets makes it foolish to make such a dominant allocation to one asset at the expense of another offering nearly identical but slightly less attractive characteristics.

We have now completed the second step in the real estate portfolio management process. We began by examining market efficiency and portfolio management approaches. We then identified the real estate investment universe and partitioned (or, segmented) it into manageable, fairly homogeneous clusters. Each cluster (or, market segment) was then examined for its risk/return characteristics through the use of various analytical tools and approaches. Finally, these results were compared, contrasted, and then reconciled with the practioner's judgments in order to arrive at the inputs needed to optimize a portfolio using MPT (i.e., to create the efficient frontier).

TARGET PORTFOLIO DETERMINATION

We began our portfolio management process by defining the investor's investment objectives and constraints. We then analyzed the real estate market conditions and expectations and derived the input estimates (i.e., expected return, standard deviation, and correlations) using several different approaches for each market segment and, through a reconciliation process, derived an efficient frontier. We are now ready to integrate these two fundamental aspects, investor needs and market conditions, into a target portfolio. The target portfolio and how it is determined is the topic of this section.

Exhibit 25–22 graphically depicts the integration of the investor's investment objectives and constraints (represented by investor risk-return indifference curves) and market conditions and expectations (represented by the efficient frontier). The investor's risk-return indifference curves are combinations of expected returns and standard deviations (risk) to which the investor is indifferent. Investors prefer higher indifference curves, as they offer greater utility (i.e., for any given risk, a higher indifference curve provides a higher return). In addition, the investor's risk-return indifference curves are upward

EXHIBIT 25–22
Target "Optimal" Portfolio Selection

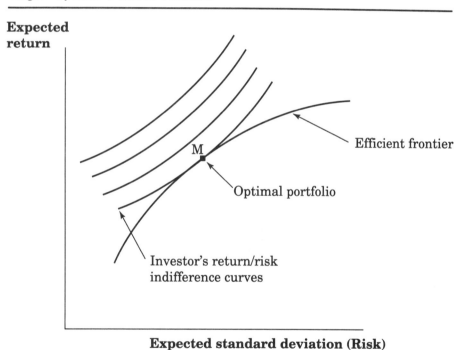

sloping to reflect the need for expected return to grow rapidly to offset increasing risk.

The tangential intersection of the investor's risk-return indifference curve and the efficient curve, at the optimal point M, represents the portfolio allocation that provides the investor with the greatest possible utility. Point M represents an exact market segment allocation. For example, if property type market segment were being allocated, it might represent a 15 percent office, 20 percent retail, 25 percent industrial, and 40 percent apartment portfolio allocation. However, to account for the uncertainty of forecasting the inputs for the efficient frontier along with the investor's objectives and constraints, allocation ranges are used to both reflect this uncertainty and provide the flexibility needed to properly manage property-level investment decisions.

Exhibits 25–23 and 25–24 show allocation ranges by both property type and economic region and a hypothetical portfolio's current allocation to each of these market segments. These allocation ranges

EXHIBIT 25–23
Hypothetical Property Type Allocation Ranges

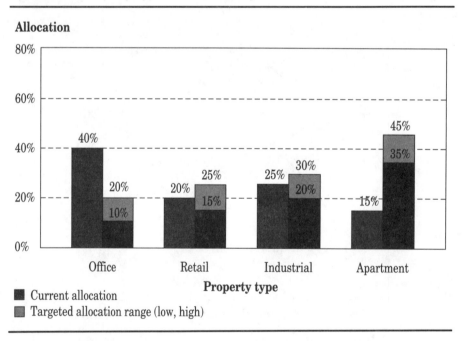

Allocation

■ Current allocation
▨ Targeted allocation range (low, high)

EXHIBIT 25–24
Hypothetical Economic Region Allocation Ranges

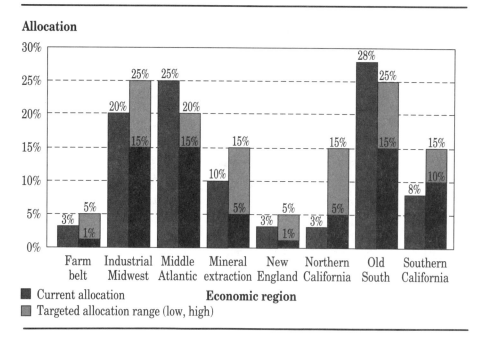

now become the guidepost the investor/portfolio manager uses when making individual property-level investment decisions. For example, from Exhibit 25–23, we can see that the hypothetical current portfolio is substantially overallocated in office and substantially underallocated in apartment, while falling within the allocation range for retail and industrial. From Exhibit 25–24, we can see that the hypothetical current portfolio is overallocated in the Middle Atlantic and Old South and underallocated in Northern and Southern California, while falling within the desired ranges for the remaining economic regions.

By taking the hypothetical portfolio example depicted in Exhibits 25–23 and 25–24 (the initial repositioning of an existing portfolio) a step further, the investor/portfolio manager now faces a very practical set of problems, specifically, the balancing of the property's existing position in the market (e.g., leasing, capital improvements, property management changes) and the market's position within its investment cycle (i.e., peak to trough to peak) within the target portfolio's designated allocation ranges. This is an important balance, because if the investor/portfolio manager allows the portfolio to stray too far from the designated allocation ranges, he or she runs the risks of losing the return, risk, and diversification benefits of the target portfolio. Likewise, if the investor/portfolio manager does not maintain an understanding of properties and the markets in which they are located, the portfolio runs the risk of generating lower returns due to an inopportune time for property sales. This balance is determined and then executed as part of the portfolio strategy determination, our next step.

PORTFOLIO STRATEGY DETERMINATION

Once the target portfolio is identified, the investor/portfolio manager must develop a portfolio strategy that will be consistent with the allocation ranges of the target portfolio and the current and expected conditions of properties in the portfolio.

If the first three steps of the portfolio management process have been completed diligently, the broad goals of the portfolio strategy should have become readily apparent (return, risk, diversification, liquidity, financing, etc.). However, the challenge now becomes translating these broad goals to be both definable and measurable. If, for example, the investor/portfolio manager has an internal real estate organization, the acquisition, asset/property management, and disposition groups will each require this translation to take place. For this type of real estate organization, Exhibit 25–25 depicts the process by which the target portfolio is translated into a single portfolio strategy and then into sub-strategies for each of the firm's functional disciplines.

It is essential that the development of each functional group's strategy be completed in conjunction with the functional group that will be responsible for its execution (i.e., an interactive, team approach). By not doing so, the investor/portfolio manager runs the risk that the functional disciplines will lack commitment and/or "buy-in" to the implementation strategy proposed. Furthermore, he or she will also miss out on a needed reality check by the individuals in the firm with the best knowledge of property and market conditions.

Each functional group's strategy thus becomes the document that communicates portfolio goals and objectives and establishes benchmarks and performance measurements, thereby providing the framework for motivating and rewarding the organization. For example,

EXHIBIT 25–25
Portfolio Strategy Determination

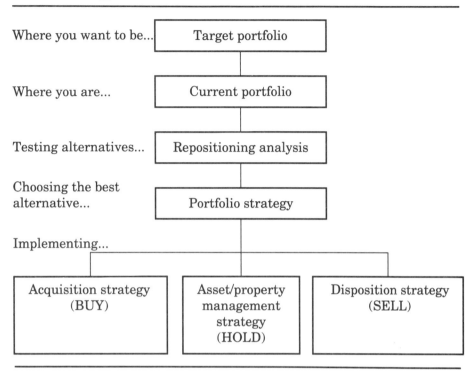

the acquisition strategy would outline acquisition goals and objectives for each portfolio (e.g., property type, location, size, age, lease structure, financing), and the performance of the acquisition group would be measured on its ability to acquire properties with these characteristics and perform as underwritten. The asset/property strategy would outline the goals and objectives for the property (market and property risk analysis, leasing objectives and guidelines, operating and capital budget, etc.). Likewise, the disposition strategy would outline the goals and objectives for the sale of properties.

For the real estate public market (i.e., REIT) investor/portfolio manager, the implementation and execution of the portfolio strategy are much simpler and more straightforward. Typically, they entail the placement and execution of a trade, which can be accomplished, depending on the liquidity of the issue, in a few minutes to a few days.

MONITORING AND REBALANCING

The concept of and need for monitoring and rebalancing goes to the very root of portfolio management. It acknowledges that the only certainty is that things will change in unexpected ways. Consequently, even the most passive investment management styles require some monitoring and rebalancing.

Monitoring and rebalancing also introduce the dimension of time into the portfolio management process. The portfolio management steps discussed thus far (investor objectives and constraints, market conditions and expectations, target portfolio determination, and portfolio strategy determination) are completed by analyzing all available information as of a point in time. The introduction of monitoring and rebalancing converts the portfolio management process from this static snapshot into a continuous, dynamic process.

This section provides a very general overview of monitoring and rebalancing. It begins with a definition and discussion of both monitoring and rebalancing, then touches on the cost of rebalancing, and concludes by examining the psychology involved in this process.

Definitions

Monitoring is the act, or process, of analyzing and understanding change and its potential impact on the performance of the portfolio. The monitoring process is represented graphically in Exhibit 25–4. That exhibit clearly shows that the monitoring process focuses on the two inputs into the portfolio management process: investor objectives/constraints and market conditions/expectations. These two inputs, knowledge of the investor and knowledge of the market, come together to determine the most appropriate target portfolio and portfolio implementation strategy.

Monitoring is also the reason we view the portfolio management process as dynamic. Essentially, monitoring captures the dynamics of change. What should be monitored for the investor? Recall the categories contained in the investment policy: portfolio size, return requirements, risk tolerance, liquidity, time horizon, and tax and legal considerations. In more technical terms, monitoring for the investor should include anything that affects the shape of the investor's risk-return preference indifference curves and their tangential intersection with the efficient frontier (see Exhibit 25–22). What should be monitored for market conditions and expectations? Recall the potential risk factors listed in Exhibit 25–9. All of these have the potential to change the risk-return trade-off for each market segment, which in effect will change the shape and composition of the efficient frontier. If conditions and/or expectations change significantly enough, the investor/portfolio manager will initiate a rebalancing of the portfolio.

Rebalancing is the process of modifying the assets within the portfolio to make them better fit the changing needs of the investor and market conditions and expectations. Rebalancing can take one of three forms: (1) allocation changes between market segments (e.g., Chicago office to Atlanta retail), (2) category or emphasis changes in a market segment (e.g., regional malls to power centers), and (3) selling a property and replacing it with another of like kind. The determination of when to rebalance and when to hold tight with the current portfolio is the operative question. To help us understand when rebalancing is worthwhile, we now introduce the concepts of rebalancing costs and psychological factors.

Rebalancing Costs

The cost of rebalancing a portfolio can take the form of trading or not trading. The costs of not trading include (1) holding onto a property that is overpriced (i.e., $V_0 < M_0$) and/or (2) holding onto a property that no longer fit the needs of the investor (e.g., changing risk tolerance). The costs of trading include (1) commissions and associated fees and (2) the impact on the market, where the impact is very difficult to measure.

Although all of the costs of rebalancing a portfolio are important, depending on the market one is trading in, they are not all equal. For example, selling and purchasing private market equity properties are expensive and time-consuming endeavors. Trading costs range from 100 to 700 basis points, depending on the size and complexity of the transaction. However, public market equity transactions (i.e., REITs) are more in line with other equity trades in the capital markets. Also, although they are just becoming available in the real estate equity market, derivatives provide an inexpensive way to change the return, risk, and diversification dynamics of a portfolio (see Chapter 27, "Application of Derivative Instruments").

Psychology of Portfolio Rebalancing

The psychology of the portfolio rebalancing decision can have a powerful impact on what the investor/portfolio manager does. In the uncertain world of investments, it is all too easy to make rebalancing decisions based on emotions and the latest investor fad. Furthermore, the investor/portfolio manager may be influenced by the portfolio rebalancing decisions of others (i.e., the herd mentality) if the portfolio is managed in a fiduciary context. The reason for this is the fiduciary constraints the portfolio manager may be required to follow (recall ERISA's "prudent man" rule). Therefore, given the substantial costs of rebalancing an equity real estate portfolio, the investor/portfolio manager must always be certain that portfolio rebalancing is being executed not for psychological reasons but for sound, fundamental reasons. Otherwise, the result is needless erosion of returns by transaction costs.

Monitoring and rebalancing are costly and time-consuming endeavors that require the dedication of the entire organization. While each firm will have its own particular method or process, the suggested approach (and theme of this chapter) is the creation, integration, and implementation of a systematic and disciplined portfolio management process. Through a disciplined approach, one moves from being overly influenced by the latest event(s) and fads to a framework that helps to identify and systematically measure how the investor and the market have fundamentally changed. Monitoring and rebalancing then become a natural part of this disciplined process.

PORTFOLIO PERFORMANCE MEASUREMENT

How skillful was the portfolio manager? Did the portfolio manager meet the investor's objectives? Were the time and resources spent on analyzing market conditions and expectations, determining the target portfolio, and completing property analysis worthwhile? More specifically, in what areas did the portfolio manager perform well, and what areas need improvement? To answer these questions, the investor/portfolio manager needs an objective means to assess the portfolio's performance.

This section provides an overview of portfolio measurement by briefly discussing (1) the ways a portfolio manager can add value, (2) return measures, and (3) performance attribution.

Adding Value

Active portfolio management can add value, via excess risk-adjusted returns, to the portfolio in one of three ways: market allocation (timing), property selection, and diversification. In essence, portfolio managers are measured on their ability to provide these three functions.

Market allocation is the percentage of the portfolio invested in each market segment (property types, economic regions, etc). When the market allocation deviates from the benchmark portfolio, it is called *market timing*. The *benchmark portfolio* is an unmanaged, or passive, portfolio (e.g., Russell/NCREIF return series) with risk equal to that of the managed, or active, portfolio. When portfolio managers engage in market timing, they assume they can affect portfolio performance by identifying and acquiring (selling) properties in markets that are expected to out- or underperform the overall market on a risk-adjusted basis.

Property selection is the impact the properties owned (or selected) have on portfolio performance. Property selection assumes the portfolio manager can affect portfolio performance by acquiring (selling) properties that are expected to outperform (underperform) the overall market segment benchmark. Here the portfolio manager is being measured on the ability to identify mispriced properties within a market segment.

Finally, *diversification* measures how completely the portfolio is diversified compared to the market portfolio. The level of diversification is important, as portfolio theory states that investors are willing to pay only for systematic (market) risk. Consequently, the portfolio manager's return performance must be adjusted for risk to provide a proper portfolio performance comparison. The degree of portfolio diversification can be determined by comparing the return of the portfolio and the returns of the market portfolio. Perfect correlation means the portfolio is completely diversified (no unsystematic risk remains).

The measurement of market allocation and property selection will be discussed more fully in the section "Performance Attribution."

Return Measures

Return measures are either historical or forecast measures of performance. Historical returns are sometimes called *performance returns,* while forecast returns are often called *expected returns.* For purposes

EXHIBIT 25–26
Various Single-Period Return Measures

1. Russell/NCREIF

   Unleveraged

   $$R_{inc} = \frac{I_t}{MV_{t-1} + .5(CI_t - PS_t) - .33I_t}$$

   $$R_{app} = \frac{(MV_t - MV_{t-1}) + PS_t - CI_t}{MV_{t-1} + .5(CI_t - PS_t) - .33I_t}$$

   $$R_{total} = R_{inc} + R_{app}$$

   Where R_{inc} = Income return.
   R_{app} = Appreciation return.
   R_{total} = Total return.
   I_t = Income during period t.
   MV_{t-1} = Market value at beginning of period t.
   MV_t = Market value at end of period t.
   CI_t = Capital improvement in period t.
   PS_t = Partial sales during period t.

2. Cash-on-cash (average book cost)

   $$R_{CC.BC} = \frac{CF_t}{(BC_{t-1} + BC_t)/2}$$

   Where $R_{CC.BC}$ = Cash-on-cash return on book cost.
   CF_t = Cash flow during period t.
   BC_{t-1} = Book cost at beginning of period t.
   BC_t = Book cost at end of period t.

3. Cash-on-cash (market value)

   $$R_{CC.MV} = \frac{CF_t}{MV_{t-1}}$$

   Where $R_{CC.MV}$ = Cash-on-cash return on market value.
   CF_t = Cash flow during period t.
   MV_{t-1} = Market value at beginning of period t.

4. Capitalization rate (market value)

   $$R_{cap} = \frac{NOI_t}{MV_{t-1}}$$

   Where R_{cap} = Capitalization rate.
   NOI_t = Net operating income during period t.
   MV_{t-1} = Market value at beginning of period t.

1050

of portfolio measurement, performance returns are used. Performance returns can be determined for a single period or multiple periods.

Returns can also be calculated using one or more of several generally accepted alternative methodologies. Exhibit 25–26 summarizes several of the more commonly used single-period performance return measures: Russell/NCREIF unleveraged return, cash-on-cash (using average book cost), cash-on-cash (using market value), and capitalization rate.

Performance returns may also be either time weighted, or dollar weighted. *Time-weighted* returns are computed for each period, multiplied together across time, and then annualized to measure portfolio performance. The *dollar-weighted* return is an internal rate of return formula that solves for the return that equates the present value of the cash flows to the initial investment. Since dollar-weighted returns are affected by the size and timing of cash flows into and out of the portfolio over the holding period, time-weighted returns are used as a measure of portfolio performance because they are independent of the timing of significant cash flow into and out of the portfolio.

Performance Attribution

The goal of performance attribution is to identify the portfolio impact of the portfolio manager's allocation and property selection decisions. Following Brinson et al. (1986), Exhibit 25–27 provides an example of a hypothetical portfolio's performance as benchmarked against the Russell/NCREIF return series for each property type.

The allocation effect measures the impact of the portfolio allocation deviating from the benchmark portfolio. It is measured as the difference between the actual portfolio return and the benchmark portfolio return. In Exhibit 25–28, the market timing effect is computed to be −3.70 percent. Using the attribution grid, it becomes readily apparent that the portfolio manager's decision to be overweighted in office and underweighted in apartments, as compared to the benchmark portfolio, has caused a significant reduction in the portfolio's overall return.

The property selection effect measures the impact of the properties actually owned in comparison to the benchmark portfolios. It measures the sum of the difference between the actual portfolio market segment returns and the returns of the appropriate benchmark portfolio. In Exhibit 25–28, the property selection effect is computed to be 2.90 percent. This reflects the portfolio manager's superior abil-

EXHIBIT 25–27
Performance Attribution: Market Timing and Property Selection

		Property (security) selection	
		Active	Passive
Market timing	Active	I $\sum W_{a,i} R_{a,i}$	II $\sum W_{a,i} R_{p,i}$
	Passive	III $\sum W_{p,i} R_{a,i}$	IV $\sum W_{p,i} R_{p,i}$

		Active	Passive
Market timing	Active	I −4.05%	II −7.80%
	Passive	III −1.20%	IV −4.10%

I–IV   = *Returns to active management*
II–IV = *Returns to market timing*
III–IV = *Returns to security selection*

ity to acquire and manage office, warehouse, retail, and apartment properties and inferior ability to acquire and manage properties compared to the benchmark portfolio.

The importance of return attribution becomes apparent when comparing the overall return for both the active portfolio (−4.05 percent) and the passive (benchmark) portfolio (−4.10 percent). Without completing a return attribution grid, one would most likely conclude the portfolio manager performed at the level of the benchmark

EXHIBIT 25–28

Example—Performance Attribution: Market Timing and Property Selection

Market Segment (Property Type)	Market Index (Benchmark)	Portfolio Allocation		Property Returns		Return Types			
		Active(A)	Passive(B)	Active(C)	Passive(D)	I(A × C)	II(A × D)	III(B × C)	IV(B × D)
Office	Russell/NCREIF (office)	55%	35%	−11%	−15%	−6.05%	−8.25%	−3.85%	5.25%
Retail	Russell/NCREIF (retail)	20	25	3	6	0.60	1.20	0.75	1.50
Warehouse	Russell/NCREIF (warehouse)	20	15	6	−4	1.20	−0.80	0.90	−0.60
Apartment	Russell/NCREIF (apartment)	5	25	4	1	0.20	0.05	1.00	0.25
		100%	100%			−4.05%	−7.80%	−1.20%	−4.10%

Performance Attribution Results

Passive return (IV)	−4.10%
Effects of property selection (III–IV)	2.90
Effects of market timing (II–IV)	−3.70
Joint effects	0.85
Active return (I)	−4.05%
Effects of active management (I–IV)	0.05%

1053

portfolio and, consequently, would fail to obtain the additional insight and benefit of understanding how the underlying investment decisions affected the portfolio's performance.

THE ROLE OF THE PORTFOLIO MANAGER

Implicit in any discussion of the real estate portfolio management process is the role of the portfolio manager. The portfolio manager provides the energy, focus, discipline, and, most importantly, the investment decisions to make the portfolio management process a reality.

Exhibit 25–29 identifies the role of the portfolio manager as one of facilitator and communicator. More specifically, at each respective step of the portfolio management process, the portfolio manager:

1. *Identifies* the investor's objectives and constraints.

EXHIBIT 25–29
Portfolio Manager's Role as Facilitator, Communicator, and Monitor

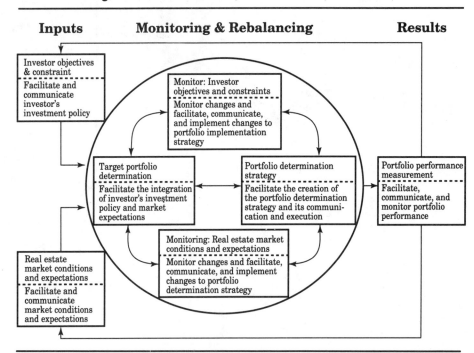

2. *Analyzes* market conditions to understand each market segment's expected return, risk, and correlations within the specified investable universe.

3. *Integrates* the investor's investment policy with market conditions and converts them into target portfolio allocation ranges.

4. *Creates* the portfolio strategy and *communicates* its goals and objectives to those responsible for its implementation.

5. *Monitors* the investor's investment objectives and constraints and market conditions, communicates these changes, and facilitates any necessary changes to the target portfolio and portfolio strategy.

6. *Measures* and *communicates* the portfolio's performance.

Moreover, the real estate investor/portfolio manager who invests in equity real estate directly, unlike the investor/portfolio manager for bonds and stocks, leads an organization and/or third-party vendors with direct management responsibilities for the properties. This requires that the portfolio manager also be an effective leader and manager. Recall Exhibit 25–7, which depicts an interactive top-down/bottom-up approach in which both approaches are interdependent. Thus, the success of the portfolio is inextricably linked to how well the portfolio manager can create a sense of mutually defined goals and esprit de corps with those responsible for implementing the real estate strategy.

CONCLUSION

This chapter attempted to show real estate portfolio management as a process, one that has individual functions (steps) that are interrelated and dynamic. The chapter began by discussing the inherent uncertainty in the market and consequent need for a disciplined portfolio management process. Then it described the industry's paradigm shift from an asset-by-asset view to a portfolio process view of investment decision making and the two market forces that act jointly to create this shift: (1) technology advances and modern portfolio theory and (2) the growth of institutional assets under a fiduciary framework.

The chapter then provided an overview of each of the six steps in the portfolio management process: (1) investor objectives and constraints, (2) real estate market conditions and expectations, (3) target portfolio determination, (4) portfolio strategy determination, (5) monitoring and rebalancing, and (6) portfolio performance measurement. Finally, the chapter discussed the role of the portfolio manager as one of communicator, implementor, monitor, and most important, investment decision maker.

As a final note, the only thing certain in the real estate market is the inevitability of change. The investor/portfolio manager thus needs to improve the chances of constructing, or repositioning, his or her real estate portfolio in anticipation of these changes. Without such a disciplined process, the investor/portfolio manager lacks the proper foundation and framework to analyze the ever-changing needs of the investor and market conditions and expectations. This chapter asserted that the best way to accomplish this is through creating, integrating, and implementing a systematic and disciplined portfolio management process.

REFERENCES

Association for Investment Management and Research. *Performance Reporting for Investment Managers: Applying the AIMR Performance Presentation Standards*. AIMR, 1991, p. 29.

Bodie, Zvi; Alex Kane, and Alan J. Marcus. *Investments*. Homewood, IL: Richard D. Irwin, 1989.

Booth, David G.; Daniel M. Cashdan, Jr.; and Richard A. Graff. "Real Estate: Hybrid of Debt and Equity." *Real Estate Review* 19 (Spring 1989), pp. 54–58.

Brinson, Gary; L. Hood; and G. Beebower. "Determinants of Portfolio Performance." *Financial Analysts Journal,* July/August 1986, pp. 38–44.

Ennis, Richard M., and Paul Burik. "The Influence of Non-Risk Factors on Real Estate Holdings of Pension Funds." *Financial Analysts Journal,* November–December 1991, pp. 44–55.

Firstenberg, Paul B.; Stephen A. Ross; and Randall C. Zisler. "Managing Real Estate Portfolios." *Real Estate Research,* November 16, 1987.

Firstenberg, Paul B., and Charles H. Wurtzebach. "Managing Portfolio Risk and Reward." *Real Estate Review* 19 (Summer 1989).

Fisher, Jeffrey; Susan Hudson-Wilson; and Charles Wurtzebach. "Equilibrium in Commercial Real Estate Markets: Linking Space and Capital Markets." *Journal of Portfolio Management,* Summer 1993, pp. 101–107.

Geltner, David Michael. "Smoothing in Appraisal-Based Returns." *Journal of Real Estate Finance and Economics* 4, no. 4 (September 1991), pp. 327–45.

Giliberto, S. Michael. *Thinking about Real Estate Risk*. New York: Salomon Brothers, Inc., May 26, 1989.

Giliberto, S. Michael. *Real Estate Risk and Return: 1991 Survey Results*. New York: Salomon Brothers, Inc., March 31, 1992.

Gold, Richard B. "Asset Allocation: The Importance of Uncertainty in Optimizing Illiquid Assets or Why the Efficient Frontier Is 'Fuzzy.'" Paper presented at the American Real Estate Society Conference, April 15, 1994.

Graff, Richard A., and Daniel M. Cashdan, Jr. "Some New Ideas in Real Estate Finance." *Journal of Applied Corporate Finance* 3 (Spring 1990), pp. 77–89.

Greig, D. Wylie, and Michael S. Young. "New Measures of Future Property Performance and Risk." *Real Estate Review* 21 (Spring 1991), pp. 17–25.

Hartzell, David; John Hekman; and Mike Miles. "Real Estate Returns and Inflation." *AREUEA Journal,* Spring 1987.

Hartzell, David; John Hekman; and Mike Miles. "Diversification Categories in Investment Real Estate." *AREUEA Journal,* Summer 1986.

Hartzell, David J.; David G. Shulman; and Charles H. Wurtzebach. "Refining the Analysis of Regional Diversification for Income-Producing Real Estate." *Journal of Real Estate Research* 2, no. 2 (Winter 1987), pp. 85–95.

Levine, Sumner N., ed. *The Financial Analyst's Handbook*. Homewood, IL: Business One Irwin, 1988.

Liang, Youguo; F. C. Neil Myer; and James R. Webb. "The Bootstrap Efficient Frontier for Mixed-Asset Portfolios." Paper presented at the American Real Estate Society Conference, April 15, 1994.

Maginn, John L., and Donald L. Tuttle, eds. *Managing Investment Portfolios: A Dynamic Process*. Boston/New York: Warren, Gorham & Lamont, 1990.

Miles, Mike, and Tom McCue. "Commercial Real Estate Returns." *AREUEA Journal,* Fall 1984.

Pagliari, Joseph L., Jr. "Inside the Real Estate Yield." *Real Estate Review* 21, no. 3 (Fall 1991), pp. 48–53.

Pagliari, Joseph L., Jr., and James R. Webb. "Past and Future Sources of Real Estate Research." *Journal of Real Estate Research* 7, no. 4 (Fall 1992), pp. 387–421.

Reilly, Frank K. *Investment Analysis and Portfolio Management*. Fort Worth, TX: The Dryden Press, 1989.

Shulman, David, and Robert E. Hopkins. *Economic Diversification in Real Estate Portfolios*. New York: Salomon Brothers Real Estate Research, November 1988.

Webb, James R., and Jack H. Rubens. "The Effect of Alternative Return Measures on Restricted Mixed-Asset Portfolios." *Journal of the American Real Estate and Urban Economics Association* 16 (Summer 1988).

White, John Robert, ed. *The Office Building from Concept to Investment Reality.* Joint Publication of the Counselors of Real Estate, the Appraisal Institute, and the Society of Industrial and Office Realtors Educational Fund, 1993.

Zisler, Randall, and Robert A. Feldman. *Real Estate Report.* New York: Goldman Sachs & Co., 1985.

CHAPTER 12

INTERNATIONAL REAL ESTATE INVESTMENT: A REALISTIC LOOK AT THE ISSUES

Helen R. Arnold
Jones Lang Wootton USA

Charles Grossman
Jones Lang Wootton Realty Advisors

INTRODUCTION

The last decade has seen the accelerated perception and acceptance of the international economic linkages that influence and constrain the American economy. Trade deficits, European and Asian investment in both real estate and major U.S. corporations, and concerns over the competitive impact of international trading blocs have all contributed to this heightened awareness. Unlike the increasing portion of international stock and bond portfolios of U.S. investors, and unlike the very substantial real estate holdings of many giant U.S.-based corporations, investment real estate has not yet become a significant component of U.S.—or, indeed, North American—institutional investor portfolios.

The late 1980s and early 1990s marked a burgeoning interest in possible international real estate investment by U.S. institutions for a variety of reasons. The weight of the evidence presented in the U.S. technical literature of the 1980s emphasized that real estate in a portfolio could enhance overall performance by increasing returns and reducing portfolio volatility, since it tended to perform inversely with U.S. stocks and bonds.[1] Moreover, the results of past return

---

[1] Earlier chapters, particularly Chapter 2, of this book provide references to the evolving technical literature.

530

histories indicated that international diversification paid off in the stock and bond arena.

The technical literature on long-term return results notwithstanding, the poor performance of U.S. real estate from 1987 to 1992 (shown vividly in the Russell/NCREIF index results) detracted from the allure of U.S. real estate as an investment just as many institutional investors had begun to increase the real estate portion of their portfolios. Consequently, investors questioned their previous assumptions about U.S. real estate as a viable investment. The flood of capital into real estate construction raised concerns about the possible recurrence of such an unusually long construction cycle; the difficulty of selling underperforming real estate heightened concerns about real estate's relatively illiquid nature; and the prospect of a long period of low inflation reduced the appeal of real estate as an inflation hedge. However, all of the above were good reasons for investors to ask whether or not international real estate investment could offer the benefit of reducing the volatility of the domestic real estate portfolio.

Economic expectations for the United States relative to the rest of the world in the 1990s also played a part in this increasing interest. The United States, burdened by public and private sector debt, was expected to suffer from an undersupply of capital available for economic expansion. The early economic forecasts for Europe in the 1990s—the economic speculation over EC '92—were for much higher rates of economic growth than those predicted for the United States. The Pacific Rim locations also seemed to offer the possibility of much higher rates of economic growth. Although there has been less publicity in the United States about the positive effects of EC '92 since the change of regimes in Eastern Europe and more discussion about the impact of potential capital shortages on worldwide development, many of the measures for European business and economic unification quietly moved forward throughout 1992 and 1993.

This institutional investor curiosity about international real estate investment has perforce remained primarily in the realm of potential action rather than followed up by a flood of investment. International real estate investment does present considerable decision-making, organizational, and managerial challenges above and beyond the problems of achieving the desired cash flows at the building level. Some of these problems would be inherent in the choice of this investment medium in any case, but they are accentuated by the time-distance gap from the United States and different socioeconomic and cultural structures associated with individual national markets.

Therefore, there is a need for a concentrated scrutiny of the problems and opportunities in international real estate investment, a scrutiny of the managerial issues an organization may face in making the decision to invest abroad and implementing that decision, as well as of the evidence available to help make such a decision. This chapter is written for the U.S. investor who is particularly interested in how various other institutional investors have approached the decision process, the quantitative evidence they have used to bolster their decisions, the criteria for the decisions, and the best mode of implementation. This generic approach is drawn from our experience with offshore institutions that have initiated this process in the last decade, when more rigorous decision procedures have become the mode in most organizations. This chapter attempts to bridge some gaps between theory and practice by providing some statistics on returns and portfolio volatility in an international real estate portfolio and evaluating the limits and actual use of such information to date.

THE DECISION PROCESS AND ITS REQUIREMENTS

The approach international institutional investors take to either their initial worldwide investment strategy or their updates and re-evaluations of worldwide real estate investment strategy follows a familiar pattern. Typically, the investor creates a working group of senior real estate officers, often in combination with international in-house equities experts and outside consultants, including economists, real estate experts, and tax and legal advisors. The working group has the assignment of determining whether or not international real estate investment has the appropriate risk-reward configuration for the investor and, if so, the overall strategy and subsequent managerial tactics to pursue. Each outside advisor is usually commissioned to report on his or her area of expertise. If we consider the roster of advisors in conceptual terms, it is heavily weighted toward those who can explain and minimize the systematic risks involved.

A major time cost is involved even in the initial decision to examine the feasibility of international real estate investment, given the requirements of fiduciary responsibility. Designated senior staff must become sufficiently familiar with all of the elements involved in reaching that decision, since ultimately it is this staff who must determine the rank ordering of criteria for country and market selection and live with the selection.

The conceptual complexities become readily apparent when one considers the difficulties of selecting the countries and the real estate markets within those countries. The problem entails

- Identifying the pertinent variables by which countries and local markets can be compared.
- Determining whether the characteristics of countries as a whole, as opposed to variables pertaining to a single market, have the greatest primacy in weighting a selection.
- Applying comparison and rank ordering, thus narrowing down the universe of nations to a small and numerically manageable sample that can then be studied in more detail.

In an abbreviated format (see Exhibit 12–1), country and local market variables can be conceived of as macro and micro issues. The macro issues conceptually relate to reducing systematic risks for portfolio allocation across particular nations. By extension, international diversification should reduce a portfolio's systematic risk, especially if that portfolio was previously composed of assets principally from one nation. The micro issues are more oriented toward those items that determine unsystematic risk. Exhibit 12–1 identifies some of these elements, both those easily quantified and those not so easily quantified. These variables are discussed more extensively in the following section.

An All-Encompassing, Systematic Approach

A common approach for first-time international investors is to utilize, with the advice of experts, a limited number of macroeconomic or political variables and select somewhat arbitrary performance cutoff points as benchmarks that serve to retain or eliminate nations. These variables can be static descriptors (size of market, per capita income, type of government) and/or trend descriptors (growth rates, frequency of change in the political party in power). Then, having reduced the investment universe to anywhere from 10 to 30 nations, the urban market selection process begins, following a somewhat similar methodology but with much greater emphasis on actual return performance.

EXHIBIT 12–1
Overview of Market Variables

Macro	Micro
National economic cycles (prices, GDP, debt, savings, household income, currency fluctuations, alternative asset returns)	Local/regional real estate returns
	Suppy/demand/vacancy rate/ absorption trends
Political stability (changing of reigning party, frequency of elections, leadership tenure, strikes)	Local economy
	Socio/political issues operating locally
Social stability (demographics, ethnic violence, popular violence or unrest, crime, etc.)	Property market structures: local planning, local companies available for management, transaction costs
Organizational/bureaucratic structures	Leasing market: lease terms and conditions
Financial system structure	
Property market structures and stability: planning, law, mode of transactions	
National real estate returns	
Political and consumer psychology and culture	

Source: JLW USA Research.

A Past Knowledge and Intuition Approach

In the case of investors with an ongoing program, those with considerable knowledge of multiple nations, or those with strong opinions, it is common to discover a selection process that moves immediately to certain urban markets and property types. Some international investors have been engaged in multination real estate investment for so long that they consciously view the world as one large economic system wherein major metropolitan areas constitute significant regional economies. National political changes and bureaucratic regulations are then simply different rules in the local game, which can be dealt with through the appropriate tax and legal advice. The focus then becomes the urban economy and local real estate market trends.

A Problem Common to Both Approaches

Above all, in the case of international real estate investors, institutional investors wish to see the kind of risk-return analysis to which they have become accustomed in the equity and fixed-income markets, in other words, the returns, standard deviations on returns, correlation coefficients, and covariances necessary to determine the impact of a new investment on a portfolio and to create the optimal portfolio. The basic premise for international investment very much rests on assumptions about reducing the variability of real estate portfolio returns. However, demonstrating the validity of those assumptions from a comparison of past return trends is formidably difficult because of the extremely mixed quality of real estate return information from the individual nations. This is easily comprehensible when one considers that the Russell/NCREIF index in the United States, a nation generally considered to be at the forefront of statistical collection and analysis, began as recently as 1978. The United Kingdom is generally considered to have the longest-running return indices comparable to the Russell/NCREIF index, and these date only to the late 1960s. By comparison, stock price data and indices in the United States have been compiled from the mid-19th century to the present.

UNDERSTANDING COUNTRY RISKS: WEIGHTING ECONOMIC AND POLITICAL/ ORGANIZATIONAL SYSTEMS

Before turning to an analysis of the evidence available on international real estate investment returns, it is useful to discuss in more detail some aspects of the way the all-encompassing systematic approach has been applied. In general, investors and their advisors are very good at identifying ways to use economic criteria to narrow down the countries to a manageable number but less accomplished at looking at the political/organizational patterns of systematic risk that may affect foreign real estate markets. Yet United States institutional investors are extremely concerned about political/organizational risk, and this aspect of international investment deserves special attention.

Some of the most common variables in the initial winnowing process used to determine the economic desirability of a nation are gross domestic product (GDP) per capita, percentage of GDP devoted to service industries, and/or per capita income. In all instances of the above, the higher, the better.

Many pitfalls lurk for the unwary investor attempting to compare multinational economic data, including the following:

- Although a national statistic may have the same name from one nation to another, it may not always be calculated or collected in the same manner.
- Concepts and/or statistics relatively unfamiliar to an American may appear and be interpreted wrongly; conversely, information that Americans automatically expect may not be available.
- Many nations are from one to three years behind in the tabulation of their national statistics. Consequently, "current" data obtained from data sellers may actually be a forecast rather than actual current information.

These issues may seem to be the kinds of problems that would crop up when dealing primarily with the lesser developed countries. Such is not the case, as anyone familiar with comparing European economic statistics may discover. Definitions published by the European Union have to be read with considerable care. For example, one of the most interesting, and frustrating concepts in the European lexicon is the one that refers to *consumption* on a national and per capita basis. Most European nations lack retail sales data and usually lack the kind of income data that are collected in the United States. The consumption data do reflect the growth in the demand for goods and services, but they are not a direct comparable for either U.S. retail sales or income.[2]

Nations such as Greece and Italy have well-known problems in the collection and tabulation of their data. Publications comparing annual European data usually have almost a three-year lag in the current quality of the data. A five-year forecast, then, may actually

---

[2] See, for example, *Eurostate: Regions: Statistical Yearbook* (Luxembourg: Office des publications officielles des communautés européennes), which is hardly annual.

be a seven-to-eight-year forecast because of the data gap. Compiling detailed time series on localized markets can also prove to be a problem, because certain nations (Greece among them again) periodically destroy their census information or surveys for reasons of confidentiality. Statistics from Eastern Europe are notoriously unreliable or biased, and presumably it may be some time before calculation methodologies are routinized.

If nothing else, these differences emphasize that an economist experienced in comparing national economies should be included in the decision process. There still remains the issue of whittling down the nations to a manageable "short list." It is, in fact, relatively easy to reduce the investment universe through the application of gross economic criteria to a list of some 30 countries. It is much more difficult to reduce that list of 30 to a short list of 5 to 10 countries, because then the investor usually scrutinizes the interrelationships among economic variables more closely and faces some difficult economic trade-offs. Typical statistics used for comparison at this stage include the savings ratio, corporate profitability, the debt-GDP ratio, household or per capita consumption, aggregate value of real estate construction, and inflation trends.

For example, a U.S. investor would probably wish to select investment locations whose basic economic cycle (measured by annual percentage change in GDP or some variation of employment growth) has been as countercyclical as possible to that of the United States. But it is questionable whether this should outweigh, for example, the importance of variables that measure the highest economic growth rates and, by extension, the expansion in demand for real estate. Even among future growth forecasts, it may be difficult to decide the appropriate level of weighting for each variable. To illustrate the differences that have appeared in rank ordering among important economic variables, Exhibit 12–2 provides forecast rankings that were tabulated in a 20-nation comparison done in early 1991.

Consider the issue of national debt, which is commonly held to be a drag on economic growth. A number of nations have fairly solid rankings in forecasts for the economic growth components noted in Exhibit 12–2 and therefore seem to be desirable locations for investment. Yet some of these nations also have a high level of public debt in relation to their GDP. Belgium, Italy, and Austria are examples of countries ranking high in the economic forecasts but having a high level of public debt. Exhibit 12–3 compares statistics on government

EXHIBIT 12–2
Rank Ordering of Forecast Growth Rates (20-Nation Study)

Real GDP Growth, 1990–94	Export Growth Forecast	Productivity Growth
Singapore	Hong Kong	Finland
Spain	Singapore	Norway
Hong Kong	United States	Italy
Germany	Spain	Belgium
Austria	Austria	France
(U.S.: 17th)		(U.S.: 12th)

Source: JLW U.K. Consulting and Research.

EXHIBIT 12–3
Government Debt as a Proportion of GDP, 1990

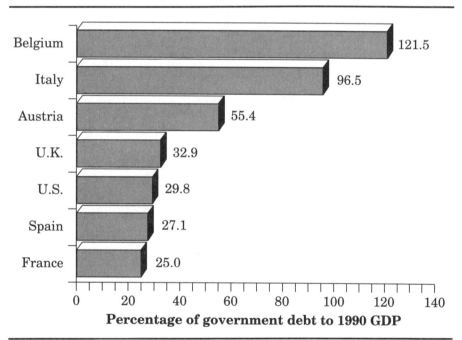

Sources: OECD, *Economic Outlook,* June 1990; JLW Consulting and Research.

debt as a proportion of GDP among various European economies and the United States.

The complicated interplay of politics and economics is reflected in any study of changing European national economic forecasts. In mid-1990, forecasts for European GDP growth rates produced by the European Community and private forecasters were extremely high; some nations were expected to see 4 to 7 percent per year growth. In the last three years, these forecasts have been drastically altered downward under the impact of recession, the slowdown in expectations for monetary union, and the economic drag expected from the diversion of resources to Eastern Europe.

A special comment should be made here about currency risk. Currency fluctuations can be treated like any other contributor to economic risk, and the volatility of nations' currencies against the dollar can be quantified and included as one of the "macro" risk elements in country comparisons. Unlike many other macro risk measures, when past real estate returns are being compared at the micro market level, the impact of currency fluctuations on real estate returns can be precisely quantified, if necessary. But in practice, international institutions seem to have been less concerned about currency risk in their decision analysis than they have been about other economic and real estate indicators. These institutions have hedging programs that apply across investments; moreover, the tax and legal structures chosen for investment often dictate the mode in which income returns can be converted or moved across national boundaries.

The Ideal Model

In an ideal research world, the results of multivariate models, with past real estate returns as the dependent variable and economic factors as the independent variables, would determine how each economic variable in the short-list comparison should be weighted. Unfortunately, the data required to construct such a model are rarely available (more on this below), and accordingly a "good fit" among the variables proves to be illusive. Moreover, even if an accurate historical model were to be created, there would be no assurance that past relationships would remain constant in the future; a forecasting model would be required. Lacking such models, the weighting attached to each economic factor is created by each investor and his or her advisors, sometimes using subjective criteria and sometimes using results drawn from other experiences.

Aspects of Political/Organizational Risk

Quantitative weights are rarely assigned to political factors in the real estate decision literature, but the literature applying quantitative techniques to a comparison of national political systems is extensive. It is possible only to highlight here certain approaches that could assist the U.S. institutional investor. These concepts assist in understanding fundamental political risks that would most heavily affect a long-term investment program. Exhibit 12–4 provides a very broad summary of the kinds of measures that quantitatively oriented social scientists use in measuring and rank ordering political volatility and organizational characteristics. The items listed under "political stability" have been the subject of extended quantitative analysis, and they are particularly useful if the investor is interested in locations other than the larger and more familiar Western European economies.

Generally, U.S. investors are most interested in the duration of governments (which generally implies stability of policy), orderly transitions between regimes, and the actual stability of economic policies pertaining to matters such as property rights and foreign

EXHIBIT 12–4
Measures of Political/Organizational Risk

Political Stability

Average durability of governments
Government effectiveness (in democracies, existence of a voting majority)
Length of tenure of major leaders
Party fractionalization
Strikes (per year, per capita)
Riots (citizens out of control destroying property)
Deaths by political violence

Bureaucratic/Managerial Behavior

Role focus (technician, advocate, broker, policymaker)
Approach to policy analysis
Attitude toward state involvement
Ideology applied to role

investment regulations and taxation. Contemplating political risks in international investment may involve rethinking some preconceptions about the stability of the United States itself vis à vis other nations and about what constitutes acceptable levels of political risk relative to potential return.

For example, duration of governments and maintenance of effective voting majorities are easily measured in years or months and compared. The United States is generally perceived by its citizens as an extremely stable regime, but when compared with the patterns of other industrial democracies, it has medium durability and a low voter participation in elections, which is ordinarily not considered consistent with high political stability.[3] Length of tenure of major leaders can also be examined. Leadership is more volatile in Latin America, North America, Europe, and Australia than in Africa, the Middle East, and Asia. Very high leadership turnover occurs in France, Portugal, Italy, Greece, and Japan.[4] When political volatility is actually quantified, nations somewhat more "volatile" than the United States may actually prove to have acceptable systems, especially given the expected holding period for a potential real estate investment.

Political violence, whether endemic to the system or occurring mainly at the change of a regime, has been measured worldwide through analyzing strikes, riots, and terrorist incidents. For another comparison that may affect American preconceptions, in the higher-technology industrialized nations, strikes have declined in Belgium, the United Kingdom, Denmark, the Netherlands, Norway, and Sweden but hovered at constant levels in the United States and Canada. The decline in strikes happens to be correlated with the increasing fraction of the national income passing through and allocated by the public sector.[5]

Bureaucratic behavior has not been the subject of as much extensive quantitative analysis, but bureaucrats do interpret their roles in government very differently from nation to nation. The international

---

[3] G. Bingham Powell, *Contemporary Democracies: Participation, Stability, and Violence* (Cambridge, MA: Harvard University Press, 1982).

[4] Henry Bienen and Nicolas Van De Walle, *Of Time and Power* (Stanford, CT: Stanford University Press, 1991), p. 78.

[5] Douglas A. Hibbs, *The Political Economy of Industrial Democracies* (Cambridge, MA: Harvard University Press, 1987).

real estate investment process requires extensive contact with bureaucratic elites, and, of course, governments are prime users of space for the most common international investment of all, the office building. In certain European nations, for instance, bureaucrats may view themselves as detached technicians and not as advocates for positions they hold.[6] Yet, in effect, these groups can be extremely powerful and can make important decisions about items concerning urban planning, construction, government location, and even currency without facing the requirements for notice and consultation that exist in the United States. Aspects of sovereign risks are often analyzed by U.S. stock and bond managers investing internationally, albeit not necessarily with the above degree of complexity. Nonetheless, the real estate portfolio manager should be able to take advantage of analyses prepared by the institutions' stock and bond managers.

A Conceptual Comparison

In addition to the above, real estate offers some special problems in immediate country comparisons relating to the use of land in a society and the density and spatial distribution of people and buildings within the finite national land mass. Moreover, there are considerable differences relating to the functions, structure, and activities of the real estate industries among various nations. There is a great difference between nations that have extremely localized markets, dominated by small familial real estate firms active in construction and brokerage, and nations where national or large regional banks, life insurance companies, or pension funds dominate the real estate market. Latin America tends to be the archetypical example of the fragmented markets, but Spain, Portugal, and Greece are not far behind. France, Germany, and Switzerland are nations where large financial institutions predominate.

A very straightforward way to conceptualize the combination of these criteria appears in Exhibit 12–5. The vertical axis reflects the percentage of the economy devoted to service industries; generally, the higher that percentage, the greater the degree of higher-technology industrialization in the society. The bars on the horizontal

[6] Joel D. Auerbach, ed., *Bureaucrats and Politicians in Western Democracies* (Cambridge, MA: Harvard University Press, 1981).

225

EXHIBIT 12–5
Stages of Urban Development

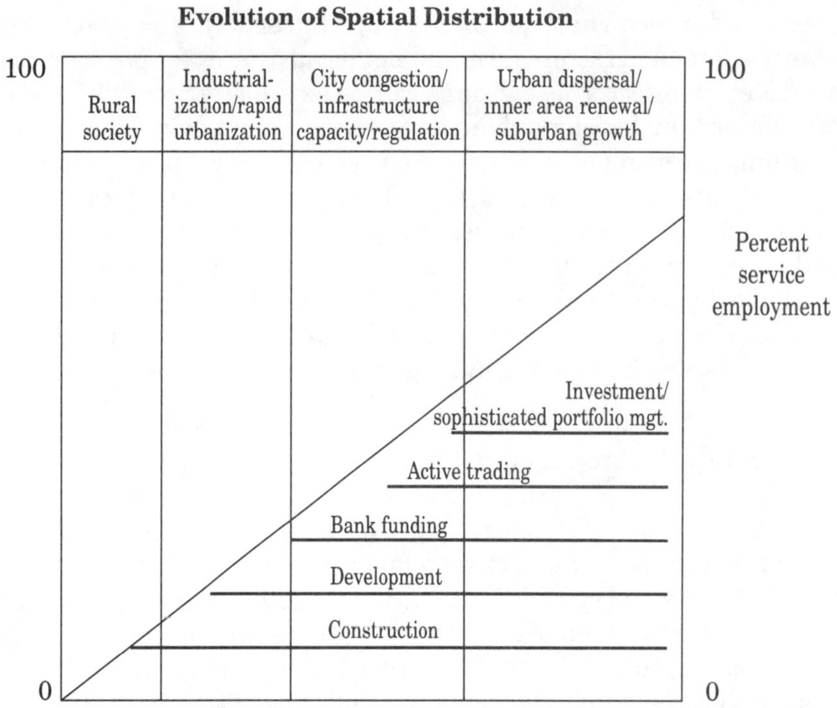

Evolution of Spatial Distribution

Source: JLW U.K. Consulting and Research.

axis illustrate four categories in the evolution of spatial distribution. Within the chart is a brief comment on the nature of the real estate activities characteristic of each level of development,[7] but these categories require elaboration.

Rural societies (grid 1) are nations still dominated by agriculture. They may have urban agglomerations, but the amount of modern, multiuse construction may be very slight, and the city street pattern may resemble a convoluted series of pathways rather than the linear or geometric focus of the more modern city. The construction that occurs tends to be small scale and financed by entities with a limited capital base.

---

[7] This grid was developed and quantified in detail by JLW U.K. Consulting and Research.

As industrialization proceeds (and manufacturing employment increases), rapid urbanization results (grid 2), often accompanied by extensive development projects, whether privately or publicly funded. These development projects focus on retail and business uses; the city layout changes to the linear or geometric focus. Specialized development companies emerge, but the capital base for real estate finance is still limited to an urban scope with a few rare exceptions. Smaller-scale local or neighborhood construction continues to occur.

Eventually, the city scene becomes more congested (grid 3). Stresses and strains are placed on the infrastructure, which must be upgraded and improved. As the service sector of the economy grows, banks or other financial institutions take a very significant role in the funding and structure of the real estate industry, and active trading of real estate properties owned by institutions of various types develops. The financial institutions have a sizable capital base and may be of national and large regional scope.

The final stage in the exhibit (grid 4) is typical of many larger U.S. and European metropolitan areas, where active trading of large real estate projects exists, institutional investors take a leading role in the market, and portfolio management becomes highly quantitative and organized. The real estate industry itself emerges as a complex hierarchy of companies with different functions, although large and small institutions exist side by side.

By and large, institutional investors prefer to focus on nations appearing in the last two grids. In the first two grids, the rates of economic development and real estate development are often very rapid, but the rapidity with which markets and investment uses emerge provides less protection for existing investment values. In grid 3, one would find nations such as Hungary, Bulgaria, Peru, Venezuela, Brazil, and Mexico. In grid 4, typical nations would include the United Kingdom, Singapore, Norway, Denmark, France, Germany, and Italy.

THE STATE OF THE EVIDENCE ON SAMPLE RETURNS

After the national selection process has reduced the world to a manageable list of target nations, the institutional investor usually wishes to contemplate the evidence on actual returns. Here the data allow very limited country comparisons, and the decision process must quickly begin to focus on target cities.

Return Indices

Very few markets—or institutional investors—possess the time-weighted rate of return real estate performance indices either on a national or an urban market basis. The Russell methodology has now spread to Canada, where a national index is approximately five years old. The United Kingdom happens to be far in advance of any other nation with respect to detailed return data for the nation and for its individual major markets, possessing at least six well-known indices.[8] Australia possesses a modified version of a national return index; one institutional investor commands such a large portion of the investment property market that the results of that portfolio may be considered an indicator of national performance. In addition, various discussions are under way in Australia regarding the formation of a national index.

On the Continent and around the Pacific Rim, even highly technocratic, information-oriented societies such as France and Germany lack performance indices from a database of actual returns. The reasons for this gap are complex and link technological development with real estate organizational issues. In certain relatively small nations, whether highly industrialized or not, the investment market is dominated by a few major players, and their own portfolio knowledge suffices for the creation of future investment strategy. In other nations, the organizations in the market are very small, very local entities acting in such a limited arena that familiarity with their neighborhood is sufficient. The proliferation of computers within the business and financial world also differentiates nations, and in many ways the United States is the most advanced nation in this respect. Generally, increased institutional participation in investment real estate is accompanied by an enhanced demand for market databases and performance analyses requiring extensive computer capability.

Mixed Transaction Returns

For almost all other nations around the world, estimates of real estate returns have to be derived from data drawn from leases in different properties and building prices and yields from actual sales transac-

---

[8] Jacques N. Gordon, "Property Performance Indexes in the United Kingdom and the United States," *Real Estate Review,* Summer 1991, pp. 33–40.

tions. Individual lease and property transaction information for any given year is not easily reduced to numbers that make sense for "average" rent and "average" capital value. The sample may be too small, and the properties may not be comparable. Creating a time series is equally difficult, since from one year to the next, the sample lease data and the sample transaction data may not be buildings that are strictly "comparable." Nonetheless, analysts do create the time series for rent and capital values by selecting those leases and those property transactions that seem most closely comparable. The final number for "rent" or "value" in a given year in a data set of this type will be as much an art as an arithmetic calculation. For convenience, such series will be called mixed transaction returns.

Beyond the methodological problems, even the assembling of the transaction data is not as simple as it may appear on the surface. For example, although actual rents in the United States are difficult to obtain, there are usually recording requirements relating to the ownership transfer of real estate and provisions for public access to information. In some other countries, very localized, "familial," noninstitutionalized practices with a strong incentive to avoid certain transfer taxes tend to make it highly difficult to discover the actual sales price. This comment applies to many South American markets. Other nations believe in more privacy than prevails in the United States, and there may be no provision for public access to transfer records. The United Kingdom and Germany, for instance, have much more stringent regulations on public access to records.

The interpretation of information on an international basis is also subject to a variety of challenges not seen in the U.S. For instance, Eastern European markets are having a problem with the general idea of "market rent." Fair pricing for the public benefit is still a prevalent political-psychological-social concept, and it can be difficult to select examples of leases or rents for real "market" rental growth.

Comparison of Returns: The Indices

Ideally, international return analyses should compare like-to-like data sets. As it happens, the Russell/NCREIF index for the United States and the various U.K. indices allow just such a comparison. This analysis is one of the first that American institutions usually

EXHIBIT 12–6
Comparison of JLW U.K. Property Index and Russell/NCREIF Index for the United States, 1978–91

	United Kingdom	United States	U.K. v. U.S.
Mean	13.2%	9.8%	
Standard deviation	10.5	7.2	
Correlation coefficient			+57%
Covariance			0.4%

Source: JLW Research.

perform when pondering international investment. When the U.S. quarterly real estate returns in the Russell/NCREIF index were compared with the U.K. quarterly real estate returns drawn from the JLW index[9] from 1978 to 1991, the results were as shown in Exhibit 12–6. U.K. returns have shown a higher average than U.S. returns, but the U.K. series shows a significantly higher variability (a standard deviation of 10.5 percent compared with the U.S. standard deviation of 7.2 percent). The two markets have a medium-strength positive correlation. If these results were to be maintained in the future, a U.S. investor might consider an investment in U.K. real estate. Two observations need to be made here. First, one should be cautious about attaching too much weight to relationships that span a limited number of economic and real estate cycles. Second, the addition of U.K. real estate may enhance the portfolio's (mean/variance) efficiency. If one accepts that these two real estate economies are moving less than perfectly together over time, then the inclusion of U.K. real estate extends the range of choices possible for optimal portfolio composition.

Some of the complexities of including international real estate investment in a portfolio can be portrayed by considering whether U.K. property has a low or negative correlation with U.S. stocks and bonds and/or U.K. stocks and bonds. The statistics in Exhibit 12–7 show that real estate returns in both nations do perform countercyclically with the stock and bond markets in either nation. Including

---

[9] The JLW index is a time-weighted rate of return index for properties managed and valued by JLW in the United Kingdom.

EXHIBIT 12–7

Correlation Coefficients for U.S. and U.K. Stock, Bond, and Real Estate Returns, 1978–91

	U.K. Property	U.S. Property
U.S. bonds	− .37	− .35
U.S. stocks	− .01	− .11
U.K. bonds	− .33	− .15
U.K. stocks	− .08	− .18

Sources: Analysis by JLW U.K. Research. U.K. returns from the JLW Property Index; U.S. returns from the Russell/NCREIF Property Index.

U.K. real estate in a U.S. real estate portfolio would enhance the countercyclical performance of real estate relative to an international U.S. and U.K. stock and bond portfolio.

Comparison of Returns: Mixed Transaction Returns

Investors who want a wider view of international returns than that which is confined to the United States and the United Kingdom and who also desire to focus on individual markets turn to the alternative return data sets that have been termed mixed transaction returns. To give an example of how these data can be used to understand international returns, a limited set of analyses has been performed on a selected number of international office markets: Los Angeles, New York, midtown, San Francisco, Washington, DC, Brussels, Frankfurt, London West End, Paris 8th, arrondissement, Hong Kong, Kuala Lumpur, Singapore, and Sydney (see Exhibit 12–8). Office is the only property type included here, because it is the only property type for which there is a data set on U.S. cities exactly comparable to the data on the non-U.S. cities.[10]

This particular data set applies to top-quality, downtown office properties suitable for purchase by major international institutions.

---

[10] These data sets were developed through a JLW international research program and at least offer a like-to-like comparison. There are probably other sources one could use for U.S. retail and industrial property rent/yield/capital value information (perhaps from the National Real Estate Index), but achieving the assurance of data comparability for such an analysis is an extensive undertaking beyond the scope of this chapter.

EXHIBIT 12–8
Comparison of Top-Quality, Prime Location, Downtown Office Returns, 1979–89

City	Average Return	Standard Deviation	Coefficient of Variation
Los Angeles	19.38%	17.8%	.92
San Francisco	16.69	29.5	1.77
New York, midtown	21.37	28.5	1.33
Washington, DC	17.96	12.4	.69
Brussels	19.11	5.7	.30
London West End	19.72	18.9	.96
Paris, 8th arrondissement	24.56	10.7	.43
Frankfurt	17.82	12.6	.71
Hong Kong	21.52	30.8	1.43
Kuala Lumpur	6.27	23.4	3.73
Singapore	25.02	65.0	2.60
Sydney	27.98	19.6	.70

Source: JLW International Research.

The annual capital value and yield data are derived from an analysis of comparable building sales in any given year. The rent data are net effective rents drawn from leases on comparable properties. Return figures for each year are composed of capital returns and income returns. These returns are calculated by taking each year's net income and applying the respective market capitalization rates to arrive at the estimated capital value for the hypothetical investment.

The returns therefore do not allow for any kind of obsolescence, whether physical or locational, and *this analysis is for illustrative purposes only*. This kind of analysis tacitly assumes an annual rent review, with all rents moving upward to market. The resulting returns thus show higher annual rental growth than would be seen in actual portfolio performance.

The time span shown here points out the limitations of this data set and, indeed, of valuation data in general. If the analysis were performed through 1992, the returns would naturally be lowered. However, the dearth of comparable sales in a number of cities since 1990, especially in the U.S., makes it extremely difficult to ascertain capital values and yields. Any such numbers would be quite hypothetical and subject to change after sales resume, whenever that might be in the 1990s. Exhibit 12–8 reports the office return results, the standard deviation, and the coefficient of variation for data from 1979 to 1989. The very high differences in variability should be noted, ranging from a low of 5.7 percent in Brussels to a high of 65 percent in Singapore. The coefficient of variation is obtained by dividing the standard deviation by the annual average return; an excellent coefficient of variation would be around .5, where the rate of return is twice the level of risk. In this instance, the coefficient of variation for the entire mix of cities equals .78.

Creating Sample International Office Portfolios

To better understand the inner workings among the office markets, it is also possible to calculate the correlations and covariances among these returns (see Exhibit 12–9). Correlations close to zero or negative are evidence of countercyclical behavior and suggest that the markets are influenced by outside factors in entirely different ways. Covariances (the product of the standard deviation and the correlation coefficient) approaching zero from the negative side are considered optimal.

The skillful portfolio manager, given perfect information, would be able to determine precise allocations of investments to various cities to achieve the desired combination of risk and return, most likely through the use of an optimization program. This program would produce the efficient frontier, that set of real estate investments which would produce the optimal return and risk mix of property investments.

Rather than create such an optimal model here, this return data set will be used to explore the potential benefits of international diversification through the creation of four simple hypothetical portfolios:

- The global portfolio consists of equally weighted investments in all of the office markets noted in Exhibit 12–8.
- The All America portfolio consists of equally weighted investments located only in New York, Los Angeles, San Francisco, and Washington, DC.
- The All Europe portfolio contains equally weighted investments in only the European cities.
- The All Asia/Pacific portfolio contains equally weighted investments in only the Pacific Rim office locations.

EXHIBIT 12–9
Correlation Coefficients of Returns, 1979–89

	LA	NY	SF	DC	Brussels	Frankfurt	HK	KL	London	Paris	Singapore	Sydney
Los Angeles	1.0000											
New York, midtown	0.8679	1.0000										
San Francisco	0.6256	0.6392	1.0000									
Washington, DC	0.4982	0.5032	0.9672	1.0000								
Brussels	0.1064	−0.2665	0.1221	0.1629	1.0000							
Frankfurt	−0.2013	−0.3538	−0.0691	−0.1382	0.2487	1.0000						
Hong Kong	0.6993	0.3431	0.5238	0.4691	0.6776	0.1890	1.0000					
Kuala Lampur	0.2047	0.0233	0.1684	0.1360	0.0269	0.5415	0.2610	1.0000				
London	0.5830	0.3690	0.3510	0.2472	0.6083	0.1366	0.7998	−0.1867	1.0000			
Paris, 8th arrondissement	0.0251	0.3016	0.2460	0.1926	−0.4334	0.3615	−0.2214	0.5141	−.2647	1.0000		
Singapore	0.7172	0.7296	0.9110	0.8124	0.1888	0.0834	0.6509	0.1791	.5641	.3346	1.0000	
Sydney	0.4924	0.5140	0.9373	0.9290	0.3212	−0.0246	0.5564	0.0274	.4807	.2208	.9052	1.0000

Source: JLW USA Research.

551

The calculations assumed a $100 million investment in the initial year, with annual rental growth and capital appreciation having occurred in accordance with the results of the mixed transaction data. Results are given in Exhibit 12–10.

The European portfolio presented the safest strategy for prudent investors, with a return of over 20 percent and a standard deviation of 6.62 percent. An investor willing to accept higher risk might have chosen the Asia/Pacific portfolio, with its higher returns but substantially higher volatility. (Since this would have increased risk dramatically for a relatively small increase in return, such an investor might pragmatically have decided to adhere to the European portfolio or focus on selected markets in the Asia/Pacific portfolio.)

Cross-regional portfolios, consisting of equally weighted investments in each of the cities within two regions, were also created for the investor looking to perhaps increase returns while decreasing risk (see Exhibit 12–11). The addition of a 50 percent investment in European offices had significant benefits for both American and Asia/Pacific investors. An investment split between the United States and Europe provided the hypothetical American investor with a higher return and a lower standard deviation than an all-U.S. portfolio. For the Asian investor, a 50/50 split between Asian/Pacific and European locations still had high returns, but considerably reduced the coefficient of variation. The European investor, however, would be helped little by such a simplistic diversification scheme. An all-European investment scheme is hurt only by dividing the portfolios between American or Asia/Pacific properties.

EXHIBIT 12–10
Comparison of Combined Downtown Office Portfolios for Different World Regions, 1979–89

Portfolio	Average Return	Standard Deviation	Coefficient of Variation
Global	20.68%	18.77%	0.91
All U.S.	18.96	19.38	1.02
All Europe	20.56	6.62	0.32
All Asia/Pacific	22.31	31.54	1.41

Source: JLW USA Research.

EXHIBIT 12–11
Comparison of Cross-Regional Downtown Office Portfolios, 1979–89

Portfolio	Average Return	Standard Deviation	Coefficient of Variation
U.S./Europe	19.78%	11.80%	0.60
U.S./Asia Pacific	20.74	24.72	1.19
Europe/Asia Pacific	21.46	19.96	0.93

Source: JLW USA Research.

Limitations of the Evidence and Statistical Techniques

How appropriate are such statistical analyses when applied to the type of data set above compared to statistics derived from time-weighted return indices based on actual portfolio performance? Under ordinary circumstances, a 10-year return series with a single-number result derived from different building comparisons and opinions, such as the above, is not statistically significant at the 95 or 99 percent confidence level. Moreover, further statistical analyses indicate that the results cannot be counted on 30 percent of the time (30 percent being the number that many social scientists think is plausible for real-world research). Adding quarterly results to annual differences would allow the analyst to eventually achieve some level of acceptable real-world probabilities, enough perhaps to justify forecast modeling or optimal portfolio modeling, but this does not resolve the basic problems stemming from the origins of the numbers for each year or quarter.

Given the limitations of the data, it is probably fair to say that the statistical calculations provide the analyst with a greater understanding of the *possible relationships among markets. The process of attempting to apply statistical techniques to even limited data necessitates thinking about portfolio composition within a rigorous framework. It is more difficult to conclude that such data should be used in forecasting actual returns for individual portfolio composition.* This in no way denigrates the value of such market trend compilation. Rather, it emphasizes that a propensity to use the quantitative methodology available should be tempered by an understanding of the limits of information.

"FUNDAMENTALS" BEHIND LOCAL MARKET CYCLES AND QUESTIONS ABOUT WHERE THE WORLD IS GOING

The preceding section on sample returns available at the national and local market levels is one component of the decision process pursued by the potential international investor. More often than not, the exercise is pursued

1. In conjunction with expert tax and legal advice to determine whether there are significant tax and legal difficulties, and in conjunction with expert tax and legal advice obtained from appropriate sources.

2. To determine whether there is sufficient evidence on overall market return trends to warrant examining individual market investment potentials more closely and individual investments themselves. Exhibit 12–12 illustrates the decision process flow-through at this point.

Assuming the weight of the return evidence is positive, major institutions have used the individual market return data as the springboard from which to proceed to a more intensive understanding of local market fundamentals. They know the return results are due to the interplay of countercyclical conditions on both the real estate supply and the real estate demand side in the local markets in question. These conditions encompass important differences in the evolution of tenant composition, significant differences in planning and development rules and regulations, and variations in the leasing structure. Yet at the same time, forces are at work to push a number of markets into a much closer relationship with one another. It is possible to give here only a few instances of these important local trends and conditions.

Similarities in Local Market Patterns

The office market provides examples of significant similarities and differences in demand trends. Although it is very difficult to obtain consistent comparative city employment and tenant data in urban markets around the world, it certainly appears that the major office markets of the world relied heavily on the expansion of the world financial markets as a source of space demand in the last decade. For instance, in the 1980s, some 60 percent of the office market demand in London stemmed from the financial sector, Frankfurt and Paris

EXHIBIT 12–12
Stages in the Decision Process for International Real Estate Investment

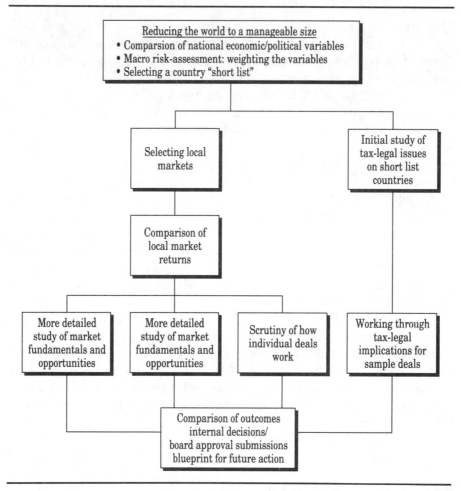

Source: JLW USA Research.

were heavily oriented toward banking and financial tenants, and New York downtown and central Chicago markets were closely tied to banking and the growth of the world securities markets. One-third of the office space in New York downtown was controlled by 50 large companies. Across the Pacific, some 40 percent of Sydney's central business district tenants were in finance and insurance industry categories.

There are markets that have served and still serve as a counterbalance to finance-based markets, markets based to a greater degree on services, government, and industrial corporations. Washington, DC, is the obvious market of this type, with its panoply of consulting firms, lawyers, accountants, and the U.S. government. New York City's midtown Manhattan has a corporation- and service-based market. Toronto also has a more diversified tenant base.

However, the recent pronounced similarity in the real estate market cycles of the United Kingdom, Canada, the United States, and Australia all point to an international investment phenomenon whose risks and outcomes would have been difficult to predict. In each of these nations, innovative financing techniques, abnormally high institutional financing available for real estate construction, and the potential for subsequent sales to Far Eastern investors (at least in the United States and Canada) largely contributed to a massive glut in real estate construction. Exhibit 12–13 illustrates the

EXHIBIT 12–13
Comparison of Selected Office Market Vacancy Rates, 1980–91

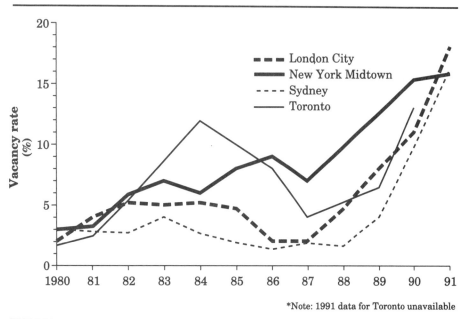

*Note: 1991 data for Toronto unavailable

Source: Jones Lang Wootton International.

confluence of their market vacancy rate trends. In many instances, the players were the same internationally. The impact of these market similarities is evident in the results of the comparison of the Russell-NCREIF index for the United States and the JLW index for the United Kingdom—a positive correlation of .57.

Despite some similarities in the tenant base, the European office markets have been following a different dynamic. The behavior of European markets has been determined by a slower pace in financial services deregulation, different industry-business mixes in the cities, and different institutional players with a much more conservative outlook on construction finance.

Various markets in Latin America and around the Pacific Rim have office markets that are tied to more trade, manufacturing, and commodities-based economies. Locations such as Jakarta, Singapore, Kuala Lumpur, and Hong Kong have the kind of volatile vacancy rates (and returns) that are characteristic of such urban areas. For example, Indonesia's main city, Jakarta, has an urban economy closely tied to oil, gas, gold-mining, and forestry corporations, and Jakarta had just begun to see the emergence of an investment market in 1987, when a few major buildings changed hands. Kuala Lumpur's tenant base is tied to exports, electronics, textiles, and rubber-based manufacturers.

Such differences in the local market office tenant base and its employment fluctuations help determine the diversification possibilities. The timing, location, and type of product demand will all vary from market to market.

Limits to New Construction

Financing practices for new construction (whether office or other property types), as well as political and bureaucratic restrictions, constitute an important factor in regulating new supply on the local scene and encouraging differences between market cycles. On the European continent, much more severe constraints are placed on construction than in the North American markets. Restrictions in North America, however, can be more severe than those in Asia. For example,

• Conservative financing practices for new construction are embodied in countries such as Germany, where insurance companies, the principal financial source, have maintained a steady, stable development program. Property funds, operated as the subsidiaries of the major banks, have had a limited role in financing development in Germany, as have pension funds.

• In countries such as France and Belgium, various limitations have been placed on new retail development (ceilings on rents and restrictions on retail leases) to protect small shopkeepers from retail mall competition. Other nations protect the supply of agricultural land, which is linked to the power of the agricultural lobby in the European Union.

• Concern for existing historical structures and restrictions on use in central cities exist across Europe and are more stringent than in North America.

• In general, land use planning in Europe is more comprehensive than in North America (although Seattle, San Francisco, and Toronto compare well with any location). Planning controls in Europe have had a longer period of evolution, and support for planning constraints is more politically acceptable. As a result, construction takes much longer.

The foregoing is not intended to suggest that Europe is a completely safe haven from cyclical construction trends. The intensive government/bureaucratic role in planning and directing urban growth in the historic cities can result in short-term overbuilding in certain areas as governments try to encourage locational shifts that will have a long-term impact. The overbuilding in the docklands area of London and the east side redevelopment of Paris are two examples. There are also signs of a market demand shift to the suburbs, which may in the future affect the focus of development financing in certain locations of Western Europe. Surveys of corporate demand in countries such as Italy, Germany, and Spain indicate that such issues as transportation access, quality of life, and technological needs are achieving primacy in corporate location thinking.

Around the Pacific Rim, regulations on new construction can be a mixture of extreme government planning combined with extreme flexibility in execution. In Kuala Lumpur, construction trends (especially in retail) indicate the relative ease of development in the country and the tendency of the sources of real estate financial supply to overanticipate the pace of demand for quality new products. Singapore land use is regulated by a master plan that is revised every five years, but the planning authorities have considerable latitude in reviewing development proposals. The burst of new construction in the late 1980s will keep vacancy rates elevated for the next four years. Appearances of some of the islands notwithstanding, Hong Kong is a highly planned agglomeration. Japan is perhaps the ultimate in restrictive land use and construction.

Lease Terms and Conditions

Lease terms and conditions are another source of important differences in local market cycles. Exhibit 12–14 illustrates differences among office, retail, and industrial properties by comparing variations in the term of the lease, lease escalation clauses, the party responsible for space improvements, special taxes on rental of space, and so on.

The international investor should be warned, though, that certain leasing practices will be under a great deal of pressure in the next decade, due to the oversupply of many types of space and the homogenization of many practices in European nations. For example, tenant concessions (or inducements) have arrived in the United Kingdom. While continuing to accept the traditional 25-year lease term, tenants are beginning to insist on having the right to cancel after a specified interval (often after 10 years) and are seeking free rent and space improvement allowances from landlords. There is some question too about whether or not the extremely protectionist laws in favor of small retail tenants (e.g., in France and Belgium) will continue to prevail under the gradual onslaught of multinational retailers and large center development.

Relative Emphasis on Different Components of Return

The analysis of local market fundamentals leads the investor to a better comprehension of the reasons for rental growth and capital appreciation (or lack thereof) in the offshore markets and the reasons for the differences in trends between U.S. real estate and markets offshore. Ultimately, the investor places the past return components in context and develops qualitative or quantitative expectations about the interrelationships among future returns. These expectations determine the relative emphasis investors have placed and still place

EXHIBIT 12–14   Commercial Leasing Practices in Western Europe

I. Office Buildings

| | | | | Responsibilities | | | | | |
Market	Lease Length	Rent Review	Rent Indexation	Operating Costs, Real Estate Taxes	Insurance	Ordinary Repairs	Structural Repairs	Tenant Right to Cancel	Tenant Right to Renew
Belgium	9 years	Every 3 years	Annual, tied to cost-of-living index	Tenant	Tenant	Tenant	Landlord	At end of each 3-year period	No
France	9 years	No	Annual or every 3 years, tied to building cost index	Tenant	Tenant	Tenant	Landlord	At end of each 3-year period	Yes, at market rent
Germany	5–10 years	Either review to market or indexation linked to cost of living, every 2 to 5 years		Tenant	Tenant	Tenant	Landlord	No	No

560

243

Market	Lease Length	Rent Review	Rent Indexation	Operating Costs, Real Estate Taxes	Insurance	Ordinary Repairs	Structural Repairs	Tenant Right to Cancel	Tenant Right to Renew
Netherlands	5–10 years	No	Annual, tied to cost-of-living index	Tenant (40%) Landlord (60%)	Landlord	Tenant	Landlord	After 5 years (both landlord and tenant)	Yes, at market rent
United Kingdom	25 years	Every 5 years, upward only	No	Tenant	Tenant	Tenant	Landlord	No	Yes, at market rent

II. Retail Properties

Market	Lease Length	Rent Review	Rent Indexation	Operating Costs, Real Estate Taxes	Insurance	Ordinary Repairs	Structural Repairs	Tenant Right to Cancel	Tenant Right to Renew
				Responsibilities					
Belgium	9 years	Every 3 years	Annual, tied to cost-of-living index	Tenant	Tenant	Tenant	Landlord	At end of each 3-year period	Yes, for 3 terms of 9 years each; rent increased by indexation
France	9 years; increasing tendency to 12–15 years	No	Annual or every 3 years, tied to building cost index; turnover rents now appearing	Tenant	Tenant	Tenant	Landlord	At end of each 3-year period	Yes; rent increased by indexation

561

EXHIBIT 12–14 *(continued)*

II. Retail Properties

				Responsibilities					
Market	*Lease Length*	*Rent Review*	*Rent Indexation*	*Operating Costs, Real Estate Taxes*	*Insurance*	*Ordinary Repairs*	*Structural Repairs*	*Tenant Right to Cancel*	*Tenant Right to Renew*
Germany	5–10 years	Either review to market or indexation linked to turnover or cost of living		Tenant	Tenant	Tenant	Landlord	No	No
Netherlands	10–15 years	Every 5 years	Annual, tied to cost-of-living index	Tenant (40%) Landlord (60%)	Landlord	Tenant	Landlord	After 5 years (both landlord and tenant)	Yes, at market rent
United Kingdom	25 years	Every 5 years, upward only	No	Tenant	Tenant	Tenant	Landlord	No	Yes, at market rent

562

III. Industrial Properties

Market	Lease Length	Rent Review	Rent Indexation	Responsibilities				Tenant Right to Cancel	Tenant Right to Renew
				Operating Costs, Real Estate Taxes	Insurance	Ordinary Repairs	Structural Repairs		
Belgium	9 years	Every 3 years	Annual, tied to cost-of-living index	Tenant	Tenant	Tenant	Landlord	At end of each 3-year period	No
France	9 years	No	Annual or every 3 years, tied to building cost index	Tenant	Tenant	Tenant	Landlord	At end of each 3-year period	Yes; rent increased by indexation
Germany	5–10 years	Either review to market or indexation linked to cost of living, every 2–5 years		Tenant	Tenant	Tenant	Landlord	No	No
Netherlands	5–10 years	No	Annual, tied to cost-of-living index	Tenant (40%) Landlord (60%)	Landlord	Tenant	Landlord	After 5 years (both landlord and tenant)	Yes, at market rent
United Kingdom	25 years	Every 5 years, upward	No	Tenant	Tenant	Tenant	Landlord	No	Yes, at market rent

563

246

on current income yield or capital growth as the dominant component of return.

For example, during the late 1980s, investors accepted low initial capitalization rates on European office properties, since there was evidence of very strong rental growth in these markets. Recession, overbuilding in some submarkets, and political and economic uncertainties have substantially slowed rental growth in the European office sector, and near-term forecasts for rental growth dropped; consequently, capitalization rates have moved upward for European offices. The 1980s and 1990s have seen U.S. office capitalization rates that are usually higher than those in the major European office centers, reflecting the lower actual rental growth and investor perceptions of higher market risk linked to fewer supply constraints. Although many forces are at work to push international markets into a similar vacancy rate and rent cyclical pattern (which may have a two-to-three-year time lag across nations), there still seem to be sufficient economic/political differences at work such that investors constantly adapt the emphasis placed on different return components.

THE AMERICAN INSTITUTION ABROAD

International Tax Laws and Restrictions, or the Way the Game Is Played

The exploration and forecasting of local market supply-demand cycles offer the institutional investor the opportunity to attempt to determine how the promise of past returns compares to present expectations of future returns. Simultaneously (referring again to Exhibit 12–12), the potential investor usually explores the legal vehicles possible for investment and the tax laws that will affect the investment. International tax laws have a major impact on whether or not the expected returns can be realized; in certain instances, the tax laws are devised to discourage foreign ownership of real property and may coincide with overt restrictions on the percentage of foreign ownership allowed.

The institutional investor can discover the mode of investment that best facilitates the flow of returns to the home base and minimizes the tax liabilities, or is "tax neutral." No short chapter could possibly do justice to the intriguing network of corporate structures and tax treaties that govern the rules for international real estate investment. Local advice from law firms and accountants familiar with the most current market practice and legal restrictions is a necessity, as are advice and assistance from locally based real estate professionals. In the learning curve for potential international investment, one common exercise is to acquire the offering brochures for various international-class properties and work through with the advisors the manner in which the legal vehicles and tax treaties would affect the ultimate choice of product and investment mode.

The need to be familiar with local practices is one reason international real estate investors often select a form of partnership, with a local entity as the preferred vehicle, for their initial investment programs. In addition to offering some protection against the risks involved in local market real estate practice, the partnership approach minimizes the costs involved in the acquisition of knowledge and hiring of expert advice. On the negative side, partnerships generally reduce the investor's control over the property and make liquidation more difficult.

During 1991 and 1992, the international real estate investment community frequently discussed the concept of swaps between institutional investor portfolios. The best-known international swap occurred between Postel and Mitsui, in which Mitsui acquired an interest in a St. James Square location in London and Postel acquired a share of the Mitsui Building in Tokyo. Up through 1992, swaps were more often discussed than consummated, since they involved interesting issues of comparative value and avoidance or minimization of taxation for both institutions. Possible legal issues may emerge if the swap does not comply with established legal procedures for transfer of property ownership.

American Advantages

U.S. domestic players can have certain advantages in the international market, advantages that are closely tied to the fact that Americans have been forced to think about real estate investment in the context of large geographic distances and rapid technological development. Europe, for example, should experience a shift in trade route patterns in the next decade that will affect the demand for all kinds of space. Analysis of product demand requires the ability to think in terms of the transition of goods and services on a continentwide basis.

For instance, the large geographic scope of unrestricted trade, combined with greater computer use, may lead to a smaller number of really significant distribution centers needed.

In the United States, the oversupply of real estate greatly overshadows the positive lessons the industry has learned about project design and market selection. If adapted to other national tastes, these lessons could have some benefit. In the next decade, many opportunities exist in Europe for the following:

• Creation and/or upgrading of suburban retail centers. U.S. retail development had used very complex methods of identifying target markets according to socioeconomic, cultural, and psychological profiles. Coupled with retail design improvements and active property management, this expertise could be used in the creation of the next generation of European retail centers.

• Development of noncentral office parks, whether suburban or city fringe. Surveys and studies of corporate Europe indicate that central congestion and demands of technology that cannot be accommodated in centuries-old (or even 30-year-old) buildings will force a demand for out-of-center locations. Suburban business park design in Europe generally does not compare with American design in terms of convenience of layout for auto and truck access, attractiveness of the site environment, or attractiveness of the finished product. As organizations are forced out of the central cities, the supplier of the right ambiance will have a competitive advantage.

Nonetheless, the astute investor will carefully make allowances for local tastes, which can cover everything from the amount of daylight, to preferences about climate control and the ability to open windows, to carpeting.

Next Steps

The great challenge, whether for a U.S. or an offshore institution, is in the arena of comparing the results of legal, tax, and micromarket issues, moving to a blueprint for real action, and implementing that action. Truly global thinking often results in the identification of so many opportunities and varying risk patterns that actually selecting the locations and product types for what is always a limited international real estate allocation greatly taxes an organization's discipline and dedication to its original location, product type, and risk-return preferences. A hypothetical strategy on paper is one thing; the lure of the visible investment with real cash flow (and real discounted cash flow projections) is another.

To date, American institutions have for the most part studied offshore real estate through advisors and consultants, but have been reluctant to engage in offshore investment themselves. Although various organizations, such as Equitable, Baring Advisors, and Jones Lang Wootton Realty Advisors, attempted to encourage American institutional investment (especially pension fund investment) in Europe in the 1990–92 period, no major shift of funds has been forthcoming. To date, the most significant amount of U.S. institutional money invested has been through the Trans-European Property Unit Trust (MIM), in the amount of approximately $50 million.

Major shifts in the international flow of real estate investment funds by U.S. institutional investors require (among other things) the acceptance of new risks and investment vehicles designed to mitigate those risks. The great shift in world political uncertainties caused by the recession appropriately gave prudent U.S. institutions cause for further thought about international real estate in the early 1990s. It is highly probable that the rest of the decade will see a refinement and adaptation of investment vehicles suitable for the appetites of U.S. institutions as those institutions gradually determine those elements of international risk that are acceptable or unacceptable to them. Such vehicles will be offered by U.S.-based organizations, but many will be created by foreign-based financial entities seeking to attract U.S. capital that has been disillusioned with poor returns in U.S. real estate and might be persuaded to invest elsewhere with the lure of higher returns.

Chapter 8

Leverage in a Private Equity Real Estate Portfolio

Susan Hudson-Wilson, CFA

Whenever interest rates fall and positive leverage conditions hold, the subject of the use of leverage in a portfolio of real estate inevitably comes up. When the cost of debt falls below the income yield on an asset or portfolio of assets, there is positive leverage and it can be used to raise the return on the asset(s). While using leverage seems trivial (how can positive leverage be a "bad" thing?), it is, in fact, quite complex and raises some philosophical and operational issues for the investor. Here the many aspects of the leverage decision are explored and a recommendation is offered. Throughout the discussion it is assumed that leverage can be applied, creating a positive spread, at least initially. The use of very aggressive leverage as an opportunistic strategy is not discussed; leverage is considered only in the context of a base real estate portfolio strategy.

REAL ESTATE LEVERAGE

Real estate leverage, in concept, is no different than any other type of leverage: it is borrowing against the collateral of an asset or portfolio of assets. The borrower may want to do so for a variety of reasons (see below), and the lender may be interested in earning a rate of return that is considered attractive on a risk-adjusted basis. While at times the provision of debt is a method used by lenders to make equity investments, and at times it becomes a de facto equity investment, typically the lender expects to receive the principal and not the property at the end of the term of the loan. In general, the lender regards itself as a fixed-income investor and the borrower behaves like the equity holder. In the discussion below it is assumed that the lender's motivations are typical.

There is one very interesting difference between some commercial real estate debt and most other kinds of debt, including residential real estate debt — the use of nonrecourse terms. Nonrecourse debt allows the lender access only to the collateral in the case of a default or other violation of the terms of the mortgage and not to the borrower or the borrower's other assets. This anomaly continues even though lenders have experienced firsthand the effects of this factor on

61

their ability to recoup value lost on their mortgage investments. This term is very useful to the borrower when times are tough since it essentially renders the mortgage a put option from the borrower to the lender. When the borrower borrows on a nonrecourse basis, it is short selling the asset: the borrower takes money out of the asset, reducing its exposure to it, and can walk away from the asset when and if it chooses to. The lender cannot force the borrower to continue the relationship with the asset or to compensate the lender for any loss of principal. In the price of the loan it is not clear what the borrower is actually paying for this option. Certainly in very low-interest-rate or in very competitive environments the borrower is not paying much, if at all, for this useful option. But it is an important consideration to an investor in determining whether or not to use leverage, and in determining the type of leverage preferred.

Mortgages may be structured as single asset, multiasset, cross-collateralized, noncrossed, recourse, or nonrecourse vehicles. The interest rate will reflect more or less appropriately, depending on the conditions in the overall debt and equity markets, the relative bargaining power of both the lender and the borrower. Loans may be interest only, amortizing or nonamortizing, short- or long-term, fixed- or floating-rate, participating or nonparticipating, and at high or low loan-to-value ratios.

Interestingly, lenders do not currently give much consideration to the true riskiness of the market within which a particular mortgage is underwritten. They tend to develop a general set of terms (rate, term, amortization, ratios) and then to apply these terms pretty evenly across all markets and, in a slightly less dogmatic fashion, to all property types. An understanding of the actual differences in market risks can be very helpful to a borrower that can essentially cherry pick its portfolio and can place debt (with the embedded put option) on its riskier assets. It can reduce its exposure to the assets more likely to present problems through the cycle.

Given the many faces of leverage, it is very important to think through the reason for using leverage (or for not using it) since the reason for using it greatly influences the type of leverage chosen.

LEVERAGE IN A REAL ESTATE PORTFOLIO

There are six principal reasons for using leverage:

1. increase the total return of the leveraged portfolio,
2. hedge the downside risk of an investment,
3. enable a certain fixed amount of funds to be spread over more individual investments,
4. increase the yield and the cash flow generated from a fixed pool of capital,

5. reduce exposure to an asset or pool of assets as a way of reducing the allocation to a class of investments (an alternative to a disposition), and

6. enhance the diversification role of real estate in the context of the overall portfolio.

Each of these reasons is discussed in turn.

Leverage, assuming that there is positive spread and assuming that the value of the collateral does not fall below the principal balance, will increase the total return on an investment. The two assumptions cited are, however, important. If those assumptions fail to hold, leverage will enhance the degree of loss on an investment in the same fashion that it enhances the degree of gain. Leverage is a two-edged sword, and so it must be used carefully and with a great deal of consideration of at what point in the cycle it is used, on what it is used, how it is structured, and at what cost. Under proper circumstances leverage will improve the performance of an asset or pool of assets, so the concept of using leverage as a return enhancer is legitimate although it is not a tool for all parts of the real estate or interest rate cycles.

Leverage is a partial sale of an investment. However, it is a sale which the borrower can essentially revoke by paying the loan off, or can choose to consummate in the case of a loss of asset value sufficient to cause the borrower to prefer to put the asset to the lender rather than pay off the loan. Alternatively, the borrower can simply keep the leverage in place, replacing it when the end of the term occurs, in order to continue the "partially sold" strategy. This partial sale aspect of leverage can be used to hedge the possible downside movement in the value of an asset (a stop loss). For example, at the top of a market cycle an investor has three choices. It can hold the asset even though there is more downside risk than upside potential, it can sell the asset in its entirety and so book the value accumulated in the asset, or it can place a mortgage on the asset and so partially book the value of the asset while leaving a portion of the value exposed to the market cycle. If the asset's value does indeed decline (below the mortgage balance), the severity of loss to the borrower will be lessened. The investor will have also lost its remaining equity, but will have hedged its exposure to the full impact of the asset's decline in value. The placing of a mortgage can be far less expensive in terms of direct and indirect costs (such as time) than a sale of the asset. Further, if the market cycle proves to be less egregious than was anticipated, the borrower still holds the asset as the market recovers and so does not have to "rebuy" the asset in order to participate in the market cycle and does not have to bear search or acquisition costs. This can be a very savvy way to time markets.

Along the same lines of using leverage on a portfolio as a hedge, is the third use of leverage: to enable the same total volume of invested dollars to be spread over more individual investments. In this way leverage is a method to increase the diversification of the portfolio (assuming that this diversification effort is effectively executed), which, in turn, reduces both the idiosyncratic and market cycle risks of the portfolio. The use of leverage increases the riskiness of the portfolio, but the enhanced diversification can readily mitigate some of that risk. One can quantitatively assess the proper amount of leverage to apply to ensure that total portfolio risk is not increased. Using leverage to increase the number and type of assets in the portfolio also allows the average value of each asset to remain at an "institutional" level and does not force the investor to enhance diversification by acquiring smaller individual assets.

The fourth way that leverage can be used is to increase the cash flow and the yield generated from a fixed pool of capital. As the capital raised from putting a mortgage on an asset is redeployed into another asset and then that asset is leveraged and the proceeds are redeployed, etc., the cash flow generated off the original pool of capital grows, as does the yield. This happens only when positive leverage exists. If the asset's yield and the cost of debt are the same, the yield does not rise and the borrower has to work very hard to even regain the level of its original unleveraged cash flow.

The fifth way that leverage can be used by an investor is to adjust, at the margin and cost effectively, the aggregate portfolio's exposure to real estate as a class of investment. When there is concern that the relative performance of the real estate portfolio might suffer (or that other assets might perform relatively better), there is a desire to reduce the allocation to real estate. One of three strategies may achieve this. The investor can liquidate certain assets within the portfolio until the real estate exposure has been pared down, can apply leverage to the total real estate portfolio and redeploy the proceeds to other classes of investment, or can apply leverage to selected assets and then redeploy the proceeds to other classes of investment. The first approach bears the cost of commissions and execution time and could upset the balance of the portfolio across market risks. The second bears fewer costs and preserves the balance of the portfolio across the markets (assuming that the portfolio was initially thoughtfully allocated across the various market cycles). The third approach allows the portfolio manager to simultaneously alter the mix and the size of the portfolio.

The final use of leverage applied to a real estate portfolio is to "short out" the debt-like behavior from the real estate portfolio and so more closely capture the pure equity-like behavior of real estate. When this is done, the leveraged equity behaves in a more complementary fashion relative to the stock and bond portions of the portfolio than does unleveraged real estate. Thus, the diversification benefits of real estate, already very useful, are strengthened. Leverage improves the correlation relationships among the assets in the portfolio, because unleveraged real estate asset behavior is comprised of greater and lesser degrees of bond-like behavior (derived from the cash flows from the leases) and equity-like behavior (derived from the marking-to-market of the residual equity value of the property). When leverage essentially removes bond-like behavior from the asset (the debt service on the leverage is "paid" from the cash flows derived from the lease payments), the leveraged asset's behavior is primarily driven by the effect of the real estate cycle on the asset — the asset is fully exposed to the incremental performance of the real estate equity market and so its value is more closely aligned with the market cycle. Thus, if the investor sees real estate's diversification benefits to be very valuable, leverage is an important means for amplifying these benefits.

LEVERAGE AND RISK

Leverage increases the risk (measured as the volatility of the return stream) of any investment to which it is applied. Period. A leveraged asset's performance will be greater as a market cycles up and lesser as a market cycles down than the performance of an unleveraged asset. This is a fact, but should not necessarily discourage the use of leverage.

In fact, it is often the case that one can apply leverage to low-risk investments and so boost their volatility, but not to a level above the volatility of a different unleveraged investment. In other words, while it is true that leverage increases the volatility of any return stream, the mere application of leverage does not mean that the volatility of an investment's return stream rises to a level above an acceptable one. It is possible to apply leverage selectively — only to assets whose volatility is generally lower than average — and judiciously. In this way the total volatility of the real estate portfolio does not need to rise above the investor's tolerance for risk.

It is also important to think about the part of the market cycle in which leverage should be applied. Leverage applied at the bottom of a cycle carries theoretical downside risk, but the likelihood of its deleterious effects is not substantial. Leverage applied as a cycle is peaking carries a substantial hazard (as does continuing to hold an unleveraged asset). Thus, the risk of leverage can be managed if one is respectful of cycles and takes a stance on cycles, market by market. If one does not believe that cycles can reasonably be predicted, the use of leverage must be regarded as simply adding risk.

MORTGAGE STRUCTURE AND LEVERAGE

Assuming that markets cycle and so introduce volatility to an unleveraged real estate investment, and assuming that leverage increases this volatility, how can the structure of a mortgage mitigate one's exposure to the negative effects of leverage? Here it is also assumed that one cannot anticipate market cycles with any degree of accuracy (a debatable assumption, but a conservative one) and so one would simply place debt on an asset or a portfolio and then ride out the cycle.

Property & Portfolio Research, Inc. has simulated the effect of different mortgage structures on the same market. One example used a typical asset in the highly volatile Phoenix office market from 1982 to 1996. A mortgage with a 70% loan-to-value ratio was compared with a mortgage with a 60% loan-to-value ratio.

All other terms were the same. The 70% mortgage went into default when the Phoenix market went south while the 60% mortgage stayed in place. This is because property values fell by more than 30% and less than 40%. In other words, the 60% borrower was able to use the good effects of the mortgage even through a deep cycle and was not forced to put the asset to the lender. The borrower certainly lost value through the cycle, as did every investor — leveraged and unleveraged. This loss of value represented a very high percentage of the borrower's equity in the asset, because the borrower had essentially executed a partial sale by placing leverage on the asset. Because the value of the asset never fell below the principal balance of the mortgage, the owner of the asset held through the cycle and was still trying to recoup some of the loss when the market turned. As market values rose again the borrower experienced a very high positive return on the remaining equity, essentially mitigating, or at least partially mitigating, the prior losses. A more highly leveraged borrower would have lost the asset and would not have been able to offset large percentage losses with large percentage gains.

Thus, the structure of a mortgage can influence the effect of a cycle on the borrower's position in the asset and on the borrower's ability to recoup a loss. Unleveraged holdings clearly allow the owner to recoup losses, but sometimes even the seemingly "safe" unleveraged owner can never make up what has been lost. The most productive leverage is perhaps that which allows the owner to ride through some downside of a cycle while acting as a stop loss through really damaging cycles. In other words, perhaps low leverage offers the owner the best of both worlds.

LEVERAGE IN A BROAD INSTITUTIONAL PORTFOLIO

There are three important factors in thinking about real estate leverage in the context of an overall portfolio. One, the enhancement of the diversification role of real estate that was discussed previously, is briefly restated below. The issues of whether an investor should ever lend and borrow at the same time, and the practicalities of institutional money management are fully discussed in this section.

As mentioned before, cross-correlations among real estate, stocks, bonds, and other assets improve when real estate returns are measured as leveraged returns. That is, leveraged real estate is a better diversifier than unleveraged real estate. If an important goal of the real estate portion of the portfolio is to reduce the riskiness of the overall portfolio, a portfolio of leveraged real estate will accomplish this objective more effectively than a portfolio of unleveraged real estate.

The second factor is that leverage is a borrowing by the investor and so begs the following question: Should an investor be borrowing in one part of the portfolio and lending (i.e., holding Treasury securities, private debt, and corporate debt securities) in another part? In particular, should an investor be lending at a lower rate than the one at which it is borrowing? (The same question might be asked with respect to the purchase of stock equities, which are typically leveraged. In the case of stock equity the investor does not borrow, the corporate entity does, but the issue is analogous. In response, stock equity portfolio managers cite the fact that they cannot purchase unleveraged company securities, so whether the question is begged or not is somewhat moot.)

If the investor is lending in the fixed-income portfolio, should the fund consider borrowing in the real estate portfolio? Or, would these two investment strategies essentially neutralize one another while incurring transaction costs? If there is an opportunity to exploit a spread sufficient to more than cover the transaction costs in the marketplace, and if it is possible to exploit the spread without incurring an unacceptable degree of risk, it would seem useful to exploit the spread. If the investor can borrow at a lower rate than the one at which it lends on a similar credit, it probably should consider doing so. Given that there is typically a positive spread between same-credit mortgages and corporate securities, traditional mortgage debt will probably not meet this standard. Portfolio-level debt, or other nontraditional approaches to real estate debt might, however, allow this type of credit spread investing.

An additional consideration is the availability of nonrecourse debt in the real estate market. The fixed-income portfolio will likely consist of recourse loans while traditional mortgages may be executed on a nonrecourse basis. This useful characteristic might be sufficient to mitigate the fact that the rate at which the borrowing would be done would likely be greater than the rate at which the lending would be done for the same credit. It may be possible to create an ideal situation where the fund could borrow nonrecourse and lend recourse. Few investors other than insurance companies and pension funds can actually execute such a strategy.

Could the debt side of an investor ever lend to the real estate side of that investor? The debt side could earn the mortgage spread over corporates that has long characterized the mortgage market. The return of the debt portfolio would rise and the return of the real estate portfolio would rise — as long as the market cycle were not too egregious. Unfortunately, if the cycle were less well behaved, the debt side would be in the difficult position of needing to negotiate a workout on the mortgage with the real estate side. Not a very practical scenario. If all went well, the borrowing and the lending would be productive. If less than well, the complexities and the conflicts would be untenable.

The final issue with respect to the context of the aggregate investor portfolio concerns an important practicality for most institutional investors — the level at which performance is measured, and the manner in which the aggregate portfolio and each asset class are managed. Typically the chief investment officer (CIO) is responsible for looking across the entire pool of assets for opportunities to create value while each asset's portfolio manager is responsible for performance within the borders of the asset. The real estate portfolio manager is certainly motivated to use, where appropriate, every portfolio management tool available. Wisely employed leverage, as has been shown, constitutes a very useful portfolio management tool. On the other hand, the CIO is concerned with the effects of the use of various tools on the performance of the aggregate portfolio. Whether the real estate and other asset portfolio managers are, or are not, granted the latitude to employ the tools available depends on how the CIO manages the portfolio. Is the portfolio managed as the sum of the individual asset pools, or is it managed in a fully integrated asset management endeavor?

In the former case a portfolio manager is expected to accomplish the objectives of his or her part of the portfolio as effectively as possible. The total portfolio's performance is the sum of these individual efforts. The CIO will be concerned with setting the objectives for each portfolio manager and with asset allocation decisions. The objectives for each asset portfolio will include guidelines for the expected return of the asset class and likely set limits on the degree of risk to be assumed to achieve the return objectives. Each portfolio manager executes strategy within these guidelines, trying to do the best possible job.

As an alternative to this approach it is theoretically possible to simultaneously manage each asset class in a fully integrated fashion. The noted portfolio strategist Bill Sharpe calls this approach "integrated asset allocation." With this approach all decisions throughout the portfolio are made with an eye to their effect at the aggregate portfolio level. This is a theoretical model because, while it is clearly a conceptually superior approach, there are numerous practical problems with its implementation. Thus, most investors use the disaggregated approach and simply set some global rules to guide each portfolio manager's actions.

It is possible that the CIO might set some constraints on the types of portfolio management tools each portfolio manager would be permitted to use, but it is more practical to simply set the required return and the permissible risk. If each portfolio manager achieves his or her bogey, the sum of the parts will create a coherent whole.

So three observations seem relevant with respect to the issue of leverage in the aggregate portfolio: (1) leveraged real estate is a better diversifier than unleveraged real estate, (2) investors can be both borrowers and lenders as long as the borrowing is done via third parties, the spread is favorable, and/or the stop loss use of leverage constitutes the reason for borrowing, and (3) there are practical issues in the management of the overall portfolio that suggest that each asset class should simply strive to best achieve its return and risk objectives as set forth by the CIO because the concepts of fully integrated asset allocation and portfolio management are very difficult to implement.

CONTEXT

Leverage constitutes a partial sale and so must be regarded as a way to raise capital, not to use capital. Before using leverage it is important to consider the need to raise additional investment capital. If an investor is not invested up to the level that has been approved for real estate, the notion of adding to the cash available for investment is a questionable one. Can additional capital be beneficially and efficiently put to use? Can the existing staff manage the incremental investments in addition to the already approved volume of investments? It may be that an investor would choose to allow the use of leverage, but only after the total existing allocation is fully employed and only if the most constructive type of leverage can be executed.

If an investor chooses to allow the use of leverage, the type of leverage used must be consistent with the return and risk requirements for the real estate portfolio, and care must be taken that the allocation of the leveraged portfolio over the various real estate investment behaviors is at least as thoughtful as the allocation of the now unleveraged portfolio. If sufficient care is not taken, the riskiness of the portfolio could very well rise beyond an acceptable level.

EXECUTION

If an investor decides that leverage is a tool that should be available to the real estate portfolio manager, several threshold questions need to be addressed before deciding on the desired approach to the problem:

- What is (are) the purpose(s) of the leverage?
- Is the stop loss useful (i.e., is nonrecourse leverage preferred to recourse)?
- Is the leverage to be placed at the asset level and/or at the portfolio level?
- What is the preferred structure of the leverage (term, prepayment, public, or private)?
- Does the cost of the leverage relative to the fixed-income side of the portfolio matter?
- Who will be responsible for placing and managing the leverage?

Investors have many options from which to choose. A few examples will be presented below, but none is intended to represent a recommendation. Before delving further into the practical questions raised above, the threshold question of the use of leverage in the real estate portfolio must be addressed.

Let's assume that an investor wishes to use leverage for the purpose of raising the prospective return of the real estate portfolio, but does not wish to raise the riskiness of the portfolio to an unacceptable level. It could evaluate the current portfolio's riskiness and then set a level of increased risk that would be acceptable. The portfolio could then be analyzed to determine which assets(s) could benefit from the application of leverage, the portfolio diversification effect of placing the leverage and deploying the proceeds, and the effect of the leverage and the incremental investments on the return of the portfolio. It is conceivable that if this were very carefully thought through in advance, the portfolio's return could be raised without adding any incremental portfolio-level risk.

Then let's assume that the investor is concerned that some of the markets in which it has investments may have reached the peak of their cycles. Rather than execute a sale in these markets, it might choose to leverage the assets in these markets as a way of placing a stop loss to ensure that if the markets were to cycle down, its gains would be preserved. In this case the analysis to select the appropriate markets would involve the identification of markets which are highly volatile and where research suggests that values may be at, or near, a cyclical peak. High loan-to-value, nonrecourse mortgages would be placed on these assets and the proceeds would be used to invest in new assets chosen to ensure that the real estate portfolio's composition is still efficient and productive.

A third approach might be to apply low loan-to-value portfolio-level leverage to the entire existing portfolio. This would preserve the current allocations across property types and geographies and would permit incremental investments to be made that would further enhance the diversification of the portfolio. Such leverage could be in the form of a securitization that could be executed either privately or publicly at quite a low interest rate.

Of course, an investor could combine various aspects of these concepts to best manage the return and the risk of the overall real estate portfolio. One very important part of the process of managing the leverage policy through time would be a frequent reevaluation of the utility of leverage for the portfolio. As discussed earlier, leverage is not appropriate for all parts of the market cycle.

BENCHMARKING

Portfolio managers who are allowed to use leverage in execution of their investment strategy should be judged on whether they used the tool effectively. Thus, benchmarking and performance attribution should be designed to evaluate the portfolio managers' performance given what they did, and then compared with what they could have done. The performance of the real estate portfolio would be the sum of the effects of asset allocation within the real estate portfolio, asset selection within the chosen property types and geographies, property management, and the chosen financial structure of the assets and the portfolio. Probably some tracking error around an appropriate benchmark would be tolerated.

It is important for the portfolio manager to get credit for the appropriate use of leverage and to not receive credit for using leverage instead of productive unleveraged strategies. In other words, the focus of the portfolio manager's attention must remain on the management of the real estate and not on the management of the capital markets.

CONCLUSIONS

If a pension fund can agree that it is reasonable and practical to be both a borrower and a lender within the overall portfolio, the real estate portfolio manager (and others) should probably be granted the latitude to use leverage in a careful and accountable fashion. It is reasonable for an investor to be both a borrower and a lender for several reasons:

1. Positive spread lending and borrowing across a credit category are productive;
2. Nonrecourse borrowing has an additional use as a stop loss, and lending recourse while borrowing nonrecourse is certainly advantageous;
3. The increase in risk that is possibly generated for the investor using leverage is possibly mitigated by both the enhanced diversification provided by a portfolio of leveraged versus nonleveraged real estate, and by the ability to use the proceeds from leverage to improve and proactively manage the diversification of the real estate portfolio;
4. Leverage is already in use within every institutional portfolio that invests in stock equities; and
5. The management of the overall portfolio must sometimes yield theoretical high ground to practical high ground, and so is likely to better produce the overall returns that it requires at the risk level it is willing to tolerate by allowing each asset type to operate somewhat independently, and as intelligently as possible.

Therefore, the real estate portfolio manager should be allowed to use conservative and thoughtful leverage as a tool for improved portfolio management of the real estate portfolio when the spread is positive and if risk management tools are carefully and empirically used. Furthermore, a system of performance measurement and attribution should be designed that can be used to ensure that portfolio managers are fully accountable for their choices, and that further study be done to determine the most effective way to design and execute a leverage strategy.

REAL ESTATE INVESTMENT PERFORMANCE AND PORTFOLIO CONSIDERATIONS

Introduction

Thus far, our discussion of risk and required rates of return has stressed a methodology or an approach that should be used when evaluating a specific project or mortgage financing alternative. In this chapter, we provide some insight into the measurement of return and risk for various real estate investment vehicles and investment portfolios.

We will apply concepts and methodologies based on financial theory and demonstrate possible applications to real estate investments. The use of many of these applications is gaining in importance to institutional investors, such as life insurance companies, investment advisors, consultants to pension funds, bank trust departments, and other entities that manage portfolios with real estate assets. Portfolio managers must be able to measure the performance of real estate assets and be able to compare it to the performance of stocks, bonds, and other investments. Also, many portfolio managers are interested in knowing how well investment portfolios perform when real estate investments are *combined* with other securities.

The Nature of Real Estate Investment Data

When measuring the investment performance of something as broadly defined as real estate, one must keep many things in mind. Ideally, to measure real estate investment performance, we would like to have data on prices for all investment property transactions—ranging from hotels to warehouses to apartment units—taking place in the economy, a detailed description of the land, improvements, and cash flows produced by these properties. We would also like to have data on repeated sales of the same properties over time. We could then calculate various measures of return on investment over time. Unfortunately, such a data series, or even an adequate sample of transactions in the many areas of real estate, is not available because the market is one in which the price for a relatively nonhomogeneous asset is negotiated between two parties. Generally, this price does not have to be disclosed

587

to any public or private agency. Hence, unlike securities markets, there is no centralized collection of real estate transactions and operating income data.[1]

Because of these limitations, current attempts to measure real estate investment performance are based on limited data that are made available from a few select sources. The available data may not be representative of (1) the many types of properties, (2) the many geographic areas in which commercial real estate is located, or (3) the frequency of transactions indicative of real estate investment activity in the economy as a whole. Consequently, you must be careful when making generalizations about real estate performance.

Sources of Data Used for Real Estate Performance Measurement

In this section, we provide information on two sources of real estate data that are used to a limited extent when measuring real estate investment performance. We also consider investment returns from data that are available on common stocks, corporate bonds, and government securities. Exhibit 20–1 summarizes the data available for these investments. We rely on two sources for real estate returns in this chapter. The first is security prices as represented by REIT shares. The second data source is based on estimates of value of individual properties owned by pension plan sponsors. Note that the primary differences in these data is that one source is based on real estate-backed securities and the other is based on estimates of individual properties.

REIT Data: Security Prices

One of the two sources of data used to produce investment returns on real estate in this chapter are based on REITs. The **NAREIT** (National Association of Real Estate Investment Trusts) REIT Share Price Index is a monthly index based on ending market prices for shares owned by REIT investors. Data for this series are available beginning with January 1972 and include all REITs actively traded on the New York and American Stock Exchanges as well as the Nasdaq National Market System.[2]

The data used in this chapter are based on only those REITs that *own* real estate, or equity REITs. NAREIT compiles a monthly index for equity REITs based on month-end prices and dividends on securities owned by investors in each equity REIT contained in the index. Hence, the prices of REIT shares are determined by how successful investors believe the trustees of an individual REIT will be in finding properties at favorable prices, managing them, and then selling them. While equity REIT share prices certainly reflect investors' perceptions of the quality, diversity, and risk of real estate assets owned, investors are also evaluating the effectiveness of trustees in their valuation of equity REIT securities. Further, when purchasing shares, investors do not give up as much liquidity as they would if they acquired and managed real estate assets directly, because a continuous auction market (e.g., NYSE) exists in which shares are traded. Thus, investing in an equity REIT may be less risky than investing directly in real estate.

Hybrid and Mortgage REITs

A mortgage REIT investment return series and a hybrid REIT return series are also shown in Exhibit 20–1. The mortgage REIT index is based on security prices of

---

[1]In some states, actual transaction prices must be disclosed to property tax assessors. However, other data relating to property characteristics and operating cash flows are generally not available.

[2]Obtained from various publications of the National Association of Real Estate Investment Trusts, Washington, DC

EXHIBIT 20-1   Common Sources of Data Used for Measuring Investment Performance

Real Estate–Equity Returns	*Description of Data*
NAREIT—Equity REIT Share Price Index and Dividend Yield Series	Monthly index computed based on share prices of REITs that own and manage real estate assets. Security prices used in the index are obtained from the New York Stock Exchange (NYSE), American Stock Exchange (AMEX), and National Association of Security Dealers Automated Quotation (Nasdaq) system. Divided data are collected by NAREIT. Properties owned may be levered or unlevered. Index values are available from 1972 to the present.
NAREIT—Mortgage REIT Share Price Index and Dividend Yield Series	Monthly index computed on share price data of REITs that make primarily commercial real estate loans (construction, development, and permanent) although some make or purchase residential loans (both multifamily and single family). Prices obtained from NYSE, AMEX, and Nasdaq market system. Dividend data are collected by NAREIT. Monthly index data available from 1972 to the present.
NAREIT—Hybrid REIT Index	Monthly index compiled by NAREIT from share prices and dividends for REITs that (1) own properties and (2) make mortgage loans. Sources of data are the same as for equity and mortgage REITs. Index values are available from 1972 to the present
NCREIF Property Index—National Council of Real Estate Investment Fiduciaries	Data are contributed by members of NCREIF, based on about 3,000 properties with an aggregate market value of about $100 billion that are owned by pension fund plan sponsors through investment managers. An index is calculated quarterly and data consist of: (1) net operating income and (2) beginning- and end-of-quarter appraised values for all properties. Actual sale prices are used, as available. Quarterly index values are available from 1978 to the present.
Common stocks— Standard & Poor's (S&P) 500	Daily index based on common stock prices for the 500 corporations with the highest market value of common stock outstanding. Data available from the financial press. Dividend data compiled by Wilshire and Associates and included in a monthly and annual total return index by Ibbotson Associates, Chicago. Daily index data available from 1926 to the present.
Corporate bonds— Salomon Brothers High-Grade Corporate Bond Index	Monthly index based on high-grade, long-term (20-year) bond prices. Interest based on bond coupons and total returns (interest, beginning, and ending index values) compiled by Ibbotson Associates, Chicago. Daily index available from 1926 to the present.
Government securities	U.S. Treasury bills and bonds. Price data obtained from *The Wall Street Journal*. A monthly total return series compiled by Ibbotson Associates, Chicago. Daily index data available from 1926 to the present.

shares outstanding in REITs that specialize in acquiring various types of mortgage loans on many types of properties. Hence, when investing in a mortgage REIT, an investor is buying equity shares in an entity whose assets are primarily mortgage loans. Hybrid REITs operate by buying real estate *and* by acquiring mortgages on both commercial and residential real estate.

NCREIF Property Index: Property Values

The NCREIF Property Index measures the historic performance of income-producing properties either (1) acquired by open-end or commingled investment funds that sell investment units owned by qualified pension and profit-sharing trusts, or (2) acquired by investment advisors and managed on separate account bases. The data incorporated in the **NCREIF Index** are voluntarily contributed and based on the performance of properties managed by members of the National Council of Real Estate Investment Fiduciaries (NCREIF).[3] Quarterly rates of return are calculated for all properties included in the index and are based on two distinct components of return: (1) net operating income and (2) the quarterly change in property market value (appreciation or depreciation). The NCREIF Index contains data on five major property categories: apartment complexes, office buildings, warehouses, office/showrooms/research and development facilities, and retail properties (including regional, community, and neighborhood shopping centers as well as freestanding store buildings). Property values are based on either appraised values or, for properties that are sold, net sales proceeds, which are entered as the final market value in the quarter in which the property is sold. The index returns represent an aggregate of individual property returns calculated quarterly before deduction of investment advisory fees. The quarterly series is calculated by summing the increase or decrease in the value of each property plus its net operating income for the quarter. To obtain changes in value, *quarterly appraisals* are made, and when sales occur, actual transaction prices negotiated by the buyer and seller are a part of the index.

Data Sources for Other Investments

In contrast to the scarcity of real estate return data, data on financial assets are plentiful and easily obtainable. In this chapter, we will also develop measures of investment performance for common stocks from the Standard & Poor's 500 Index of Common Stocks (S&P 500), U.S. Treasury bills (T-bills), longer-term U.S. Treasury bonds, and long-term corporate bonds contained in the Salomon Brothers Index of Corporate Bonds. These indexes (see Exhibit 20–1) are generally computed daily, weekly, monthly, quarterly, and annually and are published regularly in the financial press.

Cumulative Investment Return Patterns

A series of historic total return indexes (see Exhibit 20–2) have been developed to begin the discussion of real estate equity investment performance. We have included three equity indexes: the S&P 500, EREIT (equity REITs), and NCREIF Property Index. Debt securities are represented by indexes for T-bills and corporate bonds (for sources see Exhibit 20–1). These indexes are cumulative total returns based on quarterly data for each security: Each series is indexed at 100 beginning in 1985 (1Q) and is compiled through 2000 (4Q) and includes reinvestment of dividends, income, or interest as appropriate.[4]

The patterns indicate that $100 invested from the end of 1985 through 2000 would have produced the greatest total return (based on quarterly price changes and

---

[3]See the *NCREIF Real Estate Performance Report,* various issues, published by National Council of Real Estate Fiduciaries (Chicago), www.NCREIF.org.

[4]Dividends are included for the S&P 500 and EREITs. Net operating income is included in the NCREIF Index. Interest is included in the corporate bond index. T-bills include price changes only as no interest is paid on these instruments. They are bought and sold at discounts to maturity.

EXHIBIT 20–2   Cumulative Total Returns REITs, S&P 500, NCREIF, Bonds, and T-Bill Indices, 1985–2000

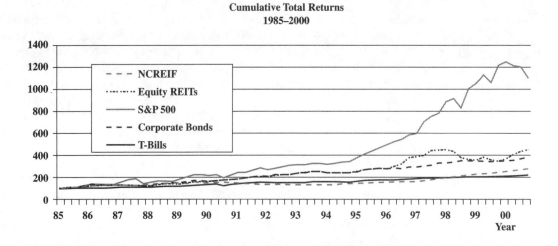

reinvestment of all dividends, interest, or income) if it had been invested in securities comprising the S&P 500 index. Total return rankings of the other indexes were as follows: Equity REITs, Corporate Bond Index, NCREIF Index, and T-bills. We stress, however, that although these return patterns are informative, it should not be implied that each investment is equivalent in *risk*. When attempting to make comparisons among different securities, cumulative return data must be broken down into an appropriate time series so that various measures of volatility can be calculated to provide some idea about the relative risk of each security. It should be stressed that when analyzing investments, returns provide us with only one-half of the information that we need. Information on the risk characteristics of investment are equally important.

Computing Holding Period Returns

While the cumulative total returns shown in Exhibit 20–2 are useful information, additional insight into the risk-return characteristics of each security can be obtained by examining returns over shorter time periods. The most fundamental unit of measure used by portfolio managers to measure investment returns for individual securities, or a class of securities in a portfolio, is the **holding period return** *(HPR)*. This is generally defined as follows:

$$HPR = \frac{P_t - P_{t-1} + D_t}{P_{t-1}}$$

where P_t is the end-of-period price for the asset, or value of an index for an investment, or index representing a class of investments, whose performance is being assessed, P_{t-1} is the beginning of period value, and D represents any dividends or other cash payouts that may have occurred during the period over which the *HPR* is being measured.

EXHIBIT 20–3   Sample Computation of Holding Period Returns (*HPRs*) and Related Statistics: Hypothetical Security

Period Ending	Index	HPR	HPR − $\overline{HPR}$	(HPR − $\overline{HPR}$)²
Quarter				
1	673.7	—	—	—
2	764.6	0.1349	0.1240	0.0154
3	787.6	0.0301	0.0192	0.0004
4	803.6	0.0203	0.0094	0.0001
5	802.5	−0.0014	−0.0123	0.0002
6	886.3	0.1044	0.0935	0.0087
7	890.6	0.0049	−0.0061	0.0000
8	855.3	−0.0396	−0.0505	0.0026
9	773.1	−0.0961	−0.1070	0.0115
10	844.3	0.0921	0.0812	0.0066
11	867.8	0.0278	0.0169	0.0003
12	878.5	0.0123	0.0014	0.0000
13	874.4	−0.0047	−0.0156	0.0002
14	895.6	0.0242	0.0133	0.0002
15	948.5	0.0591	0.0482	0.0023
16	982.6	0.0360	0.0250	0.0006
17	952.5	−0.0306	−0.0415	0.0017
18	914.5	−0.0399	−0.0508	0.0026
19	911.8	−0.0030	−0.0139	0.0002
20	780.7	−0.1438	−0.1547	0.0239
21	804.9	0.0310	0.0201	0.0004
		Σ0.2181		Σ0.0779

1st quarter $HPR = (764.6 − 673.7) \div 673.7 = 0.1349$

Mean $HPR = \overline{HPR} = \Sigma HPR \div n = 0.2181/20 = 0.0109$

Variance $= \sigma^2 = \Sigma (HPR − HPR)^2 \div n = 0.0779/20 = 0.0039$

Standard deviation $= \sigma = \sqrt{\sigma^2} = \sqrt{.0039} = 0.0624$

Coefficient of variation $= 0.0624 \div 0.0109 = 5.7219$

Geometric mean return $= \sqrt[n]{(1 + HPR_1)(1 + HPR_2)\cdots(1 + HPR_n)} − 1 = 0.0013$

An example of how holding period returns are calculated for a hypothetical security index is demonstrated in Exhibit 20–3. The first quarter's return was calculated by subtracting the end-of-period value and dividing by the beginning-of-period value. The arithmetic mean, variance, standard deviation, and coefficient of variation have also been calculated. These measures will be used in our discussion of risk later in the chapter. The *HPR* for the first quarter in the series was 13.49 percent. The mean *HPR,* or *HPR,* all quarterly returns in the series were 1.09 percent.

An alternative way of considering these return data is to calculate the **geometric mean return.** This return is calculated by finding the *n*th root of the product of each quarterly *HPR* in series multiplied together, minus 1 (see bottom of exhibit). The geometric mean return was equal to .13 percent, a measure of the quarterly *compounded* rate of return that an investor would have earned on $1 invested in the index during the period.

Although the values of the arithmetic mean and geometric mean are sometimes very close, this will not always be the case, particularly if values in the series rise and fall sharply or the series is longer than the sample shown in the exhibit. There

EXHIBIT 20–4   Summary Statistics of Performance Measures for Selected Investment Alternatives

	CPI	Corp. Bonds	S&P 500	T-Bills	NCREIF	EREIT
Arithmetic mean	1.13%	2.31%	4.06%	1.76%	2.32%	3.94%
Standard deviation	0.90%	3.80%	7.41%	0.70%	1.76%	10.26%
Coefficient of variation	0.80	1.64	1.83	0.40	0.76	2.60
Geometric mean	0.79%	2.24%	3.98%	1.40%	1.73%	2.58%

is a distinct conceptual difference between the arithmetic and geometric mean returns. The geometric mean is used by portfolio managers when considering the performance of an investment and is expressed as a compound rate of interest from the beginning to the end of a specific period of time. **Arithmetic mean returns** are simple averages (not compounded) and are widely used in statistical studies spanning very long periods of time.[5]

Exhibit 20–4 contains summary statistics for various investments that we have chosen to include in the chapter. Note that for each of the return series, we have calculated quarterly arithmetic mean and geometric mean returns and related statistics. The exhibit also includes data for the Consumer Price Index (CPI).

Comparing Investment Returns

We can now begin to compare total returns for the various investment categories contained in Exhibit 20–4. A number of patterns should be apparent from the data. The geometric mean returns (also called time weighted returns by many portfolio managers), show that from 1985 to 2000, stocks constituting the Standard and Poor's 500 Index (S&P 500) produced quarterly returns of 3.98 percent, which exceeded all other returns shown in the exhibit. Equity REIT (NAREIT) returns were 2.58 percent, followed by corporate bonds which were 2.24 percent, then by returns on the NCREIF Index, which were 1.73 percent, and T-bills (1.40 percent).

HPRs and Inflation.   All returns shown in Exhibit 20–4 may also be compared with the quarterly rate of inflation, as represented by the CPI, which was .79 percent. The comparison with the CPI provides some insight into whether returns from each investment category exceeded the rate of inflation (thereby earning *real* returns).

Comparing Risk Premiums.   In addition to returns, risk premiums may be calculated for each investment class relative to T-bills. Risk premiums may also be

---

[5]The geometric mean is considered to superior to the arithmetic mean when the past performance of an investment is being considered for a specified period of time, say from the date of purchase until the present time, or for an investment portfolio where funds are flowing in and out and the investment base is changing. For example, suppose the price of a security is 100, 110, 100 at the end of each of three consecutive years. The *HPR*s are 10 percent and − 9.09 percent. The arithmetic mean is .45 percent; however, the geometric mean is zero. The latter result occurs because the beginning and ending security prices are equal. This return better represents the performance of a security from the time of purchase until the present. Arithmetic mean returns are used in statistical studies where some inference about the future is based on averages of past performance. In these cases, an entire series of returns may be used to justify a long-term future decision and no specific time interval is considered any more important than another.

calculated for each investment relative to all other investments. For example, during the 1985–2000 period, EREITs earned an average *risk premium* of 1.18 percent per quarter, in excess of T-bills (2.58% − 1.40%). T-bills are generally used to represent a riskless investment; hence, T-bill returns provide a measure of a risk-free return. Investors in EREITs would also have earned a premium of .34 percent relative to returns on corporate bonds (2.58% − 2.24%). When compared to the NCREIF Index, which provided returns of 1.73 percent compounded quarterly, EREIT returns were higher by .85 percent. We should recall, however, that the NCREIF Index is compiled on an *unleveraged* basis; that is, the properties in the index were purchased on an all-cash basis or "free and clear" of debt. Hence, a more appropriate comparison for the NCREIF Property Index would be relative to equity REITs that purchase properties on an all-cash basis, or unleveraged basis, because EREIT returns include the effects of leverage, while the NCREIF Index does not. Hence, EREITs are more risky. Therefore, holding all else constant, a premium should be earned on EREIT shares relative to returns based on the NCREIF Index.

Risk, Return, and Performance Measurement

While comparing investment returns is an important starting point in evaluating investment performance, it represents only one part of the analysis. We know from material presented earlier that investments that produce higher returns usually exhibit greater price volatility and are generally *riskier* than investments that produce lower returns. In cases involving *individual real estate* investments, such risks may be a function of the type of property, its location, design, lease structure, and so on. Those attributes, and the attendant risks associated with those attributes, can be thought of as a type of *business risk.*

Another source of risk occurs when real estate investments are leveraged. In these cases, default risk is present. Finally, because of the relative difficulty and time required to sell property, liquidity risk is certainly present. As we know, when these three major sources of risk are compared among properties or among alternative investments, when more risk is taken by investors, a risk premium, or higher investment return should be earned by investors who bear that additional risk. One way of considering this risk-return relationship is to compute risk premiums, as we did above. A subjective assessment can then be made about whether risk premiums earned on riskier assets are adequate relative to the additional risk taken. An investor may then judge whether the premium earned on EREITs is sufficient to compensate for their added risk taken if EREITs are purchased instead of corporate bonds.

Another way of looking at the risk-return relationship is to think about the way in which business, default, and liquidity risks affect the pattern of returns that investors expect to earn. Over time, returns (dividends and price changes) on investments with more of these risks present are likely to exhibit more *variation* than investments with fewer of these risks. Recalling our earlier discussions on investment risk, we would expect a property with more risk to provide higher, but more variable investment returns than a property with less risk. The point is that greater variability in market prices and cash flows can be thought of as commensurate with increased risk because an investor owning a risky asset with a highly variable price pattern (up and down) faces having to sell it for a more unpredictable price than a less risky asset. *The assumption that variability in asset returns represents risk and that premiums over what could be earned on a riskless investment represent the price of risk is the foundation for modern finance theory.* It is also a premise that must be understood if the techniques for risk-adjusting returns that are described below are to be used.

Risk-Adjusted Returns: Basic Elements

Given that the combined effects of the sources of risk described above will be reflected in the variability in investment returns, one way of taking into account investment risk when evaluating performance is to consider the variability of returns. The variability of holding period returns for specific assets or classes of assets enables one to make a better comparison among investments exhibiting different risk.

One approach that may be used to consider risk and returns is to compute the **coefficient of variation** of the returns. This is defined as the standard deviation of returns divided by the mean return (this can be based on either the arithmetic or geometric mean returns for a given investment or investment index). This concept is sometimes referred to as a *risk-to-reward ratio* and is intended to relate total risk, as represented by the standard deviation, to the mean return with the idea of determining how much return an investor could expect to earn relative to the total risk taken if the investment was made. For example, if an investor holds a portfolio containing securities with a mean return of 2 percent and a standard deviation of 3 percent the coefficient of variation is 1.5. This may be interpreted as taking 1.5 units of risk for every unit of return that is earned.[6]

An interesting comparison may now be made between the investment performance of EREITs and the NCREIF Index. Recall from Exhibit 20–4 that the NCREIF Index produced a lower mean return compared with EREITs. However, when mean returns for both investment categories are risk-adjusted, the NCREIF Index appears to have outperformed the EREIT index on a risk-adjusted basis. When the coefficient of variation for EREITs and the NCREIF Index are compared, the NCREIF had better *risk-adjusted return* than the EREITs.

It has already been pointed out that the NCREIF Index (1) does not include the effect of leverage in investment returns, and (2) property values used to compute the NCREIF Index are based largely on quarterly appraisals plus a relatively small number of actual sale transactions. Using appraisals may have a smoothing effect on returns and reduce variability. If property appraisals are (1) significantly different from actual market values and (2) affect the variation in the index, then the NCREIF Index may not be representative of true real estate returns or volatility in those returns. For example, results in Exhibit 20–4 for EREITs indicate that the mean return was 3.94 percent and the standard deviation of returns was 10.26 percent, resulting in a coefficient of variation of 2.60. This compares to a mean return of 2.32 percent for the NCREIF Index and a coefficient of variation of .76. These results indicate a material difference in both return and risk for the two indexes. This difference also may be due to considerable differences in the types of properties (e.g., office, retail; apartment), in the geographic distribution of their locations (e.g., north, south, east, or west and suburban or urban sites); and in the investment strategies employed by investment managers (e.g., investing in raw land in predevelopment stages or in fully leased properties only). Such differences may affect the relative risk of investments

---

[6]This calculation also assumes that the risk premium, or return, is proportional to the risk taken on all investments by all investors. This assumption clearly *does not hold* for all investors, some of whom are more risk-averse than others. Even for the same investor, risk aversion cannot be considered for individual assets independently of one another. Rather, risk must be assessed in terms of the additional risk assumed relative to the total portfolio of assets owned. More will be said about this later.

in each index. Further, equity REIT shares are bought and sold in an *auction* market with continuous trading, whereas the individual properties that make up the NCREIF Index are bought and sold in a much more limited, *negotiated* market between parties. Premiums for liquidity and transaction costs when making such comparisons are really not well understood, nor have such premiums been isolated in research studies. Finally, the definition of income used in calculating the holding period returns for both indexes may not be exactly comparable because of advisory and other management fees that are deducted from REIT income, but not for properties in the NCREIF Index. More research must be done before the nature of risk and return for investments made in REIT shares versus direct investment in real estate, as represented by the NCREIF Index, is well understood.

Elements of Portfolio Theory

The preceding section dealt with one approach that may be used to compare investments by considering the investment's mean return (we used the geometric) and the standard deviation of those returns. The standard deviation was used as a measure of risk when making comparisons among investments. In addition, investors must consider the extent to which the acquisition of an investment affects the risk and return of a *portfolio* of assets. This question is very important because of the interaction between returns when investments are *combined* in a portfolio. This interaction may cause the variance of return on a portfolio to be less than the average of the individual investments. When investors add to an existing portfolio it is important to understand how the acquisition of new assets may *impact* the return and risk of the entire portfolio.

Building a portfolio by considering the return and standard deviation of returns for *individual* investments will not always ensure that an optimum portfolio will be obtained. Indeed, any new asset that is being considered as an addition to a portfolio should be judged on the grounds of "efficiency", that is, whether its addition to an existing portfolio will increase expected portfolio returns while maintaining, or lowering, portfolio risk. Alternatively, an investor may also judge whether the portfolio efficiency of an asset will lower portfolio risk while maintaining or increasing, the expected portfolio return.[7]

To illustrate how the interaction between investment returns occurs, we consider the data in Exhibit 20–5. Returns in column 1 are calculated on quarterly *HPR*s for another stock *i*, abbreviated as HPR_i. Returns in column 2 are the quarterly returns computed for stock over the same time period. The statistics presented at the bottom of the exhibit indicate that the quarterly mean return for stock *j* was 3.59 percent and the standard deviation was 9.33 percent. The mean return for stock *i* was 1.09 percent, and the standard deviation of the return was 6.24 percent (calculations not shown). Obviously, risk and returns for these two investments are very different. Stock *j* produced both a higher mean return and higher standard deviation (risk) when compared with the returns from stock *i*. Assuming that an investor was holding a portfolio *composed only* of stock *j* at the beginning of the investment period, the question to answer is, how would the addition of another investment (as represented by real estate stock *i*)

---

[7]The basis for modern portfolio theory was developed by Harry Markowitz, "Portfolio Selection," *Journal of Finance* 7, no. 1 (March 1952), pp. 77–91.

EXHIBIT 20–5   **Computation of the Mean *HPR* and Standard Deviation for a Hypothetical Portfolio Containing Stocks *i* and *j* in Equal Proportions**

	Stock i HPR	Stock j HPR	$HPR_p = .5(HPR_i) + .5(HPR_j)$	$(HPR_p - \overline{HPR}_p)$	$(HPR_p - \overline{HPR})^2$
Quarter					
1	0.1350	0.1407	0.1379	0.1145	0.0131
2	0.0301	0.0591	0.0446	0.0212	0.0004
3	0.0202	−0.0697	−0.0247	−0.0481	0.0023
4	−0.0013	0.0540	0.0264	0.0030	0.0000
5	0.1044	0.2133	0.1588	0.1354	0.0183
6	0.0048	0.0514	0.0281	0.0047	0.0000
7	−0.0396	0.0662	0.0133	−0.0101	0.0001
8	−0.0961	−0.2263	−0.1612	−0.1846	0.0341
9	0.0921	0.0587	0.0754	0.0520	0.0027
10	0.0279	0.0660	0.0469	0.0235	0.0006
11	0.0123	0.0039	0.0081	−0.0153	0.0002
12	−0.0047	0.0310	0.0132	−0.0102	0.0001
13	0.0242	0.0703	0.0472	0.0238	0.0006
14	0.0591	0.0880	0.0735	0.0501	0.0025
15	0.0360	0.1065	0.0713	0.0478	0.0023
16	−0.0307	0.0205	−0.0051	−0.0285	0.0008
17	−0.0399	−0.0302	−0.0351	−0.0585	0.0034
18	−0.0029	0.0629	0.0300	0.0066	0.0000
19	−0.1438	−0.1378	−0.1408	−0.1642	0.0270
20	0.0310	0.0895	0.0603	0.0369	0.0014
n = 20	0.2181	0.7180	0.4681		0.1100

Portfolio$_p$ holding period return $\overline{HPR}_p = 0.4681 \div 20 = 0.0234$

Portfolio variance $= \sigma^2_p = (HPR_p - \overline{HPR}_p)^2 \div n = 01100/20 = 0.0055$

Portfolio standard deviation $= \sigma_p = \sqrt{\sigma^2_p} = 0.0742$

affect the quarterly mean *portfolio* return and its standard deviation? Would the investor have been better off adding real estate securities to this portfolio?

Calculating Portfolio Returns

To demonstrate an approach that may be used to answer these questions, we will assume that both stocks *i* and *j* were *weighted equally* in one portfolio at the beginning of the period. We will then compute the mean return and standard deviation for the *combined portfolio* (see Exhibit 20–5). The mean return for the portfolio, $\overline{HPR}_p$, is calculated as:

$$\overline{HPR}_p = W_i(\overline{HPR}_i) + W_j(\overline{HPR}_j)$$
$$= .5(.0109) + .5(.0359)$$
$$= .0055 + .0179$$
$$= .0234$$

where *W* represents the weights that securities *i* and *j* represent as a proportion of the total value of the portfolio (i.e., $W_i + W_j = 1.0$). Based on this calculation, we see that the *portfolio* return would have been 2.34 percent quarterly, which is less than what would have been earned on stock *j* alone. However, we cannot really conclude much from this result until we consider how portfolio *risk* may have been affected when the two investments were combined.

Portfolio Risk   To consider how total portfolio risk would have been affected by the *addition* of stock *i* to an existing portfolio of continuing stock *i* and *j* only, the standard deviation of the *new portfolio* returns is calculated (see Exhibit 20–5). Based on those results, we can see that the portfolio standard deviation is 7.42 percent, which is far less than the standard deviation of stock *j* which was 9.33 percent.

However, it is important to note that unlike the mean *HPR* for the portfolio, the *standard deviation of portfolio returns* for the two indexes is not equal to the simple weighted average of the individual standard deviations of the two indexes; that is, [(.5)(6.24%)] + [(.5)(9.33%)] does *not* equal the standard deviation of the portfolio returns. This is because when the returns of the two assets are combined, a greater than proportionate reduction in the variance in portfolio returns is achieved. In other words, there is *interaction* between the two returns in the sense that the pattern, or direction of movement, in each of the individual *HPR*s is not the same in each period.[8] Indeed, in some quarters, the *HPR*s for EREITs are positive and the *HPR*s for the stocks are negative. Hence, when combined in one portfolio, the returns on the portfolio are less volatile than the individual assets. The nature of this interaction is important to understand when measuring the risk of an investment portfolio because it demonstrates whether a portfolio investor will benefit from diversification.

Covariance and Correlation of Returns; Key Statistical Relationships.   One important aspect of individual investment returns to consider is how the return on a prospective new asset will vary with returns on an existing portfolio. Clearly, if the asset is producing returns that move up and down in a pattern that is very *similar* to movements in portfolio returns, the inclusion of that asset in the portfolio will not reduce total variation (*risk*) by very much. This pattern, when considered with the mean of portfolio returns and mean return of the prospective asset, will give us an indication of how efficient the acquisition of an asset will be when combined with another asset or with an existing portfolio. Two statistics provide a numerical measure of the extent to which returns tend to either move together, in opposite directions, or have no relationship to one another. These statistics are the *covariance* and *correlation* between the two return series.

The **covariance** between returns on two assets is an *absolute* measure of the extent to which two data series (*HPR*s) move together over time. It is calculated for our example in Exhibit 20–6. Essentially, the covariance is computed for two investments by first finding the deviation of each investment's *HPR* from its mean ($\overline{HPR}$). These deviations for each security in each period are then multiplied and summed. The summed deviations are divided by the number of observations in each series. The result is the *covariance* or statistic that provides an *absolute* measure of the extent to which returns between two securities move together. In our example, the covariance between *i* and *j* is .47 percent.

Because the covariance was positive, the returns on the two securities tended to move *together*, or in the same direction, during the period over which we made the calculation. Hence, we have *positive covariance* between the two stocks. It is also

---

[8]As shown in Exhibit 20–5, the portfolio standard deviation can be calculated each time weights for stocks change. Another method of computation for the two-security case can be made by simply changing the weights W_E and W_S for stocks *E* and *S* in the following equation: $[(W_E)^2(S_E)^2 + (W_S)^2(S_S)^2 + 2(W_S)(W_E)(S_S)(S_E)_{pSE}]^{1/2}$ = portfolio standard deviation, where *W* = weight of security types *E*, *S* (all W_S must total 1), *S* = standard deviation of security, and p_{SE} is the coefficient of correlation between *S* and *E*. Exhibit 20–6 shows the calculations for the standard deviation for each security as well as the correlation between the securities.

EXHIBIT 20-6   **Computation of Covariance for Stocks i and j**

Period Ending	HPR Stock i	HPR Stock j	$HPR_i - \overline{HPR_i}$	$HPR_j - \overline{HPR_j}$	$(HPR_i - \overline{HPR_i}) \times (HPR_j - \overline{HPR_j})$	Stock i $(HPR_i - \overline{HPR_i})^2$	Stock j $(HPR_j - \overline{HPR_j})^2$
Quarter							
1	0.1350	0.1407	0.1241	0.1048	0.0130	0.0154	0.0110
2	0.0301	0.0591	0.0192	0.0232	0.0004	0.0004	0.0005
3	0.0202	−0.0697	0.0093	−0.1056	−0.0010	0.0001	0.0111
4	−0.0013	0.0540	−0.0122	0.0181	−0.0002	0.0001	0.0003
5	0.1044	0.2133	0.0935	0.1774	0.0166	0.0087	0.0315
6	0.0048	0.0514	−0.0061	0.0155	−0.0001	0.0000	0.0002
7	−0.0396	0.0662	−0.0505	0.0303	−0.0015	0.0026	0.0009
8	−0.0961	−0.2263	−0.1070	−0.2622	0.0281	0.0115	0.0687
9	0.0921	0.0587	0.0812	0.0228	0.0019	0.0066	0.0005
10	0.0279	0.0660	0.0170	0.0300	0.0005	0.0003	0.0009
11	0.0123	0.0039	0.0014	−0.0320	−0.0000	0.0000	0.0010
12	−0.0047	0.0310	−0.0156	−0.0049	0.0001	0.0002	0.0000
13	0.0242	0.0703	0.0133	0.0344	0.0005	0.0002	0.0012
14	0.0591	0.0880	0.0482	0.0521	0.0025	0.0023	0.0027
15	0.0360	0.1065	0.0251	0.0706	0.0018	0.0006	0.0050
16	−0.0307	0.0205	−0.0416	−0.0154	0.0006	0.0017	0.0002
17	−0.0399	−0.0302	−0.0508	−0.0661	0.0034	0.0026	0.0044
18	−0.0029	0.0629	−0.0138	0.0270	−0.0004	0.0002	0.0007
19	−0.1438	−0.1378	−0.1547	−0.1737	0.0269	0.0239	0.0302
20	0.0310	0.0895	0.0201	0.0536	0.0011	0.0004	0.0029
$n = 20$	0.2181	0.7180			0.0940	0.0779	0.1741

Stock i holding period return $\overline{HPR_i} = 0.2181 \div 20 = 0.0109$

Stock i variance $= \sigma_i^2 = 0.0779 \div 20 = 0.0039$

Stock i standard deviation $= \sigma_i = \sqrt{\sigma_i^2} = 0.0624$

Stock j holding period return $\overline{HPR_j} = 0.7180 \div 20 = 0.0359$

Stock j variance $= \sigma_j^2 = 0.1741 \div 20 = 0.0087$

Stock j standard deviation $= \sigma_j = \sqrt{\sigma_j^2} = 0.0933$

$$COV_{ij} = \Sigma[HPR_i - \overline{HPR_i}][HPR_j - \overline{HPR_j}] \div n$$
$$= 0.0940 \div 20$$
$$= 0.0047$$

Correlation between stocks i and j
$$= [COV_{ij}] \div [\sigma_i \sigma_j] = 0.8070$$

possible to have *negative covariance,* indicating that returns tend to move in opposite directions. While the covariance measure is useful, it is somewhat difficult to interpret because it is an *absolute* measure of the relationship between returns. We would expect that very large covariance values may indicate a very strong relationship (either positive or negative) between investment returns. However, the covariance statistic can take on values ranging from $+\infty$ to $-\infty$, and, as a result, it is difficult to know when a covariance value is "large" or "small." Because of this problem, we need a method to gauge the importance of the statistic on a *relative* scale of importance. The coefficient of **correlation** (ρ) is used to obtain this *relative* measure or the extent to which one set of numbers moves in the same or opposite direction with another series. The formula for the correlation statistic ρ is:

$$\rho_{ij} = COV_{ij} \div (\sigma_i \, \sigma_j)$$

In our example we have:

$$\rho_{ij} = .0047 \div (.0624)(.0933)$$
$$= .8070$$

The correlation statistic may only range between $+1$ and -1; therefore, it is a much easier way to interpret the extent to which returns are related. For example, as the coefficient of correlation approaches $+1$, two series are said to move very closely together, or be highly correlated. Hence, given a change in one of the series, there is a high likelihood of a change in the other series in the same direction.[9] Conversely, as the coefficient approaches -1, the series are negatively correlated because they move in exactly opposite directions. Hence, given a change in one series, the other would be expected to move in the opposite direction. If the correlation coefficient is close to zero, the implication is that no relationship exists between the two series. In our example, a correlation coefficient of .8070 indicates a strong positive correlation between stocks i and j over the period considered because the coefficient is equal to .8070, has a positive sign, and is much closer to $+1.0$ than it is to zero.[10]

What are some other important relationships at this point? It should be clear that if two investments are *highly positively correlated,* the reduction in the variance in portfolio returns (hence, risk) is likely to be smaller than if there were no correlation or negative correlation because, in the latter case, the distribution of two returns would be either unrelated or negatively related, and the interaction between returns would not be reinforced. If returns were negatively correlated, they would be offsetting and the sum of the deviations from the portfolio mean would be smaller after the security is added; hence, the standard deviation of portfolio returns would be lower (i.e., lower risk). Consequently, it should be stressed that anytime the correlation between returns on two assets is less than $+1$, *some* reduction in risk (standard deviation) may be obtained by combining investments, as opposed to holding one investment (or one portfolio) with higher standard deviation than the prospective investment. However, the potential for risk reduction is much greater as the correlation approaches -1.

Based on the foregoing analysis, it should be clear why the standard deviation of portfolio returns in our example is not equal to a simple, weighted average of the standard deviation of the two individual investment returns. Further, if variation in security returns is a reasonable representation of risk to investors, then it should become apparent that there may be some benefit, in the form of risk reduction, by *diversifying* an investment portfolio to include assets with returns that are negatively correlated, or assets with returns showing little or no correlation. Of course, the other critical dimension that has to be considered is how the *mean return* of the portfolio will be affected when the individual securities are combined. For example, if two securities have the *same* positive mean returns and these returns were perfectly, negatively correlated (e.g., -1), then it may be inferred that an investor could

---

[9]Obviously there would have to be an underlying cause-and-effect relationship between the two series to make an assertion that any past relationship can be used to predict a future relationship.

[10]When the coefficient of correlation has a value greater than .5, the association between two series is considered high. There are also statistical tests of significance that enable us to say with more confidence whether two series are correlated or whether the correlation statistic calculated between the series resulted from an unrepresentative sample taken from the underlying distribution of returns. For a discussion of correlation, normal distribution assumptions, and related statistics, see a standard college textbook on elementary statistics.

earn a positive portfolio return with zero risk if both investments were purchased (the standard deviation of the combined returns would be zero). The possibility that this will ever occur is slight, however, because the likelihood of finding perfectly negatively correlated (-1) securities is small. However, many investments with returns that are negatively correlated, uncorrelated, or less than perfectly positively correlated may be candidates for addition to a portfolio on the grounds of efficiency outlined above. These basic elements of portfolio analysis should make the reader aware of a framework that may be used to consider many questions regarding risk and returns.

Portfolio Weighting: Trading Off Risk and Return

In our hypothetical example, we have seen that adding stock *i* to a portfolio containing stock *j* would have reduced portfolio risk (standard deviation) by a lesser amount (percent) than the reduction in portfolio mean return. This implies that a portfolio containing both stocks (indexes) would not have been more efficient than a portfolio containing only one stock. However, in our computations, we assumed that *both assets were equally weighted.* Could a more optimal portfolio, that is, one containing some other combination of stocks that would have either increased returns relative to an increase in risk or maintained returns while decreasing risk, been attained by *varying the weight (proportion) of the two securities in the portfolio?* To answer this question, we first consider the *sample* of NCREIF and S&P 500 returns from Exhibit 20–4, or those returns that comprised the *period* 1985–2000. The arithmetic quarterly means *HPR* for the S&P 500 index was 4.06 percent with a standard deviation of 7.41 percent, and the *HPR* for NCREIF was 2.32 percent with a standard deviation of 1.76 percent. The correlation between both return series was $-.0521$ (see Exhibit 20–7).[11] Because the correlation coefficient was less than 1, some reduction in risk would have been possible by combining the two assets.

Second, we want to understand the importance of weighting securities in a portfolio. To determine the optimal *weighting, all combinations* of both assets must be considered. In our example, the weight of each security was changed in increments of 10 percent, and the mean portfolio return and standard deviation were calculated for each weighting. The result is shown in Exhibit 20–8. The diagram shows all values lying between the two extreme cases, that is, the case where the portfolio would be composed entirely of S&P 500 stocks and no NCREIF properties (100 percent in the exhibit) and the case where the portfolio would be composed of 100 percent NCREIF properties and no S&P shares (0 percent in the exhibit). Hence, the curve in the exhibit shows the *trade-off* between return and risk for the portfolio as the two asset classes are combined in varying proportions.

Note that even though the NCREIF Index had a lower mean *HPR* during this period, when compared with the S&P index (see Exhibit 20–4), diversification benefits may be realized by *combining* assets as opposed to holding only S&P 500 or NCREIF properties. This is illustrated in Exhibit 20–8.

In Exhibit 20–8, note that having a portfolio of 100 percent NCREIF has a lower return but greater risk than holding some S&P with NCREIF. This results from the diversification benefits of including both stocks (S&P) and properties (NCREIF) in a portfolio. The portion of the curve with a positive slope (returns increase as risk increases) is known as the *efficient frontier*. It represents the most

---

[11]The correlations are calculated over a longer time period to capture the long-run correlation between the different assets.

**EXHIBIT 20–7   Correlation Matrix for Selected Assets:
Quarterly Returns, 1978–2000**

	1978–2000					
	CPI	*Bonds*	*S&P 500*	*T-Bills*	*NCREIF*	*REITs*
CPI	1					
Bonds	−0.2440	1				
S&P 500	−0.1349	0.2766	1			
T-Bills	0.5868	0.1284	−0.0737	1		
NCREIF	0.3317	−0.1469	−0.0521	0.4700	1	
REITs	−0.0199	0.4862	0.5986	0.0044	−0.0642	1

EXHIBIT 20–8   Portfolio Returns of NCREIF and S&P 500 Stocks, 1978–2000

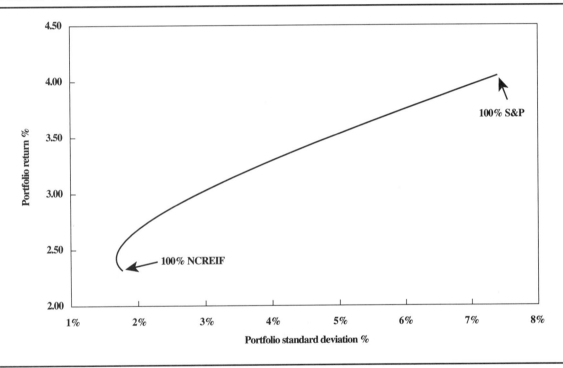

efficient combination of securities that provides investors with maximum portfolio returns as portfolio risk increases. Returns below the efficient frontier (or in the interior of the ellipse) are *inferior* because there is always a better combination of securities that will increase returns for a given level of risk. Investors will choose the combination of securities along the efficient frontier in accordance with their willingness to take risk. Investors who are risk-averse would tend to hold a mix with more properties (NCREIF) in this example. Less risk-averse investors would tend to weigh stocks (S&P) more heavily in their portfolio. Holding all stocks (100 percent S&P) has the greatest expected return but also the greatest risk.

Real Estate Returns, Other Investments, and the Potential for Portfolio Diversification

From the preceding analysis, it should be clear that there are many different assets that have the potential to be combined efficiently in a portfolio that will provide an optimal risk-return relationship for investors. Clearly, our example consisting of only NCREIFs and S&P 500 assets shows this potential. However, many other assets can be considered by investors when selecting assets. One of the key relationships that indicates the potential for combining assets in a portfolio is the correlation between asset returns. Exhibit 20–7 is a *correlation matrix,* or table, that contains the coefficient of correlation for returns on all securities listed in Exhibit 20–4. The purpose of calculating these coefficients is to consider how various *investment vehicles* might be combined efficiently with various other assets when building a portfolio.

We can gain some insight into the question of whether portfolios containing certain securities would be more efficient if *real estate investment vehicles* were added. We will focus on this more narrow question, because to consider the question of what *the* optimum portfolio *should* contain would have to include an examination of the risk and returns for the global, or worldwide set of securities and assets that are available to investors. Such a portfolio might contain bonds, stock, real estate, gold, jewelry, coins, stamps, and virtually any asset that can be owned by investors. Based on mean standard deviation of returns and covariance between returns, investors would hold portfolios containing the optimum combination of available investments. An efficient frontier, such as the one shown in our two-investment case in Exhibit 20–8, would also exist for this larger, diversified "market portfolio." If all investors made decisions based on whether or not the ratio of risk to return for the total portfolio would be improved, all investor portfolios would tend to be diversified and efficient. Returns on any additional investments would be evaluated on the basis of any incremental increases or decreases in total portfolio risk, and the risk premium paid by investors for these securities would reflect that incremental risk. In short, risk premiums for investments would be determined on the basis of the expected addition or reduction in portfolio risk and all investments would be priced in accordance with that relationship.[12]

In this section, we consider the question of portfolio performance, diversification, and real estate. Portfolio managers have seriously considered real estate as an investment class for only about 20 years. Only in recent years has equity ownership in real estate become widely available in a "securitized" form such as a REIT share or in ownership "units" in open- and closed-ended commingled investment funds. Also regulatory restrictions governing pension funds have been relaxed to include real estate as an acceptable investment. However, many institutions, which heretofore considered only government securities, corporate bonds, and common stocks have shown increasing interest in real estate.

We now consider the question of whether real estate investments are likely to provide **diversification benefits** to investors with portfolios consisting of some government securities, stocks, and bonds. In other words, we begin with some assumptions about the nature of existing investment portfolios. We then consider whether these portfolios could have benefited from diversifying by acquiring real estate investments over the period 1985–2000.

---

[12]For additional information regarding capital market theory and efficient markets, see Z. Bodie, A. Kane, and A. Marcus, *Investments,* 2nd ed. (Homewood, IL., Richard D. Irwin, 1994).

***Portfolio
Diversification:
EREITs and Other
Investments***

Looking again at Exhibit 20–7, we can see what the historical (or ex-post) correlation in quarterly returns was for each investment relative to all others for the period 1978–2000. Focusing our attention on equity investments in real estate, note, for example, that returns on EREITs tended to be positively correlated with common stocks (.5986) and corporate bonds (.4862) and a correlation of almost zero (.0044) with T-bills. This relationship suggests that because EREITs have less than perfect correlation with the S&P 500 and corporate bonds and the correlation coefficient between both EREITs and T-bills is very low, there is a good chance that if this real estate investment was combined in a portfolio containing common stock, bonds, and T-bills, diversification benefits could be achieved. Furthermore, NCREIF has a negative coefficient with the S&P 500 ($-.0521$) and bonds ($-.1469$) although it has a positive correlation with T-bills (.47). This suggests that adding direct investment in properties may provide more diversification benefits than just adding REITs.

To illustrate the diversification benefits of adding equity real estate to a portfolio of stocks and bonds, we will use the mean (arithmetic) returns from Exhibit 20–4 and the correlations from Exhibit 20–7.[13] Exhibit 20–9 shows two efficient frontiers. The lower frontier consists of only stocks (S&P 500) and bonds. The upper frontier includes stocks, bonds and private real estate investments (NCREIF Index). Note that the frontier that includes real estate has higher returns at each level of risk (standard deviation). The only exception is the highest risk/highest return portfolio which in both cases consists entirely of stocks. Including private real estate with stocks and bonds also provides a wider spectrum of risk-return combinations at the lower end of the frontier (i.e., where there is less return but lower levels of risk).

It should be noted that these results are based on historical returns over a specific time period and may not be indicative of future performance. Investors make investment decisions based on future or expected risks and returns. This example has used ex-post, or past returns to illustrate concepts. There is no assurance that these results will be repeated in the future. In practice, investors often use historic correlations as was done in this example unless there is evidence that there has been a significant change in the correlation between different assets. Similarly, historic standard deviations for securities are used unless there is a reason to believe that the underlying risk of the asset has changed. But expected future rather than historic returns are used for each asset. Historic returns are only used as one indication of what might be realistic to expect in the future.

We also used the NCREIF Index as an indication of the return and risk (standard deviation) for private real estate. The NCREIF index has a very low mean return and standard deviation of returns. As noted in the beginning of this chapter, this index may not fully capture the true variability in returns for private real estate because it is based on appraised values rather than transaction prices. Some have argued that the use of appraised values may reduce or "smooth" the variation in returns. This does not mean that the estimates of value are erroneous. Rather, the appraisal process is such that sudden shifts in the market as reflected in a few transactions are not fully captured in appraised values until the change in market conditions can be sufficiently confirmed by additional market evidence. Thus indices based on appraised values may not fully capture quarterly changes in property values in an index like the NCREIF Index.

---

[13]In practice we might use expected future returns rather than historical return for this type of analysis. We use historic returns to illustrate the diversification benefits based on what was actually achieved for each asset.

EXHIBIT 20–9   Efficient Frontiers

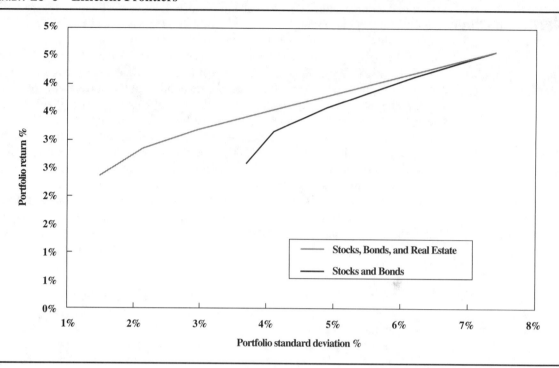

Public versus Private Real Estate Investments

We saw previously that the performance of private real estate as reflected in the NCREIF Index and the performance of REITs as reflected in the NAREIT Index were quite different in terms of historic returns, standard deviations, and correlations with other assets. For example, the standard deviation of the NAREIT Index is higher than that of the NCREIF Index. One explanation for this might be that the NCREIF Index does not capture all of the variability of returns because it is based on appraised values, as discussed earlier. An alternative explanation, however, is that when real estate is owned by publicly traded REITs, it takes on more of the risk of public markets in general. As we saw in Exhibit 20–7, REITs have a much higher correlation with the S&P 500 than NCREIF. Also, we saw that the NCREIF Index has a relatively high correlation with the CPI indicating that it may be an inflation hedge whereas the NAREIT Index has a slightly negative correlation with the CPI.

There is likely to be truth in both arguments—that appraisals reduce the variance of the true returns in the NCREIF Index but publicly traded REITs take on additional variance because they trade in more active markets that are influenced more by short-term flows of capital into and out of the stock market. To see what the difference in variability is between NCREIF and NAREIT, we have plotted the historic returns for each in Exhibit 20–10. Note that in order to better compare the returns over time, we have used a different scale for the NCREIF returns (-6% to $+6\%$) than for NAREIT returns (-20% to $+25\%$). The NAREIT Index clearly has more volatility in its returns than the NCREIF Index and the two indices perform quite differently during many time periods.

Although some people argue about which index is a better indication of the performance of equity real estate, it is quite possible that the conclusion should be that

EXHIBIT 20–10   **NCREIF versus NAREIT (REITs) Quarterly Returns, 1985–2000**

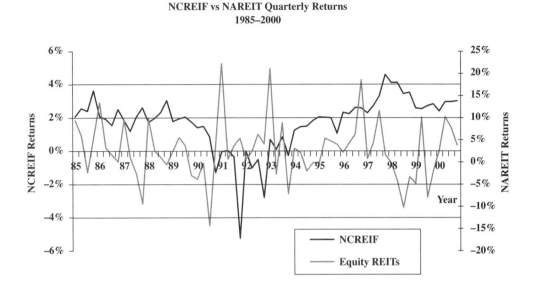

both private real estate investments (represented by the NCREIF Index) and public real estate investments (represented by the NAREIT Index) could play a role in a portfolio. Both provide diversification benefits to a pure stock and bond portfolio, and there are advantages and disadvantages of each as an investment alternative. For example, REITs are more liquid than private real estate but the investor does not have control over decisions as to when to sell individual properties as he or she would by owning properties instead of shares of stock. The purpose of this chapter is not to suggest which type of investment is better for a particular investor, but rather to illustrate what tools an investor can use to evaluate the role of either one or both ways of including equity real estate in a portfolio.

Real Estate Performance and Inflation

One final comparison of interest to portfolio managers is the relationship between real estate performance and *inflation*. More specifically, did real estate returns exceed the rate of inflation? To provide some insight into this question, we recall our earlier comparisons between the EREIT and NCREIF indexes and the CPI. In all cases, the real estate indexes exceeded the rate of growth in the CPI. This implies that at least for the period 1985–2000, real estate investments, as represented by the data used in Exhibit 20–4, exceeded the rate of inflation and produced real investment returns. Another question of importance is whether real estate returns are *correlated* with inflation. Using the correlation matrix in Exhibit 20–7, it would appear that based on the NCREIF Index and the CPI, it is. However, the same comparison with EREITs indicates that it is not. In this context it is important to realize that a *positive* correlation with inflation is desirable because it indicates that the asset is an inflation hedge. That is, if inflation increases then returns also increase which preserves the real rate of return.

Conclusion

This chapter has introduced the measurement of investment performance and the basic elements of portfolio theory. We have also dealt with the question of whether real estate investments tend to provide diversification benefits to portfolios that have traditionally consisted of government securities, common stocks, and corporate bonds.

We have stressed that the nature of real estate investment return data is very limited and may not be representative of a broad measure of real estate returns. Further, some of the data are based on a group of properties owned by investment advisors. In this case, an index is calculated on reported net operating income and appraised property values with very few actual transaction prices.

Results from the portfolio simulations conducted and reported in the last part of the chapter indicate that there appeared to be significant gains available from portfolio diversification into real estate during the period 1985–2000 based on these limited data sets. In all simulations, real estate increased portfolio efficiency. Of course, these results are based on historical data from a limited sample of real estate investments and may not be indicative of future results or apply generally to all real estate investments.

Key Terms

arithmetic mean returns   593
coefficient of variation   595
correlation   599
covariance   598
diversification benefits   603

geometric mean return   592
holding period return (*HPR*)   591
NAREIT Index   588
NCREIF Index   590

(This page intentionally left blank.)

The Economics of the Private Equity Market

Stephen D. Prowse
Senior Economist and Policy Advisor
Federal Reserve Bank of Dallas

*T*his article examines

the economic foundations

of the private equity market

and describes its

institutional structure.

The private equity market is an important source of funds for start-ups, private middle-market companies, firms in financial distress, and public firms seeking buyout financing.[1] Over the past fifteen years, it has been the fastest growing market for corporate finance, far surpassing others such as the public equity and bond markets and the market for private placement debt. Today the private equity market is roughly one-quarter the size of both the market for commercial and industrial bank loans and the market for commercial paper in terms of outstandings (*Figure 1*). In recent years, private equity capital raised by partnerships has matched, and sometimes exceeded, funds raised through initial public offerings and gross issuance of public high-yield corporate bonds. Probably the most celebrated aspect of the private equity market is the investment in small, often high-tech, start-up firms. These investments often fuel explosive growth in such firms. For example, Microsoft, Dell Computer, and Genentech all received private equity backing in their early stages. In addition, the private equity market supplied equity funds in the huge leveraged buyouts of such large public companies as Safeway, RJR Nabisco, and Beatrice in the 1980s.

Despite its dramatic growth and increased significance for corporate finance, the private equity market has received little attention in the financial press or the academic literature.[2] The lack of attention is due partly to the nature of the instrument itself. A private equity security is exempt from registration with the Securities and Exchange Commission by virtue of its being issued in transactions "not involving any public offering." Thus, information about private transactions is often limited, and analyzing developments in this market is difficult.

This article examines the economic foundations of the private equity market and describes its institutional structure. First, I briefly discuss the growth of the limited partnership as the major intermediary in the private equity market over the last fifteen years. Next, I explain the overall structure of the market, focusing in turn on the major investors, intermediaries, and issuers. I then look at returns to private equity over the last fifteen years. Finally, I analyze the role of limited partnerships and why they are a particularly effective form of intermediary in the private equity market. This entails a detailed examination of the contracts these partnerships write with their investors and the companies in which the partnerships invest.

Figure 1

Flows and Outstandings in Private Equity and Other Corporate Finance Markets

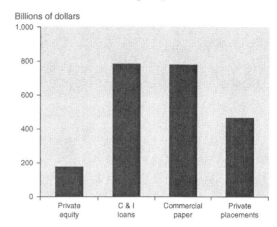

Amounts raised in 1996

Outstandings at year-end 1996

SOURCES: Federal Reserve Board flow of funds accounts; author's estimates.

THE GROWTH OF LIMITED PARTNERSHIPS IN THE PRIVATE EQUITY MARKET

The private equity market consists of professionally managed equity investments in the unregistered securities of private and public companies.[3] Professional management is provided by specialized intermediaries called limited partnerships, which raise money from institutional investors and invest it in both publicly and privately held corporations. Private equity managers acquire large ownership stakes and take an active role in monitoring and advising companies in which they invest. They often exercise as much or more control than company insiders.

The growth of private equity is a classic example of how organizational innovation, aided by regulatory and tax changes, can ignite activity in a particular market. In this case, the innovation was the widespread adoption of the limited partnership as the means of organizing private equity investments. Until the late 1970s, private equity investments were undertaken mainly by wealthy families, industrial corporations, and financial institutions investing directly in issuing firms. By contrast, most investment since 1980 has been undertaken by intermediaries on behalf of institutional investors. The major intermediary is the limited partnership; institutional investors are the limited partners, and professional investment managers are the general partners.

The emergence of the limited partnership as the dominant form of intermediary is a result of the extreme information asymmetries and incentive problems that arise in the private

equity market. The specific advantages of limited partnerships are rooted in the way in which they address these problems. The general partners specialize in finding, structuring, and managing equity investments in closely held private companies. Limited partnerships are among the largest and most active shareholders with significant means of both formal and informal control and thus can direct companies to serve the interests of their shareholders. At the same time, limited partnerships employ organizational and contractual mechanisms that align the interests of the general and limited partners.

Limited partnership growth was also fostered by regulatory changes in the late 1970s that permitted greater private equity investment

Figure 2

Private Equity Capital Outstanding, by Source of Funds, 1980 and 1995

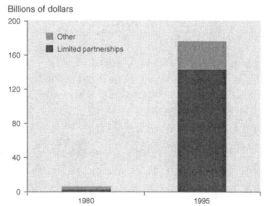

Billions of dollars

SOURCES: *Venture Economics*; Fenn, Liang, and Prowse (1997).

22

Figure 3
Organized Private Equity Market

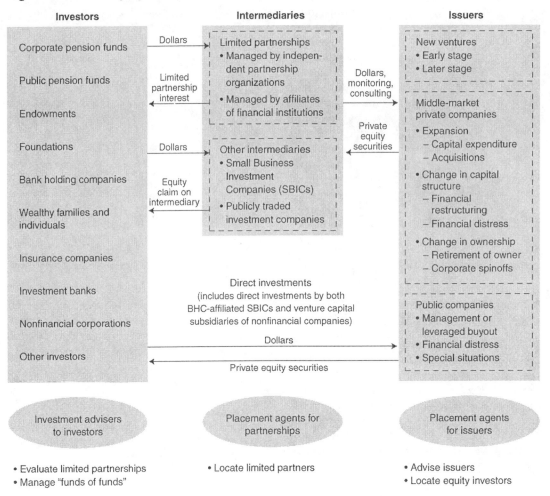

by pension funds. The results of these changes are telling: from 1980 to 1995, the amount of capital under management in the organized private equity market increased from roughly $4.7 billion to over $175 billion. In addition, limited partnerships went from managing less than 50 percent of private equity investments to managing more than 80 percent (*Figure 2*).[4] Most of the remaining private equity stock is held directly by investors, but even much of this direct investment activity is the result of knowledge that these investors have gained investing in and alongside limited partnerships.

THE STRUCTURE OF THE ORGANIZED PRIVATE EQUITY MARKET

The organized private equity market has three major players and an assortment of minor ones. Figure 3 illustrates how these players interact with each other. The left-hand column lists the major investors, the middle column lists major intermediaries, and the right-hand column lists the major issuers in the private equity market. Arrows pointing from left to right indicate the flow of dollars and other services; arrows pointing from right to left indicate the flow of private equity securities or other claims. The bottom of Figure 3 lists an assortment of agents and investment advisors that help issuers or intermediaries raise money or advise investors on the best intermediaries in which to invest. The role of each of these players in the private equity market is discussed below.

Investors

Figure 4 illustrates the total estimated private equity outstanding at year-end 1996 and the portions held by the various investor groups. Public and corporate pension funds are the largest groups, together holding roughly 40 percent of capital outstanding and currently supplying close to 50 percent of all new funds raised by partnerships.[5] Public pension funds are the fastest growing investor group and recently overtook private pension funds in terms of the amount of total private equity held. Endowments and foundations, bank holding companies, and wealthy families and individuals each hold about 10 percent of total private equity. Insurance companies, investment banks, and nonfinancial corporations are the remaining major investor groups. Over the 1980s the investor base within each investor group broadened dramatically, but still only a minority of institutions within each group (primarily the larger institutions) hold private equity.

Most institutional investors invest in private equity for strictly financial reasons, specifically because they expect the risk-adjusted returns on private equity to be higher than those on other investments and because of the potential benefits of diversification.[6] Bank holding companies, investment banks, and nonfinancial corporations may also invest in the private equity market to take advantage of economies of scope between private equity investing and their other activities. Commercial banks, for example, are large lenders to small and medium-sized firms. As such, they have contact with many potential candidates for private equity. Conversely, by investing in a private equity partnership, banks may be able to generate lending opportunities to the firms in which the partnership invests. Nonfinancial

firms typically invest in early-stage developmental ventures that may fit with their competitive and strategic objectives.

Intermediaries

Intermediaries—mainly limited partnerships—manage an estimated 80 percent of private equity investments. Under the partnership arrangement, institutional investors are the limited partners and a team of professional private equity managers serves as the general partners. Most often the general partners are associated with a partnership management firm (such as the venture capital firm Kleiner Perkins Caufield & Byers or the buyout group Kohlberg Kravis Roberts & Co.). Some management companies are affiliates of a financial institution (an insurance company, bank holding company, or investment bank); the affiliated companies generally are structured and managed no differently than independent partnership management companies.

Investment companies not organized as limited partnerships—Small Business Investment Companies (SBICs), publicly traded investment companies, and other companies—today play only a marginal role as intermediaries in the private equity market.[7] SBICs, established in 1958 to encourage investment in private equity, can leverage their private capital with loans from, or guaranteed by, the Small Business Administration.[8] In the 1970s they accounted for as much as one-third of private equity investment, but today they account for

Figure 4

Investors in the Private Equity Market, by Holdings of Outstandings at Year-End 1996

Billions of dollars

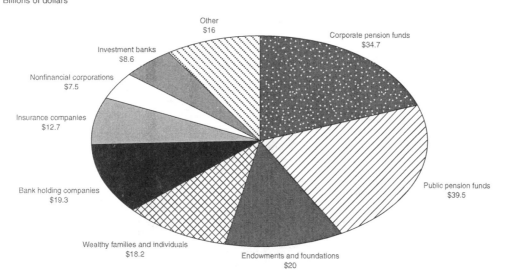

Total Private Equity Outstanding = $176.5 billion

24

Table 1

Characteristics of Major Issuers in the Private Equity Market

Characteristic	Early-stage new ventures	Later stage new ventures	Middle-market private firms	Public and private firms in financial distress	Public buyouts	Other public firms
Size	Revenues between zero and $15 million	Revenues between $15 million and $50 million	Established, with stable cash flows between $25 million and $500 million	Any size	Any size	Any size
Financial attributes	High growth potential	High growth potential	Growth prospects vary widely	May be over-leveraged or have operating problems	Under-performing High levels of free cash flow	Depend on reasons for seeking private equity
Reason(s) for seeking private equity	To start operations	To expand plant and operations To cash out early-stage investors	To finance a required change in ownership or capital structure To expand by acquiring or purchasing new plant	To effect a turnaround	To finance a change in management or in management incentives	To ensure confidentiality To issue a small offering For convenience Because industry is temporarily out of favor with public equity markets
Major source(s) of private equity	"Angels" Early-stage venture partnerships	Later stage venture partnerships	Later stage venture partnerships Nonventure partnerships	"Turnaround" partnerships	LBO and mezzanine debt partnerships	Nonventure partnerships
Extent of access to other financial markets	For more mature firms with collateral, limited access to bank loans	Access to bank loans to finance working capital	Access to bank loans For more mature, larger firms, access to private place-ment market	Very limited access	Generally, access to all public and private markets	Generally, access to all public and private markets

less than $1 billion of the $176.5 billion market. The reduced role of SBICs has resulted in part from their inability to make long-term equity investments when they themselves are financed with debt. Publicly traded investment companies also played a role in the past, but today fewer than a dozen such companies are active, and together they manage less than $300 million. Apparently the long-term nature of private equity investing is not compatible with the short-term investment horizons of stock analysts and public investors.[9]

The dramatic growth of the limited partnership as the major intermediary in the private equity market is a result of the limited partnership's success in mitigating the severe information problems that exist in the market—both for institutional investors looking for appropriate partnerships in which to invest and for partnerships looking for appropriate portfolio company investments. The mechanisms the limited partnerships use to control these problems are explored in detail in a following section.

Issuers

Issuers in the private equity market vary widely in size and their motivation for raising capital, as well as in other ways. They do share a common trait, however: because private equity is one of the most expensive forms of finance, issuers generally are firms that cannot raise financing from the debt or public equity markets.

Table 1 lists six major issuers of private equity and their main characteristics. Issuers of

Table 2

Average Internal Rates of Return for Venture and Nonventure Private Equity Limited Partnerships and for Public Small-Company Stocks

Average annual return (percent)

Partnerships formed in:	Venture capital	Nonventure capital	Public small-company stocks
1969–79	23.3	—	11.5*
1980–84	10.0	24.8	15.3†
1985–89	15.2	15.3	13.4‡
1990–91	24.1	28.9	15.6§

* Over the period 1969 to 1988.
† Over the period 1980 to 1993.
‡ Over the period 1985 to 1996.
§ Over the period 1990 to 1996.

SOURCE: Fenn, Liang, and Prowse (1997).

traditional venture capital are young firms, most often those developing innovative technologies that are predicted to show very high growth rates in the future. They may be early-stage companies, those still in the research and development stage or the earliest stages of commercialization, or later stage companies, those with several years of sales but still trying to grow rapidly.

Since 1980, nonventure private equity investment—comprising investments in established public and private companies—has outpaced venture investment, as illustrated in Figure 5. Nonventure investments include those in middle-market companies (roughly, those with annual sales of $25 million to $500 million), which have become increasingly attractive to private equity investors. Many of these companies are stable, profitable businesses in

low-technology manufacturing, distribution, services, and retail industries. They use the private equity market to finance expansion—through new capital expenditures and acquisitions—and to finance changes in capital structure and in ownership (the latter increasingly the result of private business owners reaching retirement age).

Public companies also are issuers in the nonventure sector of the private equity market. Such companies often issue a combination of debt and private equity to finance their management or leveraged buyout. Indeed, between the mid- and late 1980s such transactions absorbed most new nonventure private equity capital. Public companies also issue private equity to help them through periods of financial distress, to avoid registration costs and public disclosures, and to raise funds during periods when their industry is out of favor with public market investors.

Agents and Advisors

Also important in the private equity market is a group of "information producers" whose role has increased significantly in recent years. These are the agents and advisors who place private equity, raise funds for private equity partnerships, and evaluate partnerships for potential investors. They exist because they reduce the costs associated with the information problems that arise in private equity investing. Agents facilitate private companies' searches for equity capital and limited partnerships' searches for institutional investors; they also advise on the structure, timing, and pricing of private equity issues and assist in negotiations. Advisors facilitate institutional investors' evaluations of limited partnerships; they may be particularly valuable to financial institutions unfamiliar with the workings of the private equity market.

RETURNS IN THE PRIVATE EQUITY MARKET

A major reason for the explosive growth of the private equity market since 1980 has been the anticipation by institutional investors of returns substantially higher than can be earned in alternative markets. Of course, private equity investments are regarded as considerably more risky and more illiquid than other assets. For those institutional investors that can bear such risk and illiquidity, however, the high expected returns are a major attraction.

Available data indicate that returns to private equity have at times far exceeded returns in the public market. Table 2 shows internal

Figure 5

Private Equity Capital Outstanding, by Type of Investment, 1980 and 1995

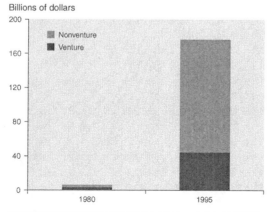

Billions of dollars

SOURCES: *Venture Economics*; Fenn, Liang, and Prowse (1997).

26

rates of return on venture and nonventure private equity partnerships during the period in which the partnership was formed. These returns are those experienced by the limited partners; they are measured net of management fees and other partnership expenses. Returns to partnerships that have not yet been liquidated reflect the valuation of a residual component comprising investments whose market values are unknown but are often reported at cost. This may bias downward the returns reported for the funds formed from the mid-1980s onward.

Overall, Table 2 suggests that returns to private equity have generally been above those experienced in the public equity market. The fourth column of Table 2 shows the annual average returns on a portfolio of public small-company stocks over various periods. These periods are intended to be roughly comparable with the ones during which the partnerships listed were earning the bulk of their returns.[10] Except for the early 1980s, returns to both venture and nonventure private equity are greater than returns to public small-company stocks, sometimes substantially so. Whether this is enough to compensate investors for the increased risk of such investments is, of course, another matter. However, as mentioned above, returns for more recent partnerships may be biased downward.

Table 2 also suggests that returns have been higher for nonventure than for venture partnerships. This pattern may partly explain the faster growth of the later stage and, particu-

Table 3

Mechanisms Used to Align the Interests of Participants in the Private Equity Market

Limited partners – general partners	Partnership – portfolio companies
Performance incentives	Performance incentives
Reputation	Managerial ownership
General partner compensation	Managerial compensation
Direct means of control	**Direct means of control**
Partnership covenants	**Voting rights**
Advisory boards	**Board seats**
	Access to capital

NOTE: Most important mechanisms are in bold type.

larly, nonventure sectors of the private equity market over the past fifteen years.

To a certain extent, returns are driven by capital availability. For venture investments, for example, returns have been greatest on investments made during periods when relatively small amounts of capital were available (*Figure 6*). Conversely, there is concern, if not a large amount of evidence, that periods of greater capital availability depress future returns.

THE ROLE OF LIMITED PARTNERSHIPS IN THE PRIVATE EQUITY MARKET

Accompanying the rapid growth of the private equity market in the 1980s was the rise of professionally managed limited partnerships as intermediaries, as illustrated in Figure 2. In certain respects, the success of limited partnerships is paradoxical. Funds invested in such partnerships are illiquid over the partnership's life, which in some cases runs more than ten years. During this period, investors have little control over the way their funds are managed. Nevertheless, the increasing dominance of limited partnerships suggests that they benefit both investors and issuers.

Table 3 provides an overview of the mechanisms that are used to align the interests of (1) the limited and general partners and (2) the partnerships and the management of the companies in which they invest. These mechanisms can be categorized under the broad headings of performance incentives and direct means of control.

As shown on the left-hand side of Table 3, performance incentives that align the interests of the limited and general partners are twofold. First, the general partners must establish a favorable track record to raise new partnerships. Second, they operate under a pay-for-performance scheme in which most of their expected compensation is a share of the profits earned on

Figure 6

Capital Raised by Venture Capital Partnerships and Internal Rates of Return as of 1995

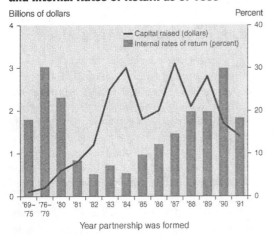

SOURCE: Fenn, Liang, and Prowse (1997).

investments. These provisions are the principal means by which the interests of the general and limited partners are harmonized. Of secondary importance are direct control mechanisms such as partnership agreements and advisory boards composed of limited partners. Partnership agreements give limited partners restricted direct control over the general partners' activities. These agreements consist mainly of restrictions on allowable investments and other partnership covenants, which the advisory board can waive by majority vote.

In contrast, the direct means of oversight and control are the principal mechanisms for aligning the interests of the partnership and portfolio company management. The most important of these mechanisms are a partnership's voting rights, its seats on the company board, and its ability to control companies' access to additional capital. Performance incentives for company management, including managerial ownership of stock, are also important but are secondary to direct partnership control.

Information Problems in Private Equity Investing

Two types of problems frequently occur when outsiders finance a firm's investment activity—sorting problems and incentive problems. Sorting (or adverse selection) problems arise in the course of selecting investments. Firm owners and managers typically know much more about the condition of their business than do outsiders, and it is in their interest to accent the positive while downplaying potential difficulties (see Leland and Pyle 1977; Ross 1977). Incentive (or moral hazard) problems arise in the course of the firm's operations. Managers have many opportunities to take actions that benefit themselves at the expense of outside investors.

Private equity is used in financing situations in which the sorting and incentive problems are especially severe.[11] Resolving these problems requires that investors engage in intensive preinvestment due diligence and postinvestment monitoring. These activities are not efficiently performed by large numbers of investors; there can either be too much of both types of activities because investors duplicate each others' work, or too little of each owing to the tendency for investors to free ride on the efforts of others. Thus, delegating these activities to a single intermediary is potentially efficient.

The efficiency of intermediation depends on how effectively the sorting and incentive problems between the ultimate investors and intermediaries can be resolved.[12] In the private equity market, reputation plays a key role in addressing these problems because the market consists of a few actors that repeatedly interact with each other. For example, partnership managers that fail to establish a favorable track record may subsequently be unable to raise funds or participate in investment syndicates with other partnerships.[13]

Overview of Private Equity Partnerships

Private equity partnerships are limited partnerships in which the senior managers of a partnership management firm serve as the general partners and institutional investors are the limited partners. The general partners are responsible for managing the partnership's investments and contributing a very small proportion of the partnership's capital (most often, 1 percent); the limited partners provide the balance and bulk of the investment funds.

Each partnership has a contractually fixed lifetime—generally ten years—with provisions to extend the partnership, usually in one- or two-year increments, up to a maximum of four years. During the first three to five years, the partnership's capital is invested. Thereafter, the investments are managed and gradually liquidated. As the investments are liquidated, distributions are made to the limited partners in the form of cash or securities. The partnership managers typically raise a new partnership fund at about the time the investment phase for an existing partnership has been completed. Thus, the managers are raising new partnership funds approximately every three to five years and at any one time may be managing several funds, each in a different phase of its life. Each partnership is legally separate, however, and is managed independently of the others.

A partnership typically invests in ten to fifty portfolio companies (two to fifteen companies a year) during its three- to five-year investment phase. The number of limited partners is not fixed: most private equity partnerships have ten to thirty, though some have as few as one and others more than fifty.[14] The minimum commitment is typically $1 million, but partnerships that cater to wealthy individuals may have a lower minimum and larger partnerships may have a $10 million to $20 million minimum.

Most partnership management firms have six to twelve senior managers who serve as general partners, although many new firms are started by two or three general partners and a few large firms have twenty or more. Partnership management firms also employ

28

associates—general partners in training—usually in the ratio of one associate to every one or two general partners. General partners often have backgrounds as entrepreneurs and senior managers in industries in which private equity partnerships invest and, to a lesser extent, in investment and commercial banking.

RELATIONSHIP BETWEEN A PARTNERSHIP AND ITS PORTFOLIO COMPANIES

Partnership managers receive hundreds of investment proposals each year. Of these proposals, only about 1 percent are chosen for investment. The partnership managers' success depends upon their ability to select these proposals efficiently. Efficient selection is properly regarded as more art than science and depends on the acumen of the general partners acquired through experience operating businesses as well as experience in the private equity field.

Investment proposals are first screened to eliminate those that are unpromising or that fail to meet the partnership's investment criteria. Private equity partnerships typically specialize by type of investment and by industry and location of the investment. Specialization reduces the number of investment opportunities considered and reflects the degree of specialized knowledge required to make successful investment decisions.

This initial review consumes only a few hours and results in the rejection of up to 90 percent of the proposals the partnership receives. In many cases, the remaining proposals are subjected to a second review, which may take several days. Critical information included in the investment proposal is verified and the major assumptions of the business plans are scrutinized. As many as half the proposals that survived the initial screening are rejected at this stage.

Proposals that survive these preliminary reviews become the subject of a more comprehensive due-diligence process that can last up to six weeks. It includes visits to the firm; meetings and telephone discussions with key employees, customers, suppliers, and creditors; and the retention of outside lawyers, accountants, and industry consultants. For proposals that involve new ventures, the main concerns are the quality of the firm's management and the economic viability of the firm's product or service (Gladstone 1988). For proposals involving established firms, the general objective is to gain a thorough understanding of the existing business, although the precise focus of the investigation varies with the type of investment. With distressed companies, efforts are focused on discussions with the company's lenders; for buyouts of family-owned businesses, management succession issues will warrant greater attention; and for highly leveraged acquisitions, efforts will focus on developing detailed cash-flow projections.

Extensive due diligence in the private equity market is needed because little, if any, information about issuers is publicly available and in most cases the partnership has had no relationship with the issuer. Thus, the partnership must rely heavily on information that it can produce *de novo*. Moreover, the management of the issuing firm typically knows more than outsiders do about many aspects of its business. This information asymmetry, combined with the fact that issuing private equity is very expensive, has the potential to create severe adverse selection problems for investors. In the private equity market, this problem is mitigated by the extensive amount of due diligence and by the fact that alternative sources of financing for private equity issuers are limited.

Information asymmetries between investors and managers of the issuing firm give rise to a potential moral hazard problem, whereby management pursues its own interests at the expense of investors. Private equity partnerships rely on various mechanisms to align the interests of managers and investors. These mechanisms can be classified into two main categories. The first category comprises mechanisms that relate to performance incentives, including the level of managerial stock ownership, the type of private equity issued to investors, and the terms of management employment contracts. The second comprises mechanisms that relate to direct means of control of the firm, including board representation, allocation of voting rights, and control of access to additional financing. These mechanisms are examined in turn.

Performance Incentives

Managerial Stock Ownership. Private equity managers usually insist that the portfolio firm's senior managers own a significant share of their company's stock, and stock ownership often accounts for a large part of managers' total compensation. In venture capital, management stock ownership varies widely depending upon the management's financial resources and the company's financing needs and projected future value. It also depends upon the number of rounds of financing, as dilution typically occurs with each round. Even in later stage companies, however, management ownership of 20 percent is not unusual. For nonventure companies, managerial share ownership usually ranges between 10 percent and 20 percent.

A common provision in both venture and nonventure financing is an equity "earn-out" (Golder 1983). This arrangement allows management to increase its ownership share (at the expense of investors) if certain performance objectives are met.

Type of Private Equity Issued to Investors. Convertible preferred stock is the private equity security most frequently issued to investors. The major difference between convertible preferred stock and common stock is that holders of preferred stock are paid before holders of common stock in the event of liquidation. From the partnership's standpoint, this offers two advantages. First, it reduces the partnership's investment risk. Second, and more important, it provides strong performance incentives to the company's management because management typically holds either common stock or warrants to purchase common stock. If the company is only marginally successful, its common stock will be worth relatively little. Thus, the use of convertible preferred stock mitigates moral hazard problems. Subordinated debt with conversion privileges or warrants is sometimes used as an alternative way of financing the firm: it confers the same liquidation preference to investors as convertible preferred equity and, thus, the same performance incentives to management.

Management Employment Contracts. In principle, management's equity position in the firm could induce excessive risk taking. However, management compensation can also be structured to include provisions that penalize poor performance, thereby offsetting incentives for risk taking. Such provisions often take the form of employment contracts that specify conditions under which management can be replaced and buyback provisions that allow the firm to repurchase a manager's shares in the event that he or she is replaced.

Mechanisms of Direct Control

Although managerial incentives are a very important means of aligning the interests of management and investors, a private equity partnership relies primarily on its ability to exercise control over the firm to protect its interests.

Board Representation. In principle, a firm's board of directors bears the ultimate responsibility for the management of the firm, including hiring and firing the CEO, monitoring and evaluating the firm's performance, and contributing significantly to the firm's business and financial planning process.

General partners can be extremely influential and effective outside directors. As large stakeholders, they have an incentive to incur the expense necessary to monitor the firm. Moreover, they have the resources to be effective monitors—in the form of their own staff members, information acquired during the due-diligence process, and the expertise acquired while monitoring similar companies.

Private equity partnerships in many cases dominate the boards of their portfolio companies. Lerner (1994) reports that general partners hold more than one-third of the seats on the boards of venture-backed biotechnology firms, which is more than the share held by management or other outside directors. Even if it is a minority investor, a private equity partnership usually has at least one board seat and is able to participate actively in a company's management.

Allocation of Voting Rights. For early-stage new ventures, leveraged buyouts, and financially distressed firms, the investment is often large enough to confer majority ownership. In other situations, the partnership may obtain voting control even if it is not a majority shareholder. Even if the partnership lacks voting control, however, it is generally the largest non-management shareholder. Thus, it has a disproportionate degree of influence on matters that come to a shareholder vote.

In general, a partnership's voting rights do not depend on the type of stock issued. For example, holders of convertible preferred stock may be allowed to vote their shares on an "as-converted" basis. Similarly, subordinated debt can be designed so that investors have voting rights should a vote take place. The issue of voting control can also be addressed by creating separate classes of voting and nonvoting stock.

Control of Access to Additional Financing. Partnerships can also exercise control by providing a company with continued access to funds. This is especially the case for new ventures. Venture capital is typically provided to portfolio companies in several rounds at fairly well-defined development stages, generally with the amount provided just enough for the firm to advance to the next stage of development. Even if diversification provisions in the partnership agreement prevent the partnership itself from providing further financing, the general partners have the power, through their extensive contacts, to bring in other investors.

30

Conversely, if the original partnership is unwilling to arrange for additional financing, it is unlikely that any other partnership will choose to do so; the reluctance of the original partnership is a strong signal that the company is a poor investment.

Nonventure capital is also provided in stages, though to a lesser extent. For example, middle-market firms that embark on a strategy of acquisitions periodically require capital infusions to finance growth; that capital is not provided all at once. Similarly, companies that undergo leveraged buyouts are forced to service debt out of free cash flow and subsequently must justify the need for any new capital (Palepu 1990).

Other Control Mechanisms. Other mechanisms by which partnerships control and monitor the activities of the companies in which they invest include covenants that give the partnership the right to inspect the company's facilities, books, and records and to receive timely financial reports and operating statements. Other covenants require that the company not sell stock or securities, merge or sell the company, or enter into large contracts without the approval of the partnership.

RELATIONSHIP BETWEEN THE LIMITED PARTNERS AND THE GENERAL PARTNERS

By investing through a partnership rather than directly in issuing firms, investors delegate to the general partners the labor-intensive responsibilities of selecting, structuring, managing, and eventually liquidating private equity investments. However, limited partners must be concerned with how effectively the general partners safeguard their interests. Among the more obvious ways in which general partners can further their own interests at the expense of the limited partners are spending too little effort monitoring and advising portfolio firms, charging excessive management fees, taking undue investment risks, and reserving the most attractive investment opportunities for themselves.

Private equity partnerships address these problems in two basic ways: by using mechanisms that relate to performance incentives and mechanisms that relate to direct means of control. Performance incentives are the more important means of aligning general partners' interests with those of the limited partners. These incentives involve the general partners' need to protect their reputations and the terms of the general partners' compensation structure, such as their share of the profits. These incentives can significantly curtail the general partners' inclination to engage in behavior that does not maximize value for investors. Direct control mechanisms in the partnership agreement are relatively less important means of controlling the moral hazard problem between general and limited partners.

Performance Incentives

Reputation. Partnerships have finite lives. To remain in business, private equity managers must regularly raise new funds, and fund raising is less costly for more reputable firms. In fact, to invest in portfolio companies on a continuous basis, managers must raise new partnerships once the funds from the existing partnership are fully invested, or about once every three to five years.

Raising partnership funds is time consuming and costly, involving presentations to institutional investors and their advisors that can take from two months to well over a year, depending on the general partners' reputation and experience. A favorable track record is important because it conveys some information about ability and suggests that general partners will take extra care to protect their reputation. Also, experience itself is regarded as an asset. To minimize their expenses, partnership managers generally turn first to those who invested in their previous partnerships—assuming, of course, that their previous relationships were satisfactory.

Certain features of a partnership enhance the ability of the general partners to establish a reputation. These features essentially make both the partnership's performance and the managers' activities more transparent to investors than might be the case for other financial intermediaries. One such feature is segregated investment pools. By comparing one partnership's investment returns with those of other partnerships raised at the same time, it is easier to account for factors that are beyond the control of the general partners, such as the stage of the business cycle or the condition of the market for initial public offerings, mergers, and acquisitions. By contrast, if private equity intermediaries did not maintain segregated investment pools, earnings would represent a blend of investment returns that occur at different stages of the business cycle or under different market conditions.

Another feature is the separation of management expenses and investment funds. In a limited partnership, management fees are specified in the partnership agreement (described below). Thus, the amount of investment capital that can be consumed in the form of manager salaries and other perquisites is capped. Moreover, because such expenses are transparent, it is easier to compare expenses across partnerships. Other types of financial intermediaries pay expenses and finance investments out of the same funds raised from investors; although expenses are reported, they are difficult to control before the fact and are not always transparent after the fact.

Compensation Structure. General partners earn a management fee and a share of a partnership's profits, the latter known as carried interest. For a partnership that yields average returns, carried interest may be several times larger than the management fees (Sahlman 1990). This arrangement—providing limited compensation for making and managing investments and significant compensation in the form of profit sharing—lies at the heart of the partnership's incentive structure.

Management fees are frequently set at a fixed percentage of committed capital and remain at that level over the partnership's life. Fee percentages range from 1 percent to 3 percent. Carried interest is most often set at 20 percent of the partnership's net return.

Direct Control Mechanisms

Partnership agreements also protect limited partners' interests through covenants that place restrictions on a partnership's investments and on other activities of the general partners. Restrictions on investments are especially important because a considerable portion of the general partners' compensation is in the form of an option-like claim on the fund's assets. This form of compensation can lead to excessive risk taking. In particular, it may be in the interest of the general partners to maximize the partnership's risk—and hence the expected value of their carried interest—rather than the partnership's risk-adjusted expected rate of return.

To address the problem of excessive risk taking, partnership covenants usually set limits on the percentage of the partnership's capital that may be invested in a single firm. Covenants may also preclude investments in publicly traded and foreign securities, derivatives, other private equity funds, and private equity investments that deviate significantly from the partnership's primary focus. Finally, covenants usually restrict the fund's use of debt and in many cases require that cash from the sale of portfolio assets be distributed to investors immediately.

Partnership covenants also limit deal fees (by requiring that deal fees be offset against management fees), restrict coinvestment with the general partners' earlier or later funds, and restrict the ability of general partners and their associates to coinvest selectively in the partnership's deals.

Finally, partnership agreements allow limited partners some degree of oversight over the partnership. Most partnerships have an advisory board composed of the largest limited partners. These boards help resolve conflicts involving deal fees and conflict-of-interest transactions. They do so by approving exemptions from partnership covenants. Special committees are also created to help determine the value of the partnership's investments. However, these two types of bodies do not provide the kind of management oversight that a board of directors can for a corporation; indeed, their power is limited by the legal nature of the partnership, which prohibits limited partners from taking an active role in management.

CONCLUSION

This article has presented an economic analysis of the private equity market. In particular, it has detailed how the contracts that limited partnerships write with investors and portfolio firms address many of the adverse selection and moral hazard problems that face investors considering investments in small and medium-sized firms.

The private equity market's success in addressing these problems is evidenced by the large number of successful firms that received initial financing in this market. This success has been much admired in the rest of the industrialized world, particularly in Japan and Germany. In these countries, private equity markets of the U.S. kind do not exist, primarily due to the heavily regulated nature of their securities markets, and so firms rely much more on bank financing. While such bank-centered systems may have had advantages in the past, there is an increasing feeling that such systems may not adequately provide funds for small and medium-sized firms that are the engine of future economic growth and innovation. Both Japan and Germany have recently taken steps to deregulate their financial markets. By fostering the growth of U.S. private equity market practices, these countries hope to solve the informational and governance problems of small firms looking for capital.

32

NOTES

1. This article draws selectively from a longer, more comprehensive research paper on the private equity market by Fenn, Liang, and Prowse (1997).

2. Some studies have been made of particular market sectors, such as venture capital and leveraged buy-outs (LBOs) of large public companies. On venture capital, see Sahlman (1990) and special issues of *Financial Management* (1994) and *The Financier* (1994). For a summary of the LBO literature, see Jensen (1994).

3. An equity investment is any form of security that has an equity participation feature. The most common forms are common stock, convertible preferred stock, and subordinated debt with conversion privileges or warrants.

4. The emergence of limited partnerships is actually more dramatic than these figures indicate. As recently as 1977, limited partnerships managed less than 20 percent of the private equity stock.

5. These and other figures in this section are my estimates based on information from a variety of sources. See Fenn, Liang, and Prowse (1997) for details on how these estimates are constructed.

6. Private equity is often included in a portfolio of "alternative assets" that also includes distressed debt, emerging market stocks, real estate, oil and gas, timber and farmland, and economically targeted investments.

7. Two other types of private equity organizations are SBICs owned by bank holding companies and venture capital subsidiaries of nonfinancial corporations. Both types were extremely important in the 1960s, and they still manage significant amounts of private equity. However, these organizations invest only their corporate parent's capital. In this sense, neither is really an intermediary but rather a conduit for direct investments. I treat the investments by these organizations as direct investments, not as investments by intermediaries.

8. See the *Venture Capital Journal*, October 1983.

9. This, of course, raises the question of why private equity investments haven't proven to be ideal for closed-end mutual funds, wherein the fund invests money for the long term but investors can get out in the short term.

10. For example, partnerships in the first row were formed between the years 1969 and 1979. These funds would have invested and earned returns on their capital between the years 1969 and 1988. The first row/fourth column thus shows the annual average return to public small companies over this 20-year period. Returns for small-company stocks for the other periods are similarly calculated. Returns for small-company stocks are after transactions costs (Ibbotson 1997).

11. In venture investing, for example, the firm is often a start-up with no track record. In a leveraged buyout, while there may be ample information about the firm, management may have little or no incentive to act in equityholders' best interests.

12. If, for example, investors must investigate the intermediary to the same extent that they would investigate the investments that the intermediary makes on their behalf, using one may be *less* efficient (Diamond 1984).

13. Intermediaries are also important because selecting, structuring, and managing private equity investments require considerable expertise. Gaining such expertise requires a critical mass of investment activity that most institutional investors cannot attain on their own. Managers of private equity intermediaries are able to acquire such expertise through exposure to and participation in a large number of investment opportunities. Although institutional investors could also specialize in this way, they would lose the benefits of diversification. Finally, intermediaries play an important role in furnishing business expertise to the firms in which they invest. Reputation, learning, and specialization all enhance an intermediary's ability to provide these services. For example, a reputation for investing in well-managed firms is valuable in obtaining the services of underwriters. Likewise, specialization allows an intermediary to more effectively assist its portfolio companies in hiring personnel, dealing with suppliers, and helping in other operations-related matters.

14. Many partnerships that have a single limited partner have been initiated and organized by the limited partner rather than by the general partner. Such limited partners are in many cases nonfinancial corporations that want to invest for strategic as well as financial reasons—for example, a corporation that wants exposure to emerging technologies in its field.

REFERENCES

Diamond, Douglas W. (1984), "Financial Intermediation and Delegated Monitoring," *Review of Economic Studies* 51 (July): 393–414.

Fenn, George, Nellie Liang, and Stephen D. Prowse (1997), "The Private Equity Market: An Overview," *Financial Markets, Institutions and Instruments* 6 (4): 1–105.

Financial Management 23 (1994), May.

The Financier 1 (1994), Autumn.

Gladstone, David (1988), *Venture Capital Handbook* (Englewood Cliffs, N.J.: Prentice Hall).

Golder, Stanley (1983), "Structuring and Pricing the Financing," in *Guide to Venture Capital*, ed. Stanley Pratt (Wellesley, Mass.: Capital Publishing Corp.).

Ibbotson, Roger (1997), *Stocks, Bonds, Bills, and Inflation 1997 Yearbook* (Chicago: Ibbotson Associates).

Jensen, Michael C. (1994), "The Modern Industrial Revolution, Exit, and the Failure of Internal Control Systems," *Journal of Applied Corporate Finance* 6 (Winter): 4–23.

Leland, Hayne, and David Pyle (1977), "Information Asymmetries, Financial Structure and Financial Intermediation," *Journal of Finance* 32 (May): 371–87.

Lerner, Joshua (1994), "Venture Capitalists and the Oversight of Private Firms" (unpublished working paper, Harvard University).

Palepu, Krishna (1990), "Consequences of Leveraged Buyouts," *Journal of Financial Economics* 27 (September): 247–62.

Ross, Stephen A. (1977), "The Determination of Financial Structure: The Incentive-Signalling Approach," *Bell Journal of Economics* 8 (Spring): 23–40.

Sahlman, William A. (1990), "The Structure and Governance of Venture Capital Organizations," *Journal of Financial Economics* 27 (Spring): 473–521.

Venture Capital Journal (1983), "SBICs After 25 Years: Pioneers and Builders of Organized Venture Capital," October.

34

The Reality of Hedge Funds

DAVE PURCELL AND PAUL CROWLEY

DAVE PURCELL
is the founder and managing member of Continental Advisors LLC, a Chicago-based asset management firm. At the time this article was first published, Mr. Purcell was a Managing Director responsible for U.S. equity and equity derivative distribution at Warburg Dillon Read.

PAUL CROWLEY
is an Executive Director and Global Head of Equity Derivative and Quantitative Research at Warburg Dillon Read in Stamford, Connecticut.

This article was originally published in October 1998 as a Warburg Dillon Read research report.

The hedge fund industry has grown rapidly, whether measured by number of funds available or by aggregate assets under management, and anecdotal evidence suggests that hedge funds have earned attractive returns. As a result, hedge funds have attracted considerable interest from the investing community in general and the financial press in particular. Yet significant confusion about hedge funds—what they are and how they work—persists.

This article seeks to bring clarity to the debate. We examine typical hedge fund structures and strategies in some detail, and analyze the available data on historical hedge fund performance. We conclude that hedge funds are attractive investment vehicles, particularly when viewed in a portfolio context.

Some press reports have vilified hedge fund managers as rank speculators making excessive use of leverage and, in so doing, risking the collapse of global capital markets. We believe the typical press reports convey a very inaccurate impression of hedge fund experience. In fact, hedge fund performance was attractive compared to many common perfor-mance benchmarks in mid- and late 1998. Furthermore, very few hedge funds actually failed or encountered serious financial distress during that period.

Clearly, a small number of funds have used far too much leverage, given the risks in their positions. Others appear to have underestimated the probability of extreme events. Still others appear to have deviated significantly from their core skills in search of expanded opportunity sets and increased diversification. These funds, however, are a very small minority of the overall population of funds.

Remember too that investment tools—such as leverage, shorting, and derivatives—are neither good nor bad. Rather, they may be used either appropriately or inappropriately.

Some believe that we may be witnessing the end of the hedge fund phenomenon. We feel that the reverse is true. We believe the hedge fund industry is still in the early stages of a secular growth trend. Although events may lead to a cyclical reversal in the industry, as investors become understandably nervous in the face of negative press reports, we are confident that the historical growth trend will be reestablished before long.

We see parallels between the recent press coverage of hedge funds and press coverage of program trading at the time of the October 1987 market crash; junk bonds around the time of the Drexel failure in 1990; and derivatives around the time of the Procter & Gamble, Gibson Greetings, and Metallgesellschaft debacles. Pundits forecast the end of program trading, junk bonds, and derivatives at those times, and yet program trading, junk bonds, and derivatives continue to thrive and grow. We believe that the hedge fund community will similarly survive the turmoil of recent months, and will go on to grow.

We focus largely, although not exclusively, on hedge funds investing in equity and equity derivative securities, including convertible bonds. We believe that our comments apply equally to hedge funds investing in the bond and currency markets. We also focus largely on the U.S. marketplace. Again, however, we believe our comments are largely applicable to hedge funds based abroad, as well as to investors domiciled abroad. The sections on regulation deal with U.S. regulation only.

In our discussion of characteristics commonly shared by hedge funds, we make the point that many funds currently referred to as hedge funds do not fit the traditional definition of the term.

Hedge funds are primarily distinguished by their use of short-selling, leverage, derivatives, and portfolio concentration. We suggest a scheme for segmenting the universe of funds that may help bring some order to an otherwise confusingly diverse array of funds.

The risks inherent in hedge fund strategies may be greater (relative to capital) and often more complex than those experienced by traditional investment managers. Hedge fund managers typically use sophisticated risk management techniques to control these risks.

In analysis of the past performance of hedge funds, we find that hedge funds have generally delivered on their promise, which is to provide attractive returns not strongly correlated to moves in the market in general. Hedge funds as a group did not suffer catastrophic losses in August and September 1998, but in fact outperformed most major benchmarks. Only a handful of funds actually encountered serious financial distress, and these few situations were highly publicized.

DEFINING THE TERM "HEDGE FUND"

The term "hedge fund" is traditionally defined as:

- A privately organized, pooled investment vehicle.
- Investing primarily in publicly traded securities and derivatives on publicly traded securities.
- Using short positions, long positions, and leverage in combination to reduce exposure to moves in the broad market and focus on profiting from security selection.

Specifically, a classic hedge fund holds gross long positions in excess of capital, but also holds offsetting short positions so that the net is a long position between zero (or perhaps slightly short) and 100% of capital. Some hedge funds attempt to eliminate market exposure entirely as a matter of policy. Such funds, which are called market-neutral funds, are a small minority of the overall hedge fund universe.

Excluded from this definition are funds investing primarily in private investments—such as venture capital funds and LBO funds—real estate funds, and funds investing primarily in commodities (i.e., CTAs and CPOs).

Some hedge funds have deviated from the classic definition by taking positions that on net have been more than 100% long or, in rarer cases, substantially short. Although this has been an understandable response to the recent strong performance of stock and bond markets globally, it has opened such firms to significantly greater risk. We would argue that such funds really should not be called hedge funds, because they are more speculative than hedged.

Nonetheless, as a result of this recent trend, the definition of the term "hedge fund" currently in use is effectively:

- A privately organized, pooled investment vehicle.
- Investing primarily in publicly traded securities and derivatives on publicly traded securities.
- Using leverage.

Beyond these basic characteristics, hedge funds commonly share a variety of other structural traits.

They are typically organized as limited partnerships or limited liability companies. They are often domiciled offshore, for tax and regulatory reasons. They are not burdened by regulation like that limiting the activities of entities registered under the Investment Company Act of 1940. In return, they pay a penalty; they cannot raise funds from investors via public offerings of their securities. In practice, this has several implications.

Hedge funds cannot have more than 100 accredited investors or 500 super-accredited investors. In order to qualify as an accredited investor, an individual must have a net worth (including principal residence) in excess of $1 million U.S., or income of US$200,000 in each of the past two years (US$300,000 for a married couple) and a "reasonable expectation" of earning the same in the current year. To qualify as a super-accredited investor, an individual must have a net worth (excluding principal residence) in excess of US$5 million. Other definitions apply to investing entities other than individuals.

No more than 25% of funds may be contributed by ERISA plans.

Hedge funds may not advertise broadly or engage in "general solicitation" of the investing public.

Because hedge funds are not limited by regulatory or contractual limits on investment discretion, they enjoy almost unlimited freedom to invest across a wide array of asset classes and geographic areas; to use leverage and derivatives; and to short securities.

Compared to traditional asset managers, they charge aggressive fees—typically 1% or 2% of assets under management, and 20% of cumulative profits (although in recent years fee structures have become more varied). Hedge funds often require advance notice for redemptions of as short as one month and as long as three years. Such notice periods are designed to limit the impact of fund redemptions on investment strategy.

Hedge fund investors are thus predominantly wealthy individuals and, to a lesser degree, foundations and endowments. ERISA plans and state and local pension plans have not historically been significant investors in hedge funds, although they appear to be becoming more interested of late. Appendix A describes more of the legal and regulatory environment governing hedge funds.

Hedge fund managers are usually general partners in their respective funds, and often invest a large proportion of their own personal net worth in their funds. This practice is viewed as an expression of the managers' confidence in their own abilities, and has the effect of unifying the interests of the managers with those of the outside investors. Hedge fund investment staffs tend to be small, and organized in flat reporting structures to facilitate rapid and decisive responses to market opportunities.

Hedge funds are commonly viewed as a phenomenon of the late 1980s and 1990s, but they have a considerably longer history than that. The first hedge fund on record, the Jones Hedge Fund, was established by Alfred Winslow Jones in 1949. The fund invested in U.S. stocks, both long and short, in an attempt to reduce market risk and focus on stock selection. (Thus, Jones' fund fits our classic definition quite well.)

Jones generated very strong returns while managing to avoid significant attention from the general financial community until 1966, when an article in Fortune led to increased interest in hedge funds (see Loomis [1966]). Two years later in 1968, the SEC estimated that approximately 140 hedge funds were in existence.

Many funds perished during the market downturn of 1969, apparently having been unable to resist the temptation to be net long and levered during the prior bull market. By the early 1970s, hedge funds had lost their popularity, not to gain it back until the mid-1980s.

Since then, hedge funds have once again grown dramatically in terms of numbers of funds as well as aggregate funds under management. The driving forces behind this growth appear to be the following:

- The total pool of capital available in the high net worth segment has grown rapidly, fueled by the recent long economic expansion and particularly by high compensation packages in the high-tech and financial fields and the success (and, in many cases, sale) of many family-owned and entrepreneurial businesses.
- The markets for securities borrowing and lending and derivatives have grown tremendously in size and liquidity.

- The business proposal offered by hedge funds has certain appealing characteristics, including the notion that much of the managers' net worth is at risk alongside that of their investors. Hedge fund managers have come to enjoy a reputation as the savviest players in the marketplace; many hedge fund managers started their funds after completing successful careers as portfolio managers for traditional asset management firms.

- Hedge fund returns have been rumoured to be very high. More on this later.

- The low degree of correlation thought to exist between hedge funds and traditional, long-only funds has attracted investors looking for diversification. Toward the end of the recent bull market, for instance, many investors came to fear a market reversal, and therefore desired investments that would generate attractive returns but not suffer if the broad market were to turn down.

HEDGE FUND STRATEGIES AND SEGMENTATION

Hedge funds employ a diverse array of strategies, but some general approaches are common to a good proportion of them. We suggest a segmentation scheme that we feel helps make sense out of the differences among funds.

Common Features

A large proportion of hedge funds share common elements in their investment strategies.

Shorting. One of the defining characteristics of hedge funds, as discussed above, is the regular use of both long and short positions. The objective in shorting securities is twofold. First, short positions are used to offset the systematic market risk common to long positions. Hedge funds have typically sought to profit primarily from selection of securities, and only to a lesser degree from taking broad market risk and timing their market exposure. By reducing broad market risk, the overall risk of the portfolio is reduced, and the return earned from security selection becomes larger relative to total portfolio risk. This in turn enables the fund manager to lever the portfolio, thus increasing the expected returns relative to the total capital. In this manner, managers focus risk-taking in areas where they feel they can add the most value.

Second, the use of short positions in a sense doubles the hedge fund manager's opportunity to profit from security selection; the manager can profit by holding long positions in stocks that rise in price, as well as by holding short positions in stocks that fall in price.

Leverage. By definition, many hedge funds apply leverage in an attempt to increase return on their capital. (In other words, they often control securities that, in aggregate value, significantly exceed their total capital.) Of course, leverage is a two-edged sword; both positive and negative returns are magnified. Leverage is typically obtained via margin loans or derivative positions; unsecured bank loans are far less commonly used, but are not unheard of.

Hedge funds apply widely differing degrees of leverage. Ideally, the degree of risk is matched to the risk characteristics of the investment strategy.

Several models of leverage usage are depicted in Exhibit 1. The Jones model involved going long about 110% of capital and short about 40% of capital, resulting in a net long exposure to the market of about 70% of capital. Jones varied these proportions, depending on his expectations for future market direction. (Jones was, to some degree, a market timer.)

Market-neutral managers go long and short in equal measures, resulting in a net exposure to the market of zero. Some managers adopt a levered directional position. An example might be 300% long and 40% short, resulting in a net market exposure of 260%. Clearly this is likely to produce a high degree of risk relative to capital. Still other managers adopt an extremely levered position. An example might be 1000% long (i.e., ten-times levered) and 930% short, resulting in a net market exposure of 70%.

Although this last approach may seem to be no riskier on net than the Jones model, in fact it almost certainly is. The reason is that the long and short sides of the strategies are unlikely to be perfectly correlated. Combinations of these strategies can also be applied.

Concentration. Many hedge funds hold portfolios that are significantly more concentrated than a typical, traditionally managed portfolio. Hedge fund

EXHIBIT 1
Several Models of Leverage Usage

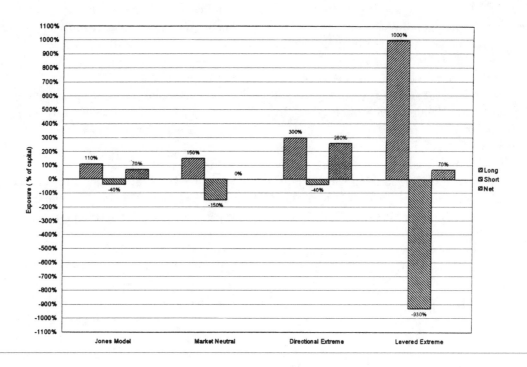

managers typically seek to focus their bets on a smaller number of investment opportunities in which they have a high degree of certainty. The result is higher risk of course, but also higher expected return (assuming the views are accurate).

Conversely, traditional asset managers seek broad diversification as a way of reducing risk. The consequence, of course, is reduced expected returns, since the strongest views are diluted by less strongly held views.

Derivatives. Many hedge fund managers use derivative securities—options, futures, forwards, swaps, and convertible bonds—in addition to stocks and bonds. Derivatives serve as an alternative source of leverage, and as an alternative method for obtaining short positions. Derivatives also present opportunities to more precisely express a view.

For example, a hedge fund manager who likes a stock at its current price—let's say, hypothetically, $50—and who is furthermore very confident the stock will move above $55 in the near future, might buy a call struck at $55. In this example, the manager would feel very confident of profiting on the

trade, and any profit would likely be large relative to the premium invested.

Efficient execution. Finally, many hedge fund managers focus considerable attention on trading their positions as efficiently as possible. In many cases, hedge funds trade large gross positions in an attempt to capture relatively small profit opportunities. Therefore, they are acutely aware of the negative impact that transaction costs can have on fund performance.

Segments in the Hedge Fund Universe

Beyond their common features, hedge funds are a diverse lot. Among the universe as a whole, many different and often complex strategies are employed. Many funds use a mix of several strategies; in truth, there are probably as many hedge fund "styles" as there are hedge funds.

It is nonetheless edifying to divide the funds into segments as we outline the various strategies used.

Fundamental long/short funds. Fundamental long/short funds trade securities that seem mispriced based on analysis of the business prospects for the firms issuing those securities. In this sense, they are similar to traditional asset managers. The difference is that they short stocks that seem to offer poor return prospects, and they apply leverage to their positions.

Some managers in this segment focus their activities narrowly in one industry or in several closely related industries. Others specialize in distressed securities, the securities of firms in financial difficulty. Here the bet is on the likely value of the securities in question after the issuer resolves its difficulties.

As we have said, hedge funds typically take long and short positions so that their net positions are somewhere between slightly short and 100% (of capital) long. Most funds in this category meet this generalization. Market risk (relative to gross positions) can be minimized by adopting equal gross long and short positions, i.e., by becoming market-neutral. Even tighter risk control can be achieved by matching longs and shorts within industry groups, to eliminate any net industry exposures. In general, funds that practice tighter risk control also employ more leverage to squeeze higher returns (relative to capital) out of the risks they do take.

In recent years, however, consistent strong returns to the market have led some managers in this category to adopt net long positions exceeding 100% of capital. Not surprisingly, such funds were badly hurt by the 1998 corrections in markets globally. Other funds have emerged that are systematically biased toward being net short on the order of 100% of capital. Clearly being long-only or short-only *and significantly* levered is potentially a recipe for disaster, as risk relative to capital can become extremely high indeed.

Quantitative long/short funds. Quantitative long/short funds apply statistical analysis to historical data (historical asset prices as well as "fundamental" or accounting data) to identify profitable trading opportunities. The traditional discipline entails hypothesizing the existence of a particular type of systematic opportunity for unusual returns, and then backtesting the hypothesis.

Backtesting essentially entails gathering the historical data and performing the calculations neces-

sary to determine whether the opportunity would have been profitable had it been pursued in the past. Simple hypotheses are preferred to complex hypotheses; the intricate trading rules favored by technicians and chartists are generally avoided. Normally, analysts hope to bolster their empirical findings with intuitive explanations for why the hypothesized opportunity should exist.

Once a successful strategy is identified, it is normally implemented relatively mechanically. That is, the strategy is traded according to a limited set of clearly defined rules (the rules that were backtested), which are only rarely overridden by the subjective judgment of the manager.

"Quant" fund strategies are often closely related to work published by finance academics in peer-reviewed academic journals. In many cases, the fund managers come from academic backgrounds and, in some cases, created the academic research themselves.

Quant fund managers are not very forthcoming about their strategies, as their trading rules are potentially prone to theft. A partial list of specific strategies thought to be employed by quantitative hedge funds is provided in Appendix B.

Users of quantitative strategies expect to identify small but statistically significant return opportunities, often across large (for hedge funds) numbers of stocks. High degrees of leverage are used to make these return opportunities significant relative to capital. Risk control is therefore critical.

Quantitative managers typically balance their longs and shorts carefully to eliminate all sources of risk except those that they expect will create return. Since they are often trading long portfolio lists, they are able to dramatically reduce not only broad market risk, but also industry risk and aggregate stock-specific risk.

Quantitative funds are more likely than any other type of hedge fund to be market-neutral; they are also among the most aggressive users of leverage as a result. They appear to be less likely than fundamental managers to adopt substantial long or short biases.

Arbitrage/relative value funds. Arbitrage/relative value funds seek to identify mispricings or expected return differentials between closely related securities where these differentials are not attributable to the business prospects of the issuers of the securities. Typically such funds participate only when they perceive a very high probability that the mispricing will be corrected or the expected return differential will be realized.

Note, however, that the term "arbitrage" is used loosely here to mean that risk is low; the term is traditionally defined to mean that there is no risk at all. The term "relative value" is probably a better one for this reason.

Merger arbitrage, which entails betting on the likelihood that announced mergers will actually be consummated, is probably the form of arbitrage most widely known to traditional investment managers, but there are many other forms of arbitrage and relative value trades. One of the largest, and paradoxically the most obscure, is convertible bond arbitrage, which entails buying (selling) a convertible bond and selling (buying) the associated stock in appropriate proportions. Here the investor is essentially betting that the option to exchange the bond for the stock is mispriced.

Some common arbitrage and relative value trades are described in Appendix C.

The returns to be expected in these trades tend to be small relative to the values of the securities involved, so arbitrage/relative value funds are also among the most aggressive users of leverage. Risk is controlled by the very nature of the trades themselves, which involve taking offsetting long and short positions in closely related securities. The aggregate position is largely protected from broad moves in the market as a result. Nonetheless, events that affect the prices of the two securities differently can still have deleterious effects on returns.

Macro funds. Macro funds take positions based on their views about global macroeconomic events. Normally they use futures and forwards to bet on the currencies, bond markets, or equity markets of whole countries. Perhaps the most highly publicized type of trade that macro funds use involves betting against the currency of an economically weak country that attempts to stabilize its exchange rate at a fixed level or within a certain band.

Many macro funds were hurt by long positions in Russian government bonds, and by the so-called yen carry trade, which entails borrowing at low interest rates in yen (by shorting Japanese money-market instruments) and buying U.S. Treasury bills offering higher interest rates. The risk, of course, is that yen appreciates, which it did in October 1998.

Because of the relatively low degree of correlation between the currencies and indexes in which macro funds trade, they are unable to exercise strict risk control. Macro funds therefore often use less leverage than other types of funds.

Many macro funds also engage in strategies typical of funds in other segments, such as merger arbitrage or fundamental long/short investment in stocks. Such funds are therefore actually hybrids of several segments. In fact, many macro funds started life as fundamental long/short funds, diversified their activities to include stocks globally, and then made the natural leap to macro strategies. In fewer cases, the evolution proceeded in the opposite direction.

Macro funds tend to be the largest funds by capital, and also tend to be the most widely known in the broad financial community. Their large bets on macro events often attract headlines in the financial press.

Funds of funds. Funds of funds gather investor assets and invest them in other hedge funds. Such funds seek to add value by choosing hedge funds that will be successful in the future. Normally, they seek to enhance diversification by selecting several funds of divergent style. They tend to be among the lowest-risk funds as a result.

FOCUS ON RISK IN HEDGE FUNDS

The risks inherent in hedge fund strategies may be larger (relative to capital) and are often more complex than those inherent in more traditional accounts. Furthermore, risks can become extremely large if hedges are inappropriate or mismanaged. Therefore, most hedge funds use sophisticated analytics to characterize, measure, and manage the risks in their portfolios.

Many of these analytics were pioneered by major investment banks, and have subsequently been adopted by hedge funds. Using these tools, hedge funds are generally able to keep their risks within reasonable, or at least known, levels. The experience of late-1998 shows, however, that potential for disaster, albeit small, does exist.

There are a variety of sources that contribute to risk in hedge fund portfolios.

Market risk. Although hedge funds typically reduce market risk, most do not eliminate it entirely. Moreover, after a long bull market such as we have seen recently, many funds are unable to resist the temptation to get net long the market on a levered basis, effectively shifting their focus from security selection to market timing. Also, macro funds often find that they are unable to identify hedges to their positions.

How, for example, would one hedge a long position in Russian GKOs? No other asset is closely correlated.

Security-specific risk. Security-specific risk is the risk remaining after the effects of common risk factors have been removed. Security-specific risk is clearly non-zero, and thus even portfolios with closely matched long and short positions experience risk. Even in a concentrated portfolio, aggregate security-specific risk is normally small compared to position sizes.

Yet, when managers apply leverage to their capital, aggregate security-specific risk can become large relative to capital. In practice under normal market circumstances, however, hedge fund security-specific risk is not large relative to capital.

Non-market, common factor risk. Between market risk and security-specific risk lies non-market, common factor risk, risk that arises from factors common to some, but not all, securities. Hedge funds take on such risk by taking large positions in certain types of securities, such as stocks in specific industries, low-grade debt instruments, or "deal stocks."

The classic example is merger arbitrage funds, which, as described above, buy and sell stocks in announced or rumored mergers and acquisitions. Although such portfolios are normally well-balanced long and short, and well-diversified across industry groups, they are subject to the systematic risk of merger and acquisition transactions as a group.

As we have seen, significant declines in the market or in the economy often cause corporate management teams to reconsider proposed deals. In such environments, merger arbitrage funds may find that a significant proportion of their bets suddenly turn against them.

Liquidity risk. Hedge funds often take very large positions relative to market liquidity. In the event that a given fund needs to exit a large position quickly, it may be unable to do so, at least without impacting prices significantly. Since liquidity has a tendency to dry up during periods of market turmoil, and since it is during such periods that funds are likely to seek to unwind trades, this problem has the potential to be disastrous. Readers will recognize this dynamic in the events of August and September 1998.

"Herd" risk. The hedge fund community is a surprisingly tightly linked one. Many hedge fund managers know one another personally. Additionally, since many share common investment styles, they often seek to exploit the same opportunities. Thus, when the time comes to exit a trade, there is a tendency for a large proportion of fund managers to attempt to exit simultaneously. This effect magnifies the liquidity risk already discussed.

Herding among hedge funds is discussed in detail in Eichengreen and Mathieson [1998]. It appeared to be in evidence in October 1998, when it was rumored that many hedge funds sought to exit their yen carry trades simultaneously, causing the yen to appreciate suddenly and precipitously against the U.S. dollar, and causing substantial losses for some funds.

"Greeks" risk. The use of options can produce risk that changes radically as the prices of the securities underlying the options change. Additionally, options can change in value substantially even in the absence of a change in the price of their underliers if, for example, market implied volatilities or interest rates change, or even simply with the passage of time.

These risks are often referred to as "greeks" risk, for the Greek letters for which five of them are named: delta, gamma, vega, rho, and theta.

Borrow and counterparty credit risk. Shorting leads to borrow risk, the risk that the borrowed security is called in by the lender. If replacement borrow cannot be found, the short position has to be closed out or the borrower will be in default. If the short is closed out, any offsetting hedge positions also need to be closed. If this happens before the trade moves in the fund's favor, it may realize a loss.

Use of leverage and OTC derivatives creates counterparty credit risk that must be monitored.

Credit crunch risk. To the extent that hedge funds use leverage aggressively, they can fall victim to sudden tightening of credit in the marketplace. In such circumstances, funds with positions that go against them even to a small degree may find they have difficulty extending their credit facilities to cover, especially if they had previously been at the limits of those facilities. This may force them to liquidate positions rapidly, resulting in further degradation of the value of their positions.

This dynamic was in evidence, or at least rumored to be in evidence, in the marketplace in September and October 1998. We should note, however, that although fear was rampant at the time that many hedge funds might fall victim, even to the point of threatening systemic collapse, in fact very few funds defaulted or even suffered substantial losses.

Operational risk. Hedge funds also face operational risk. Hedge funds often run very complicated portfolios in which capital is often levered, sometimes heavily, and positions are carefully balanced to keep risk in check. Errors in analyzing, trading, or recording positions can be very damaging.

Many hedge funds are like securities dealers in this regard, and face many of the same operational issues, albeit on a smaller scale.

Redemption risk. Hedge funds typically allow redemptions only infrequently, and at specified times, such as quarter-ends. (Mutual fund managers by contrast have to deal with daily inflows and outflows.) While this is convenient between redemption dates, it can be massively inconvenient on redemption dates, when an entire period's redemptions must be implemented simultaneously. This can force managers to unwind trades at inopportune times.

HEDGE FUND PERFORMANCE

In the end, the proof of the hedge fund concept is in the performance of the group. Unfortunately, exhaustive and completely reliable data on hedge funds are impossible to obtain. Nonetheless, the imperfect data that are available make it clear that hedge funds have been very successful during the 1990s.

Sources and Quality of Data

As we have noted, hedge funds are private partnerships and corporations. They are sold through private offerings of securities, and are subject to no direct regulation beyond the basic securities regulations to which all investors are subject. Most relevant to our discussion in this section, they are not required to report to any public regulator. Additionally, they are not allowed to advertise. As a result, no source of exhaustive, audited data on hedge fund performance or assets under management exists.

Several private organizations do gather and sell data on hedge funds. Often these organizations also advise prospective investors in hedge funds, particularly helping them select from the universe of available funds. Their activities in the former area exist primarily to support their activities in the latter.

Such organizations include Managed Accounts Reports, TASS Management, Hedge Fund Research, Van Hedge Fund Advisers, Hennessee Fund Advisory Group, and Financial Risk Management Ltd. Doubtless there are others.

The data vendors gather their data by surveying the hedge fund managers themselves. This introduces several systematic imperfections into the resulting data. The vendors generally acknowledge these imperfections.

Definition of the universe. Some data vendors seek to exclude funds that do not use either leverage or short-selling; others do not. Some include so-called managed futures funds; others do not. The latter often trade futures on commodities as well as on securities and financial indexes, and are often set up as CTAs or CPOs. We exclude such funds from our definition of hedge funds, but some vendors do not. In any event, the distinctions are often blurred.

Completeness of the universe. Since there is no single, exhaustive source even for identities of funds, the data vendors can never be certain they have captured all funds in their surveys. New funds come into existence quite frequently, and vendors become aware of them only through word of mouth.

Thus, the databases are almost certainly not complete, and vendors will, if pressed, estimate the portion of the total universe they capture. Figures regarding total numbers of funds and total assets under management within the industry have to be grossed up to reflect this coverage issue.

Participation in surveys is purely voluntary on the part of the fund managers, and it is known that certain funds choose not to participate. Such funds fall into one of at least two classes: funds that have performed poorly and do not wish to advertise the fact, and funds that have performed well, are now closed to new investment, and therefore are no longer interested in promoting themselves to new investors. Omission of the former group tends to cause average performance to be overstated, while omission of the latter tends to cause average performance to be understated.

Additionally, data vendors seek to compile lists of funds currently available for investment. Therefore, they typically drop funds from their data bases if and when they go out of existence. Thus, the histories remaining reflect only the funds that have survived, which in turn tend to be funds that have performed well. (The majority of funds that go out of existence presumably do so as a result of poor performance, although other motivations also exist.) This phenomenon tends to cause the historical performance of hedge funds as a group to be overstated.

Several biases thus clearly exist in the historical performance data, some upward and some downward. It is not immediately obvious whether the net bias is upward or downward. Consensus seems to be that the net bias is mildly upward (i.e., historical results are mildly overstated).

Accuracy of reported values. Since the data are not collected as part of any regulatory process, the accuracy of the data that are collected is questionable. Reported performance may be unaudited. Reporting standards may be unclear, at least to the individual at the fund who responds to the survey request. (For example, should performance be reported gross or net of fees?) Additionally, to the extent that hedge funds trade in illiquid securities (such as long-dated OTC index options), accurate marks may be difficult to obtain, particularly during times of market stress.

Despite the acknowledged imperfections in the data, it is generally agreed that they are of sufficient quality to support several conclusions. We feel comfortable in using the information partly because the data confirm conclusions we have reached independently in our role as broker and dealer to the hedge fund industry. All hedge fund data used in this article are from Managed Account Reports (hereafter MAR), except for returns for September 1998, which were obtained from Hedge Fund Research (hereafter HFR). Data for September were not available from MAR at the time of writing.

Conclusions Drawn from the Data

Exhibit 2 depicts the growth of hedge funds as a class during the 1990s. MAR, like all data vendors, openly admits that it is unable to capture all funds in its data base. Clearly, many small funds escape notice, and certain large and well-known funds choose not to report.

To reflect these facts, we apply a gross-up factor of 3.0 to the raw data. We choose this factor so that our resulting estimate of aggregate funds under management matches current consensus, $300 to $400 billion.

Our gross-up factor is roughly the same as that suggested by Eichengreen and Mathieson [1998]: 2.7. They base their selection of gross-up factor on discussions with several data vendors. In any event, the gross-up factor is constant in time, and so does not contribute to the pattern of rapid growth that is obvious in the data.

Exhibit 2 reveals that hedge funds as a class have grown very rapidly during the 1990s, measured either by number of funds in existence or by aggregate assets under management. In this particular sense, it is clear that hedge funds have been very successful.

Exhibit 3 depicts the risk/return performance of hedge funds during the 1990s, compared to several major performance benchmarks. The data used are for the 142 funds that are represented in the MAR data base continuously from January 1991 through August 1998. We calculate results for all 142 funds as a group, as well as for each of the subgroups that match the segments discussed above.

For the hedge fund universe and segments, monthly fund returns are averaged on an equal-weighted basis, and then geometric averages and

EXHIBIT 2
Growth of Hedge Fund Industry over Time

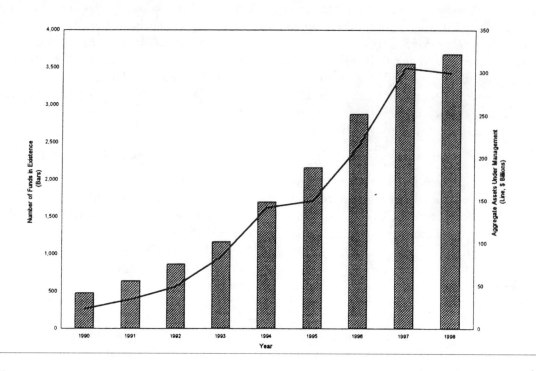

EXHIBIT 3
Risk/Return Performance of Hedge Funds as a Class over Time

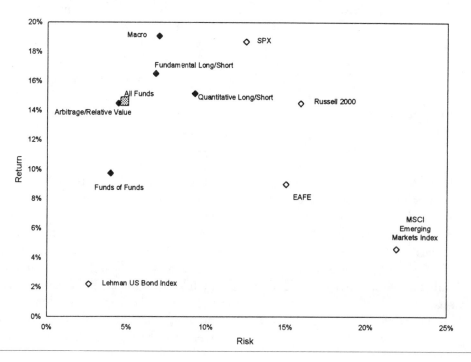

standard deviations are calculated across time. Results are multiplied by twelve and $\sqrt{12}$ respectively, to convert them to an annual-equivalent basis.

The benchmarks used are the S&P 500 (SPX in Exhibit 3), the Russell 2000, MSCI EAFE, the MSCI Emerging Markets Index, and the Lehman US Bond Index. All hedge fund returns are net of fees. No adjustments are made to the published returns to the benchmark though, so our analysis is arguably slightly biased in favor of the benchmarks.

Exhibit 3 supports the assertion that hedge funds have exhibited strong risk/return performance during the 1990s. The hedge fund universe outperformed all benchmarks except the S&P 500, and at lower risk than all benchmarks but the Lehman U.S. Bond Index. Furthermore, the ratio of return to risk is clearly higher for the hedge fund universe than for any of the benchmarks.

Among the hedge fund segments, the macro funds turned in the highest return, while funds of funds exhibited the lowest risk. Funds of funds also exhibited the lowest return of any segment. This is surprising, given that funds of funds seek to select funds that will turn in the strongest performances.

Statistically sophisticated readers will recognize that the mathematics of Exhibit 3 subtly but significantly favor hedge funds. By calculating the average return and standard deviation through time of the average monthly return across all funds in each category, we have implicitly evaluated an equal-weighted investment in 142 hedge funds simultaneously. Such an investment is of course not feasible. If it were feasible, such an investment would benefit from significant diversification effects. These effects are particularly strong in portfolios of hedge funds, because hedge funds tend to be largely uncorrelated with one another.

Exhibit 4 presents hedge fund performance in a more critical light. Here, we calculate the average and standard deviation through time of monthly returns to each hedge fund individually, and then average across all funds within each class. Thus,

EXHIBIT 4
Risk/Return Performance of Hedge Funds on Average over Time

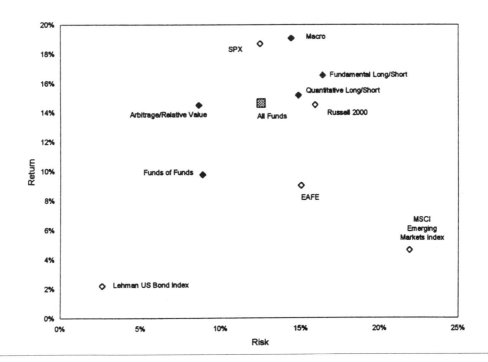

Exhibit 4 represents the risk and return experienced by the average fund in each class, rather than by the class as an aggregate.

Average returns are unchanged, but risk estimates are significantly increased. Graphically, the effect is to shift all hedge fund points to the right, while leaving the benchmark points fixed.

As Exhibit 4 shows, the average hedge fund experienced about the same risk as the S&P 500, but delivered lower return. Hedge fund risk continues to be lower than all other benchmarks except the bond benchmark, and returns are higher than all the other benchmarks.

While Exhibit 4 does not appear to make a dramatic case for hedge funds, consider these observations. First, the reality of hedge fund investing lies somewhere between the depictions in Exhibit 3 and Exhibit 4. Although investors cannot practically invest in 142 funds simultaneously, they can very reasonably invest in three or four. By doing so, risk levels can be moved from those depicted in Exhibit 4 toward those depicted in Exhibit 3.

Second, comparison to the S&P 500 over this period is a bit unfair. During the 1990s the S&P 500 experienced unusually high returns and unusually low volatility. (Hedge funds did not participate fully in this experience because they tend to be less than 100% net long most of the time.) This historical pattern of risk and return for the S&P 500 is not a reasonable estimate of its expected risk and return for the future.

So far, we have looked at performance statistics for hedge funds, and compared them to analogous statistics for several performance benchmarks. While interesting, these analyses do not really answer two questions: Should I incorporate hedge funds into my portfolio? Do they enhance risk and return in a portfolio setting? We address this question in Exhibit 5.

Exhibit 5 depicts the efficient frontier of the set of feasible portfolios under two assumptions: that hedge funds are available for investment, and that hedge funds are not available for investment. The other available assets are the benchmark assets used above: the S&P 500, the Russell 2000, MSCI EAFE, the MSCI Emerging Markets Index, and the Lehman U.S. Bond Index.

Expected returns and covariances are calculated on the basis of monthly returns from January 1991 through September 1998, the same time window used in the other exhibits. The hedge fund asset used is the *average* hedge fund as discussed above. (That is, diversification benefits potentially derivable by investing in several hedge funds are not considered.)

EXHIBIT 5
Estimated Efficient Frontiers with and without Hedge Funds

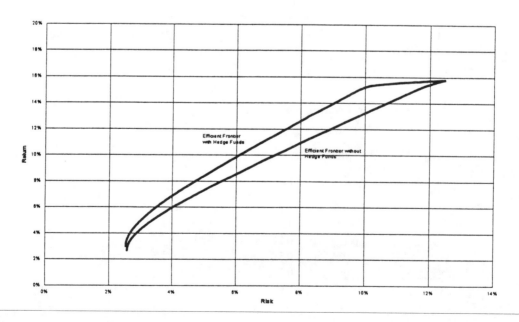

Optimizations are performed subject to a full investment constraint as well as prohibitions on shorting.

As Exhibit 5 clearly reveals, the set of feasible portfolios is expanded significantly when hedge funds are available. Depending on the investor's risk preference, the inclusion of hedge funds increases expected portfolio return by as much as 200 basis points.

Both frontiers terminate on the right in the single highest return asset, the S&P 500. It is interesting to note that the frontiers on the left terminate at different points. These points are the portfolios that minimize risk under the respective assumptions.

The points are different because the average hedge fund, if available, enters into the minimum-risk portfolio. These effects are more pronounced if several hedge funds are assumed available for investment.

The results of Exhibit 5 can be explained by three factors: risk, return, and correlation. As we have already seen, the average hedge fund has experienced risk slightly below that of the S&P 500, and return somewhat less than the S&P 500. Both have had lower risk and higher return than have any of the other benchmarks except the bond index, which offers both lower risk and lower return.

Moreover, as depicted in Exhibit 6, hedge funds offer low correlations with all the other asset classes, including the S&P 500. Thus in this analysis, hedge funds constitute an asset class with volatility and return expectations similar to those of the S&P 500 (i.e., very attractive), but that is not highly correlated with the S&P 500 or any other asset class.

This is a very powerful combination. It enables the investor to lower risk without significantly degrading return by forming portfolios combining both hedge funds and the S&P 500.

This low degree of correlation is a major advantage for hedge funds in a portfolio context. It is therefore not surprisingly used as a key point in many hedge fund marketing presentations. An additional selling point, closely related to the correlation issue, is performance during market downturns. As Exhibit 7 indicates, hedge funds tend to significantly outperform the market during periods of poor market returns.

Exhibit 7 shows quarterly returns to the S&P 500 for the calendar quarters since fourth quarter 1987 during which the index suffered negative returns. Also shown are returns to the average hedge fund during the same time periods. Here, rather than using only the 142 hedge funds in existence since January 1991, we use the set of all funds in existence for the length of each quarter depicted.

Exhibit 7 clearly demonstrates that hedge funds tend to outperform the market during periods of poor market performance. In the eleven quarters shown here, the average hedge fund outperformed the S&P 500 in ten, including Q3 of 1998. The sole exception is Q4 1994, when the average hedge fund underperformed the S&P 500.

The fact that hedge funds outperformed the S&P 500 from June through September 1998 is an interesting one, as this was a time period of particular turbulence in the capital markets and one that featured the highly publicized difficulties of several

EXHIBIT 6
Correlations between Hedge Funds and Major Benchmarks

	Average Hedge Fund	SPX	Russell 2000	MSCI EAFE	MSCI Emerging Markets Index	Lehman US Bond Index
Average Hedge Fund	1.00	0.29	0.13	0.03	−0.08	−0.01
SPX	0.29	1.00	0.24	0.54	0.59	0.06
Russell 2000	0.13	0.24	1.00	0.21	0.36	0.21
MSCI EAFE	0.03	0.54	0.21	1.00	0.47	0.11
MSCI Emerging Markets Index	−0.08	0.59	0.36	0.47	1.00	0.09
Lehman US Bond Index	−0.01	0.06	0.21	0.11	0.09	1.00

EXHIBIT 7

Performance of Hedge Funds during Down Quarters in S&P 500

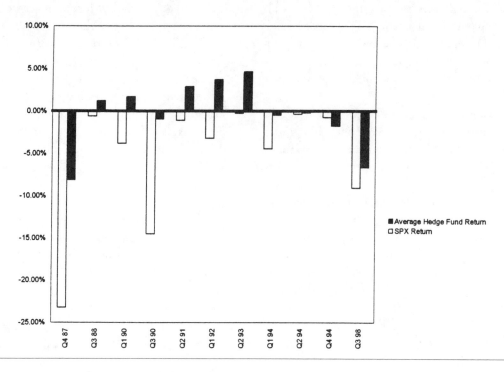

funds. Despite impressions that may be left by press coverage, hedge funds as a group weathered the third quarter 1998 reasonably well, turning in a loss of 6.7% to the S&P 500's 9.1% loss.

Exhibit 8 looks at hedge fund average performance relative to the benchmarks for each of several time periods ending September 30, 1998. Hedge fund performance for the first nine months of 1998 was slightly negative, while the return to the S&P 500 was slightly positive. Losses in the hedge fund sector were small, however, relative to losses in the Russell 2000 and in emerging markets. For Q3, we have

EXHIBIT 8

Recent Hedge Fund Performance Compared to Major Benchmarks

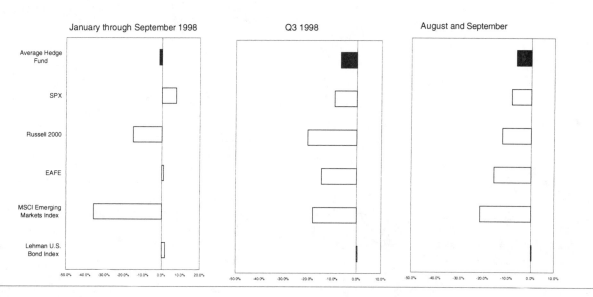

already seen that hedge funds outperformed the S&P 500 by a small margin. Hedge funds outperformed the Russell 2000, EAFE, and the MSCI Emerging Markets Index by larger margins during the quarter. Interestingly, the period painted by the press as most troublesome for hedge funds—August and September—also saw funds outperform all the benchmarks with the exception of U.S. bonds.

Although the evidence demonstrates that hedge funds *on average* have performed well during the recent turmoil, *a subset* of the funds in the universe are known to have suffered severe financial distress. These several examples have been the subject of extensive coverage in the financial press. As a result, many investors appear to have concluded that a large proportion of funds are either insolvent or in danger of becoming so.

This impression is not supported by the facts. The hedge fund industry, now believed to number in excess of 3,000 funds, saw fewer than five failures among funds of significant size in late-1998. (It is not possible to know how many very small, obscure funds may have failed.) Most if not all of these seem to have been concentrated among bond arbitrage funds, which were surprised by the sudden and precipitous widening of credit spreads throughout the world.

We believe that the funds that suffered severe distress did so for one of three reasons:

- They took on far too much leverage, and therefore too much risk relative to capital.
- They grossly underestimated the potential for extreme moves in values or relative values of assets, a classic error in risk management.
- They deviated from their core competence, in an attempt to improve their opportunity set and diversify their risk.
- Clearly mistakes were made. Other funds will likely make these or other mistakes in the future. We believe, however, that the risk of outright failure of hedge funds is actually quite small.

SUMMARY AND CONCLUSIONS

Our basic point is quite simple. Typical hedge fund strategies constitute reasonable approaches to profiting in modern capital markets. While risks clearly exist, so too does the technology for manag-

ing those risks. Most important, the historical performance of the hedge fund community has been attractive. Hedge fund patterns of risk, return, and particularly correlation make them an attractive addition to a traditional, diversified portfolio. We expect the hedge fund community to continue its rapid growth.

APPENDIX A

U.S. Legal and Regulatory Distinctions Between Hedge Funds and Registered Mutual Funds

It is not correct to speak of hedge funds as unregulated. More accurately, the legal structure and limited distribution of hedge funds make them eligible for exemptions from the Securities Act of 1933, the Investment Company Act of 1940, and the Investment Advisers Act of 1940. While the exemptions allow hedge funds to escape the rigorous requirements otherwise imposed on regulated mutual funds, hedge funds must meet certain legal and regulatory restrictions in order to be eligible for exemption.

From the perspective of hedge funds, however, the restrictions imposed as a condition for the exemptive relief are more tolerable than the daily regulatory obligations of registered investment vehicles, which include restrictions on margin, leverage, disclosure, reporting, tax treatment and compensation for fund performance.

Legal and Regulatory Considerations for Registered Mutual Funds

As private investment partnerships subject to the private placement exemption of the Securities Act of 1933, hedge funds are able to avoid requirements on regulated securities as follows:

- **Compulsory Transparency.** Regulations require the timely submission of accurate information about management, holdings, fees, and expenses.
- **Registration and Prospectuses.** Funds subject to registration are compelled to comply with SEC filing and registration requirements, an expensive and time-consuming process.
- **Restrictions on Investments.** Both holdings and strategies are subject to the limitations imposed by the 1940 Act.
- **Limitations on Fees and Sales Charges.** Registered funds are subject to specific limits imposed by the National Association of Securities Dealers as well as

12b-1, and are required to disclose all fees and expenses with specificity.

- **Restrictions on Leverage.** The Investment Company Act restricts leverage in a mutual fund to $1 for every 2 under management; hedge funds have no such restriction.
- **Restrictions on Derivative Strategies.** Certain specific limitations are placed on the use of derivatives.
- **Daily Valuations.** Open-ended mutual funds are marked to market on a daily basis at fair value, and net asset value must be reported to the NASD shortly after the close of markets each business day.
- **Greater Liquidity.** SEC regulations require a minimum amount of cash to be maintained at all times for the purpose of meeting investors' demands for redemptions.

Legal and Regulatory Considerations for Hedge Funds

To qualify for exemption from the federal securities laws, hedge funds must comply with a variety of constraints.

Limitations on number of investors. In order to remain eligible for the private investment company exclusion under Section 3(c)(1) of the Investment Company Act (ICA), a hedge fund must have no more than 100 beneficial owners of its securities or interests (otherwise known as the "100-investor test"). An investing entity of numerous investors will count as a single investor for purposes of the 100-investor test, unless the entity controls 10% or more of the outstanding voting securities of the fund. In the latter case, the statute requires the fund to "look through" the investing entity, and count each investor toward the 100-investor limit.

As of April 1997, amendment of the ICA in the form of the National Securities Markets Improvement Act of 1996 permits creation of hedge funds that allow an unlimited number of "qualified purchasers." Among the hedge fund legal community, a self-imposed rule of thumb has developed that limits the number of qualified purchasers to 500.

Limitations on type of investors. The Section 3(c)(1) exempt fund is generally composed of "accredited investors," as defined in Rule 501(a) of Regulation D. The statutory definition of accredited investors includes individuals whose net worth (or joint net worth inclusive of the person's spouse) exceeds $1 million, or whose income was in excess of $200,000 in each of the two preceding years (or, together with the person's spouse, in excess of $300,000 in each of the two preceding years) and who

reasonably expect to reach the same income level in the current year.

The Regulation D private placement safe harbor under Section 4(2) of the 1933 Securities Act permits thirty-five of the investors to be "non-accredited." Rule 506, however, requires each non-accredited investor to receive the same level of disclosure documentation as if the fund had been conducted as a registered offering. Therefore, as a practical matter, most hedge funds do not permit any non-accredited investors.

If a hedge fund seeks to take advantage of the 500-investor exemption afforded by the National Securities Markets Improvement Act, all investors in the fund must meet the "qualified purchaser" asset test.

Limitation on method and extent of placement. Rule 502(c) of Regulation D prohibits offers or sales of securities by any form of general solicitation or advertising. Although the concepts of general solicitation and general advertising are left undefined in Regulation D, an offer directed personally to the offeree will not be deemed a general solicitation.

Hedge funds must limit the extent of directed selling efforts and, to the extent possible, solicit potential investors with whom it can demonstrate a preexisting relationship, such as participants in other offerings.

Restrictions on use of solicitors under Investment Advisers Act of 1940. Rule 206(4)-3 of the Investment Advisers Act relates to the use and payment of solicitors in the purchase and sale of partnership units. As "unregistered advisers," hedge funds are not covered by the regulation, and no exemption exists permitting the use of solicitors. To do so would imply the hedge fund is presenting itself as a registered advisor, which would require registration under Section 203(b)(3). While it may be possible to structure a solicitation arrangement so that the hedge fund does not present itself as a registered advisor, most funds avoid the use of independent solicitors entirely.

Commodity Exchange Act Registration. The Commodity Exchange Act defines a Commodity Pool Operator (CPO) as a person who solicits, accepts, or receives from others funds, securities, or other property (either directly or through capital contributions, the sale of securities, or otherwise) for the purpose of trading commodity or financial futures contracts. From the perspective of the Commodity Futures Trading Commission (CFTC), any activity by a hedge fund in exchange-traded futures or options on futures triggers a CPO registration with the National Futures Association.

Most hedge funds that trade futures contracts qualify for the exemption from CPO registration and are, accordingly, subject to the mandatory registration, disclosure, and promotional compliance mandated by CFTC and NFA rules.

State blue sky considerations. A hedge fund is subject to the laws and regulations of each state in which it solicits interest in partnership units. Most states have adopted the Uniform Securities Act of 1956 and the Revised Uniform Securities Act of 1985, but substantial differences may exist in the regulatory scheme from state to state. For the most part, hedge fund offerings are generally exempt from registration in most states that have adopted a form of the Uniform Limited Offering Exemption, which is modeled after the Regulation D safe harbor in both form and substance (no general solicitation permitted, no more than thirty-five non-accredited investors, and so on). Nevertheless, certain states may require registration of the offering itself or of the general partners of the fund, as well as a license to do business in the state.

Summary

When they comply with the various exemptions from state and federal laws and regulations, hedge funds enjoy enormous advantages over their registered siblings, the mutual funds. Hedge fund managers are exempt from registration as an investment advisor under the 1940 Investment Adviser Act, pursuant to Section 203(b)(3). Hedge funds are generally exempt from the Advisers Act Rule 204-2, which requires copies to be maintained as follows: written agreements, certain investor communications, brokerage records, advertisements, records of personal trades, solicitation, accounting records, and written disclosure statements. Incentive compensation may be significantly higher for funds that are exempt from Section 205(a) of the IAA, which prevents compensation structures based upon capital gains or appreciation of the fund.

Consequently, the investor in a hedge fund partnership is subject to the risk and rewards attendant on the hedge fund manager's potentially limitless ability to use leverage, shorting, and derivatives to enhance returns.

APPENDIX B
Some Quantitative Strategies

A partial list of quantitative strategies thought to be used currently by hedge funds includes:

- Buy "value" stocks and sell "growth" stocks; buy "momentum" stocks and sell the others; and buy small-caps while selling large-caps. These strategies have been heavily researched in academic journals, particularly following a seminal article published by Fama and French in 1992.
- Buy (sell) stocks after positive (negative) earnings surprises in the expectation of stock appreciation (depreciation) over the following weeks and/or more positive (negative) earnings surprises to come.
- Buy (sell) stocks after positive (negative) earnings revisions in the expectation of stock appreciation (depreciation) over the following weeks and/or more positive (negative) earnings revisions to come.
- Hold stocks over ex-dividend dates, on the expectation that the stock price will drop by an amount less than the dividend paid out.
- Buy stocks after dividend split announcements, in the expectation of stock appreciation over the subsequent weeks.
- Trade negative serial correlation in stock residual returns at the daily frequency.
- Use neural networks to detect patterns in historical data.
- Use chaos theory to detect patterns in historical data.
- Use genetic algorithms to detect patterns in historical data.

APPENDIX C
Arbitrage/Relative Value Strategies

Here are examples of arbitrage and relative value trades that hedge funds engage in. Merger arbitrage and convertible bond arbitraged are discussed in the body of the article. Note that many of these trades are far from riskless.

- **Cash/futures arbitrage,** which entails buying (selling) futures and selling (buying) the underlying security or securities in an attempt to capture small mispricings between the two.
- **Share class structure arbitrage,** which entails buying and selling two or more securities of the same company in an attempt to exploit a perceived mispricing between them. A-share (voting)/B-share (non-voting) arbitrage and ordinary/preferred arbitrage are classic examples.
- **Holding company arbitrage,** which involves buying and selling securities of two companies that have ownership interests in a single asset. The classic example of this is the Reed-Elsevier trade. Reed is a British company; Elsevier is a Dutch company. Both hold interests in a third company, Reed Elsevier, as their sole assets. Thus, there should be a very close relationship between the prices of Reed and Elsevier, but

small discrepancies arise regularly, and offer opportunities for profit. Although the profit opportunities are small relative to the prices of the securities involved, so are the risks. Thus, positions can be levered extensively to increase the magnitude of profit relative to capital.

- **Index reconstitution trades**, such as buying stocks to be added to the S&P 500, and shorting the S&P 500 itself using futures. Trading activity around such reconstitutions is partly predictable, since index funds normally rebalance their positions on or very close to the market closing time on the effective date of the reconstitution. Hedge funds buy stocks to be added to the index shortly after the announcement of the reconstitution in expectation of a run-up in price as index funds buy closer to the effective date. Several variants of this trade exist, such as shorting into the close on the effective date in expectation of a subsequent decline in price.
- **Volatility arbitrage**, which entails buying and selling options and hedging the positions using the underlying security or securities.
- **Credit spread trades**, such as buying (selling) corporate bonds and selling (buying) Treasury bonds of like

maturity, on the expectation that credit spreads will narrow (widen).
- **Duration arbitrage**, which entails buying (selling) the long end of a yield curve and selling (buying) the short end in expectation that the curve will flatten (steepen).
- **"Carry" trades**, such as the yen carry trade.
- **Bond option arbitrage**, which involves buying (selling) bonds with embedded options (such as call features) and selling (buying) bonds of similar maturity and credit quality without embedded options. Here the bet is that the options are priced cheap (rich).

REFERENCES

Eichengreen, Barry, and Donald Mathieson. 1998. "Hedge Funds and Financial Market Dynamics." International Monetary Fund Occasional Paper, 1998.

Fama, Eugene F., and Kenneth R. French. "The Cross-section of Expected Stock Returns." *Journal of Finance*, 47 (1992), pp. 427–465.

Loomis, Carol J. "The Jones Nobody Keeps Up With." *Fortune*, (April, 1966), pp. 237–247.

Controlled Risk Strategies

Bruce I. Jacobs
Principal
Jacobs Levy Equity Management

Long–short investing provides investors the opportunity to enhance returns and control risk, but investors need to understand the basics and operational considerations of long–short before they can benefit from this controlled risk strategy. Integrated long–short management notably frees the manager from benchmark constraints and allows the manager to act on *all* of his or her insights. Long–short also provides investors the flexibility to restore equity market exposure with futures or transport the spread to other asset classes.

This presentation discusses controlled risk strategies and specifically focuses on a world of equity investing where short selling is permitted. It starts with a brief summary of the basics: What is long–short? How is long–short implemented, and why do it? Next, it elaborates on some of the advantages of using long–short, such as return benefits, taking advantage of market inefficiencies, and risk control. The presentation then discusses integrating long–short and shows that long–short is not, optimally, two portfolios (one long, one short) but rather a single integrated portfolio. The presentation continues by explaining how to equitize a long–short portfolio using stock index futures—a value-added equity strategy—and how to transport the spread. The long–short value added, or the spread between the long and short positions, can be transported to any asset category. The presentation also discusses the notion of equitizing the long–short portfolio in an integrated fashion to achieve optimality. Finally, the presentation reviews the operational considerations of long–short, specifically margin and liquidity requirements, trading and shorting issues, and ERISA and tax concerns.

Basics

To profit from a long–short strategy, investors need to understand what long–short is, how to implement it, and why to do it. This section shows that long–

short is an innovative method of portfolio construction; it is not a new asset class or category. Its implementation requires several operations that occur simultaneously. The primary motivations for using the strategy are return enhancement and improved risk control relative to a long-only or short-only portfolio.

What Is Long–Short? Long–short is a portfolio-construction process in which the portfolio manager buys high-expected-return securities, sells short low-expected-return securities, and balances the average betas of the long and short positions to neutralize market risk. Long–short can take various forms. It can be market neutral, in which case the systematic risk, or beta, is zero. It can also be equitized, so that market exposure is restored with stock index futures. At Jacobs Levy Equity Management, we find that long–short adds flexibility in pursuing high returns, controlling risk, and allocating assets.

How to Implement Long–Short. The various steps shown in **Figure 1** illustrate how long–short is implemented in practice, but keep in mind that all these steps actually occur simultaneously.

The center box shows that the short stocks are housed in a margin account at a prime broker. The prime broker acts as custodian, keeping track of margin, borrowing the stocks to short, and clearing the trades.

Step 1 is the initial funding, in which money comes to the prime broker from the client. For simplicity, the funding amount is shown to be $10. In Step 2, 90 percent of that initial funding is allocated

Figure 1. Implementing Long–Short

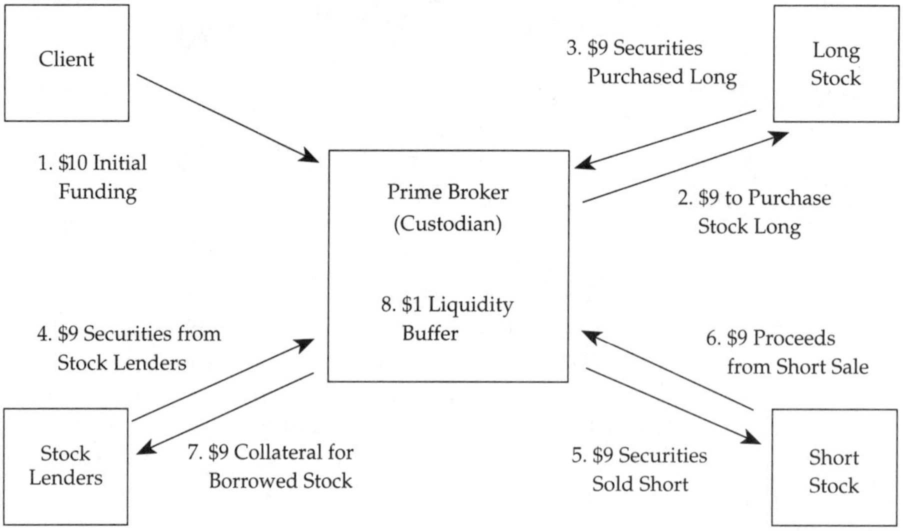

Source: Jacobs and Levy (1997).

to purchase stocks long. (See Jacobs and Levy 1993a for a note on leverage in long–short portfolios.)[1] In Step 3, the $9 of securities purchased long is delivered to the prime broker. In Step 4, $9 of securities are borrowed from the stock lenders. In Step 5, those borrowed securities are sold short. In Step 6, the sale of those securities gives rise to short-sale proceeds in the amount of $9. In Step 7, that $9 is transferred to the stock lenders as collateral for the borrowed shares.

Of the $10 initial funding, $9 is allocated long and $9 short, so 90 percent of the initial capital is allocated, which leaves a 10 percent (or $1) liquidity buffer. The liquidity buffer is needed to meet the marks to market on the shorts.

Why Do Long–Short? A long–short portfolio offers investors return and risk advantages. Using a long–short strategy provides return advantages because managers are able to use all their insights, including insights about poor performers as well as good performers. Long positions in stocks that are undervalued and short positions in stocks that are overvalued make use of all available market information to enhance returns. Not being able to use insights about overvalued as well as undervalued stocks is like tearing the *Wall Street Journal* in half and reading only the good news.

Using long–short strategies can result in risk advantages. Systematic risk can be eliminated. Addi-

tionally, managers can control risk without being held hostage by the capitalization weightings of the stocks in the underlying benchmark index—a key advantage of long–short.

Advantages of Long Plus Short

Some of the return advantages of a long–short strategy can be illustrated by comparing the return payoff of a very basic long-plus-short portfolio with that of a long-only portfolio (see also Jacobs and Levy 1993b).

Long Portfolio Payoff. Figure 2 shows the payoffs to a long-only portfolio. The line for the market portfolio can be viewed as the return to a long passive position in the market. The benefit of active management is presumably an excess return, or alpha. This excess return shifts the active long portfolio's payoff upward relative to the long market portfolio.

Short Portfolio Payoff. Figure 3 shows the payoffs for the short portfolio. The short market portfolio can be viewed as the return to a short passive position in the market. When an investor sells short, however, proceeds are generated, and those proceeds earn interest. The short market portfolio line can thus be shifted upward by the amount of interest, as shown in the figure. Active management should produce an excess return, or alpha, on top of the market-return-plus-interest line. The payoff line for the active short portfolio thus recognizes the short passive market

---

[1]For full reference citations, see the reference list at the end of the book on pp. 105–106.

Figure 2. Payoff: Long Portfolio

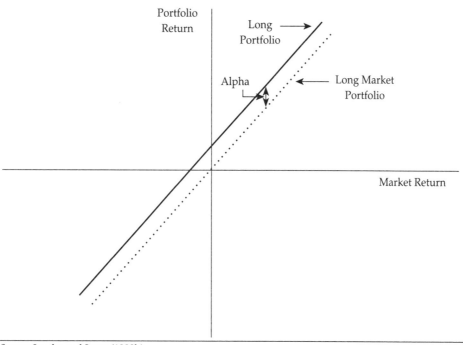

Source: Jacobs and Levy (1993b).

Figure 3. Payoff: Short Portfolio

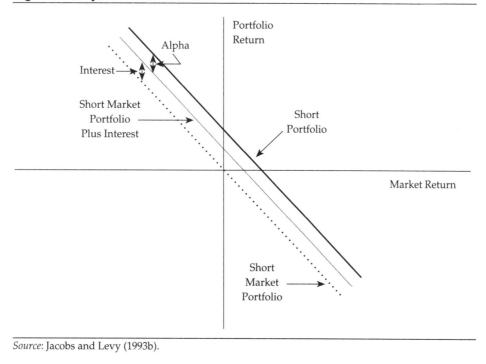

Source: Jacobs and Levy (1993b).

return, the interest received on the short-sale proceeds, and the short active portfolio alpha.

Market-Neutral Long-Plus-Short Payoff. A market-neutral long-plus-short portfolio combines the long portfolio and the short portfolio just dis-

cussed. **Figure 4** shows that the payoff, or value added, for this market-neutral long-plus-short portfolio equals the alpha from the short portfolio plus the alpha from the long portfolio plus the interest earned on the proceeds from the short sales.

Figure 4. Payoff: Market-Neutral Long-Plus-Short Portfolio

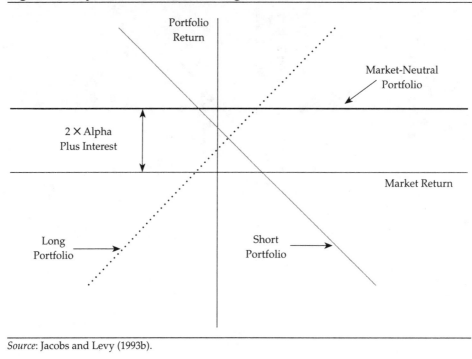

Source: Jacobs and Levy (1993b).

Greater Inefficiencies on the Short Side. There are reasons to believe that greater inefficiencies may exist on the short side of the market than on the long side. **Exhibit 1** shows a world divided according to whether short selling is restricted or unrestricted and whether investor opinion is uniform or diverse. When short selling is restricted and investor opinion is diverse, market prices are no longer efficient, and the capital asset pricing model (CAPM) and arbitrage pricing theory (APT) do not hold. When investors have diverse opinions, some will be more pessimistic than others. Without complete freedom to sell short, the pessimism of these investors will not be fully represented in security prices, and some stocks will tend to be overpriced.

Security overpricing may be supported by fads or bubbles. Overpricing may also be supported by corporate publicity, which tends to favor good news over bad. Good news tends to be publicized in a timely manner, whereas bad news is subject to delay, window dressing, and actual fraud.

Also, analysts and brokers tend to favor buy over sell recommendations. Brokers have more to gain from buy recommendations than from sell recommendations; after all, anyone may buy, thus generating commissions for the broker, but only those who already own a stock (and a relatively small number of short sellers) are likely to sell. Analysts are often swayed by their firms' investment banking relationships and are reluctant to issue negative reports that might offend current and potential corporate clients.

Market Risk Neutralization. The long-plus-short portfolio eliminates systematic risk. **Figure 5** illustrates this risk reduction by using the example of the $10 account from Figure 1. In Panel A, the S&P 500 Index rises 30 percent. The long portfolio rises 33 percent and the short portfolio 27 percent, producing a return spread of 6 percent.

In addition to the long–short spread of 6 percent, the long-plus-short portfolio earns a short rebate on the proceeds from the short sales, which is assumed to be 5 percent. It also earns interest on the cash liquidity buffer; again, a rate of 5 percent is assumed. Adding these interest earnings to the long–short spread produces a total return of 10.4 percent. Of that 10.4 percent return, 5.4 percent, not 6 percent, is value added. Remember, only 90 percent of the capital was deployed long and short, so 90 percent of 6 percent, or 5.4 percent, is the value added.

Now consider the bear market case, shown in Panel B, in which the S&P 500 declines 15 percent. The spread is the same as in the bull market case, 6 percent. Adding the interest component to this long–short spread produces a return of 10.4 percent, the same as in the bull market scenario. Again, the value added is 5.4 percent. The market's return has been neutralized.

Exhibit 1. Short-Side Inefficiencies

Investor Opinion

	Uniform	Diverse
Unrestricted	Market Portfolio Efficient CAPM and APT Hold (No One Shorts)	Market Portfolio Efficient CAPM and APT Hold
Restricted	Market Portfolio Efficient CAPM and APT Hold	Market Portfolio Not Efficient CAPM and APT Do Not Hold

Short Selling

Source: Jacobs and Levy (1993b).

Integrating Long–Short

The preceding section focused, for simplicity, on a basic view of long–short, one in which (as in Figure 4) the portfolio is viewed as a combination of two portfolios, one short and one long. This view of long–short is a prevalent one that arises from the tendency to see long–short through the lens of long-only investing (see also Jacobs and Levy 1996).

A common assumption is that the return and risk of the long side of long–short is essentially the same as the return and risk of a long-only portfolio and that the return and risk of the short side of long–short is essentially the same as the return and risk of the long side of long–short. Because a long-only portfolio is index constrained, by definition, this assumption is equivalent to assuming that the long and short components of long–short are separate, index-constrained portfolios.

Within this framework, the performance of the longs and the shorts of long–short can be measured as excess returns, or alphas, relative to their underlying benchmarks. Such a long-plus-short portfolio offers no benefits over a long-only portfolio (assuming equal leverage) except to the extent that the correlation between the long and short portfolio alphas is less than one. The risk–reward trade-offs for the long side of long–short and the short side of long–short are identical to the risk–reward profile of long-

only. A benefit may arise because of a less-than-one correlation between the long and short alphas, but this benefit offers nothing that could not be gained by introducing any uncorrelated portfolio—basic Markowitz diversification theory.

Optimally, long–short is not at all a two-portfolio strategy. Neither the longs nor the shorts should be index constrained. In addition, performance measurement should not be dichotomized into how the longs perform relative to a benchmark plus how the shorts perform relative to a benchmark. Long–short does not give rise to two separately measurable alphas but, rather, to a single long–short spread. The benefits of long–short are not then dependent on a less-than-one correlation between separately measurable alphas.

Only with integrated optimization can the real benefits of long–short be realized (see also Jacobs and Levy 1995c). These benefits become apparent by comparing long-only management with integrated long–short management (see also Jacobs and Levy 1997).

Long-Only Management. With long-only management, the portfolio is exposed to market, or systematic, risk. Controlling residual risk requires holding benchmark-like weights; the further the portfolio departs from benchmark weights, the more residual risk it incurs. Long-only's ability to under-

Figure 5. Performance of Long–Short Portfolio in Bull and Bear Markets

A. Bull Market

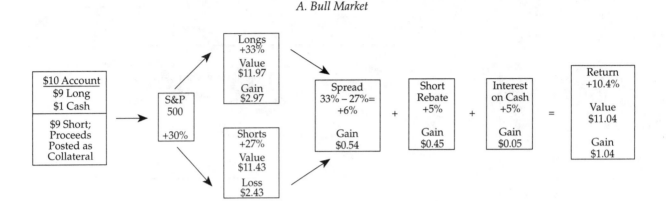

B. Bear Market

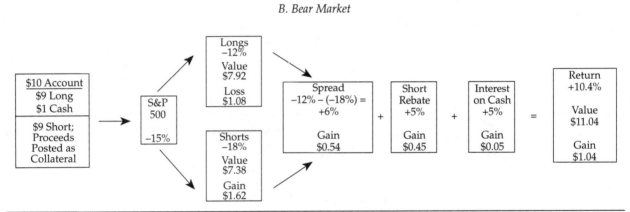

Source: Jacobs and Levy (1997).

weight securities is also severely limited.

Consider, for example, a median-capitalization security, which would constitute about 0.01 percent of the market's capitalization. A long-only manager can underweight such a security by, at most, 0.01 percent (accomplished by not holding any shares). Imagine if a manager were constrained to hold no more than a 0.02 percent long position in a median-cap security (an overweight of 0.01 percent), no matter how attractive its expected return. Most long-only managers would consider such a limit a material impediment to their ability to add value.

Integrated Long–Short Management. As mentioned previously, market-neutral long–short eliminates systematic risk. More importantly, however, integrated long–short eliminates the need to hold stocks merely to control portfolio risk relative to a benchmark. The balance of long and short positions in

effect eliminates the benchmark as a constraint in security selection and security weighting.

The real benefit of integrated long–short is this freedom from index constraints. The manager can overweight and underweight stocks by as much as his or her insights, and the client's risk considerations, allow. The manager has no inherent restrictions on security underweighting and does not have to make the portfolio converge to benchmark security weights to control residual risk. In fact, the manager can use offsetting long and short positions to hedge security risks, thereby fine-tuning overall portfolio risk.

For example, suppose a manager does not have the ability to discriminate between good and bad oil stocks, or believes that no oil stocks will significantly outperform or underperform the market in the near future. In a long–short design, the manager's portfolio could exclude oil stocks without incurring any risk. By contrast, a long-only manager may need to hold some oil stocks, if only to control the portfolio's risk relative to the oil stock exposure of the benchmark.

The added flexibility of long–short, the manager's enhanced ability to implement insights and control risk, should be reflected in the long–short portfolio's information ratio, or the ratio of the portfolio's return to its risk. For an integrated long–short portfolio, return is measured not as an alpha for the short portfolio plus an alpha for the long portfolio (as Figure 4 implied) but as the spread between the returns on the long and short positions (the weighted returns of the securities, long and short, in the long–short portfolio). Risk is measured by the variability, or standard deviation, of the long–short return spread.

Equitizing Long–Short

As discussed, and as Figure 5 illustrated, market-neutral long–short eliminates the portfolio's exposure to market risk and to market return. This exposure can be added back via the purchase of stock index futures in an amount equal to the initial investment. The return on the overall portfolio will reflect the change in the price of the futures plus the underlying long–short portfolio's interest income and its long–short return spread. This long–short spread should reflect the flexibility advantages of long–short construction.

Figure 6 shows how to equitize a long–short portfolio. Again, for simplicity, an initial funding of $10 is used. The manager purchases an equal amount of stock index futures, collateralized by $0.40 in T-bills. This expenditure reduces the liquidity buffer to $0.60, which is ample in an equitized strategy because the marks to market on the long futures can offset the marks to market on the short stocks.

Figure 7 shows that equitized long–short performance, unlike market-neutral performance, does reflect market movements. Here, as in Figure 5, the S&P 500 rises 30 percent in the bull market case (Panel A) and declines 15 percent in the bear market case (Panel B). In Figure 7, however, returns differ between the two scenarios. Total returns are 35.4 percent in the bull market example and –9.6 percent in the bear market example. In each case, however, the value added is the same. That is, the market-relative excess return is 5.4 percent—90 percent of the 6 percent long–short spread—in both bull and bear market cases.

Transporting the Spread

The long–short spread captures the return from security selection; it is independent of the return to the overall market from which the securities are selected. Thus, the return from stock selection is separable from the asset class return, which suggests that security selection can be separated from asset allocation.

Figure 6. Equitizing the Long–Short Portfolio

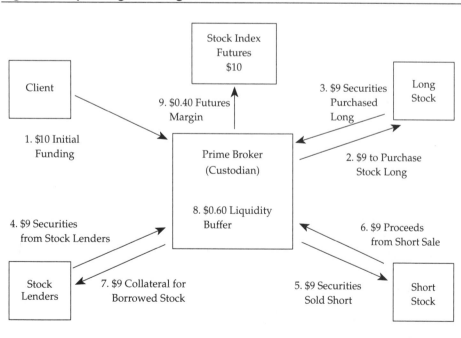

Source: Jacobs and Levy (1997).

Figure 7. Performance of Equitized Long–Short Portfolio in Bull and Bear Markets

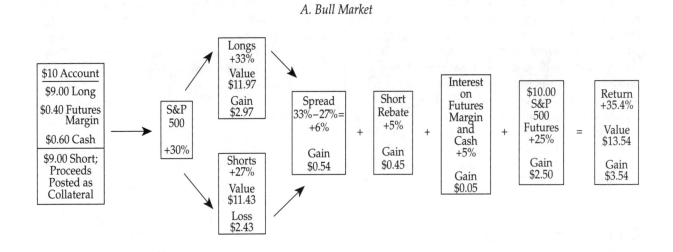

A. Bull Market

B. Bear Market

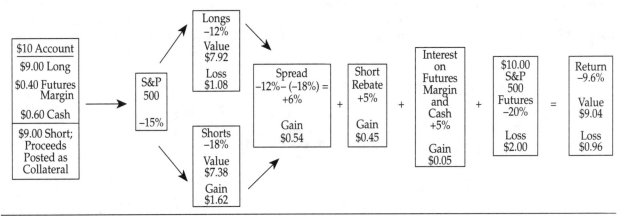

Source: Jacobs and Levy (1997).

In fact, with long–short, the talents of the stock selector are not confined necessarily to the equity market but are transportable to other asset classes. Although a basic market-neutral portfolio, for example, offers a return from security selection on top of a cash return (with some additional risk exposure), an equitized long–short strategy offers the return from security selection on top of the equity market return. The long–short spread can be transported to other asset classes by combining the underlying long–short portfolio with other derivatives, such as futures or swaps. For instance, fixed-income return patterns can be achieved with fixed-income swaps.

Whether long–short offers an absolute return relative to cash or a relative return vis-à-vis domestic equity, international equity, fixed income or any other asset class is determined by the decision as to whether and what derivatives overlays are appropriate. This decision can be made by the investor, independent of the investor's selection of a long–short manager.

The transportability of the long–short spread underscores the fact that long–short is not a separate asset class and should not be treated as such in asset allocation analyses (see also Jacobs, Levy, and Starer 1998). Long–short is, rather, a portfolio-construction method.

Equitizing Plus Integrating

So far, equitization has been considered as an add-on to an underlying market-neutral long–short portfolio. But as it is optimal to construct a long–short portfolio in an integrated fashion, so it is optimal to equitize a long–short portfolio in an integrated fashion. Thus, although managers may typically set the average beta or dollar value of the longs equal to that of the shorts, this equalization is not necessary and may not be optimal. In fact, the requirement for long–short balance merely imposes a constraint not unlike the constraint on short selling, which long–short eliminates. And constraints have costs.

An integrated optimization that considers long and short positions plus stock index futures frees up the manager's ability to implement insights. If the short side of the market does indeed have more or larger inefficiencies, for example, the manager can pursue them more freely if not constrained by a need to balance long and short positions. The manager can offset any net beta exposure and, in fact, obtain any desired market exposure by using the appropriate amount of equity futures. For example, the manager could allocate 50 percent long and 150 percent short without violating margin requirements. To establish market neutrality, the manager would then invest an amount equal to 100 percent of capital in stock index futures.

Balancing long and short positions, either by beta or dollar amounts invested, is nevertheless the typical fashion in which long–short is implemented. And it has some real and perceived advantages. For example, deploying capital both 100 percent long and 100 percent short takes advantage of the full amount of leverage allowed by regulation. Furthermore, it requires no borrowing of funds to collateralize the shares sold short. Under the U.S. IRS Revenue Ruling 95-8, borrowing funds to purchase stock on margin can give rise to unrelated business taxable income for tax-exempt investors.

Some investors may favor equal dollars long and short because the balance seems to afford a tangible measure of the market neutrality of the portfolio. Their sense of comfort may be false, however. If the beta of the long positions is 1.3 and the beta of the short positions is 0.8, the portfolio is not market neutral, no matter the equality of the dollar amounts invested long and short.

Finally, a preference for long–short balance may reflect aspects of investor psychology, such as "mental accounting." For an investor who wants to separate the security selection decision from the derivatives overlay decision, for example, using a beta- or dollar-balanced long–short portfolio may seem to make more sense. The security selection process implicit in the long–short portfolio is distinct, in this investor's mind, from the asset allocation decision implicit in the derivatives overlay. No necessary rationale exists, however, for separating the two, even if separate managers are employed for each; the manager responsible for the derivatives overlay can be instructed to set it so as to offset or augment any market exposure associated with the long–short manager's portfolio.

Operational Considerations

Establishing a long–short investment account involves operational issues, such as margin requirements and short-sale implementation problems not usually encountered in long-only management. Trading costs, management fees, and ERISA and tax considerations may also be of concern to investors who are contemplating the use of long–short. As this section will show, none of these issues represents an insurmountable obstacle.

Margin Requirements. U.S. Federal Reserve Board Regulation T requires that in order to borrow shares to sell short, the resulting portfolio must be at least 50 percent collateralized. Thus, the $10 in initial funding in the earlier examples could, in theory (without the liquidity buffer), have supported borrowing $10 of stocks to sell short. Once positions are established, maintenance margin requirements apply. NYSE Rule 431 sets maintenance margins at 25 percent of the stock price for long positions, at the greater of $5 or 30 percent of stock price for short positions when the stock is more than $5 a share, and at the greater of $2.50 or the stock price for short positions when the stock is less than $5 a share. Individual brokers generally require more than 30 percent collateralization.

Liquidity Buffer. Short positions are marked to market daily; increases in a stock's price require that the borrower deposit additional collateral with the stock lenders, and declines release collateral from the stock lenders to the borrower's margin account. The liquidity buffer serves as the pool for meeting and receiving these obligations. When a long–short strategy is equitized, marks to market on the long futures position can offset the marks to market on the short stock positions. The liquidity buffer can thus be smaller in an equitized long–short portfolio, as shown in Figure 6, than in a nonequitized one.

Long–short portfolios also need to reimburse stock lenders for dividends paid on the borrowed stock. From a cash flow perspective, these payments can often be met from the dividends on the long positions. When the dividend yield on the longs is less than that on the shorts, however, reimbursements can come from the liquidity buffer.

Determination of the size of the liquidity buffer is a balancing act. Investors will want to be able to invest as much capital as possible and hence have the smallest liquidity buffer practical. At the same time, they will want to avoid having to borrow from the broker to meet required payments. Borrowing at the broker call rate can be costly and may have tax repercussions, even for a tax-exempt investor. At Jacobs Levy, we find that a liquidity buffer equal to 10 percent of capital is generally adequate.

Changes in Long–Short Values. Although a market-neutral long–short portfolio is designed to be neutral to market movements in terms of its ultimate risk and return, changes in the values of the long and short positions can necessitate trading because market movements can lead to margin violations, long–short imbalances, and draw-downs of the liquidity buffer.

Table 1 illustrates the consequences of the long and short positions either falling 50 percent or rising

100 percent in price. That is, positions either fall by half or double in value. The "Action" column shows that, when positions fall in value by one-half, the manager needs to buy more long and sell more short to restore the liquidity buffer. If values double, the manager has to sell longs and cover shorts to restore the liquidity buffer and meet margin requirements. Table 1 also shows that a market crash, cutting security values in half, increases the liquidity buffer by $4.50. So, crashes actually create liquidity for long–short.

No trading actions are required with an equitized long–short portfolio when all securities (longs, shorts, and futures) rise by 100 percent. As **Table 2** shows, the manager has the benefit of those offsetting marks to market on the long futures and short stock positions.

One might expect that, in a market-neutral world, a long–short spread that is in the manager's favor should not give rise to any trading. But it does. As **Table 3** shows, a positive spread of 2 percent requires selling some of the long positions and covering some of the short positions to restore long–short balance.

Table 1. Market-Neutral Long–Short: Trading Required when Long and Short Positions Fall 50 Percent or Rise 100 Percent

Position	Initial Values (Fall or Rise)	Return (Fall/Rise)	Gain/Loss (Fall/Rise)	Owe/Owed (Fall/Rise)	New Values (Fall/Rise)	Action (Fall/Rise)	After-Action Values (Fall or Rise)
Long	$9.00	–50%/+100%	–$4.50/+$9.00		$4.50/$18.00	Buy $4.50/ Sell $9.00	$9.00
Short	9.00	–50/+100	+4.50/–9.00	Owed $4.50 by lenders/ Owe lenders $9.00	4.50/18.00	Sell short $4.50/ Cover $9.00	9.00
Cash	1.00				5.50/–8.00		1.00
Equity	10.00				10.00/10.00		10.00
Margin	55.6%				111.1%/27.8%		55.6%

Source: Jacobs and Levy (1997).

Table 2. Equitized Long–Short: Trading Required when Securities (Long, Short, and Futures) Rise 100 Percent

	Initial Values	Return	Gain/Loss	Owe/Owed	New Values	Action	After-Action Values
Long	$9.00	+100%	+$9.00		$18.00		$18.00
Short	9.00	+100	–9.00	Owe lenders $9.00	18.00		18.00
Cash	0.60				1.60		1.20
Equity	9.60				19.60		19.20
Margin	53.3%				54.4%		53.3%
Futures	$10.00 + $0.40 in T-bills	+100	10.00	Owed $10.00 on mark to market	$20.00 + $0.40 in T-bills	Buy $0.40 in T-bills	$20.00 + $0.80 in T-bills

Source: Jacobs and Levy (1997).

79

Table 3. Two Percent Long–Short Spread

	Initial Values	Return	Gain/Loss	Owe/Owed	New Values	Action	After-Action Values
Long	$9.00	+4%	+$0.36		$9.36	Sell $0.198	$9.162
Short	9.00	+2	−0.18	Owe lenders $0.18	9.18	Cover $0.018	9.162
Cash	1.00				0.82		1.018
Equity	10.00				10.18		10.180
Margin	55.6%				54.9%		55.6%

Source: Jacobs and Levy (1997).

Difficulties with Shorting. As mentioned previously, shorting requires establishing a margin account at a prime broker. Dealing with a prime broker is somewhat different from dealing with a traditional master trustee or custodian that is totally divorced from the risk-taking activities at investment banks. Most importantly, the manager must perform due diligence when evaluating prime broker candidates to ensure that the broker chosen is capable and creditworthy.

Short sales may be thwarted because some shares, especially those of small-cap stocks, are not always available for borrowing. Furthermore, shares that have been borrowed may be recalled by the lender, in which case either the manager or the prime broker has to cover the shares.

Brokers will charge for securing and providing lendable stocks. Intermediation costs, which average 25 to 30 basis points (but can be higher for hard-to-borrow shares), are incurred as a "haircut" on the short rebate received from the interest earned on the short-sale proceeds.

With equitized strategies, a duration mismatch might exist between the short rebate, based on overnight rates, and the stock index futures contracts, which are priced off equivalent-term LIBOR. The manager may be able to negotiate a term deal that mitigates such mismatches.

Finally, uptick rules may prevent or delay short sales and result in opportunity costs, especially if the short trades are urgent. Uptick rules will be less costly for less-urgent, or patient, trades. For instance, if the manager has a trading strategy of selling on upticks and buying on downticks, he or she will not be affected by the rules.

Trading Costs. A fully levered long–short portfolio will generally engage in twice as much trading as a long-only portfolio, hence its trading costs will run higher. But these costs are largely a function of leverage. The investor can choose the desired level of leverage in either long–short or long-only, going with an unlevered long–short portfolio or a levered long-only portfolio. Thus, trading costs need not differ significantly between long–short and long-only investing.

With long–short, trading may be required to maintain long–short balance, meet margin requirements, and restore the liquidity buffer, as discussed previously. With an equitized strategy, because of offsetting marks to market on futures and short positions, these incremental trading costs will be minimized.

Management Fees. Management fees need not be higher in long–short than in long-only, especially if one considers the fee per active dollar invested. Investors need to consider whether they are getting what they pay for in terms of the level of active management provided. Long-only portfolios implicitly have a sizable passive component; only the overweights and underweights relative to the benchmark are truly active. Virtually the entire long–short portfolio is active. The management fees associated with long–short may thus be far less than those associated with long-only management when measured per dollar of active positions taken. Furthermore, long–short management is almost always offered in a performance-fee context.

Risk Levels. One aspect of risk in long–short management that differs fundamentally from long-only management is that the loss on a short position can theoretically be unbounded. That is, as a security's price rises, the loss on a short position in that security can rise without limit. In long-only management, a security cannot sell at a negative price, so the investor cannot lose more than the price paid for the security. In terms of a sharp market rise, losses in the value of short positions should be offset, at least approximately, by gains in the value of long positions. To guard against the event risk of an individual shorted stock rising precipitously, however, having small positions in a large number of stocks, both long and short, is best. The rebalancing that takes place in long–short management should also assure that as a shorted stock rises in price, and its weighting in the portfolio increases, the short position will be partially covered by scaling back its position size. So, short covering will diminish the portfolio's exposure to individual security risk.

In general, risk levels may be higher for long–short than for long-only but only to the extent that long–short engages in more leverage or more active management. Again, the investor makes a conscious choice about the levels of leverage and active management desired. Beyond those decisions, integrated optimization controls risk and ensures that the risk incurred is compensated by expected return. Consider this: The riskiest long-only portfolio holds a 2:1 levered bet on one stock, whereas the riskiest long–short portfolio holds full positions in two stocks.

ERISA and Tax Concerns. ERISA's prudence and diversification requirements are fully consistent with the responsible use of long–short. Optimization can control risk and ensure the proper diversification of long–short portfolios.

Some concerns about the tax treatment of shorting were cleared up in January 1995 with the IRS ruling that borrowing shares to initiate short sales does not constitute debt financing. Any profits resulting from closing out shorts do not give rise to unrelated business taxable income (UBTI). By contrast, buying stocks on margin can result in UBTI.

In August 1997, the short-short rule was rescinded. Mutual funds can now short without jeopardizing their tax pass-throughs, which has prompted mutual funds to offer long–short strategies. More taxable investors will now be able to benefit from the added flexibility of long–short management.

For the taxable investor, long–short may result in higher turnover and in tax consequences not encountered in long-only management. Investors should always evaluate strategies net of all costs, whether they are trading costs, fees, or taxes.

Conclusion

Long–short has the ability to enhance portfolio returns by maximizing implementation of investment insights. Whether or not long–short will enhance returns will depend ultimately on the goodness of those insights. Besides analyzing the operational considerations of long–short, investors need to evaluate carefully the value-adding potential of the manager's security selection system.

Market Neutral: Engineering Return and Risk

David Steyn
Chief Executive Officer
Quaestor Investment Management

Much like satellite management, market-neutral investing offers investors the opportunity to pursue high returns, but investors must match these returns with the risk. Managers that use the market-neutral portfolio-construction technique are free of index constraints and are free to allocate resources where markets are most inefficient and where manager skill can add the most value. Of course, if the manager believes markets are efficient and if the manager does not have the skill to offset the transaction costs, the manager/client should be a passive investor in that market.

The benefits and usefulness of market-neutral investing are clearly described by Nobel Laureate William Sharpe:

> I favor market-neutral strategies for certain kinds of active management, if the costs can be kept low, since they allow separation of asset allocation decisions from stock-picking decisions. Thus an investor can use index funds and/or derivatives to achieve a desired asset allocation, then invest in market-neutral funds to the extent that he believes some of them can add value without excessive added risk.[1]

Given the benefits of market-neutral investing, I listened with great interest to Scott Lummer's presentation, in which he summarized the pitfalls of alternative investment strategies—lack of data, survivorship bias, short track records, inadequate risk models, bad risk models.[2] I thought about international market-neutral investing, and every single one of those problems is writ large across the international market-neutral field. This presentation discusses how we address some of those problems at Quaestor Investment Management and devise appropriate solutions.

The presentation is organized into three parts. The first covers the identity of market neutral. Market neutral is not a new asset class but a portfolio-construction tool. Practitioners now appear to be in agreement on this point. The problems of market neutral are portfolio-construction problems, and in particular, they are risk problems. The second part of the presentation discusses the fact that the purpose of a market-neutral strategy is to engineer manager skill to maximize returns. And third, the presentation goes into how risk should be engineered to complement manager skill. This part of the process is often forgotten in the treatment of market neutral.

Portfolio Construction

Changes in market dynamics have led to the growing appeal of market-neutral portfolio-construction techniques. Starting in the United States and now mirrored in the United Kingdom, the Netherlands, Switzerland, Scandinavia, Australia, Hong Kong, and even Japan, balanced management has been declining and is being replaced by specialized management and increasingly by passive or semipassive core management run in tandem with satellite management.[3] Core management offers the plan sponsor low turnover, low costs, and low risk. Satellite management offers the plan sponsor higher returns but at the same time higher turnover, higher costs, and higher risk.

This evolution in process has been accompanied by an evolution in the importance of risk control in

---

[1]E-mail to author, February 1998.
[2]See Mr. Lummer's presentation, pp. 5–12.

[3]For further reading on core/satellite management, see John L. Maginn, "Investment Policies and Practices of U.S. Life Insurance Companies," in *Investment Policy*, edited by Jan R. Squires (Charlottesville, VA: AIMR, 1994).

---

the entire portfolio-construction process, as **Figure 1** shows. In many respects, this change represents a revolution in thought, in which core management focuses on achieving market exposure and satellite management focuses on capitalizing on manager skill to achieve higher returns. Today's plan sponsor has the ability to allocate assets or gain market exposure at a minimal or even zero cost, if the plan is big enough, and then make an allocation to skill. Market-neutral investing is the ultimate skill allocation.

Engineering Manager Skill

As Bruce Jacobs mentioned, market neutral is not a conventional long portfolio with a mirror-image short portfolio added to it. The entire portfolio-construction process in a market-neutral fund is different from that of a conventional portfolio, the long part as well as the short part. The key to engineering manager skill is the process of allocating client and management resources to where the markets or segments of markets are most inefficient and where the manager has the most skill and can offer added value.

Market Inefficiencies. Equity market inefficiencies arise as the result of buy-side and sell-side biases. On the buy-side of the equity market, investment banking relationships and the propensity to favor good news over bad can corrupt the views of brokers. Because potential buyers are more numerous than potential sellers, behavioral biases also exist within the market. No one likes realizing losses or getting hit with transaction costs as a result of realizing losses; all those costs lead to inefficiencies on the sell side. Inefficiencies are found in the United States and even more so outside the United States, where transaction costs are higher and markets are less efficient.

Other factors, such as manager concentration, are also at work to create sell-side inefficiency. Currently in Japan, the vast majority of assets are run by a small number of trust banks and insurance companies. In Germany, a vast majority of assets are run by five or six banks. In the United Kingdom, five pension fund managers have more than 50 percent of the pension fund market. So, a large number of clients and a large number of assets are run by a small number of players who tend to make decisions in committee. They take longer to make a decision by working in committee, but when they do, the market impact is greater. Thus, sell-side inefficiency is greater internationally than in the United States.

International markets are more inefficient and have greater potential alpha to exploit than the U.S. market does. After having doubled our market opportunities by going to the sell side, we double it again by the number of securities available in global markets. As **Table 1** shows, measured by the number of stocks, twice as many investment opportunities lie outside the United States as in the United States alone. Short selling in international markets, however, is not necessarily cheap. The "haircut" of 25 or

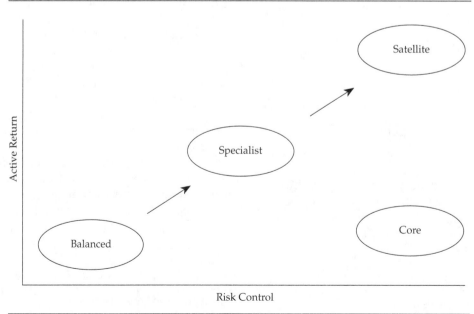

Figure 1. Evolution of Portfolio-Construction Process

30 basis points (bps) "haircut" on U.S. short selling that Bruce Jacobs mentioned for the U.S. market turns into a multiple in international equity markets, where borrowing costs might be 200, 300, or 400 bps and, of course, trading costs are also much higher.

Table 1. Global Equity Market Investment Opportunities by Market Capitalization and Number of Stocks

Market	Percent of Total Market Capitalization	Percent of Total Number of Stocks
Europe	29%	29%
Pacific	15	36
United States	51	26
Other	5	9

Source: Financial Times/S&P All World Index, December 31, 1997.

International market-neutral investing has great return potential, but the trading costs of accessing it and the borrowing costs of short selling dwarf anything a market-neutral practitioner experiences in the United States. Over time, those costs should change. The growth of passive management internationally, which is 10–15 years behind passive management in the United States, is creating liquidity pools that will ultimately drive down short-selling costs. But currently, if investors go into that market with eyes closed to the costs, they are in trouble.

Focus and Freedom. The case for market neutral is particularly interesting when one looks at the manager's focus and freedom to act, in relation to long-only investing. Imagine a universe of five stocks, as shown in **Table 2**, each with a 20 percent weighting. The manager has insight on four of them; he or she has a positive view on two (B and D) and a negative view on two (A and C). The manager has no view about Stock E. Perhaps the manager's models do not work in that sector of the market. In a long-only portfolio, the manager's freedom to act on his or her insight on Stocks A and C is constrained by their weights in the index. Furthermore, the manager

Table 2. Stock Weightings versus Benchmark in Long-Only and Market-Neutral Portfolios

Stock	Long-Only Portfolio		Market-Neutral Portfolio	
	Portfolio	Benchmark	Portfolio	Benchmark
A	10%	20%	–10%	0%
B	30	20	10	0
C	10	20	–10	0
D	30	20	10	0
E	20	20	0	0

essentially has to gain exposure to and be paid to gain exposure to a segment of the market in which he or she has no expertise (Stock E) or has a negative view (Stocks A and C). Conversely, market-neutral fund managers can take full advantage of all of their insights (short and long), and where they have no insight (e.g., Stock E), they have no exposure, as shown in Table 2. No insight, no costs, no fees.

Take that process one stage further: same portfolio, same five stocks. Assume that they are U.S. stocks. Say that the manager has insight in two additional stocks (F and G), shown in **Table 3**, and that they are Japanese car companies. If the manager has the insight, he or she is no longer constrained. The manager has the freedom to go where the opportunities

Table 3. Stock Weightings versus Benchmark in Domestic and Global Market-Neutral Portfolios

Stock	Domestic		Global	
	Portfolio	Benchmark	Portfolio	Benchmark
A	–10%	0%	–10%	0%
B	10	0	10	0
C	–10	0	–10	0
D	10	0	10	0
E	0	0	10	0
F	0	0	–10	0
G	0	0	10	0

are and to gain full exposure in his or her portfolios to reflect that insight. All of this change leads to a provocative new paradigm in which engineered returns are a function of market efficiency and manager skill. If the market is highly efficient and the manager has no skill, go passive, as shown in **Figure 2**. If the market is inefficient and the manager has enough skill to compensate for the trading and borrowing costs involved, then go market neutral because it is the most efficient way to gain exposure to and capitalize on that manager's skill.

Engineering Risk

This description of market neutral makes the process seem quite easy. But if it were easy, all managers would be using it. I have left out the part of the process that I think is the most important—risk control. Far too much of the treatment of market neutral, and indeed alternative investments in general, focuses on the opportunities and the returns. This focus on returns acts as a glorified sales pitch and does not focus on the inherent risk. International market neutral is no exception.

The following example helps to illustrate the point. Imagine that market neutral is a car. All of us (managers and investors) are interested in returns,

Figure 2. Engineering Return Paradigm

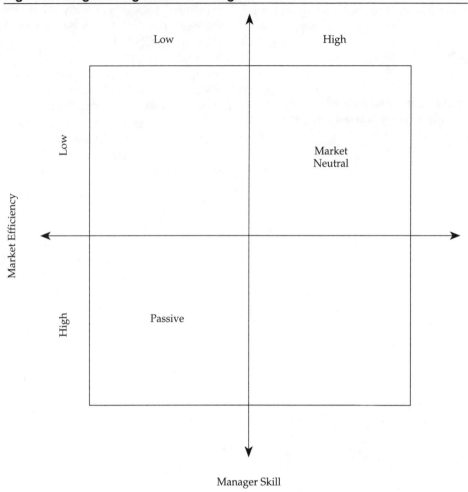

so we are on the straightaway with our foot down on the accelerator. We accelerate from 50 miles per hour to 100 miles per hour. We have the radar detector on, and we think that radar detection constitutes risk control. Then we hit a curve. We put our foot on the brakes, but they do not work. Now we discover that we lack true risk control. Focusing only on returns in market neutral is dangerous. That focus is the sales pitch of market neutral, and attached to that sales pitch should be an equal focus on risk control.

In reality, the risk-control techniques for market-neutral fund management are very similar to those for long-only portfolio management. Risk control for market neutral does not require a new set of rules for how markets work or a new definition of variance or a new explanation of correlation. It uses the same tools as conventional long-only management. For example, the tracking error of a market-neutral portfolio is described by the same formula that applies to the tracking error of a long-only portfolio, as shown by the following equations:

$$\omega^2_{\text{long-only}} = \text{Variance (Portfolio return} - \text{Benchmark return)}$$
$$= \sigma^2_P + \sigma^2_B - 2\rho\,\sigma_P\,\sigma_B$$

$$\omega^2_{\text{market neutral}} = \text{Variance (Long return} - \text{Short return)}$$
$$= \sigma^2_L + \sigma^2_S - 2\rho\,\sigma_L\,\sigma_S$$

where

ω^2 = tracking error
P = portfolio
B = benchmark
L = long position
S = short position

Although the techniques used for risk control in market neutral are not different in kind from those used in conventional management, the application of those techniques has to be much more flexible for market neutral.

The majority of the risk for a long-only portfolio manager lies in market risk, which is reasonably stable, easily identified, and easily modeled. Portfolios held by global market-neutral fund managers, or indeed by any market-neutral fund manager, are dominated by active-return risk. To model that risk, the manager must adapt standard risk-control techniques to match manager skill. Active-return risk models are the mirror images of the long-only risk models, but the models must be applied with a degree of flexibility that matches the dynamics of the active-return strategy. The whole purpose of active-return management is to free oneself from the constraints of the index. So, the manager is going to the extremes by definition, and those extremes and the associated risks are intrinsic to the manager's strategy. Risk-control techniques must be tailored to the strategy.

At Quaestor, we use three general techniques for risk engineering in global market-neutral portfolios: pair diversification, strategy diversification, and leverage. I will not debate the merits of pair trading versus optimization. As a firm, we do not think that the two techniques are irreconcilable. The difference is one of emphasis. Indeed, we use both techniques at the same time, but the further we move away from the mainstream U.S. market, the more we gravitate toward pair trading techniques and away from optimization.

Pair Diversification. Pair trading itself is strictly a misnomer. It makes one think of one long and one short stock. Although that is an example of a pair trade, so is three long and one short with equal aggregate value or an optimized basket of securities held long and an optimized basket of securities held short. I combine all of these variations into the generic term of pair trading. Think of pair trades as subportfolios with zero exposure, or as close to zero exposure as possible, to the main risk factors. The overall portfolio can be seen as the aggregate of these subportfolios.

Our use of pair trading is driven by practical considerations. First, we analyze the pairs in the baskets individually, and we trade them individually, which means we can be very responsive to some of the problems we encounter. If we were to go to a prime broker with 20 Japanese securities we wanted to short in the current market conditions, the prime broker would likely come back and say, "Fifteen fine, no problems. Three are going to cost you an arm and a leg, and two we could not borrow at the cost of both of your arms and both of your legs." Rather than go back and reoptimize the entire process, pair trading allows a flexible response to such situations.

Another reason we use pair trading instead of optimization in certain markets is that optimization requires the allocation of a numerical value to an alpha. Many managers have methodologies consistent with that approach. In our particular case, we do not allocate numerical values to alphas, although our methodology is primarily quantitative. A lot of soft information influences active returns, and we believe that reducing all that information to a single number loses much of that information and corrupts the active-return process.

With pair trading and pair diversification, two components are present. First, we are looking to minimize the risk within each pair, which requires a high correlation between the long and short returns. The high correlation is achieved by matching systematic factors on the long and short positions to minimize the return variation from unwanted sources. Having done that, the second thing we want is to diversify the strategy by constructing a portfolio consisting of a number of such pairs with a low correlation between pair returns.

Table 4 gives an example of matching systematic factors to minimize return variation. Because Ford Motor Company and General Motors are very similar, pair trading them is easy. The similarities of these companies can easily reduce the unwanted factor exposure. We start out with a fairly equal split between factor risk and specific risk. By pair trading, we can get the factor risk down to about 2 percent.

Aggregating a number of pairs with low mutual correlation into a portfolio reduces risk. If all pairs have the same risk characteristics and the pairs are not correlated, then as the number of pairs increases, the level of risk decreases. **Figure 3** illustrates how this relationship works with actual pairs. These results are not loaded; they are fairly representative. The solid line shows the effect on risk of increasing the number of pairs, assuming no correlations between returns on the pairs and equal risk for all pairs. The points show the results for actual pairs. Because the actual pairs did not have equal risk, they were ordered from high to low risk, which explains why the first few data points lie above the solid line and subsequent points lie below the line. But the

Table 4. Pair Diversification

Risk[a]	Ford	General Motors	Ford/GM Pair	Contribution to Total Variance
Factor risk	16.40%	17.21%	2.09%	3%
Nonfactor risk	16.77	17.29	12.05	97
Total risk			12.22	

[a]Risk is measured as standard deviation.

Figure 3. Portfolio Risk versus Number of Pairs

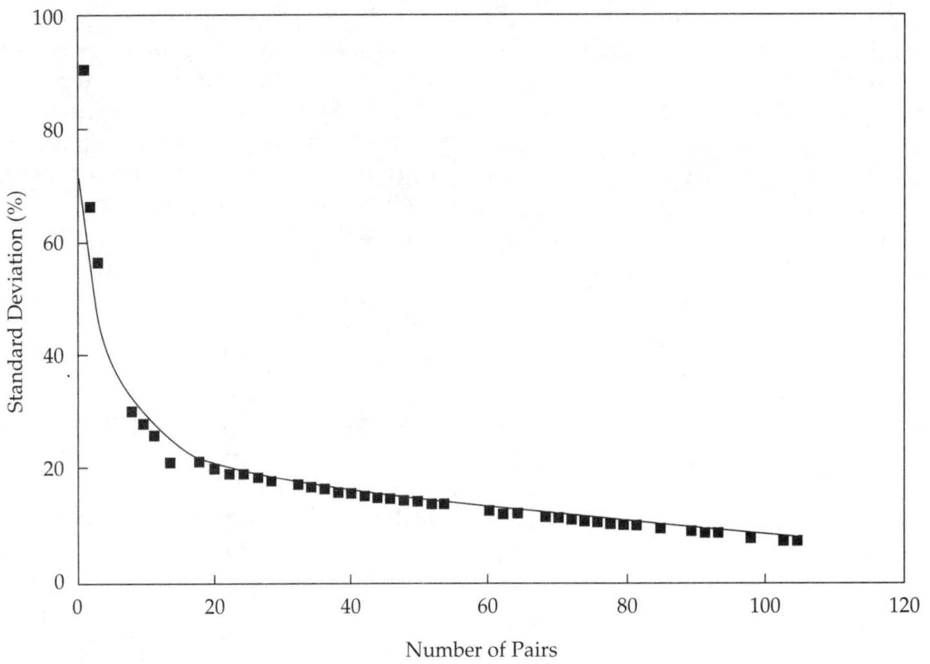

important point is that Figure 3 shows an extremely low correlation between pairs, which is logical and intuitive. Once systematic factors have been eliminated, why should a correlation exist between the value added from a GM/Ford pair and that from a pair of oil companies? We are not interested in the correlations of the underlying companies. They have been removed. We are interested in the correlations of our trading strategy.

Strategy Diversification. The diversification argument is simple: Diversifying across strategies reduces portfolio risk. Diversification can, of course, be achieved within a single market (e.g., we might have Strategy 1 for the U.S. market and run in tandem a small substrategy trading against it), but it also works when we start introducing other countries. The primary purpose of introducing other countries is exactly the same as in the diversification of long-only portfolios—to reduce risk. International diversification also works in market neutral, but it requires a low correlation between strategy returns, rather than a low correlation between market returns.

Table 5 shows the hypothetical risk profile of a domestic long–short portfolio; an international long–short portfolio, which has higher risk (16.0 percent) than the domestic portfolio (12.6 percent); and an equal-weighted combination of the two (the "Global Long–Short" column). The overall risk of the global portfolio (10.2 percent) is the lowest of the three, which is exactly what one would expect.

Some actual data may help to illustrate the diversification argument. A Japanese client of ours had a U.S. long–short strategy. Curiously, the client wanted to add a Japanese component to it for risk diversification purposes. We started running the money on October 3, 1997, which was probably the worst possible starting time because of market conditions. **Figure 4** and **Figure 5**, respectively, show the performance of the U.S.-only long–short portfolio and the Japanese-only long–short portfolio on a daily and cumulative basis. The Japanese market was incredibly volatile in October 1997, clearly a terrible trading environment.

Table 5. Hypothetical Strategy Diversification

Domestic Long–Short		International Long–Short		Global Long–Short (50 percent domestic + 50 percent international)	
STD (long)	= 20.0%	STD (long)	= 20.0%	STD (domestic)	= 12.6%
STD (short)	= 24.0%	STD (short)	= 24.0%	STD (international)	= 16.0%
CORR (long, short)	= 0.85	CORR (long, short)	= 0.75	CORR (domestic, international)	= 0.0%
STD (long–short)	= 12.6%	STD (long–short)	= 16.0%	STD (domestic + international)	= 10.2%

Note: STD = standard deviation; CORR = correlation.

Figure 4. Portfolio Return for U.S. Long–Short Portfolio, October 3, 1997–February 4, 1998

A. Daily Return

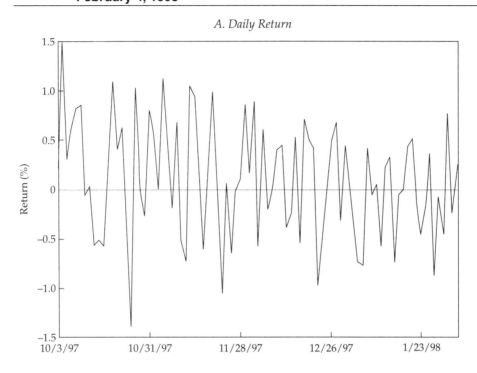

B. Cumulative Return

Figure 5. Portfolio Return for Japanese Long–Short Portfolio, October 3, 1997–February 4, 1998

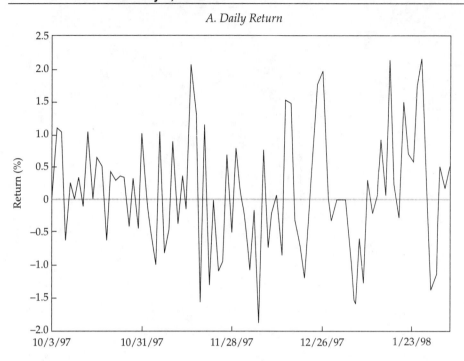

A. Daily Return

B. Cumulative Return

By combining the two strategies, we found that the overall risk of the client's portfolio shot down, even in what was an extremely difficult environment. In this case, the portfolio was not optimally mixed. It was 50/50; equal dollars in the United States and in Japan. Thus, the reduction in total risk to 9 percent shown in **Table 6** is not the optimal figure. As **Figure 6** shows, the optimal split between the Japanese and the U.S. allocation is not 50/50 but rather 30 percent Japan and 70 percent United States.

Table 6. Standard Deviation of Long, Short, and Long–Short Portfolio by Position

Position	Long	Short	Total
United States	23.3%	19.0%	9.3%
Japan	45.1	36.8	14.5
United States + Japan	26.6	22.3	9.0

Leverage. The final component of risk control is leverage within a strategy (to control the strategy risk) and then leverage across strategies (to control the portfolio risk). Using the numbers in Table 6, **Table 7** illustrates the effects of leverage. Without margin requirements, a value of 1 for leverage means that for $100 invested, the investor is $100 short, $100 long, and has $100 in a cash position.

Leverage can be extremely useful to dampen the volatility of international portfolios. For example, consider a Japanese portfolio in which we want to reduce risk. Long–short trading in Japan is very efficient. Without leverage, and over the volatile period in question, we can get the annualized volatility of the Japanese long positions to 45 percent, the Japanese short position to 37 percent, and the combined Japanese long–short position down to 14.5 percent, which is a considerable reduction but one that leaves volatility still too high. With a leverage factor of 0.6, we dampen the volatility of the Japanese portion. So, out of 100 units invested in Japan, 60 would be long, 60 short and 100 in cash. In that way, the risk of the Japanese long–short portfolio is brought down to 8.7 percent, and the overall risk of the global portfolio is 6.4 percent.

Matching Risk and Return. Matching risk and return is the greatest hurdle that an international market-neutral fund manager faces. For a long-only portfolio manager, the potential to deviate from the index is strictly constrained. Insofar as a long-only U.S. manager does deviate from the index, by and large that manager will be going into securities that share many of the same characteristics as the index. The manager has the freedom to go where the opportunities are and will likely go into securities that are not representative of the index.

Risk models can, in principle, be extended to

Figure 6. U.S. and Japanese Weighting versus Risk

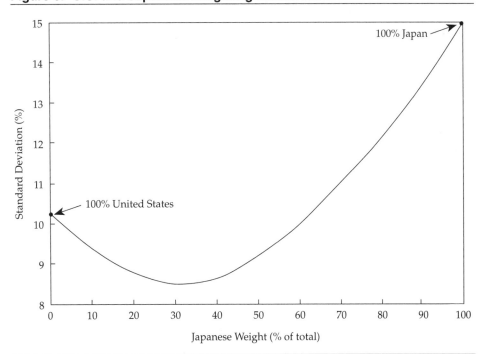

©Association for Investment Management and Research

337

Table 7. Leverage

	Domestic	International (unleveraged)	International (leveraged)	Global Long–Short (50% domestic + 50% leveraged international)		
Leverage	1.0	1.0	0.6			
STD (long)	23.3%	45.1%	45.1%	STD (domestic)	=	9.3%
STD (short	19.0%	36.8%	36.8%	STD (international)	=	8.7%
CORR (long, short)	0.92	0.96	0.96	CORR (domestic, international)	=	0.0%
STD (long–short)	9.3%	14.5%	8.7%	STD (domestic + international)	=	6.4%

Note: STD = standard deviation; CORR = correlation.

cover this new opportunity universe. Extending the risk models might sound easy, but it is actually very hard and the pitfalls can be disastrous. The irony of the situation is that as the global market-neutral fund manager deviates further and further from the index, the manager gets more and more dependent on risk models to control the process, but the risk models that the manager depends on are less and less robust. Put another way, the best active-return opportunities exist in neglected areas, but those are the areas in which the data are sparse, inaccurate, out of date, or unavailable—a state of affairs frequently encountered in non-U.S. markets. In general, risk models represent the influence of many variables as the influence of relatively few factors. The aggregation of many influential variables into a few factors relies on regularities that may not be present.

Although fewer market-neutral investors exist than traditional investors, the downside of the market inefficiency is that competitors may have better information than we do. The situation we find ourselves in is that the neglected areas in which we want to invest are the areas least amenable to risk modeling. But market-neutral fund managers cannot give up on modeling risk. They have to go through the process of matching their risk models to their active-return processes. The factors that managers use in their risk models must be consistent with the factors they use in their active-return process to avoid corruption of active returns. If a factor adds value to the returns, it must also be incorpo-

rated into the risk model. Conversely, a dynamic factor should not be in the risk model if it is totally extraneous to the manager's search for active returns. In addition, the time scales of those factors have to be compatible.

Finally, another downside to market inefficiency is that a manager's competitors may also follow a market-neutral strategy. William Sharpe notes:

> Of course, on average, active managers will not add value. This is especially apparent if all are market neutral since they will simply take long and short positions with another.[4]

Conclusion

Market-neutral investing provides for manager focus and manager freedom, but concomitant with that focus and freedom is (1) a need for a clear understanding of the sources of active return and return variation and (2) an ability to model those sources of return in the risk models. Market-neutral investing is not a new asset class but, rather, a new approach to portfolio construction that gives rise to new portfolio-construction problems. The upside is that managers are free to do what they do best—chase returns. The downside is that they need far better risk models in the international marketplace than are currently available.

---

[4]E-mail to author, February 1998.

Global Equity Research

www.ubswarburg.com/researchweb

In addition to the **UBS Warburg** web site our research products are available over third-party systems provided or serviced by: Bloomberg, First Call, I/B/E/S, IFIS, Multex, QUICK and Reuters

UBS Warburg is a business group of UBS AG

Alexander M Ineichen CFA
+44-20-7568 4944
alexander.ineichen@ubsw.com

The Search for Alpha Continues

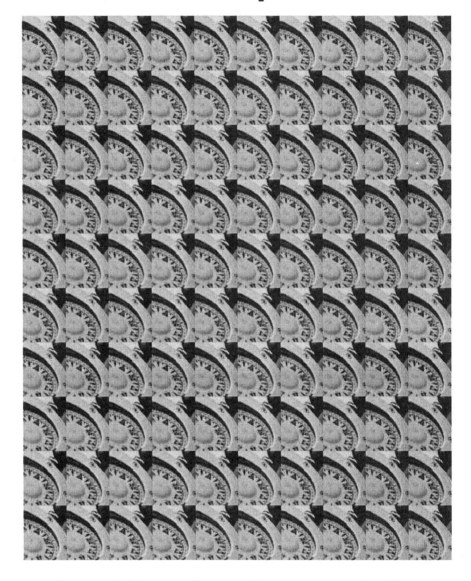

Do Fund of Hedge Funds Managers Add Value?

⚜ UBS Warburg

An Introduction to Funds of Hedge Funds

"Either you understand your risk or you don't play the game."
Arthur Ashe[1]

Introduction

Definition

A fund of funds is a fund that mixes and matches hedge funds and other pooled investment vehicles, spreading investments among many different funds or investment vehicles. A fund of funds simplifies the process of choosing hedge funds, blending together funds to meet a range of investor risk/return objectives while generally spreading the risks over a variety of funds. This blending of different strategies and asset classes aims to deliver a more consistent return than any of the individual funds.

Diversification still makes sense as long as assets are not perfectly correlated

A fund of hedge funds is a diversified portfolio of hedge funds. Most often the constituents are uncorrelated. However, a fund of funds can be widely diversified, as well as have a focus on a particular style, sector of geographical region. The fund of funds approach has been the preferred investment form for many pension funds, endowment funds, insurance companies, private banks, family offices and high-net-worth individuals.

Fund of Funds Ain't That Simple

The operation of a fund of funds manager is complex and its process iterative

Table 10 on page 27 is one way of looking at the tasks and risks of a fund of funds managers. We believe that selecting and monitoring hedge fund managers and monitoring and managing hedge fund exposures is complex. Although conceptually simple, the implementation is difficult. It – the fund of funds operation – involves quantitative as well as (and more importantly) qualitative processes and projections. In addition it requires the knowledge, insight and experience of getting a qualitative interpretation of the quantitative analysis. The whole process is iterative because there is no beginning or end to the process of manager selection, portfolio construction, risk monitoring and portfolio rebalancing.

The heterogeneity of skill sets of a fund of funds operation might be a first, crude indication of its competitive strength

By assessing and selecting a fund of funds manager, the investor will have to judge whether the fund of funds manager has fundamental skill and, ideally, an edge in all variables. Obviously, there will be differences in fund of funds operations as every manager might have different objectives, strengths and weaknesses. The point we would like to highlight here is that a fund of funds operation is a business which will include huge diversity in individual skill sets.

---

[1] From Barra advertisement

(original pp. 2–25 were intentionally omitted)

Table 10: Investment Risk Matrix

Investment activity	Potential areas of risk		
Asset allocation (strategic/tactical)	Selection of asset classes/proxies	Market shocks	Underlying models
	Return/correlation projections	Market structures	Long term versus short term
	Sufficient diversification	Economic assumptions	Costs when changing policy
	Liquidity	Tax	Cash flows
			Liability projection
Benchmark determination	Selection - weight bias	Costs	Rebalancing
	updates/changes		
Manager selection	Style - past, present, future	Guidelines	Concentration
	Misfit to benchmark	Trading instruments	Performance
	People	Philosophy	Process
	Compliance	Controls	Separation of functions (Trading/back office)
Manager monitoring	Guidelines/controls	Models	Data
	Systems		
Performance reporting	Calculation	Presentation	
Custody	Independence	Subcustodian	Capital
Accounting	Methodology	Separation of duties	
Valuation	Modelling risk	Process	Pricing source
	Size of position	Seasonality	
Operations	Business interruption	Staffing	Internal controls
	Record-keeping	External relationships	Technology
	Insurance	Systems	Legal/regulatory
Business/event	Currency convertibility	Reputation	Legal/regulatory
	Credit rating shifts	Taxation	Disaster
	Market disruptions		

Source: Miller II (2000), p. 55

Fund of Funds Industry Characteristics

Size and Market Share

Soon to be a multi-US$100bn industry

Based on data from Quellos there were 444 funds of funds officially or unofficially reporting returns as of December 2000.[1] We estimate that funds of hedge funds manage around 20-25% of the whole hedge funds universe of cUS$500bn assets under management.

Liquidity

Chart 14 shows the distribution of funds of funds by withdrawals (left axis). We found withdrawal information on 235 funds of funds. The right axis of the graph shows the average monthly return by withdrawal for the 96 fund of funds that were in existence during January 1996 and December 2000. Chart 15 shows the distribution by contribution. The sample size for Chart 15 was 189 funds of funds. The average monthly return was drawn from 78 funds of funds in existence over the five-year period ending in 2000. The overlapping sample size was 177 funds of funds (information on withdrawals as well as contributions).

Chart 14: Withdrawals

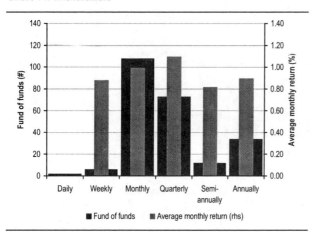

Chart 15: Contributions

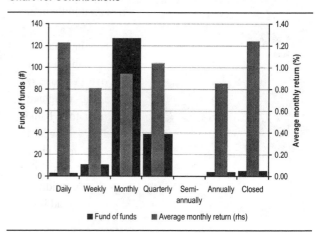

Source: Quellos, UBS Warburg calculations
Return (rhs) only shown for funds of funds in existence between January 1996 and December 2000.

Source: Quellos, UBS Warburg calculations
Return (rhs) only shown for funds of funds in existence between January 1996 and December 2000.

- 77% of the funds of funds had a withdrawal period of either monthly or quarterly (Chart 14). 88% took monthly or quarterly contributions (Chart 15).

- 69% of 177 funds of funds where we had information on withdrawals as well as contributions had a match between withdrawals and contributions. 17.5% took monthly contributions and had a longer withdrawal period. 28% had longer withdrawal period than contribution period. No fund of funds had a shorter withdrawal period than contribution period.

[1] For description of data please refer to page 81.

Relationship between Liquidity And Performance

Liquidity is a theoretical concept with little practical value

Whether there is correlation between liquidity and performance on a fund of funds level[1] and whether a fund of funds manager can have a duration mismatch between his investors (liabilities) and his investments in individual hedge funds (assets) is open to debate. In addition, liquidity on a single fund or fund of funds level is to some extent a theoretical issue. Most managers will have provisions to extend redemptions, either buried in the fine print of the offering memorandum or via some other legal recourse. In other words, liquidity is not necessarily as it appears at first sight.[2]

Liquidity terms of skilful hedge fund and fund of funds managers will probably get tougher

Since the hedge funds with the greatest skills will generate returns in less efficient markets, and demand going into hedge funds is expected to increase at a pace faster than new skilled managers can supply new capacity, skilled managers potentially will continue to be in the position to tighten (and dictate) liquidity terms. Thus we might expect more 2+20 fee structures for single hedge funds, tougher liquidity terms, and more lockup provisions. Potentially some managers may face a moral hazard of opening their doors to new money once having closed. Nevertheless, one could argue that the truly skilled managers would not add capacity beyond what is optimal in their field of expertise and with their operational setup.

Liquidity has a tendency to disappear exactly then when most demanded

Assuming that fund of funds managers must match the duration of their assets with their liabilities, they will have to tighten their liquidity terms as a result of the above. A counterargument to this view is that the fund of funds manager need only manage weighted average terms and probabilistic redemptions. This would be similar to a bank that only needs fractional reserves since a run on the banking industry is seen as unlikely. In addition, funds of funds, as banks or hedge funds themselves, in such catastrophic situations could refuse to pay redemptions. Nevertheless, in the long run, funds of funds will have to tighten their weighted average liquidity terms by either replacing old investors with new investors facing lockups or adding new vehicles with tougher terms.

Flight-to-quality scenarios such as in autumn 1998 do not happen often. In other words, a duration mismatch between assets and liabilities will not be a problem in most market situations. However, shocks to the system do happen. We believe that sound funding and matching asset/liability duration are advisable.

---

[1] Liquidity on a single hedge fund level is a different matter. For example, currencies, interest rate and equity index instruments are the most liquid and also the most efficiently priced. Thus, funds specialising in these instruments could easily offer weekly liquidity. Distressed and convertible bonds are relatively illiquid. Managers focusing here need quarterly redemptions if not longer. In general, the efficiency of an asset is highly correlated to its liquidity. Since we are trying for inefficient markets, this necessitates less liquid investments.

[2] One could argue that liquidity in itself is a theoretical or at least ephemeral concept. Liquidity tends to evaporate when most needed. For example, there was no liquidity during the 19 October 1987 crash. According to the *Report of the Presidential Task Force on Market Mechanisms,* market makers possessed neither the resources nor the willingness to absorb the extraordinary volume of selling demand that materialised. (Swensen (2000), p. 93) Just when investors most needed liquidity, it disappeared. Swensen (2000) quotes Keynes (1936) who argued that *"of the maxims of orthodox finance none, surely, is more anti-social than the fetish of liquidity, the doctrine that it is a positive virtue on the part of investment institutions to concentrate their resources upon the holding of 'liquid' securities. It forgets that there is no such thing as liquidity of investment for the community as a whole."* Swensen (2000) suggests that investors should purse success, not liquidity, ie fear failure, not illiquidity. If private, illiquid investments succeed, liquidity follows as investors gain interest. In public markets, as once-illiquid stocks perform well, liquidity increases as investors recognise progress. In contrast, if public, liquid investments fail, illiquidity follows as interest dries up. Recent trading turnover patterns in telecom stocks might be an example of the latter point.

Fee Structure

In this section we examine the fee structures of some of the funds of hedge fund on which we have information. One caveat of this analysis is that we are not necessarily comparing them on a like-for-like basis. A fund of funds specialising in constant absolute returns will most likely have different fee structure than a fund of funds shooting for the moon, ie with a strong directional bias. In addition, we have no information on trail fees, kickbacks and retrocessions.[1]

From the whole sample of funds of funds data available to us, we found information on base fee, hurdle rate and performance fee for 118 funds, of which 51 were in operation as of December 2000. Chart 16 and Chart 17 (cumulative) show the distribution by flat fee.

Chart 16: Distribution by Flat Fee

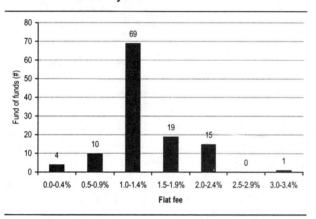

Source: Quellos

Chart 17: Flat Fee of Funds of Funds

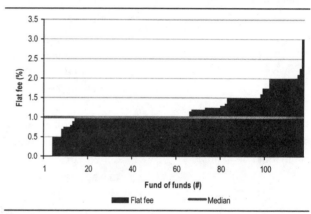

Source: Quellos

- 58% of the funds had a flat fee between 1% and 1.4%. 75% of the flat fees were between 1% and 1.9%. From the 118 funds of funds the median manager had a flat fee of 1% where the average was 1.2%. The range was between 0% (four funds) and 3% (one fund).

- Of the 88 funds with a flat fee between 1% and 1.9%, only eight (9.1%) did not have an incentive fee. The incentive fee varied between 2% and 25%. 20 funds of funds (22.7%) had a hurdle rate[2] of some sort in place.

- Of the 88 funds with flat fee between 1% and 1.9%, the median incentive fee was 10% and the average 12%. The hurdle rate varied from 0% to S&P 500

---

[1] Kickback: Some fund of funds get a fee from the hedge fund's clearing broker, eg a fund of funds manager insisting that a hedge fund clears with a broker of their choosing and that broker then gives a percentage back to the fund of funds. Another kick back idea is for the hedge fund to give a percentage of their total fee income and a percentage of their hedge fund business for being an initial investor. Both of these things are rarely announced. A trail fee is usually payable on mutual funds and seen as a payment to an intermediary for ongoing client servicing and monitoring on the fund. Retrocession is a fee-sharing arrangement whereby a portion of the fees charged by the hedge fund or fund of funds is given back either to marketers or other agents in consideration for their efforts in raising money for the product, or given back directly to the client as a form of compensation (mainly true of retail-distributed products).

[2] The return above which a hedge fund manager begins taking incentive fees. For example, if a fund has a hurdle rate of 10%, and the fund returns 25% for the year, the fund will only take incentive fees on the 15% return above the hurdle rate.

returns. Chart 18 below shows flat fee in relation to incentive fee from the whole universe of 118 funds of funds.

■ The most common structure is a flat fee of 1% and incentive fee of 10%. 28 (21.5%) funds of funds had this structure. Of these 28, nine had a hurdle rate of 10%, six had no hurdle rate and five had a hurdle rate associated with T-bills or other short-term interest rate benchmark. From the remaining eight funds of funds with a 1+10 structure, three had a hurdle rate of 8%, two of S&P 500 returns, and the remaining three had hurdle rates of 7%, 7.5% and 8% respectively.

Chart 18: Flat Fee versus Incentive Fee

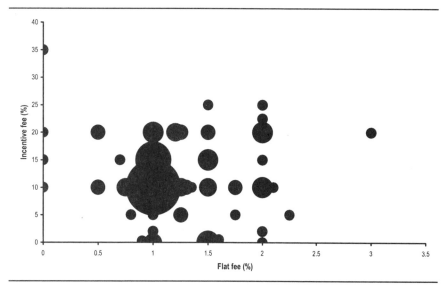

Source: Quellos
Bubble size measures number of funds of funds with same fee structure.

■ The second most common structure was a 1% flat fee and a 15% incentive fee. 12 funds had this structure. However, all of these 12 funds had a hurdle rate ranging from T-bills to S&P 500 returns. Four funds had 1% plus 20%.

Chart 19 below estimates the total fee from the universe of 118 funds of funds. The graph has been sorted by ascending total fees. We assumed a hedge fund gross return of 20%. For the benchmarked hurdle rate, we assumed a three-month rate of 6% and an equity return of 10%. The equity hurdle benchmark rate was either the S&P 500 or MSCI World.

Chart 19: Total Fee Structure

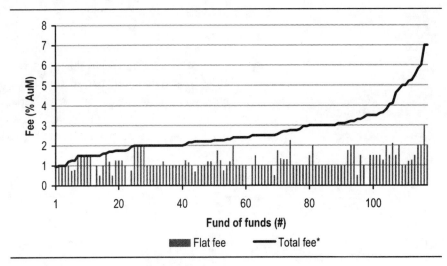

Source: Quellos, UBS Warburg estimates and calculations

* Assumptions: Hedge fund gross return of 20%, 3-month rate 6%, equity hurdle was set 10%.

■ For the total fee the median was 2.4% and the average was 2.7%. The range was from a total fee of 0.935% to 7.0% given our assumptions outlined above.

■ The lowest total fee was in a fund of funds with a flat fee of 0.9% and an incentive fee of 0.25% above a hurdle rate of two-year T-notes. The highest fee structure was 2% flat fee and 25% incentive fee with no hurdle rate.

Volatility of Funds of Funds

Different funds of funds have different volatility targets

Different funds of funds have different objectives and, as a result, different portfolios with different volatilities. Chart 20 shows the dispersion of volatility for 475 funds of funds where we had at least 36 months of continuous monthly returns. A chart with only 286 funds of funds with at least 60 months of returns (not shown) looks nearly the same as Chart 20. The two extreme outliers on the right-hand side of the volatility distribution were missing, if we only look at funds of funds with 60 months of returns. This, in theory, could be a function of a smaller sample size.

Chart 20: Volatility of Funds of Funds

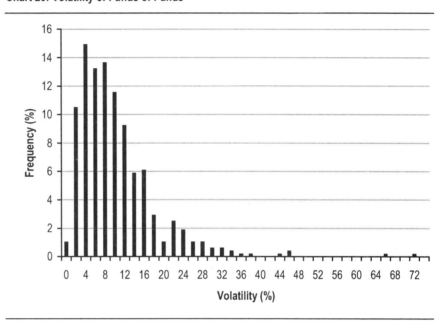

Source: Quellos, UBS Warburg calculations

- 19.4% of funds of funds had volatilities that were 5% or lower, 34.1% were between 5% and 10%, 24.6% were between 10% and 15%, and 11.2% were between 15% and 20%. 10.7% of the funds of funds had annual volatilities higher than 20%.

- Five funds of funds (1.1% of sample size) had a volatility lower than 2%. The lowest volatility was 1.17% (based on 48 monthly returns to December 2000).

- Five funds of funds had volatilities above 45%. The two most volatile funds had volatilities of 72.7% and 66.3% respectively (based on 36 and 48 monthly returns, respectively).

Chart 21 below shows the most volatile compared with the least volatile funds of funds. We only screened funds with continuous monthly returns of five years or more. The fund with the highest volatility had an annual standard deviation of monthly returns (volatility) equal to 47.6% (based on 180 returns to December 2000) whereas the lowest was 1.72% (based on 72 returns to December 2000).

Chart 21: Most and Least Volatile Funds of Funds

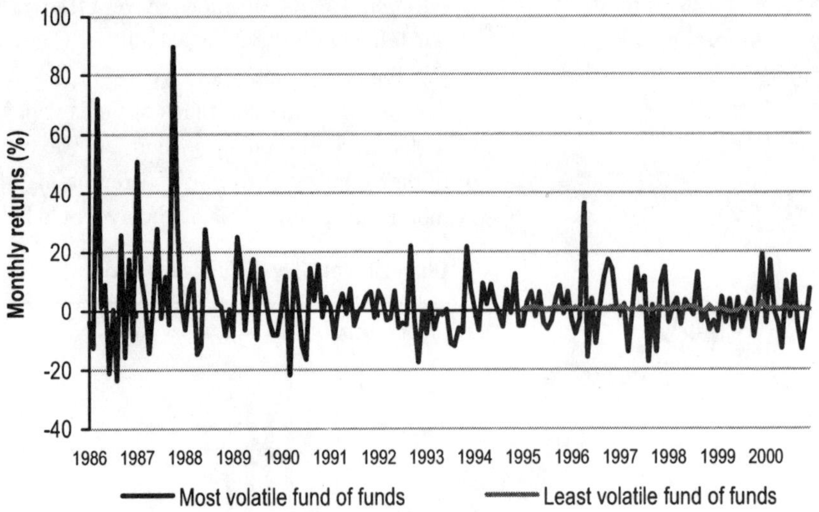

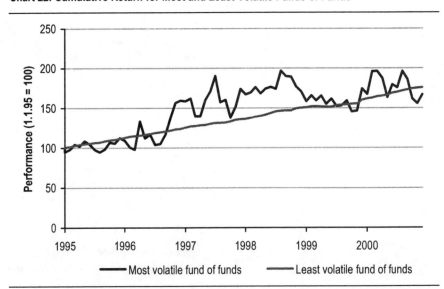

Source: Quellos, UBS Warburg calculations

■ The conclusion we draw from Chart 20 and Chart 21 is that the fund of hedge funds industry is probably as heterogeneous as is the hedge fund industry.

Occasionally our hedge fund research is criticised for being biased towards the non-directional spectrum of the hedge fund industry, for which, obviously, we apologise. Our at times agnostic remarks and digressions on market timing do not go down well all the time. Therefore, for the time being we leave it to the reader to judge which of the following two investments in Chart 22 is superior.

Chart 22: Cumulative Return for Most and Least Volatile Funds of Funds

Source: Quellos, UBS Warburg calculations

Domicile

Chart 23 looks at fund of funds domicile. The chart is based on 130 funds of funds in operation in the two-year period from 1999 to 2000.

Chart 23: Fund of Funds Domicile

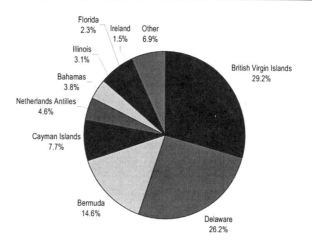

Source: Quellos

Other: One fund each in British West Indies, California, Connecticut, Curaçao, Guernsey, Isle of Man, Luxembourg, Pennsylvania, and Texas

■ 63% of the 130 funds of funds universe are in domiciles renowned as tax havens and boast a fair amount of sunny days per year.

■ Many funds of funds are registered in Delaware. There are some advantages to registering in Delaware:

— No minimum capital is required to form a Delaware corporation.
— There is no corporate income tax on companies formed in Delaware and not doing business in the state.
— Corporate records can be kept anywhere in the world.
— No formal meetings are required and shareholders need not be US citizens.
— Any legal business may be conducted in Delaware.
— Ownership of a Delaware corporation is strictly confidential.
— One person can act as the sole officer, director and shareholder of a corporation.
— It is inexpensive.

Minimum Investment

The following charts show the distribution of fund of hedge funds by minimum investment requirement. From a universe of 929 existing and distinct funds of funds we have minimum investment information on 395 funds of funds.

Chart 24: Distribution by Minimum Investment

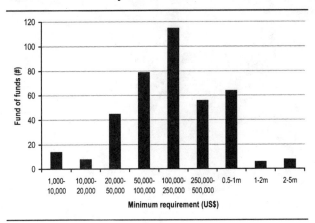

Source: Quellos

Chart 25: Minimum Investment of Funds of Funds

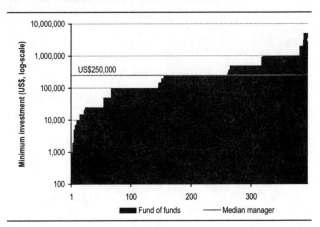

Source: Quellos

- The median fund of funds had a minimum requirement of US$250,000. The range varies from US$1,000 to US$5m.

- 66.1% of the funds of funds had a minimum investment requirement of US$250,000 or less and 37.0% of US$100,000 or less. Only 3.5% of the funds of funds had a requirement of more than US$1m.

- We believe that Chart 24 could have a slight bias to the left as some requirements of older funds of funds might not have been updated.

This concludes our brief analysis on fund of funds industry characteristics. Performance is discussed on page 81. In the following two sections we will contrast what we believe are the advantages of investing in funds of funds, with some obvious and less obvious disadvantages.

Advantages and Disadvantages of Investing in Funds of Funds

"The man who does not read good books has no advantage over the man who cannot read them."
Mark Twain

Summary

- We believe that all investors without a competitive advantage in the inefficient hedge fund industry should invest with funds of funds.

- The main advantage of investing in a fund of funds with an edge is that the manager is able to add value through manager selection, portfolio construction and monitoring investments and managers.

- The main disadvantage is that most fund of funds managers are not purely charitable organisations, ie they most often charge a fee on top of the fees of the individual hedge funds.

Advantages

Value-added

Alpha potential is inversely related to efficiency

We believe that the potential to add value, ie generate alpha, is somewhat inversely proportional to the efficiency and/or liquidity of the underlying instruments. We elaborated this point in our report from last October.[1]

Chart 26: Potential Alpha Generation

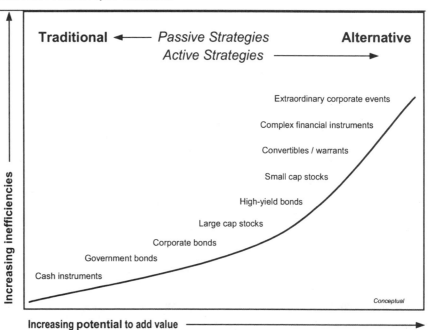

Source: Quellos

---

[1] UBS Warburg research (2000), pages 54-56 and 156-157.

■ Chart 26 shows conceptually what we referred to earlier as two trends in asset management. Where markets are price-efficient, more and more investors adopt a passive approach since the potential for an active manager to add value is limited.

■ The greatest potential for adding value is where information is not freely available, ie in inefficient markets. There, we believe, the potential for active management is larger. Note that there is a difference between adding value in an *informationally inefficient* market through achieving an informational advantage or adding value by picking up a premium for liquidity in an *informationally efficient* market. Absolute return managers are involved in both.

Hedge fund selection is value-added

Given that the hedge fund industry is opaque, ie inefficient, the more experienced and skilled fund of funds managers should have an edge over the less experienced and skilled. Given the high dispersion of returns between managers (Chart 1 on page 4), hedge fund selection is most likely a value-added proposition. Investing with the first quartile of hedge fund managers differs widely from investing with the lowest quartile. In Chart 27 below we show conceptually the expected dispersion of market-based strategies in contrast with skill-based strategies.

Chart 27: Expected Return Dispersion of Market-based and Skill-based Strategies

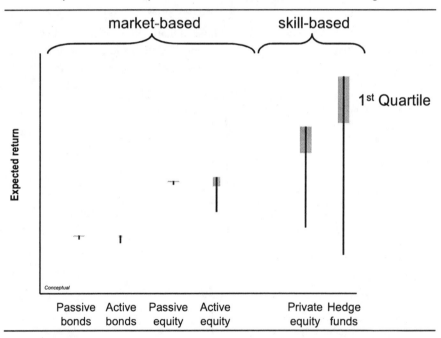

Source: UBS Warburg
Private equity is probably a hybrid between market- and skill-based strategies as the performance of private equity is very dependent on the risk appetite for Nasdaq-like investments.

Wide dispersion is an opportunity for some and a risk to others

The dispersion of returns with skill-based strategies is much higher than with market-based strategies where tracking error constraints drives the range of dispersion. The dispersion for passive bond funds, for example, with the same benchmark is probably minimal. Also, actively managed equity funds on, say, the

FTSE All-Share index will have a relatively low dispersion.[1] A wide dispersion means that the lower quartile will do much worse than the upper quartile. To an investor with no edge this is a risk. To an active investor with a competitive advantage this is an opportunity to add value.

Picking a fund of funds manager is becoming more difficult

As the number of hedge funds increases, the number of fund of funds managers is also increasing as a result of increasing demand for exposure to hedge funds. The lack of longevity of some of the newer funds of funds is a risk to the investor as is the low level of experience relative to fees by those fund of funds managers. We therefore believe that the selection of a fund of hedge funds manager will become more difficult and costly over time.

Differing growth rates

The accepted wisdom in the hedge fund industry is that it is a demand-led business. But 'quality hedge funds' – ie those with superior business models, investment philosophies and risk management capabilities – are actually driven by supply (capacity) rather than demand. We believe there is an imbalance between the demand for hedge fund exposure in general (increasing fast) and the supply of quality hedge funds (increasing slowly).

Some hedge funds close rapidly to new investors

Quality hedge fund managers are making their funds less attractive to new investors either by increasing fees, increasing redemption periods or simply closing to new money. It seems to us that these hedge funds close at a continuously faster pace than normal hedge funds.[2]

Returns in the hedge fund industry might fall

One possible outcome of this supply and demand imbalance it that the quality of the median manager falls. If the current acceleration of demand for hedge funds should quicken, the deterioration of quality could accelerate and those investors last to jump on the bandwagon will likely invest with the least talented hedge fund managers.[3] An experienced and established fund of funds manager, however, is probably more likely to invest with the most talented managers. This, we believe, is a strong value proposition.

---

[1] There is a strong incentive not to deviate too widely from the benchmark, as those asset managers who were following the wrong investment style (and/or were measured against the wrong benchmark) and lost business as a result during the late 1990s will know.

[2] There is the distinction between hard and soft close. Hard close means that a fund is officially as well as unofficially temporarily not taking new funds from any investors. Soft close means that the fund is 'officially' not open to new money. However, an allocation by a large long-term investor is still possible. Note that quality hedge funds are in a position to 'manage' their client base, ie not all investors are treated equally. Sophisticated long-term investors are preferred over unsophisticated short-term investors.

[3] One interesting aspect of the LTCM period is that initial investors had an 18% annual return over the life of the firm because LTCM returned more funds back to investors in 1997 than it initially had invested. Investors who were paid out fully had an even higher return. However, investors who entered last, ie at the peak, lost money. See Lowenstein (2000), p224.

Diversification

Diversification reduces idiosyncratic risk

Portfolio diversification is probably the main reason why institutional investors invest in AIS in general and hedge funds in particular.[1] The main reason for investing in a portfolio of hedge funds instead of a single hedge fund is diversification. Investing in a portfolio of hedge funds significantly reduces individual fund and manager risk.

Schneeweis and Spurgin (2000) differentiate between different degrees of diversification, as shown in Table 12.

Table 12: Classification of Hedge Funds by Diversification Characteristics

Classification	Characteristics	Examples
Return Enhancer	High return, high correlation with stock/bond portfolio	Equity market-neutral, CB arbitrage
Risk Reducer	Lower return, low correlation with stock/bond portfolio	Merger arbitrage, distressed securities, long/short equity
Total Diversifier	High return and low correlation with stock/bond portfolio	Global asset allocation
Pure Diversifier	Low or negative return with high negative correlation with stock/bond portfolio	Short seller

Source: Schneeweis and Spurgin (2000)

Diversification is probably the main reason to invest in hedge funds

A fund of funds is normally not a random composition of hedge fund strategies. The fund of funds manager aims to deliver more stable returns under most market conditions through portfolio construction, ie combining the various hedge strategies. Most often hedge fund portfolios are constructed in a way to reduce the volatility of traditional asset classes such as equities and bonds.[2]

Efficient Exposure

Due diligence is important, laborious, important, costly, and important

Analysing hedge funds is laborious. Once the information is collected, which in itself is difficult, due diligence begins. What are the annual net returns of the fund? How consistent are the returns, year-on-year? Are audited returns available? What reputation does the principal have and what objective references (investors, not friends) can the manager provide? How much of the managers' money is at risk in the fund? Are any investor complaints on file with local or national authorities? Does the investing style make sense? Has the fund performed well in relative as well as absolute terms? What is the risk of losing the principal? How leveraged is the fund?

---

[1] After hedge funds have become mainstream and institutionalised there will be new forms of alternative investments. The goal of this search will be positive returns with low correlation to equities and bonds. The future of AIS, therefore, could include exposure to, for example, Bordeaux wine. Euronext is in the process of launching futures on a basket of clarets (launch was scheduled for June 2001 but postponed to 14 September 2001 because of its IPO). As the connoisseur will know, the 2000 vintage achieved high prices which were, therefore, negatively correlated to the Nasdaq. The reason Bordeaux wine is weakly correlated with equity markets is because one variable is weather in France, which by definition is not affected by investor sentiment. (There is some causality between equity returns and Bordeaux wine because the price for Bordeaux is also a function of general wealth, which to some extent is dependent on the level of the stock markets.) Further alternative investments could include other commodities which are dependent on weather (as opposed to economic conditions for commodities) or weather risk itself.

[2] At this stage of the document we should be showing the classic 'hedge-funds-are-good-for-you' graph, ie the potential portfolio efficiency improvement when hedge funds are added to a traditional portfolio in mean-variance space. We, however, assume that the reader, like ourselves, has seen this graph so often over the past 12 months that we will refrain.

Large universe of opportunities

There are around 2,000-6,000 hedge funds available.[1] Certainly, many of them are closed or do not meet certain basic criteria. However, picking hedge funds from a small, easily accessible universe is probably similar to building a diversified equity portfolio with pulp and paper stocks only.

Finding and hiring investment staff could be difficult and expensive

There are two aspects with respect to staff analysing and selecting hedge fund managers: finding and hiring. Since the hedge fund industry is relatively young, there is no oversupply of investment professionals who have the necessary skill set and experience to analyse the investment philosophy and quality of business franchise and management. Given the opaqueness of the industry, someone from within the industry will probably have a competitive advantage over someone from outside. We believe experience is an important variable in ex-ante manager evaluation. Finding investment staff is not equal to hiring. Location probably matters. One could make the point that a plan sponsor located in the suburbs of Helsinki will not appeal equally to all investment professionals with hedge fund manager selection experience. In other words, the costs of setting up one's own hedge fund selection process could exceed those charged by fund of funds managers.

Low administration costs

A fund allows easier administration of widely diversified investments across a large variety of hedge funds.

Reduced minimum investment requirement

Private and small institutional investors are not able to diversify properly by investing in single hedge funds. The fund of funds approach allows access to a broader spectrum of hedge funds than may otherwise be available due to high minimum investment requirements.

Providers of Capacity

Fund of funds managers are the gatekeepers of capacity

The notion that fund of funds managers are gatekeepers of capacity is not entirely uncontroversial. An established fund of funds manager is quick to spot talent and can secure a certain capacity in a new fund, even when the fund closes for new money. On the other hand, many hedge fund managers are only *soft-closed*, ie they officially announce they are closed but are still open for high-quality investors.

Most swords are double-edged

The term *high-quality investors* is obviously subjective. However, hedge fund managers prefer sophisticated long-term investors who understand the merits and risks of the strategy. This reduces the risk that the investor will pull out of the fund at the worst possible moment. In other words, a hedge fund manager might prefer a professionally managed pension fund over a fund of funds. Although the fund of funds manager might understand the merits of the strategy, this might not necessarily be true for the investors in the fund of funds. In this respect, the capacity argument for fund of funds managers is a double-edged sword.

---

[1] This is a pretty wide spread. The reason is that there is no consensus as to what a 'fund' is. We assume that some vendors, to exaggerate the size of their database, list for example Class A shares (leverage 2:1) and Class B shares (leverage 3:1) as two separate funds. We would consider these two separate share classes. By this reckoning, the number tranches joined by pari passu approaches (hot issues/no hot issues, onshore/offshore, leveraged/non-leveraged, US$/other currency, etc.) suggest only about 2,000 different 'funds', with probably 8,000 different share classes.

There is probably a difference whether the end-investor of a fund of funds is retail or institutional

We believe the capacity argument has been diminishing over time because the allocation from institutional investors into funds of funds has been increasing relative to hot (short-term) money. In other words, a hedge fund manager will distinguish between a fund of funds marketed to retail investors or a fund of funds where the client base is institutional or sophisticated or both.

Conclusion

We believe the hedge fund industry is inefficient as information on managers is not available for all market participants at the same time and at the same price. This means a fund of funds manager with a competitive advantage should be able to add value through manager selection.

The hedge fund industry is heterogeneous. This means different hedge fund strategies have different *expected* returns, volatilities and correlation characteristics. Unlike with equities, portfolio volatility can be reduced to below 5% through portfolio construction. A fund of funds manager is probably more likely to estimate return, volatility and correlation, and is therefore in a position to construct more efficient portfolios.

Probably every investment decision can be broken down to balancing the advantages and disadvantages. In the following section we will discuss some of the disadvantages of investing in fund of funds. The main disadvantage is probably cost.

Disadvantages

Double Fee Structure

Paying the farmer as well as the milkman

With funds of funds, fees are charged twice. The individual hedge fund collects fees from the fund of funds manager and the fund of funds manager collects additional fees from the distributor or investor. The double fee structure is often seen as a negative aspect of investing in hedge funds.[1]

The hedge fund industry is not efficient

The double fee argument does not relate fees to the value added by the fund of funds manager.[2] If a random selection of hedge funds yields the same gross risk-adjusted returns as the fund of funds approach, then we would have to question the double fee structure. However, we doubt that the hedge fund industry is efficient. Most likely it is quite the opposite. Information is still scarce and costly. Institutions have just begun to think about hedge funds on a grander scale. Someone once said with respect to investing and dealing with uncertainty:

> *"We are all in a dark room. However, the one who has been in the room for some time will have an advantage over someone who just entered."*

A massive increase in liquidity has reduced to lower costs of exposure to beta

In theory, an active fee should be paid on active management and a passive (lower) fee for passive management. The main reason for passive management having lower fees is that the costs of getting exposure to efficient markets such as the US or UK stock market have continuously been falling. In other words, an active fee should be charged on exposure that is not available through indexation or other passive investment strategies. Put differently, excess returns attributed to skill are scarce and costly while market exposure is not.

Distinction between alpha and beta is becoming more important

We believe that performance attribution is becoming more and more important to the fee-paying investor base. The distinction between performance attributable to beta and performance from alpha is, therefore, becoming increasingly important. Chart 28 below shows the results of a study conducted by Fung and Hsieh (1997a) based on a sample of 3,327 US mutual funds and 409 hedge funds/CTAs. The authors compared the performance attribution of mutual funds with the performance attribution of hedge funds. Although this example applies to individual hedge funds, the logic should apply to active and passive fees in general.

Hedge fund returns are not driven by the market

Chart 28 shows the percentage of performance attributable to traditional asset classes for long-only funds and hedge funds. In the chart, a reading of 100% indicates that 100% of the return is attributable to asset classes whereas a reading of 0% indicates that performance is not attributable to any asset class.[3] While more than half the mutual funds have R^2s above 75%, nearly half (48%) of the hedge funds have R^2s below 25%. This means that whatever is driving hedge fund returns it is not the stock market or any other efficiently replicable variable. We believe it is

---

[1] Some investors still regard the fee structure of a single hedge fund as excessive. However, fees are probably positively correlated with skill. An unskilled manager will not be in a position to demand high fees. Liang (1999), for example, finds that average hedge fund returns are positively correlated with incentive fees, fund assets, and the lockup period. In addition, excess returns cannot be explained by survivorship bias.

[2] We have discussed the difference of paying a fee for alpha or beta on page 14 of this report as well as on pages 84-87 of UBS Warburg (2000) *In Search of Alpha*.

[3] The asset classes were US equity, non-US equity, emerging markets, US bonds, non-US bonds, high-yield corporate bonds, the US dollar, gold, and cash.

primarily differences in the skill and flexibility of hedge fund managers' mandates that allow them to deliver an uncorrelated set of returns.[1] We discuss the Fung and Hsieh (1997a) article and other related, more recent papers in more detail in the Appendix on page 92.

Chart 28: Performance Attribution

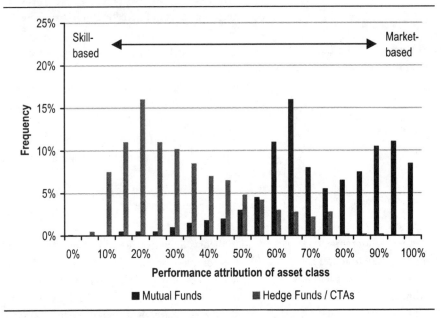

Source: Fung and Hsieh (1997a), UBS Warburg

Note: Terms 'skill-based' and 'market-based' are not in the original by Fung and Hsieh (1997a).

There is normally no passive alternative in inefficient markets

We believe that the high fees of hedge funds and the double layer of fees of the fund of funds manager have to be put in context with the value added on an after-fee basis. Exposure to price-efficient markets is most efficiently accessed through passive vehicles such as index funds or total return swaps or any other variant. Exposure to price and informationally inefficient markets do not normally have a passive alternative.

Lack of Transparency

Black-box syndrome

Some investors find it unnerving not to know what they are investing in when investing in a hedge fund since transparency is lower compared with traditional managers. When we visited him, one pension fund manager asked us the (rhetorical) question:

> "So you suggest we invest in a venture which is not regulated, its positions and investment philosophy are not transparent, is illiquid and is run by a bunch of 30-year olds?"

In some cases, transparency is diminished still further when investing in funds of funds because not all fund of funds managers disclose the names of the funds they invest in. However, quite often fund of funds managers have greater transparency of

---

[1] This is, obviously, not the full story. The flexibility comes at a cost. In addition, hedge fund returns are not normally distributed, adding an extra layer of complexity and calling for greater efforts in due diligence, portfolio construction and risk monitoring. We have added an essay entitled 'Who's long?' at the end of this document (page 100). This touches on the subject of performance attribution of market-neutral, long/short and long-only managers.

the positions of a hedge fund manager they invest in than any other investor. Hedge fund managers might be more willing to disclose information to market participants who do not trade in the same markets and securities as they do.

Most hedge funds have little or no name recognition

Again, we attempt to challenge this disadvantage: How many hedge funds does the reader know by name? Hedge funds are not like stocks with respect to brand recognition. Every investor, or every person for that matter, has knowledge of companies because they affect our daily lives. Hedge funds, in most cases, do not. The industry itself is opaque to most investors. Even an investor who can name 20 different hedge funds still only 'knows' a fraction of the industry. Fund of funds managers specialise and operate in a field where knowledge is only attainable at high cost.

Asset management firms that specialise in AIS in general or hedge funds in particular are not usually household names. This is a disadvantage for two reasons: Unfamiliarity and information cost.

Unfamiliarity

Banks in Gualeguaychu also have no brand recognition

In the most general sense, everything else being equal, something unfamiliar has more subjective risk than something familiar, ie uncertainty is perceived as higher.[1] For example, most people would prefer banking with an established Swiss bank rather than with a small and new private bank in Gualeguaychu (Argentina).[2]

Alternative asset managers are less established than traditional asset managers

Many fund of funds managers are not well known to the decision-maker in an institutional setup. However, today there is a core of asset management firms that have a track record of five years or more. Given that the hedge fund industry is newer than the traditional long-only industry, investors are familiar with the large asset management institutions but unfamiliar with the newer alternative asset management firms.

Mergers between traditional asset management and alternative management houses are likely

Going forward we will probably witness combinations of traditional asset management firms with niche alternative asset management firms in general and funds of hedge funds in particular. That way the traditional asset manager can market a product where demand is increasing and margins are high while the fund of funds manager gets distribution power.

Cost

Due diligence is costly

The cost of information in the hedge fund industry is high. The main reason is the persistent opaqueness of the industry. An institutional investor will have to go through a lengthy due diligence process before the fiduciaries and plan sponsors are prepared to invest the OPM (Other People's Money) they were entrusted to manage. The decision-making process for non-institutional investors is faster and less rigid, ie cheaper, than it is for fiduciaries.

---

[1] Unfamiliarity is not a very scientific and sophisticated way of expressing risk. Note, however, that LTCM was, without a shadow of a doubt, the most scientific and sophisticated risk managers with honours and high-flying reputations in both academia as well as Wall Street. The point is that it is probably healthy to practice some degree of conservatism to anything new, even if we cannot model it econometrically.

[2] Although the boom in banking with online startups in 1999/2000 would indicate otherwise.

Limited Liquidity

Liquidity on a Single Hedge Fund Level

Allocations to AIS in general or hedge funds in particular are long-term investments

Some investors might find comfort in the fact that most hedge fund managers have a large portion of their net wealth tied to the fund, ie the same long redemption periods as the investor. A more pragmatic argument for low liquidity is the fact that hedge funds exploit inefficiencies and therefore are by definition in markets that are less liquid than the bluest of blue chips. In other words, exploiting inefficiencies by its nature involves some degree of illiquidity.

Liquidity on a Fund of Hedge Funds Level

Liquidity is best optimised, not maximised

Limited liquidity in a fund of funds is certainly a detraction, especially when compared with single hedge funds offering superior liquidity or traditional investments offering daily withdrawal/redemption terms. Limited liquidity comes with a cost, and this cost ought to be compensated with proper returns for the investor. Earlier (page 29) we examined the issue of liquidity of fund of funds managers in relation to performance. Skilful fund of funds managers should not only be able to construct portfolios that outperform, but also be able to target a liquidity horizon that is optimal both for hedge fund investments as well as the needs of the investors in the fund of funds.

Caveat emptor

Some funds of funds nonetheless offer opportunities for withdrawal on a weekly or daily basis, though mainly with penalties attached. We however would regard a fund of funds manager who aggressively provides liquidity free of charge with suspicion. Non-marketable securities are by definition illiquid. Our suspicion for such an operation is based on two assumptions:

1. A fund of funds manager could be investing in hedge funds which are only trading in liquid markets. These funds are traditionally directional and their performance more volatile. We would view this as negative because market inefficiencies are by definition to be found in smaller, less liquid and less efficient markets. Long-term investing in hedge funds, therefore, is to some extent about picking up a liquidity premium.

2. *'Beggars can't be choosers'*. We do not believe that the most talented managers in the alternative investment arena make compromises. At least not at this stage in the cycle. We assume these managers can resist the temptation of being part of a retail product that offers high-frequency, eg daily, liquidity.

No 'Learning-by-doing' Effect

'What They Don't Teach You at Harvard Business School'

A further disadvantage of investing in a fund of funds instead of investing in hedge funds directly is a lack of knowledge transfer. One could argue that, at the most general level, investing involves a 'learning-by-doing' effect. Mark McCormack's classic *What They Don't Teach You at Harvard Business School* could have easily been addressed to investment management as opposed to marketing sport celebrities. Success in investment management is to some extent a function of experience.[1]

Sticking a toe into the water

This argument has two sides to it. Many institutions use funds of funds to get acquainted with the asset class,[2] for example by investing some of the allocation with the fund of funds manager and, at the same time, investing with the hedge fund manager directly. This implies that the fund of funds manager is part fund manager and part advisor. The investor, therefore, benefits from the experience of the fund of funds manager in the field of alternative investments.

Conclusion

The main disadvantage of investing in funds of funds is the double fee structure. Fund of funds managers charge a fee on top of the fee structure of the hedge fund manager. We believe investors should relate the double fee structure with the value added of the fund of funds manager. However, to a minority of institutional investors the total amount of fees charged is unacceptable, irrespective of the net value added.

---

[1] The counterargument to this notion is that from 1995 until March 2000 inexperienced investors loading up on internet stocks were outperforming the establishment which, to a large extent, thought that the market was 'overpriced.' Most 'seasoned' investment veterans probably agreed with Alan Greenspan and Robert Shiller that the market was 'irrationally exuberant.' That was in December 1996, ie many years before the peak.

[2] Whether hedge funds are a separate asset class or not is open to debate. Normally, investment vehicles with different risk, return and correlation attributes are classified into different asset classes. This would suggest that hedge funds are a separate asset class as their risk, return and correlation attributes are different from equities and bonds. However, value and growth investing have different attributes but are not separate asset classes. One could argue that long-only, market-neutral or long/short strategies are simply other investment styles (but not different asset classes) as are value, growth and small-cap investing.

Investment Process of Fund of Funds Manager

"To us who think in terms of practical use, the splitting of the atom means nothing." British science writer Lord Richie Calder, 1932.

Summary

■ The investment process of a fund of hedge funds manager is dynamic and can be classified into two selection processes (manager selection and portfolio construction) and two monitoring processes (manager review and risk management).

■ Initial and ongoing due diligence of the hedge fund managers is probably the single most important aspect of the investment process for anyone investing in hedge funds.

■ Portfolio construction and managing the risk of the hedge fund portfolio are mission-critical in the hugely heterogeneous hedge fund industry.

Portfolio Mandate and Investment Process

Portfolio Mandate

The hedge fund industry is heterogeneous and portfolio tilts vary widely

The first step in starting any business is probably setting the objectives. Different fund of funds managers will have different objectives. Different portfolio designs will serve different purposes. Given the breadth of the hedge fund industry it is likely that fund of funds managers might specialise in a certain investment style. We believe that some fund of funds managers might be closer to the non-directional arena, whereas other managers might have an implicit or explicit bias towards directional hedge fund managers and strategies. The difference between directional and non-directional is probably the most general classification of the strategies in the hedge fund industry.

Investment Process

Once the fund of funds manager has set up his business and knows what objectives are to be met, the actual investment process begins. At the most general level there are two variables and two processes. The two variables are the hedge fund manager and the portfolio of the fund of funds. The two processes are a selection and a monitoring process.[1] Most important aspect, in our opinion, is that these two variables and processes are dynamically interrelated. There is little chance of success in a 'let's-go-home-the-work-is-done' approach.[2]

---

[1] To some extent this is similar to creating a stock portfolio. In a stock portfolio there is a selection process (picking constituents) and a monitoring process (managing the portfolio, ie, aggregate of individual constituents).

[2] We are inclined to argue that a fund of funds manager who does not have dark rings under his eyes is probably too relaxed on at least one of the processes.

Chart 29: Dynamic Investment Process of Fund of Funds Manager

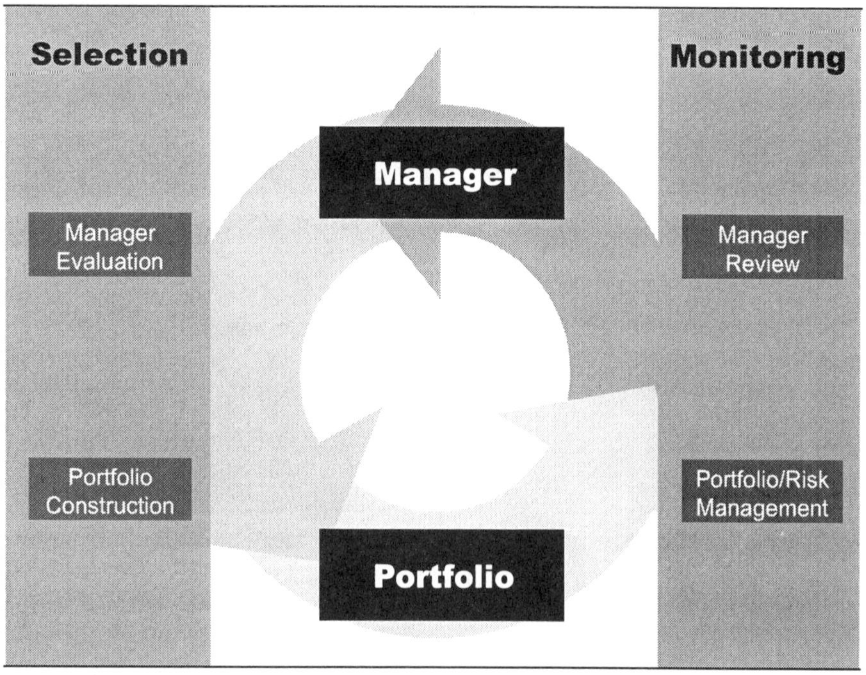

Source: UBS Warburg

Manager Selection and Monitoring

Manager Evaluation

The hedge funds industry is a 'people business'

Manager identification and evaluation is probably the key to success. Investing in hedge funds is essentially a people business. By allocating funds to a manager or a group of managers, the investor expects to participate in the skill of the manager or managers and not necessarily in a particular investment strategy or process. Allocating funds to a convertible arbitrage manager, for example, does not necessarily imply participation in the classic trade of buying the bond and managing the delta through selling the stock. The expectation is to participate in inefficiencies and opportunities in the convertible bond (CB) market where a skilled and experienced manager has a competitive advantage over the less skilled, ie the rest of the market.

Manager data is difficult to obtain

Manager evaluation is not only the most important step but also the most cumbersome. Commercial databases on hedge funds are a starting point but are incomplete. The difficulty and effort of collecting information probably puts in place significant barriers to enter the fund of funds business in a serious entrepreneurial fashion. Put differently, this means that fund of funds managers with an operating history of a couple of years might have a competitive advantage over those fund of funds managers who entered the game last year.

Qualitative as well as quantitative information is important

Due diligence is probably the single most important aspect of the investment process for an investor investing in a hedge fund directly or a fund of hedge funds. Due diligence includes quantitative as well as qualitative assessment. Quantitative analysis of (imperfect) data, however, is not everything. We believe that qualitative analysis is at least as important as quantitative analysis. We also believe that this view is the consensus in the industry. Due diligence includes a thorough analysis of the fund as a business and a validation of manager information, and covers operational infrastructure, financial and legal documentation, affiliates, investment terms, investor base, reference checks etc.

"The due diligence process is an art, not a science"[1]

Martino (1999) also stresses the point of prudence and integrity in an unregulated market where the hedge fund structure provides a manager with a great deal of freedom.[2]

Due diligence is value added

We believe the due diligence done by the fund of funds manager is part of their value proposition. Whether a fund of funds manager is able to pick the best manager is, by definition, uncertain. As most bottom-up equity fund managers will claim to have superior stock-picking skill, most fund of funds managers will equally claim to have superior hedge fund picking skill.[3] However, an investor can assess the due diligence capabilities of the fund of funds manager in advance by assessing the level of experience of the fund of funds managers in the field of absolute return strategies. This is the reason why most fund of funds managers will list the fund managers' number of years in the industry in the marketing prospectus.

There is no definitive guide to manager evaluation. Below we show an incomplete list of some factors we consider important:

- Intangibles: integrity, lifestyle and attitude
- Strategy: identifiable opportunity sets, embedded market risks, definition of investment process, market knowledge in defined strategy
- Experience: portfolio management ability, risk assessment and management ability, strategy implementation, experience of different market conditions, understanding of the impact of market flows, overall trading savvy
- Assets: size (critical mass versus manageable amount), ability to manage growth, quality of investors
- Operation: back office infrastructure and reliability; fee structure; decision and execution process; quality, stability, compensation and turnover of staff

Manager Review

Manager review is a dynamic and iterative process

The due diligence process never ends. As mentioned before, we believe this to be the consensus among investors and hedge fund professionals. Our belief is based on speaking with hundreds of institutional investors, and several hedge fund and fund of funds managers over the past year. The qualitative nature of the due diligence process is also flagged at most of the hedge fund conferences we attended over the year.

---

[1] Martino (1999), p. 281.

[2] See also section 'On Prudence, Trust and Integrity' on page 69 of this document.

[3] This is slightly unfair, because the hedge fund picker is operating in an opaque and inefficient market whereas a stock picker in, say, US large caps is operating in a transparent and price-efficient market. The opportunity to add value is, by definition, larger in an inefficient market than in an efficient market. The value propositions of the two, therefore, are diametrically opposed.

Acknowledging the importance of due diligence and questioning the business model of a fund of funds manager is a paradox

What we find amazing is that the value added of a fund of funds manager is often put in doubt (or the extra layer of fees determined as excessive and/or unnecessary). This is, in our opinion, a paradox: On the one hand, investors agree that seeing hundreds (from a universe of thousands) of hedge fund managers on a regular basis is important, yet on the other hand they postulate that fund of funds managers do not add value. Who else is in the position of doing the due diligence other than experienced investment professionals who are in the loop of the information flow? The industry itself is opaque, ie information does not flow efficiently, so scarce resources must be expended to find and analyse the information. Shouldn't fund of managers be compensated for performing a service that investors both need and want? We doubt that the information advantage of a top-quartile fund of funds manager over a less informed investor will deteriorate any time soon.

Portfolio Selection and Monitoring

Portfolio Construction

There are probably more roads not leading to Rome than there are roads leading to Rome

Most portfolio construction will probably blend bottom-up (manager selection) and top-down (asset allocation) approaches. Different fund of funds managers will have different biases. These biases can be in terms of geographical focus, investment style or strategy. Some managers might put more weight on their personal network in the industry, while others have a more scientific approach to portfolio construction. We are quite confident that there many wrong ways of approaching portfolio construction. There are many potential conflicts of interest which have to be addressed. However, we also believe that there is no single right way of constructing a portfolio of hedge funds.

Hedge fund exposure can involve optionality

As outlined earlier, the mandate and purpose of the portfolio determine the first step. For example, a fund of funds manager who believes that market timing[1] in efficient capital markets does not work is tempted to ignore Commodity Trading Advisors (CTAs) funds from the start, despite their potential attractive diversification and (exploding) gamma features.[2]

---

[1] Until a couple of decades ago, scientists viewed the world as an orderly place governed by immutable laws of nature. Once uncovered, it was believed, these laws would enable scientists to determine the future by extrapolating from historical patterns and cycles. This approach worked well for Sir Isaac Newton. Once he discovered the mathematics of gravity, he was able to predict the motions of our planets. This line of thinking, called *determinism*, is based on the belief that future events unfold following rules and patterns that determine their course. Current science is proving this deterministic view of the world to be naïve. The theories of chaos and complexity are revealing the future as fundamentally unpredictable. This applies to our economy, the stock market, commodity prices, the weather, animal populations, and many other phenomena. Sherden (1998) analysed sixteen different types of forecasting. He found that from the sixteen, only two – one-day-ahead weather forecasts and the ageing of the population – can be counted on; the rest are about as reliable as the fifty-fifty odds of flipping a coin. An interesting view is that only one of the sixteen – short-term weather forecasts – has any scientific foundation. The rest are typically based on conjecture, unproved theory, and the mere extrapolation of past trends. "...*something no more sophisticated than what a child could do with a ruler (or perhaps a protractor).*"

[2] CTAs had a stunning quarter in Q3 98, ie, when everyone else had a difficult period. One could argue – assuming history repeats itself – that exposure to CTAs, to some extent, is similar to being long gamma in a stress scenario: the market (long) exposure is decreased as markets fall, or, in plain English, losses are reduced. Edwards and Caglayan (2001b) examined the returns of CTAs and hedge funds in bull and bear markets. They found that CTAs have higher returns in bear markets than hedge funds, and generally have an inverse correlation with stock returns in bear markets. Hedge funds typically exhibit a higher positive correlation with stock returns in bear markets than in bull markets. The authors also found that three hedge fund styles – market-neutral, event-driven, and global macro – provide fairly good downside protection, with more attractive returns over all markets than commodity funds.

In the following pages we examine some aspects of hedge fund portfolio construction. In the absence of perfect foresight, we use historical data. Table 13 shows the historical returns, volatility and correlation of a selection of hedge fund strategies.

Table 13: Return, Volatility and Correlation for a Selection of Hedge Fund Strategies

	Return (%)	Volatility (%)	Equity Market Neutral	CB Arbitrage	Fixed Income arbitrage	Risk Arbitrage	Distr. Securities	Macro	Equity hedge	Equity non-hedge	Emerging markets
Equity Market-Neutral	11.6	3.5	1								
Convertible Arbitrage	12.1	3.5	0.12	1							
Fixed Income Arbitrage	8.9	4.9	0.04	0.12	1						
Risk Arbitrage	12.8	4.5	0.12	0.46	-0.06	1					
Distressed Securities	15.4	6.6	0.16	0.60	0.37	0.52	1				
Macro	18.1	9.0	0.24	0.40	0.11	0.28	0.46	1			
Equity Hedge *	21.7	9.3	0.38	0.47	0.05	0.41	0.58	0.60	1		
Equity Non-Hedge **	18.4	14.8	0.22	0.48	0.09	0.47	0.64	0.59	0.89	1	
Emerging Markets	14.6	16.4	0.13	0.46	0.28	0.42	0.66	0.61	0.64	0.70	1
Off-diagonal correlation			0.18	0.39	0.13	0.33	0.50	0.41	0.50	0.51	0.49

Source: HFR, UBS Warburg calculations
Calculations based on monthly US$ total returns: January 1990 - May 2001.
The off-diagonal correlation measures the average correlation of one subject with all subjects in the correlation matrix except itself (correlation of 1).
*Equity Hedge investing consists of a core holding of long equities hedged at all times with short sales of stocks and/or stock index options. Some managers maintain a substantial portion of assets within a hedged structure and commonly employ leverage. Where short sales are used, hedged assets may comprise of an equal dollar value of long and short stock positions. Other variations use short sales unrelated to long holdings and/or puts on the S&P 500 index and put spreads. Conservative funds mitigate market risk by maintaining market exposure from 0% to 100%. Aggressive funds may magnify market risk by exceeding 100% exposure and, in some instances, maintain a short exposure. In addition to equities, some funds may have limited assets invested in other types of securities.
**Equity Non-Hedge funds are predominately long equities although they have the ability to hedge with short sales of stocks and/or stock index options. These funds are commonly known as 'stock-pickers.' Some funds employ leverage to enhance returns. When market conditions warrant, managers may implement a hedge in the portfolio. Funds may also opportunistically short individual stocks. The important distinction between equity non-hedge funds and equity hedge funds is that equity non-hedge funds do not always have a hedge in place. In addition to equities, some funds may have limited assets invested in other types of securities.

- Fixed income arbitrage has the lowest off-diagonal average correlation of 0.13 from the selection in Table 13. This is intuitive as fixed income arbitrageurs (most often) trade in non-equity spreads. We show more detailed correlation analysis in the Appendix on page 98.

- Equity market-neutral has lower volatility, lower correlation and lower returns than long/short equity (equity hedge). Off-diagonal average correlation with other hedge fund strategies in Table 13 was 0.18.

- Equity non-hedge and emerging markets have higher volatility, equal correlation and lower returns than equity hedge. This means these strategies add little value in terms of efficiency improvement in mean-variance space.

In Table 14 we contrast three hedge fund portfolios with four equity indices and one global government bond index. The three hedge fund portfolios were optimised for lowest volatility, 5% volatility and highest return and were rebalanced monthly. Again we used historical data as a proxy for expectations. We show monthly returns of these three portfolios in the Appendix on page 92.

Table 14: Skill-based Portfolios versus Market-based Portfolios

	Skill-based			Market-based				
	Minimum Risk Portfolio	5%- volatility portfolio	Maximum return portfolio	MSCI World	S&P 500	MSCI EAFE	MSCI Europe	JPM Global Gov't Bonds
Return	11.38	16.26	21.74	8.33	14.36	3.96	10.31	6.67
Volatility	2.32	5.00	9.31	14.51	14.32	17.07	15.14	5.82
Sharpe ratio (5%)	2.75	2.25	1.80	0.23	0.65	-0.06	0.35	0.29
Worst month (%)	-2.65	-6.06	-7.96	-14.30	-15.64	-14.97	-13.42	-3.35
Worst month (date)	Aug-1998	Aug-1998	Aug-1998	Aug-1998	Aug-1998	Sep-1990	Aug-1998	Feb-1999
Worst 12-months (%)	1.64	0.71	-5.02	-28.59	-24.42	-29.67	-25.49	-6.37
Worst 12-months (date, 12m to)	Apr-1999	Jan-1995	Mar-2001	Mar-2001	Mar-2001	Mar-2001	Mar-2001	Jan-2000
Skew	-1.37	-0.21	-0.02	-0.58	-0.69	-0.26	-0.60	0.16
Excess kurtosis	5.89	2.65	1.36	0.78	1.43	0.49	0.70	0.10
Correlation MSCI World (all)	0.32	0.61	0.59	1.00	0.83	0.94	0.86	0.34
Correlation MSCI World (down)*	0.44	0.49	0.40	1.00	0.73	0.88	0.81	0.04
Correlation MSCI World (up)*	0.06	0.30	0.33	1.00	0.58	0.85	0.69	0.23
Correlation JPM Global Gov't Bonds	-0.06	0.07	0.07	0.34	0.20	0.38	0.37	1.00
Negative months (%)	6.6	21.2	25.5	38.7	34.3	42.3	37.2	40.9
Average monthly return (%)	0.90	1.32	1.64	0.67	1.12	0.32	0.82	0.54
Average positive monthly return (%)	1.02	1.95	2.79	3.29	3.32	3.15	3.04	0.98
Average negative monthly return (%)	-0.68	-1.03	-1.70	-3.49	-2.37	-4.15	-2.71	-0.16

Source: HFR, Datastream, UBS Warburg

Calculations are based on monthly US$ total returns between January 1990 and May 2001.

*Measures correlation in months when MSCI World is down or up respectively.

By comparison: statistics for an equally weighted skill-based portfolio (nine strategies): return 14.9%, volatility 6.1%, Sharpe ratio 1.6x, correlation MSCI World 0.66, worst 12-month performance –6.5%.

- The minimum risk portfolio[1] outperformed the maximum return portfolio in the (difficult) years of 1994 (by 112 basis points), 2000 (435bp) and 2001 to May (263bp). This is not surprising, as one would expect less volatile portfolios to outperform in falling markets and underperform in rising markets.

- The three skill-based portfolios have, for what it's worth, much higher Sharpe ratios than the market-based strategies. If risk were equal with volatility of returns and, therefore, the Sharpe ratio a measure for risk-adjusted returns, the hedge fund portfolios would be superior by a wide margin.

- The worst month in the 11½-year period was August 1998 except for bonds and the MSCI EAFE index.[2] This implies that in a stress-test scenario, correlation moves towards 1 for all portfolios. The worst monthly loss for the skill-based portfolios is a fraction of the equity indices.

---

[1] We use the terms *minimum risk portfolio*, *minimum volatility portfolio* and *minimum variance portfolio* interchangeably to describe the portfolio with the lowest possible expected volatility in mean-variance space. The terms could be misleading as, in the real world, risk is not equal to volatility and variance.

[2] The MSCI EAFE index measures the performance of Europe, Australasia and Far East, ie essentially the developed world ex-Americas.

■ The worst 12-month period for the equity indices and the maximum return skill-based portfolio ended in March 2001. Note that the maximum return skill-based portfolio has an equity-long bias. The minimum risk skill-based portfolio had its worst 12-month period in April 1999, ie the period including Q4 98.

■ Excess kurtosis is highest for the minimum risk portfolio, which constitutes only strategies based on a spread (arbitrage strategies). In the rare event of all the spreads blowing up at the same time, these strategies are prone to outliers on the left-hand side of the return distribution.

Chart 30 shows the three skill-based portfolios discussed above. We have added the portfolio in between in 1% volatility increments.

Chart 30: Mean-variance Optimal Hedge Fund Portfolios

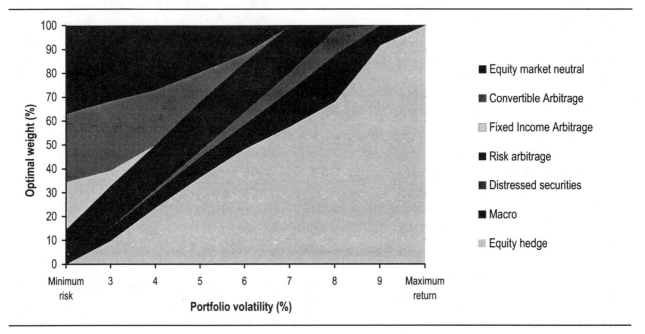

Source: HFR, Datastream, UBS Warburg calculations

All efficient allocations have zero weight in Equity non-hedge (long/short with long bias) and Emerging markets.

The weights floated between 0% and 100% (short positions constrained).

Calculations are based on monthly US$ total returns: January 1990 - May 2001.

Returns, volatility and correlation matrix from Table 13 on page 52.

■ Depending on the fund of funds manager's objectives, the hedge fund portfolio will be biased towards directional or non-directional, ie towards the left-hand or right-hand side of Chart 30. Note that the maximum return portfolio contains a 100% allocation to long/short equity strategies (equity hedge).[1]

---

[1] Fund and Hsieh (2001) point out that the 'spread risk' inherent in a long/short portfolio, for example, often overwhelms the market directional component of the portfolio's exposure. The authors make reference to the former Tiger Fund favouring value stocks on the long side and being negative on growth stocks which led to the dissolution of the fund in February 2000. The authors also note the destiny of George Soros' Quantum Group of funds which experienced substantial losses in a period where the Wilshire 5000 index showed positive returns. In other words, volatility of returns can substantially underestimate the risk of a dynamic trading strategy.

Minimum risk portfolio is biased towards spread-based strategies

If low portfolio volatility, ie stable positive returns are the main objective, the hedge fund portfolio will include high Sharpe ratio strategies such as market-neutral, convertible arbitrage, and risk arbitrage. These are all spread-based strategies. Traditionally, these portfolios were for wealthy individuals who wanted to grow their wealth steadily with little downside volatility. We believe institutional investors use low-volatility hedge fund exposure to diversify exposure to equities and bonds, ie traditional assets. Schneeweis and Spurgin (2000) call these strategies 'risk reducers' (see Table 12 on page 40).

The maximum return portfolio consists of 100% long/short equity

The maximum return portfolio consists of 100% in long/short equity (equity hedge). These portfolio have a long bias, ie correlation with equities is higher than portfolios constructed with arbitrage strategies.[1] The assumption is that these portfolios will not yield positive returns in a bear market, ie not diversify portfolios of traditional risks as well as hedge funds portfolios with non-directional exposure. We believe that in the past these portfolios had more appeal to investors seeking high equity-like returns as opposed to diversification opportunities and stable income.[2] The superiority of long/short equity strategies in the high-return spectrum in mean-variance space is one of the reasons why we believe that absolute-return investment styles are as much a new paradigm as they are a bubble. Schneeweis and Spurgin (2000) call these strategies 'return enhancers'.

Chart 31: Mean-variance Optimised Hedge Fund Portfolios versus Traditional Indices

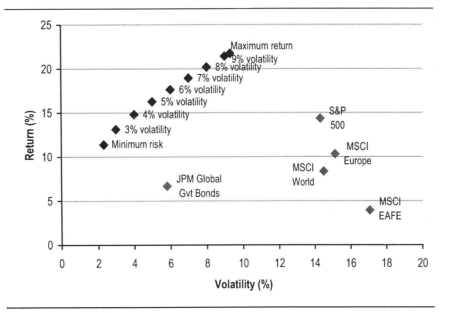

Source: HFR, Datastream, UBS Warburg calculations
Calculations are based on monthly US$ total returns: January 1990 - May 2001.

Chart 31 compares the mean-variance optimised hedge fund portfolios from Chart 30 from page 54 with traditional asset classes.

---

[1] We apologise for using the term 'arbitrage' quite loosely. However, we believe the term has somewhat lost its original meaning of a riskless profit. Today the term is used, it seems, for any investment style involving a spread.

[2] If we optimise using historical returns, volatility and correlation from the past five years ending May 2001 instead of 11.5 years, the maximum return portfolio remains 100% equity hedge. The minimum risk portfolio only changes slightly. The weight in convertible arbitrage increases at the expense primarily of fixed income arbitrage. Fixed income arbitrage was able to use much lower leverage to amplify returns in the post-LTCM era.

■ This or a similar looking graph is probably the most often shown graph at any hedge fund conference. Some speakers even go as far as to describe the horizontal axis as 'risk' instead of standard deviation of returns or volatility.

Survivorship bias in hedge fund data is a problem but not a major issue

The following graph (Chart 32) indicates that even when we shave off 300-400 basis points off the returns due to survivorship or any other bias, little changes when compared with traditional asset classes. Survivorship bias[1] is a problem with any fund data.[2] However, it is unlikely to be a rational reason for not investing in hedge funds.

For the sake of argument, we have subtracted 300bp from the historical returns (to account for any positive biases in the data) and doubled volatility (to account for non-normality of returns, the 'unfamiliarity aspect' and limited liquidity and transparency) for the nine mean-variance efficient hedge fund portfolios in Chart 31.

Chart 32: Return versus Volatility (Hedge Fund Return −300bp and Volatility Doubled)

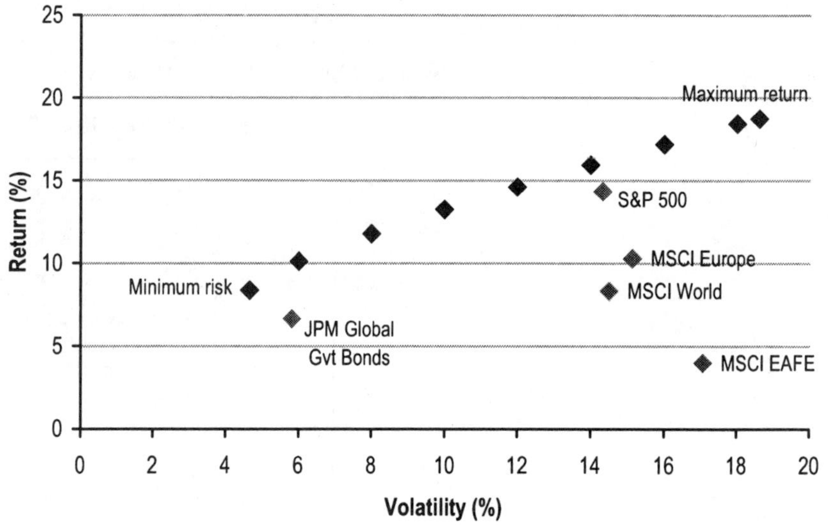

Source: HFR, Datastream, UBS Warburg calculations
Calculations are based on monthly US$ total returns: January 1990 - May 2001. 300bp was subtracted from historical returns to account for any imperfection in the data and volatility was doubled, potentially to account for imperfection in calculating standard deviations of non-marketable financial instruments.

■ We were admittedly surprised to see the superiority of these non-traditional portfolios. Mean-variance efficiency remained intact, even when subtracting 300bp for any upward bias from returns and doubling the volatility. Note that

---

[1] Survivorship bias occurs when data samples exclude markets or investment funds or individual securities that disappeared. The data sample of survivors describes an environment that overstates the real-world return and understates the real-world risk.

[2] Park, Brown and Goetzmann (1999), Brown, Goetzmann and Ibbotson (1999) and Fung and Hsieh (2000) estimated survivorship bias in hedge fund data to be 2.6% and 3% respectively. Survivorship bias is not a phenomenon exclusively in hedge funds performance data. Grinblatt and Titman (1989); Brown, Goetzmann, Ibbotson, and Ross (1992); Malkiel (1995), and Elton, Gruber, and Blake (1996) found that survivorship biased mutual fund returns upward by 0.5-1.4% a year.

Fung and Hsieh (1999) suggest that using a mean-variance criterion to rank hedge funds and mutual funds will produce rankings which are nearly correct.

In Chart 33 below we have normalised some variables from Table 14 on page 53 (skill-based portfolios versus market-based portfolios). We normalised relative to a global equity portfolio. In this case we used the MSCI World Index (including dividends). The graph also shows differences between the different hedge fund portfolios. The MSCI World was normalised to 100. A reading at 200 or 50, therefore, indicates that the variable for the hedge fund portfolio is double or half that of MSCI World. Note that the vertical axis is on a log scale.[1]

Chart 33: Hedge Fund Portfolios Compared with a Global Equity Portfolio (MSCI World)

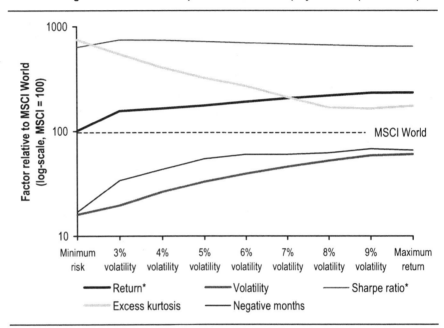

Source: HFR, Datastream, UBS Warburg calculations
* Historical return minus 300bp

■ The minimum risk portfolio, ie the hedge fund portfolio with the lowest possible volatility, has the same historical total return (after subtracting 300bp) as the MSCI World Index. The return increases as the volatility of the hedge fund portfolio is increased.

■ The volatility of the minimum risk portfolio is less than one-sixth (2.3% versus 14.5%) that of the global equity index. The Sharpe ratio, in theory a measure for risk-adjusted returns, for all skill-based portfolios is substantially higher than the Sharpe ratio of the market. Portfolios with a volatility of around 3% have the highest Sharpe ratios.

■ Excess kurtosis is 7.5 times higher (5.9 versus 0.8) for the so-called minimum risk portfolio. Excess kurtosis is negatively correlated with volatility, ie as volatility increases excess kurtosis is reduced.

---

[1] We have subtracted 300bp from the historical returns, primarily to avoid further debates about survivorship bias in hedge fund data and potential conspiracies of the providers of hedge fund data to sell hedge funds.

■ The number of negative months is lower for all skill-based portfolios. As volatility increases, the number of negative months increases as a result.

Conclusion

In conclusion we believe that portfolios of different fund of funds managers will have similar allocations depending on their volatility preference. Standard mean-variance optimisation is far from being a perfect portfolio construction tool.[1] Risk assessment cannot be done accurately using a second-order, ie mean-variance, approach. However, until a superior model is found it most likely will continue to be the industry standard.

Portfolio/Risk Management

Expectations matter

The second monitoring process, next to reviewing the manager, is monitoring the portfolio or managing the risk of the portfolio on an ongoing basis. The analysis above is ex-post. The key to success of any portfolio construction exercise is to estimate return, volatility and correlation, ie the three input variables of the mean-variance optimisation process, and to combine the variables to construct a mean-variance efficient portfolio. It is therefore obvious that different fund of funds managers will have different portfolios, as their estimates for the future differ. Some might be more reliant on the past and others might try to 'call the market,' ie try to pick the strategy which will perform best over the next 12-24 month period.

Little variance in strategy allocations is favourable

The picking of strategies and the resultant portfolio rebalancing is probably not entirely independent of the fund of funds managers' marketing effort. A fund of funds involved in marketing to retail investors, for example, has an incentive to bias the portfolio constituents towards the current darlings of the industry. This would have meant having large allocations in convertible arbitrage and risk arbitrage in the beginning of 2001.[2] These two strategies performed extremely well in 2000. In other words, there are fund of funds managers who are opportunistic with respect to portfolio construction and rebalancing and those who accept less variance in their strategy allocations. We would favour the latter over the former on the grounds that it is probably difficult to time strategies. In addition, short-term trading of skill-based strategies is, in our opinion, counterintuitive and probably expensive to execute.

Assessing risk management capability is more subjective than assessing risk measurement skill

Risk management is not the same as risk measurement. The measurement of portfolio risk is to a large extent a quantitative process. However, risk management is judgmental. Any investor investing in a fund of funds will probably find it easier to assess whether the fund of funds manager can measure risk. This can be achieved by examining the models, the data and the skill and experience of the fund of funds management operation. These input parameters are more objective. The judgement to take action based on the changing risk parameters is more subjective. Whether a fund of funds manager takes action according to its objectives is uncertain. One layer of comfort from the investors' perspective is when the fund of funds manager

---

[1] That said, Fung and Hsieh (1999) analysed whether the mean-variance analysis of hedge funds approximately preserves the ranking of preferences in standard utility functions. Their results suggest that using a mean-variance criterion to rank hedge funds and mutual funds will produce rankings which are nearly correct. The authors also examine the usefulness of the Sharpe ratio to measure risk-adjusted returns. They concluded that the Sharpe ratio works poorly when the investor's risk aversion is low, but works reasonable well when risk aversion is high.

[2] This would also have meant no allocation to hedge funds operating in emerging markets and global macro.

is also a principal. This is not a guarantee of prudently executed and continuous risk management. However, at least it should align the interests of the investor with those of the manager.

This concludes our general thoughts on hedge funds in general and funds of funds in particular. In the following section we attempt to define the 'edge' of a fund of funds manager. Ideally, this should allow investors to pick fund of funds managers with a competitive advantage.

The Edge

"As an investor, as long as you understand something better than others, you have an edge."
George Soros

Summary

We believe an investor interested in funds of funds should search for the following attributes when seeking in a manager selecting hedge funds. The manager should:

- understand all hedge fund strategies,

- understand all instruments used by hedge funds,

- emphasise qualitative aspects relative to quantitative variables,

- be in the 'information loop' and have extensive proprietary data,

- be of highest integrity, as there is little regulation or reputational risk of large corporates to assist investors.

- Ideally, the interests of the managers are aligned with those of their investors.

Investment Philosophy of Fund of Funds Manager

Industry's heterogeneity results in opportunities as well as risks

The hedge fund industry is heterogeneous when compared with the traditional long-only asset management industry. This heterogeneity allows one to pursue different strategies. The two extreme choices are to (1) minimise portfolio volatility or (2) maximise expected return. The former aims to capture stable returns in the region of 12%. The latter expects returns in the low twenties. We believe that most funds of funds will opt for a blend of the two extremes with a bias either towards directional or non-directional strategies.

Does market timing work or not?

Among important considerations is whether the fund of funds manager believes in market timing or not. We find that many investment professionals in a risk management discipline or professionals with a bias to academia have developed an aversion to market risk, which they perceive as being exposed to chance.[1] Those investors will find attraction in strategies where the manager's alpha is isolated from beta, ie from timing the market.[2] The other extreme will be biased towards timing the market. These managers will include more opportunistic, ie directional strategies. Note that the goal of the first hedge fund (Alfred Jones) was to reduce exposure to chance (market risk) and increase exposure to skill (stock selection). Note also that the hedge fund boom of the early 1970s ended because funds were long and leveraged, ie the industry disappeared after departing from its origins.

---

[1] Behaviourists argue that we have a hard time discerning probabilities of events and cannot distinguish a long-shot prediction from something that is likely to occur by pure chance. Or as Warren Waver, author of the book *Lady Luck*, observed, *"The best way to lose your shirt is to think that you have discovered a pattern in a game of chance."* From Sherden, p121.

[2] Peter Lynch was quoted as saying, *"I don't believe in predicting markets,"* and that market timers *"can't predict markets with any useful consistency, any more than the gizzard squeezers could tell the Roman emperors when the Huns would attack."* From Sherden (1998), p106.

At the end of the day, a fund of funds manager will offer what his clients demand

A fund of funds manager might also elaborate the demand structure of its clientele. Retail investors are probably more likely to be in 'get-rich' mode and high-net-worth private investors in 'stay-rich' mode, while institutional investors might seek diversifiers to their equity stake. Fund of funds managers targeting a specific client type have an incentive to structure a fund of funds that matches what their clients demand.

Not utilising the full spectrum of hedge fund strategies is probably similar to playing the piano by only using the ebony keys

One of the first decisions a fund of funds manager either implicitly or explicitly will do, therefore, is focus on the left- or right-hand side of Chart 34. Strategies on the right-hand side include market timing, strategies on the left do not, or do so to a much lesser extent.[1] We believe the more sophisticated fund of funds managers will blend either directional with non-directional or non-directional with directional strategies. The diversification benefits due to low correlation is, simply put, too great not to be utilised in constructing a portfolio of hedge funds.

Chart 34: Dispersion of Quarterly Returns

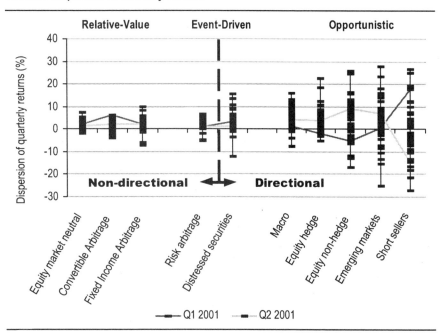

Source: HFR, UBS Warburg
Horizontal marks measure quarterly total return in US$; vertical line measures dispersion of quarterly returns from January 1990 to June 2001. Q1 and Q2 01 are marked with lines.

All fund of funds managers have absolute return and risk targets

Most fund of funds managers will aim for absolute returns and low volatility when compared with the traditional asset classes such as equities and bonds. Capital preservation or the protection of wealth is also the goal of most fund of hedge funds managers. Not only is the return target defined in absolute levels but the long-term risk target is also defined in absolute terms.

---

[1] A convertible arbitrageur, for example, will occasionally time both market direction as well as volatility. It could be argued that to some extent all hedge fund strategies are opportunistic.

Due Diligence and Track Record

Quantitative versus qualitative assessment

Most investors are familiar with the phrase 'past performance is no guide to future performance'. However, many investors seem to focus on track record when evaluating investment in the hedge fund industry as highlighted by the aforementioned Golin/Harris Ludgate survey. We believe that quantitative analysis has its limitations when evaluating and selecting hedge fund managers. At best it should be used to support in-depth qualitative research and rigorous due diligence. We believe that quantitative analysis is more relevant for risk monitoring than for manager selection.

Quantitative assessment is cheap when compared with qualitative analysis

The advantage of quantitative research is its relatively low cost and easy access. Anyone can buy a database for a couple of thousand US dollars and screen for top quartile performers. However, many top performers in the hedge fund industry do not appear in commercially available databases.

A proprietary database including qualitative and quantitative information is essential

We believe a proprietary database, which includes qualitative information, is important. The qualitative information can be scored and used in a ranking process to compare different managers within a strategy. A ranking process also allows elaborating on the strengths and weaknesses of each manager. The weakness of one manager can then be balanced through the strength of another manager in the portfolio construction process. This option is not available to the fund of funds manager who does not have qualitative information.

Due diligence and corporate governance are qualitative processes

Given the importance of qualitative research and due diligence, an investor evaluating a fund of funds manager will want to assess whether the manager is equipped to manage the laborious task of due diligence on an increasing number of funds. One could argue that the job of the fund of funds manager used to be to pick one outstanding manager per quarter from ten new managers. Today this task is probably more picking one or two managers out of c200 new funds per quarter; manager selection has probably become more difficult over time.

Risk and Performance Monitoring

Transparency

There are no patents on investment strategies

Transparency is among the hottest topics discussed at fund of funds conferences and in the minds of institutional involvement in hedge funds. A hedge fund manager has an incentive not to reveal the fund's positions for two main reasons. First, the market can trade against the manager if the position is in an illiquid security or spread and the position is revealed to the market. Inefficiencies are found in illiquid markets, not liquid markets. The period of autumn 1998 was a showcase example of the market trading against LTCM once the company was in distress and positions were revealed to the market. Second, most managers believe they have an edge relative to the market. In other words, they are making money by doing something the market does not know or by doing it better than the market does. This 'edge' is their whole value proposition and justification for being in business. It is only rational that they protect what they believe is most valuable.[1]

---

[1] This point might be open to debate. We took the view that someone investing in a hedge fund invests in the skill of the manager and not in a mechanical investment process.

(original pp. 62–72 were intentionally omitted)

The costs of attaining transparency of complex strategies might be higher than the risk monitoring benefits

There are additional reasons why a hedge fund manager might not want to reveal positions to a prospective or existing investor. A rude cynic might argue that most investors will not understand the real-time or daily positions of an arbitrage fund in any case. The information given to the investor would give transparency but would, in the cynic's view, cause more harm than good. We obviously do not share this view. However, as mentioned before, a fund of funds manager having full access to a manager's positions but not understanding the underlying strategies and instruments has a competitive disadvantage relative to the fund of funds manager who does.

In *Sound Practices for Hedge Fund Managers* (2000) the authors[1] recommend that investors should receive periodic performance and other information about their hedge fund investments. According to the report, hedge fund managers should also consider whether investors should receive interim updates on other matters in response to significant events. Hedge fund managers should negotiate with counterparties to determine the extent of financial and risk information that should be provided to them based on the nature of their relationship in order to increase the stability of financing and trading relationships. They should also work with regulators and counterparties to develop a consensus approach to public disclosure. Agreements and other safeguards should be established to protect against the unauthorised use of proprietary information furnished to outside parties.

Manager Risk Factors

The standard deviation of returns is the tip of the iceberg

We believe that one of the most important factors in terms of risk is that risk is not synonymous with volatility.[2] This is especially true when investing in non-marketable securities or ventures. When managing the risk of a manager, Jaeger (2000) distinguishes between portfolio market and non-market related factors as well as operational factors. We believe these factors also apply for someone investing with a fund of funds manager.

(1) Porfolio factors: non-market related.
  -Leverage
  -Concentration
  -Illiquidity
  -Trading behaviour

(2) Portfolio factors: market-related.
  -Directional factors: long bias, short bias, neutral, etc.
  -Technical factors: volatility
  -Spread-related factors: sector tilts, style tilts, credit spreads

---

[1] Caxton Corporation, Kingdon Capital Management, Moore Capital Management, Soros Fund Management, and Tudor Investment Corporation.

[2] Rahl (2000) uses the term 'iceberg risk' in connection with the lessons learnt from LTCM. The visible tip of the iceberg (for example the volatility of returns) is not necessarily a clear indication of the full risk. A long/short equity manager, for example, normally has lower beta risk. This means volatility of returns is lower. However, the manager is also exposed to 'spread risk'. Spread risk is not necessarily captured be measuring the standard deviation of returns. Returns from beta are fairly normally distributed. Returns from taking spread risk are not normally distributed. The returns from spread risk are leptokurtic, ie narrowly distributed around the mean with (usually) negative outliers (when spreads blow up). Favouring one form of distribution over the other is subjective depending on personal preference or tolerance of risk. However, what is not subjective is the fact that the combination of different return distributions driven by different factors reduces portfolio volatility.

---

(3) Organisational factors:
    -Length of record
    -Assets under management (rate of growth, nature of client base)
    -Ownership/compensation structure
    -Risk monitoring/control systems

High degree of sophistication is required

We believe that a fund of funds manager needs the sophistication and the operational setup to assess and weigh all of these factors. We do not believe that policies such as 'no-leverage-only' or 'five-year-track-record-required' make a lot of sense.

Market risk is only one source of risk

In *Sound Practices for Hedge Fund Managers* (2000) the authors distinguish between three categories of risk that are quantifiable – 'market risk', 'credit risk', and 'liquidity risk' – and on the less quantifiable 'operational risk'. Market risk relates to losses that could be incurred due to changes in market factors, ie prices, volatilities, and correlations. Credit risk relates to losses that could be incurred due to declines in the creditworthiness of entities in which the fund invests or with which the fund deals as a counterparty. Liquidity risk relates to losses that could be incurred when declines in liquidity in the market reduce the value of the investments or reduce the ability of the fund to fund its investments.

The authors of the report recommend that while current market practice is to treat the risks separately, it is crucial for hedge fund managers to recognise and evaluate the overlap that exists between and among market, credit and liquidity risks. This overlap is illustrated in the following diagram (recognising that the relative sizes of the circles will be different for different strategies):[1]

Chart 38: Risk Monitoring Function

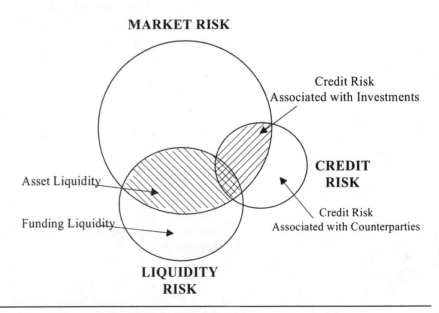

Source: *Sound Practices for Hedge Fund Managers* (2000)

---

[1] *Sound Practices for Hedge Fund Managers* (2000), p16.

Consequently, any risk-monitoring activity should monitor three interrelated variants of market, liquidity and credit risks in combination:

- Market risk – including asset liquidity and the credit risk associated with investments

- Funding liquidity risk

- Counterparty credit risk

In this framework, the risk sometimes referred to as 'sovereign risk' would be included as 'credit risk', if the potential loss is related to the financial solvency of the sovereign, or as 'market risk', if the potential loss is related to policy decisions made by the sovereign that change the market value of positions (eg currency controls). The term 'event risk' is broader and could incorporate aspects of 'credit risk' and 'operational risk', as well as some elements of 'market risk'.

Funding liquidity is important

Funding liquidity is critical to a hedge fund manager's ability to continue trading in times of stress. Funding liquidity analysis should take into account the investment strategies employed, the terms governing the rights of investors to redeem their interests and the liquidity of assets, eg all things being equal, the longer the expected period necessary to liquidate assets, the greater the potential funding requirements. Adequate funding liquidity gives a hedge fund manager the ability to continue a trading strategy without being forced to liquidate assets when losses arise.

Dealing with the complexity of monitoring manager risk is labour intensive

The reason why we are highlighting this is to show the complexity of the task. If we are in a hedge fund bubble, as some are suggesting,[1] it is because shortcuts are being taken. We believe only a team of dedicated and experienced full-time financial professionals are equipped to implement and monitor these risk variables. The use of leverage adds a further layer of complexity.

Leverage

Fund of funds manager must monitor accounting-based and risk-based leverage

One of the consistently hot topics in the hedge funds arena is the use and misuse of leverage. However, leverage is not a concept that can be uniquely defined, nor is it an independently useful measure of risk. Nevertheless, leverage is important to investors, counterparties and fund managers because of the impact it can have on the three major quantifiable sources of risk: market risk, credit risk and liquidity risk. A fund of funds manager, must therefore, have the ability to monitor accounting-based and risk-based leverage. We believe that the aforementioned fund of funds manager who declared arbitrage strategies as too risky because of the use of leverage has not spent a lot of time thinking about the different aspects of leverage.

Accounting- versus risk-based leverage

The variety of 'leverage' measures used in banking and finance is evidence that leverage is not a uniquely defined concept.[2] These measures may be accounting-based (also referred to as 'asset-based') or risk-based. The accounting-based measures attempt to capture the traditional notion of leverage as 'investing

---

[1] See Footnote 1 on page 7.

[2] *Sound Practices for Hedge Fund Managers* (2000)

borrowed funds'. Using borrowed money (or its equivalent) enables an investor to increase the assets controlled for a given level of equity capital. Accounting-based measures of leverage relate some measure of asset value to equity. Both returns and risk, relative to equity, are magnified through the use of traditional, accounting-based leverage. The risk-based measures of leverage capture another aspect associated with leverage, namely, the risk of insolvency due to changes in the value of the portfolio. The risk-based measures relate a measure of a fund's market risk to its equity (or liquidity). Although useful in this capacity, risk-based leverage measures do not convey any information about the role that borrowed money plays in the risk of insolvency.

No single measure captures all of the elements that market participants, regulators, or market observers attribute to the concept of leverage. Indeed, the authors of *Sound Practices for Hedge Fund Managers* 2000 show examples in which a risk-reducing transaction increases some leverage measures while decreasing others. This leads to the observation that leverage is not an independently useful concept, but must be evaluated in the context of the quantifiable exposures of market, credit and liquidity.

Leverage viewed in isolation is not an indication of risk

While continuing to track and use accounting-based measures of leverage, the authors of *Sound Practices for Hedge Fund Managers* (2000) recommend that hedge fund managers focus their attention on measures of leverage that relate the riskiness of the portfolio to the capacity of the fund to absorb that risk. These measures must include elements of market risk (including the credit risk associated with the assets in the portfolio) and funding liquidity risk. Hedge fund managers should focus on such measures because traditional accounting-based leverage by itself does not necessarily convey risk of insolvency. To say that one fund is levered 2-to-1 while another is unlevered does not necessarily mean that the levered fund is more risky or more likely to encounter liquidity problems. If the levered fund is invested in government securities while the unlevered fund is invested in equities, accounting-based leverage would lead to erroneous conclusions about the riskiness of the two funds. In this sense, accounting-based measures of leverage are arguably deficient since they convey the least information about the nature and risk of the assets in a portfolio.

Risk-based measures present a measure of market risk (usually VAR) relative to a measure of the resources available to absorb risk (cash or equity).[1] However, in doing so, risk based measures effectively condense several dimensions of risk into a single number. The result of this compression is that some of the detail is lost; the specific effect of leverage is intertwined with dimensions of market, credit and liquidity risk. To illustrate, consider two funds with identical risk-based leverage. One fund employs 2-to-1 accounting leverage while investing in 'low-risk' strategies (eg long/short strategies) using borrowed funds, while the other fund uses no accounting leverage but employs 'high-risk' strategies (eg macro directional) and large cash reserves. One is 'high risk' and 'high cash' and the other is 'low risk' and 'low cash/high borrowing', yet each achieves the same risk-based leverage. This comparison highlights the second reason why leverage measures are not independently useful: more comprehensive measures that blend the effect of

---

[1] *Sound Practices for Hedge Fund Managers* (2000)

multiple risk dimensions are required. To assess the contribution of leverage requires additional information.[1]

Risk-based leverage relates the riskiness of a portfolio to the ability to absorb that risk

The authors of the report argue that managers and investors alike must recognise that leverage is important, not in and of itself, but because of the impact it can have on market, credit and liquidity risk. In other words, leverage influences the rapidity of changes in the value of the portfolio due to changes in market, credit, or liquidity risk factors. Consequently, the most relevant measures of leverage are 'risk-based' measures that relate the riskiness of a portfolio to the ability of the fund to absorb that risk. Recognising the impact that leverage can have on a portfolio's exposure to market, credit, and liquidity risk, the fund of funds manager or investor should assess the degree to which a hedge fund is able to modify its risk-based leverage in periods of stress or increased market risk. Traditional, accounting-based measures of leverage should also be examined. This can provide insights into the source of risk-based leverage and how that leverage could be adjusted.

The Risk of Style Drift

Defining style drift is difficult

A further ongoing risk factor to be monitored by the fund of funds manager is style drift. Style drift is the risk to the investor that the hedge fund manager drifts away from his area of expertise where he has an edge into a field where he has a competitive disadvantage. Historical examples have been fixed income arbitrageurs investing in non-domestic equity markets or equity managers investing in Russian debt.

There are probably two types of style drift: a short-term opportunistic style drift as well as a continuous departure of a manager's area of expertise. A permanent shift will force reassessment of the investment. We are inclined to argue that a short-term opportunistic drift into a related area is probably not as negative for the investor as a permanent shift. The short-term shift is both a risk to the investor as well as entrepreneurial expansion through exploiting economies of scale, ie an opportunity. A convertible arbitrage manager, for example, has a competitive advantage in areas of analysing changes in credit and volatilities. There are, potentially, related trading opportunities to make money by exploiting inefficiencies left behind by less informed investors.

Diversification results in a more stable stream of returns

Over the years, there has been an increasing tendency for hedge fund managers to employ multiple strategies.[2] The value of creating a more stable stream of returns over different market cycles has attracted hedge funds to adopt a multi-strategy approach. By investing in a manager attempting to achieve absolute returns, one automatically invests in the skill of the manager, ie not in an asset class or mechanical execution of an investment technique, strategy or process. This implies a higher degree of flexibility for the manager. In other words, the hedge fund manager is not restricted to replicate a benchmark but has a mandate to exploit opportunities. The basic question is how far a hedge fund manager should be allowed to drift away from his initial area of expertise.

---

[1] See *Sound Practices for Hedge Fund Managers* (2000), p 50-55.

[2] From Fung and Hsieh (2001a), p7.

Restrictions are a double-edged sword

Restrictions work in both ways. On one hand restrictions reduce risk; on the other they limit the set of opportunities to add value. Every market changes over time. Change, and its derivative, uncertainty, are the most certain variables in any social science. Market inefficiencies, for example, have a tendency to disappear as they become known to the market and attract capital. If manager restrictions were too tight, the manager would not be able to exploit inefficiencies in a neighbouring or related market as they appear, thereby missing out on *first-mover* advantage.

Handcuffs and Opportunism – a Trade-off

An active fund manager with very tight restrictions is essentially running an enhanced index fund (charging an active fee)

Our belief that a high degree of freedom is good is based on the assumption that a large portion of the value added in the hedge fund industry is attributable to flexibility and not purely to skill.[1] If ex-ante value added is defined as manager skill times the square root of breadth, then handcuffing an active manager does not make a lot of sense.[2]

Loose restrictions potentially could essentially increase portfolio volatility and correlation

A high degree of freedom causes many challenges in terms of monitoring risk on an ongoing basis.[3] In addition, investors construct portfolios of hedge fund strategies according to their own risk tolerances and return preferences. A high degree of flexibility means that the investor's portfolio of different hedge fund managers could occasionally experience a higher degree of overlap. This would result in higher volatility and higher correlation of the hedge fund portfolio.

There are no guarantees

One important aspect that aligns the interests of the investor with those of the manager is the fact that many hedge fund managers have large portions of their net wealth tied to their fund. Often hedge fund managers view their fund as the safest place for their wealth to compound. An aversion to market risk exposure was the main reason why hedge funds started back in 1949 in the first place. To some extent, this alignment of interest is a hedge against the manager leaving his area of competence by risking his and his investors equity. However, human nature does not always work that way. There are no guarantees for a prudent assessment of new opportunities. Judgement is omnipresent in pure active management, ie hedge fund investing. The degree of tolerable style drift will remain in the eye of the beholder.

Legal and Compliance

A fund of funds manager's legal/compliance personnel must have the authority and resources to operate independently and effectively. This function should seek to actively manage the legal risks presented by the hedge fund manager's trading, focusing on the documentation governing trading relationships and individual transactions. A fund of funds manager will have to ensure that the hedge fund managers pursue a consistent and methodical approach to documenting transactions so that the legal consequences of periods of market stress or performance declines

---

[1] Other restrictions include the use of derivatives. According to Kosky and Pontiff (1999), 79% of the researched sample of 679 equity mutual funds do not use derivatives.

[2] More formally: Information ratio = information coefficient (skill or correlation between forecast and realised active returns) times the square root of the breadth or scope (number of independent forecasts of exceptional return a manager can make a year). Grinold and Kahn (2000a), p 148. The formula is often regarded as the law or sine qua non of active money management. If one of the two variables (skill or breadth) is zero, the product of the equation is also zero. In other words, a skilled manager stripped of all opportunities to add value has an expected information ratio of zero and cannot add value.

[3] Note that there is a controversy surrounding long/short investing. See page 108 in the Appendix.

may be more clearly anticipated and managed. The legal aspect should allow risk monitoring with useful input in the evaluation of a hedge fund's projected liquidity in stressed environments, including inputs derived from the fund's transaction documentation (eg terms regarding termination, collateral and margining).

Data and Information

Data on hedge funds is not perfect

Generally speaking, data on hedge fund performance in general is bad and information is difficult and costly to obtain. Hedge fund data suffers from various biases, of which survivorship bias is the most often quoted deficiency.[1] The hedge fund industry is still opaque. This means information flow is not efficient and transparent.

The lack of information and transparency is a risk to the investor

The lack of transparency, the poor quality of available data and the high cost of information are a risk to some investors. It is essentially is a risk to investors who are not in the information loop. However, information and high-quality data are among the competitive advantages of the fund of hedge funds manager.

This concludes our search for 'edge' in the fund of funds business. In the following chapter we analysed data on a 929 funds of funds from a proprietary database.

---

[1] Probably the most extreme example of survivorship bias in capital markets today is the notion that equities outperform bonds in the long term, ie the widely touted equity risk premium puzzle. The term 'equity risk premium puzzle' refers to the puzzling high historical average returns of US stocks relative to bonds. Mehra and Prescott (1985) show that standard general equilibrium models cannot explain the size of the risk premium on US equities, which averaged 6% over the period 1889-1978. The view that stocks outperform bonds could be because most analysis is based on a surviving stock market, ie the US stock market. However, the standard error of such an analysis is high. Unfortunately, one cannot test the equity premium by rerunning US market history to see what would have happened along other sample paths. However, one can look at other stock markets. Jorion and Goetzmann (1999) did exactly that. They examined the 20th century returns of 39 stock markets around the world, including several with experiences vastly different from the US stock market, such as Russia (disappeared in 1917) and Germany and Japan (experienced discontinuities). The authors reported that the US market was the best performing market of all 39 markets. The belief that equities outperform bonds in the long run, therefore, is founded on some debatable assumptions.

(This page intentionally left blank.)